The College of Arms

JOHN VANBRUGH

by Richardson

A
BIOGRAPHICAL
DICTIONARY

OF

Actors, Actresses, Musicians, Dancers,

Managers & Other Stage Personnel

in London, 1660–1800

Volume 15: Tibbett *to* M. West

by
PHILIP H. HIGHFILL, JR., KALMAN A. BURNIM
and
EDWARD A. LANGHANS

SOUTHERN ILLINOIS UNIVERSITY PRESS

CARBONDALE AND EDWARDSVILLE

Publication of this work was made possible in part through a
grant from the National Endowment for the Humanities.

Library of Congress Cataloging-in-Publication Data
(Revised for Vol. 15)

Highfill, Philip H.
  A biographical dictionary of actors, actresses,
musicians, dancers, managers & other stage personnel in
London, 1660–1800.

  Includes bibliographical references.
  1. Performing arts—England—London—Biography—Dictionaries. 2. Actors—England—London—Biography—Dictionaries. 3. Theatrical managers—England—London—Biography—Dictionaries. 4. London (England)—Biography—Dictionaries. I. Burnim, Kalman A., joint author. II. Langhans, Edward A., joint author. III. Title.
PN2597.H5   790.2'092'2 [B]   71-157068
ISBN 0-8093-1802-4

Volume 15

Tibbett *to* M. West

1   **TIDSWELL**

Tibbett. *See* TIBET.

Tibet, William   *c. 1756–1832, instrumentalist.*

Born about 1756, William Tibet (or Tebbit, Tebbett, Tibbett) was recommended for membership in the Royal Society of Musicians on 7 April 1782. At that time he was described as about 25, married, (without children), proficient on the violin and viola, and a private musician to the Duke of Marlborough. Tibet played first violin in the Handel Memorial Concerts at Westminster Abbey and the Pantheon in May and June 1784 and viola or violin in the benefit concerts for the clergy at St Paul's in May 1785, 1789, and 1791. Doane's *Musical Directory* of 1794 noted that Tibet also played the violoncello. He was living "at the Duke of Marlborough's."

Mee in *The Oldest Music Room in Europe* states that Tibet played first violin in the band of the Oxford Musical Society in 1808, but notices of him in the nineteenth century are rare. Tibet petitioned the Royal Society of Musicians for aid on 6 April 1817, and he received a guinea for medical bills in September 1828. The Society granted him £3 for medical aid on 6 March 1831. Jackson's *Oxford Journal* of 19 May 1832 reported that Tibet had died on 16 May at Headington at the age of 77. The obituary notice declared that Tibet had been in the service of the late Duke of Marlborough for 48 years.

Tice, Mr *fl. 1795–1800,* *house servant.*

The Drury Lane accounts and benefit bills mention Mr Tice, one of the house servants, from 5 June 1795 to 14 June 1800.

Tickell, Mrs Richard the first. *See* LINLEY, MARY.

Tidd, Mr *fl. 1760,* *billsticker.*

A Covent Garden Theatre paylist dated 22 September 1760 cites Mr Tidd as a billsticker earning 2s. daily.

Tidswell, Charlotte *1760–1846, actress.*

Charlotte Tidswell was born in 1760 and, according to the notebooks of W. J. Lawrence, performed at the Crow Street Theatre in Dublin as early as 1768–69. Kathleen Barker places her at Bristol, playing pages, in 1776. The first time Miss Tidswell was mentioned in a London playbill was on 24 January 1783, when she played Scentwell in *The Busy Body* at Drury Lane Theatre. She went on that season to act Leonora in *The Mourning Bride*, Miss Flack in *A Trip to Scotland*, Isabella in *The Revenge*, Jenny in *The Tender Husband*, a Beggar in *The Ladies' Frolick*, a Chambermaid in *The Clandestine Marriage*, Lucy in *The Adventures of a Night*, and a Chambermaid in *Imitation*. Her benefit tickets were accepted on 23 May.

That first season was fairly typical of the rest of Charlotte Tidswell's long career. With the Drury Lane troupe over the next 39 years she played such parts as Lettice and Eliza in *The Plain Dealer*, Miss Frolick in *The Absent Man*, a Shepherdess in *Cymon*, Prudentia in *A Duke and No Duke*, Honoria in *Love Makes a Man*, Night in *Amphitryon*, Mrs Foresight in *Love for Love*, Gymp in *Bon Ton*, Penelope in *The Natural Son*, Colombine in *The Cauldron*, Diana and Jenny in *The Humorist*, Myrtilla and Trusty in *The Provok'd Husband*, Lady Clifford in *The Earl of Warwick*, Alithea in *The Country Girl*, Marmalet in *All in the Wrong*, Galatea in *Philaster*, Tiffany in *The Heiress*, Cephisa in *The Distrest Mother*, Lady Freelove in *The Jealous Wife*, Kitty in *The Lyar*, Madge in *The Gentle Shepherd*, Altea in *Rule a Wife and Have a Wife*, Florella in *The Orphan*, Mrs Fulmer in *The West Indian*, the Player Queen in *Hamlet*, Erixene in *The Grecian Daughter*, the Duchess of York in *Richard III*, Arante in *King Lear*, Bianca in *Catherine and Petruchio*, Charmion in *All for Love*, Toilet in *The Jealous Wife*, Lucetta in *The Suspicious Husband*, Parley in *The Constant Couple*, and Lettice and Lady Loverule in *The Devil to Pay*.

Other parts were Lady Scroop in *Mary Queen of Scots*, Mrs Slammekin in *The Beggar's Opera*, Jenny and the Nurse in *Love for Love*, Lamorce in *The Inconstant*, Margaret in *Much Ado about Nothing*, Miss Ogle in *The Belle's Stratagem*, Tag in *Miss in Her Teens*, Gipsy in *The Beaux' Stratagem*, Mrs Clogget and Mrs Amlet in *The Confederacy*, Situp in *The Double Gallant*, Jaqueline in *The Count of Narbonne*, Dorcas in *The Jew*, Lady Sneerwell in *The School for Scandal*, Nelly in *No Song No Supper*, Anna in *Douglas*, Mrs Coupler in *A Trip to Scarborough*, Confidant and Mrs Dangle in *The Critic*, Lady

Harvard Theatre Collection

MISS TIDSWELL as Corinna, JOHN BANNISTER as Young Philpot, and
WILLIAM PARSONS as Old Philpot

artist unknown

Capulet in *Romeo and Juliet*, Francisca in *Measure for Measure*, Ursula in *Robinson Crusoe*, Delia in *Theodosius*, Deborah in *The Will*, Miss Pickle in *The Spoil'd Child*, Lucy in *The Gamester*, Betty in *A Bold Stroke for a Wife*, Winifred in *The Children of the Wood*, and Mrs Caddy in *The Prize*.

In the nineteenth century she added such parts as the Hostess in *Honeymoon*, a Maid in *She Stoops to Conquer*, Cicely in *The Midnight Hour*, Leonarda in *The Pannel*, Mrs Ramsey in *Turn Out*, Lucy in *The Recruiting Officer*, Dame Spriggins in *Orange Boven*, Lady Macsycophant in *The Man of the World*, Sarah in *The School for Friends*, Galna in *The Ninth Statue*, Dame Hawbuck in *Town and Country*, Mrs Ledger in *The Road to Ruin*, and Mrs Maggs in *The London Hermit*.

For her labors at Drury Lane, usually in sec-

ondary and tertiary roles, Charlotte Tidswell earned £2 10s. weekly in the 1790s and the early years of the nineteenth century; she seems not to have risen above £3 weekly. Over the years she was given benefit tickets to peddle, and by 1792 she was sharing benefits. The bills occasionally provided her address: No 8, Martlet Court, Bow Street, in 1790; in Stanhope Street, Clare Market, in 1791; No 3, Little Charles Street, St James's, in 1793; in Lisle Street about 1800; and No 12, Tavistock Row, Covent Garden, in 1814.

With the Drury Lane company Miss Tidswell appeared at the King's Theatre and the Haymarket while the new Drury Lane was under construction, but she also acted with other troupes. In 1793–94 she joined other Drury Lane folk at the Haymarket under Colman's management, playing some of her old parts but also the Marquis's Maid in *Harlequin Peasant*, Lucy Welldon in *Oroonko,* a Chambermaid in *Heigho for a Husband!,* and Dorothy in *All in Good Humour.* At the Haymarket in the summer of 1794 she acted a few of her regular parts, as she did in the summers of 1795 and 1796. Over the years she also performed away from London. She acted in Brighton in the summer of 1788 and in Liverpool in September 1791 and apparently in earlier summers. She was evidently in Manchester in 1806.

Hildebrand in his biography of Edmund Kean collected most of what is known about Charlotte Tidswell's private life, for early sources used sometimes contradictory information about the parentage of Kean—information gained from Miss Tidswell herself. She was supposedly the daughter of an army officer, tried the stage when he died and left her destitute, was protected by the Duke of Norfolk, and looked after Kean in his early years—so attentively, in fact, that Kean later supposed she must have been his mother. Rumor had it for a while that she was the wife of Moses Kean. Hildebrand believes that she was probably not the mother of Edmund Kean but that she may have been his aunt and was certainly a great help to the boy in his early years.

James Winston in his *Drury Lane Journal* wrote in 1826 of Edmund Kean about 1800: "He was then a boy in Drury Lane. He says he had a common dog's collar about his neck, engraved . . . 'Bring this boy to Miss Tidswell, Lisle Street, etc.' No hat, scarce any shoes or stockings. He used to run away from Tidswell for a week, sleep in trees or anywhere." Winston also wrote of Miss Tidswell's farewell benefit, at Drury Lane on 21 May 1822: "At end of play, before the curtain dropped, Kean fetched on Tidswell from prompt side. She addressed a few lines written by Knight which nearly overpowered her, and then curtain dropped."

Given the humble parts she played during most of her career, it is surprising that the critics paid so much attention to her. *The Secret History of the Green Room* in 1790 noted that she had been educated in France by her army officer father but that he was a spendthrift. Since her debut she had "officiated in any little characters that the Manager chose to give her." In Liverpool, where she acted in the summers,

she does not figure in the first line upon the boards, yet she maintains in private life a very respectable character. We frequently see her in parts the most obnoxious to human nature; such as Courtezans, and those of the most sanguinary kind, as Lamorce in the Inconstant, and Louisa in Love makes a man, &c. &c. Though we must hold in abhorrance those characters, however chaste the person who represents them, yet as they certainly must be represented by somebody and when we consider that the Manager is absolute, we should separate the Actress from the woman, and applaud her discretion for not displaying those wanton gestures which naturally distinguish that description of women, and would prove extremely offensive to female delicacy.

The *Authentic Memoirs of the Green Room* in 1801 noted that Miss Tidswell had played subordinate characters in both comedy and tragedy. "Another range of characters which generally falls to her lot, is that of profligate and abandoned females; such, for instance, as Corinna in the Citizen; Mrs. Fulmer, in the West Indian, &c. The latter character, in particular, we saw her perform on the recent revival of that excellent comedy, with considerable talent and address."

John Williams in his *Pin Basket to the Children of Thespis* in 1797 put it in verse:

> Her Nell, *and her* Tomboy—*her* Hoyden, *and*
>   Prue,
> *Make my happiness stronger the oft'ner I view:*
> *But her Juliet! oh, zounds, what a Mantuan pat-*
>   *tern!*
> *Would a man, damn his kindred to grapple a slat-*
>   *tern?*
> *Her coif seem'd so greas'd, and her vestment so*
>   *worn,*
> *In the rage of the fete she look'd—finely forlorn.*

He concluded, ". . . make her genteel, and her usefulness ends."

Charlotte Tidswell died at the age of 86 on 3 September 1846, according to Giles Playfair's *Kean.*

Miss Tidswell appears as Corinna, with William Parsons as Old Philpot and John Bannister as Young Philpot, in an engraving by an unknown artist of a scene from *The Citizen.* An example is in the Harvard Theatre Collection. She also is depicted with others, including James G. Raymond, Samuel Arnold, and Harriot Mellon, in a satirical print entitled "Management—or—Butt & Hogsheads," engraved by Cruikshank and published by W. N. Jones, 1 December 1812. The print is reproduced in this *Dictionary* 12: 272, and is described in that volume, p. 273, item No 6, and also in the *Catalogue of Political and Personal Satires in the British Museum,* No 11940.

Tidwell. *See* TIDSWELL.

Tifer. *See* TYFER.

Tildsley, Mr ₁*fl. 1799–1804*₁, *doorkeeper.*
The Drury Lane accounts cite Mr Tildsley as a gallery doorkeeper in December 1799 earning £1 1*s.* (probably per week). He was mentioned occasionally through 1803–4.

Tillemans, Peter *1684–1734, scene painter.*
Peter Tillemans was born in Antwerp in 1684, the son of a diamond cutter. He and his brother-in-law Peter Casteels came to England in 1708 with the dealer Turner and worked for him as copyists of masters such as Teniers. Tillemans was especially skilled as a landscape painter, and works by him can be seen in such places as Chatsworth, Thoresbury House, and Knowsley House. He was a student at Kneller's academy and a teacher of William, Lord Byron, according to *The Dictionary of National Biography.* Mist's *Weekly Journal* on 10 August 1717 reported that Tillemans's musical picture of the royal court, with the muses above, was exhibited at the actor William Pinkethman's booth at Bartholomew Fair, and it was shown again in a room next to the Richmond Theatre in the summer of 1718.

In 1724–25 Tillemans and Joseph Goupy were employed by the King's Theatre to paint scenery for operas, and at Drury Lane Theatre Tillemans helped paint the scenery for Thurmond's *The Miser,* which opened on 30 December 1726; working with him were Devoto, Eberlin, and Domonic. Deutsch in his *Handel* has Tillemans and Goupy painting scenery for Handel's *Riccardo I,* which was first presented at the King's Theatre on 11 November 1727.

PETER TILLEMANS
engraving by Chambers, after Hysing

Most of Tillemans's work was done outside the theatre. He executed some 500 drawings for Bridge's *History of Northampton.* Tillemans lived in Richmond, Surrey, for a number of years, but when he died on 5 December 1734 he was working for Dr Cox Macro of Norton Haugh, Suffolk. Tillemans was buried at Stow Langtoft, near Bury St Edmunds.

A portrait of Peter Tillemans holding a palette and brushes was engraved by T. Chambers, after H. Hysing, and published as a plate to Walpole's *Anecdotes,* 1762.

Tilley, Samuel ₁*fl. 1794–1810?*₁, *violist?*
Doane's *Musical Directory* of 1794 lists Samuel Tilley, of No 4, Northampton Buildings, Rosoman Street, Clerkenwell, as a tenor (i.e., violist, probably) and a music engraver. Tilley was a member of the Handelian Society and performed in the oratorios at Covent Garden Theatre and in the Handel concerts at Westminster Abbey. Humphries and Smith in *Music Publishing in the British Isles* list the music engraver S. Tilley as having a shop about

1800 at No 2, Booth's Court, Oxford Street. He was active there until about 1806. The Tilley who in the summer of 1810 had recently joined the band at the Haymarket Theatre was probably our subject.

Tillman, Mr *fl. 1722–1727₁*, *door-keeper.*

The gallery doorkeeper Tillman was first noticed on 28 May 1722 when he and two others shared £83 1s. in benefit receipts at Lincoln's Inn Fields Theatre. He shared similar benefits through 1726. On 27 April 1727 he served as a boxkeeper at Glover's benefit.

Tilly, John *fl. 1702₁*, *stroller.*

Two John Tillys, Senior and Junior, were listed in the *Post Man* of 8 September 1702 as required to pay town constables 2s. daily when they performed.

Tilly, John Jr *fl. 1702₁*, *stroller. See* TILLY, JOHN.

Tilman. *See* TILLMAN.

Tilson, Gertrude. *See* MAHON, MRS GILBERT.

"Timbertoe, Captain." *See* FOOTE, SAMUEL.

"Timbertoe, Mons" *fl. 1752–1754₁*, *dancer.*

At the Haymarket on 21 and 23 May 1752 "Mrs Midnight" (Christopher Smart) presented an entertainment that included dancing by "M Timbertoe, from the Opera House in Paris." Timbertoe appeared again on 5 September 1753, dancing a hornpipe at Bartholomew Fair, again as part of a production by Mrs Midnight, this one called "La Je Ne Sca Quoi [*sic*]; or, Wooden Spoons à la mode." At the Haymarket in 1752–53 Timbertoe offered a hornpipe on several occasions. On 7 March 1754 at the Haymarket there was dancing by "The Great New Timbertoe," who may or may not have been the same performer. On the eleventh he joined Signora Mentorini in an *English Ballet,* and the pair entertained with a *Burlesque Ballet* on 30 March. On 1 April they were principal performers in *The Adventures of Fribble;* on 22 April Timbertoe offered *Grand Burlesque Dances;* and on 2 May he shared a benefit with Signora Gapatoona.

"Timbertop." *See* LACY, JAMES *1696–1774.*

"Tincture Laudanum, Count" *fl. 1748₁*, *dancer.*

"Mr Foote the second, late arrived from Copenhagen" announced in the *Daily Advertiser* on 20 October 1748 that at Marshalsea Prison, Southwark, he would exhibit a collection of pictures and offer *The Murder of the Dragon of Wantley* and a *Sleepy Dance* by "Count Tincture Laudanum." The event was obviously capitalizing on Samuel Foote's *Auction of Pictures* at the Haymarket.

Tindal, Mr *fl. 1740₁*, *tumbler.*

Tindal, a tumbler, performed at Hallam's booth at Bartholomew Fair on 23 August 1740.

Tindal, Charles *fl. 1761–1767₁*, *actor.*

Mr Tindal was said to be making his first appearance on any stage when he came on as Marcian in *Theodosius* at Covent Garden on 25 April 1761. Evidently he met the test, for he returned as a regular company member the following 3 October, when his name was entered in Covent Garden's account book for 15s. per week.

Tindal remained at Covent Garden until May 1765 and acted at the Haymarket during the following summer. He amassed a number of tertiary and secondary roles: at Covent Garden in 1761–62 he played Exeter in *Henry V,* Mowbray in *2 Henry IV,* Pandulph in *King John,* Cassander and Polyperchon in *The Rival Queens,* an unspecified character in *The Twins,* Old Pilgrim in *The Pilgrim,* Sir Harry Beagle in *The Jealous Wife,* and Humphrey in *The Conscious Lovers;* in 1762–63, Lodovico in *Othello,* Duke Frederick in *As You Like It,* and a Member in *The Apprentice;* in 1763–64, Dervise in *Tamerlane* and Carlos in *Love Makes a Man;* and in 1764–65, Macduff in *Macbeth,* Offa in *The Royal Convert,* and Portius in *Cato.* In the summer of 1765, at the Haymarket, he was Harpy in *The Commissary,* Quildrive in *The Citizen,* Loader in *The Minor,* and Cape in *The Old Maid.*

Tindal evidently spent the winter season of 1765–66, or some part of it, acting at Edinburgh, and he returned there in 1766–67, only to be caught up in the riot and destruction when adherents of the dismissed actor George Stayley gutted the theatre. He joined two managers and ten actors in signing a letter of protest distributed on a handbill dated 12 January 1767, which brought on the final destructive act of the mob. (John Jackson, in *The History of the Scottish Stage* [1793], who described that action, furnished Tindal's first name, Charles.)

A "Tyndall," probably our man, was playing minor parts at Bristol later in 1767.

Tinker, Philip. *See* TYNCHARE, PHILIP.

Tinley, Mr *fl. 1794–1804₁*, *prompter.*
The Covent Garden Theatre accounts show that Mr Tinley was a prompter in 1794–95. He was paid £15 for himself and a boy, probably a call boy, for an unspecified period. Tinley was named in the accounts again in 1802–3 and 1803–4. Mrs Tinley was cited in 1794–95 as working in the women's wardrobe for 10s. 6d. weekly.

Tinley, Mrs *fl. 1794–1795₁*, *dresser.*
See TINLEY, MR.

Tinns, Mrs *fl. 1750s₁*, *dresser.*
George Ann Bellamy in her *Apology* wrote that Mrs Tinns was the dresser she left behind at Drury Lane Theatre when she finished her engagement there. Mrs Tinns therefore must have been active at the theatre in the 1750s.

Tinte (or Tinti) Rosa, later Mme ₁Carlo?₁ Rovedino *fl. 1778–1780₁*, *dancer, singer?*
Signora Tinte (sometimes, and perhaps correctly, "Tinti") was an Italian dancer whose first recorded appearance in London was at the King's Theatre on 31 October 1775. At the end of *La sposa fidele* she, with four others, danced in the "New Grand Pantomime Ballet" *Pigmalion Amoureuse de la statue*. Other dances she participated in during the 1775–76 season were the incidental dances in the opera *Didone; Il filosofo amoroso* (on 16 November, with Paladini in his first appearance), *Les Evenemens imprevues*, *Les Deux soeurs rivales*, *Le Générosité de Scipion*, *La Fête du village*, *Le Re-*

tour des matelots, Les Maissoneurs distresses and *Le Triomphe de la magie.*

On 23 October 1776, for the benefit of Anne Catley, Rosa Tinte and Palladini made their first appearance at Covent Garden, dancing a *New Rural Ballet*. Signora Tinte remained at Covent Garden through the season of 1778–79 and in that season divided her time between Covent Garden and the King's Theatre. Among the ballets, pantomimes, and specialty dances she appeared in, usually with several other dancers, were: at Covent Garden in 1776–77, pastoral dances, rural dances, and a *Minuet de la cour* teamed with the dancing master Bishop, and a minuet with Dumay; at Covent Garden in 1777–78, a part in *The Humours of New Market and the Poney Races, La Soirée à-la-mode, The Garden of Love*, the dancing in the new Messink afterpiece *The Norwood Gypsies*, Columbine in *Mother Shipton*, and a part in *The Russian Light Infantry and Cossack Camp*; at Covent Garden in the fall of 1778, a "Principal Character" in *The Medley; or, Harlequin At-All*, and dancing in *Les soirée à-la-mode*; at the King's Theatre in 1778–79, the opera dances in *Demofoonte*, a *Pas de deux anacréontique*, a *Ballet by the Fairies of the Court of Azore*, Feora in *La Fête du ciel*, and *Le paysano vales*. Her last London appearance was at the opera on 15 June 1779, dancing some quadrilles, which were advertised as having been presented at the Pantheon on the previous evening, with Slingsby and others.

Taddeo Wiel, in *I Teatri musicali Venesiani del Settecento* (Venezia, 1897) cites her after 1780 as Tinti Rovedino, i.e., as if she had married [Carlo?] Rovedino. But that citation is puzzling, inasmuch as the sole appearance in London of a Signora Rovedino, so far as extant opera bills show, was at the King's Theatre on 26 March 1778 as one of the "Principal Characters"—thus a singer—in the opera *Il Marchese villano*. If she became Carlo Rovedino's wife, then she was probably the mother of two, perhaps three, musicians who are discussed in Rovedino's entry.

Tinti. *See* TINTE.

Tioli, John Baptist *fl. 1757–c. 1760s₁*, *dancer.*
Neither the date of John Baptist Tioli's first arrival in London nor that of his departure for

Dublin are known. He was advertised as "late first dancer of the Opera" (in London) on the Smock Alley Theatre's bill of 19 October 1757. W. S. Clark's manuscript records show him at the Crow Street Theatre in 1759–60. By the fall of 1760 he was again in London.

David Garrick wrote to Joseph Austin, his assistant prompter, on Sunday, 12 October 1760, urging him to make a substitution in the planned playbill at Drury Lane on the following Tuesday. "I have thought of something better than y^e *beggar's Opera*. . . . let it be y^e *Careless Husband* wth Dancing by Sign^r Tioli. . . ." Tioli's "first appearance" on that stage duly occurred on 14 October, when he danced with Mary Baker in "a new pantomime dance called *The Mad Doctor.*" He danced again, with the corps de ballet, on 13 December. He teamed with Mary Baker again on 24 January 1761 in *The Enchanted Peasant,* another "pantomime dance," and was seen once more with her and others for the benefit of the ballet master Leviez on 18 April 1761 in *The Venetian Gondolier.*

According to the record of the proceedings in a law suit—presumably of 1761—in the British Library (MS 1890.e.5), the entrepreneur Anthony Minelli recruited Tioli again for Smock Alley in that year, promising him and Master Goodwin his pupil a salary of £65 to dance in a series of burlettas.

Julia Curtis, in her dissertation "The Early Charleston Stage," states that Tioli was dancing and teaching in Philadelphia in the 1760s and that one of his pupils was the actor-dancer James Verling Godwin.

[Tior], Mr   ₁*fl. 1795*₁,   *house servant?*
A person whose name appears to be Tior is cited in the Drury Lane accounts on 25 April 1795 at a salary of £1 10s., presumably per week. He may have been one of the house servants.

"Tirenello"   ₁*fl. 1754*₁,   *dancer.*
At "Mrs Midnight's New Carnival Concert" at the Haymarket Theatre on 15 August 1754, one of the dancers was named "Tirenello." Since the concert was a concoction by Christopher Smart, we cannot tell whether the dancer was a human or a trained animal.

Tirrell, Mr. *See* TIRRELL, MRS.

Tirrell, Mrs   ₁*fl. 1799–1808*₁,   *singer, impresario?*
The Drury Lane Theatre accounts first named Mrs Tirrell on 8 June 1799, when she was paid 13s. 4d. for singing in the chorus for four days. She served as an extra in the chorus during the summer, and on 12 October she was paid, again 13s. 4d., for teaching the chorus. The Tirrell named in the benefit bill of 14 June was probably Mrs Tirrell. By 1801, when she was last mentioned in the accounts, Mrs Tirrell was earning £1 weekly. She seems to have been the Mrs Tirrell who in 1806, 1807, and 1808 was granted a license to present an entertainment at the Haymarket Theatre. In 1810 a similar license was granted to Mr Tirrell.

Tirrevette, Mons   ₁*fl. 1722*₁,   *dancer.*
Monsieur Tirrevette danced the role of the Valet de Chambre in the pantomime *The Magician* at Lincoln's Inn Fields in January and February 1722, beginning on 13 January.

Tirrill, Mr   ₁*fl. 1727*₁,   *boxkeeper.*
Though Mr Tirrill seems not to have been on the regular house staff at Lincoln's Inn Fields Theatre, he worked as one of the boxkeepers at Mrs Barbier's benefit on 16 March 1727.

Tisdall, Mrs   *d. 1779, actress, singer.*
Mrs Tisdall (or Twisdale) played Molly in *The Beggar's Opera* in Samuel Foote's troupe at the Haymarket Theatre from 12 July to 29 August 1769 and was presumably the Mrs Tisdale who had acted Lucy in *The Devil to Pay* at the Haymarket on 22 May 1769. In *The Irish Stage in the County Towns* W. S. Clark traced Mrs Tisdall to Smock Alley Theatre in Dublin in 1774, Cork in 1775, and Belfast in 1778 and 1779. She died in Belfast in 1779.

Tisdall, John   ₁*fl. 1660s*₁,   *musician.*
Among the professional musicians in London in the 1660s was John Tisdall, who took on Thomas Watson as an apprentice but died before the lad's seven years were completed. Tisdall's widow had, according to the Middlesex County records, married a seaman who had no skill in music, so young Watson was released from his apprenticeship.

Titter, Sarah, later Mrs John Henry Colls

fl. 1778–1803₁,   actress.

The bills and other records of John Palmer's ill-starred attempt to establish a third winter playhouse, the Royalty Theatre, in London in 1787 and 1788 are few and scattered. The fluctuating roster was composed of defectors from the patent houses and adventurers from country theatres who played at the Royalty on short contracts. Apparently one such person was Sarah Titter, who as Mrs John H. Colls became a familiar face in various provincial houses.

The evidence is slight but apparently conclusive. A letter, now in the Huntington Library, dated at London on 12 January 1788, from Sarah Titter to the influential and aristocratic poet and dramatist Edward Jerningham

beg[s] to submit to your Judgment, as I cannot accede to any proposal at the hazard of your displeasure, [an offer] from Mr. Barrett the Manager of the Norwich Theatre, wherein he proposes my playing *five* or *six* Nights to share the produce of the seventh with him. I went to Mr Palmer to consult with him on the subject, he advises me to go, if Mr. Barrett will give me a *clear* Benefit—as otherwise it would be paying *Him* for *My* exertions— Mr Palmer told me in confidence *he* would soon be in Norwich and would play any character on my Night—and assured me, he should petition Parliament [for a permanent license] before the 8th Inst. February.

Palmer's petition failed, though the Royalty staggered on until April 1788. But Miss Titter had made her Norwich debut on 14 February 1788, according to the *Norwich Mercury* of 9 February, billed as "from the Royalty."

The letter is part of an extensive file, now in the Huntington Library, from Sarah Titter and John Henry Colls to Jerningham, their friend and patron. Sarah was evidently already the mistress of Colls, a poet and aspiring playwright, and on 4 June 1789, according to the register of marriages at St James's Church, Bath, she became his wife.

Nearly all of the rest of what we know about Sarah Titter and her husband comes from the letters to Jerningham: one from Colls to Jerningham from "Crown Court, Elm Hill," Norwich, 14 March 1788, shows her to have been successful at Norwich in "the Characters of Lady Townly [in *The Provok'd Hus-*

band], Letitia Hardy [in *The Belle's Stratagem*], Beatrice [in *Much Ado about Nothing* and], . . . Indiana [in *The Conscious Lovers*]," among others. She gained "encomiums," and her sixth benefit night "exhibited a more splendid and numerous Audience than has been seen here for several years." Colls and wife returned to town within a fortnight, hoping that Jerningham's "kind recommendation to the Summer Theatre will be thankfully acknowledged" and that success at the Haymarket would lead to "the Winter Houses." It was not to be; she never again appeared on stage in London, though the couple did return to town sometime late in March, when she was living at No 27, King Street, Holborn.

John Colls wrote to Jerningham from Bath on 4 May 1788 informing him that the sudden departure of Mrs Goodall from the Bath-Bristol company for Drury Lane had opened up a place at Bath for Sarah. Colls had written an "address" for her debut. She had been successful.

Long years later, in 1803, and again in a letter to Jerningham, the Bath editor and newspaper proprietor William Meyler recalled that he had twice at Bath given Sarah "a name":

The Managers conceiving that "Titter" was a most inpropitious name for their first Tragic Actress I was consulted—& to avoid the little Wits of the City making it a subject of ridicule, & still to preserve an affinity of Sound I called her "Tittore", and by that appellation she passed, till at the Altar I again changed her name by giving her hand to the then happy Colls!

Progress reports continued to come to Jerningham, sometimes with a poem that Mr or Mrs Colls had written. She continued to act with some success at Bath and Bristol in 1788–89. Jerningham exerted his influence with letters to local magnates, evidently to some effect on her benefit night—"she had *Eighty Places* in the Boxes (thanks to *you* Sir), this, added to the liberality of the Town made the House Seventy One Pounds." But the managers believed she needed seasoning, so she engaged with the Swansea company for the summer, opening with Portia in *The Merchant of Venice*.

The Swansea engagement went well, but Sarah did not return to the Bath-Bristol company. She signed for a spring season with Brunton at Norwich early in 1790, acting until a week or two before the birth of a son, named Edward (for Jerningham). After that came Yarmouth in August 1790, an autumn in London (where Colls was trying to place an opera at Covent Garden), Norwich again in the 1790–91 season, and then in 1791–92, she was with the company serving the circuit embracing Lichfield, Wolverhampton, Shrewsbury, Worcester, and Bewdley. She remained in that troupe until at least 1797.

The letters reflect the constant struggle required of these people of modest talents. Almost all are penned by Colls, who boasts affectionately of his wife's accomplishments and diffidently of his own, which include one or two dramas produced in small towns and numbers of poems printed in provincial newspapers. It was a losing fight. Evidently Colls had a share in the Worcester circuit but sold it and failed in his efforts to buy into a publishing firm. But in 1795 he reported "much connubial felicity . . . we have enjoyed these six years. . . . More 'tis hardly possible to experience—for bating our lack of independence—I think we are objects that even Angels might envy."

In 1797, Mrs Colls joined a small company in Lancashire. A letter from Plymouth on 9 August 1798 from Granville Leveson-Gower, first Earl Granville, to Jerningham assures him that Colls will immediately be given an ensign's commission in the earl's regiment. The last letter from Colls to Jerningham places Ensign and Mrs Colls at Winchester in June 1799. Meyler's letter to Jerningham of 29 April 1803 mentions the death some weeks before of Colls, praises him as "virtuous, manly & friendly," and pledges to assist his "Orphan Family."

Tittore. *See* TITTER.

Tivio, Mr ₁fl. 1782₁, *acrobat.*
The Bristol papers on 3 February 1782 advertised performances by Andrews's troupe "from *London*" at Coopers' Hall in King's Street. Participating in *Egyptian Pyramids* was a Mr Tivio, who presumably had appeared in London.

Tobin, Mr ₁fl. 1732₁, *dancer.*

Mr Tobin was a member of Madame Violante's troupe at the Haymarket Theatre in the fall of 1732. On 4 September he danced *Two Pierrots* with Lalauze, and on 11 September he was an Old Woman in a dance called *The White Joke*. On 12 September the troupe was at Richmond Wells, where Tobin and Lalauze again danced.

Todd, James *d. 1736, actor.*
At Covent Garden Theatre on 27 March 1736 James Todd played Skin'em in *A City Ramble*. He appeared at Southwark Fair as a Chimney Sweep in *The Innocent Wife* on 7 September. On 1 October *The Necromancer* was presented and Todd was standing in for Salway as the Miller's Man in a flying scene. The *Daily Post and General Advertiser* described what happened:

Last Night in the Entertainment of Dr Faustus . . . when the Machine wherein were Harlequin, the Miller's Wife, the Miller and his Man, was got up to the full Extent of its flying, one of the Wires which held up the hind part of the Car broke first, and then the other broke, and the Machine, and all the People in it fell down upon the Stage; by which unhappy Accident the young Woman who personated the Miller's Wife had her Thigh broke, and her Kneepan shattr'd, and was otherways very much bruised, the Harlequin had his Head bruised, and his Wrist strained; the Miller broke his Arm; and the Miller's Man had his Scull so fractured that his Life is despaired of.

The *Daily Advertiser* on 4 October reported:

Yesterday Morning Mr James Todd, who represented the Miller's Man on Friday Night . . . and fell in one of the flying Machines from the very top of the Stage by the breaking of the Wires, by which accident his Skull was fractur'd, died in a miserable manner. Susan Warwick, who represented the Miller's Wife, lies at the point of Death. . . . The two other Persons who fell in the same Machine are like to recover.

All four of those who were in the accident were "Servants belonging to the Theatre, and only Representatives ["doubles"] in the different Characters of Mr Lun [John Rich], Mr Nivelon, Mr Salway, and Mrs Moreau."

Todi, Signora Francesco Saverio, Luiza Rosa, née d'Aguiar *1753–1833, singer.*
The mezzo-soprano Luiza Rosa d'Aguiar was born in Setubal, Portugal, on 9 January

Civica Raccolta Stampe A. Bertarelli, Castello Sforzesco,
Milan

LUIZA ROSA TODI

engraving by DePian, after Bini

1753, according to the notice in *The New Grove Dictionary of Music and Musicians,* from which many of the facts for this entry are taken. Her first appearances in Lisbon were in straight comedy, in 1768, when she was only 14. In Lisbon she studied music with David Perez and married Francesco Saverio Todi, leader of the band at the theatre. She made her opera debut at Lisbon in 1770, in Scolari's *Il viaggiatore ridicolo.*

In 1777–78, as Signora Todi, she appeared in London, singing parts unspecified in Paisiello's *Le due contesse,* Grassman's *L'amore artigiano,* the pastiche *Il marchese villano,* and Piccini's *La buona figliuola,* and the original Ottavina in Andrei and Sacchini's *L'amore soldato.* At the time of her benefit, 2 April 1778, her address was No 12, Haymarket. Lord Mount-Edgcumbe in his *Musical Reminiscences* (1824) recalled that she had "failed to please here," and Charles Burney in *A General History of Music* (1782), observed, "She must have improved very much since she was in England,

or we treated her very unworthily, for, though her voice was thought to be feeble and seldom in tune while she was here, she has since been extremely admired in France, Spain, Russia and Germany as a most touching and exquisite performer."

Signora Todi was certainly sensationally successful at the Concert Spirituel in Paris in 1778. She returned in 1779 to Lisbon but was again acclaimed in Paris in 1781. In 1782 she was engaged for the Berlin Opera at a yearly salary of 2000 thaler, but her "French" mannerisms were unsatisfactory to the Berlin public, and she returned again to Paris. There at the Concert Spirituel she and Madame Gertrude Mara appeared together, dividing the audience into contending factions of "Maratistes" and "Todistes."

In Berlin again in 1783 Signora Todi attracted the notice of the King as Cleofide in *Lucio Papirio.* He urged her to remain in Prussia, but she had signed a contract with the opera in St Petersburg. There she was greatly successful in Sarti's *Armida e Rinaldo* and developed a warm and influential relationship with Catherine the Great after publishing *Pollinia,* dedicated to the Empress.

The King of Prussia lured her back to Berlin with extravagant offers in 1787, and she remained there until 1789, except for a few months more in Russia. In the latter part of her career she sang at Mainz, Hanover, Venice, Prague, Turin, and Madrid. She retreated to Portugal in 1793. Her last lengthy engagement was at the San Carlo theatre in Naples, 1797 to 1799.

Signora Todi spent the rest of her long life in Lisbon, dying there on 1 October 1833. (The account in Grove's fifth edition reported that "She was twice married [but Grove did not give the name of her second husband] and left to her husband and her eight children who survived her a sum of 400,000 francs, besides jewels and trinkets worth a fortune.") The *New Grove* gives an analysis of her bravura style and furnishes a considerable bibliography.

A portrait of Signora Todi engraved by De Pian, after Bini, was published at Venice in 1791. *Grove's Dictionary* cites "a pretty and scarce portrait [engraving] of her in character, singing, called 'L'Euterpe del secolo XVIII' (1791)." She also appears in a large group of singers on a plate engraved by the studio of Rainaldi, after a design by Antonio Fedi, published at Florence, 1801–7.

"Toe, Mr" [*fl. 1752–1758*], *actor, singer.*

"Mr. Toe," another of Christopher Smart's pseudonyms for a performer working in his "Mrs Midnight" entertainments, delivered a new prologue at the Haymarket Theatre on 1 April 1752. On the eighteenth, Toe's benefit night, he spoke and sang a prologue and epilogue, as he did again on 5 May. Toe received another benefit on 31 March 1753, sang "The Just Cart" on 10 April (accompanied by "Bombasto"), and was in Smart's *Old Woman's Oratory* on 18 May 1758.

Tofts, Catherine, later Mrs Joseph Smith *1685?–1756, singer.*

Catherine Tofts was probably born about 1685, if Mollie Sands's guess in *Theatre Notebook,* 20, is correct; *The Dictionary of National Biography* suggests about 1680. Catherine was said to have been connected with the family of Bishop Burnet and to have had her early vocal training in England. Her first known appearance was at Drury Lane Theatre on 30 November 1703, when she sang several songs in Italian and English, "accompany'd by the best Masters in England." She sang again on 21 December, this time at Lincoln's Inn Fields. "Mrs" Tofts was at Drury Lane again on 4 January 1704, singing songs by Henry Purcell from *The Fairy Queen, King Arthur, The Prophetess* (*Dioclesian*), and *Bonduca* and an ode on the accession of Queen Anne by Daniel Purcell. On 18 January she sang Pallas in *The Judgment of Paris.*

Mrs Tofts's chief rival was Margherita de l'Épine, who sang for the first time at Drury Lane on 29 January 1704. When she repeated her songs on 5 February Ann Barwick, who was a maid to Mrs Tofts, created a disturbance in the audience. Mrs Tofts wrote to the *Daily Courant* the following day, addressing her note to the manager of Drury Lane, Christopher Rich:

I was very much surpriz'd when I was inform'd that Ann Barwick, who was lately my servant, had committed a Rudeness last Night at the Play-

house, by throwing Oranges, and hissing when Mrs l'Epine, the Italian Gentlewoman Sung. I hope no one can think that it was in the least with my Privity, as I assure you it was not. I abhor such practices; and I hope you will cause her to be prosecuted, that she may be punished, as she deserves.

On the eighth the *Daily Courant* reported that "Ann Barwick having occasioned a disturbance at the theatre-royal Drury-lane on Saturday night last, the 5th of February, [was] thereupon taken into custody. . . ." On 16 January 1705 Mrs Tofts sang the title role in *Arsinoe.*

A year later, on 3 March 1705, a poem on Mrs Tofts by Samuel Phillips appeared in the *Diverting Post:*

> How are we pleas'd when beauteous Tofts appears,
> To steal our Souls through our attentive Ears?
> Ravish'd we listen to th' inchanting Song,
> And catch the falling Accents from her Tongue:
> With Raptures entertain the pleasing Sound,
> Whose very Softness had a Pow'r to Wound:
> Pleasure and Pain she does at once impart,
> Charms every Sense, and peirces every Heart,
> Each Word's a Salve, but every Shake's a Dart.

The scribblers were busy that summer. On 16 June the *Diverting Post* printed an "Epilogue for the Theatre Royal" that complained of small audiences, split between the two rival acting companies, while Signora de l'Épine and Mrs Tofts, both at Drury Lane, "sneak off with all our Gains." Another poem, "The Power of Musick," suggested that the members of Parliament were not doing their jobs because they were too busy listening to de l'Épine and Tofts.

John Hughes suggested in one of his poems that there were political overtones to the followings that Mrs Tofts and Signora de l'Épine each inspired:

> Music has learn'd the discords of the state,
> And concerts jar with Whig and Tory hate.
> Here Somerset and Devonshire attend
> The British Tofts, and every note commend,
> To native merit just, and pleas'd to see
> We've Roman arts, from Roman bondage free.
> Then fam'd L'Epine does equal skill employ,
> While list'ning peers crowd to th' ecstatic joy:
> Bedford, to hear her song, his dice forsakes,
> And Nottingham is raptur'd when she shakes.

Mrs Tofts was still singing at Drury Lane in 1705–6, but in midseason she stopped, hav-

ing encountered difficulties with the tyrannical Christopher Rich. Her "case," hand-dated
8 January 1706, is among the Lord Chamberlain's papers. She said that on 30 December
1704 she had agreed to sing for Rich at Drury
Lane for one year, beginning on 5 January
1705. A dispute later arose about a gift of £60
which Mrs Tofts had received from the nobility; Rich, typically, wanted half. When he
lost that squabble, according to Mrs Tofts,

He tooke all the Opportunity he could to be Revenged on her: which was in calling her to Sing
oftner than She was Able to performe. . . .
Through his ill Nature he called her to sing on a
Tuesday, Thursday, and Saturday in the same
week, not in hopes of getting audiences (it being
after Midsumer the Weather Excessive hott and the
Towne very Empty) but only to shew his ill will.

She lost her voice one Tuesday, and at the end
of the season Rich held back £20 of her £100
salary because of that; he refused to let her
have the £20 until she had sung twice, on 10
July and 29 October 1705.

She claimed that she had spent a great deal
of money on doctors, and

after all her Care and Expences the time being near
that she was to performe again She desired him to
gett Cloathes fitt for her to appear in the Opera,
these that she had before being not only worne out,
but were never made fitt for her, To which he an-
swered he supposed She had a mind to improve
herself that she might be in a Condition to Raise
her price.

She called Rich "a Man unfitt to deale with
for his ill Manners & Management of them
which are in his power."

The musician Charles Dieupart on 28 January 1706 delivered Mrs Tofts's proposals. She
wanted a salary of £100, release from past for-
feitures, 22 guineas "for what is past," and
jewels (Rich could keep the clothes). New articles were to be entered into, for three
months; Mrs Tofts would sing 12 times for
£200 (£16 13s. 4d. for each performance), and
she wanted the money before the curtain went
up. She would make up any missed performances at a later date. She was to be provided a
harpsichord accompanist and "that Roome
called the Practicing Roome to Dress in," with
two women dressers. Rich was to provide her
with "two Bottles of Wine every time she
Sings to be for her Use to dispose of them to

the Gentlemen that practice with her." She
would not be obliged to sing more than twice
in one day. Finally, she demanded a benefit on
19 February.

How many of those demands were met cannot be determined; she did not get the benefit
she asked for on 19 February 1706, and, in
fact, the bills do not show any benefit for her
that spring, so she may have had to settle for
far less than she wanted. She sang the title
role in *Camilla* on 30 March and "her own
part" in *Arsinoe* on 14 June.

Among Vice-Chamberlain Coke's papers at
Harvard are a number of documents pertaining to the opera singers, who, in 1706–7,
were at Drury Lane but in 1707–8 shifted in
mid-season to the Queen's Theatre. One of the
documents is a request to the Vice-
Chamberlain, submitted by Mrs Tofts and
other members of the opera troupe, for assistance against Christopher Rich. They pointed
out that their season, compared with the regular theatrical season, was short, but they had
the added expense of keeping their voices in
shape, an especially difficult task in English
weather—hence their need for higher than
usual salaries. Mrs Tofts complained that she
had her own clothes made for her role in *Camilla* at a cost of 80 guineas. Rich had not made
more than three suits of clothes for her,
though she had performed in four operas. Because of the importance of her parts she had
extra expenses for jewelry, ribbons, veils,
gloves, and the like, for the purchase of which
£100 was not sufficient for a season. Added to
the complaint was a note that several of the
singers, as of 31 December 1707, were owed
money by Rich; Mrs Tofts claimed her arrears
came to £24 10s.

In A. M. Broadley's "Annals of the Haymarket" at the Westminster Public Library is
yet another letter from Mrs Tofts, probably
written on 18 December 1707, to Vice-
Chamberlain Coke:

I have Seen yᵉ ordʳˢ you have Sent to Mr Dieupart and am very Sorry that I should be put to yᵉ
necessity of dining [*sic,* perhaps declining] I am
convinced that none but Mr Rich's frinds could
prevail upon my Lᵈ & you have Thomyris down
wᵗʰout having matters Settled So that we may be
Seckeurd from farther trobles Put [But] if it is my
Lᵈˢ pleasure that I Should be Sylent I willingly
Submit to his LᵈShips commands and am con-

tented to wait for a better oportunity in hops that in case fresh orders Should come that I must Sing again 80 guines that I laid out last winter for Camilla's Cloths by ye order of a Noble man who is Mr Riches best friend wth Mr Richs consent Shall be payd to me otherwise I am resolvd never to Sing Sett my foot upon ye Stage again Since it is to my great loss that I have done it hitherto by reason of ye expence that I have been att and must Daily to make a tollerable appearance Since Mr Ritch won't allow necessary's Therefore I humbly beg of my Ld Chamberlain not to depend upon my performance in Thomyris on Saturday next Since I am resolved not to do it till I have 80 guineas Sent to me by Mr Rich beside what I must have for my days Performance. . . .

Early in 1708 Mrs Tofts sent Sir John Vanbrugh the following articles of agreement:

In obedience to y^r Lord^ps comand I humbly propose to sing upon ye following terms
1st I obleige myself to sing as often as required for twenty Guinneys each time
2^d In Consideration ye year is so far advanc'd I offer to sing as often as Operas shall be performd till ye first of July for four hundred Guinneys
3^d I humbly propose to sing for Tenn Guinneys A time till ye first of July next upon condition ye Under taker obleige themselves to call me to sing twice a week
4^ly That I may not be debard singing at a Play wch is comeing out upon condition it does not interfere wth an Opera All wch is humbly offerd to y^r Lord^ps consideration. . . .

That she may have been a difficult artist to deal with goes without saying, but she was apparently a fine singer, the first singer of English birth to sing Italian opera. She held her own against native Italians, usually receiving the leading roles. In addition to Camilla and Arsinoe, she sang Queen Elinor in *Rosamond* (Drury Lane, 4 March 1707), Cleora in *Thomyris* (Drury Lane, 1 April 1707), Licisca in *Love's Triumph* (Queen's, 26 February 1708), Climene (or, according to a document in the Harvard Coke papers, Deidamia) in *Pirro e Demetrio* (14 December 1708), and Isabella in *Clotilda* (2 March 1709).

Colley Cibber was perhaps no expert on music, but he admired Mrs Tofts:

Mrs. *Tofts,* who took her first Ground of Musick here in her own Country, before the *Italian Taste* had so highly prevail'd, was then not an Adept at it: Yet whatever Defect the fashionably Skilful might find in her manner, she had, in the general

Sense of her Spectators, Charms that few of the most learned Singers ever arrive at. The Beauty of her fine proportion'd Figure, and exquisitely sweet, silver Tone of her Voice, with that peculiar, rapid Swiftness of her Throat, were Perfections not to be imitated by Art or Labour.

Dr Burney never heard Mrs Tofts, but on the basis of the music written for her he was able to draw some conclusions. She

seemed to have endeared herself to an English audience by her voice, figure, and performance, more than any preceding singer of our own country whose name and excellence have been recorded. . . .

This performer had songs given to her in all styles; her compass, however, did not surpass the common limits of a *soprano,* or treble voice. With respect to her execution, of which we are still enabled to judge by the printed copies of her songs, it chiefly consisted in such passages as are comprised in the shake, as indeed did that of most singers at this time. In *Arsinoe* and *Camilla* not one division occurs of great length or difficulty; but in *Pyrrhus and Demetrius* many. However, those of Mrs. Tofts are, in general, easy and common, except in one song. . . .

She and Signora de l'Épine were the highest-paid singers in the opera company, receiving, according to the Coke papers, £7 10s. each daily, or £400 for a season (another document lists Mrs Tofts at £500 and Signora de l'Épine at £400). Those were extraordinary salaries for the time—far beyond what the best actors received—and they set a pattern for singers for the rest of the century.

An epigram, attributed to Pope but probably not by him, goes:

So bright is thy beauty, so charming thy song,
As had drawn both the beasts and their Orpheus along;
But such is thy avarice, and such is thy pride,
That the beasts must have starved, and the poets have died.

In addition to her opera roles, Mrs Tofts sometimes offered entr'acte songs, but she seems rarely to have appeared at concerts or other musical events. One exception was a performance at the disused Dorset Garden Theatre on 30 October 1706, when an anonymous group of women presented *Pastor Fido,* with Mrs Tofts singing between the acts. Lady Wentworth in a letter dated 10 December 1708 told of a rehearsal of *Pirro e Demetrio* the day before, apparently at the Duchess of Marl-borough's house; the Duchess had persuaded Nicolini, the *castrato,* to sing, "but Mrs. Taufs huft and would not sing because he had first put it ofe; though she was thear yet she would not, but went away. I wish the house would al joyne to humble her and not receav her again." On 13 March 1709 at a party at the Duke of Somerset's, Mrs Tofts sang, and kisses were sold at a guinea each.

At the end of the 1708–9 season Mrs Tofts left the stage, for what reasons we cannot tell; she may have carried her haughtiness too far, but there was a revolution at the theatres and she may have fallen a victim to it. Christopher Rich was ousted at Drury Lane, and the new management, at first under Aaron Hill, may not have cared to keep so expensive and tem-peramental a singer. There was also a story that Mrs Tofts became mentally disturbed for a while. Her last stage appearance was prob-ably on 21 May 1709 as Camilla. Steele wrote of Mrs Tofts, calling her Camilla, in the *Tatler* on 26 May, describing

the distresses of the unfortunate Camilla who nas had the ill luck to break before her voice, and to disappear at a time when her beauty was in the height of its bloom. This lady entered so thor-oughly into the great characters she acted, that when she had finished her part, she could not think of retrenching her equipage, but would appear in her own lodgings with the same magnificence that she did upon the stage. This greatness of soul has reduced that unhappy Princess to an involuntary retirement where she now passes her time among the woods and forests, thinking on the crowns and sceptres she has lost, and often humming over in her solitude

> *I was born of royal race*
> *Yet must wander in disgrace.*

In the summer of 1711 Mrs Tofts, calling herself Smith, went to Rotterdam. She by then may have married Joseph Smith, a gen-eral merchant who later became the British consul in Venice, though some evidence sug-gests a wedding years later. In the *Huntington Library Quarterly* in November 1961 Robert Schafer transcribed a letter from Anthony Hammond to James Brydges (later the Duke of Chandos) dated 25 July 1711, Rotterdam:

This leads me to another point, wch. I wd. not presume to trouble you with, but fear you may hear it misrepresented. In another Pacquet came over at ye same time with me a Lady who went by ye name of Smith, at Helvoestsluys we met & I had once seen her for half an hour in her Pacquet boat where an impertinent fellow had pin'd himself upon her, he was it seems a Page to ye Count Tar-ouca. . . . In short I take him little better than a Pimp to ye Count his Master. . . . The impudence of this fellow & my civility prevail'd with this Lady to go with us to ye Hague, as we were going along examining her face, and considering her shape more exactly, I discover'd her to be M^{rs}. Tofts. That first scene was pleasure enough, but too long to relate. At ye Hague we lodg'd in ye same House, & being discover'd like a mine, she show'd her riches, & now & then gave me a piece of a Song & a conversation agreable enough, but here our officer declar'd himself, & ply'd her so close in favour of the Count his Master, that She was Sick, frighted & tir'd out worse than if she had been still in ye Pacquet. While I was preparing to go to this place, he prevail'd with her the other day to show her ye House in ye Wood where ye Count follow'd in his Caleche, & in a proper part of ye House, he & two friends more appear'd, she was so startled that he had not ye reception he hoped for, wch. rebutted him. He & his friends withdrew, but our Officer for this Stratagem She treated roughly & yesterday beg'd to come with me to Rotterdam. I saw no inconvenience, because I make it no charge to bring her hither, where She is now in private lodgings, expecting some friends from England to go with her to Hanover, where Valentini [the singer] meets her, upon some design of an Opera, wch. is a secret to me.

Mrs Tofts was probably in Venice by De-cember 1711. Mollie Sands suggests that she may have gone there because of her acquaint-ance with the opera impresario Owen Swiney, who was there in 1710 or 1711. One of Swi-ney's friends in Venice was Joseph Smith.

On 25 April 1712 the *Daily Courant* in London was able to report from Venice:

An English Gentlewoman named Mrs. Tofts hath been much applauded here for her fine singing, wherein she hath succeeded all the excellent voices on the stage of Venice. This lady hath sung in all the great Assemblies that were held at the Elec-toral Prince of Saxony's, and Signor Grimani hath endeavoured by all means to prevail upon her to remain here to sing in the Theatre of Chrysostome, but it is believed she will rather chuse to return to her own Country, and the rather seeing the Opera's at London are better served at present than any in Europe. . . .

But she did not return to England.

15 TOFTS

"Camilla" wrote to the *Spectator* on 29 July 1712:

Mr. SPECTATOR.

"I TAKE it extremely ill, that you do not reckon conspicuous Persons of your Nation are within your Cognizance, tho' out of the Dominions of *Great-Britain*. I little thought in the green Years of my Life, that I should ever call it an Happiness to be out of dear *England;* but as I grew to Woman, I found my self less acceptable in Proportion to the Encrease of my Merit. Their Ears in *Italy* are so differently formed from the Make of yours in *England*, that I never come upon the Stage, but a general Satisfaction appears in every Countenance of the whole People. When I dwell upon a Note, I behold all the Men accompanying me with Heads enclining, and falling of their Persons on one Side, as dying away with me. The Women too do Justice to my Merit, and no ill-natur'd worthless Creature cries, *The vain Thing*, when I am wrapp'd up in the Performance of my Part, and sensibly touch'd with the Effect my Voice has upon all who hear me. I live here distinguished, as one whom Nature has been liberal to in a graceful Person, an exalted Mein, and Heavenly Voice. These Particularities in this strange Country, are Arguments for Respect and Generosity to her who is possess'd of them. The *Italians* see a thousand Beauties I am sensible I have no Pretence to, and abundantly make up to me the Injustice I received in my own Country, of disallowing me what I really had. The Humour of Hissing, which you have among you, I do not know any thing of; and their Applauses are utter'd in Sighs, and bearing a Part at the Cadences of Voice with the Persons who are performing. I am often put in Mind of those complaisant Lines of my own Countryman, when he is calling all his Faculties together to hear *Arabella;*

Let all be hush'd, each softest Motion cease,
Be ev'ry loud tumultuous Thought at Peace;
And ev'ry ruder Gasp of Breath
Be calm, as in the Arms of Death:
And thou, most fickle, most uneasy Part,
Thou restless Wanderer, my Heart,
Be still; gently, ah! gently leave,
Thou busy, idle Thing, to heave.
Stir not a Pulse; and let my Blood,
That turbulent, unruly Flood,
   Be softly staid:
Let me be all but my Attention dead.

The whole City of *Venice* is as still when I am singing, as this polite Hearer was to Mrs. *Hunt*. But when they break that Silence, did you know the Pleasure I am in, when every Man utters his Applause, by calling me aloud the *Dear Creature*, the *Angel*, the *Venus; What Attitude she moves with!*—

Hush, she sings again! We have no boisterous Wits who dare disturb an Audience, and break the publick Peace meerly to shew they dare. Mr. SPECTATOR, I write to you thus in Haste, to tell you I am very much at Ease here, that I know nothing but Joy; and I will not return, but leave you in *England* to hiss all Merit of your own Growth off the Stage. I know, Sir, you were always my Admirer, and therefore I am yours,

Camilla.

'P.S. I am ten times better dress'd than ever I was in *England*.'

On 18 September 1716 Alexander Cunningham wrote (in a letter now at the Public Record Office), "As for Mr. Smith he is so much in love wt. Mrs. Tofts he is fitt for nothing at present. . . ." Mollie Sands believes that Smith probably married Mrs Tofts at the end of 1716 or in 1717. He was born about 1674, was in Venice by 1709, and was a lover and in time a patron of the arts. He amassed a formidable library, doted on opera and drama, and seems not to have been very well-liked by Englishmen who knew him.

The Smiths' home in Venice was the Palazzo Balbi (now the Argentine Consulate), and they had a villa at Mogliano. Possibly their son was the John Smith (1721–1727) who was buried at the Church of the SS Apostoli, near the Palazzo Balbi. Mrs Smith's mental illness returned, according to Hawkins in his *General History*. She lived "sequestered from the world, in a remote part of the house, and had a large garden to range in, in which she would frequently walk, singing, and giving way to that innocent frenzy which had seized her in the earlier part of her life."

According to the inscription on her tombstone in the Protestant Cemetery of San Nicolò del Lido, Mrs Smith died in 1756. Under the Tofts coat of arms was inscribed "Catherine Tofts / uxori incomparabili / de se bene merenti / quae obiit anno MDCCLVI / diutino vexata morbo / nec unquam displicuit nisi erepti / Joseph Smith Consul Britannicus / moerens fecit." In *Odes of Importance* (1794) by "Peter Pindar" is the statement that Catherine Tofts had 20 cats and left a legacy to each one.

Joseph Smith was married about 1757 to Eliza Murray. He died, aged about 96, on 6 November 1770.

At Castle Howard is a picture by Marco Ricci of an opera rehearsal of *Pirro e Demetrio* in which Mrs Tofts is shown with Margherita de l'Épine, Dr Pepusch, Nicolini, and others. There are some six versions of the painting, which are discussed by Eric Walter White in *Theatre Notebook,* 14, and by Mollie Sands in the same number of that journal (Autumn 1964). It is suggested to us by Joanne Lafler (author of *The Celebrated Mrs Oldfield*) that a portrait by an unknown engraver which has been identified in the Harvard Theatre Collection catalogue as Mrs Oldfield as Rosamond (published with an edition of *Rosamond* in 1778) is not Mrs Oldfield but possibly could be Mrs Tofts.

Tognioni. *See* TAGNONI.

Tokely, James *1790–1819, actor, dancer, singer.*

The 1814 edition of *Authentic Memoirs of the Green Room* gives a sketch of the first 24 years of the life of James Tokely. He was born on 31 October 1790 of respectable parents in London in a neighborhood near Russell Street. A relative, "being concerned in the mechanical part" of one of the theatres, "young Tokely early imbibed a predilection for the stage; and at the infantile age of three years made his first appearance in the character of a Cupid, in a piece called Jack of Newbury, brought out the first season of the late Drury-lane theatre, in 1794." The bills do not reflect his participation (the piece opened in May 1795). They give Cupid instead to Master Welsh, but perhaps Tokely was somewhere among the numerous "Loves, Graces," and chorus members, not all of whom are named.

Tokely is supposed by the *Authentic Memoirs* account to have continued in such parts—the playbills offer no proof—until Benjamin Thompson's drama *The Stranger* was produced, when, indeed, the bills do show him in the part of the Stranger's Son, on 24 March 1798 and for 26 nights during that season. On 5 June 1798 he had a part unspecified in John O'Keeffe's new interlude *The Eleventh of June.* He was one of the *Children in the Wood* at the Haymarket on 28 June, a part he resumed the following winter season at Drury Lane. He played Goliah in *The Young Quaker* on 22 November 1798. The following summer he returned to the Haymarket as Harry in Henry Neuman's new drama *Family Distress* on 15

June and played one of the Children again on 18 June; that part he repeated at Drury Lane on 26 September 1799. His only other roles that season were the Child in *The Embarkation,* Andrew Franklin's new afterpiece, on 3 October, and the Child in *Isabella,* on 22 November 1799.

Though the playbills before the century's end reflect only those tiny parts, he was likely pushed on in others, for he was credited by the *Authentic Memoirs* with "the Page in *The Purse,* and the Duke of York, and Prince of Wales" in *Richard III,* probably before the end of the century. When the brief mass infatuation for child performers, centering on Master William Betty, began around 1804, "young Tokely played the Prince [of Wales] to [Betty's] Richard [III]; and the likeness, both in face and figure, was so striking, that, but for the difference in dress, they might have been brothers." But, alas, "growing too stout for children's characters," Tokely moved into Servants' roles and "was after knocked about by the Clown in comic pantomimes, and now and then engaged in desperate theatrical broad-sword combats."

Growing discouraged at his prospects, he "wisely determined to try the country." That must have been after 1807–8, when his name disappeared from the Drury Lane lists at the Folger Library and the British Library. He had been paid £1 5s. 0d. in 1806–7 and £1 10s. 0d. in 1807–8. (In 1801–2 a sweeper named Tokely was earning 6s. per week and in June 1807 another "Tokeley" was listed among the house servants. We cannot say what connection they may have had to James.)

James Tokely is said by the *Authentic Memoirs* to have acted at Brighton and then to have joined Hughes's management "as a low comedian, in which line he continued with great success at the different theatres of Exeter, Weymouth, and Guernsey, for more than five years." He came back to Drury Lane at Christmas season, 1813, to play Robin Roughhead in *Fortune's Frolic* and Tony Lumpkin in *She Stoops to Conquer* with approbation. As late as the season 1813–14, William Cotton in *The Story of the Drama in Exeter* confirms that Tokely had sung comic entr'acte songs, played Scaramouche, and acted such parts as Artaxominous in *Bombasto Furioso* on the Exeter circuit.

Harvard Theatre Collection

JAMES TOKELY, as Dick Hatterick
by De Wilde

By permission of the Trustees of the British Museum

JAMES TOKELY, as Peter Pastoral

by Cruikshank

We do not know how long Tokely remained at Drury Lane after his return. He had been on the Haymarket summer list every season from 1804 through 1810, at least, and James Winston's transcripts at the Folger Library show him there also in summers from 1815 through 1817, in which years Mrs Tokely was also engaged, as a dresser, at 9*s.* per week. The register of St Giles in the Fields shows that at some time in 1816 James "Tokeley" of 2 Denmark Street, "Comedian at the Theatre Royal, Covent Garden," and his wife Mary baptized a child, whose name was not given in the register.

The *Theatrical Inquisitor* (1814) found that Tokely had "considerable powers of vulgar humour: . . . The person of Mr. Tokely is ungraceful, his stature low, and his face expressive only of contented stupidity; but in characters like those he has selected . . . these imperfections are scarcely observable. . . ."

The *European Magazine* for February 1819 reported that James Tokely, of Covent Garden Theatre, had died on 9 January.

A watercolor drawing by Samuel De Wilde of James Tokely as Dick Hatterick in *Guy Mannering* is in the Harvard Theatre Collection. A watercolor by De Wilde, September 1817, of Tokely as Peter Pastoral in *Teasing Made Easy* is in the Garrick Club (No 59B); it shows a stout man, standing full-length, with a hat in his right hand. An engraved portrait by I. R. Cruikshank of Tokely as Peter Pastoral, standing, full-length, holding a hat and flowers, was published as a plate to *British Stage,* 1817.

Tollard, Mons *fl. 1723₁*,   *acrobat.*
At the Richmond Theatre on 2 September 1723 the actor-manager William Pinkethman presented, among other entertainments, tumbling by Monsieur Tollard, recently arrived from Madrid.

Tollet, Mr *fl. 1714₁*,   *actor.*
Mr Tollet was a member of a company that called themselves the Duke of Southampton and Cleaveland's Servants. In the summer of 1714 they presented *Injured Virtue* at Richmond; they repeated the work on 1 November at the King's Arms Tavern, Southwark.

Tollett, Mrs *fl. 1731–1732₁*,   *actress.*
Mrs Tollett played Betty (and Miss Tollett played Mrs Lovely) in *A Bold Stroke for a Wife* at Fielding's booth at Southwark Fair on 28 September 1731. One supposes the two women were mother and daughter. The younger one in time married Samuel Crisp, and as Mrs Crisp she is entered in this dictionary. In 1731–32 the two women were at Goodman's Fields Theatre, and the bills did not distinguish them carefully. The younger Tollett, whose Christian name was Henrietta Maria, was sometimes called Miss but sometimes Mrs; she had recently reached her majority, and in such cases young women were addressed as either Miss or Mrs for a year or two.

In any case, we believe the elder Tollett was the one who played the Mother to Cadiere (Colombine) in *Father Girard* on 2 February 1732, Catherine in *The Footman* on 7 March, a Countrywoman in *The Stratagem* on 23

March, and Mrs Motherly in *The Provok'd Husband* on 17 May.

Tollett, Mrs ₁*fl. 1793*₁. *See* FOLLETT, MRS JOHN.

Tollett, Charles ₁*fl. 1668?–1717*₁, *musician.*

A Lord Chamberlain's warrant dated 7 September 1715 authorized livery payments to instrumentalists in the King's Musick, among whom was Charles Tollett. His annual salary was £40, but he did not enjoy it for long: on 20 August 1717 he was replaced by Talbot Young. There was a Charles Tollett who, with two other Tolletts, Thomas and John, was a member of the Dublin City Music from 1668 or 1678 to 1688, but we cannot tell if he was our subject.

Tollett, Henrietta Maria. *See* CRISP, MRS SAMUEL.

Tollett, Thomas *d. 1696?, musician, composer.*

W. J. Lawrence found that Thomas, John, and Charles Tollett (brothers?) were members of the Dublin City Music from 1678 to 1688 (the *New Grove* says between 1669 and 1688). In 1689 or 1690 Thomas came to London, and in 1691 he set a song for D'Urfey's *The Marriage-Hater Match'd*. He composed other theatre tunes for *The Cheats* (c. 1693) and *The Virtuous Wife* (1699) (and Grove adds *The Lover's Luck* [1696]). In 1692 Tollett and John Lenton published *A Consort of Musick in Three Parts,* and Tollett wrote *Directions to Play on the French Flageolet.* By 22 June 1694 Tollett's name began appearing in the Lord Chamberlain's accounts in connection with a place for him in the King's Musick. On 27 March 1695 he received an appointment, but it was without fee, and he had to wait for a vacancy. He replaced Robert Carr on 9 January 1696, but the following 2 September it was agreed that upon Tollett's death his livery and wages were to go to John Eccles. That suggests that Tollett was then old or in poor health. By 1697 Eccles received his appointment, but the records do not indicate whether Tollett died or retired. Grove guesses that he may have died in 1696.

In addition to the *Consort,* Tollett composed a farewell piece for the Queen's funeral in 1695. Some of his manuscript music is at the Bodleian Library.

Tollett, William ₁*fl. 1664*₁, *piper.*

The Lord Chamberlain appointed William Tollet a "bag-piper in ordinary" in the King's Musick on 23 February 1664.

Tolly, Thomas ₁*fl. 1724*₁, *house servant.*

The Lincoln's Inn Fields Theatre accounts show that Thomas Tolly worked as an attendant in the lobby during November 1724 at 8s. weekly. On 21 December he was paid 16s. for 12 days' work as "street keeper."

Tolman, Mr ₁*fl. 1794*₁, *messenger.*

The Drury Lane Theatre accounts cite Mr Tolman as a messenger on 3 May 1794. Surely the same person was the messenger "Tottman" mentioned on the following 8 November.

Tolman, John ₁*fl. 1763–1770*₁, *musician.*

John Tolman was bound apprentice to John Ward on 8 June 1763 and became a freeman of the Worshipfull Company of Musicians on 3 April 1770.

Tolve, Francesco ₁*fl. 1736–1737*₁, *singer.*

As a member of Porpora's opera troupe at the King's Theatre, Francesco Tolve sang Cosroe in *Siroe* on 23 November 1736, Polifonte in *Merope* on 8 January 1737, Fenicio in *Demetrio* on 12 February, and (advertised as "Signora Frances Tolve") the title roles in *Tito* on 12 April and *Demofoonte* on 24 May.

"Tom Fool." *See* BANISTER, JOHN.

"Tomasino, Signor." *See* LOWE, THOMAS.

"Tomaso." *See* GABRIELLI, TOMASO.

Tomasselli, Vincenzo. *See* GALEOTTI VICENZO.

Tombs, Mr ₁*fl. 1784*₁, *singer.*

Mr Tombs of Winchester sang bass in the Handel Memorial Concerts at Westminster

Abbey and the Pantheon in May and June 1784.

Tomes, Miss   *fl. c. 1786–1787₁,*   *dancer.*
Miss Tomes danced in a piece called *Nobody* at the Royal Circus, probably in the spring of 1786. She was named again in a Royal Circus bill in April 1787.

Tomkins, Mr   *fl. 1798–1802₁,*   *actor, singer.*
A Mr Tomkins acted for Tate Wilkinson at Hull in 1798. James C. Dibdin, in *The Annals of the Edinburgh Stage,* places that Mr Tomkins in the Liverpool theatrical company in 1798 and at the Theatre Royal, Shakespeare Square, Edinburgh, acting under the name Walpole, at some time in the 1798–99 season. Norma Armstrong's manuscript Edinburgh calendar preserves one character for him: Edwin in *Robin Hood* on 23 January 1799.

When the actor appeared first in London, at Drury Lane on 1 May 1799, as Pantaloon in the harlequinade *Robinson Crusoe,* he had reverted to his real name, Tomkins. It was his only notice in the bills that season. He went to Brighton for the summer and acted there as "Mr Walpole."

After the opening of the following season, 1799–1800, Tomkins somehow talked the Drury Lane management into bringing him on in a leading character, Lord Aimworth in *The Maid of the Mill,* and under the usual description "A Gentleman (First Appearance)." The *Monthly Mirror* for November identified him:

A Mr. Tomkins, who performed at the Brighton theatre, last summer, under the name of Walpole, was introduced, this evening, in the part of Lord Aimworth.—If this character did not require to be well spoken, beside being well sung, we should have little else than praise to bestow upon the present candidate, who has an agreeable tenor voice, of very ample compass, which he modulates with a more than ordinary degree of taste,—but, like nearly all young singers, he is unmeaning in action, awkward in deportment, and hurried, indistinct, and injudicious in delivery.

Management and the public agreed. Tomkins was seen no more in London. Apparently he went back to the provinces and assumed his old identity as Walpole. The *Monthly Mirror* for December 1802 reports

Liverpool benefit receipts of £54 for Mr Walpole.

Tomkins, Miss   *fl. 1750₁,*   *actress.*
Miss Tomkins played Jenny in *The Constant Couple* at Phillips's booth at Southwark Fair on 7 September 1750.

Tomkins, Miss   *fl. 1788₁,*   *actress.*
Miss Tomkins played Millener in *Harlequin's Frolic* at Bartholomew Fair in 1788.

Tomkins, Giles   *d. 1668, player on the virginal, organist, composer.*
Giles Tomkins, the sixth son of the musician Thomas Tomkins of St David's (c. 1545–1627), was appointed organist of King's College, Cambridge, in 1624. In 1629 he succeeded John Holmes as organist of Salisbury Cathedral. Tomkins was appointed "musician for the Virginalls" in the King's Musick on 2 April 1630, at a salary of £40 annually and a livery allowance of £16 2s. 6d. yearly. He was reappointed on 9 June 1660 and evidently attended the King in London from time to time even though his primary duties were in Salisbury. The Lord Chamberlain's accounts mentioned Giles Tomkins numerous times, usually in connection with livery payments long overdue. He died at Salisbury in April 1668

His will, dated 20 March 1668, when he was "sicke in body," described him as of the Close of Sarum, Wiltshire. Tomkins's servant Elizabeth Hewlett was left 30s. To his daughter Elizabeth Sinedmore (?) he left £50 or the equivalent in household goods. To his sister Elizabeth Blagden he gave 20s. for a ring. To his daughter Jane Siser and son John he left 20s. each, and to Jane's son Roger he left 40s. Giles Tomkins's wife Elizabeth was given 5s. His son William, "which I had by her," was to receive £5 when he reached his majority.

Any money due Tomkins from the King was to be equally divided among his five children, Thomas (b. 1631), Giles (1633–1725), John (b. 1637), Jane Siser, and Elizabeth Sinedmore. Any remainder was to be divided between Thomas, Giles, John, and Jane. Tomkins left his organ books to the Cathedral Church of Sarum (Salisbury Cathedral). The will was proved on 24 May 1669 by Tomkins's son Thomas. Tomkins composed some church music, but little has survived.

Denis Stevens's *Thomas Tomkins* includes a section on the Tomkins family generally, many of whom were musicians.

Tomkins, John   *fl. 1723₁*,   *doorkeeper.*
John Tomkins, doorkeeper at the King's Theatre, was given a benefit at the Haymarket Theatre on 15 April 1723.

Tomlenson. *See* TOMLINSON.

Tomlings, Mr   *fl. 1752–1761₁*,   *house servant?*
Mr Tomlings shared benefits at Drury Lane on 2 May 1752 and 20 May 1757 and may have been one of the house servants. The "Tom" cited in the benefit bill of 8 May 1761 was surely Tomlings and not Tomlinson (as *The London Stage* conjectures), since Tomlinson was named in another benefit bill later that month.

Tomlins, Mr   *fl. 1791₁*,   *actor.*
Mr Tomlins acted Elliot in *Venice Preserv'd* at the Haymarket Theatre on 24 October 1791.

Tomlinson, Mr   *fl. 1747–1781₁*, *house servant, actor.*
Mr Tomlinson shared a benefit with five others at Drury Lane Theatre on 14 May 1747. He was cited similarly in the years that followed, and on 10 May 1750 the bill indicated that he was one of the boxkeepers. On 9 May 1751 at his shared benefit he acted Simon Pure in *A Bold Stroke for a Wife* and spoke the following epilogue:

> After long strutting on and off the stage,
> One night a prelate, and the next a page;
> A soldier, senator, a clown, a lord,
> And all the while, ne'er spoke a single word;
> At length, surcharg'd with these, and favours past,
> My thanks burst from me, and I speak at last.
> But thanks are all, alas! I have no merit;
> A grateful heart is all that I inherit.
>   Could I, like our commander here in chief
> Raise up your joy, or sink you down in grief;
> Like him, had power to captivate the soul;
> Like him, to you I should devote the whole.

The commander in chief was, of course, David Garrick.

Most of the benefit bills mentioning Tomlinson give no indication of his performing,

but Garrick gave him occasional opportunities to do something other than walk-ons. On 20 May 1761 Tomlinson delivered another epilogue—or perhaps the old one, revised; he described himself (according to *The London Stage*) as the habitual stage mute who had played dumb-show prelates, senators, pages, and soldiers. The bill for 18 May 1762 advertised "*A New Sketch of his own picture drawn* from the life by way of *Epilogue*—Mr Tomlinson, his second time of attempting to speak on the Stage." The management had evidently forgotten his performance of 1751.

On 13 May 1763 Tomlinson essayed Sir Charles in *The Stratagem,* and on 17 May 1764 he delivered "A New Panegyri-Satiri-Serio-Comic Epilogue upon Epilogues." At some point Tomlinson's house duties changed from boxkeeper to dresser, for on 9 February 1765 the paylist has him so identified at a daily wage of 1*s. 6d.,* and the accounts in later years show payments to him for men's clothes. On 17 May 1765 he assumed the character of a Buck and spoke an epilogue, and on 27 May 1767 Silas Neville saw Tomlinson, in the character of a Beggar, deliver an epilogue which received so much hissing by some patrons and clapping by others that it could scarce be heard. The bills reveal shared benefits for Tomlinson through 25 May 1781; and the accounts in 1774–75 show that he still served as a supernumerary.

Tomlinson, Mr   *fl. 1794₁*,   *musician.*
Doane's *Musical Directory* (1794) notices a Mr Tomlinson of Talbot Court, Grace Church Street, "Tenor" (viola or voice?), who had performed in one of the "grand performances" celebrating Handel at Westminster Abbey after 1784.

Tomlinson, Mr   *fl. 1795₁*,   *house servant.*
Bills for the Royal Circus in April 1795 noted that places for the boxes could be had from Mr Tomlinson, a house servant at the Circus.

Tomlinson, Kellom (Kenelm)   *fl. 1715–1743₁*,   *dancer, dancing master, choreographer.*
In the preface to his treatise *The Art of Dancing* (1734), our subject sought to rectify

KELLOM TOMLINSON

engraving by Morellon la Cave, after Van Bleeck

"the Disadvantage to which I have been exposed by going accidentally under two different Names, *Kellom* and *Tomlinson. . . .*" He explained that

During the Time of my Apprenticeship I went generally by the name of *Kellom,* a Corruption of *Kenelm* my true Christian Name; . . . At the Expiration of my Apprenticeship, several of my Friends out of Respect called me by my Sur-Name of *Tomlinson;* but, being unwilling to decline the Advantage I might probably receive from the Reputation of having learned the Art of Dancing under so great a Master as Mr. *Caverley,* I chose rather to retain the Name of *Kellom. . . .* This Duplicity of Appellation turned afterwards to my great Disadvantage: many of the Nobility and Gentry, who would have had their Children taught by Mr. *Kellom,* refusing to employ Mr. *Tomlinson . . .*

and vice versa. Therefore he wished to be called in the future "by both conjunctly, *Kellom Tomlinson.*" The only other information that Tomlinson gave in the preface about his training was that he had been instructed also in theatrical dance by René Cherrier, a choreographer in the London theatres between 1699 and 1708.

If Tomlinson performed on the stage, no record remains. But John Topham, advertised as "Kellom's Scholar," danced at Drury Lane Theatre between 1716 and 1718, and Miss Francis (fl. 1719–1723) was Tomlinson's pupil when she made her debut at Lincoln's Inn Fields Theatre on 19 March 1719 in a "new Passacaille." Tomlinson also choreographed dances for the London theatres, several of which he listed in his preface: *The Passepeid Round O* in 1715; *The Shepherdess* in 1716; *The Submission* in 1717 (which, by the name of Mr Kellom's New Dance was performed by Sallé and Mlle Sallé at Lincoln's Inn Fields in February of that year); *The Prince Eugene* in 1718; *The Address* in 1719; *The Gavot* in 1720; and *The Passacaille Diana* in 1721 (danced by Miss Tenoe at Drury Lane on 10 May 1721?). Those six dances were published in a collection by Tomlinson in 1720 and were sold for a guinea and a half at his house in Devonshire Street, "the last but one on the right hand going to Queens Square by Ormond Street." The collection was embellished with 36 plates. Between 1715 and 1717 Tomlinson had lived at Mr Smith's, coach maker, at the corner of King's Gate Street, Holborn.

In 1734 Tomlinson published *The Art of Dancing,* with 37 plates. In his preface Tomlinson claimed that the book had been finished by 1724 and that he had advertised for subscribers several times between 1726 and 1728, without success. He accused the publisher of Rameau's *The Art of Dancing* of undercutting his potential subscribers by "assuming thus the very Title and Form of the Book proposed to the Publick by me."

Little else is known of Tomlinson's activities. At Covent Garden Theatre on 9 April 1743 a *New Ball Dance* composed by Tomlinson was performed by Villeneuve and Mrs Delagarde. Possibly he was related to the actor and house servant named Tomlinson who worked at Drury Lane Theatre from 1747 through 1781.

A portrait of Kellom Tomlinson was painted by Peter van Bleeck in 1716, but its location is unknown. An engraving of it by F. Morellon de la Cave was published as frontispiece to Tomlinson's *Art of Dancing,* 1754.

Tomlinson, Richard   *d. 1691, violinist.*

Richard Tomlinson (or Thomlinson, Tomleson) was a violinist in the King's Musick as early as 22 September 1674, when he accompanied the King on a trip to Newmarket. He spent much of his career on such journeys, going to Windsor or Newmarket or both almost every year through 1690. He received extra money for such services; his base salary as of March 1676, when he became a musician in ordinary, was £46 12*s.* 8*d.* He and three other court musicians were suspended on 22 November 1681 because they "neglected their duty in attending at ye play acted before his Ma^{te} at Whitehall" on the fifteenth.

Tomlinson was reappointed to the King's Musick under James II and again under William III, but the prudent William reduced his violinists' monthly salaries to £30. On 8 December 1690 Tomlinson was selected to accompany the King on a trip to Holland in January 1691, but he did not live to make the voyage. His will was dated 5 January 1691 and proved by his widow Elizabeth ten days later. The violinist left a shilling to his son Thomas and everything else to his wife. The will described Tomlinson as from the parish of St Clement Danes.

Tommasino, The. *See* LINLEY, THOMAS
1756–1778.

"Tommy." *See* LOWE, THOMAS.

Tomosein, Signor   ₁*fl. 1741*₁,   *dancer.*
Signor Tomosein, advertised as recently arrived from Italy, played Harlequin in *The Adventures of Harlequin in Spain* at Tottenham Court Fair on 4 August 1741.

Tompson, Mr   ₁*fl. 1797*₁,   *actor.*
Mr Tompson played Pillage in *The Romance of an Hour* at the Haymarket Theatre on 10 May 1797.

Toms, Mr   ₁*fl. 1790–1807*₁,   *actor.*
The actor Toms was reported by W. C. Oulton in *Authentic Memoirs of the Green Room* (1799) to be the son of a fishmonger.
On 4 October 1790 at Covent Garden Theatre, a "Young Gentleman," said to be making his first appearance on any stage, played the title character in *Douglas.* The *European Magazine* for October 1790 identified him as "Mr Turner," but both the *Morning Herald* and the *London Chronicle* subsequently (1795) and correctly called him Toms. He did not play in London again for nearly five years.
Toms turned up on the roster of the company of the Theatre Royal, Shakespeare Square, Edinburgh, on 29 January 1791, as Lord Gayfield in *The Heiress.* He finished the season at Edinburgh, adding to his repertoire Orlando in *As You Like It,* Sir George Euston in *I'll Tell You What,* Frederick in *The Miser,* Young Meanwell in *Tit for Tat,* and Oswald in *Arthur and Emmeline.*
On 30 January 1792 he acted (as "from Edinburgh") at the theatre in Waterford in Ireland and was still there on 21 March, according to W. S. Clark. Later in 1792 he played at Norwich. In June 1794 the *Thespian Magazine* reported him at Leominster. From Leominster he moved on to Weymouth, a royal resort, where, said the *Authentic Memoirs,* "he had the honor of meeting their Majesties' approbation; this afforded him another opportunity of trying the metropolis."
On 21 September 1795 the Covent Garden playbill announced that Mr Toms from Weymouth was making his first appearance on the Covent Garden stage, as Romeo in *Romeo and*

MR TOMS, as Titus
engraving by Wilson, after Graham

Juliet. The following day the *Morning Herald,* speaking of the "probationary essay last night in the character of Romeo," corrected that assertion: "his unsuccessful attempt in Young Norval [in *Douglas*], about five years ago, on the same boards, is perfectly within our recollection."
Toms remained at Covent Garden for three seasons, filling the following roles: in 1795–96, Tressel in *Richard III,* the Ghost in *Hamlet,* Pylades in *The Distrest Mother,* Raymond in *The Widow of Malabar,* Charles Davenant in *The Mysterious Husband,* Captain Pendant in *Arrived at Portsmouth,* the Earl of Northumberland in Richard Cumberland's new melodrama *Days of Yore,* Captain Arable in *Speculation,* Fenton in *The Merry Wives of Windsor,* Rodonsko in *Zorinski,* Bellcamp in *The Positive Man,* and Lord Edmond in *The Prisoner at Large;* in 1796–97, the Prince in *Romeo and Juliet,* Ganem in *The Mountaineers,* Albany in *King Lear,* Sir Walter Blunt in *I Henry IV,* Sey-

mour in *The Irishman in London*, Lodovico
in *Othello*, Octavio in *Two Strings to Your Bow*,
Neville in *The Dramatist*, Bellamy in *The Suspicious Husband*, Count Montoni in *The Mysteries of the Castle*, Sir Charles Danvers in *Fortune's
Fool*, Trueman in *The London Merchant*, Captain Absolute in *The Rivals*, Captain Douglas
in *Fashionable Levities*, and Saville in *The Belle's
Stratagem;* and in 1797–98, Horatio in *Hamlet*, Claudio in *Much Ado about Nothing*, Juan
in *Rule a Wife and Have a Wife*, Edrick in *Percy*,
Captain Manley in *The Honest Thieves*, Paris in
Romeo and Juliet, Charles Stanley in *A Cure for
Heartache*, Albany in *King Lear*, Henry Mor-
land in *The Heir at Law*, a Greek Herald in *The
Grecian Daughter*, the French Prince in *England Preserv'd*, and Uberti in *Disinterested
Love*.

The list is by no means contemptible,
either as to numbers, magnitude, or length of
the "sides" to be memorized, and it marked
Toms as a quick study, willing, and a "useful"
actor. But his country habits had not been
eradicated. They rubbed the critic John Williams the wrong way. Williams had "seen him
in *Romeo*—ah me, what a sight!," and Toms's
shortcomings precipitated a tirade about the
life of the country actor in *A Pin Basket to the
Children of Thespis* (1797), including the following:

> *When Chance draws a barn-door bred actor to
>   town,*
> *Who's been beating the drum through each burgh
>   up and down;*
> *Who has swell'd the crack'd clarion announcing
>   the fare,*
> *And distributed play-bills to charm away Care*
> ....
> *When such are brought forth to tragedize here,*
> *They should undergo quarantine ere they appear.*

The Hull correspondent for the *Monthly
Mirror*, reporting in December 1798 the arrival "lately" of the actors on the York circuit,
of whom Toms was one, agreed with Williams, in prose and with specifics. Sometimes
Toms acts well, but generally "In deliberation
he is formal and uninteresting; in declamation, rapid, indistinct, and inaccurate; his
voice is hollow, hoarse, and feeble; his feelings
are expressed without energy and without effect; and, in action, he is exuberant, ungraceful, and incessant. But—he may yet prove to
be satisfactory." Perhaps the criticism stimu-

lated reformation, for a year later a *Monthly
Mirror* correspondent applauded Toms's sound
judgment, perfect accuracy, and care of dress
and appearance.

Toms was at York in 1799, 1800, and some
part of 1801. He was also at Liverpool in the
summer of 1802. But in the winter seasons
(beginning in January and running into the
following June or July) of 1800 and 1801, and
from 1802 through 1807, he returned to
Edinburgh, where, apparently, he gained his
best acceptance. In addition to playing his
London characters he added some 65 others in
the same lines (some doubtless tried out on
provincial audiences elsewhere), such as Altamont in *The Fair Penitent*, Henry in *Speed the
Plough*, Iachimo in *Cymbeline*, Leonard Mel-
moth in *Folly as It Flies*, Aubrey in *The Fashionable Lover*, Caesario in *Alfonso, King of Cas-
tile*, Captain Faulkner in *The Way to Get
Married*, Count Romaldi in *A Tale of Mystery*,
Frank Rochdale in *John Bull*, Malfort in *The
Soldier's Daughter*, Woodville in *The Chapter of
Accidents*, Arvida in *Gustavus Vasa*, and Sir Os-
win Mortland in *To Marry or Not to Marry*.
Nothing is known of Mr Toms after the Edin-
burgh winter season of 1807.

A portrait of Mr Toms as Titus in *Lucius
Junius Brutus* engraved by Wilson, after J.
Graham, was published as a plate to *Bell's
British Theatre* by Cawthorn in 1796. The
original painting by Graham was sold at
Leigh & Sothebys on 25 May 1805, lot 271.

Toms, Edward   *d. 1775, trumpeter.*

Edward Toms, who became Serjeant-
Trumpeter to the King in 1774, was placed
among the "non-musicians" and "court fa-
vourites" in the article about that office in
Grove's Dictionary (fifth edition) by Henry
George Farmer. But that assertion seems to be
erroneous, for a document of the Lord Chamberlain's department dated 1759, in the Public Record Office, establishes him as a trumpeter in ordinary in the royal music, replacing
Joseph Goodman; and the *Biographia Dramatica* (1812) says that he was "celebrated for his
performance on the trumpet." He was admitted to the Royal Society of Musicians on 3
September 1762.

A comic opera, *The Accomplished Maid*, was
adapted by Toms from the Goldoni-Piccini
opera *La buona figliuola* and was performed at

Covent Garden nine nights on and after 3 December 1766. It was published in 1767. Toms was referred to in a notation in the Covent Garden account book dated 16 April 1770: "Receiv'd of Messrs Toms and Arnold for the use of the Organ [in 11 oratorios] this season £21." On 3 February 1772 the account book noted, "Paid Toms for [rental of?] Trumpeter's coats and Banners £34 13s."

Toms died 12 April 1775, according to Isaac Reed's "Notitia Dramatica" in the British Library and Fawcett's notebook in the Folger Library. His will, signed on 4 April 1775 at Angel Court in Windmill Street in the parish of St James, Westminster, directed all his effects to be sold to pay his creditors, any residue to pass to his friends and executors Samuel Howard, Doctor of Music, of Norfolk Street in the Strand and the musician Redman (Redmond) Simpson of Broad Court, Covent Garden. The will was proved by Howard and Simpson on 22 April, but Tom's directions had still not been carried out completely when Simpson signed his own will on 4 July 1786, directing Samuel Arnold the musician to sell "all the Manuscript and printed Musick in the closet of my first floor one pair of stairs" to satisfy Toms's creditors.

Toms, William *fl. 1699–1706₁,* actor.

William Toms (or Tomms) played Eurybates in *Achilles* in December 1699 as a member of Christopher Rich's troupe at Drury Lane Theatre. He was then seen as Adrastus in *The Grove,* Careless in *The Reformed Wife,* Ned Chollerick in *Courtship à la Mode,* Grandfoy in *Love at a Loss,* Don Manuel in *Love Makes a Man,* Du Croy in *The Unhappy Penitent,* Freeman in *The Humours of the Age,* Accestes in *The Virgin Prophetess,* Cabinet in *The Funeral,* Adelan in *The Generous Conqueror,* probably Acustes in *Cassandra,* Manuel in *All for the Better,* Frederick in *The Lying Lover,* probably Dormantle in *Love the Leveller,* a Merchant in *The Royal Merchant,* and, about April 1706— the last mention of him—Peregrine in *The Fashionable Lover.*

Tomson. *See also* THOMPSON and THOMSON.

Tomson, Mr *fl. 1784₁,* singer.

A Mr Tomson was said by Charles Burney to have been among the bass singers participating in the Handel Memorial Concerts at Westminster Abbey and the Pantheon in May and June 1784.

Tomson, Mrs *fl. 1733₁,* actress.

Mrs Tomson acted Mrs Sullen in *The Beaux' Stratagem* at the Haymarket Theatre on 19 March 1733.

Tonioli, Signor *fl. 1779–1780₁,* singer.

In the Burney papers at the British Library (938.d.16) a Signor Tonioli is named as second tenor and third buffo for the opera at the King's Theatre in 1779–80. The *Public Advertiser* on 21 October 1780 announced that Tonioli had been engaged to sing the ensuing season at the King's. His name, however, is not in any bills or advertisements extant for these seasons.

Tonioli, Vicenzo *fl. 1783–1791₁,* violist.

A musician named Tonioli is listed on a document in the Public Record Office as an employee at the King's Theatre in 1783. Probably that person was Vincenzo Tonioli, who was engaged as a violist at the Pantheon in 1791.

A Tonioli's name is found on a "List of Persons" at the opera in 1791. *The London Stage* and William Smith in *The Italian Opera and Ballet in London, 1789–1820* identify him as the librettist Girolamo Tonioli and call him poet at the Pantheon. Indeed, several operas written or adapted by Girolamo Tonioli were produced at that theatre in that season, but we believe that it is the violist who was intended as the Tonioli on the "List of Persons." Perhaps Vicenzo and Girolamo Tonioli were related.

Tonson, Mr *fl. 1790₁,* actor.

At the old Yates and Shuter booth at Bartholomew Fair in 1790 *The Spaniard Well Drub'd* was performed with Mr Tonson as Will Bowsprit.

Toogood, Miss   *b. 1745, dancer, actress.*

The *Daily Advertiser* reported the debut of Miss Toogood as the Duke of York in *Richard III* at the Richmond Theatre on 28 July 1750. She repeated the role at Twickenham on 11 September and was given a benefit at Richmond on 26 September. With her in the Richmond-Twickenham company that summer was Mrs Sarah Toogood, who was probably her mother. When Miss Toogood presented a *Pastoral Dance* at Covent Garden Theatre on 23 April 1755, she was described as ten years of age, an apprentice to the dancing master Lalauze, and making her second (*sic*) appearance on stage. Through 25 April 1759 she was seen at Lalauze's spring benefits, sometimes dancing a minuet and louvre with him. She also appeared in a solo *Pastoral Dance*, a *Harlequin Dance*, and a *Fingalian Dance*.

Toogood, Sarah   *d. 1755, actress, dancer.*

Sarah Toogood shared a benefit at Drury Lane Theatre on 5 May 1747 and had presumably been performing throughout the season in minor roles. In the summer of 1750 she was a member of the Richmond-Twickenham troupe, acting Galatea in *Philaster* on 3 July at Twickenham for her initial appearance. She went on to play King Edward V in *Richard III* at Twickenham and several parts at Richmond: Lavinia in *The Fair Penitent,* King Edward (again), Lucinda in *Don Quixote,* and Jenny in *The Tender Husband.* In the troupe with her was Miss Toogood, a child of five, who was probably her daughter.

In 1750–51 Mrs Toogood worked at Drury Lane, dancing in *Bird Catchers* on 27 November 1750 and then serving as Colombine in *Queen Mab,* a Lady in *A Bold Stroke for a Wife,* a dancer in *La Minuet à quatre,* Gipsy in *The Stratagem,* Milliner in *The Suspicious Husband,* Mincing in *The Way of the World,* Winifred in *Eastward Hoe,* a character in *Harlequin Ranger,* Beleza in *The Comical Lovers,* Dorothea in *The Man of Taste,* Honoria in *Love Makes a Man,* Miss Dawdle in *Bayes in Petticoats,* Dainty Fidget in *The Country Wife,* Prince Henry in *King John,* and Margery in *The King and the Miller of Mansfield.* After acting Mincing on 8 May 1755, she appears to have left the stage. In his diary on 19 September 1755 the

prompter Cross noted that Mrs Toogood died, apparently on that date. She was buried at St George, Bloomsbury, on 21 September. She had been living in Longacre Street. *The London Stage* occasionally cites her as Miss Toogood.

Toole, Mr   [fl. 1745–1747], *dancer, actor.*

On 14 February 1745 Mr Toole was a Demon in *The Tempest* at Goodman's Fields Theatre, and on 1 May his benefit tickets were accepted. Toole stayed at Goodman's Fields through 16 January 1747, rarely being noticed in the bills, yet on 20 February 1746 he was granted a benefit with one other. His role in *The Tempest* is the only one we have found in the bills.

Toosey, William   [fl. 1783–1804], *house servant.*

In 1783 William Toosey was the pit doorkeeper at the King's Theatre. By 1799–1800 he was pit office keeper at Drury Lane, a position he retained until 1803–4 and perhaps later. His weekly salary as of 1801 was £2 2s. In the Enthoven Collection at the British Theatre Museum are some manuscript Chancery proceedings dated 28 October 1801 in which Toosey's full name is given and he is also identified as a builder.

Tooth, Mr   [fl. 1794], *singer.*

Doane's *Musical Directory* of 1794 listed Mr Tooth, of Birmingham, as a bass who sang in the Handel concerts at Westminster Abbey.

Topham, Mr   [fl. 1796], *union pipe player.*

Mr Topham played the union pipes, with Weippert on the harp, in *The Lad of the Hills* at Covent Garden Theatre on 9 April 1796.

Topham, H.   [fl. 1718–1725], *dancer, dancing master.*

Two Tophams danced in London in the second and third decades of the eighteenth century; H. Topham seems to have been the one sometimes cited in the bills as Topham Junior, and the other, John Topham, was usually called just Topham and had the longer career. They were brothers, as the first notice of the younger Topham indicated: a new comic dance was presented at Drury Lane Theatre on 12 August 1718 and again on the twentieth by Topham, "Topham's Brother," and others. The younger Topham was not mentioned in the bills again until 7 March 1720, when he danced at Lincoln's Inn Fields Theatre. He performed regularly from March to June and received a solo benefit on 29 April. After that his name disappeared from the bills until 27 January 1724, when he danced a Follower of Mars in *The Loves of Mars and Venus* at Drury Lane. He had a role in *The Escapes of Harlequin* on 2 May and danced in *Foresters* on 12 May. H. Topham was named in the bills at Drury Lane in November 1724 and May 1725, and on 6 May 1725 he shared a benefit with Mrs Walter. After that he seems to have left the stage; the Topham who continued his dancing career was, we believe, John Topham. The sporadic appearances of H. Topham and his benefits suggest that he may have served theatres more as a dancing master than as a performer.

Topham, John *fl.* 1717–1740], *dancer, actor.*

If we have separated the two dancing Tophams correctly, John Topham was first noticed in Drury Lane playbills on 25 October 1717, when he danced in *Four French Peasants*. He continued as an entr'acte dancer throughout the 1717–18 season, sharing a benefit with Ray on 22 May 1718 and being featured with Mrs Bicknell in *Swedes* on 27 May and with Miss Tenoe in *Fairbank's Maggot* on 13 June. Topham remained at Drury Lane through the 1719–20 season, dancing frequently between the acts, usually in pieces not given titles in the bills. But occasionally we find *Comic Dance* or *Pastoral Dance of Myrtillo*, and on 12 February 1719 he played Octave in *The Dumb Farce*, a pantomime-like piece by the dancer Thurmond.

Topham was not mentioned in London bills in 1720–21 and 1721–22, though John Weaver in his *Anatomical and Mechanical Lectures upon Dancing* lists Topham as an active dancing master in 1721. Topham was again at Drury Lane from 1722–23 through 1724–25, often dancing with his younger brother, H. Topham. Among the few named characters John had during that period were Pierro in

The Escapes of Harlequin, a Follower of Mars in *The Loves of Mars and Venus* (Topham junior was also a Follower of Mars), and a Countryman and Pan in *Apollo and Daphne.* He danced briefly in September 1725 at Drury Lane, and then his name disappeared again from the bills. During that second engagement at Drury Lane, John and his wife Cornelia had a son, Richard, who was christened at St Paul, Covent Garden, on 9 September 1724.

Topham's name did not turn up again in Drury Lane bills until 24 September 1733, when he was Sir Polidorus in *Aesop.* He worked at Drury Lane until mid-October 1734, playing such parts as a Constable in *Harlequin Doctor Faustus,* Mittimus in *The Harlot's Progress,* a Constable in *The Recruiting Officer,* a Triton, Gardener, Miller, and Mandarin Gormogon in *Cephalus and Procris,* Butts in *Henry VIII,* Isander in *Timon of Athens,* a Wind, a Waterman, and Sycorax in *The Tempest,* Iphicrates in *Timon in Love,* Punch and a Peasant in *The Country Revels,* Charino in *Love Makes a Man,* Slap in *The Intriguing Chambermaid,* Charon in *The Author's Farce,* Plumb, a Satyr, Bacchus, an Old Woman, and a Sylvan in *Cupid and Psyche,* Clip in *The Confederacy,* a Follower of Mars in *Love and Glory,* a Follower of Mars in *Britannia,* and an Old Woman in *Columbine Courtezan.* His last appearance at Drury Lane seems to have been on 23 October 1734.

Unless there was another Topham performing in London in 1734 (a possibility if H. Topham returned to the stage, but we have found no clear evidence of that), John Topham began appearing at other theatres when he was not needed at Drury Lane. On 5 April he played Brief in *Don Quixote in England* at the Haymarket with Drury Lane performers; on 23 May he was Major Rakish in *The School Boy* at Lincoln's Inn Fields for his shared benefit; on 27 May he acted Bardolph in *1 Henry IV* and Galoon in *The Covent Garden Tragedy* at the Haymarket for Hewson's benefit; on 31 May he was James in *The Miser* at the James Street tennis-court playhouse for Norris's benefit (the performance had been intended for Lincoln's Inn Fields); and in late September and early October (before Drury Lane required his services) he was a Londoner in *Britannia* at Goodman's Fields Theatre. The rebellion of some of the Drury Lane performers in 1733–34 was the cause of many Drury Lane people appearing at other theatres. Only once, on 17 October 1734, do the bills show Topham at Drury Lane and another theatre; and either he was swift enough to make both engagements or there was an error in the bills.

Topham began the 1734–35 season at Drury Lane, but evidently he enjoyed his visits to Goodman's Fields, then under the management of the ingenious Henry Giffard, and from 21 October 1734 on Topham performed regularly at Goodman's Fields. He was Punch and a Haymaker in *The Necromancer,* a Witch and a Follower in *Jupiter and Io,* and a Waterman in *Britannia.* He appeared at the Haymarket in the summer of 1735, playing Mrs Midnight in *The Twin Rivals,* Simon in *The Anatomist,* the Chaplain in *The Orphan,* Sir Jasper in *The Mock Doctor,* Blunder in *The Honest Yorkshireman,* and Tipple in *The Beggar's Opera.* On 25 August, after his Haymarket engagement concluded and before the fall season began at Goodman's Fields, Topham acted the Toyman in *Bartholomew Fair* at Lincoln's Inn Fields.

His 1735–36 season was not a busy one, but he managed appearances at both Goodman's Fields and the Haymarket. At his home theatre he was seen as a Waterman in *Britannia,* a Fury and a Pierrot Man in *The Necromancer,* a character in *King Arthur,* a Swain, Triton, and Country Lad in *Harlequin Shipwrecked,* and a Follower in *Jupiter and Io.* At the Haymarket he was Bullock in *The Recruiting Officer,* Old Mirabel in *The Inconstant,* and Sir Henry Fox Chase in *Pasquin.*

Again Topham's name dropped from London bills, and one supposes that he busied himself as a dancing master. In 1734 he had described himself that way when he subscribed to Kellom Tomlinson's *Art of Dancing.* Topham had been Tomlinson's student. Our subject turned up at Southwark Fair on 9 September 1740 to play Pluto in *Harlequin Doctor Faustus,* and the Covent Garden Theatre accounts show him as a member of the company there beginning on 24 November 1740 at 3s. 4d. daily—but his name did not appear in the bills. Perhaps he served the theatre as a dancing master, but the accounts do not mention him after November.

Topham, Thomas   *c. 1710–1749, singer, strong man, actor.*

Thomas Topham was a favorite subject of several early biographical works; Caulfield's *Remarkable Persons* contains as good a description as any. Topham was born about 1710, the son of a London carpenter, under whom Tom trained. He worked as a carpenter until he was about 24 and, having put aside some money, took over a public house, the Red Lion, opposite St Luke's Hospital at the corner of City Road. He failed, partly because of his wife's coquettish behavior and his consequent inattention to business.

His first public exhibition of his remarkable strength, Caulfield says, was in Moorfields,

where he opposed his own personal strength against that of a young and vigorous horse, which he accomplished, by placing his feet against the dwarf-wall, dividing Upper from the Lower Moorfields. . . . He afterwards pulled against two horses, but as his legs were placed horisontially [*sic*], instead of rising parallel to the traces of the horses, he was jerked from his seat, and had one of

THOMAS TOPHAM

engraving by Toms, after Leigh

his knees much bruised and hurt. By the strength of his fingers he rolled up a very strong and large pewter dish; and broke seven or eight short pieces of a tobacco-pipe by the force of his middle finger, having laid them on his first and third.

Among Topham's other feats were lifting with his teeth a table six feet long with half a hundred weight hanging on the end of it and keeping it horizontal, lifting two hundred weight with his little finger, lifting Mr Chambers of Derby with one hand (Chambers, vicar of All Saints, Derby, weighed 27 stone), and bending a one-inch diameter iron bar that was struck against his bare arm.

The greatest of Topham's exploits was performed before some thousand people in Bath Street, Cold Bath Fields, on 28 May 1741. The spectators presumably paid a shilling each, his usual fee. Topham lifted three hogsheads of water weighing a total of 1,836 pounds. Remarkably, Topham was not a giant of a man; he is reported to have been five feet ten inches tall, well made, "but nothing singular." Alderman Cooper at Derby, said Caulfield, was amazed at Topham's strength and "requested him to strip, that he might examine whether he was made like other men; when he discovered, that the usual cavities under the arms and hams of others were in him supplied with ligaments."

At some point Topham took over the Duke's Head in Islington, where he was apparently more successful than he had been at the Red Lion. Pinks in his *History of Clerkenwell* says that Topham kept The Apple Tree at the corner of Dorrington Street, Clerkenwell, a pub frequented by men recently discharged from the nearby Cold Bath Fields Prison. We take it that the Topham who in February 1729 had a Great Room in York Buildings, where concerts were held, was the strong man, for Topham was known not only for his immense strength but also for his singing.

He made his stage debut at Drury Lane Theatre playing the giantess Glumdalca in *The Opera of Operas* on 7 November 1733, and he subsequently appeared at concert rooms. On 10 July 1734, for example, he and Cecilia Young sang at Hickford's Room for Topham's benefit, and then Topham showed his prowess as a strong man. At Lincoln's Inn Fields Theatre on 6 September Topham, described in the bill as from Islington, sang in English and

Italian and "at the Particular Desire of the King" performed "all the Experiment of his surprising strength." So, too, at the Haymarket Theatre on 22 March 1735 for his benefit.

He appeared in Dublin, and Irish audiences, said the *Daily Gazetteer* in June 1737, were "inconsolable for the deportation of Thomas Topham, a Performer most excellent in his Way" who was going to England. In 1739 and 1740 he performed in Edinburgh, where the newspaper on 5 July 1739 stated that Topham, for his benefit, would exhibit "several extraordinary feats of strength, in the same manner he did before the Royal Society." He twisted an iron poker around his neck, broke a rope that would bear two thousand weight, rolled up a dish of hard metal of seven pounds weight by the strength of his fingers, and then entertained the audience with "several diverting songs, such as Mad Tom of Bedlam, &c." But by January 1740 the town had lost interest in him.

On 26 May 1741 Topham sang at Drury Lane Theatre in London, and he performed also at Spitalfields on 28 May 1741. His voice, by some reports, was "more terrible than sweet," but his appearances at concert rooms and theatres suggest that he was a passable singer. His temper, on the other hand, must have been frightening, for on 8 August 1749 he quarreled with his wife Sarah over her infidelities, stabbed her in the breast, and then stabbed himself. Topham died on 10 August from his wounds and was buried at Shoreditch. His wife survived, and on 13 November 1749 administration of his estate was granted to his widow. Topham was described in the administration as of the parish of St Leonard, Shoreditch.

A picture by C. Leigh of Topham at Spitalfields, standing on a scaffold lifting three hogsheads of water, was engraved by W. H. Toms and published in 1741. A copy by an unknown engraver was published as a plate to Caulfield's *Remarkable Persons,* 1820.

Toping. *See* TOPHAM and TOPPING.

Topott, Robert *fl.* 1660–1667?₁, *actor*

The London Stage lists Robert Topott (or Topatt) as a member of the King's Company at the Vere Street Theatre in 1660–61 on the basis of his being listed on a Lord Chamberlain's warrant of 12 December 1660. In their *Register of English Theatrical Documents* Milhous and Hume cite a warrant dated 8 June 1665 naming Topott. *The London Stage* index indicates that Topott was in the King's Company in 1666–67 as well; the roster for that season names (in error?) Thomas, not Robert Topott.

Topott, Thomas. *See* TOPOTT, ROBERT.

Topping, Mr ₍*fl.* 1736–1737₎, *actor.*
Mr Topping (or Toping) worked with Henry Fielding at the Haymarket Theatre, playing Phoebus in *Tumble Down Dick* on 29 April 1736, a Politician and a Patriot in *The Historical Register* on 21 March 1737, and an Actor in *Eurydice Hiss'd* on 13 April. There were numerous performances of the last two works.

"Torangin." *See* FRANCO, FRANCESCO.

Torinese, Checo ₍*fl.* 1742–1743₎, *dancer.*
On 8 November 1742 at Drury Lane Theatre the dancer Signor Checo Torinese (sometimes just Checo or Chico) made his first English appearance after his arrival from Italy.

He performed regularly as an entr'acte dancer throughout the 1742–43 season and was granted a benefit on 19 March 1743. Among his dance numbers were *Les Moisoneurs de la Styrie, La Recrue des houssars, The Italian Gardeners, Neopolitan Punch, Les Chasseurs, New Sicilian Peasant, La Mascarade de Florana,* and a *Hussar's Dance*—perhaps *La Recrue des houssars* with an English title.

Torré, Morel ₍*fl.* 1751–1792₎, *pyrotechnist, entrepreneur.*
The earliest known production of the Italian pyrotechnist Morel Torré appears to have been a display erected at Versailles on 30 December 1751 to celebrate the birth of the Duke of Burgundy. Alan St H. Brock, in his *History of Fireworks,* says that "The 'machine' was on a scale, both of size and elaboration, that has never been exceeded. Indeed, it is difficult to realize that the building depicted was of a temporary nature."

E. Campardon, in his *Spectacles de la foire,* quotes *Mémoires sur les spectacles de la foire,* which calls our subject, apparently incorrectly, Jean-Baptiste Torré, but identifies him as the "artificier italien, directeur d'un spectacle pyrique ouvert en 1764 sur le boulevard Saint-Martin, et fondateur de l'établissement

Courtesy of Harrap Ltd and the Folger Shakespeare Library

Fireworks at Versailles, 1751

by Torré

connu sous le nom de Wauxhall de Torré," near the Porte St Martin. Torré had been struck with admiration for London's Vauxhall Gardens. But though he was said to have modeled his Paris establishment on the London original, the description given by Campardon of the Parisian copy was of an immense building, one in which were displayed what Leathers, in *British Entertainers in France,* called "pyrotechnical pantomimes." In 1766 Torré gave there two successful scenic displays with firework effects called *The Forge of Vulcan* and *Eurydice in the Underworld,* but householders in the neighborhood were alarmed, so those spectacles were terminated. In 1768 Torré opened a new entertainment entitled *Les Fêtes foraines,* which involved more acting, trick lighting, musical concerts, and gambling. But success bred envy, and in 1771, when two politically powerful former directors of the Opéra Comique decided to compete in the pleasure-garden business, a monopoly was declared in their favor, despite the fact that Torré had risen so high in his profession as to have supervised the fireworks exhibition at the marriage of the Dauphin to Marie Antoinette in 1770.

Jean Monnet, the theatrical producer, an old friend of David Garrick's, wrote to him in Torré's behalf. On 24 September 1771 Garrick wrote to Samuel Foote in Paris, asking him to tell Monnet that "the Person *Le Sieur Torré* is desir'd to come over, to make his bargain upon ye Spot, ye Sooner ye better." Torré came and devised a licopodium torch for use on the stage. Garrick introduced him to the managers at Ranelagh Gardens, with whom Torré was unable to come to terms, and then to Samuel Arnold at Marylebone Gardens, where he was an immediate sensation, increasing the attendance manyfold. Warwick Wroth, in *Pleasure Gardens,* says:

Torré's masterpiece, often repeated at the Gardens, was called the Forge of Vulcan. After the fireworks were over, a curtain rose, and discovered Vulcan and the "Cyclops" at the forge behind Mount Etna. The fire blazed, and Venus entered with Cupid, and begged them to make arrows for her son. On their assenting the mountain appeared in eruption.

On his own benefit night in 1772 Torré gave a representation of Hercules delivering Theseus from Hell.

But Torré soon ran into trouble. There were attacks on him in the newspapers, like the one of 8 June 1772. The writer excoriated him—one of a "Nest of foreign papists, now employed at Marybone Gardens"—for his insolence in supposing himself the equal of Englishmen at the art of fireworking. More seriously, as at Paris, neighbors of Marylebone Gardens were fearful for their property, and they added their squibs in the papers. One Mrs Fountayne (wife of Handel's friend Dr Fountayne, according to Wroth) produced a rocket-case that she had found in her garden. The proprietor Arnold was summoned to Bow Street and arraigned before Justice Fielding "to shew cause why he should not pay the penalty of £5 which is inflicted by Act of Parliament on those who cause fireworks to be made. . . ." Apparently that charge did not stick, and it was then recommended by Justice Kynaston that Arnold be cited as a nuisance. The whole matter was finally dropped, according to the accounts in the *London Chronicle* cited in *The Letters of David Garrick.*

Mollie Sands, in her history of Marylebone Gardens, describes several of the elaborate spectacles, involving music and dramatic performance as well as pyrotechnics, which Torré directed there. (In 1774 he was employing some of the best-known fireworkers: Mons Caillot, lured from Ranelagh in 1773; Samuel Clanfield; and Benjamin Clitherow.) The *Chronicle* for 18–20 August 1774 described "a most brilliant firework" conducted by Torré during the fête champêtre held, as a delayed celebration of the Garricks' wedding anniversary, at their villa at Hampton on 19 August.

By 1774, however, Torré had diversified his activity, according to John Thomas Smith in *A Book for a Rainy Day,* forming a partnership in a print shop with a man named Thane. He was then living in Market Lane, Haymarket. Charles Humphries and William Smith, in *Music Publishing in the British Isles,* cited Torré & Co., printsellers, of No 132, Pall Mall, who were also in the business of importing sheet music from Vienna in 1784. Also, according to Mollie Sands, Torré was an instrument artificer. He had been taught by Réaumur to make barometers, and in 1778 he had supplied the Paris Observatoire with two of his thermometers.

But Torré continued to turn occasionally

from other concerns to ignite his displays. In 1792 Ranelagh Gardens brought him in to produce his old "Mount Etna" and "Vulcan" spectacles. Thomas Brock was put in charge of the pyrotechnic part of that presentation.

Frank Hedgcock, in *Garrick and His French Friends,* described Torré as an eccentric and a mystic. The Forster Collection at the Victoria and Albert Museum contains letters from Torré to Garrick in which Torré offers to reveal the secret of the cabala and to give instructions "for harvesting the Celestial Manna."

Two signed watercolor drawings by Torré of sets and machines for fireworks at Versailles on 30 December 1751, in celebration of the birth of the Duke of Burgundy, are in the possession of the family of Alan St Hill Brock; these were handed down from some eighteenth-century Brocks, John and Thomas, who worked with Torré in London. (See the Brocks in volume 2 of this *Dictionary.*)

Tortoriti, Giuseppe, called "Pasquariello"   *d. c. 1697, actor.*

Giuseppe Tortoriti played Pasquariello in the *commedia dell'arte* troupe which performed at the court of Charles II between November 1678 and February 1679. Campardon in *Les Comédiens du roi de la troupe Italienne* states that "Pasquariello," as he was called, was born at Messina and made his debut at the old Comédie Italienne in March 1685 in capitano roles, which he could perform in either Italian or French. He gave up that line for Scaramouch in May 1694 and, to distinguish him from the famous Tiberio Fiorilli, he was called "The Young Scaramouch." After the Comédie Italienne was suppressed in 1697, Tortoriti formed a troupe of his own, but it was not successful, and the failure may have hastened his death, which came, apparently, that year.

Tortoriti had married the actress Angelica Toscano, who had made her debut at the Comédie Italienne about 1685 and specialized in soubrette roles. The couple had four children, two boys and two girls; one of the girls became the wife of Pierre Paghetti and the other of Pierre-François Biancolelli, called "Dominique."

Toscano, Monsieur   *fl. 1739?–1767?, actor, manager.*

Fuchs in his *Lexique* and Gueulette in *Le*

théâtre Italien are uncertain about the identity of a performer called Toscano—whether one performer was active from 1739 (or perhaps 1737) to 1767 or more than one person of that name was cited in the bills. In any case, a Toscano made his debut on 7 April 1739 at the Théâtre Italien in Paris, and he may have been the Toscano who managed a troupe in Rouen in September 1742. Toscano and his wife, born Delamotte, were in Le Havre in 1743, and Toscano was a harlequin in Lille in 1748. He was a member of Monnet's company at the Haymarket Theatre in London on 14 November 1749, performing in *Les amans réunis,* but the company met with such strong anti-Gallic sentiment that Toscano had to settle for £189 7s. 10d. instead of his promised £289 7s. 10d. because the engagement was cut short. A Toscano was in Nevers in 1760 and, with his wife, managed a troupe in Le Havre in 1766–67.

Tosi, Pier Francesco   *c. 1653–1732, singer, composer.*

The *castrato* Pier Francesco Tosi was born in Cesena about 1653, according to the *New Grove Dictionary of Music and Musicians,* the son of the musician and diplomat Giuseppe Felice Tosi. He traveled much when young, but by 1693 he had settled in London, presenting concerts. Elkin in *The Old Concert Rooms of London* quotes an advertisement dated 3 April 1693: "On next Thursday, being the 6th of April, will begin Signior Tose's [*sic*] Consort of Musick, in Charles Street, Convent Garden. . . ." His first one at York Buildings was on 2 November; concerts were to be held weekly throughout the winter. From 1705 to 1711 Tosi was a composer and sometime diplomat at the Viennese court. He was in Dresden in 1719 and Bologna in 1723, after which he returned to England. After 1727 he returned to Italy, where he took holy orders in 1730. According to Grove (fifth edition) Tosi died at Faenza, Italy, in April 1732.

Tosi is remembered now as a teacher, and his *Opinioni de' cantori antichi e moderni* of 1723 (translated by Galliard into English in 1742 as *Observations on the Florid Song*) still stands as a fine practical treatise on singing. In his edition of Tosi's *Observations* Galliard (presumably) spoke of Tosi's wit and vivacity, his fine voice "full of Expression and Passion, chiefly in the Stile of Chamber Music." He was a special favorite of the Earl of Peterborough, to whom his book was dedicated.

Toten, Mr *(fl. 1758–1761₁,* *pit office-keeper.*

Mr Toten's benefit tickets were accepted at Covent Garden Theatre annually from 12 May 1758 to 15 May 1761. He was identified on a paylist dated 22 September 1760 as one of three pit officekeepers, Henning being his superior. Toten's daily salary was 1*s*. 8*d*. His name disappeared from the theatre accounts after 3 October 1761.

Totnam, Mrs *(fl. 1795₁,* *singer, actress.*

Mrs Totnam was named in the advertisements as playing the Wife in *The Recruiting Serjeant*, a new burletta that was performed at Hughes's Royal Circus in St George's Fields on 17 April 1795 and other times that season.

Tottman. *See* TOLMAN.

Totty, The Masters *(fl. 1738₁,* *actors?*

In Latreille's manuscript at the British Library is a transcription of a bill (not included in *The London Stage*) for a benefit held at the James Street Theatre on 2 May 1738 for Miss Charke, Charlotte Charke's daughter. Among the performers were "The two Masters Totty." But were they live actors or two of Mrs Charke's puppets?

Toubel, Philippe. *See* ALCIDOR.

Touchbury, Mr *(fl. 1735–1746₁,* *singer, dancer, actor.*

It appears that references in playbills to Touchbury, Stichbury, and Stitchbury are all to the same person, whom we have arbitrarily identified as Touchbury. At Goodman's Fields Theatre on 17 December 1735 he sang in *King Arthur*, and on 20 February 1736 he began appearing as Proteus and a Shepherd in the pantomime *Harlequin Shipwrecked*. He was Inachus in *Jupiter and Io* on 3 March, and he had benefit tickets out on 16 April. Touchbury was in *King Arthur* again on 28 September at Lincoln's Inn Fields Theatre. During the rest of the 1736–37 season there he played a Fol-

lower and Proteus in *Harlequin Shipwrecked*, a Gamester and an Attendant on Polly in *The Beggar's Pantomime*, an Attendant in *Britannia*, and a High Priest in *Hymen's Triumph*. With Miss Jones on 4 May 1737 he sang "Since times are so bad."

At Goodman's Fields on 19 February 1741 Touchbury sang again in *King Arthur*, and on 3 March he was Tenebroso and Mars in *Harlequin Student*. He was Luna in *The Rehearsal* on 3 February 1742 and had benefit tickets out on 10 and 18 May. At Lincoln's Inn Fields on 6 December he was again Luna in a dance accompanying *The Rehearsal*. At Goodman's Fields on 15 March 1746 he acted Bonniface in *The Stratagem*.

Touche, Pierre de la *1684–1769,* *dancer.*

The *Public Advertiser* of 24 November 1769 announced that the dancer Pierre de la Touche had died at Seven Dials on 21 November at the age of 85.

Tour, La. *See* LA TOUR.

Towers, Mr *(fl. 1735–1736₁,* *dancer.*

Mr Towers danced in pantomimes at Drury Lane Theatre, appearing as a Drawer in *Harlequin Restored* on 7 October 1735 and subsequent dates, a Monkey in *Columbine Courtezan* on 3 May 1736, and Monsieur Flip-Flap in *Taste à la Mode* on 12 May. On 24 May he and others performed a turn from the last work as an entr'acte entertainment.

Towers, Samuel *(fl. 1676–1682₁,* *scene painter.*

Samuel Towers and Robert Aggas evidently worked as scene painters for the King's Company at Drury Lane Theatre in 1676–77. The Lord Chamberlain ordered the players to pay their debt of £40 to the two painters in a warrant dated 8 August 1677. The following April 1678 the debt still had not been paid, and the Lord Chamberlain ordered the leading actors of the troupe to appear before him. The players seem to have put off payment again, and on 2 December 1682 they were still obliged to pay Towers and Aggas £32.

Townley. *See* TOWNLY.

Townly, Mr   *fl. 1744–1745₁,   actor.*

The first known appearance of Mr "Townley" (usually thereafter "Townly") was as Young Fashion in *The Relapse* at the Haymarket on 6 April 1744. On 10 May following he played Frederick in *The Miser* and Harry in *The Mock Doctor.* (Mrs Townly was Mrs Wisely in *The Miser,* her only recorded appearance). Townly played Archer in *The Stratagem* on 16 May and Claudius in *Hamlet* on 29 June.

In the 1744–45 winter season Townly went to Goodman's Fields Theatre, opening on 11 December as Gayless in *The Lying Valet.* He followed that, during the season, with Valentine in *Love for Love,* Gonzalez (*sic*) in *The Tempest,* and, for his benefit on 21 March 1745, the title role in *Othello.* Seemingly, that was his adieu to the London stage. He had acted only ten times altogether.

Townly, Mrs   *fl. 1744₁,   actress. See* TOWNLY, MR.

Townsend. *See also* TOWNSHEND.

Townsend, Edward (or Edmund) Evans *1766–1809, actor, singer.*

The Mr Townsend (or Townshend) who was listed by Charles Burney among the bass singers at the Handel Memorial Concerts at Westminster Abbey and the Pantheon in May and June of 1784 was probably the young Welshman Edward Evans Townsend, born in 1766. He came first to theatrical notice as a young aspirant at Hull on the York circuit in 1789. Tate Wilkinson, the manager there, recalled in his *Wandering Patentee* (1795) that "A Mr. TOWNSHEND made his entrée that season; he promised remarkably well as a singer: His ear was not nice it is true, but his person was good for many parts, and his voice was more than commonly excellent." He may have been briefly at Norwich the previous season. He was certainly there in 1791–92 and 1792–93.

On 14 November 1793 Townsend, advertised as from the Theatre Royal, Norwich, took the title role in the comic opera *Robin Hood* at Covent Garden Theatre. From then through the season of 1801–2 he spent his winters at Covent Garden and his summers apparently in a variety of provincial places. (In the summer of 1790 he was at the Crow Street Theatre, Dublin, his debut occurring 30 June. He was at Norwich again in the summer of 1794. In the summer of 1796 he was at Dublin, Cork, and Limerick; in the summers of 1795 and 1797 he was at Birmingham.)

Manuscripts in the Folger Library and British Library show his salary increments at Covent Garden: from £4 per week in 1793–94, to £5 the following season, to £8 in 1801–2, to £9 in 1801–2 and 1802–3. Folger MS. T.a.64 records that he "had a Ben[efit] & quitted the St[age] 14 Dec [1802]."

Townsend's roles as he accumulated them at Covent Garden, year by year, were: in 1793–94 Arviragus in *Cymbeline,* Thomas in *Marian,* Medley in *The Woodman,* Hawthorn in *Love in a Village,* Asmodius in *Harlequin and Faustus,* Antonio in *The Duenna,* Selim in *A Day in Turkey,* Balthazar in *Much Ado about Nothing,* a Bard in *Oscar and Malvina,* Philippo in *The Castle of Andalusia,* the original Fisherman in Henry Bate's comic opera *The Travellers in Switzerland,* Osmond in *The Two Misers,* Allen O'Dale in *Robin Hood,* a "Principal Character" in *Naples Bay,* Grapple in *Love and Honor,* Roger in *The Gentle Shepherd,* Lindor in *The Sicilian Romance,* Captain Belville in *Rosina,* and Rundy in *The Farmer.*

In 1794–95 Townsend added Jeffery in *Netley Abby,* Peter in *Hartford Bridge,* a Bowman in *Robin Hood,* Noodle in *Tom Thumb,* the original Major Drummond in William Pearce's musical farce *Arrived at Portsmouth,* Damoetas in *Midas,* Mervin in *The Maid of the Mill,* Charley in *The Highland Reel,* the original Robin Hoofs in John O'Keeffe's comedy *Life's Vagaries,* the Butler in *The Devil to Pay,* the Drummer in *The Battle of Hexham,* Hippy in *How to Grow Rich,* the original Tim in William Macready's comedy *The Bank Note,* Freakish in *The Poor Sailor,* a Bacchanal in *Comus,* and Lieutenant Easy in *The Frolics of an Hour.*

In 1795–96, Townsend added to his repertoire a Witch in *Macbeth,* Tester in *The Suspicious Husband,* Eustace in *Love in a Village,* Denis in *The Midnight Wanderers,* Jack Haulyard in *The Shipwreck,* David in *The Rivals,* Mr Vermillion in *The Wives Revenged,* Eugene in *The Agreeable Surprise,* Squire Shenken in *Crotchet Lodge,* a Gambler in *Harlequin's Treasure,* Biondello in *Catherine and Petruchio,* the original Devereux in O'Keeffe's comic opera *The Lad of the Hills*, Amalekite in *Zorinski*, Medley in *The Woodman*, Rimenes in *Artaxerxes*, and Stern in *The Positive Man;* in 1796–97, Sadi and one of the Muleteers in *The Mountaineers*, Sir Hugh Evans in *The Merry Wives of Windsor*, the Postman in *Harlequin and Oberon*, Gibbet in *The Beaux' Stratagem*, Westmoreland in *I Henry IV*, the original Lieutenant Hamilton in George Reynolds's musical entertainment *Bantry Bay*, Crop in *No Song, No Supper*, Peter the Preacher in *The Village Fête*, the Scotch Pedlar in *Oscar and Malvina*, and, on an evening, 5 October 1796, when his sister made her only London appearance, William in *Rosina*.

In 1797–98 his new roles were Farmer Blackberry in *The Farmer*, Don Caesar in *The Castle of Andalusia*, Durazzo in *Diamond Cut Diamond*, both a Principal Druid and a Fisherman in J. C. Cross's ballet pantomime *The Round Tower*, Farmer Giles in *The Maid of the Mill*, Bluff in *Abroad and at Home*, Compton in *The Agreeable Surprise*, the original Inca in Cross's pantomime *Harlequin and Quixotte*, the original Jack Junk in Cross's pantomime *Harlequin's Return*, Campley in *Inkle and Yarico*, Jenkins in *Lionel and Clarissa*, the Mail Coach Guard in *Voluntary Contributions*, Moggy in *Unanimity;* in 1798–99, Faithless in *Reformed in Time*, Mac Rusty in *A Day at Rome*, the original Jack Junk in T. J. Dibdin's musical interlude *The Mouth of the Nile*, Hecate in *Macbeth*, the original Bertolt in Samuel Birch's melodrama *Albert and Adelaide*, Fitzroy in *The Poor Soldier*, Costly in *Laugh When You Can*, Captain Wilson in *The Flitch of Bacon*, a Sailor in *The Magic Oak*, a Lieutenant in *The Death of Captain Cook*, Iskouriah in *The Princess of Georgia*, Tim Tingle in *The Paradox*, Le Sage in *The Adopted Child;* and in 1799–1800, the original Firelock in Dibdin's musical interlude *The Naval Pillar*, the original Binnacle in Dibdin's musical farce *True Friends*, the Captain in *The Hermione*, Drill in *The Camp*, and the original Tropic in Cobb's musical farce *Paul and Virginia*.

In 1803 Townsend took a lease of the Horns Tavern, Kennington, but was almost immediately "articled for three Seasons, at a salary of 12 pounds per week" by Charles Dibdin, the new manager of Sadler's Wells. Dibdin says in his *Memoirs* that "Townshend played the principal character" in the two works that Dibdin composed especially for the theatre's "opening": *New Brooms: or, the Firm Changed*, and "an operatic piece in rhyme," *Edward and Susan, or the Beauty of Buttermere*. Yet, notwithstanding the large salary and the starring roles:

During the Season, Mr. Townshend [*sic*] had neglected the Business, so much, and taken, repeatedly, so many unwarrantable liberties with the audience, as well as the Proprietors; and appeared so dissatisfied with the business of the Horns Tavern very materially; that I proposed to him to cancel the Article on both sides, and he as readily agreed—said I to myself,
"For this relief much thanks."
He was of great service to us at the commencement of the Season, but after about 8 or 10 weeks, his conduct really injured us: we had allowed him the privilege of taking two Benefits; both of which failed, through his paying not the least attention to them.

Townsend's most popular service at Covent Garden had been in comic opera, ballad opera, and musical divertissements full of sentiment and hearty roaring about the tars of old England and hearts of oak. It was a similar service to which he was called at Vauxhall Gardens, the Crown and Anchor Tavern and, finally, at Sadler's Wells—the Serjeant in Charles Dibdin's burletta *Barbara Allen*, and Starboard in the latter's musical *Edward and Susan*. But he could also furnish an excellent entertainment all alone, as part of an evening's bill, as that of 17 October 1803 at the Royal Circus, demonstrates. Between the equestrian exercises he delivered "his much-admired IMITATIONS of the Principal Performers of both [patent] Theatres" and sang "the popular Song of the 'Tight Little island,'" and the Comic Song, called 'The Horns, or Towns-end at the End of Town,' with two additional Verses written by himself." Numbers of songs were published "as sung by" him, like Reeve's *Briton's Glory, The Beggar*, and *The Wind Blew Fresh*, and Hook's *Be Merry and Wise*.

Townsend's wife made her debut at Covent Garden on 8 May 1795. The couple shifted their lodgings several times, as benefit bills show: to No 249, High Holborn, in June 1794; to No 153, Drury Lane, in June 1795; to No 9, Leicester Place, in May 1799; and to No 127, the Strand, in May 1800. He died at the Horns Tavern, Kennington Common, on 22 March 1809 according to the *Gentleman's Magazine* for March. The *European Magazine* added his age—43—but called him *Edmund* Evans Townsend. He was buried at St Mary, Lambeth, on 26 March.

Administration of whatever property Townsend had was granted to his creditors, Christopher Dunkin, Thomas Vincent, and John Henley, apparently leaving nothing for "Elizabeth Townsend widow the relict . . . the natural and lawful mother [of] . . . Elizabeth Townsend spinster a minor & Ellen Townsend [and] Georgiana Townsend infants & only children of the said deceased."

Townsend, Mrs Edward Evans, Elizabeth, née Bunn   *fl. 1789–1837*], *actress*.

Elizabeth Bunn was either the daughter or (more probably) the younger sister of James Bunn, scene painter at Norwich and later at Manchester. It was predicted by the *Norwich Mercury* of 24 January 1789 that she would make her "second appearance on any stage" at the Theatre Royal, Norwich, on 26 January, but her role in that performance is not known. She appeared in Tate Wilkinson's York troupe at Hull, as "from Norwich," on 1 December 1789, and she was with that company in the 1790 season, according to Sybil Rosenfeld's manuscript calendar of York playbills.

The Diary; or Woodfall's Register for 15 February 1790 announced the marriage ("last week") of Miss Bunn to the Norwich actor Edward Evans Townsend. Mrs Townsend, with her husband, continued at Norwich from 1791 through the fall of 1793, when Edward Townsend secured a place in the Covent Garden company. Elizabeth remained at Norwich through the 1793–94 season, her husband returning to act there in the summer of 1794. The *Theatrical Journal* for December 1794 found Mrs Townsend also acting that month at the Ipswich Theatre as Adeline in *The Battle of Hexham*, taking also some role in *The Midnight Hour*.

On 8 May 1795 Mrs Townsend made her Covent Garden debut as Angelina in *Love Makes a Man* for the benefit of Joseph Munden, when she was advertised as "from Norwich." Evidently she satisfied, for she secured a regular place in the Covent Garden company

ELIZABETH TOWNSEND, as Christina

engraving by Audinet, after Roberts

for the 1795–96 season. On 16 September 1795, she played Miss Courtney in *The Dramatist;* then, in September and October, she was Emma Hall in *The Bank Note; or a Lesson for Ladies,* Louisa in *The Irishman in London,* Jacintha in *The Suspicious Husband,* Flora in *The Farm House,* and Lady Grace in *The Provok'd Husband.* During the remainder of the season she was almost equally busy, adding Lucilla in *The Fair Penitent,* Cleone in *The Distrest Mother,* Fatima in *The Widow of Malabar,* Dian in *The London Hermit,* Emily in *Cross Purposes,* Belinda in *Modern Antiques,* Rachael in *The Prisoner at Large,* Nerissa in *The Merchant of Venice,* Florimel in *The Positive Man,* and Lydia in *The School for Arrogance.* She ended her season on 7 June with some "Principal Character," undisclosed by the bill, in *The Way to Get Married.* Despite her apparent willingness and quickness of study, that performance was the last one of her London career, though her husband would continue at Covent Garden until December 1800.

Mrs Townsend was acting at the Birmingham Theatre with her husband in the summer season of 1795. She turned up there again on 21 September 1797, said to be making her first appearance "on this stage" for two years. She apparently acted there throughout the summer season of 1799.

Edward Townsend leased the Horns Tavern in Kennington in 1803 and turned almost immediately to singing for Dibdin at Sadler's Wells but, according to Dibdin, neglected both duties. In 1809 Townsend died in debt, and his creditors seized upon whatever he had left for Elizabeth and their children, "Elizabeth Townsend spinster a minor & Ellen Townsend [and] Georgiana Townsend infants & only children of the said deceased."

We do not know how the small family then survived. Perhaps the widow returned to the stage. The Lord Chamberlain's records for 1809 in the Public Record Office show a license granted "to the Widow and children of the late Edwd. E. Townsend for play & entertainment at Haymarket for Oct." But at some point the theatrical orbits of the humble secondary player and the celebrated star Harriet Mellon had coincided. When Miss Mellon, now Duchess of St Albans and generous mistress of the millions of her former husband, the banker Thomas Coutts, added to her will the codicil dated 14 March 1837, it provided to "Mrs Elizabeth Evans Townsend, of the Corn Exchange, an annuity or clear yearly sum of one hundred pounds for her life."

A portrait of Elizabeth Townsend as Christina in *Gustavus Vasa*, engraved by P. Audinet, after James Roberts, was published as a plate to Cawthorn's *British Library*, 1796. The original painting by Roberts, intended for *Bell's British Theatre*, was sold at Leigh & Sotheby's on 25 May 1805 (lot 263).

Townsend, James *fl.* 1685–1719?₁, *singer, organist, composer.*

James Townsend marched in the coronation procession of James II in 1685 as one of the children of the Chapel Royal. By 25 September 1690 his voice had broken and he had left the Chapel, but he was granted £20 a year and a suit of clothes. He was still cited in the Lord Chamberlain's accounts as a former Chapel

boy in 1697. He was very likely the James Townsend cited twice in the 1719 edition of *Wit and Mirth:* as composer of songs called "The Mistress" and "Fly Damon Fly." He was identified as organist of "Lyn Riges"—that is, Lyme Regis, Dorsetshire. We cannot be certain he was still active in 1719, however.

Townshend. *See also* TOWNSEND.

Townshend, Mr *fl.* 1800–1814₁, *doorkeeper.*

A Mr Townshend (sometimes "Townsend") was called "doorkeeper" in the manuscript treasurer's account of Drury Lane Theatre, now in the Folger Library, in June 1800 and again several times in 1801. In the 1803–4 season he was a balcony doorkeeper and was paid 9s. per week. He or another house servant named Townshend was employed at Drury Lane in the 1802–3, 1811–12, 1812–13, and 1813–14 seasons.

Townshend, Miss ₗG. S.?₁ *fl.* 1796–1801₁, *actress, singer.*

On 5 October 1796 "A Young Lady," making her first appearance "on any stage," sang the title role in the comic opera *Rosina* at Covent Garden Theatre. She was identified by the *European Magazine* for October as Miss Townshend. The *Monthly Mirror* called her a "cousin" of Mrs William Heard, a Drury Lane actress, observing that "she speaks very like her relation, and is a genteel figure; her voice, at present, is extremely confined, and under no regulation of taste or science." The role of William in *Rosina* was assumed by Edward Evans Townsend on the night of her debut; he had come to Covent Garden from Norwich in 1793. He was probably her brother, for he was too young to have been her father. (He seems to have preferred to spell his name "Townsend.")

Miss Townshend seems not to have appeared again in London. She may have taken her talents to the provincial stage. A Miss Townshend, doubtless our subject, sang Rosina at the Theatre Royal, Shakespeare Square, Edinburgh, on 29 June 1801, played Jessica in *The Merchant of Venice* on 6 July, and was a Singing Witch in *Macbeth* on 20 July.

Hogan in *The London Stage* concludes that Miss Townshend was the person who signed a Covent Garden receipt laid into a volume of Genest in the Harvard Theatre Collection: "Mr Townsend for season [of 1796–97] £201/0/0 (settled G. S. Townshend)."

Tradge, Mr   ₍fl. 1734₎,   actor.
Mr Tradge played Cato and spoke an original prologue (written by him?) at the James Street Theatre on 23 May 1734.

Trafuse. See TREFUSIS.

Trajana, Signor   ₍fl. 1791₎,   singer.
At Salomon's concert at the Hanover Square Room on 11 March 1791, Signor Trajana was one of the singers; Haydn presided at the keyboard.

"Trampwell, Mrs"   ₍fl. 1757₎,   actress?
At the Haymarket Theatre from 29 August to 12 September 1757, "Mrs Trampwell" provided introductions at "Mrs Midnight's" (Christopher Smart's) Medley concerts. The name was a pseudonym for some performer, possibly Theophilus Cibber, who appeared on the programs.

Trancart, Antoine   ₍fl. 1761–1792₎,
dancer, ballet master, manager.
Antoine Trancart was a dancer in Noverre's company at Stuttgart by 1761. Between 1772 and 1776 he was ballet master at the Munich Hofoper. By 1772 he had married the dancer Nancy Leviez, whom he had met at Stuttgart. On 4 December 1790 the Times announced that Antoine and Nancy Trancart were engaged as "Danseurs pour les Ballets d' Action" at the Pantheon for the coming season. Antoine signed a contract for and was paid £400, according to information provided to us by Judith Milhous, but the Trancarts' names do not appear on any bills for performances given by D'Auberval's troupe at the Pantheon from 17 February to 19 July 1791. Perhaps Trancart helped with rehearsals and administration. In the following season, 1791–92, the Pantheon was under Trancart's management. When the Pantheon burned down on 14 January 1792 the company finished its season at the Haymarket Theatre. After that season the feud between the Pantheon and King's Theatre was terminated and opera production was reestablished at the King's in 1793, but without Trancart, who had disappeared from London accounts.

Trancart, Mme Antoine, Nancy, née Leviez   ₍fl. 1755–1792?₎,   dancer.
The dancer Nancy Leviez (sometimes Levier) was born in London. Though identified by Marian H. Winter in her Pre-Romantic Ballet as the daughter of the London ballet master Charles Leviez (d. c. 1778), Nancy was probably his niece: early in 1755 Noverre wrote to David Garrick, "I have made an excellent dancer of Levier's niece." On 27 July 1761 she was re-engaged in Noverre's company at Stuttgart, according to the ducal archives of that date, "from Easter for so long as she wishes to remain in the Service at a new yearly wage of 2,200 florins tax free instead of 1,000 florins hitherto, but to include shoe money she has always drawn." In her portrayal of Medée, "apart from her amazing dancing talent," wrote Joseph Uriot in his Description des Fêtes at Stuttgart (1763), she succeeded "in showing in her acting all the soul and expression of that incomparable actor, the celebrated Garrick, in England, where this dancer, trained by Mr. Noverre, was born."

By 1772 Nancy Leviez married the dancer Antoine Trancart, who had also been in Noverre's company at Stuttgart. Probably she performed at the Munich Hofoper during the period her husband was ballet master there, between 1772 and 1776. Little is known to us of their careers until the Times on 4 December 1790 announced that they were engaged for D'Auberval's troupe at the Pantheon in London from 17 February through 19 July 1791. But, though Trancart was paid £400, their names appeared in no Pantheon bills that season. In 1791–92 Trancart served as manager at the Pantheon, and after it burned on 14 January 1792 the company moved to the Haymarket Theatre. Though we do not find her name in bills Mrs Trancart probably danced in the company that season, after which the names of both her and her husband disappeared from London accounts.

Travers, John   c. 1703–1758, organist,
composer, copyist.
John Travers was born about 1703 in Windsor, according to the New Grove, the son of Joseph Travers, a Windsor shoemaker. John

was probably given his first musical training at St George's Chapel in Windsor, and he was apprenticed to Maurice Greene in 1719. He copied many of Greene's works between 1722 and 1728, and he also studied with Pepusch. Travers became active in the Academy of Ancient Music, copying for it a good deal of music. He was appointed organist of St Paul, Covent Garden, on 24 November 1726 at £30 annually and later became organist at Fulham. He was made an organist of the Chapel Royal on 10 May 1737.

Travers lived in King Street, Covent Garden, from 1747 to 1758. He was one of the original subscribers to the Royal Society of Musicians on 28 August 1739. The *New Grove* lists his compositions, most of which were religious in nature. Travers died in London in June 1758. He was buried at St Paul, Covent Garden, on 11 June 1758.

Travis, Mrs ₍fl. 1794₎, singer.

Doane's *Musical Directory* of 1794 lists Mrs Travis of Lancashire as a singer in the Handel concerts at Westminster Abbey. Perhaps she was related to Deborah Travis, of Shaw, near Oldham, Lancashire, who married the musician William Knyvett in 1826. According to Grove, Mrs Travis was one of the Lancashire chorus singers engaged in London in the Concert of Ancient Music.

Travis, Deborah. *See* KNYVETT, MRS WILLIAM THE SECOND.

Trearly[?], Mr ₍fl. 1777₎, performer?

A Mr Trearly (if we have transcribed his name correctly) was taken off the Drury Lane Theatre paylist for two weeks on 11 October 1777. After his name in the accounts was written the amount £8 6s.—presumably the money the theatre saved while Trearly was off the list. He was thus earning a weekly salary of over £4, which was considerable.

Trebbi, Giuseppe ₍fl. 1775–1782₎, singer.

The tenor Giuseppe Trebbi, a native of Bologna, was engaged in 1775–76 as first buffo for the opera at the King's Theatre, where he made his first appearance on 31 October 1775

as Marchese in *La sposa fedele*. He sang in *La buona figliuola* on 12 December, and during the remainder of the season was heard in *Il bacio, Le ali d'amore, L'isola d'amore, Alcina, Caio Mario* (the title role), *Piramo e Tisbe,* and *Antigono.* When Onofreo died suddenly in January 1776, Vento's new serious opera *La vestale* was postponed from the twenty-seventh in order to give Trebbi time to study the tenor part, which he played when the opera was sung on 6 February 1776. On 14 March 1776 Trebbi took his benefit in *Le ali d'amore.* Trebbi, who had been engaged to replace Lovattini, did not impress Dr Burney: "his voice was not so sweet, his taste so good, or his humour so risible, as those of predecessor."

In 1776–77, his second season at the King's Theatre, Trebbi appeared on 2 November 1776 as Fenicio in *Astarto* and then sang Nardone in *La Frascatana* on 5 November. His subsequent roles that season were Alarico in *Germondo,* the title role in *Antigono,* Damone in *L'ali d'amore,* Giannino in *I capriccio del Sesso,* Enopione in *Orione,* and parts in *Il geloso in Cimento, La schiava,* and *Telemaco.* For his benefit on 10 April 1777, when he sang in *La schiava,* tickets could be had from Trebbi at Stephenson's in the Haymarket.

After an absence of two years, Trebbi returned to the King's Theatre in 1779–80, reappearing on 27 November 1779 in the title role of *Alessandro nelle Indie.* He sang in *La contadina in corte* on 14 December, and on 22 January 1780 he was heard as Lucio Papirio in *Quinto Fabio.* Subsequently he sang Don Faustino in *L'amore soldato,* a principal part in *L'Olimpiade,* Ubaldo in *Rinaldo,* and Capocchio in *Il Duca d'Atene.* His new roles in 1780–81 were the title part in *L'Arcifanfano,* Giannino in *Le serve rivali,* the title part in *Mitridate,* Armidoro in *Il Barone di Torre Forte,* Ali in *Zemira e Azore,* Eupalte in *Piramo e Tisbe,* a principal part in *L'Omaggio,* and Creso in *Euriso.* Trebbi's full name appeared in the printed libretto of *Piramo e Tisbe* in 1787.

Dr Burney stated that Trebbi's performance "was never very attractive," and his engagements in London did little to rescue comic opera from "a languid and declining state." Michael Kelly visited Trebbi in the fall of 1782 at Bologna, where the tenor had retired from public life "with very ample means."

Trebeck, Andrew   *d. 1715, singer.*

Andrew Trebeck, a bass singer from Worcester, was sworn a Gentleman of the Chapel Royal on 5 October 1671. By the time of the coronation of James II on 23 April 1685 Trebeck was a Clerk of the Chapel. He continued to serve under William and Mary as both a singer and a cleric, and under Queen Anne he made regular trips to Windsor and Hampton Court for periods ranging from three weeks to three months.

Trebeck died on 19 November 1715. His will, written on 11 June 1715 and proved on 5 December, stated that in addition to his duties in London in the Chapel Royal, Trebeck was a Clerk of the Cathedral Church of Worcester. He wished to be buried at St Peter's, Worcester, should he die there, and his inscription should identify him as a vicar of that church. His late wife's grave was at St Peter's. But should he die in London, Trebeck wished to be buried in the cloisters of Westminster Abbey and be identified as a Presbyter of the Chapel Royal. Trebeck evidently died in the country.

In his will he left £5 to the poor of St Peter's, Worcester; many of his books and clothes to his son Andrew; his exchequer orders and tallies to his daughters Sarah and Elizabeth; £100 to Sarah "on account of her having been my housekeeper and very carefull in attending upon me in my old age"; £5 to his maid Nan; and his household goods, divided equally, to his son and four daughters. The name of the third, and evidently youngest, daughter was Mary. The eldest seems to have been named Newton (her husband's name?). (Mrs) Newton and the younger Andrew Trebeck, according to the will, had already received their portions when they married.

A Mary Trebeck was buried at St Margaret, Westminster, on 22 July 1717 and may have been our subject's daughter. The younger Andrew Trebeck was cited in the Calendar of Treasury Books as receiving £30 for reading prayers at St James's Chapel from 1 August 1714 to 1 August 1716. The baptismal records of St Margaret, Westminster, reveal that Mary, the daughter of Andrew and Mary Trebeck, was baptized on 19 November 1719; their daughter Alicia was born on 29 January

and baptized on 17 February 1721. In the latter entry Andrew was identified as "Rev Trebeck, Clerk."

Treeble, Joseph   *fl. 1794₁,   singer.*

Doane's *Musical Directory* of 1794 lists Joseph Treeble, of No 43, St Martin's Lane, as a bass who sang for the Choral Fund, the Handelian Society, and the Longacre Society and performed in the oratorios at Drury Lane Theatre and the Handel concerts at Westminster Abbey.

Trefusis, Joseph   *fl. c. 1675–1720₁, actor, dancer.*

Joseph Trefusis acted at the Smock Alley Theatre in Dublin beginning about 1675, his earliest known part being the First Gentleman in *Othello*, which was presented in the 1670s or 1680s. The registers of St John the Evangelist contain four entries concerning Trefusis. On 20 July 1684 Jane, the daughter of Joseph "Trefuse," was christened; on the following 10 August, Jane, the daughter of Jane Trefuse, was christened. That surely was the same child, and one supposes that Joseph's wife's name was Jane. But the double christening is baffling. Little Jane died in her infancy; she was buried on 6 November 1687. Sara, daughter of Joseph "Trefewses," was buried on 24 November 1688.

In 1688 Smock Alley closed, and Joe Trefusis came to London to join the United Company at the Drury Lane and Dorset Garden theatres. His earliest identified role was Whimsey in *The Widow Ranter* on 20 November 1689 at Drury Lane. Then he played Toby and perhaps the Constable in *Madam Fickle* in 1690–91, Secret in *Edward III* in November 1690, Bernardo in *The Mistakes* in mid-December 1690, MacBuffle in *The Marriage-Hater Match'd* in January 1692, Hickman in *A Very Good Wife* in late April 1693, Bernardo in *2 Don Quixote* in late May 1694, and Alderman Fur in *The Canterbury Guests* in late September 1694.

When the United Company split, Trefusis chose to join Thomas Betterton's rebel players at Lincoln's Inn Fields Theatre, where he was seen as Trapland in *Love for Love*, which opened the theatre on 30 April 1695. Before he returned to Dublin in 1698 he played Pettifog in *The City Bride,* Old Hob in *The Country Wake,* Squire Illbred in *Love's a Jest,* Pantalone in "Natural Magick" (a part of *The Novelty*), an English Countryman in *Europe's Revels,* Actwell in *The Deceiver Deceived,* and Broakage in *The Pretenders* (in March 1698, his last London role).

Trefusis returned to Dublin where, according to W. S. Clark in *The Early Irish Stage,* he performed until about 1720. In 1707–8, according to the promptbook of the Smock Alley Theatre, he had a role in *The Spanish Wives,* and in 1715 he is known to have played Aelius in *Timon of Athens* and Obadiah in *The Committee.*

The prompter Chetwood, in a pamphlet on Anthony Aston quoted in Percy Fitzgerald's *New History,* wrote of Trefusis:

Mr. Joseph Trefusis was the original Trapland in "Love for Love," and a well-esteemed low comedian (a theatrical term to distinguish that branch from the genteel), and was famous for dancing an awkward country clown. He was an experienced angler. As he was fishing by the Liffy side, some friends of his were going in a boat in order to embark for England. Jo seeing them, called to them to take him in that he might see them safe on board. He gave his fishing-rod to a friend on shore to take care of till his return; but Jo, it seems, was prevailed upon by his companions to make the journey to London with them, with his fishing-clothes upon his back, not a second shirt, and but 7s. in his pocket. His companions left him in London, and Mr. Wilks found him gazing at the dial in the square of Covent Garden. He hardly knew him at first (as Mr. Wilks told me) but by his particular gait, which was beyond imitation. When he asked him how he came there, and in that pickle: "Hum! ha! why, faith, Bobby," replied Jo, "I only came from Dublin to see what it was a clock at Covent Garden." However, Mr. Wilks new clothed him, supplied him with money, and sent him back. . . .

Jo was so inimitable in dancing the clown, that General Ingoldsby was so well pleased that he sent him five guineas from the box where he sat. Jo dressed himself the next day, and went to the castle to return thanks. The general was hard to be persuaded it was the same person; but Jo soon convinced him by saying, "Ise the very mon, and please your Excellency," and at the same time twirling his hat, as he did in the dance, with his consummate foolish face and scrape. "Nay, now I am convinced," replied the general, laughing, "and thou shalt not show such a face for nothing here"—so gave Jo five guineas more, which so well

pleased him, that he paid his compliments in his awkward clownish manner, and, as Shakespeare says, set the table on a roar. So exit Jo.

Trelawny, Miss *fl.* 1774₁, *singer.*
Wroth in *The London Pleasure Gardens* notes that Miss Trelawny sang at Marylebone Gardens in 1774.

Tremells, Roger ₁*fl.* 1766?–1800₁, *impresario?*
Roger Tremells was granted a license for seven concerts at the Pantheon between 24 February and 1 June 1779. He may have been no more than an agent for the Pantheon proprietors or he may have been the impresario organizing and promoting the concerts. In 1781 he was granted a similar license for two masquerades and ten concerts, and in 1782, 1784, and 1800 he received permission to present one concert each year. Perhaps he was the Roger Tremells, bachelor, who married Sarah Whitby at St Marylebone on 28 May 1766.

Trenti, Mme. *See* CORNELYS, TERESA.

By permission of the Trustees of the British Museum

HENRY TRESHAM
engraving by Turner, after Chinnery

Tresham, Henry   *c. 1749–1814, scene painter, costume designer?*

Henry Tresham was born in Dublin about 1749, according to some accounts, and in 1756, according to others. Possibly he was related to James Tresham, a boxkeeper at Smock Alley Theatre, Dublin, who died on 5 January 1784. He studied under W. Ennis and then under Robert West at the Dublin Society's Drawing School. For three years Tresham exhibited his work in Dublin, including chalk drawings in 1771, allegorical designs for a ceiling in 1772, and "Andromache mourning for Electra" in 1773. In that last year he assisted in decorating transparent ceilings in the Fishamble Street Music Hall.

In 1775 Tresham came to London, where he found employment for a time drawing small portraits; soon he obtained the patronage of John Campbell (later first Baron Cawdor), whom he accompanied on travels throughout Europe for 14 years. At Rome, where they stayed much of the time, Tresham studied the paintings and style of the antique Roman school. He became a member of the academies of Rome and Bologna, and at Rome in 1784 he published *Le Avvenature di Saffo,* consisting of 18 subjects designed and engraved in aquatint, not the best examples of his draughtsmanship.

In 1789 Tresham returned to England and in that year sent 12 works, mostly drawings, to the Royal Academy. He took up residence for some years at No 9, George Street, Hanover Square, and thereafter at No 26, Brook Street.

When the Pantheon housed the opera in 1791 (the King's Theatre having burned),

By permission of the Trustees of the British Museum

A scene in *Antony and Cleopatra*

engraving by Facius, after Tresham

Tresham decorated the front of the stage, painted a curtain with figures representing the sciences, and painted some scenery. The bills for the opera *Armida* on 17 February 1791 state that the dresses were executed by Lupino from original drawings by Tresham and Bartolozzi; evidently neither artist created special costume designs but rather Lupino used some of their published historical works as his models.

Tresham was elected an associate of the Royal Academy in 1791 and a full member in 1799. From 1789 to 1806 he exhibited some 33 works, mostly on scriptural, Roman, and English history. Two illustrations by him inspired by *Antony and Cleopatra* appeared in Boydell's *Shakespeare* and another from the same play in the large Boydell's *Shakespeare Gallery*. Frontispieces by him appeared in various publications, including Sharpe's *British Classics*. Tresham became professor of painting at the Royal Academy in 1807, succeeding John Opie, but ill health obliged him to resign the post in 1809. He retired on a life annuity of £300 settled upon him by Frederick, first earl of Carlisle and father-in-law of Lord Cawdor, Tresham's early patron. Tresham also continued to receive income for writing the descriptive text of the *British Gallery of Pictures,* a series of engravings which he had helped to select; the collection was issued by Longman & Co until 1818. Tresham was a collector of pictures and art objects, and he profited by a sale of some Etruscan vases (once belonging to Sir William Hamilton) to Samuel Rogers for £800. Tresham also published five volumes of verse: *The Sea-Sick Minstrel,* 1796; *Rome at the Close of the Eighteenth Century,* 1799; *Britannicus to Buonaparte: an Heroic Epistle,* 1803; *Recreation at Ramsgate,* 1805?; and *A Tributary Lay to the Memory of the Marquis of Lansdowne,* 1810.

In the last several years of his life Tresham was infirm and feeble. He died at his house in Bond Street on 17 June 1814. In his will, made only two days earlier, he described himself as an "historical painter" of No 43, Bond Street, in the parish of St George, Hanover Square. He ordered all his valuables and property to be sold at auction by Mr Christie. To Miss Charlotte Whitsell (a servant?) he left £10, and he bequeathed several mourning rings to acquaintances. The remainder of his estate went to his nephew William Harris (or Jarris?). The will was proved at London on 18 August 1814 when administration was granted to his attorney.

Portraits of Henry Tresham include:

1. Drawing by J. Chinnery, location unknown. An engraving was made by Mrs D. Turner.

2. Crayon drawing by G. Dance, location unknown. An engraving was made by W. Daniell.

3. By A. Pope (the actor), location unknown. An engraving by A. Cardon was published in *Contemporary Portraits,* 1814.

4. A pastel drawing (35″ × 40″) by H. D. Hamilton shows Tresham and Canova looking at the latter's sculpture of Cupid and Psyche. Once owned by Lady Bentinck, eldest daughter of Marquess Wellesley, the picture passed to her great-niece Hyacinthe Wellesley and then to the latter's grandson Hugh Farmar, the present owner. It is illustrated in Anne Crookshank and the Knight of Glin's *Irish Portraits 1660–1800* (1969), No 61. A damaged version is in the collection of the Earl of Cawdor, Stackpole Hall, and was published in the *Connoisseur,* December 1959, when it was erroneously attributed to Gawin Hamilton and called a picture of Colonel John Campbell (later first Baron Cawdor) and Canova. The Farmar version was also erroneously described in *Art Bulletin,* 44 (June 1962). One of the versions had been exhibited at the Royal Academy in 1791.

5. By John Opie. Exhibited at the Royal Academy in 1806, but now evidently lost. An engraving of it by S. Freeman was published as a plate to the *Monthly Mirror,* 1809.

Tresswell. *See* CRESSWELL.

Trevor, Mrs, née Kelly ₁*fl.* 1800₁, *singer, actress.*

Mrs Trevor was one of 14 children of Thomas Kelly, a wine merchant in Mary Street and Deputy Master of Dublin Castle. Her mother, formerly Miss McCabe, was from a respectable family of Westmeath. At least three of our subject's brothers became performers: Joseph Kelly (d. 1817), who acted in

Ireland for several seasons in the 1790s; Mark Kelly (1767–1833), who acted and sang in the provinces in the 1790s and at Drury Lane Theatre in 1794–95; and Michael Kelly (1762–1826), the very popular performer and musical director in whose notice more information about the family will be found.

Mrs Trevor's name was first noticed in the Covent Garden bills as a chorister in Cumberland's *Joanna,* which had its premiere on 16 January 1800 and was performed a total of 14 times before the season ended. Her salary was listed as £4 4*s.* per week.

Her career was brief. On 24 May 1800 she arranged an evening of performances for her own benefit and met with audience disapproval of her presumption. Her characters were Zelma in *Ramah Droog* (her first appearance in a speaking role) and Patrick in *The Poor Soldier.* According to Thomas Dutton's report in his *Dramatic Censor,* Mrs Trevor became the victim of a "settled, preconcerted plan" to injure her, for "The moment the lady made her appearance on the boards, before she even opened her mouth, before a single note furnished an opportunity of appreciating her abilities, opposition began to manifest itself in all the various forms which malice on such occasions is wont to resort to." As the hisses grew louder, the theatre "absolutely assumed the appearance of a riot, rather than that of a civilized company, assembled for the purpose of amusement." The *Monthly Mirror* of June 1800 predicted that the ill-advised attempt would prove fatal to Mrs Trevor's career:

We cannot speak favourably of the lady's exertions . . . nor can we afford her any hopes of future success. It is but justice, however, to mark that, the ridicule with which the audience seemed to treat Mrs. Trevor, whenever she appeared, was sufficient to 'quail the stoutest', and to deprive her of that degree of courage and self-possession of which a novice and especially a *singer,* stands so particularly in need.

Tickets for her benefit could be had from "Mrs Trevor, sister to Mr Kelly of Drury-lane Theatre," at No 31, Bedford Street, Covent Garden. The gross receipts that night amounted to £268 12*s.*

Trevor, George   ₁*fl.* 1711₁,   *musician.*
George Trevor shared a benefit concert with

one other musician on 25 April 1711 at Clothworkers' Hall.

Trew, Mr   ₁*fl.* 1780–1786₁,   *actor.*
The "Young Gentleman" who acted Varanes in *Theodosius* at Covent Garden Theatre on 24 November 1780, advertised as making his first appearance on any stage, was identified by J. P. Kemble on his copy of the playbill as Mr Trew. In a press clipping in the O. Smith collection at the British Library, Trew was said to possess many necessary powers to act tragedy, particularly in the line of the tender and pathetic lover. He needed, however, a "more expressive" face, and he imitated too much the late Spranger Barry, "especially in those breaks which had so happy an effect in that uncomparable tragedian."

Trew's second appearance at Covent Garden was on 24 September 1781, when, still billed as "a Gentleman," he acted Romeo. Appearing yet again anonymously (and again identified by Kemble on the playbill), Trew acted Orestes in *The Distrest Mother* on 14 March 1782. When he played Dumont in *Jane Shore* on 26 April 1782, his name was given in the bill; the performance was for his benefit, and tickets were available from him at No 9, Great Square, Gray's Inn. Possibly Trew was the "Gentleman" who acted Orlando (his "first appearance in that character") in *As You Like It* on 17 May 1783. The last notice of Trew at Covent Garden was on 24 May 1783, when he played the title role in *Alexander the Great* and shared benefit tickets with the dancer Peter Harris.

On 22 March 1786 Mr Trew delivered "English readings and recitals" at Free Masons' Hall, Great Queen Street, Lincoln's Inn Fields. He shared the performance with the singer Sedgwick and the musician Percy. Tickets were available from Trew at No 50, Frith Street, Soho.

Triggs, James   ₁*fl.* 1669–1676₁,   *scenekeeper.*
James Triggs served the King's Company at the Bridges Street Theatre from 1669–70 if not earlier. The Lord Chamberlain's accounts cite Triggs as a scenekeeper. He was last cited on 3 January 1676, when the company was at their new Drury Lane Theatre.

Trimuer, Mr *fl. 1728₁,* *actor.*
Mr Trimuer was in Signora Violante's troupe at the Haymarket Theatre playing an Egyptian in *The Rivals* on 21 February 1728.

"Trincalo." *See* UNDERHILL, CAVE.

Tring, Thomas *fl. 1792₁,* *performer.*
In the Drury Lane Theatre accounts is a note dated 11 October 1792 indicating a payment, amount unspecified, to Thomas Tring for his performance in *Cymon.* But *Cymon* was not presented that fall, and the only recent performance was a single one on 21 September 1791—not at Drury Lane but at Covent Garden. Perhaps Tring was loaned by Drury Lane to the rival patent house to play some bit part.

Tringer. *See* FINGER.

"Tripe." *See* HAMILTON, MRS JOHN.

Triulzi, Signor *fl. 1746–1747₁,* *singer.*
Signor Triulzi sang at the King's Theatre in 1746–47 but, according to Dr Burney, was not distinguished. On 4 November 1746 Triulzi had a part in *Annibale in Capua,* and he sang on 14 April 1747 at the benefit for indigent musicians and their families. He probably had other singing assignments, but the bills do not reveal them.

Troas, Christopher *fl. 1726–1755?₁,* *musician.*
Christopher Troas was active as a harpsichord teacher as early as 11 May 1726, when his pupil Miss La Tour played at the Lincoln's Inn Fields Theatre. On 28 August 1739 Troas became one of the original subscribers to the Royal Academy of Musicians. A benefit concert for Troas was held at the Haymarket Theatre on 29 January 1748. He may have remained active in the Royal Society to 1755.

Troba. *See* TROWA.

Troche, Gervaise *fl. 1791₁,* *dancer.*
Mlle Gervaise Troche was hired in Paris for a season's salary of £500 and danced at the Pantheon in the spring of 1791, appearing first on 17 February, when the reconstructed building opened, as a Student of Terpsichore in the pantomime ballet *Amphion et Thalie; ou, L'Élève des muses.* Beginning on 19 March she was a Nymph (companion to Calypso) in *Telemachus in the Island of Calypso,* and on 24 March she danced a Niece in *The Deserter of Naples.* Her last part was Adonis in *Le Siège de Cythère* beginning on 9 May. She also danced in the opera *Idalide,* which opened on 14 April, for her name appeared in the libretto published that year. Mlle Troche's last notice came on 10 June 1791, when she danced in *La Fille mal gardée.* She had experienced difficulty in collecting her salary, according to Judith Milhous, citing the Bedford Opera Papers, and she did not return to the Pantheon the following season.

Troke, The Messrs *fl. 1783₁,* *boxkeepers.*
Two men named Troke, one identified as Junior, were boxkeepers at the King's Theatre in 1783, according to the accounts.

Trombetta, Signor *fl. 1755₁,* *manager. See* MATTEI, COLOMBA.

Trombetta, Signora. *See* MATTEI, COLOMBA.

Trossy *fl. c. 1785₁,* *performer?*
In the Lord Chamberlain's accounts is a note dating about 1785 indicating a payment of £50 to one Trossy in connection with the opera at the Kings Theatre. The only names that come close to that are those of Mme Rossi, who danced at the King's in 1784–85, and of Spozzi, who danced there in 1785–86.

Trott, John *d. c. 1764, house servant.*
A Drury Lane Theatre memorandum dated 10 September 1726, from the managers to the treasurer, ordered that the name of John Trott (or Trot) be stricken from the daily charge. How long Trott had been working at the playhouse is not known. As playbills and accounts show, Trott served John Rich at Lincoln's Inn Fields and Covent Garden from as early as 7 October 1726 until his death about 1764. In 1727–28 he filled in as an extra boxkeeper at Lavinia Fenton's benefit, but his regular assignment was as a lobby doorkeeper. In 1726 he was earning 2*d.* daily, and in 1735–36 his salary for 179 days was £17 18*s.* He shared in

benefits regularly each spring. On 12 May 1764 his widow was granted some benefit tickets, so one guesses that Trott had died recently, his last mention in the benefit bills being 26 May 1763 (as Trout).

Trott, Mrs John *fl. 1764–1775₁, house servant?*

John Trott's widow was given benefit tickets to sell on 12 May 1764, and since she was still being granted tickets on 30 May 1775, perhaps Covent Garden Theatre provided her with a house servant's position. Her husband had been a lobby doorkeeper.

Trotter, Mr. *fl. 1743₁, house servant.*

A Mr Trotter is called a "servant" to Drury Lane Theatre in the players' petition to the Lord Chamberlain against the patentee Charles Fleetwood in September 1743. Fleetwood was said to owe Trotter money, but no sum is specified.

Trotter, Mr *fl. 1775–1777₁, actor.*

Mr Trotter played Eustace in *Love in a Village* at the Haymarket Theatre on 2 February 1775. On 2 May 1776 he was Charles in *The Jealous Wife* and Beaufort in *The Citizen*. At China Hall, Rotherhithe, on 18 June 1777 Trotter played Rossano in *The Fair Penitent*, and between then and 23 July he appeared as Sir Jacob Jollup in *The Mayor of Garratt*, Catesby in *Jane Shore*, Henry in *The Mock Doctor*, Don Lopez in *The Wonder*, Beau Trippet in *The Lying Valet*, Harry Bevil in *Cross Purposes*, Cook in *The Devil to Pay*, Montano in *Othello*, and Sir Philip Modelove in *A Bold Stroke for a Wife*.

Trotter, Mrs *fl. 1777–1787?₁, actress.*

Mrs Trotter acted Betty in *A Bold Stroke for a Wife* at China Hall, Rotherhithe, on 23 July 1777. Also in the cast was Mr Trotter, who had been acting in London since 1775. Perhaps she was the Mrs Trotter who was cited on 25 January 1787 in the Covent Garden Theatre accounts as receiving 15s. for six half-tickets returned.

Troughton, John *fl. 1767–1769?₁, proprietor.*

The solicitors Joseph Beaumont and John Troughton, "on the part of themselves and other creditors," in 1769 acquired the lease of Marylebone Gardens from the bankrupt Thomas Lowe, according to Mollie Sands in *The Eighteenth-Century Pleasure Gardens of Marylebone*. The partners had expended of their "own proper Monies" £263 10s. 5d. The lease had at that time still 11 years to run. In March 1769 the *London Chronicle* declared that Troughton and the violinist and conductor Thomas Pinto had purchased the lease of the Gardens for £755.

Trout. *See also* TROTT.

Trout, Mr *fl. 1696–1707₁, actor.*

Mr Trout's first known part was Humphrey Doddipole in *Love's a Jest* in June 1696 with the Betterton troupe at Lincoln's Inn Fields Theatre. Trout remained at that house until the opening of the Queen's Theatre in 1705, playing Symon in *The Anatomist*, Nicholas in "Natural Magick" (part of *The Novelty*), Sir Walter Blunt in *Henry IV*, the Elder Clerimont in *The Beau Defeated*, a Plebeian in *Julius Caesar*, Supple in *The Ladies Visiting Day*, Hearty in *The Different Widows*, Tom Joly in *The Stage Coach*, Sir John Single in *Love at First Sight*, and Grumble in *The Biter* (on 4 December 1704). In the early years of the new century Trout could command an annual salary of only £30, very close to the lowest wages offered.

He may not have joined the company at the Queen's Theatre when it opened, for his next advertised parts were in 1707: Humphrey in *Wit Without Money* on 4 January and a Citizen in *Caius Marius* on 18 February—both at the Queen's.

Trowa, Joseph *fl. 1752–1759₁, horn player, trumpeter.*

The *Royal Society of Musicians* (1985) lists Joseph Troba as joining the organization on 2 February 1752. We believe that he was the musician Trowa or Trova active later in the decade. The treasurer's minutes at the Foundling Hospital list Trowa as a horn player in the *Messiah* in May 1754 at a fee of 10s. 6d. On 27 April 1758 he was cited as a trumpeter at the same salary. "Trova" played in the *Messiah* again in 1759.

Trowd. *See* FROUD.

Trowell, Mr *fl. 1774₁*, *actor.*

When a special benefit was given the actors Jacobs and Owenson at the Haymarket Theatre on 21 September 1774, a Mr Trowell, otherwise unknown, took a role unspecified in *The Duellist.*

Trowell, Miss *fl. 1770–1773₁*, *actress.*

Miss Trowell was first seen in London playbills when she acted Mrs Bruin in *The Mayor of Garratt* with Samuel Foote's company at the Haymarket Theatre on 28 May 1770. She remained with Foote during the rest of that summer season, acting Arante in the Tate *King Lear*, Lucy in *The Devil to Pay*, Gypsy in *The Stratagem*, Venus in *Midas*, Blanch in *King John*, Florella in *The Orphan*, and Corinna in *The Citizen*. On 5 October following she returned to the theatre to assist in a special benefit for Vandermere, playing Miss Biddy in *Miss in Her Teens*. She was probably the Miss "Trowel" who was acting with the York company in 1771, 1772, and 1773.

Trowion, Mr *fl. 1791₁*, *house servant?*

On 26 May 1791 the benefit tickets of Mr Trowion, probably a house servant, were accepted at Covent Garden Theatre.

Trueman, Mr *fl. 1756₁*, *actor.*

On 20 September 1756 a Mr Trueman acted Don Alonzo in *The Intriguing Captains* in Bence's booth on the Bowling Green at the time of Southwark Fair. The piece was repeated on 22 and 23 September.

Trueman, Mr *fl. 1793–1817₁*, *actor, singer.*

An actor named Trueman (not to be confused with Thomas Trueman) was a chorus singer at the Haymarket Theatre at the end of the century. He was first noticed in the bills as one of the chorus of Witches and Spirits in *Macbeth*, Kemble's inaugural production at the new Drury Lane Theatre, on 21 May 1794. He appeared regularly in 13 performances of that play until the season ended on 7 July, and he earned £1 10s. per week. On 1 May 1794 he acted the Lord Chamberlain in *Henry VIII*, and was seen that summer as a Courtier in *The Miller of Mansfield*, one of the Lazzaroni in *The Pirates*, a Polander in *Lodoiska*, Anthony in *The Chances*, Trueman in *The Clandestine Marriage*, and Freeman in *High Life below Stairs*. Probably this actor was the Mr Trueman who had been at the Theatre Royal, Manchester, in December 1793 and January 1794, prior to his engagement at Drury Lane.

In his second season at Drury Lane, 1794–95, in which he continued to earn £1 10s. per week, Trueman added to his modest repertoire Vasquez in *The Wonder*, the Duke of Burgundy in *Henry V*, Gustavus in *Lodoiska*, Pedro in *Isabella*, a Goatherd in *The Mountaineers*, a Servant in the premiere of Mrs Inchbald's *The Wedding Day* on 1 November 1794, a Citizen in *The Roman Father*, a Sailor in *Othello*, an unspecified role in *Nobody*, the Jeweller in *A Trip to Scarborough*, Calippus in *The Grecian Daughter*, a chorus role in *The Cherokee*, a Gentleman in *Measure for Measure*, Captain Loveit in *Miss in Her Teens*, Michael in *Lodoiska*, Mat o' the Mint in *The Beggar's Opera*, a Servant in *The Wheel of Fortune*, the English Herald in *King John*, Kenred in *Edwy and Elgiva*, Granada in *The Child of Nature*, Octavio in *The Pannel*, Sir Bertrand in *The Adopted Child*, a Chorister in *The Triumph of Hymen* (the masque in *Jack of Newbury*), a Servant in *First Love*, Col Modish in *A Quarter of an Hour before Dinner*, and vocal parts in *Britain's Glory* and *A Masonic Melange*.

Continuing in a similar line of roles, most of them tertiary and obscure, Trueman remained at Drury Lane through 1802–3. Some of his more important roles included the Earl of Leicester in *The Critic* on 9 June 1797, Macheath in *The Beggar's Opera* on 5 July 1799, and Count Floreski in *Lodoiska* on 17 April 1800. As Floreski he replaced Michael Kelly at very short notice and was favorably received. He repeated the role the following night. On 10 May 1800 he sang "a pleasing glee" with Dignum and Danby. For his benefit on 5 June 1800 he acted Lovewell in *The Clandestine Marriage* for the first time, and according to Thomas Dutton in the *Dramatic Censor* Trueman played "with great ability." Dutton's approbation perhaps might have been expected, for Trueman also sang "Secure within her sea-girt reign," a song written by Dutton in commemoration of the King's providential escape from the recent attempt on his life. Benefit tickets were available from Trueman at No 38, Norfolk Street, the Strand. When he took his benefit on 4 June 1801 his address was No 18, Queen Street, Bloomsbury; that night he appeared for the first time as Don Philip in *She Wou'd and She Wou'd Not*. By 1798–99 his salary was £2 10s. per week.

Michael Kelly reminisced about seeing Trueman perform in a provincial company at Plymouth in 1796; but Kelly's memory may have been faulty. That engagement perhaps occurred earlier, for in the summer of 1796 Trueman was playing at the Haymarket Theatre in London, where he made his first appearance on 11 June 1796 as Goodwill in *Bannian Day*. The next night he and several other performers appeared at both Drury Lane and the Haymarket; Trueman acted Hortensio in *Catherine and Petruchio* at Drury Lane and the Drummer in *The Battle of Hexham* and Goodwill again at the Haymarket. During the rest of the summer at the Haymarket, Trueman appeared as John in *The Agreeable Surprise*, Solarino in *The Merchant of Venice*, Apathy in *The London Hermit*, Alcade in *The Spanish Barber*, a character (probably Odune) in O'Keeffe's *The Magick Banner* (also known as *Alfred*), which premiered on 22 June 1796, a Muleteer in *The Mountaineers*, Saunders in *The Jew*, Canteen in *The Deaf Lover*, Rustic in *Rosina*, Boquet in *The Son-in-Law*, Charles in *The Village Lawyer*, Frederick in *No Song No Supper*, a Stockbroker in *A Bold Stroke for a Wife*, Lubin in *The Quaker*, Jemmy in *Love and Money*, John d'Aire in *The Surrender of Calais*, the Butler in *The Devil to Pay*, a Mate in *Inkle and Yarico*, Ignacio in the premiere of Cumberland's *Don Pedro* on 23 July 1796, Lord Rake in *The Provok'd Wife*, Rosencrantz in *Hamlet*, Sir Walter Blunt in *1 Henry IV*, Omar in *A Mogul Tale*, Gregory in *The Iron Chest*, Naclo in *Zorinski*, Thomas in *The Virgin Unmask'd*, Patent in *A Peep behind the Curtain*, and the Prince in *Romeo and Juliet*.

Some of Trueman's more important roles in his summer engagements at the Haymarket, which continued at least through 1804, were Lenox in *The Rival Soldiers* on 6 July 1797, Belville in *Rosina* on 12 July 1797, Carlo in the premiere of Boaden's *The Italian Monk* on 15 July 1797, Don Manuel in the premiere of Holcroft's *The Inquisitor* on 23 June 1798,

Harmon in *Lionel and Clarissa* on 5 July 1798, Capt Greville in *The Flitch of Bacon* on 20 June 1800, and Gossip in *My Grandmother* on 27 June 1800.

In 1801 he was described in the *Authentic Memoirs of the Green Room* as:

A very useful, diligent, punctual, and respectable performer. To higher claims he does not aspire. His original sphere was the counting-house; but possessing a good voice, with a tolerable knowledge of music, he was induced to exchange the mercantile for the theatrical profession. . . . His cast of parts at Drury-Lane is very humble, consisting principally of singing characters; but at the Haymarket he sustains a weightier line of business. Few performers, at either theatre, have a more respectable and extensive range of connexions.

In 1803–4 Trueman joined the Kemble family's exodus from Drury Lane to Covent Garden, where he continued, according to the *Thespian Dictionary* (1805), as "one of those prudent, unassuming performers, who never appears in a part above his abilities."

In the summer of 1807 Trueman went north to engage at the Theatre Royal, Edinburgh, where he first appeared on 24 July as Tom Tug in *The Waterman*. At Edinburgh he remained at least through 1816–17, being last mentioned in Dibdin's *Annals of the Edinburgh Stage* as playing on 14 July 1817. Among his numerous roles at Edinburgh, several notches above any he ever played in London, were Aimwell in *The Beaux' Stratagem* on 3 April 1817, Benvolio in *Romeo and Juliet* on 21 November 1814, Careless in *The School for Scandal* on 23 December 1815, Duke Orsino in *Twelfth Night* on 4 February 1815, Faulkland in *The Rivals* on 24 December 1814, the title role in *Julius Caesar* on 24 March 1817, Claudius in *Hamlet* on 16 December 1816, Major Oakly in *The Jealous Wife* on 28 December 1816, and Aufidius in *Coriolanus* on 13 March 1815.

Trueman, Thomas   *fl.* 1800–1810], *singer, actor.*

Thomas Trueman was a chorus singer at the Haymarket Theatre in the summer of 1800. His name appeared in the bills as the 2nd Negro Robber in *Obi* on 21 July. In that production another performer named Trueman acted the Overseer; this latter Trueman, though also a minor performer, had a more substantial career in London. On 16 September "T. True-man" entertained at the end of the mainpiece with "A Variety of Imitations." Thomas was again at the Haymarket in 1801. In 1801–2 he seems to have begun an engagement at Covent Garden Theatre, where he remained for a number of years an obscure chorus singer. His salary in 1802–3 was £1 10*s.* per week. In the British Library is a signed receipt by Thomas Trueman for pay at Covent Garden in 1808. In 1808–9 and 1809–10 a Mr "Tru-man," probably our subject, was earning £2 10*s.* per week.

A Mrs "Truman" was on the paylist at Covent Garden from 1810–11 through 1812–13, earning in the latter two seasons £3 per week. The "Truman" who was paid £4 on 30 May 1801 for four weeks as a call boy at Covent Garden was probably related.

Trufler. *See* TRUSLER.

"Trumpeter, Charles the Merry." *See* "CHARLES THE MERRY TRUMPETER.".

Trusler, John *d. 1766, proprietor, manager.*

About 1746 John Trusler, a cook by trade, succeeded Daniel Gough as landlord of the Rose Tavern (on the site of the present Nos 35–37, Marylebone High Street) and proprietor of Marylebone Gardens. Trusler was in partnership with John Sharratt (who seems to have overseen the entertainments) from 1749 to 1753 and with a Mr Sweedes in 1755–56. At mid-century, Marylebone Gardens, like the more sophisticated Ranelagh and Vauxhall, offered pleasant walks and refreshments on a summer evening, along with concerts and fireworks. Trusler advertised at the beginning of his 1756 season:

MARYLEBONE GARDENS are now open'd for the Reception of Company, where Gentlemen and Ladies may every Morning breakfast on Tea, Coffee, or Chocolate, with the finest Butter, Cream, and new Milk, Cows being kept for that Purpose; and Afternoons and Evenings be entertain'd. with Coffee, Tea, Cakes, Pastry, and all sorts of Wine and other Liquors.

There are two large Rooms, genteely fitted up, for Assemblies, Balls, Concerts, or publick Dinners; and the Proprietor being by Profession a Cook; any publick or private Entertainment will,

Harvard Theatre Collection

BERTHA (?) TRUSLER
artist unknown

upon proper Notice, be provided and dress'd in the best Manner.

Trusler ran the establishment until 1763, when he was succeeded by the singer Thomas Lowe. But Trusler continued to reside at the Gardens until 1764 and then took his family to the Gold Lamp, Boyle Street, Saville Row, where he died on 2 April 1766. His confectionery business was carried on by one of his daughters, probably Bertha Trusler.

Trusler's widow, Elizabeth Trusler, died a few months after her husband, on 9 October 1766. In her short will, made on 7 October 1766, she described herself as of St James's parish, Westminster. She left a guinea each to her son John Trusler and her daughter Elizabeth Storace and five pounds each to her daughters Mary, Sarah, and Catherine. The residue of her unspecified estate she bequeathed to her daughter Bertha Trusler, whom she also named as sole executrix and to whom administration was granted on 16 October 1766.

John Trusler became a man of means, gained from his attention to the commissariat of Marylebone Gardens. His son John, born in London in July 1735, was educated at a fashionable seminary in Marylebone and was sent to Emmanuel College, Cambridge. With the elder Stephen Storace, who became his brother-in-law, the younger John Trusler translated and adapted Pergolesi's *La serva padrone,* which became the first burletta given at Marylebone Gardens; it had its first performance on 8 June 1758 and proved exceptionally popular. Young Trusler became an Anglican priest in 1759 and was also an author, literary compiler, and bookseller. He is noticed in *The Dictionary of National Biography.*

One of the elder of John Trusler's daughters, Elizabeth, in 1761 married Stephen Storace, a Neapolitan musician who was sometimes engaged as a double-bass player at the King's Theatre. She became the mother of the celebrated vocalist Anna Selina Storace and the composer Stephen Storace. Her will, dated September 1817, contains information about several of Elizabeth Trusler Storace's sisters, the daughters of our subject John Trusler. Sarah Trusler was still a spinster in 1817; Catherine Trusler was by then the wife of the Reverend Joseph Legg of Mabbington. It is likely that the Miss Trusler (mistakenly and variously given in *The London Stage* as Trotter, Trufler, or Truster) who baked the pastries at Marylebone Gardens between 1758 and 1760 and carried on the bakery at Saville Row after Trusler's death was Bertha, since she became the executrix and legatee of the residual estate. *The London Stage* cites an advertisement for 14 August 1758 (similar to others until 1760):

Mr Truflers [*sic*] daughter continues to make the Rich Seed and Plomb Cakes, so much admired by the Nobility and Gentry. They are made in a square Form, and will cut out in as large Slices as those of four Times the price. They are always kept ready made, and will be sent to any Part of the Town when bespoke, at Half a Crown each.

No portrait of the proprietor John Trusler is known. In an extra-illustrated volume of J. T. Smith's *Book for a Rainy Day,* in the Harvard Theatre Collection, is a rare print, 1760, of Miss (Bertha?) Trusler, with a turban on her head, seated at a table upon which is a pie.

Trussler, Mr ₁*fl.* 1778–1779₁, *double-bass player.*

The Drury Lane Account Book at the Folger Shakespeare Library lists Mr Trussler as a double-bass player in the band in 1778–79, with a salary of £2 per week.

Truster. *See* TRUSLER.

"Trusty Anthony." *See* ASTON, ANTHONY.

Trye, Mr ₁*fl.* 1748₁, *actor.*

At Southwark Fair on 7 September 1748 Mr Trye played Ferdinand in *The Tempest.*

Tubbs, Mrs Charles. *See* ARNOLD, MRS HENRY.

Tubman, Mr ₁*fl.* 1722–1749₁, *house servant.*

Mr Tubman shared a benefit with two others on 29 May 1722 at Lincoln's Inn Fields Theatre. The gross receipts came to more than £128. He was similarly cited at benefit time and in the account books through 1728–29, first as a gallery doorkeeper and then as a slips keeper. (Slips are seats on the top gallery level at the sides of the auditorium, near the proscenium opening.) Tubman was paid 5s. 4d. for four days' work on 29 May 1747 and was last mentioned in the accounts on 29 September 1749. He presumably served John Rich's troupe for 27 years.

Mrs Tubman, probably his wife, was paid 1s. 4d. daily for 179 days in 1735–36 as a boxkeeper. Her benefit tickets were accepted in May 1744 and May 1746, and on 17 November 1746 she was earning 8s. weekly as a "stepkeeper."

Tubman, Mrs ₁*fl.* 1735–1746₁, *house servant. See* TUBMAN, MR.

Tuckells. *See* ZUCHELLI, SIGNORA.

Tucker, Mr ₁*fl.* 1743–1745₁, *actor.*

At Lincoln's Inn Fields Theatre on 4 April 1743, the title role in *The Lying Valet* was acted by "a Gentleman who never appear'd on any Stage before." When that comedy after-piece was performed on 23 April 1744 at the Haymarket Theatre, the bills listed in that role a Mr Tucker, who was identified as the person who had acted it at Lincoln's Inn Fields. The Haymarket performance, adver-tised under the subterfuge of "A Concert," was for Tucker's benefit, and in the mainpiece he played Brazen in *The Recruiting Officer*.

The following season Tucker was with the company at Goodman's Fields Theatre, where he acted Antonio in *The Tempest* (and Meph-istopheles in the masque) on 14 February 1745, Sparkle in *The Miser* on 7 March, and Usher in *The Rehearsal* on 14 March. On 15 April 1745 he was replaced as Antonio by Nailor, and his name was omitted from the masque in *The Tempest*.

Mrs Tucker, perhaps our subject's wife, played Mrs Highman in *The Indian Merchant* in Phillips and Yates's booth in West Smith-field on 25 August 1742 at the time of Bar-tholomew Fair.

Tucker, Mrs *fl. 1742*₁, *actress. See* TUCKER, MR. ₁1743–1745₁.

Tucker, William *d. 1679, singer, com-poser.*
William Tucker, a Gentleman of the Chapel Royal, was installed a Petty Canon at West-minster Abbey on 16 February 1661, accord-ing to the Precentor's Book. Tucker was occa-sionally mentioned in the Lord Chamberlain's accounts, usually in connection with trips he made to Windsor to attend the King. He was the composer of a number of services and an-thems. Tucker died on 28 February 1679 and was buried on 1 March in the Abbey cloisters. Administration of his estate was granted his widow Elizabeth on 29 May 1679. At some point after that Mrs Tucker was paid £15 out of Secret Services funds for her husband's 15 books of "Anthems with Symphonies for King Charles the 2nds use in his Chappell Royal. . . ."

Tucket, Mr *fl. 1794–1795*₁, *carpenter.*
The Covent Garden Theatre accounts for 1794–95 show a payment of £1 1s. for one week's work to Mr Tucket, one of the theatre carpenters.

Tude, Mr *fl. 1745*₁, *flutist.*
At the Castle Tavern on 14 January 1745 a concert was presented at which Mr Tude played the German flute.

Tudway, Thomas *c. 1650–1726, singer, composer.*
Thomas Tudway was probably the son of Thomas Tudway (d. 1671), a lay clerk at St George's Chapel, Windsor. He was born about 1650 (according to the *New Grove*) and edu-cated under Captain Henry Cooke at the Chapel Royal; with him as fellow students were John Blow, Michael Wise, William Tur-ner, and Pelham Humphrey. Samuel Pepys heard the boys singing at Whitehall on 22 November 1663. In his *Biographical Dictionary* Pulver states that Tudway was admitted as a tenor at Windsor on 22 April 1664, and on that evidence argues for Tudway's having been born no later than 1646. But if he was born that early, he might have been too old in 1663 to be one of the Children of the Chapel Royal (his fellow students were born in 1649, c. 1648, 1651, and 1647 respectively).

In any case, by 8 January 1669 Tudway had

Faculty of Music, Oxford

THOMAS TUDWAY
by Hill

left the Chapel Royal. In 1670 he was appointed organist of King's College, Cambridge, and in 1679 he was made instructor to the choristers there. He served also as organist at Pembroke College. In 1681 he received his bachelor's degree in music, and on 30 January 1705 he was appointed Professor of Music and granted a doctorate. Queen Anne made Tudway composer and organist extraordinary (without fee, presumably) to the Queen on 16 April 1705, but he was suspended a year later for speaking ill of the monarch and her administration. He recanted and was restored in March 1707. From 1714 to 1720 Tudway worked on the collection of cathedral music for which he is today remembered. It includes some of his own compositions. The collection is now at the British Library. Thomas Tudway died at Cambridge on 23 November 1726.

A portrait of Thomas Tudway by Thomas Hill depicts him holding in his hand a paper inscribed with the words and music of an anthem performed "on the occasion of her majesty's presence in King's Coll. Chapel, Cambridge, April ye 16, 1705." It was bought in Lord Oxford's sale in 1742 by Dr Rawlinson, with another picture, for a guinea. Rawlinson left it to Oxford University in 1757 and it is now with the Faculty of Music.

Tully,   James   *fl.   1714?–1734*, *dancer.*

It is very probable that the Mr Tully who danced at the Lincoln's Inn Fields Theatre on 22 December 1714 and subsequent dates was James Tully, who in 1734 subscribed to Tomlinson's *Art of Dancing.* Tomlinson was also active in the second decade of the century. Tully (or Lully, once) continued dancing at Lincoln's Inn Fields through the spring of 1719, usually between the acts, but he was named for at least two pantomime roles: Scaramouch in *Mars and Venus* on 22 November 1717 and a Fury in *Amadis* on 24 January 1718.

Tumoth,   Daniel   *fl.   1739–1744*, *musician.*

On 28 August 1739 Daniel Tumoth became one of the original subscribers to the Royal Society of Musicians. He remained active to 1744.

Tunbridge, Mr   *fl. 1756*,   *actor.*

Mr Tunbridge played Don Juan in *The Intriguing Captains* at Bence's booth at Southwark Fair on 20 September 1756.

Tunstall, Mr   *fl. 1789–1793*,   *actor, singer.*

In a performance of *Inkle and Yarico* given by a small company at the King's Head Inn, Southwark, on 16 September 1789 Mr and Mrs Tunstall played the title roles. At the end of the comic opera Tunstall recited *British Loyalty; or, A Squeeze for St. Paul's.* Several months later they were at the White Hart Inn, Fulham: on 9 November 1789 Tunstall played Curry and Mrs Tunstall reappeared as Yarico in *Inkle and Yarico,* and he was also the title character in *Chrononhotonthologos,* in which she played Fadladinida. On 11 November Tunstall acted Faddle and his wife acted Fidelia in *The Foundling;* in the afterpiece *The Deuce Is in Him* he played Colonel Tamper.

No doubt he was the Tunstall who was with Brooke's touring company at St Albans in November 1792 and in Butler's troupe at Harrogate on 23 July 1793. Perhaps he was the father of the singing actress Catherine Tunstall (1796–1846), a prominent member of the younger Charles Dibdin's company at Sadler's Wells between 1817 and 1826. She also performed at Drury Lane and Vauxhall during those years; in the 1830s she was with the Edinburgh theatre.

Tunstall, Mrs   *fl. 1789*,   *singer, actress. See* TUNSTALL, MR.

Turbutt, Benjamin   *fl.   1734–1735*, *actor.*

The P. Turbutt who acted a Bridewell Keeper in *The Harlot's Progress* at Drury Lane on 21 October 1734 was (supposing a misprint) Benjamin Turbutt. On 22 January 1735 "Turbutt Sr" acted Porter in *The Plot;* also in the cast was the actor Robert Turbutt. "Benj. Turbutt" was Bagshot in *The Stratagem* at the Haymarket Theatre on 26 August 1735 and a Bravo in *Harlequin Grand Volgi* at Drury Lane on 13 November.

Turbutt, Robert   *d. 1746, actor, singer, manager.*

ROBERT TURBUTT, as Sosia
engraving by Miller, after Bisse

Robert Turbutt was probably the son or brother of Benjamin Turbutt, who acted briefly in the 1730s. Robert was first noticed in London bills on 23 August 1733, when he acted Sir Robert "Brockenbury" in *Jane Shore* at the Mills-Miller-Oates booth at Bartholomew Fair. He then joined the Drury Lane company, making his first advertised appearance on 1 October 1733 as Alonzo in *Rule a Wife and Have a Wife*. He went on that season to play Antonio in *The Tempest*, Wilmot in *The Fatal Falsehood*, Axalla in *Tamerlane*, Neptune in *Cephalus and Procris*, the Surveyor in *Henry VIII*, the Singing Master in *Timon in Love*, Hotman and perhaps Jack in *Oroonoko*, Manuel in *Love Makes a Man*, Lucius in *Theodosius*, Story in *The Committee*, Harry in *The Livery Rake*, Bantamite and the Manager in *The Author's Farce*, Neptune and Plumb in *Cupid and Psyche*, Giffard in *The Albion Queens*, La Tour in *The Country House*, Stocks in *The Lottery* (with Drury Lane players at Lincoln's Inn Fields on 1 April 1734), the Mayor in *Don Quixote in England* (at Lincoln's Inn Fields), Lodovico in *Othello* (at Lincoln's Inn Fields),

Peachum in *The Beggar's Opera*, and Young Rakish in *The School Boy* (for his shared benefit).

In the summer of 1734 at the Haymarket he attempted such new characters as Westmoreland in *1 Henry IV*, Lockit in *The Beggar's Opera Tragedized*, Falstaff in *The Humours of Sir John Falstaff*, Jobson in *The Devil to Pay*, Moody in *The Provok'd Husband*, Aboan in *Oroonoko*, Horatio in *The Fair Penitent*, Aimwell in *The Stratagem*, Sir John in *The Non-Juror*, Cleavar in *Penelope*, Chaunter in *The Beggar's Wedding*, Buffskin the Tanner in *The Humorous Election*, James in *The Miser*, and Old Melton in *The Cobler's Opera*.

Turbutt remained at Drury Lane through 24 January 1746, just before his death. He was a hard-working performer who played mostly secondary and tertiary roles year in and year out. Among his new parts were Alonzo in *The Mourning Bride*, James and Jasper in *The Mock Doctor*, Decoy and Mother Midnight in *The Harlot's Progress*, Metellus Cimber in *Julius Caesar*, Ruffus in *Junius Brutus*, the Player King and Marcellus in *Hamlet*, Phillipo in *The Rover*, Sir Sampson in *Love for Love*, Demetrius in *Timon of Athens*, Ratcliff and Catesby in *Richard III*, Strato in *The Maid's Tragedy*, Fairbank and Balderdash in *The Twin Rivals*, Poundage in *The Provok'd Husband*, Corydon in *Damon and Phillida*, a Constable in *The What D'Ye Call It*, Aristander and Perdiccas in *The Rival Queens*, Mat and Lockit in *The Beggar's Opera*, a Forester in *The King and the Miller of Mansfield*, Decius and Syphax in *Cato*, the Chaplain in *The Orphan*, the Second Murderer and Angus in *Macbeth*, Hackem and Lolpoop in *The Squire of Alsatia*, Quack in *The Country Wife*, Lovewit, Sir Epicure, and a Neighbor in *The Alchemist*, Spinosa in *Venice Preserv'd*, Goodwill and Blister in *The Virgin Unmask'd*, Campeius and Cranmer in *Henry VIII*, Waitwell and Sir Wilful in *The Way of the World*, and Omar in *Tamerlane*.

He also played Gripe in *The Confederacy*, Jacques in *The Pilgrim*, Sir Harry in *The Tender Husband*, Cacafogo in *Rule a Wife and Have a Wife*, Sir Jealous in *The Busy Body*, Sosia in *Amphitryon*, Periwinkle in *A Bold Stroke for a Wife*, the Orangewoman and Old Bellair in *The Man of Mode*, Cornwall and Albany in *King Lear*, an Alderman in *The Plain Dealer*, Morton in *The Albion Queens*, Wade in *Sir Wal-*

ter *Raleigh*, the French Ambassador and the Bishop of York in *2 Henry IV*, the Host in *The Merry Wives of Windsor*, Old Atall in *The Double Gallant*, Jacques in *As You Like It*, the Captain in *Twelfth Night*, Sullen in *The Stratagem*, the First Merchant in *The Comedy of Errors*, Reynaldo in *All's Well that Ends Well*, King Arthur in *Tom Thumb*, the Governor in *Oroonoko*, Slap in *The Intriguing Chambermaid*, Dr Crisis in *The Wedding Day*, Simon in *The Anatomist*, Pyracmon in *Oedipus*, Oldrents in *The Jovial Crew*, Humphrey in *The Conscious Lovers*, a Constable in *The Recruiting Officer*, Alphonso in *The Spanish Fryar*, and Chatillion in *King John*.

Turbutt made occasional appearances away from Drury Lane. In June 1735 he played Cacafogo in *Rule a Wife and Have a Wife* at Lincoln's Inn Fields; in July and August of that year he acted a few roles at the Haymarket: Thorogood in *The London Merchant*, Trueman in *The Twin Rivals*, Crispin in *The Anatomist*, and Peachum in *The Beggar's Opera*. In June 1736 he played Bonniface in *The Beaux' Stratagem* at Lincoln's Inn Fields; at Richmond on 21 August 1736 for a benefit of Turbutt and Mrs Pritchard he presumably played in *The Wonder* or *The Devil to Pay* or both; in August 1741 he operated a booth at Bartholomew Fair and played Jocula in *Thamas Kouli Kan;* on 8 September 1741, when he was not scheduled at Drury Lane, he played Blister in *The Virgin Unmask'd* and a Constable in *The Recruiting Officer* at Goodman's Fields; at Southwark on 30 March 1743 he acted Balance in *The Recruiting Officer* at a charity benefit; and in June 1743 he was Sir Jealous in *The Busy Body* at Lincoln's Inn Fields.

On 30 July 1743 at Richmond, Turbutt played Lockit in *The Beggar's Opera*, according to a note from A. H. Scouten. With Dove in August 1743 Turbutt operated a booth at Bartholomew Fair at which *The Glorious Queen of Hungary* and *Harlequin Dissected* were presented. His last stage appearance was as a Constable in *The Constant Couple* on 28 December 1745 at Drury Lane. *The Lottery* was also performed that night, but Turbutt did not play his usual role of Stocks.

Robert Turbutt died on 26 February 1746, according to the *General Advertiser*, after a "lingering illness." He was described as belonging to the Theatre Royal, Drury Lane,

and master of the Swan Tavern in Smithfield. He was, the paper said, "a facetious and agreeable companion, greatly and justly esteem'd by all that knew him for his Sincerity where he profess'd a friendship." He left a widow and children who were supposed to receive a benefit at Drury Lane on 29 April 1746, but it was deferred and may never have taken place. David Garrick's letters tell us that Turbutt was a glutton and was taunted by his fellow actors for his passion for food. Turbutt's son, Benjamin Robert Turbutt, according to the *Gentleman's Magazine*, was to be executed for theft in 1765 but was respited after the intercession of powerful friends, including Garrick.

Robert Turbutt was shown as Sosia in *Amphitryon* in an engraving by A. Miller, after T. Bisse, published 1740. He (or possibly Dunstall) is depicted, as figure "O," in the anonymous satirical print called "The Theatrical Contest," published on 24 October 1743 (*Catalogue of Political and Personal Satires in the British Museum*, No 2599).

Turk   *fl. 1800*], *trained horse.*
James De Castro recorded in his *Memoirs* that the equestrian William Davis, for the summer production of *The Magic Flute; or, Harlequin Champion* in 1800, "taught the noble Horse Turk to rear up, seize hold of, and tear down a streaming banner from the rampart walls, at the representation of a grand tournament in the opening scene. . . ."

"Turk, The." *See* CARATTA, MAHOMET.

"Turkey Horse." *See* "BLACK PRINCE, THE."

Turkins. *See* FURKINS.

Turner, Mr *See also* TOMS, MR.

Turner, Mr   *fl. 1718–1740?*], *actor, dancer, singer.*
A Mr Turner played a Fury in *Amadis* at the Lincoln's Inn Fields Theatre beginning on 24 January 1718; he repeated the role—a dancing one, probably—in the spring of 1719.

Turner played Catesby in *Jane Shore* at the Haymarket Theatre on 28 June 1722. He was

probably the Turner who was active later in
the 1720s and 1730s. At the Haymarket on
15 October 1728 Turner acted Cheatley in *The
Metamorphosis* and danced; after that he was
seen as Capreol in *The Lottery,* Macheath in *The
Beggar's Opera,* and the Duke in *Venice Preserv'd.* On 30 December he and Miss Careless
shared a benefit. After the 1728–29 season
Turner's name disappeared once more from the
London bills.

On 7 April 1735 Turner (the same one, we
are guessing) turned up at Southwark to play
Brazen in *The Recruiting Officer.* On 28 May he
was at Tottenham Court acting Tinsel in *The
Drummer;* in July he played three characters at
Lincoln's Inn Fields Theatre: Blunt in *The
London Merchant,* Basset in *The Provok'd Hus-
band,* and Sir Politick Staunch in *Politicks on
Both Sides.* On 4 August he was at the Hay-
market as Leander in *The Mock Doctor* and
Polydore in *The Orphan;* between 6 August
and 5 September at Lincoln's Inn Fields he
played Doodle in *The Tragedy of Tragedies,*
Cinna in *Caius Marius,* Silence in *Bartholomew
Fair,* Filch in *The Beggar's Opera,* and Veroni in
The Carnival; and he was Dumont in *Jane Shore*
at the Haymarket on 17 September, Brainless
in *The Art of Management* at York Buildings on
24 September, and the title character in *George
Barnwell* at York Buildings on 1 October. At
the Haymarket he acted Sir George Friendly
in *The Female Rake* on 26 April 1736 and a
Manager in *Tumble Down Dick* on 29 April.
Possibly our Mr Turner was the "Gentleman,
with a large Family, who has suffered very
great Losses" and was given a charity benefit
at Covent Garden Theatre on 19 December
1740.

Turner, Mr *fl. 1755–1768?₁, actor.*
Mr Turner played Trippet in *The Lying Valet*
at the Haymarket Theatre on 1 September
1755. On 9 September he was a Footman in
The Devil to Pay and on 11 September one
of the Kings of Brentford in *The Rehearsal*
and Tattoo in *Lethe.* At Bartholomew Fair
on 5 September 1757 Turner appeared as a
Clown in *The Restoration and Adventures of
Harlequin.* He was perhaps the Turner in
Durravan's troupe in Derby from 25 April to
7 July 1760 and the Turner who acted Montano in *Othello* at Covent Garden Theatre in
London on 23 June 1761. Turner per-

formed at Bath in 1763–64 and was Sir
Jasper Wilding in *The Citizen* at the Haymarket in London on 13 July 1764. A Turner was at Bath in 1765–66 and at Kilkenny,
Ireland, in 1768.

Turner, Mr *fl. 1778–1792₁, actor.*
Mr Turner played Burgundy in *King Lear* at
the Haymarket Theatre on 7 September 1778.
There on 22 January 1781 he was in *The
Sharper's Last Shift,* and on 26 March he acted
Lyrick in *Love and a Bottle.* At the Haymarket
on 12 December 1791 Turner played Lord
Randolph in *Douglas,* and on 26 December
1792 he repeated that role.

Turner, Mr *fl. 1798–1802₁, actor,
singer?*
Mr Turner, from the Norwich company, attempted Macbeth for his London debut at
Covent Garden Theatre on 15 December
1798. The *Monthly Mirror* took his performance apart:

This gentleman did not appear to us to possess, in
any sufficient degree, a single requisite for the profession of an actor; and we think, of all characters,
that of Macbeth is the last he should have chosen.
His figure is low, and not moulded with that elegance which will sometimes compensate for a deficiency in height; his voice, though loud and extensive, is coarse, hollow and monotonous; his
action and deportment are under no restraint of
grace or propriety.

Yet Turner received friendly support from "a
vast number of professional gentlemen" of his
fraternity, the law.

That was Turner's only recorded appearance
in London in the eighteenth century, but he
made his Bath debut on 28 September 1799,
according to Genest, and perhaps he was the
Turner, a soprano, who was a member of the
Bath Harmonic Society in 1799. Turner
played second leads in Bristol in 1799–1800
and on 13 January 1800 was advertised in
Salisbury as from the Bath theatre. He was at
Bath again in 1800–1801, and we believe
he was the Turner who performed in Manchester in 1801. A Manchester report on 16
February 1801 said that Turner was to play
Hamlet and Macbeth, among other characters, but his "voice is not yet matured,
and I must add, not sufficiently distinct, to

give the requisite energy and pathos the characters require." Yet he made £75 at his Manchester benefit. The *Monthly Mirror* noted that Turner did not make a second attempt in London until 27 October 1802, when he acted at Drury Lane.

Turner, Mrs, later Mrs Tame *fl. 1728–1743₁, actress, dancer.*

Mrs Turner, presumably the wife of the Turner who was active in London theatre from 1722, danced at the Haymarket Theatre on 5 October 1728 and then went on during the rest of the season to play Serena in *The Orphan,* Sylvia in *The Lottery,* Eboli in *Don Carlos,* and Venus in *The Humours of Harlequin.* In the company that season was Mr Turner, and after that, both left the London stage for several years.

When Mrs Turner played Tom Thumb in *The Tragedy of Tragedies* at the Haymarket on 13 December 1735 for her benefit, she was advertised as making her stage debut—but that kind of dissembling in playbills was not uncommon. We have guessed that the Mr Turner who had suffered losses and was given a benefit at Covent Garden Theatre in 1740 may have been our subject's husband. Coincidentally, the next time she appeared on the London stage she had become Mrs Tame. On 15 April 1743 Mrs Tame, "late Mrs Turner, of Bow Street" played Tom Thumb again for her benefit, postponed from 9 April because of her illness.

Turner, Miss *fl. 1735₁, actress.*

A Miss Turner played Emilia in *Othello* at York Buildings on 19 March 1735.

Turner, Miss *fl. 1745–1755₁, singer, harpsichordist.*

The "youngest Miss Turner" sang in a concert at the Devil Tavern on 14 March 1745. On 27 January 1753 she sang in a concert at the Great Room in Dean Street, Soho, and on 26 March 1754 a benefit was held there for her, at which *Solomon* was performed. She had another benefit on 11 March 1755, when *Esther* was given and Miss Turner played a concerto on the harpsichord. She was, according to Otto Deutsch in *Handel,* the daughter of Dr William Turner.

Turner, Miss *fl. 1782₁, actress.*

Miss Turner had a principal but unspecified role in *The Lawyer Nonsuited* at the Haymarket Theatre on 6 May 1782.

Turner, Ann. *See* BELFILLE, MRS, and ROBINSON, MRS JOHN THE FIRST.

Turner, Anthony *fl. 1622–1660₁, actor.*

Anthony Turner's pre-Restoration career is outlined in G. E. Bentley's *The Jacobean and Caroline Stage.* Turner was a member of Lady Elizabeth's troupe at the Cockpit (or Phoenix) in Drury Lane in 1622. His roles there were Justice Landby in *The Wedding* in 1626, "A kitching Maid" in the first part and Bashaw Alcade in the second part of *The Fair Maid of the West* about 1630, Old Lord Bruce in *King John and Matilda* in 1634, and Piston in *Hannibal and Scipio* in 1635.

There are nontheatrical references in the pre-Restoration period to an Anthony Turner who may have been the actor. On 23 October 1624 Dorothy Turner was ordered to appear at court "for cruelly beatinge and abusinge her husband Anthony Turner." In the registers of St Giles in the Fields, which contain the names of other actors of the time, are several citations for an Anthony Turner: his daughter Mary was buried on 26 November 1636, his wife Jone on 8 February 1640, his daughter Mary on 1 October 1641, his daughter Jane on 4 April 1642, and a "Crisom Child" on 19 March 1651.

Just before the Restoration our Turner was active in the theatre again. On 12 and 17 May 1659 he and Edward Shatterell were summoned before the Sessions of the Peace for putting on "Stage playes and enterludes att the Redd Bull in St. John's Street." That would have been the group of actors headed by John Rhodes, several of whom later became members of the Duke's Company under Sir William Davenant. Turner, Shatterell, Eaton, and Wintershall were charged on 12 May 1660 with performing illegally at the Red Bull. After 5 November theatrical records are silent about Anthony Turner, though he may have done more acting than we know. Two parish register entries may concern him, though identification is not certain: an Anthony Turner was buried at St Clement Danes on 31 August 1661; an Anthony Turner was executed for treason (he was a Jesuit) and buried at St Giles in the Fields on 20 June 1679.

Turner, John   d. c. 1776? trumpeter.

John Turner earned £40 annually as a trumpeter in the King's Musick from 1749 to 1759. On 5 February 1759 he was admitted to the Royal Society of Musicians, and the records in *The Royal Society of Musicians* (1985) show that Turner was married in November 1760 at St James, Marylebone. He was probably the Turner who was paid 5s. on 13 November 1761 by the management of Covent Garden Theatre for playing in *The Coronation* and £2 5s. by the management of Drury Lane Theater on 24 March 1774 for serving as an extra trumpeter for six nights. John Turner died before December 1776.

Turner, M.   fl. 1799–1815₁,   inventor.

The *Monthly Mirror* in July 1799 reported on the "Naumachia" being shown in Silver Street, Fleet Street: "This sublime exhibition, which gives a more correct representation of the battle of the Nile than can be imagined, continues to draw crowded audiences every evening, who are anxious to pay their tribute of applause to the ingenuity and invention of Mr. Turner." Turner exhibited his show at the Theatre Royal in Bath during the year and at Manchester in 1801. Charles Dibdin in his *Memoirs* wrote of Turner's work in March 1815:

A Gentleman who had invented a very extraordinary naumachial exhibition, illustrative of the Battle of the Nile, and which had attracted all the curiosity hunters in London, proposed to produce a similar exhibition on *our* Nile; for which we were to pay him a considerable sum of money if it succeeded; and be ourselves at the charge of all the Ships, machinery, etc. etc. necessary to the purpose. The preparations employed many hands, and much time, and occasioned us much expense; and we advertised it in the most effective manner; the public curiosity was highly excited, and completely disappointed.—It was entirely a failure. But it is necessary to say in justice to the artist, that it failed from the same defect as my heretofore mentioned *aquatic Fantoccini* failed, viz. the objects exhibited were too minute to be understood, or appreciated, by the audience, from the great distance between them; and they had been so accustomed to our large ships,—which every naval and

marine character allowed to be the *ne plus ultra* of that species of exhibition—that the Ships produced in *this* Battle of the Nile, appeared in comparison like Children's toys; and were, therefore, not at all *ad captandum*. Yet if our Artist did not ensure success, he certainly deserved it.—But the public mandate, in a Theatre, is imperative; and we immediately withdrew. The remuneration to be given to the Artist as the thing had failed, was settled between two private friends, one on each side; and what they awarded, we paid; and altho' we had lowered our flag, did not suffer it to lower our Spirits.

Dibdin was at the time at Sadler's Wells Theatre, which had featured aquatic spectacles.

Turner, Purbeck   fl. 1706–1720?₁, singer, actor.

A Mr Turner sang at the Queen's Theatre and then Drury Lane in the early eighteenth century, and it seems unlikely that he was Dr William Turner, the court singer, or Mr William Turner, the composer (who is not known to have been a singer). Our guess is that the theatre singer was Purbeck Turner, who was twice mentioned in printed songs as singing at the Theatre Royal. The 1706 edition of the opera *Camilla* has Turner down for the role of Latinus, which he may have sung on 30 March 1706, when the work was first presented at Drury Lane. Vice Chamberlain Coke's papers at Harvard show Turner to have been at the bottom of the list of singers at the Queen's Theatre about January 1708: his daily salary was 10s. (whereas Mrs Tofts was paid £7 10s). In 1707–8 and 1708–9 the singers performed first at Drury Lane, where Turner sang Latinus in *Camilla* on 6 December 1707, and then at the Queen's, where he was Arbantes in *Pirro e Demetrio* on 14 December 1708.

A Mr Turner—Purbeck presumably—had a benefit concert at Stationers' Hall on 30 November 1709 at which he and Reading sang a two-part song by John Blow. Turner was described in the advertisement as being he "who sets the Musick for the British Apollo." For a few years Turner's name did not appear in any advertisements, but beginning on 28 October 1715 he sang regularly at Drury Lane between the acts and in musical-theatre pieces. On 10 November he sang Mars in the second interlude in *Venus and Adonis,* and when the song

Beauty now alone shall move him from that work was separately published about 1715, the singer was identified as Mr Turner. An entr'acte song, *No, no, no; I will no more believe thee,* was also published about 1715 (according to the *Catalogue of Printed Music in the British Museum,* where the conjectural dates for undated publications are sometimes a few years off); the song was sung at Drury Lane by the "late Mr. Purbeck Turner." But we believe that the other references to a singing Mr Turner are to Purbeck and that the dating in the *Catalogue* could be two years off. Another song, *Wanton Cupids cease to hover,* published about 1720, names Purbeck Turner as the singer, at the Theatre Royal, and does not suggest that he was deceased. Our guess is that Turner died sometime after May 1717, when he was last mentioned in the bills.

In 1715–16, in addition to singing Mars in *Venus and Adonis,* Turner sang in an English cantata composed by Pepusch, was Peneus in *Apollo and Daphne,* sang "The Genius of England" between the acts, was Mercury in *The Death of Dido,* sang a "Mad Song" and "Mad Dialogue" by Purcell with Mrs Willis and spoke a prologue on 30 May 1716 (at Turner's benefit, shared with Robinson), acted the Mad Scholar in *The Pilgrim* (his first attempt at acting, on 19 July), and sang Neptune in *The Tempest.*

His 1716–17 season was not as busy. He sang between the acts on occasion, was again Neptune in *The Tempest* and the Mad Scholar in *The Pilgrim,* and sang Purcell's "Mad Dialogue" with Mrs Fitzgerald. He and Mrs Boman sang between the acts on several occasions, the last being on 22 May 1717, after which Turner's name dropped from the bills.

Turner, Robert *fl. 1660–1694?]*, *actor.*
On 5 November 1660 an agreement was drawn up between Sir William Davenant and his actors at the Salisbury Court Theatre; among the players signing on with Davenant was Robert Turner. The Lord Chamberlain's accounts mentioned Turner from time to time. On 4 July 1662, for example, Turner was one of the members of the Duke's Company who beat a messenger from Sir Henry Herbert's Office of the Revels; on 20 May 1669 Sir Henry sued Turner, Jacob Hall the rope dancer, and John Perin the actor; and

Nicholas Butler was given leave to sue Turner, probably for a debt, on 25 May 1669.

Theatrical notices of Turner are rare. He is only known to have played Joan in *The Slighted Maid* on 23 February 1663 at the Lincoln's Inn Fields Theatre. *The London Stage* confuses him in the 1673–74 season with the court singer William Turner. A Henry Turner (error for Robert?) was named in December 1694 as a former actor with the Duke's Company. Similarly, there is no way of telling whether or not the Turner mentioned in the *Satyr on the Players* about 1684 was Robert:

> Currer [*the actress*] 'tis time thou wert to Ireland
> > gone
> Thy utmost Rate is here but half a Crown
> Ask Turner if thou art not fulsom grown—

Turner, Samuel   *fl. 1773–1799]*,   *violinist, violist.*
Samuel Turner of Rochester became a member of the Royal Society of Musicians on 7 February 1773. He played tenor (viola) in the Handel Memorial Concerts in Westminster Abbey and the Pantheon in May and June 1784 and was cited in Doane's *Musical Directory* of 1794 as also a member of the Academy of Ancient Music. The minutes of the Royal Society mention Turner a few times in 1791 and 1792: he was ill, and the organization granted him some financial assistance. He was still on the membership list in 1799.

Turner, William   *1651–1740, singer, lutanist, composer.*
William Turner was born in Oxford in 1651, the son of a cook at Pembroke College. Turner received his musical education, first in the choir of Christ Church, Oxford, from Edward Lowe, and then from Captain Henry Cooke at the Chapel Royal in London. Samuel Pepys heard Captain Cooke's boys singing at Whitehall on 22 November 1663; with young Turner were Michael Wise, John Blow, Thomas Tudway, and Pelham Humphrey. He joined with Blow and Humphrey in the quick composition of a "Club Anthem," Turner writing the middle part, which was a bass solo. After his voice changed he left the Chapel, but he developed an excellent countertenor and became master of the choristers at Lincoln Cathedral.

On 11 October 1669 Turner, described as from Lincoln, was sworn a Gentleman of the Chapel Royal, a position he held until his death 71 years later. He received an unspecified annual salary and a yearly livery fee of £16 2s. 6d.—which was rarely paid on schedule. Whenever he accompanied the King on a trip out of London he was given additional pay— usually 8s. daily, which is what he received for service at Windsor in the summer of 1671. At the death of Henry Cooke in 1672 Turner was granted his place in the private music of Charles II. Turner, as Cooke's replacement among the singers and lutenists in the private music, was to receive £40 annually (that dropped to £30 under William III) and an allowance of £20 annually for strings (which may have been for all the lutes in the private music).

Like many court musicians, Turner had connections with the public theatres, one of his earliest being participation in the Duke's Company production of *The Tempest* at Dorset Garden Theatre in 1674. The "opera" was presented on 30 April and subsequent dates, and on 16 May the Lord Chamberlain issued an extraordinary notice concerning participation by court singers:

Chappellmen for ye theatre
It is his Majesty's pleasure that Mr. Turner and Mr. Hart or any other men or boys belonging to his Majesty's Chappell Royall that sing in ye Tempest at His Royal Highnesse Theatre doe remaine in towne all the weeke (during his Majesty's absence from Whitehall) to performe that service, only Saturdayes to repaire to Windsor and to returne to London on Mundayes if there be occassion for them. And that [they] also performe ye like service in ye opera in ye said theatre or any other thing in ye like nature where their helpe may be desired upon notice given them thereof.

Turner may have been involved in other theatrical productions, but we have the record of only one, at court: on 15 and 16 February he sang the Genius of England and Coridon in the masque *Calisto*.

By 1675 Turner had begun composing for the theatre. He contributed music to *The Libertine* in 1675, *Madam Fickle* and *Pastor Fido* in 1676, and *A Fond Husband* in 1677. He composed a number of songs and catches and many pieces of church music. After his flurry of activity connected with the theatres in the

mid-1670s Turner apparently gave up composing for the stage.

References to William Turner in the Lord Chamberlain's accounts over the years are many. Most of them concern livery payments (or nonpayments); on 22 January 1677, for example, he was to be paid £80 12s. 6d. for livery allowances for the previous five years. The accounts also name him from time to time for trips out of London: to Windsor in the summer of 1678, for instance, or to the Hague with the King in January 1691.

Turner was one of the select few chosen to sing for the Queen's birthday in the 1690s. He did so on 30 April 1690 and again in 1693. He also sang in the St Cecilia's Day celebration on 22 November 1692. In 1696 he was granted a Doctor of Music degree by Cambridge, after which he seems regularly to have been identified as Dr Turner, though some sources still confused him with Mr William Turner, who composed some theatre music in the first quarter of the eighteenth century and wrote a poor treatise called *Sound Anatomiz'd* in 1724.

The *London Gazette* reported that "On Wednesday next, the 4th of May [1698], will be performed in York-Buildings, the Song which was Sung before her Royal Highness on Her Birth Day last; With other Variety of New Vocal and Instrumental Musick, Composed by Dr Turner, and for his Benefit." Turner may well have had other benefit concerts, the records of which have been lost. A song set by Dr Turner, "Peace, peace, peace, peace," was published in *Mercurius Musicus* in June 1699, and it is probable that he was the composer, identified in that periodical as W. T., who wrote other songs published in 1699 and 1700.

Queen Anne held court at Windsor and Hampton Court frequently, and the Lord Chamberlain's accounts for the early years of the new century regularly cited Dr Turner as attending Her Majesty—23 days in 1702, 43 days in 1703, 55 days in 1708, 72 days in 1713. The tradition was continued by George I. The last notice we have of Turner's court service is a warrant dated 20 April 1725 authorizing payment to Dr Turner for attending at Windsor in the summer of 1724 for 20 days.

Dr Turner died on 13 January 1740 at his

house in Duke Street (*The Dictionary of National Biography* says King Street), Westminster. His wife Elizabeth had died on the ninth; she had been 85, he 90. They were buried in the same grave at Westminster Abbey on 16 January. He had written his will on 4 January 1728, cutting off his children with one shilling each. They were William Partheriche Turner, Edward Turner, Elizabeth Jenkins, Catherine Gardiner, and Ann Robinson (Mrs John). He left his estate to his wife Elizabeth. The will was proved on 14 February 1740 by Ann Robinson, but we do not know how the estate was divided. Ann Robinson had married the organist John Robinson on 6 September 1716.

The *New Grove Dictionary of Music and Musicians* has an extensive list of Turner's compositions.

Turner, William   *fl.* 1785–1803?], *scene painter.*

When *Omai* was presented at Covent Garden Theatre on 20 December 1785 a Mr Turner was listed as one of the scene painters. The accounts show a payment to him of over £27 on 25 January 1786. Curtis Price in *Turner Studies* (Winter 1987) reports that in the Bedford Estates archives are records of a William Turner serving as a scene-painting assistant at the Pantheon from as early as 30 April 1791. On 14 May Turner was paid £9 9s. for two weeks' work. The accounts reveal that he sometimes worked from seven in the morning until seven at night and was in attendance on at least one Sunday. Payments to him continued through 18 June. He may have been the Turner cited in the Covent Garden accounts in 1802–3.

Could the Pantheon painter have been the great Joseph Mallord William Turner (1775–1851)? Price shows the signature of the Pantheon painter William Turner and that of J. M. W. Turner and points out similarities. He also notes that William Turner's activity at the Pantheon came during the Plaister Academy's Easter vacation, when J. M. W. Turner would have been free. Price observes other coincidences but admits that the evidence is not conclusive. Indeed, had *the* Turner (an inveterate theatre-goer) had early experience as a scene painter one would suppose that biographers like Jack Lindsay (*Turner: The Man and His Art,* 1985) and John Gage (*J. W. M. Turner,* 1987) would have found certain evidence of it. Without further evidence we can only report Price's interesting speculation.

Turner, William   *fl.* 1794], *singer.*

Doane's *Musical Directory* of 1794 lists William Turner of No 27, Stangate Street, Lambeth, as both a tenor and a bass who sang in the Handelian performances at Westminster Abbey.

Turrschmidt, Mr   *fl.* 1786], *horn player.*

Mr Turrschmidt and Mr Palsa played French horns at concerts on 13 March 1786 at the Tottenham Street Music Room and on 8 April 1786 at the Ancient Concert Rooms on Tottenham Street.

Tursleton. *See* TWISLETON.

Turtle, Mr   *fl.* 1782–1789], *singer.*

Mr Turtle was named with many others on benefit bills for Covent Garden Theatre from 8 May 1782 through 16 June 1789. He was evidently a member of the singing chorus, for in May and June 1784 at Westminster Abbey and the Pantheon he was one of the tenors singing in the Handel Memorial Concerts.

Tutton, James   1761–1817, *clarinetist, violinist.*

When James Cornish recommended James Tutton as a member of the Royal Society of Musicians on 4 January 1784, he certified Tutton to be "a proper person to be a Member. . . . He is a single man, plays claronett [*sic*] and violin—23 years of age. . . . Plays in the [Guards] 1st Regiment Band and at the Royal Circus."

Tutton played violin in the Society's annual May benefit concerts at St Paul's Cathedral in 1791, 1792, and 1794. By 6 April 1817 he was in poor health and was granted 15 guineas for medical aid. By 1 June following he had died, and Mrs Tutton was granted a pension and £8 toward funeral expenses, it being established by "M. Simcock, Collector," that Tutton "had before his decease paid his Subscription to this Fund to Xmas 1817." The Tuttons were said to have had no children.

During years following, Tutton's widow

was granted (or refused) sums for "additional relief." On 2 April 1820 she was "granted the usual dowry of 30 guineas" when she presented a certificate of her marriage to James Carew. On 5 November 1826 she again applied for relief but was refused because she had remarried. But on 1 January 1832, her second husband now dead, she was readmitted as a pensioner. She was still receiving medical relief in November 1838.

The James Rufus Tutton, harpsichordist and violinist, son of Rufus Tutton, who was declared by his father to have been born on 16 August 1799 and who was admitted to the Society on 5 July 1829 was probably a nephew of James Tutton.

Twaites, Miss   *fl. 1797₁,   actress.*

A Miss Twaites played Corinna in *The Citizen,* the afterpiece of a performance given under special license at the Haymarket Theatre on 4 December 1797.

Twaits, William   *1781–1814,   actor, singer, dancer, manager.*

The authority for the early life and provincial English career of William Twaits is William Dunlap, who wrote in his *History of the American Theatre* (1832):

Mr. William Twaits was born on the 25th of April 1781. His father died when he was very young, and he obtained admittance behind the scenes of Drury-lane, through the influence of a playmate, the son of Phillemore [John Phillimore], one of the performers. Having determined to be an actor, he stuck to the point, as [George] Colman [the younger] says, "like a rusty weathercock," and we suppose, like most of our heroes, ran away. He commenced acting at a place called Waltham Abbey.

Dunlap mentioned no London experience for Twaits. But *The London Stage* cites two performances, a year apart, both in the humble precincts of Wheatley's Riding School, Greenwich. On 8 June 1798 nine provincial actors staged a performance as a benefit for five of them, Twaits included. He played Glenalvon in *Douglas* and Tom Tug in *The Waterman* and sang between the acts. The effusive appeal on the bill informed the gentry of Greenwich, "with the utmost Deference and Respect," that the actors were giving only one perform-

Harvard Theatre Collection

WILLIAM TWAITS, as Sir Adam Contest
engraving by Smith

ance, "being compelled to answer their engagements in another town."

On 17 May 1799, again at the Riding School, a group including some of the previous summer's players acted *She Stoops to Conquer* and *The Agreeable Surprise.* Twaits was Tony Lumpkin ("with a *song* in character") in the mainpiece. After that performance Twaits retreated again—to the Midlands, presumably, where, wrote Dunlap, "he had been the Richard and Romeo of many a barn, when he had the promise of the highest salary in the company, nine shillings per week, and was obliged to be content with two-and-sixpence; when he feasted upon a hog's heart and vegetables (cost ninepence, baking a penny) for a week. . . ."

Twaits apparently was not given a chance at the London patent theatres, even though W. B. Wood reported that he was "considered one of the best burletta singers in England." Wood imported him to Philadelphia from Birmingham, where he had been a favorite in the elder Macready's company, and gave him the equivalent of four guineas a week. But Twaits proved so valuable that in a short while that salary was raised to six guineas.

Dunlap described Twaits's singular appearance:

Short and thin, yet appearing broad; muscular yet meagre; a large head, with stiff, stubborn, carroty hair; long colourless face, prominent hooked nose, projecting large hazel eyes, thin lips, and large mouth, which could be twisted into a variety of expression, and which, combining with his other features, eminently served the purposes of the comic muse—such was [his] physiognomy. . . .

Twaits made his American debut at the Chestnut Street Theatre in Philadelphia as Dr Pangloss in *The Heir at Law* on 14 December 1803 (according to Dunlap; T. Allston Brown gives 23 November), when his success was so decisive that every print-shop in the city displayed engravings of him in the part.

After two seasons in Philadelphia, Twaits went to New York, appearing at the Park Street Theatre for the first time on 21 June 1805, for Dunlap's benefit, as Caleb Quotem in *The Wags of Windsor*. Mrs Eliza A. Westray Villiers—whom Twaits would marry in May 1808—played Leonora that night. The *Post* next day found Twaits's performance "the most spirited laughter-provoking piece of low comedy we ever yet witnessed. His song was ludicrous beyond conception; it was given with such effect, and excited such a tumult of applause, as seemed to threaten to bring the walls of the theatre about our ears." The managers were advised to "detain Mr. Twaits, . . . if anything short of compulsion can do it."

The managers did "detain" him through the summer season of 1805, while he increased his popularity in such roles as Megrim in *Blue Devils*, Dominique in *Paul and Virginia*, Stave in *The Shipwreck*, Shelty in *The Highland Reel*, Goldfinch in *The Road to Ruin*, Trudge in *Inkle and Yarico*, Ruttekin in *Robin Hood*, and Dick Dashall in *The Way to Get Married* and scored frequently with comic songs like "The Origin of Old Bachelors" and "Giles Scroggins's Ghost." But he spent the

1805–6 season performing at Boston, coming again to New York for a summer of acting and singing in "musical divertissements" in the new summer theatre called Vauxhall in 1806.

Twaits went on acting broad comedy in New York, at the Park Theatre or the Olympic, in the winter seasons (except 1810–11) through 1813–14. But he insisted, many times, on trying tragedy, somewhat to the diminution of his reputation: "Twaits," observed Dunlap, "seriously thought that his features were fitted for tragedy, and that he only wanted height to be like John Kemble." Shylock, Lear, and, particularly, Richard II were fatally seductive to Twaits when, on his benefit nights, he had a choice of parts, despite scoldings such as that from the *Rambler* in October 1806 over his Richard: "Mr. Twaits's peculiar physiognomy, his awkward gait, nasal twang, and *petite* form, all disqualify him for those parts where dignity of person, and gracefulness of carriage are essential concomitants."

Twaits was a leading actor and one of six manager-shareholders of the theatre at Richmond, Virginia, from August 1810 until the calamitous fire of 26 December 1811, which took 77 lives. After that tragedy he hastened back to New York. On 14 July 1812 the *Columbian* advertised the opening in Anthony Street, New York, of the Olympic Theatre, managed by Twaits, Placide, and Breschard.

Twaits's wife, Eliza Westray Villiers Twaits, who had never performed in England, was a considerable success in New York and Philadelphia. Twaits was himself declining rapidly in health when, on 13 December 1813, Mrs Twaits died suddenly, and her death seemed to accelerate his decline. Dunlap said of Twaits's malady that "frequent exertions of his lungs in public and private, ultimately changed asthma into consumption." But Dunlap hints also that Twaits was "a great . . . favourite with convivialists," so it may be that drinking hastened his death, which occurred on 22 August 1814, in New York. He was buried there in St Paul's churchyard, according to *Miscellanea Genealogica et Heraldica*.

William Twaits is pictured as Sir Adam Contest in *The Wedding Day* in an engraving by J. R. Smith. An anonymous engraving of him as Dr Panglos in *The Heir at Law* was also published.

"Twangdilo, Signor"   *fl.* 1752–1760₁, Jew's harp player.

"Signor Twangdilo" was Christopher Smart's pseudonym for one of the performers in the exceedingly popular *Old Woman's Oratory*, which began at the Haymarket Theatre on 7 December 1752 and continued, with variations, all season. On the opening night Twangdilo was identified only as a casuist; he played the Jew's harp. His specialty was omitted beginning 18 December but Twangdilo was named on the bill for 13 March 1753— presumably to play the Jew's harp again. On 29 March the Jew's harp was played by Mr Church. Among Smart's ("Mrs Midnight's") "band of originals" at the Haymarket on 14 February 1760 was, again, Signor Twangdilo, but the bill did not indicate what he did.

"Twanglyre, Shadrach"   *fl.* 1774₁, Jew's harp player.

On 15 March 1774 at the Haymarket Theatre a benefit was held for Dr Arne. The evening consisted of catches, glees, *Timotheus*, a comic ode, and instrumental music. Within the comic ode, written by Bonnell Thornton, was introduced a musical piece for saltbox, Jew's harp, marrow bones and cleavers, and hurdy-gurdy. "Shadrach Twanglyre" played the Jew's harp.

Tweedale, Miss, later Mrs Austin   *fl.* 1787–1792₁,   *actress.*

"A Young Lady" making her first appearance "on any stage" played Louisa in *The West Indian* at Covent Garden Theatre on 14 November 1787. She was identified in the *European Magazine* for that month as a Miss Tweedale. She had a considerable vogue over the next two seasons, even though in *A Trip to Parnassus* (1788) Apollo was made to chide her gently:

> With a person whose charms o'er each heart might
>   prevail
> Now forth from the crowd step'd the lovely
>   TWEEDALE.
> Apollo discern'd, from her manner and air,
> She thought it was merit enough to be fair.
> "Charming creature (he cried) it gives me much
>   pain,
> "To see one so lovely, so thoughtless and vain:
> "Your beauty might warm the cold bosom of age,
> "But beauty alone will not do on the stage.

> "You must have animation, must feel what you
>   speak.
> "Call a tear to your eye, or a blush to your cheek.
> "It is wrong on the stage, when performing a part,
> "Like a school girl, to con o'er your lesson by
>   heart."

—and so on.

Her other roles were nearly all comic ones and good ones: in 1787–88, Lady Touchwood in *The Belle's Stratagem*, Julia in *Which Is the Man?*, Constantia in *The Man of the World*, Lucinda in *The Conscious Lovers*, Narcissa in *Tantara Rara, Rogues All!*, Rosa in *Fontainebleau*, and Harriet in *The Jealous Wife;* and in 1788–89, Louisa in *The West Indian*, Harriet in *The Devil upon Two Sticks*, Miss Ogle in *The Belle's Stratagem*, Serina in *The Orphan*, Miss Leeson in *The School for Wives*, and Arabella in *A School for Widows.*

Her subsequent history seems to have been distressed. Evidently she went to Ireland and fell in with a man, perhaps an actor, named Austin. The London *Diary* of 2 March 1790 carried the news that her nominal husband Austin had been convicted in the Old Bailey of petty larceny. In 1792 *An Answer to the Memoirs of Mrs Billington* reported that our subject had engaged with the abominable Richard Daly in Dublin, that he had "starved" her into an affair with him (his frequent practice), and that she had contracted a "violent disorder" which had marred her beauty. She was said to have gone to Cork and there to have met a Quaker sea captain who took her to America.

"Twelve-Bell Man," The. *See* FRANKLIN, Mr.

Twiddy, Miss   *fl.* 1787–1789₁,   actress, singer.

A Miss Twiddy acted and sang some "principal character" unspecified in Giardini's new burletta *The Boarding School* at Hughes's Royal Circus in St George's Fields, according to a playbill dating about mid-summer of 1787. Probably she was the same Miss Twiddy who played Elmira in the farce *The Sultan* at the Margate Theatre on 11 August 1789.

Perhaps Miss Twiddy was related to Thomas Twiddy, a trumpeter who was connected to the Norwich playhouse from about 1769 until

1803, and to William Twiddy, an actor at Norwich from about 1781 who died there on 2 April 1798, according to the *Norwich Mercury* of 7 April.

Twiford. *See* TWYFORD.

Twisdale. *See* TISDALL.

Twiselton, Mr ₍*fl.* 1713₎, *trumpeter.*
Mr Twiselton, advertised as "Trumpet to his Excellency the Duke of Aumont," played a benefit concert at Caverley's Academy, Chancery Lane, on 20 March 1713. His selection was a sonata for trumpet composed by Corelli "on purpose for Mr. Twiselton when he was at Rome."

Twisleton, Mrs Thomas James, Charlotte Ann Frances, née Wattell, later Mrs Thomas Sandon, sometime stage name Mrs Stanley *c. 1770–1812, actress.*
Charlotte Ann Frances Wattell, daughter of John Wattell, Esq, and niece of Sir John Stonehouse, was about 18, and Thomas James

CHARLOTTE TWISLETON (when Mrs Stanley)
engraving by Snyder

Twisleton, second son of Lord Say and Sele, was 19 and still a student at Westminster School when their interest in amateur theatricals brought them together. Twisleton was already a veteran of Latin school plays and of some modern works that he had acted with his mother and sister and other amateurs at Adlestrop House near Stow-in-the-Wold. On 9 May 1788 he took the role of Mentevole in Jephson's tragedy *Julia* at Freemasons' Hall in London. Miss Wattell was assigned the title role. (Sybil Rosenfeld describes the performance in *Temples of Thespis*.)

The young couple fell quickly in love, eloped to Scotland, and were married there on 28 September 1788. There was a more regular ceremony at St Marylebone Church in London on 4 November. The mild interest shown by the newspapers in the union of the second son of a peer to a minor provincial heiress was quickened when both Twisleton and his bride continued to be prominent in amateur evenings and then began to act in public for money. They were under no necessity to do so, if news reports of her fortune are to be be-

CHARLOTTE TWISLETON
engraving by Ridley, after Naish

lieved. One clipping, dated 8 October 1788, suggested that "Mr. TWISLETON by his marriage with Miss WATTLE, has got possession of an amiable little girl, that must make any man the happiest of TRIFLERS:—The lady's age is about eighteen and her fortune about £4,000."

The *Morning Post* of 22 January 1789 reported further participation of the young couple in the Adlestrop theatricals as Edwin and Matilda in *Matilda,* Raymond and Hortensia in *The Count of Narbonne,* Pierre and Belvidera in *Venice Preserv'd,* Lord Minikin and Miss Tittup in *Bon Ton,* and Gradus and Charlotte in *Who's the Dupe?* A clipping dated 6 December 1789 contains the information that "Mr. and Mrs. TWISLETON are talked of as auxiliaries to the drama of Richmond-house [residence of the Prince of Wales]—the gentleman in *Pierre*—the lady in *Lady Macbeth."*

Records of the Twisletons' activities are sparse for several years after 1789. On 5 June 1790 "The Lady of the Hon. Thomas James Twisleton was safely delivered of a son, at his house in Portland-street." There were hints of their forays into the provinces to perform in both amateur and professional companies. But the satisfactions of acting before small aristocratic audiences with amateurs of small talent eventually palled. Gradually they became professionals—at least she did. She had attracted the attention of J. G. Holman, and he had hired both her and her husband to act with him in Liverpool in July 1793, according to the *World* of 27 July 1793. At Holman's behest she was given an audition by Harris at Covent Garden. Evidently she was approved, but her engagement was delayed, for a Winston excerpt in the Folger Library, dated only 1793, reads, "The Hon. Mrs. Twisleton is not yet recov'd fr a recent Encouchem^t The Rumor of Her appce at C. G. may therefore be consid^d as unfounded."

A news report of 29 January 1794 that "The Hon. Mr. TWISSELTON and his Lady are to be the new Pierre and Belvidera, on Saturday next [1 February] at Covent-Garden Theatre" was corrected two days later: "The Hon. Mr. TWISSELDON has, it seems, suddenly declined appearing on the *Stage,* and turned his thoughts more *devoutly* towards the

Pulpit:—His Lady, however, pursues the bent of her theatrical genius. . . ." (The Dowager Viscountess Say and Sele, despite her own fascination with acting, had applied pressure, and her son had fled to the ancient refuge of second sons, the Church. A transcript dated only February 1794 tells us "The Hon. Mr. Twisleton has been to Oxford to take a Degree previous to going to Orders. By availing himself of the Prerogative of Birth he is entitled to that of M.A. He in that manly Manner with wh[ich] he always acts chose only to take the Bachelors & disdain'd to profit by accidental Advantages." His noble restraint was rewarded by 22 March following: "The Hon. Mr. Twisleton of St. Mary Hall Oxfd is admitted to the Deg. of B.A.").

J. G. Holman played Jaffeir when he brought his protegée Mrs Twisleton forward at Covent Garden as Belvidera on 1 February 1794. Her notices were mixed. The *Morning Chronicle* found her a "beautiful miniature" but felt that her "voice wants musical sweetness" and "does not touch the heart." The *European Magazine* judged that "This lady's features are agreeable and her person possesses peculiar symmetry and elegance, but the latter is rather *petite* and the former wants expression. Her voice wants variety, and, possibly from too much exertion, in order to fill so large a theatre, it came upon the ear with a loud monotony, destructive of all possibility of pathetic effect." It was evident that she had "watched Mrs. Siddons." Yet "It was an effort which entitles the lady to no inconsiderable share of commendation."

She filled out the rest of her contracted nights, scattered from February to 6 May, as Calista in *The Fair Penitent,* Euphrasia in *The Grecian Daughter,* Cordelia in *King Lear,* Juliet in *Romeo and Juliet* (on 30 April, for her benefit; tickets to be had of her at No 2, James Street, the Adelphi), and, for Holman's benefit, Statira in *Alexander the Great.* A Covent Garden ledger sheet in the Harvard Theatre Collection notes that her pay for her exertions that season was the clear profit from her benefit: £172.

In the summer of 1794, Mrs Twisleton was engaged for six nights at the Crow Street Theatre, Dublin, billed as "the Hon. Mrs Twisleton from Covent Garden." She moved on from

Dublin to the Bath-Bristol company in the 1794–95 season. It was reported that spring, according to a Winston extract, that "This Lady has not quitted the Stage, but does not enter into any regular Articles, making (like Palmer) a Kind of theatrical Tour, & playing a certain Number of Nights at diff: places." And indeed in the summer of 1795 she exploited her tenuous association with nobility before curious audiences at Bristol, Bath, Birmingham (including Holman's benefit at Birmingham on 24 August), Margate, and Brighton. She had been the center, at Bath, of a brief flurry of charge and refutation in the newspapers. A clipping dated 17 March 1795 contains a defense of her conduct:

The Bath edict, prohibiting public performers from frequenting the [Assembly] Rooms, has been said to originate from Mrs. TWISLETON claiming her right of precedence in a dance.—Another statement attributes it to her being seated on the bench of Honourables. Both these assertions we find to be erroneous. Mrs. TWISLETON never stood up to dance in a Bath ball-room, and never was seated on the benches of precedency. A love of truth impels us to say so much:—had [she] claimed her rank, she would only have asserted an undoubted right.

In September she went to Newcastle, summoned by the northern manager Stephen Kemble who, unable to secure Ann Brunton Merry as his leading tragedienne for the coming winter, decided to take a chance with a newcomer who had been drawing good houses. Mrs Twisleton went on with Kemble to Edinburgh in December and on 23 January 1796 opened the season there as Calista in *The Fair Penitent*. She played there through mid-April, attaining great popularity and sustaining many new leading roles: Alicia in *Jane Shore*, Berinthia in *A Trip to Scarborough*, Catherine in *Catherine and Petruchio*, Charlotte Rusport in *The West Indian*, Clarinda in *The Suspicious Husband*, Emily in *The Wheel of Fortune*, Emmeline in *Speculation*, Lady Anne Mordent in *The Deserted Daughter*, Lady Emily Gayville in *The Heiress*, Lady Randolph in *Douglas*, Lady Racket in *Three Weeks after Marriage*, Lady Ruby in *First Love*, Leonora in *Lovers' Quarrels*, Lydia Languish in *The Rivals*, Miss Woodburn in *Every One Has His Fault*, Olivia in *The Man of Ten Thousand*, Queen Elizabeth

in *Richard III*, Roxana in *The Rival Queens*, and the Widow Belmour in *The Way to Keep Him*. Kemble asked her to return the following season.

In May 1796 the *Monthly Mirror* found Mrs Twisleton performing in Hull, and bills in the Birmingham Public Library show that she was still in Hull in July. She and Twisleton had almost certainly recently separated, though two news reports point to the fact that she was again pregnant. The first, dated 22 August 1796, declared that she had "declined her Edinburgh and Newcastle engagements" and that Miss Gough had been hired in her place. The second, dated 18 November, crudely expected her "to be in the *straw* early in the next month."

The popular actress Elizabeth Farren had at last married the Earl of Derby and retired from the stage on 8 April 1797, and there was speculation that Mrs Twisleton might succeed her at Drury Lane. One newspaper reported that she, "the tragedian, who aspires to be the *comic* successor of *ci-devant* FARREN, is sweating down for *shapes* accordingly," a reference to Miss Farren's meager figure and Mrs Twisleton's now maternal one. But the speculation about the ascent was idle.

Twisleton, his wife's career faltering and her money gone, had found even the formal connection with her an impediment to his progress in the Church, and he had petitioned Parliament for a bill of separation. On 3 March 1798 the newspapers reported that he had obtained a divorce at Doctors' Commons. Apparently a bill had also been proposed in Parliament containing some language prejudicial to Mrs Twisleton's reputation, and her family had objected. A news account dated 21 April 1798 is of interest in interpreting Mr Twisleton's character as well as his wife's:

A petition was presented from Mrs. Twisleton's mother against an allegation contained in the preamble of the Bill, respecting a child born seven months after a deed of separation had taken place between Mr. Twisleton and his wife; but the Counsel had already been instructed to omit that part of the allegation.
The usual forms were then gone through, and a witness proved that a Mr. Steele and Mrs. Twisleton had lived together as man and wife. A deed of separation was then read, by which Mr. Twisleton

had settled an annuity of £100 per annum upon his wife during her life, and in consequence of which an actual separation took place . . . previous to any criminal conduct on her part.

Mr. Twisleton, agreeable to the late adopted standing orders for Divorces, was called to the Bar, and examined upon oath as to his motives for having granted this deed of settlement, which, he said, was on account of her extravagance threatening him with ruin; and her extreme partiality for the Stage depriving him of all domestic happiness, and on which she had actually appeared, much against his will.

The Duke of NORFOLK thought evidence ought to be given at the Bar of the legitimacy of all the children, as the allegation in the preamble tended to call some doubts upon them.

The Duke was overruled by the Lord Chancellor.

On 9 June 1798 the newspapers carried the announcement of the marriage of Twisleton ("the Hon. and Rev.") to Ann Ashe, daughter of Benjamin Ashe, Esq, "formerly in the East India Company's service." Equipped with a nabob's daughter, Twisleton was on his way to a D.D. and, eventually, to the archdeaconship of Colombo.

On 11 July 1799, "Thomas Sandon, Esq., of this parish {St George, Hanover Square], B[achelor}, & Charlotte Anne Frances Wattell, of St George, Southwark, Surrey, single woman (her marriage with the Hon. Thomas James Twiselton having been dissolved by Act of Parl[t]) were married by license," according to the church register. The former Mrs Twisleton had already dramatically renounced her "Honourable" in a notice to the London papers on 21 January 1799: "Miss Wattell (late Mrs. Twisleton) respectfully informs her Friends, and the Public in general, that, through an unintentional mistake of Mr. Palmer, the playbill for his benefit gave her a name which she had not the smallest wish of retaining. . . ." Future bills would call her Miss Wattell.

But there were no more bills carrying any of her names in London. She, with her new husband, underwent another name-change, to "Stanley," under which both were seen acting at York in 1800. A clipping dated 26 May 1802 speaks of her returning with a female companion from France in the "elegance of Parisian costume." Another, of December 1802, alludes vaguely to a difficulty over child support. On 12 February 1803 her counsel obtained for her a discharge from the custody of the warden of the Fleet Prison. She had passed herself off as "the Honorable Mrs Sandon," daughter of a peer, "and by such artifice obtained articles to the value of £7 which she pledged {pawned] to support her husband Mr Sandon confined in the Fleet for debt. . . ."

The fate of Thomas Sandon is not known. Charlotte Anne Frances Twisleton Sandon was hired, somewhere in the English provinces, for the Federal Street theatre in Boston, Massachusetts. On 26 October 1806 "Mrs Stanley" made her first American appearance there, playing Letitia Hardy in *The Belle's Stratagem*. In his *Retrospections*, Bernard admired her face and figure and compared her favorably to Mrs Abington, Miss Farren, and Mrs Merry. She remained at Boston for two seasons, was briefly at the Chestnut Street Theatre in Philadelphia, and then at the Park Street Theatre in New York in 1808. Bernard wrote of her re-arrival in Boston in 1809, "from a country circuit she had been taking; but as we could not agree upon terms, she quitted us for a lucrative and agreeable situation in the Canadas, to perform there in private with military amateurs."

S. M. Oland has called our attention to the performance of a Mrs Stanley in Halifax, Nova Scotia, on 5 March 1811. According to the *Columbian Centinel* of 26 December 1812, Mrs Stanley had recently died in Burlington, Vermont.

A portrait of Charlotte Twisleton, engraved by Ridley, after W. Naish, was published in the *Monthly Mirror*, April 1796. An engraved portrait of her by Snyder was published as a plate to *The Polyanthus*, January 1807.

Twiss, Mrs Francis. *See* KEMBLE, FRANCES.

Twiss, John. *See* TWIST, JOHN.

Twisselton or **Twistleton.** *See* TWISLETON.

Twist, Mr ₁*fl.* 1772₁, *violinist.*
In his *Diary*, Sylas Neville reported that on Saturday, 22 August 1772, he "was at a very genteel concert at the Assembly room. A Mr. Twist, a gentleman of this city, plays remarkably well upon the violin. He played a solo."

Twist, Mr *fl. 1794–1795₁,   carpenter.*

On a manuscript (Add 29949) in the British Library a Mr Twist is listed as a carpenter at Covent Garden Theatre in 1794–95.

Twist, Miss   *fl. 1777–1787₁,   actress, singer.*

On 9 June 1777 at the Haymarket Theatre, "A Young Gentlewoman," announced as making her first appearance on any stage, acted Nysa in O'Hara's *Midas.* That burletta was repeated on 13 and 18 June and 1 July, and then at the fifth performance on 14 July Miss Twist was named in the bills. On 18 July she played a Fairy in *The Fairy Tale,* and on 24 July appeared as Isabel in *The Portrait.* Her other roles were Cephisa in *April Day* on 22 August and Patience (with a song) in *Henry VIII* on 29 August.

The following season she made her debut at Covent Garden Theatre on 8 January 1778 as Mandane in *Artaxerxes,* again billed anonymously as "A Young Lady" making her first appearance on that stage. The *Morning Post* of 9 January identified her as Miss Twist from the Haymarket, as did that month's *Westminster Magazine,* where it was also reported that she was the sister of the late Dolly Twist (d. 1774) of Covent Garden. (That relationship would also make her the sister of the dancer Sukey Twist and probably of Charlotte and Mary Twist, two supernumerary walk-ons in 1769–70.) *Artaxerxes* was not repeated that season, but very likely Miss Twist was the unidentified pupil of the late Dr Arne who on 1 May 1778 played Polly in *The Beggar's Opera* and Sabrina and a Pastoral Nymph in *Comus.*

In the summer of 1778 Miss Twist returned to the Haymarket, where she performed Margery in *Love in a Village* on 22 May. Subsequently she appeared again as Nysa and Patience, and as Buxom Joan in Willet's burletta of that name. When she played Theodosia in *The Maid of the Mill* on 9 and 10 July, the critic in the *Morning Chronicle* of 11 July reported that "as a musical performer she has undoubted merit; as an actress we fear she never will acquire much reputation." That summer Miss Twist also played Isabella in the premiere of Dibdin's comic opera *The Gipsies* on 3 August 1778, and repeated her roles of Isabel in *The Portrait,* Cephisa in *April Day,* and Buxom Joan.

The next two summers also were spent by Miss Twist at the Haymarket. In 1779 she played her familiar roles—Margery, Nysa, and Patience—and on 31 August appeared in an unspecified part in the premiere of Colman's *The Separate Maintenance.* Her roles in 1780 included Nysa, Margery, and Theodosia again, and Sabrina and a Pastoral Nymph in *Comus* on 24 June.

The remainder of Miss Twist's career was passed in the provinces, mainly at Bath and Bristol, where she appeared regularly in a similar repertory from 1781–82 through 1786–87. Among her roles at Bath in the spring of 1782, for example, were a Shepherdess in *The Maid of the Oaks,* Peggy in *The Gentle Shepherd,* and Dollalolla in *Tom Thumb the Great.* On 28 May 1782 she sang "With Hound and with Horn" in a forest setting and dressed in the character of Diana. She also was advertised to sing in a number of benefit concerts at the Bristol Assembly Room in Princes' Street, including those given on 16 April 1783, 7 April 1784, 6 July 1784, 2 November 1784, 26 September 1785, and 21 October 1786.

Twist, Charlotte   *fl. 1769–1770₁,   supernumerary.*

On 26 April 1770 the Covent Garden treasurer paid Charlotte and Mary Twist £1 10s. each for "walking 12 nights" in *Man and Wife.* Colman's comedy about the Shakespeare Jubilee had opened on 7 October 1769. These two Twists were probably related to Dorothy and Sukey Twist, regular performers at Covent Garden during that time. It is possible that either Charlotte or Mary Twist was the Miss Twist (fl. 1777–1787) who made her "first appearance on any stage" at the Haymarket on 9 June 1777 as Nysa in *Midas.*

Twist, Dolly   *d. 1774, dancer, actress, singer.*

Between 1757 and 1774 the name of a Miss Twist appeared regularly in the Covent Garden bills as a dancer; and in several seasons, specifically 1759–60, 1762–63, 1766–67, 1768–69, and 1769–70, there were two Misses Twist dancing at that theatre. The first names of Dolly and Sukey Twist are in the Covent Garden account book on 24 September 1768; each was paid £1 5s. per week through 1769–70. They signed their surnames and first initials to a public letter from the Covent Garden performers, addressed to Colman, that was printed in the *Theatrical Monitor* on 4 November 1768.

Presumably Dolly and Sukey Twist were sisters. It is nearly impossible to separate their careers, because their modest repertoires were similar. We have arbitrarily determined that Dolly was the Miss Twist who performed in the seasons 1756–57 through 1758–59, before the second Miss Twist appeared. We know that when Dolly Twist died in 1774 she was described as of Covent Garden Theatre. So perhaps it can be assumed that Dolly was the one who continued to perform there after 1769–70 (the last season both were in the company) through 1773–74.

If our assumptions are correct, then Dolly was the Miss "Twiste" who danced a minuet with Master Settree at Covent Garden on 25 May 1757. Several weeks later at the Haymarket Theatre she appeared in a new comic ballet called *The Marine Boys Marching to Portsmouth.* Her partners were Masters Settree, Cowley, Hussey, and other young performers, so it is likely that she was a teenager at the time. That summer at the Haymarket she also danced with young Settree in such specialty numbers as *Blind Man's Buff* and *The Tailors.* Those dances were included in a program called *A Medley Concert,* which was offered by Theophilus Cibber regularly from early summer through October, and in November the title of the entertainment was changed to *Mrs Midnight's Medley Concert.* On 31 October 1757 Miss Twist played Colombine in a production by youngsters of *The Farmer Trick'd.* On 6 March 1758 she and Master Settree danced *Colin and Phebe.* They returned to Covent Garden on 20 April 1758 to perform a comic dance and a piece called *The Prussian Sailors,* at which time they were advertised as scholars of the elder Settree. Announced as making their first appearance on the Drury Lane stage they danced at that theatre on 1 June 1758 in *The Prussian Sailors* and *The Faggot Binders.*

In 1758–59 Miss Twist was engaged at Drury Lane, where on 16 September 1758 she and Master Settree performed a new comic dance. She appeared in a new *Grand Dance* on 9 May 1759 and in a *New Dutch Dance* on 15

May (when she shared in benefit tickets). In a special summer performance at that house on 12 July 1759, she danced in *The Threshers.*

The following season Miss Twist's name was in the bills very infrequently. At the Haymarket on 2 June 1760 some unspecified dancing was performed by "the Misses Twist," indicating that Dolly's sister Sukey, probably younger, had begun her career. No doubt it was Dolly who was at Drury Lane on 19 June 1760 to dance in a program given "by the Richmond Company for the Benefit of Distress'd Actors."

In May 1761 Miss Twist, presumably Dolly, danced her *Provincial Sailors* at Covent Garden on the eighth and then joined the Haymarket company for the summer. She had a benefit on 22 August 1761; the bill gave her address as No 10, Wild Court, Wild Street. In the fall of 1761 she began a long-term engagement at Covent Garden, at a salary of 3s. 4d. per day, or £1 per week. On a paylist dated 26 November 1761 she is down for £25 for the season and is classified in the lowest grade of salary. In 1762–63 her sister Sukey joined her at Covent Garden, and both their names appeared in the bills on 26 January 1763 as Followers of Ceres in *The Rape of Proserpine, with the Birth and Adventures of Harlequin,* a pantomime ballet that was repeated often. That season Dolly's partner in a minuet specialty was Dumai, so probably she was maturing into a young woman.

Except for several occasional appearances at the Haymarket, Dolly spent the remainder of her career at Covent Garden, dancing there through 1773–74 in her familiar but modest repertoire. In the summer of 1765 she performed at Richmond, Surrey, and during August she sang as well as danced. When she returned to Covent Garden that fall she made her first London attempt as a singing actress as Margery in *Love in a Village* on 4 October 1765. She also returned to Richmond in the summer of 1766.

In 1766–67 both Misses Twist were at Covent Garden. They appeared together in a ballet called *The Wapping Landlady* on 26 April 1767. In 1767–68 Dolly earned 4s. 2d. per day. On 2 October 1769 she played the Miller's Wife in *Harlequin Doctor Faustus,* a part she retained over the next four years. On 8 May 1771 she played, for the first time,

Southern Pr.
Illinois

Sally in *Thomas and Sally,* another singing role. In her last season at Covent Garden, 1773–74, she performed Columbine in *Harlequin Sorcerer* and in *Mother Shipton* and danced in *The Fair* and *Elfrida.* On 22 September 1773 she acted Patience (with a song) in *Henry VIII,* and on 16 October she played both Sabrina and a Pastoral Nymph in *Comus;* those three roles, it should be noted, were also in the repertoire of a Miss Twist, probably a relative, who made her "first appearance on any stage" as Nysa in *Midas* at the Haymarket on 9 June 1777.

Notations in the Burney papers and the Jerome obituary collection in the British Library report that Miss Dolly Twist died on 23 September 1774; corroboration of her name and date of death is found in the Fawcett "Notebook" in the Folger Shakespeare Library.

In addition to her sister Sukey Twist and the above-mentioned Miss Twist (fl. 1777–1787), Charlotte and Mary Twist, no doubt also related, appeared as walk-ons at Covent Garden in 1769–70.

Twist, John   *d. 1687, violinist.*

John Twist (or Twiss, Twisse) was appointed to the King's Musick as violinist on 6 November 1671 at 20*d.* daily plus livery. He was frequently named in the Lord Chamberlain's accounts after that date, several times in connection with trips out of London to attend the King. He was in Newmarket or Windsor or both almost every year through 1686, usually at a fee of 5*s.* daily. A warrant dated 10 April 1677 indicates that Twist was serving at court without a salary, though his appointment in 1671 clearly stated that he was appointed to a salaried post. At any rate, when Thomas Fitz died in 1677, Twist was to receive wages of £46 12*s.* 8*d.* annually for life.

John Twist died between 14 April 1687, when he made his will, and 25 April, when he was replaced in the King's Musick. He evidently had amassed a nice fortune (if he did not exaggerate), for he made some generous bequests. He gave £500 each to his two nieces, Elizabeth and Mary Borome, his sister's daughters, when they should reach their majorities; should both die before coming of age, the £1000 was to go to Twist's cousin, Anne Burton, wife of Mr Burton, blacksmith, of Blackman Street, Southwark. In any case,

Anne Burton was to receive £50. To the poor of the parish of St Andrew, Holborn, he left £20 (that was not his own parish, for Twist described himself as of St Martin-in-the-Fields, gentleman). To John Harwood "if he survives me" £20 was to be given. Another £50 was bequeathed to Edward Farrer. Twist left twenty-shilling mourning rings to a number of friends, including his fellow court musicians John Blow, Henry Purcell, and John Lenton. To the 24 members of the band of violins at court, "the musicke," he left gloves and favors. He gave his maid Rebecca £2. The rest of his estate went to Elizabeth and Mary Barome. The will was proved on 4 May 1687 by Twist's executor, Edward Farrer.

Twist, Mary   *fl. 1769–1770]*,   *supernumerary. See* TWIST, CHARLOTTE.

Twist, Sukey (Susannah?)   *d. 1780?, dancer.*

Sukey Twist seems to have been the Miss Twist whose name appeared occasionally in Covent Garden bills between 1759–60 and 1769–70. The other Miss Twist, Dolly, we believe for the reasons suggested in her notice, was the Miss Twist who was at the same theatre from 1757 through 1773–74. Sukey's career was more modest than that of Dolly, who was probably her elder sister.

The first notice of a second Miss Twist occurred when some unspecified dancing was performed by "the Misses Twist" at the Haymarket Theatre on 2 June 1760. In 1762–63 Sukey joined Dolly at Covent Garden Theatre. Both of their names appeared in the bills as Followers of Ceres in *The Rape of Proserpine, with the Birth and Adventures of Harlequin* on 26 January 1763. Both were engaged at Covent Garden in 1766–67, appearing together in a dance called *The Wapping Landlady* on 27 April 1767. The Covent Garden account books list both, with first names, for salaries of £1 5*s.* on 24 September 1768, and each was paid that amount, it seems, through 1769–70. Sukey and her sister signed their names with first initials to a letter from Covent Garden performers to Colman that was printed in the *Theatrical Monitor* on 4 November 1768. On 4 November 1769 both appeared again in the *Rape of Proserpine.*

Sukey perhaps was the Susannah Twist who

was buried at St Paul, Covent Garden, on 19 November 1780; she was described in the burial register as "from St. Ann's Westminster." Dolly Twist had died on 23 September 1774.

Twyford, Timothy _fl. 1664?– c. 1684?_₁, _actor?_

In his possibly unreliable "History of the British Stage" at Harvard, John Payne Collier quoted three stanzas from "a ballad in my possession" titled "A new ballad, shewing how one Tim Twyford, a player of the King's Company was carried to the Marshalsea for money he owed to his laundress, and what he did there" dated, said Collier, 1674:

> _Beware, ye players all, beware_
> _Of poor Tim Twyford's fate,_
> _And learn to live upon your share,_
> _Although it be not great._
>
> _For players, too, must pay their debts,_
> _Or in cold prison lie,_
> _At which each proud stage-strutter frets,_
> _And some do almost cry._
>
> _No longer can they strut and huff,_
> _Though once they could do so,_
> _And smooth or rough, they get enough_
> _To pay the debt they owe._

In _All the Kings Ladies_ John Harold Wilson points out the dangers in trusting Collier but notes that in this case the evidence may be valid. "A Satyr on Players" (c. 1684) speaks of the actress Mrs Twyford's husband "being close in Custody," and that confirming piece of evidence seems not to have been seen by Collier. Timothy Twyford, then, may well have been a minor actor in the King's Company about 1674.

As Wilson observes, there was a Timothy Twyford, bookseller and publisher within Inner Temple Gate in the early 1660s. Plomer's _Booksellers and Printers_ states that Twyford may have been the son of the publisher Henry Twyford, who ended in prison in 1664 for illegally selling law books. Timothy "Twiford" published a law book in 1660, and in 1664 the title page of Stapylton's _The Step-Mother_ stated that the play was to be sold at "T. Twyford's" shop. He seems not to have been a very successful businessman, and perhaps he tried the stage.

Twyford, ₁Mrs Timothy?₁ _fl. 1673?– 1689₁, actress._

The prompter Downes in his _Roscius Anglicanus_ of 1708 wrote that about 1673–74 Mrs Twyford (or Twiford) joined the Duke's Company, but the first known role for her is Emilia in _The Man of Mode_ on 11 March 1676. The information in Timothy Twyford's entry indicates that the actress may have been his wife, and we guess that because of his imprisonment for debt she turned to the stage for a living. With the Duke's troupe at Dorset Garden Theatre Mrs Twyford played Osmida in _Circe_ on 12 May 1677, Aurelia in _The Royalist_ on 23 January 1682, and doubtless other parts of which we have no record.

With the United Company at Dorset Garden and Drury Lane she acted Beatrice in _Dame Dobson_ on 31 May 1683, Meriel in _The Jovial Crew_ in December, Flametta in _A Duke and No Duke_ in mid-August 1684, Mildred in _Cuckold's Haven_ in July 1685, Menalippe in _The Commonwealth of Women_ in mid-August, Christina in _The Banditti_ in January 1686, Lettice in _The Devil of a Wife_ on 4 March, and Lucia in _Madam Fickle,_ Carolina in _Epsom Wells,_ and Clara in _The Libertine_ about 1686–87. _The London Stage_ lists her as a member of the United Company in 1688–89 but gives no roles for her.

She was the subject of some unflattering lines in "A Satyr on the Players" about 1684:

> _Once Twyford had som modesty, but she_
> _Her Husband being close in Custody_
> _Wou'd be unkind to let him famish there_
> _So F——ks for Guineas, to provide him Fare._

Twyste. _See_ TWIST.

Tyers, Jonathan _1702–1767, proprietor._

Nothing is known of the life of Jonathan Tyers before he obtained from Elizabeth Masters in 1728 the lease of the Spring Gardens at Vauxhall for £250 per year. Tyers eventually became the owner of the property, purchasing a portion for £3,800 from George Doddington in 1752 and the remainder in 1758. After making a considerable investment in alterations and improvements, he opened the establishment, renamed Vauxhall Gardens, on 7 June 1732 with a _ridotto al fresco._ That type of special fête, attracting the _haut ton,_ most of whom wore masks, became the tradition by

JONATHAN TYERS the elder

artist unknown

which the gardens inaugurated subsequent seasons each April or May.

Tyers had built supper boxes and a bandstand, called the Orchestra, and several years later he added the Rotunda, which accommodated concerts in wet weather, and, in later years, a supper room. By 1745 he added vocal music to the instrumental concerts. During its heyday, Vauxhall Gardens hosted such singers as Mrs Baddeley, Mrs Arne, Mrs Weichsell, Mrs Wrighten, Mrs Martyr, Mrs Vincent, Vernon, Incledon, Arrowsmith, Rheinhold, and Lowe; and the instrumentalists Hook, Morgan, Barthélemon, Snow, and Wilson, among many others, regularly played there. Among the many composers who worked and played for Tyers was Thomas A. Arne, who churned out dozens of songs for the approbation of many different kinds of listeners at the Gardens and was the period's most prolific and gifted composer of popular music.

To the pleasant natural environment Tyers added thousands of lamps, which amplified the enchantment of the place. In May 1738 he placed in a prominent space the large statue of Handel seated in a loose robe, striking a lyre, which he had commissioned from Roubiliac.

(The statue is now in the Victoria and Albert Museum and is reproduced in this *Dictionary* 7:80.) In the *London Magazine* of June 1738 was printed an ode to Tyers, the "Maecenes" (*sic*) who sponsored this remarkable statue in Carrara marble, which the *Daily Post* of 2 May 1738 described as "in very elegant taste." (For a full account of the Vauxhall Handel see Terence Hodgkinson, "Handel at Vauxhall," *Victoria and Albert Museum Bulletin,* I, October 1965.) Until his death in 1751, Frederick Prince of Wales was a frequent patron of the gardens, usually bringing a lively company of followers who arrived by water from Kew. Tyers had built for his convenience, opposite the Orchestra, the Prince's Pavilion. In the mid-1740s Tyers commissioned Hayman and Hogarth's series of pictures, many on Shakespearean subjects, which ornamented the alcoves of the Pavilion.

An account of Vauxhall Gardens published in *England's Gazetteer* in 1751 described some of the delights offered to fashionable society during three months each summer:

Here are fine pavilions, shady groves, and most delightful walks, illuminated by above one thousand lamps so disposed that they all take fire together, almost as quick as lightning, and dart such a sudden blaze as is perfectly surprising. Here are, among others, two curious statues of Apollo, the god, and Mr. Handel the master of musick, and in the center of the area, where the walks terminate, is erected the temple for the musicians, which is encompassed all round with handsome seats, decorated with pleasant paintings, on subjects most happily adapted to the season, place and company.

Views of Vauxhall Gardens in 1754 and 1785 are reproduced in this *Dictionary* 3:515 and 516.

In 1734, two years after he opened Vauxhall Gardens to the public, Tyers purchased from a Mr Wakefield an estate called Denbies, which consisted of a farmhouse and grounds in a fine position on the crest of the North Downs, about a mile northwest of Dorking. Over the years he converted the farmhouse to a mansion and created gardens, the principal feature of which was an eight-acre wood that he called "Il Penseroso." One of the structures in the garden was "The Temple of Death"; an iron gateway led to the "Valley of the Shadow of Death," a macabre setting that reflected Tyers's somewhat melancholy nature and was

Yale Center for British Art

John Wood, JONATHAN TYERS the elder, and Elizabeth Tyers Wood
by Hayman

in marked contrast to the lively ambience of Vauxhall. At Denbies, however, there were also pleasing walks and an open building with life-size figures painted by Hayman. (For details and views, see Brian Allen, "Jonathan Tyers's Other Garden," *Journal of Garden History,* vol 1, 1981) Tyers passed Sundays and holidays at Denbies; otherwise he lived in his house on the Vauxhall grounds. After his death in 1767 Denbies was sold by the family to Peter King, who removed Tyers's "grave conceits."

Tyers's enterprising management of Vauxhall Gardens brought him prosperity and respect. In *Amelia,* Fielding paid tribute to his "excellency of heart" and "truly elegant taste."

Jonathan Tyers is usually believed to have died on 1 July 1767, the date reported by the *Gentleman's Magazine.* But entries in the Minet Library's copy of "Lists of Songs and Instrumental Music perform'd at Vaux-Hall 1790–91" indicate that 26 June was observed each year as "The Anniversary of Mr. Tyers's Death." Reed's "Notitia Dramatica" in the British Library also claims 26 June 1767 as his death date. It is said that just before his death he asked to be carried into "The Grove" for a farewell look at his pleasant domain.

By his wife Elizabeth he had two sons and two daughters. The eldest child seems to have been Margaret (1724–1786), who married George Rogers (1718–1792) of Southampton, a sometime proprietor of Vauxhall Gardens, and, as his will reveals, a wealthy man. (Rogers is noticed in this *Dictionary,* vol 13.) The next child and elder son was Thomas Tyers (1726–1806), a barrister and lyricist, who upon his father's death became joint proprietor of Vauxhall Gardens with his younger brother, Jonathan Tyers (d. 1792). The younger Jonathan married Margaret Rogers (c. 1722–1806), the sister of George Rogers, thereby uniting the Rogers and Tyers families a second time. The younger daughter and evidently youngest child of Jonathan Tyers and his wife Elizabeth was Elizabeth, who married John Wood of Abchurch Lane about 1750.

In his will drawn on 4 June 1758, with codicils on 18 July 1758 and 6 May 1765, Jonathan Tyers bequeathed to his wife Elizabeth all his real and personal estate, including his property freehold and copyhold, on condition that she pay to their son Thomas Tyers £200 per year, in quarterly installments. After Elizabeth's death the payments to Thomas were to cease and he was to receive the freehold in Barnaby Street. The remainder of Tyers's estate he directed to be sold by and with the consent of his daughters Margaret Rogers and Elizabeth Wood, in order to purchase government securities, the proceeds of which were intended for his wife Elizabeth and afterwards were to be transferred to his son Thomas and his brother-in-law Edmund Farmer of Wandsworth in trust for the sole use of his daughters.

The most curious part of the will concerns his son Jonathan Tyers the younger, to whom he gave £100 per year during his life "in case my son Jonathan shall happen to survive his present wife the ffirst payment to be made the ffirst quarter day after her decease." Jonathan was immediately upon his father's death to sign a release on all claims to property, and if he refused to do so, then all intended for him (after his wife's death) was to revert to his mother. In the first codicil of 18 July 1758 Tyers directed that, since he had recently purchased "the other moiety of Mrs. Jennings and Mr. Atkins of the Spring Gardens," that was to be devoted to the same uses and purposes "as the other moiety of the same premises mentioned in the within will." There was, however, no specific mention of Spring Gardens (or Vauxhall Gardens) in the will, so that property was intended to be included with the other property bequeathed to his wife. The will was proved at London on 7 July 1767, soon after Tyers's death.

Vauxhall Gardens continued to prosper under the management of Tyers's sons Thomas

and Jonathan. In 1785 Thomas sold his interest to Jonathan, who carried on until his death in 1792. Vauxhall remained a popular and fashionable resort for many years. In 1792 the younger Jonathan's son-in-law, Bryan Barrett, took over and conducted affairs until 1809, when he was succeeded by his son George Barrett. In 1821 the Barrett family sold Vauxhall for £30,000 to a syndicate of Bish, Gye, and Hughes, who opened it in June 1822 under the new name of the Royal Gardens, Vauxhall. The last evening's entertainment was held there on 25 July 1859, and several weeks later the trees were cut down and the site prepared for buildings. Books devoted to Vauxhall include W. S. Scott, *Green Retreats: The Story of Vauxhall Gardens* (1955), James G. Southworth, *Vauxhall Gardens: A Chapter in the Social History of England* (1941), and Warwick Wroth, *London Pleasure Gardens* (1896).

Portraits of Jonathan Tyers include:

1. By Francis Hayman, 1740. Jonathan Tyers and his family, including, from left to right, Thomas Tyers, Jonathan Tyers, Elizabeth Tyers (daughter), Jonathan Tyers the younger, Elizabeth Tyers (wife), and Margaret Tyers. The painting was with the Wood family until 1949, when it was acquired from the dealer Morton Lee by Robert Tritton. It was offered at Christie's on 15 July 1983 but was not sold. Later that year it was acquired by the National Portrait Gallery, a gift from the estate of Mrs Robert Tritton. For additional details see John Ruch, "A Hayman Portrait of Jonathan Tyers's Family," *Burlington Magazine,* 112 (August 1970).

2. By Francis Hayman, c. 1750–52. Jonathan Tyers with his daughter Elizabeth and her husband John Wood. This painting was sold at Sotheby's on 23 November 1966 (lot 79) as "The property of a Lady" and was bought for £2400 by M. Bernard. In 1968 it was acquired from Arthur Tooth & Sons by Paul Mellon and is now in the Yale Center for British Art. See Brian Allen, *Francis Hayman* (Yale University Press, 1987), No 23.

3. By J. F. Nollekens. A painting of a musical conversation piece, showing Jonathan Tyers and other members of the family on a garden terrace with view of a country house beyond. The painting was sold by the Curry family at Christie's on 7 June 1884 (lot 100).

It was sold as the property of a gentleman at Sotheby's on 31 March 1976 for £800 and was illustrated in the sales catalogue.

4. By Louis Joseph Watteau. A portrait of Tyers by this artist was owned in 1855 by Frederick Gye, according to the *Numismatic Chronicle,* 1856.

5. By unknown artist. Sepia drawing in the British Museum, called a copy from a painting (perhaps No 4 above?). An anonymous engraving of it is in the Harvard Theatre Collection.

6. By unknown artist. Seated outdoors, right elbow on table, with book. Pantomime figures in background landscape. In the Fitzwilliam Museum, Cambridge.

7. By Louis François Roubiliac. Marble bust. In the City Art Gallery, Birmingham. Roubiliac's terra cotta model for the bust of Tyers is in the Victoria and Albert Museum.

8. A print of the Gardens engraved by Romano and published by Bickham in May 1744 shows a group of frequenters, with Tyers grumbling at his check-taker.

Tyers, Jonathan   *d. 1792, proprietor.*

Jonathan Tyers was the younger son and one of the four children of the elder Jonathan Tyers (1702–1767) by his wife Elizabeth. Little is known of his early life and education, especially in comparison to information available on his better-known brother Thomas Tyers. Some information on his sisters is given in the notice of his father.

Jonathan's relationship with his father seems to have been strained, but few details are known. In his will dated 4 June 1758 the elder Jonathan Tyers left the younger one £100 per year (compared to £200 and a freehold house to Jonathan's brother Tom) for use during his lifetime "in case my son Jonathan shall happen to survive his present wife with the ffirst payment to be made the ffirst quarter day after her decease." Upon his father's death Jonathan was obliged to sign a release on all claims to property, and if he refused to do so all intended for him would revert to his mother.

After their father's death in 1767, Jonathan and Thomas Tyers jointly managed Vauxhall Gardens until 1785, when Thomas, who seems not to have taken a major role in the affairs of the place, sold his share to Jonathan.

Jonathan continued as sole proprietor until his death on 21 March 1792.

In his will drawn on 14 December 1787, Jonathan Tyers directed that £150 be paid to his wife Margaret (who was also his executrix) as soon as possible, and she was instructed to place that money with trustees Hugh Meares, Esquire, of Lambeth, and George Keir, oilman, of Bridge Street, Westminster, for the benefit of his daughter Elizabeth, the wife of Bryant Barrett. The rest of his estate he left to his widow, who proved the will at London on 24 July 1792.

Jonathan's wife Margaret was the sister of George Rogers (1718–1792), a sometime proprietor of Vauxhall who died on 26 September 1793. Rogers had married Jonathan's sister, also named Margaret, in the 1740s. After Jonathan's death, his son-in-law Bryant Barrett carried on the management of Vauxhall until 1809; his son George Barrett then managed until 1821, when the family sold Vauxhall Gardens to Bish, Gye, and Hughes.

Jonathan Tyers is shown standing behind his mother in a painting by Francis Hayman of the elder Jonathan Tyers and his family in 1740. The painting is now in the National Portrait Gallery.

Tyers, Thomas   *1726–1787, proprietor, lyricist.*

Thomas Tyers, born in 1726, was the second child and elder son of Jonathan Tyers (1702–1767), proprietor of Vauxhall Gardens, and his wife Elizabeth. Some information on his siblings is given in his father's notice. In 1742 he was graduated B.A. at Pembroke College, Oxford, where he matriculated on 13 December 1738, and he became M.A. at Exeter College in 1745. In 1757 he was admitted barrister-at-law at the Middle Temple, but his temperament was too vivacious and capricious to be restrained by legal practice, and, as Boswell in his *Life of Johnson* described him, he "ran about the world with a pleasant carelessness," telling amusing anecdotes. Johnson, who called him Tom Tyers, described him in *Idler,* No 48 (1759) as "Tom Restless," the "ambulatory" student who looked for his ideas in coffee houses and debating clubs rather than in books. But Johnson conceded that he always learned something from Tyers.

Upon his father's death in 1767 Thomas was left well off, receiving £200 a year, a freehold in Barnaby Street, and joint managership with his brother Jonathan, of Vauxhall Gardens. But he seems not to have taken a large part in the management, preferring to indulge his interests in literature and music. He did provide the words for many songs performed there and contributed an account of the Gardens to Nicholas's *History of Lambeth*. In 1785 he sold his share in Vauxhall to his brother, who carried on as proprietor until his death in 1792.

Tyers kept apartments in Southampton Street, Covent Garden, and acquired a villa at Ashtead, near Epsom, driving back and forth seemingly at whim: "just as the humour hits I'm there or here," he was quoted in a character sketch, supposedly written by himself, in which he was described as "inquisitive, talkative, full of notions and quotations, and, which is the praise of a purling stream, of no great depth."

Thomas Tyers died at Ashtead, Surrey, on 1 February 1787, in his sixty-first year, after a long illness. He never married. In his will, signed on 26 March 1785, he requested to be buried in the church or churchyard of St Paul, Covent Garden, and directed "that I may not [be] interred until the body begins to putrify and that my funeral consist only of a hearse and pair and one mourning coach and pair and I desire my servants may attend . . . and that I may be buried as privately silently and frugally as may be." His remains were deposited in the vault under the communion table at St Paul, Covent Garden, on 17 February 1787.

Tyers left £500 to Elizabeth Norman of Southampton Street, Covent Garden (sister of Mary Norman of the same place). All the furniture and effects in his apartments he gave to his relation Mary Farmer. To his brother Jonathan Tyers, his sister Elizabeth Wood (widow), and his brother-in-law George Rogers of Southampton, he left £500 in trust to be invested in government securities, and he directed that the dividends thereof be paid to Mrs Rachel Waller independent of her husband, and if she should die before her husband the capital stock of £500 was to return to Tyers's estate for proper distribution. He bequeathed a year's wages to his servants, and to Daniel Bloss, probably his manservant, "if liv-

THOMAS TYERS
engraving by Hall, after Taylor

ing with me at my decease," he gave £100 instead of a year's wages. (In a codicil dated 18 January 1787 Tyers added another £100 to the bequest for Bloss.) Mourning rings were left to Mrs Page of Newbury, John Harris, and Daniel Beaumont of Bedford House, Bloomsbury (who also received five guineas). Jonathan Tyers, his sisters Elizabeth Wood and Margaret Rogers, and the latter's husband George Rogers were named joint executors. They proved the will at London on 24 February 1787.

Tyers was a good-natured man, known for his many acts of kindness. He was also a shy and dilettante author. He printed only 50 copies of his *Historical Essay on Mr Addison*, 1782, with a second edition of 100 copies in 1783. Only 25 copies of his *Conversations, Political and Familiar* were issued in 1784 with the stipulation that "this pamphlet may not be lent. A very few copies are printed for the perusal of a very few friends." His other publications included *Political Conferences between great men in the last and present century*, 1780, with a second edition in 1781; *An Historical Rhapsody on Mr. Pope*, 1781, with a second edition in 1782, each edition having 250 copies;

National Portrait Gallery, London

THOMAS TYERS, JONATHAN TYERS the elder, Elizabeth Tyers (daughter), JONATHAN TYERS the younger, Elizabeth Tyers (wife), and Margaret Tyers

by Hayman

and "A Biographical Sketch of Dr. Samuel Johnson," published in *The Gentleman's Magazine*, vol 54, 1785: 899 and 982.

Thomas Tyers is shown, standing on the left behind his seated father, in a painting by Francis Hayman of Jonathan Tyers and his family in 1740. The painting is now in the National Portrait Gallery. A portrait of Thomas Tyers was engraved by J. Hall, after a drawing by J. Taylor.

Tyfer, Mr ₁*fl. 1723–1741*₁, *gallery doorkeeper.*

Mr Tyfer (or Teyfer, Tifer) was the second-gallery doorkeeper at Lincoln's Inn Fields and then Covent Garden Theatre, his first mention in the benefit bills being on 6 June 1723, when he shared with two others. Receipts that day came to a little over £82 before house charges. Some of his later benefits brought in more money: about £114 in 1725, for example, and almost £150 in 1731. He was last named in the bills on 8 May 1741.

Working with Tyfer for a few years was his wife. She was paid £1 2s. 6d. on 14 October 1726 for attending in the upper gallery for 15

days. Her name appeared on the free list in 1728–29.

Tyfer, Mrs ₁*fl. 1726–1729*₁, *gallery keeper. See* TYFER, MR.

Tyldesly, Mr ₁*fl. 1736–1737*₁, *box-keeper.*

The Latreille transcriptions in the British Library cite a Drury Lane playbill for 28 May 1736 that is not in *The London Stage:* the benefit tickets of a Mr Tyldesly and others were accepted on that date. He was a boxkeeper and was still at Drury Lane in 1736–37. A Mrs "Tyldsley" was paid £10 10s. for a woman's robe on 23 October 1766; she seems not to have been on the regular theatre staff, but she may have been a relative of our subject.

Tyler, Mr ₁*fl. 1791–1793*₁, *tumbler, equestrian.*

A Mr Tyler is named on several bills for Astley's Royal Amphitheatre from 6 May 1791 through 21 August 1793, on the first date as a tumbler and on all thereafter as an equestrian.

Tyler, Miss ₁*fl. 1748*₁, *actress.*

From 24 through 27 August 1748, during Bartholomew Fair, a Miss Tyler played Madge in *The Volunteers* at the Great Theatrical Booth in the George Inn Yard, run by Bridges, Cross, Burton, and Vaughan. From 7 through 13 September she played Madge in *The Northern Heroes* at the same proprietors' booth at Southwark Fair.

Tymms, ₁L.?₁ ₁*fl. 1755–1758?*₁, *singer.*

A Mr Tymms sang at the Haymarket Theatre on 11 September 1755. Perhaps he was the L. Tymms named in a 1758 Edinburgh broadside among the playbills preserved in the Harvard Theatre Collection.

Tynchare, Philip *d. 1673, singer.*

There were a number of people in the parish of St Margaret, Westminster, named Tynchare (or Tynshare, Tinker, Tinchard), and most of them when named in official documents were described as "alias Littleton." Similarly, people named Littleton were usually designated as "alias Tynchare." The interrelationships are bewildering, and one does not quite know what to do about such parish register entries as this one from Westminster Abbey: Littleton Taylor married Mary Littleton, alias Tynchare, on 24 November 1692. Mary was the daughter of Rev John Tynchare, alias Littleton, who was the son of our subject, Philip Tynchare, alias Littleton.

Philip Tynchare matriculated at Oxford on 2 November 1621, receiving his B.A. from New College on 21 June 1625 and his M.A. on 3 July 1628. He was a Petty Canon at St Paul's in London in 1632, Rector of Old Radnor from 1636 to 1640, and Vicar of Overbury, Worcestershire, from 1640 to 1663. He was installed a Chanter of Westminster Abbey on 11 February 1661 and also in 1661 became a Confessor to the King's household. As one of the Gentlemen of the Chapel Royal he attended the King at Windsor in June and July 1671 for 8s. daily over his regular salary (which was not specified in the Lord Chamberlain's accounts). In addition to his duties as a singer and clergyman, Tynchare was the keeper of the early burial registers at Westminster Abbey.

Philip Tynchare died on 9 May 1673 and was buried at the Abbey on 12 May. He had written his will on 20 February 1673, describing himself as clerk and chanter of the Collegiate Church of Westminster. To the poor of St Margaret's parish "who attend my funeral" he left a total of 10s. To his children he bequeathed various heirlooms with the stipulation in each case that they were not to be sold: to his eldest son, John, his best piece of plate and some furniture; to his second son, Philip, a plate; to his third son, Edward (an earlier son, William, had died), his second best piece of plate; to his eldest daughter, Mary, relict of Thomas Ellis, £4 and a piece of plate; to his second daughter, Anne, wife of Robert Blondell, a tankard; to his third daughter, Elizabeth, wife of Robert Powell, a silver cup; and to his fourth daughter, Sarah, two silver spoons.

Tynchare noted that Robert Blondell owed him £20; he was to use it to help support Tynchare's widow. To each of his grandchildren Tynchare left 5s., and to his grandchild Edward Ellis he left all of the household goods bought for his father with Tynchare's money. Everything else, including arrears in salary from the Chapel Royal, Tynchare left to his wife, Mary. She proved the will on 30 May 1673, signing herself Mary "Tinchard alias Littleton."

Tyndall. *See* TINDALL.

Tynte, Miss [*fl.* 1722–1730], *actress, singer?*

The young woman variously cited from 1722 through 1730 as Miss or Mrs Tent or Tynte was apparently a member of the company at Drury Lane when a manuscript list of performers at both playhouses was drawn up on 12 April 1722. Her earliest known role came on 20 January 1725 when she played Lucia in *The Squire of Alsatia* at Drury Lane. Then she was seen as the Page in *The Orphan,* Prue in *Love for Love,* and Sylvia in *The Old Bachelor* before the season ended. On 19 May she shared a benefit with two others. The following season she added Isabella in *The Stage Coach* to her small repertoire of named parts. Her next new characters came in 1728, by which time she had left Drury Lane. On 20 June at the Haymarket Theatre she was seen as Lady Trueman in *The Drummer,* and on 25 June at Lincoln's Inn Fields she acted Feliciana in *The Successful Strangers.* On 16 January 1730 at the Haymarket she replaced Mrs Lindsay in *The Village Opera,* but we do not know whether or not Miss Tynte sustained a singing role.

"Tyrant." *See* AICKIN, FRANCIS.

Tyrawley, Lady. *See* WEWITZER, SARAH.

= U =

Uhl, Anthony *fl. c. 1727–1737*, trumpeter, horn player.

Anthony Uhl was named in several warrants in the Lord Chamberlain's accounts as a trumpeter in the King's Musick, his earliest notice dating about 1727. At Hickford's Music Room on 21 February 1735 Uhl played the French horn. On 30 May 1737 Uhl was replaced in the King's Musick by Hezekiah Hopkins.

"Uncle, Mr." *See* CLEVELAND, THOMAS.

Uncles, Mr *fl. 1786*, exhibitor.

At the Pantheon on 18 May 1786, according to a theatrical cutting at the British Library, Mr Uncles exhibited an air balloon in the shape of a fish 56 feet long, complete with a triumphal car, a "Ballast Piece" in imitation of a timepiece, and "eagles wings." The four eagles that were to propel the machine had been trained by Uncles to guide the machine or return to the car. They were "to be perfectly subservient to his pleasure." The balloon was taken to Ranelagh for a test on 18 July. Uncles "mounted his seat with eagles harnessed, and made an effort to ascend." He managed to rise about eight feet before he plumped to the ground.

Courtesy of the Garrick Club

CAVE UNDERHILL, as Obadiah
by Bing

Underhill, Cave *1634–1713*, actor, singer, playwright?

The registers of the Merchant Taylors' School show that Cave Underhill (his real name) was born in the parish of St Andrew, Holborn, on 17 March 1634, the only son of Nicholas Underhill, clothworker. Nicholas may have been related to the Nicholas Underhill who was one of the King's musicians and thus protected from arrest by Master of the Revels Sir Henry Herbert on 27 December 1624 or the Nicholas Underhill who acted for the old King's Company in the 1620s. Cave was admitted to the Merchant Taylors' School in January 1645. *The Dictionary of National Biography,* following Daniel Hipwell's article in *Notes and Queries* in September 1890, states that Cave married Elizabeth Robinson at St James, Clerkenwell, on 17 November 1664. She was the widow of Thomas Robinson, a vintner in Cheapside, and died in October 1673, when Underhill was evidently living in Salisbury Court. Salisbury Court is in the parish of St Bride, Fleet Street, and we believe that the Cave Underhill cited several times in the registers there was probably our man. If so, he may have been married twice before he married Elizabeth Robinson.

Cave "Vndrill" and Sarah Kitter were granted a certificate on 31 August 1655 and permitted to marry wherever they chose. Their daughter Mary was born and baptized (at St Giles's) on 29 February 1656; their daughter Sarah was buried on 5 April 1657, and Cave's wife Sarah was buried on 30 October 1657. She evidently died in childbirth, for an unnamed child of Cave Underhill was buried on the following 4 November. The registers show that Cave married again but apparently in another church; his new wife was named Rebecka, and their daughter Rebecka was born and baptized on 22 September 1661. Cave's wife Rebecka "Hunderhill" of New Street, was buried on 29 November 1662.

In 1659–60 Underhill was a member of the acting troupe headed by Rhodes at the Cockpit in Drury Lane. On 5 November 1660 he signed on with Sir William Davenant as one of the original members of the Duke's Company. His first known part was Sir Morgly Thwack in *The Wits*, which was performed at Lincoln's Inn Fields Theatre on 15 August 1661. He then played the First Gravedigger in *Hamlet* on 24 August, Feste in *Twelfth Night* on 11 September, the title role in *Cutter of Coleman Street* on 16 December, and Gregory in *Romeo and Juliet* on 1 March 1662. He established himself that season as a droll comedian, a popular speaker of prologues and epilogues, and, in *Twelfth Night,* a singer. On 4 July 1662 he was involved in a fray at the theatre: he and several other actors beat a messenger from the Office of the Revels, for which offense each player was fined 3s. 4d.

Underhill's other roles before the plague closed the theatres in 1665 were the Parson in *The Witty Combat*, the title role in *Ignoramus* (at court), Diego in *The Adventures of Five Hours*, Peralta in *The Slighted Maid,* Tetrick in *The Step-Mother,* Gardiner in *Henry VIII,* Palmer in *The Comical Revenge,* the Duke of Bedford in Boyle's *Henry V,* and Cunopes the Jailor in *The Rivals.* Between 15 August 1667 and the union of the Duke's and King's companies in 1682 Underhill was seen as Old Moody in *The Feigned Innocence,* Trincalo in *The Tempest* (which earned him the nickname Trincalo), Jodolet (the Man) in *The Man's the Master,* Pedagog in *Mr Anthony,* Timothy in *Sir Salomon,* Sir Adam Meridith in *The Six Day's Adventure,* Sir Simon Softhead in *The Citizen Turned Gentleman* (on 4 July 1672, his first recorded role at the new Dorset Garden playhouse), Fullam in *The Morning Ramble,* Justice Clodpate in *Epsom Wells,* the Tutor in *The Reformation,* Booby in *The Country Wit,* Snarl in *The Virtuoso,* Sanco in *The Wrangling Lovers,* apparently Jacomo in *The Libertine,* Old Jollyman in *Madam Fickle,* Blunt in *The Rover,* Phaeax in *Timon of Athens,* Sir Noble Clumsey in *Friendship in Fashion,* Fabio in *The Counterfeits,* Pimpo in *Squire Oldsapp,* Ajax in *The Destruction of Troy,* Tickletext in *The Feign'd Curtizans,* Thersites in *Troilus and Cressida,* Brainworm or possibly Amble in *The Virtuous Wife,* Sulpitius in *Caius Marius,* Circumstantio in *The Loving Enemies,* Pedro in *The Spanish Fryar,* Ned Blunt in 2 *The Rover,* Guzman in *The False Count,* Wiseacre in *The London Cucklods,* Timothy Turbulent in *Mr Turbulent,* and Copyhold in *The Royalist.* He continued to be a popular speaker of prologues and epilogues.

During that period Underhill was once sued, by Will Allen on 31 May 1673, for debt. That case may have dragged on for years, for on 3 April 1677, when Cave was confined in the Poultry Compter, his liberty was demanded by Sir Allen Apsley, since Underhill was technically a servant of the Duke of York. We have no record of Underhill acting between March 1677 and January 1678.

Yet Cave was one of the leading members of the Duke's Company and probably well paid. He was also the holder of 1.5 shares in the troupe. In the *Register of English Theatrical Documents* Milhous and Hume cite a Chancery document of 10 November 1705 containing testimony given by Cave Underhill: he claimed that he once owned 2s. 10d. in Dorset Garden rent but about 1688 sold 11s. of it to Anne Shadwell and the remainder to Alexander Davenant. He said that he also once owned three-fourths of one of the actors' shares in the United Company.

Cave Underhill's name has been connected (incorrectly?) with a sermon on the burial of Titus Oates, *Vox Lachrymae* (1681), "By Elephant Smith, Claspmaker, an unworthy Labourer, in the Affairs of the Good Old Cause." Elephant Smith is identified as Cave Underhill in the British Library *Catalogue,* and that identification was picked up in Wing's *Short Title Catalogue.* The catalogue of the Huntington Library, however, lists the work as by Francis Smith.

Underhill's new parts with the United Company—usually at Drury Lane Theatre but sometimes at Dorset Garden—began with the Curate in *The Duke of Guise* on 28 November 1682. After that he played Daredevil in *The Atheist*, a Plebeian in *Julius Caesar*, the Cook in *The Bloody Brother*, Hothead in *Sir Courtly Nice* (in rehearsal on 6 February 1685; it was Underhill, according to John Dennis, who gave the news to the author Crown that the King was dead, the theatre closed, and his play sure to fail), Don Diego in *The Banditti*, Dr Baliardo in *The Emperor of the Moon*, a Soldier in *The Injured Lovers*, Lolpoop in *The Squire of Alsatia*, Oldwit in *Bury Fair*, Timerous Cornet in *The Widow Ranter*, Mufti Abdalla in *Don Sebastian*, Guzman in *The Successful Strangers*, Old Ranter in *The English Friar*, Bernardo in *The Amorous Bigot*, Smug in *The Merry Devil of Edmonton*, Sir Rowland Rakehell in *Love for Money*, Sassafras in *Greenwich Park*, Justice Shallow in *The Merry Wives of Windsor*, Sir John Oldfop in *Win Her and Take Her* (in the writing of which he may have had a hand; it was given at Drury Lane in 1691–92), Hiarbas in *Regulus*, Captain Drydrubb in *The Maid's Last Prayer*, Setter in *The Old Bachelor*, Dick Stockjobb in *The Richmond Heiress*, Sir Maurice Meanwell in *The Female Vertuosos*, Lopez in *Love Triumphant*, Sampson in *The Fatal Marriage*, Sancho Pancha in *2 Don Quixote*, and Sir Barnaby Buffler in *The Canterbury Guests*.

Underhill was again in financial trouble in the 1680s. On 17 January 1684 Ann Allen (related to the Will Allen of 1673?) sued him for a debt, and a Lord Chamberlain's warrant of 17 January 1684 directed Underhill to pay her in yearly installments. At the Public Record Office is a complaint against Cave Underhill dated 20 November 1684; in 1666 he had agreed to pay Endymion Lanyer (i.e., Lanier) of East Greenwich for some paintings, but Underhill reneged. The epilogue to *The Royalist* (January 1682) has Cave speak of himself as ". . . Tory Cave; / Who rores in Coffeehouse, and wasts his Wealth, / Toping the Gentleman in Scotland's Health." A poem ridiculing the lavish production of *Albion and Albanius* (June 1685) devotes a verse to Cave:

> *Damme, says* Underhill, *I'm out of two hundred*
> *Hoping that Rainbows and Peacocks would do;*
> *Who thought infallible* Tom Betterton *could have*
> *blunder'd,*
> *A plague upon him and Monsieur* Grabu [*the*
> *composer*].

And the anonymous *Satyr on the Players* about 1684 took Underhill to task for his drinking:

> *Roaring Mad Cave is ye Reproach o'th'Age;*
> *Scandall to all, but ye leud Shameless Stage;*
> *The Coffee houses, and the Taverns Scum,*
> *Drunk every night, ye lobby* [*booby?*] *Tumbling*
> *home,*
> *Alarms ye Watch, his chiefest Eloquence*
> *Does lye in many Oaths, & little sence*
> *I Gad, he'd make a Swinging Evidence.*

Cave Underhill is sometimes listed as co-author of *Win Her and Take Her;* he signed the dedication to the Earl of Danby. Anthony à Wood ascribed the play to John Smyth. The epilogue, spoken by Mrs Butler, seems to treat Underhill as the author, who would receive the third day's receipts:

> *This here had been without an Epilogue,*
> *If Underhill that Comicall old Dog,*
> *Had not with a grimace that made me laugh,*
> *Desir'd me to speak something in's behalf.*
> *What is't cry'd I? why faith (say'd he) to pray*
> *The audience to be kind to my third day.*
> *The friendly Author lik'd my Phizz so well,*
> *That I the Oyster get, he but the shell.*
> *The money's mine, that's gotten by the Cause,*
> *And he good Soul's contented with applause.*

In December 1694 Underhill signed a list of grievances that he and many of the older actors in the United Company had against the tyrannical management of Christopher Rich. In the patentees' reply it was noted that Underhill had been earning £3 weekly even though he seldom acted. The period is so ill-documented that there is now no way of knowing if that was a correct statement; what records of performances we do have seem to show that Underhill acted fairly regularly. In any case, Thomas Betterton and the other unhappy players received a license to set up a new company, and on 30 April 1695 they opened with *Love for Love* at Lincoln's Inn Fields Theatre. Underhill acted Sir Sampson Legend.

He continued with the troupe through

1704–5, but he was in his sixties, and he apparently began to lighten his schedule as the years went on. At Lincoln's Inn Fields his new characters were Alderman Whim in *The Lover's Luck,* Sir Toby Cusifle in *The She-Gallants,* Sir Thomas Testie in *The Country Wake,* Sir Topewel Clownish in *Love's a Jest,* Cacafogo in *Rule a Wife and Have a Wife,* the Doctor in *The Anatomist,* Bevis in *The City Lady* (December 1696; the curtain was delayed because of "Mr Underhill's violent Bleeding," and he was not able to finish the performance), Sir Blunder Bosses in *The Intrigues at Versailles,* Flywife in *The Innocent Mistress,* Sir Wealthy Plainder in *The Pretenders,* Merryman in *The Amorous Widow,* Sir Willful Witwoud in *The Way of the World,* Obadiah in *The Committee,* and Kent in *King Lear.*

On 23 November 1700 Underhill played his role of Archbishop Gardiner in *Henry VIII;* that representation and the ridiculing of a christening by the actors caused offense, according to Luttrell in his *Brief Relation.* The players were again in trouble in December for blaspheming on the stage. Underhill was accused of using the name of God jestingly and profanely on the public stage on 5 and 20 December (in what plays we do not know); other players were similarly accused. They pleaded not guilty to the offenses, and the litigation dragged on into the reign of Queen Anne. The players were finally acquitted.

A proposed company roster in the Lord Chamberlain's accounts, dating about 1703, lists Cave Underhill at £60–£80 per year "besides a guiney a time when he acts. . . ." He was not listed with the regular members of the proposed troupe but, with Doggett, Johnson, Pinkethman, and others, on a second list. His salary scale was below those three but above such minor players as Trout, Pack, Bright, and Norris.

Tom Brown in his *Letters from the Dead to the Living* had Anthony Leigh write to Cave from the shades:

Brother Cave,

 . . . I must confess, when I left you you were a good sociable sort of a Drunkard, and a pretty little pedling sort of a Whoremaster, but I hear since you have droop'd within a few Years into such a dispirited condition, that 'tis as much as a plentiful Dose of the best Canary can do to remove the *Hyppocon* for a few Minutes, that you may entertain your friends With a little of your Comick Humour, Grac'd with that agreeable Smile that has always render'd what you say delightful, and that it is not in the subtile Power of intoxicating *Nantz* to add new Life to that decay'd Member, which has in a manner taken leave of this World before the rest of your Body: You have so often been us'd to a Grave in your Life-time that I think you never wanted a *Memento Mori* to put you in mind of Mortality: Death sure can be no Surprize to a merry Mortal who has so often Jested with him upon the Stage, and I long to hear when the grining Skeleton shall shake you by the Hand, and say, *Come old Duke* Trinculo, *thy last Sands are running, thy ultimate Moment is at hand, and the Worms are gaping for thee.* What a Jocular Answer you will make to the thin-jaw'd Executioner, for every Comedian ought to die with a Jest in his Mouth to preserve his Memory, for if he makes not the Audience Laugh as he goes off the Stage, he forfeits his Character, and his Fame dies with his Body; therefore I wou'd advise you to set your wits on work to prepare yourself, that as you have always liv'd by repeating other People's Wit, you may not make your Exit like a Fool, but show you have some remains of your own Juvenile sparklings to oblige the World with at your last Minute.

I hear the effects of your Debauches are tumbled into your Pedestals, and make you walk with as much deliberation as Mr. *Cant* Preaches, when a Man is once so founder'd by the Iniquity of his Life, that his full Speed is no faster than a Snail's Gallop, and that his Memory and his Members both equally fail him, it is full time that he travel'd to his Journey's end; for with what Comfort can a Man live when the World is grown weary of him: Young Men I know look upon you as Superanuated Conversation, and had rather see a Death's-head and an Hour-glass in their Company, than see you make wry Faces at your Rheumatick Twitches, or hear you banter upon your Gouty Pains and the past Causes thereof between Jest and Earnest. . . .

Yet Underhill continued acting. When the Queen's Theatre opened in 1705, the players moved from Lincoln's Inn Fields. Underhill may not have acted in 1705–6, for his first recorded part at the Queen's was Sir Joslin in *She Wou'd if She Cou'd* on 5 December 1706. He was Blunt in *The Rover* on 20 January 1707 and had a benefit on 28 May. He evidently went into retirement after that season; the next theatrical notice for him came on 3 June 1709, when he played the Gravedigger in *Hamlet* for his benefit at Drury Lane (the Queen's by then was used for operas). Underhill said in the newspapers that he had suffered losses of nearly £2500 and needed whatever income the benefit could bring him. The *Tatler* puffed his benefit in the issue of 31 May:

My chief business here this evening was to speak to my friends on behalf of honest Cave Underhill, who has been a comic for three generations: my father admired him extremely when he was a boy. There is certainly nature excellently represented in his manner of action; in which he ever avoided the general fault in players, of doing too much. It must be confessed, he has not the merit of some ingenious persons now on the stage, of adding to his authors: for the actors were so dull in the last age, that many of them have gone out of the world, without having ever spoke one word of their own in the theatre. Poor Cave is so mortified, that he quibbles and tells you, he pretends only to act a part fit for a man who has one foot in the grave, viz. a grave-digger. All admirers of true comedy, it is hoped, will have the gratitude to be present on the last day of his acting, who, if he does not happen to please them, will have it even then to say, that it is his first offence.

We do not know how well Underhill did at his benefit.

He acted in *Hamlet* again on 23 February 1710; when the work was repeated on 9 May his part was omitted, perhaps because he was preparing for his benefit on 12 May, when he played Trinculo in *The Tempest*. The *Daily Courant* on 11 May had called him "that Ancient Comedian Cave Underhill." He acted just once more, on 26 August 1710 at Greenwich, as Ned Blunt in *The Rover*. His activity in 1710 has baffled historians, for in the registers of St Andrew, Holborn, is recorded the burial of Cave Underhill, from Carter Lane, on 14 October 1709. That Cave Underhill was, we believe, the son of the actor. Cave Underhill, from Carter Lane, was buried at St Andrew's on 26 May 1713.

Both Colley Cibber and Tony Aston left descriptions of Underhill. Aston was remarkably unkind. He said Underhill was more admired by his fellow actors than by the audience. Aston thought Ben Johnson, who took over such parts as the Gravedigger, Judge Gryphus in *Amphytrion* (which Underhill is not otherwise known to have played), and Jacomo in *The Libertine*, did those roles better. Underhill's

best character, Aston believed, was Lolpoop in *The Squire of Alsatia*. Aston described Underhill as six feet tall, long- and broad-faced, and somewhat corpulent. His face was "very like the *Homo Sylvestris*, or *Champanza;* for his Nose was flattish and short, and his Upper Lip very long and thick, with a wide Mouth and short Chin, a churlish Voice, and awkward Action, (leaping up with both Legs at a Time, when he conceived any Thing waggish, and afterwards hugging himself at the thought)."

Aston found Underhill "the most confin'd Actor I ever saw" and noted that he was not good at serious characters. Underhill could barely be brought to speak a short bit of Latin in *Don Quixote:* "Sir Bonus Populus, bonus ero Guberator" came out "Shit bones and bobble arse, Bones, and ears Goble Nature." But Underhill had no rivals, Aston said, in his "dry, heavy, downright Way in Low Comedy."

Cibber was warmer in his admiration for the comedian. Cibber probably did not see Underhill in his prime, but he remembered Cave's benefit in 1709: he was "so worn and disabled, as if himself was to have lain in the Grave he was digging; when he could no more excite Laughter, his Infirmities were dismiss'd with Pity: He dy'd soon after, a superannuated Pensioner in the List of those who were supported by the joint Sharers under the first Patent granted to Sir *Richard Steele*."

Underhil was a correct and natural Comedian, his particular Excellence was in Characters that may be called Still-life, I mean the Stiff, the Heavy, and the Stupid; to these he gave the exactest and most expressive Colours, and in some of them look'd as if it were not in the Power of human Passions to alter a Feature of him. In the solemn Formality of *Obadiah* in the *Committee*, and in the boobily Heaviness of *Lolpoop* in the *Squire of Alsatia*, he seem'd the immoveable Log he stood for! a Countenance of Wood could not be more fixt than his, when the Blockhead of a Character required it: His Face was full and long; from his Crown to the end of his Nose was the shorter half of it, so that the Disproportion of his lower Features, when soberly compos'd, with an unwandering Eye hanging over them, threw him into the most lumpish, moping Mortal that ever made Beholders merry! not but at other times he could be wakened into Spirit equally ridiculous—In the course, rustick Humour of Justice *Clodpate*, in *Epsome Wells*, he was a delightful Brute! and in the blunt Vivacity of Sir *Sampson*, in *Love for Love* he shew'd all that true perverse Spirit that is commonly seen in much Wit and Ill-nature. This Character is one of those few so well written, with so much Wit and Humour, that an Actor must be the grossest Dunce that does not appear with an unusual Life in it: But it will still shew as great a Proportion of Skill to come near *Underhil* in the acting it, which (not to undervalue those who soon came after him) I have not yet seen.

A portrait by Robert Bing of Underhill as Obadiah in *The Committee* is at the Garrick Club (No 273). An engraving of it by J. Faber, Jr, was published in 1712. Other engravings after Bing include by R. B. Parkes, by W. Parsons, in reverse, 1798; and by an anonymous engraver, published by J. Caulfield, 1825.

Underhill, William   ₁fl. c. 1714₁, *drummer.*
William Underhill was a drummer in the King's Musick about 1714; his annual salary was £40.

Underwood, William   ₁fl. 1797–1815₁, *machinist, scene painter, carpenter, tailor.*
William Underwood worked at a variety of technical theatre trades in London from 1797 (and perhaps earlier) to at least 1815. His name was in the bills for designing the machinery for the premiere of *Julia of Louvain* at the Royal Circus on 15 May 1797. All subsequent notices of him concern his work at Drury Lane Theatre.

His first noticed assignment at Drury Lane was for the execution, along with Johnston, Gay, and Miss Rein, of the machinery, decorations, and dresses for the premiere of the younger Colman's extravagant *Blue-Beard* on 16 January 1798. The following season his work included new decorations for a refurbished *Blue-Beard* on 6 October 1798, assistance in the execution of machinery, dresses, and decorations for *Feudal Times* on 19 January 1799, and the same assignments for *Pizarro* on 24 May 1799. On 19 May the treasurer paid him £14 14s., apparently in connection with expenses for materials for *Pizarro;* on 12 March he had been given £15 15s. for timber.

In 1799–1800 Underwood prepared the machinery, dresses, and decorations for the premiere of *The Egyptian Festival* on 11 March 1800 and the premiere of *De Montfort* on 29 April. He seems never to have been respon-

sible for the designs but functioned much as a modern technical director does, carrying out the various jobs of building, painting, and sewing. His salary for such services remained a constant £3 3s. per week between 1802–3 and 1814–15, the last year in which we note his name in the account books. He was described variously as carpenter and painter. By 1805 he was also being paid a summer salary of about £40, covering some ten weeks. His full name appears on a collection of facsimile signatures of the Drury Lane company and staff owned by the New York Public Library.

Undril. *See* UNDERHILL.

Unwin, Mrs. *See* ERWIN, MRS.

Uphill, Anne   ₁fl. c. 1673–1675₁, *actress. See* UPHILL, SUSANNA.

Uphill, Susanna   ₁fl. 1669–1676₁, *actress.*
Susanna Uphill acted with the King's Company at the Bridges Street Theatre, playing Erotion in *Tyrannick Love* on 24 June 1669 and Livia in *The Generous Enemies* in June 1671. After that playhouse burned in early 1672 the troupe took up temporary quarters at Lincoln's Inn Fields Theatre, where Susanna probably acted Artemis in *Marriage à la Mode* about May 1672, certainly appeared as Rosella in *The Spanish Rogue* in March 1673, and probably played a Maid in *The Maides Revenge* sometime in 1673–74. A Lord Chamberlain's warrant dating about 1673–74 and cited by Milhous and Hume in their *Register of English Theatrical Documents* lists both "Susan" and "Anne" Uphill as members of the King's company. Of Anne nothing else is known, and there is a possibility that both references were to the same woman.

Susanna's first role at the new Drury Lane Theatre was Syllana in *Nero* on 16 May 1674, after which she was seen as Parhelia in *Love in the Dark* on 10 May and Zayda in *Aureng-Zebe* on 17 November 1675.

On 28 August 1675 at Dorset Garden Theatre, operated by the rival Duke's Company, Susanna was in the audience, masked, to see *Macbeth*. Among the Verney manuscripts is a letter from John to Sir Ralph Verney reporting on a fight that ensued between Sir Thomas

Armstrong and the younger brother of Sir Carr Scroope: "Their quarrel is said to [be] about Mrs Uphill, the player, who came into the house maskt, and Scrope would have entertained discourse with her, which Sir T. Armstrong would not suffer, so a ring was made wherein they fought." Scroope was killed. In Sir Francis Fane's manuscript Commonplace Book at the Shakespeare Memorial Library in Stratford-upon-Avon is a scrap of related conversation: "S\(^r\) Oliver Butler sade to S\(^r\) Tho: Stiles betweene you and I neighbour M\(^{rs}\) Uphil is with child."

For some years Susanna Uphill was confused with Mary Uphill, mistress and later third wife of Sir Robert Howard. But Oliver in his biography of Howard explains that there is nothing to connect Howard's Mrs Uphill with the theatre.

Uploe, Mrs   *fl. 1735–1736₁,   dancer.*

The accounts for Lincoln's Inn Fields Theatre at the British Library cite a dancer, Mrs Uploe, who received a benefit at Lincoln's Inn Fields on 16 February 1736. She was engaged at that house from 18 December 1735 to 28 February 1736. *The London Stage* does not mention her and, indeed, Lincoln's Inn Fields is not shown in the calendar of performances to have been in use that winter.

Upsdell, Mrs, née Palmer   *fl. 1796–1832₁,   actress.*

A manuscript note in the Folger Library informs us that, sometime in 1796, "Mrs. Upsdell (Dtr to Mr. Palmer the Actor)" was to perform Olivia in *Twelfth Night* at the private theatre of the Margravine of Anspach on the occasion of the Margravine's birthday, in a company composed principally of amateurs.

"A Young Gentlewoman," identified in a manuscript at Harvard as Mrs Upsdell, came on at the Haymarket Theatre as Cecilia in *The Chapter of Accidents* on 6 July 1796. The comedy was repeated on 12 July. The critic of the *Monthly Mirror* wrote:

Her figure is tall and elegant; her face handsome; though not very expressive; her voice is thin and delicate; her conception of the character appeared to be just. On the whole, it was an interesting first appearance, and as Mrs. U. performed the part with increased effect we may hope that she will rise in the profession.

The hope was forlorn. Mrs Upsdell did not appear again in London. Her later years were tragic. A news clipping in the British Library, hand-dated 26 August 1832, contains a letter addressed to an unidentified newspaper editor:

A short time since, Mrs Upsdell (a daughter of John Palmer, the celebrated actor) applied at one of the police offices for relief, her husband having died of cholera, and left her at an advanced age, about 70, without a shilling in the world. . . . The magistrate kindly gave her a sovereign; this, and one more forwarded to the Sunday *Times,* are all she has to live upon. Since that period she has been residing with her sister, Mrs. Collier, who, from a large fortune has been reduced to the lowest state of wretchedness; she was the widow of the late T. Collier, Esq., of Lloyd's. In addition to their other misfortunes, their brother, Mr. E. Palmer, lately committed suicide. Immured in an obscure lodging, and unable to obtain any employment, those unfortunate ladies have existed for days together on a small quantity of bread and water. . . .

The account details clinically the protracted agonies of the old women and their fruitless applications to various persons for relief. After a period of "five days entirely without food," Mrs Collier had died. "Mrs. Upsdell still survives."

The only acting Palmer who could be called "celebrated" within memory in 1832 (and the most celebrated of all) was John "Plausible Jack" Palmer (1744–1798). Besides, we know from other testimony that one of his daughters was Mrs T. Collier. But Mrs Upsdell could not have been quite 70 years old in 1832, even if she was the eldest of Palmer's 11 children; for her father and mother apparently did not meet until 1764. (She also was not Nell Palmer, as we suggested in her father's entry, for John Palmer sent Nell a letter, addressed to Miss Nell Palmer, in 1798, by which time our Miss Palmer was Mrs Upsdell.)

Upton, Mr   *fl. 1781–1802?₁,   singer, actor.*

Mr Upton sang at Astley's Amphitheatre, Westminster Bridge, on 27 February 1781. He was probably the Upton who acted (with songs) Colonel Bully in a specially licensed performance of *The Humours of Sir John Brute* at the Haymarket Theatre on 26 December

1791. It is also likely that he was the Upton who was still performing at Astley's in 1802. In the *Monthly Mirror* that year, it was reported that "Mr Upton, of whose genius we have so often had cause to speak, has again given further specimens to strengthen our opinion in favour of his talents."

Urbani, Valentino. *See* "VALENTINI."

Ursler, Barbara. *See* VAN BECK, MRS MICHAEL.

Urwin, Mrs. *See* ERWIN, MRS.

Usher, Miss, later Mrs Weston
fl. 1800–1812, *actress, singer.*
Miss Usher, advertised as "A Young Lady" making her first appearance on any stage, acted Maria in *The Citizen* at Drury Lane on 14 June 1800. She was identified in a manuscript notation on J. P. Kemble's playbill and soon after in Thomas Dutton's *Dramatic Censor* (1800):

A Young Lady, of the name of USHER, made her debut this evening in the character of Maria. Short, as is the part it admits of great scope and variety of talent; and may therefore be considered as a difficult essay for a first appearance. The young candidate, however, for Theatrical honours wanted not *confidence;* and, upon the whole, acquitted herself better than we expected. She seemed to form her style of acting upon the model of Mrs. JORDAN.

Miss Usher may, indeed, have been a younger cousin to Dorothy Jordan, whose mother Grace Phillips was sister to the Miss Phillips who married the longtime London actor Howard Usher. A daughter of the Ushers acted in Bristol in 1778–79 and then in Ireland between 1784 and 1790, but she seems never to have appeared in London.

After her single London appearance, Miss Usher became by June 1801 a member of the company at the Theatre Royal in Shakespeare Square, Edinburgh. On 29 June 1801 she acted Jacintha in *The Suspicious Husband* and then played Maria in *The Citizen* (her London role) on 6 July, a Singing Witch in *Macbeth* on 20 July, and Celia in *As You Like It* on 21 July.

By the following season at Edinburgh Miss Usher had married a Mr Weston, also an actor in the company. In *The Theatre* (Edinburgh) on 12 February 1802 she was called Mrs Weston, late Miss Usher. When she acted Lucy Waters in *The Brothers* on 20 February 1802 she was billed as Mrs Weston. Her other known roles at Edinburgh in 1802 included Miss Bridgemore in *The Fashionable Lover* on 24 March, Julia in *The Prize* on 29 March, and Clarinda in *Which Is the Man?* on 16 April. In 1803 she played Mrs Caroline Dormer in *The Heir-at-Law* on 22 January and Margaretta in *Rule a Wife and Have a Wife* on 3 February. Her husband acted such roles as Balthazar in *Much Ado about Nothing,* Compton in *The Agreeable Surprise,* Hodge in *Love in a Village,* and the Second Gravedigger in *Hamlet.*

Mrs Weston was still at Edinburgh in 1805. Perhaps she was the actress of that name who was a member of the Covent Garden company from 1809–10 through 1811–12, earning £6, £7, and £8. According to the *Authentic Memoirs of the Green Room* (1804), her husband Mr Weston was "of theatrical parentage, and, we understand, a relation of Thomas Weston, who performed at all the London theatres, and died January 18, 1776." Mr Weston was brought by Colman to the Haymarket in 1804, when he made his London debut as John Lump in *The Review.*

Usher, Howard   *d. 1802, actor.*
Little is known about the details of Howard Usher's life, though his journeyman career on the London stage spanned 60 years. He began at Drury lane Theatre in 1739–40 playing tertiary or supernumerary roles, and seldom did his repertoire rise above that status. His first known appearance was on 20 October 1739 as Phoebus in *The Fall of Phaeton.* After several performances in that role he appeared on 15 January 1740 as Mittimus in the premiere of *The Fortune Tellers,* an anonymous pantomime that enjoyed numerous performances that season. He also acted Tackum in *The Tragedy of Tragedies* on 30 April 1740 and several other nights. In 1740–41 he played a Peasant in *The Rural Sports: With the Stratagems of Harlequin* on 27 October 1740 and other nights, but his name appeared in no other bills that season or in the following two seasons.

Usher's name reappeared in Drury Lane bills on 22 October 1743, when he acted the

Priest in *Aesop*. That season he was also seen as Mirvan in *Tamerlane*, a Councellor in *Women Pleased*, Bull in *The Relapse*, an unspecified role in *The Rehearsal*, Meleager in *The Rival Queens*, Gower in *2 Henry IV*, and the Second Ambassador in *Regulus*. The following season, 1744–45, he added to his repertoire a Soldier in *The Committee*, Marcellus in *Hamlet*, the English Herald in *King John* (a revival on 20 February 1745 in which Garrick acted the title role), Blunt in *Richard III*, and the Cook in *Chrononhotonthologos*.

Usher remained engaged at Drury Lane through 1749–50 playing an extensive repertoire of roles, a small selection of which will exemplify his service to the theatre: Young Gerald in *The Anatomist*, the Serjeant in *Henry VIII*, Jacques de Boys in *As You Like It*, and Guildenstern in *Hamlet* in 1745–46; Crookfinger Jack in *The Beggar's Opera*, Poundage in *The Provoked Husband*, and a Gentleman in *All for Love* in 1746–47; Scruple in *The Recruiting Officer* and Buckle in *The Suspicious Husband* in 1747–48; Albany in *King Lear*, Valentine in *Twelfth Night*, Benvolio in *Romeo and Juliet*, and Father Peter in *Measure for Measure* in 1748–49; and Euricles in *Merope*, Conrade in *Much Ado about Nothing*, and Alberto in *A Duke and No Duke* in 1749–50.

In the summer of 1748, and perhaps in other summers, Usher performed at the London fairs. On 24 August 1748 he appeared as Charles XII in *Northern Heroes* at the George Inn Yard, during Bartholomew Fair. Later that summer he played the same role in a booth on the Bowling Green during Southwark Fair on 7 September and at least five other days through the thirteenth.

On occasion Usher also acted at Richmond, Surrey. He had a benefit there in early October 1748. In his diary the Drury Lane prompter Richard Cross wrote that on 11 October, "Miss Pitt went to play in the Beggars Opera for Mr. Usher at Richmond & was deliver'd of a fine girl—NB; She was a virgin." Usher had acted the Gentleman in *Jane Shore* at Drury Lane on 2 October but did not appear there again until he played Valentine in *Twelfth Night* on 9 October, and no doubt he had played the intervening week at Richmond. He also acted in the company at the Jacob's Wells Theatre in Bristol in the summers of

1749 (with a benefit on 31 July as Macbeth), 1750 (benefit on 6 August as King Lear), and 1756, and perhaps others.

After a decade or more at Drury Lane, Usher left that theatre at the end of the 1749–50 season. He passed the summer at Bristol, and in the autumn began a four-year engagement at Covent Garden Theatre, appearing there for the first time on 25 October 1750 as Rosencrantz in *Hamlet*. Subsequently that season he acted the Lieutenant in *Richard III*, Ratcliff in *Jane Shore*, Heli in *Tamerlane*, Seyton in *Macbeth*, Westmoreland in *1 Henry IV*, the Dauphin in *Henry V*, Luis in *She Wou'd and She Wou'd Not*, Rossano in *The Fair Penitent*, Decius Brutus in *Julius Caesar*, and Suffolk in *Henry VIII*. During the following three seasons his lot improved little, as he played many of the roles he had acted at Drury Lane. At Covent Garden he added, among others, Chatilion in *Zara*, Aranthes in *Theodosius*, Sergius in *The Siege of Damascus*, and the Governor in *The Pilgrim* in 1751–52; Rake in *The Provok'd Wife*, Frederick in *The Miser*, Cornwall in *King Lear*, Rovewell in *The Fair Quaker of Deal*, Solarino in *The Merchant of Venice*, Dorilant in *The Country Wife*, and Octavius in *Julius Caesar* in 1752–53; and Vainlove in *The Old Bachelor*, Amphialus in *Philocles*, and Raleigh in *The Earl of Essex* in 1753–54. In the summer of 1752 he had played again at Richmond, one of his roles being Heartfree in *The Provok'd Wife* on 23 September.

In the autumn of 1754 Usher was not at Covent Garden but returned to Drury Lane, where he remained for four seasons through 1757–58, playing almost nightly in his indispensable but undistinguished line.

After having been employed at a London theatre regularly for some 18 years, Usher found himself without a job at Drury Lane. In the autumn of 1758 he was to be found under Benjamin Victor's management at the Smock Alley Theatre in Dublin, where he appeared for the first time on 16 November as Archer in *The Beaux' Stratagem*. With him was his wife, who appeared as Mrs Sullen. Mrs Usher was the former Miss Phillips, daughter of a Welsh clergyman and the sister of the actresses Maria Phillips (d. 1782) and Grace Phillips. Mrs Usher and her sisters were all members of the Smock Alley company in 1758–59.

On 23 November 1758 Benjamin Victor wrote to Charles Macklin in London about the difficulties Usher was causing him. The actor had sent his wife to tell Victor that he did not intend to act until the arrival of Theophilus Cibber, and indeed Usher never set foot in the theatre during he first three weeks it was open. When the news came that Cibber had perished off the Scottish coast on 27 October, Usher decided to make his Irish debut but insisted on playing Archer, a role for which he was "entirely without one Requisite," wrote Victor. His voice was "one continued Monotone and that Harsh," and his countenance was "Severe and ill natur'd, and without one Grain of Humour." The theatre lost £30 by Usher's first appearance, at which he was universally disliked. Victor told Macklin that he intended to employ Usher in the grave parts of comedy.

Usher told Macklin in a letter on 7 December 1758 that he had received an offer from Barry to act at the Crow Street Theatre in Dublin. He accused the manager of Smock Alley of repudiating all financial agreements with him and said that he found himself penniless and in despair. But Usher and his wife remained at Smock Alley, it seems, through 1760–61. In June 1761 they played for a month at "the Vaults" in Belfast. Their whereabouts are unknown for several seasons until they resurfaced in Dublin in 1764–65 at Crow Street, where they remained engaged through 1767–68. In September and October 1765 Usher acted at Cork and returned there for a similar period in 1766.

After 1767–68, we lose track of the Ushers for several years. Mrs Usher made an unsuccessful debut at Drury Lane on 5 May 1772 as Alicia in *Jane Shore* but never reappeared in London. She was at York in 1773–74, so perhaps her husband was similarly employed. No doubt he was struggling to eke out small wages in the provinces during those years.

In a pattern not unusual in the profession during the eighteenth century, Usher's fortune brought him back to the stage of a London theatre as abruptly as he had left. Engaged by Garrick for 1774–75, he reappeared at Drury Lane on 14 October 1774 as Stockwell in *The West Indian*. Audiences now were to see him in a somewhat more mature repertoire. In 1774–75 he also performed the Governor in *Oroonoko*, Borachio in *Much Ado about Nothing*, Bonniface in *The Stratagem*, Old Wilding in *The Lyar*, Alonzo in *Rule a Wife and Have a Wife*, Belford in *Isabella*, Lucius in *Cymbeline*, Worthy in *The Fair Quaker*, Phoenix in *The Distrest Mother*, Lemos in *Braganza* (in the premiere of Jephson's tragedy on 17 February 1775), Sir Toby Fuz in *A Peep behind the Curtain*, Duncan in *Macbeth*, Lord Brumpton in *The Funeral*, Chaunter in *Phebe*, and Friar Peter in *Measure for Measure*. In 1775–76 he added Belfield Senior in *The Brothers*, Humphrey in *The Conscious Lovers*, the Player King in *Hamlet*, the Captain in *Macbeth*, Dawson in *The Gamester*, the Chaplain in *The Orphan*, and Ramble in *Old City Manners*.

Usher's salary at Drury Lane in 1774–75 was £3 per week. According to notations by Winston in the Drury Lane Fundbook (in the Folger Shakespeare Library), Usher subscribed £1 1s. to the Fund in 1775 and left that theatre in 1777. His name, however, appeared in no Drury Lane bills in 1776–77. In 1777 he was a member of the summer company at Richmond, Surrey.

In the summer of 1778 Usher, who must have been then in his late fifties at least, began an engagement with the Colmans at the Haymarket Theatre that was to last 21 years. He appeared on 19 June 1778 in the title role of *Henry VIII*, a more important part than usual for him in London. On 30 July he acted Nennius in Colman's version of *Bonduca*. He performed Classick in *The Englishman in Paris* on 10 September and the Butler in *Piety in Pattens* and Manly in *The Provok'd Husband* on 18 September. In 1779 his roles were Owen in *The English Merchant*, Spurious in the premiere of Jodrell's *A Widow and No Widow* on 17 July, King Henry in the premiere of Mrs Cowley's *Albina, Countess of Raimond* on 31 July, Bonniface in *The Stratagem*, and Bates in *The Irish Widow*.

Among the original roles acted by Usher over the years at the Haymarket, in addition to the above-mentioned, were the Landlord in Colman's *The Genius of Nonsense* on 2 September 1780, Dennis in O'Keeffe's *The Dead Alive* on 16 June 1781, Simpson in Frances Burney's *The East Indian* on 16 July 1782, the Steward in O'Bryen's *A Friend in Need, Is a*

Friend Indeed! on 5 July 1783, a Planter in the younger Colman's *Inkle and Yarico* on 4 August 1787, Paul Peery in the younger Colman's *Ways and Means* on 10 July 1788, Beedle in Wewitzer's pantomime *The Gnome* on 5 August 1788, Sancho in O'Keeffe's (?) *A Key to the Lock* on 18 August 1788, Sir Walter Manny in the younger Colman's *The Surrender of Calais* on 30 July 1791, Barleycorn in O'Keeffe's *The London Hermit* on 29 June 1793, a Moor in the younger Colman's *The Mountaineers* on 3 August 1793, and Baron Fitz-Allen in Cross's *The Apparition* on 3 September 1794.

In 1799 the entry for Usher in *The Authentic History of the Green Rooms* read: "This gentleman seems to be retained through compassion, though his services are but little worth. He has been may years on the stage without acquiring any fame." Usher's last performance at the Haymarket was on 10 September 1799, as Sir Walter Manny in *The Surrender of Calais*.

Howard Usher died in April 1802, between the fourth, when he made his will, and the tenth, when it was proved by his executor. In his will he described himself as "Howard Usher late of the Theatre Royal in the Haymarket but now Lodging at N° 12 Cross Street Carnaby Market." He directed that all his debts and funeral expenses should be paid and that £5 should be given to Sarah James, "who has nursed me in my illness." The residue of his unspecified estate he left to his executor Edwin William Ayrton of Red Lyon Square for his own use. Ayrton was probably related to the eminent musician and concert organizer Edmund Ayrton and other musicians of that name. Usher signed the will by his mark, being at that time, as Sarah James testified, too ill to sign his name.

In his *Records of My Life* (1832) John Taylor wrote at some length, though sometimes mistakenly, about Usher:

This gentleman was respected for his literary talents & according to report, was author of an elegant little tract, entitled "Clio, or a Discourse on Taste." [Taylor was wrong: it was written in 1767 by James Usher, a schoolmaster.] . . . He never rose to eminence in his profession, but the parts assigned to him he always supported with judgment, & was particularly attentive to dumb show. . . . He seemed to be of very reserved disposition, &, instead of mingling in the green-room with the rest of the performers, always retired to the back of the stage during the intervals of the performance. Hence one of the performers designated him by the title of "The Recluse of the Lake" [a recent novel]. . . . I was acquainted with him, & held him in great respect, though his station on the stage was always a very subordinate description. I found him modest, attentive, and intelligent. He had a daughter who was a provincial actress of some repute, but I believe never made her way to the London boards. I knew her also for a short time while she resided in London, & considered her a very sensible woman. She was too unwieldy for the stage when I knew her.

According to Taylor, Usher had "devised a strange expedient" to better his fortune by selling fruit. He purchased "a great number of wheelbarrows, which he lent every day to the itinerant daughters of Pomona, who drive these carriages through the streets of London." The scheme failed, however, through the dishonesty of the barrow borrowers.

Little is known about the career of Mrs Usher. She was in the York company as late as 1783, but since she was not mentioned in Usher's will, she probably died before he did. The daughter mentioned by Taylor was probably the Miss Usher who acted pathetic heroines at Bristol in 1778–79 and performed at Belfast in 1784, appearing there on 10 December as the heroine in *The Grecian Daughter;* she also acted at Ennis in 1790. She seems not to have been the Miss Usher, who, billed as "A Young Lady" making her first appearance on any stage, acted Maria in *The Citizen* at Drury Lane on 14 June 1800. The two women may have been related. In the first decade of the nineteenth century the latter Miss Usher, then known as Mrs Weston, acted at Edinburgh and then at Covent Garden.

In his history of the Brighton stage Porter reports the presence in that company in 1776 of a Mr and Mrs "R." Usher, but possibly that identification is a mistake for the Howard Ushers, whose whereabouts that year are otherwise unknown to us. Several other performers with the surname Usher may have been related to Howard Usher in some manner, though there is no evidence to that effect. The well-known clown Richard Usher (1785–1843), the son of a traveling showman of mechanical exhibitions, appeared at the Liverpool amphitheatre by 1807 and in 1809 came out at Astley's in London, where he continued as a popular favorite for many years. He was, according to his notice in *The Dictionary of National Biography*, "known in the profession as the John Kemble of his art, and in the [circus] ring was the counterpart of Grimaldi on the stage." Richard Usher appeared at Bristol in September 1820 with his large family of performers, who danced, mimed, and walked rope. They included his wife (probably his second, who was a sister of James W. Wallack) and their daughters Miss H., Miss J., and Miss L. Usher. When he performed at Brighton in 1828 he was accompanied by his daughter Charlotte, according to Porter.

Also likely to have been related to our subject was Luke Usher, who may have had some provincial experience in the Three Kingdoms before he went, in 1790, to act in America. His son, Noble Luke Usher, first appeared in Boston in 1799. The latter, about 1804, married Harriet Snowden, widow of a young Philadelphia merchant; her father, Joseph L'Estrange, acted in London between 1774 and 1788 and then in America, with his wife, from 1796 to his death in 1804. Noble Luke and Harriet Usher remained in Boston until 1807–8 and eventually settled in Kentucky, where he established theatres in Lexington, Frankfort, and Louisville. Both died in 1814.

Usher, Mrs Howard, née Phillips
fl. 1756?–1784, *actress.*

The Miss Phillips who married the actor Howard Usher was, according to Robert Hitchcock's *Historical View of the Irish Stage,* the sister of the actresses Maria and Grace Phillips. They were the daughters of a Welsh clergyman. Maria Phillips's career is noticed separately in volume 11 of this *Dictionary.* Grace Phillips, whose main distinction was becoming the mother of the famous Dorothy Jordan, did not act in London but had a busy career, mainly in Ireland.

It is possible that our subject was the Miss Phillips who acted Ismene in *Phaedra and Hippolitus* at Covent Garden Theatre on 5 February 1756 and who, when she played Zara in *The Mourning Bride* for her benefit on 3 May following, was said to be "first time in that character and fourth time on any stage." We

have, however, in the notice of Maria Phillips credited that actress with those performances at Covent Garden and with being the Miss Phillips who acted at the Jacob's Wells Theatre in Bristol during the summer of 1756.

When Howard Usher joined the Smock Alley Theatre company in the autumn of 1758, he was accompanied by Mrs Usher, who no doubt had had previous provincial experience. She appeared at Smock Alley on 16 November 1758 as Mrs Sullen in *The Beaux' Stratagem;* her husband acted Archer, a role for which he was most unsuited. Also members of the company that season were Mrs Usher's sisters, Maria and Grace Phillips.

Mrs Usher and her husband remained at Smock Alley through 1760–61. They also played during June 1761 at "The Vaults" in Belfast. Between 1764–65 and 1768 they were at the Crow Street Theatre in Dublin. She acted at Cork in the summers of 1765 and 1766. Mrs Usher was at York early in 1772.

On 5 May 1772 Mrs Usher came to London to act Alicia in *Jane Shore* at Drury Lane Theatre. She was announced as making her first appearance there. It proved to be her last. The prompter Hopkins wrote in his diary, "Alicia by Mrs Usher,—bad figure,—and play'd worse." The critic in the *Theatrical Review* hoped that "the Managers will never attempt to *usher* her on the Stage in so capital a Character again." She was seen again at York in 1773.

Though her husband returned to London to play at Drury Lane in 1774–75 and 1775–76 and at the Haymarket in the summers from 1778 through 1799, Mrs Usher was never again seen in the capital. The record of her activity elsewhere is sparse. She was in the York company in 1773 and 1783. Probably she died before her husband, who died in April 1802 and did not mention her in his will. Her daughter, according to John Taylor's *Records of My Life* (1832), was "a provincial actress of some repute." Probably she was the Miss Usher who performed at Bristol in 1778–79 and in Ireland between 1784 and 1790. Information on other possible relatives is given in the notice of Howard Usher.

"Utility, Miss." *See* KNIGHT, MRS THOMAS.

Uttini, Vincenzo ₍*fl.* *1783–1784*₎, *singer.*

On 29 November 1783 Vincenzo Uttini sang the title role in *Silla* at the King's Theatre. He went on to sing Don Bartolo in *L'albergatrice vivace,* Narduccio in *Le gelosie villane,* and a role in *Issipile* during the remainder of the 1783–84 season. His last appearance in London seems to have been on 29 May 1784. He may have been related to the dancers Francesco Antonio Uttini and Mons and Mme Charles Uttini, who were active in Sweden in the latter half of the eighteenth century.

= V =

V.,S. *fl. 1761₁*, *performer.*

The Covent Garden accounts at the Folger Shakespeare Library list a female performer, "S. V.," at £2 weekly in 1761. The woman was not Vallois, Vernon, Vincent, or Vivier, who were active at the time.

Vachon, Pierre *1731–1802, violinist.*

The violinist and composer Pierre Vachon (or Vasson or Waschon) was born in Arles in June 1731. At the age of 20, according to Fétis, he went to Paris to become the student of (Carlo?) Ciabrano. Jean Harden in the *New Grove* suggests that our subject was the violinist Vasson who was a member of the orchestra of the Comédie Italienne in 1754. At the Concert Spirituel in Paris on 24 December 1756 Vachon played one of his own concertos, and in 1758 he played at the Concert repeatedly and with great acclaim. In 1761 he was made leader of the Prince de Conti's band. In 1765 he gave concerts at the court in Fontainebleau.

In 1772 Vachon came to London. He was probably employed in the band of the opera of the King's Theatre, but we can find him on only one bill, that of the Haymarket Theatre for 27 April 1772 cited by *The London Stage*, when he played two concerts for the benefit of the violoncellist Jean Pierre Duport. Harden claims that Vachon went briefly to Paris, then returned to London in 1774 or 1775 and remained there for ten years, publishing some of his chamber music.

Vachon toured Prussia in 1784, was concertmaster in Berlin in 1786, and was pensioned in 1798. He died in Berlin on 7 October 1803. Harden gives a brief discussion and a comprehensive list of Vachon's compositions in the *New Grove*.

A pastel by L. Carmontelle showing a French musical group depicts Pierre Vachon on the violin, Jean Pierre Duport on the violoncello, Johann Joseph Rudolphe on the horn, and M. Provers holding music. The picture is in the Musée Condé, Chantilly.

Val, Mlle de la *fl. 1704–1705₁*, *dancer.*

The *Diverting Post* on 16 December 1704 reported that the dancer "Madame De La Valle" had performed at Drury Lane Theatre and was considered better than Mme Subligny. *The London Stage* calls her Mlle de la Val and has her dancing at Lincoln's Inn Fields Theatre ("lately arriv'd in England") on 12 December. She had a benefit there on 13 January 1705 and continued appearing until the end of March.

Valcour, Miss *fl. 1758–1759₁*, *dancer.*

Miss Valcour danced a minuet with Noverre at Drury Lane Theatre on 27 April 1758. Benefit tickets for "Mrs" Valcour were accepted that day, but that may have been a misprint in the bills for Miss Valcour. Our subject danced in *Comus* on 3 November 1758, danced a minuet with Noverre in *Romeo and Juliet* on 8 and 26 December, and shared a benefit with two others on 15 May 1759.

Vale, Isaac *b. 1765, singer.*

Born in 1765, Isaac Vale was listed in Doane's *Musical Directory* of 1794 as a basso who was secretary to the Choral Fund and sang for the Cecilian Society and in the oratorios at Drury Lane Theatre. He was then living at No 14, "Bethlem Court, Old Bethlem." Tickets for the Choral Fund performance of the *Messiah* at the Haymarket Theatre on 15 January 1798 were available from "the Secretary, J. Vale, Old Bethlem, Bishopsgate." In 1800, when Vale at the age of 35 was initiated into the Masonic Lodge called Union, at St Catherine's near the Tower, his address was given as No 74, Bishopsgate Street. Information on Vale's Masonic con-

Musée Condé, Chantilly

M. Provers holding music, JOHN PIERRE DUPORT on violoncello, Johan Joseph Rudolphe on horn, PIERRE VACHON on violin, and Mr Vernier on oboe

by Carmontelle

nection comes from John M. Shaftesbury's "Jews in Regular English Freemasonry" in the *Transactions of the Jewish Historical Society of England*, 25.

Valenti, Signor   *fl.*   *1745–1747₁*, *dancer.*

Judith Milhous finds a Signor Valenti cited in volumes 4 and 5 of *Comic Tunes,* the annual booklets published by John Walsh listing music for theatrical dances. Apparently Valenti danced at the King's Theatre in the 1745–46 and 1746–47 seasons, if we judge from his partners: Mechel, Salamon (Salomoni), and Nardi in 1745–46 and Nardi and Sodi in 1746–47. Valenti is otherwise unknown.

Valentine, Henry   *fl. c. 1790–1794₁*, *oboist, music seller.*

Henry Valentine of Leicester sold a collection of anthems and psalms by Thomas Collins about 1790. Doane's *Musical Directory* of 1794 noted that Valentine was an oboist and had played at the Handelian concerts at Westminster Abbey. He was probably a relative of John Valentine.

Valentine, John   *1730–1791, violist, composer.*

John Valentine was born in Leicester on 7 June 1730, the son of John and Sarah Valentine, according to Martin Medforth in *Musical Times* in December 1981. (The *New Grove* states that our subject was born in 1710, but that was a different John Valentine from another branch of the family, as Medforth's genealogical chart shows.) Our John Valentine published a number of musical works from about 1765 to about 1785: marches, minuets, psalm tunes, music for *Isabella, or the Fatal Marriage,* and symphonies. He came to London to play viola in the Handel Memorial Concerts at Westminster Abbey and the Pantheon in May and June 1784. The *Gentleman's Magazine* reported that Valentine died in Leicester on 10 September 1791. He and his wife Tabitha had six children: Thomas, Elizabeth, Ann, John, Sarah, and Charles (whose last name is given by Medforth as Simpson).

Valentine, Mary. *See* TAYLOR, MRS. THOMAS?

Valentine, Robert   *1674–c. 1735, oboist, flutist, composer.*

Robert Valentine was very likely the son of Thomas and Sarah "Follintine" who was christened on 16 January 1674 at St Martin's, Leicester, according to Martin Medforth in *Musical Times* in December 1981. (The *New Grove* says our subject was born about 1680.) Robert may have gone to Italy as early as 1707 and was probably the Roberto Valentino (or Valentini) who played oboe at the Ruspoli Palace in Rome in April 1708. Valentine performed in London in 1731. The *Catalogue of Printed Music in the British Museum* lists many compositions by Valentine, published in London from about 1710 to 1735. Most of his airs and sonatas used a flute or flutes (probably recorders). Grove suggests that Robert may have been a cousin of the musician John Valentine. Robert Valentine died about 1735.

Valentine, Thomas   *1759–c. 1800, violinist.*

Thomas Valentine was born in 1759 and was single when he was admitted to the Royal Society of Musicians on 4 July 1784. The previous May and June he had played second violin in the Handel Memorial Concerts at Westminster Abbey and the Pantheon and was then cited as Valentine junior, perhaps to distinguish him from John Valentine of Leicester. Thomas was performing at Covent Garden Theatre in 1784 as well. He played violin in the Society's St Paul's concerts in May of 1792 and 1793. Thomas Valentine must have died about 1800, for his widow, Margaret, on 4 May 1800 was granted an allowance of over £6 monthly for herself and her five children. On 5 July she asked the Society if her son (unnamed) could be apprenticed to his aunt, an organist in Leicester. The proposal was rejected, for some reason. By 1801 Mrs Valentine was living in Wrexham, Denbighshire. The Society Minute Books contain a number of references to Mrs Valentine and the apprenticing of her children Henry, Sarah, and Anna. The names of the other children were not mentioned. Mrs Valentine was still alive in July 1837.

Valentine, Thomas   *fl. 1777₁*, *musician.*

Thomas Valentine was admitted to the Royal Society of Musicians on 5 January 1777. He was single at that time. His relationship, if any, to the Thomas Valentine who was born in 1759 is not known.

Valentini. *See also* MINGOTTI, SIGNORA PIETRO.

"Valentini," stage name of Valentino Urbani ₍fl. 1690–1719₎, *singer.*

The male contralto (later high tenor) Valentino Urbani, called "Valentini," was a native of Udina and, according to Galliard's notes to Tosi's *Observations,* was trained under Pistocchi before going into the service of the Duke of Mantua. He sang in Venice and Parma in 1690, in Bologna in 1691 and 1695, in Rome in 1694, and in Venice again in 1695. From 1697 to 1700 he sang for the Electress of Brandenburg in Berlin. He was in Mantua in 1703.

Montague Summers, in his editions of the works of both Congreve and Wycherley, states that Valentini sang at the premiere of the opera *Camilla* in London on 29 or 30 March 1706 at Drury Lane Theatre, though *The London Stage,* quoting the 1706 edition of the work, does not list him. The role of Turnus, which Valentini certainly sang later, was listed as sung by Hughes. The Italian *castrato* is cited by *The London Stage* as singing Turnus on 8 March 1707; the *New Grove* calls that performance Valentini's debut. On 6 December 1707, when he sang in Italian, "The Baroness" and Margherita de l'Épine sang partly in Italian, and the rest of the cast sang in English.

Valentini had come to England with the music and Italian text of *Il trionfo d'amore;* he gave the text to Peter Motteux to translate for 50 guineas (plus an additional 30 guineas on the sixth performance day). While that was being arranged, Valentini was negotiating with Vanbrugh for his singing contract. Among the Coke papers at Harvard are several documents pertaining to Valentini. One is an agreement for Valentini to sing from 13 January to 13 June (1708?; but 13 June that year fell on a Sunday) for 400 guineas; he also bargained for 100 guineas for the opera *The Triumph of Love.* Another document has him asking 420 guineas for singing 40 times, or

Art Gallery of Toronto, A. R. Gellman Collection

"VALENTINI"

artist unknown (Ricci?)

ten and a half guineas per evening. That note, in French, was followed by another, in English, suggesting that Valentini may have settled for 350 guineas. A paylist shows Valentini at £7 10s. nightly, less than the 350 guineas for the season that the earlier document suggested.

Still another document outlines the reasons why Valentini, Signora de l'Épine, and Mrs. Tofts needed higher salaries: the shortness of the opera season, the cold and damp English weather, the cost of clothes, and so on. A note dated 31 December 1707 says that Valentini was owed £25 17s, 3d. by the Drury Lane manager Christopher Rich for costumes for the opera *Thomyris*—plumes, a turban, shoes, lace, and the like—for his character of Orontes.

Love's Triumph, as *Il trionfo d'amore* was finally called in English, was scheduled to open on 26 February 1708 at the Queen's Theatre with Valentini as Liso. Addison wrote to the Earl of Manchester on 24 February:

The Gay part of the town is in high Expectation of a New opera that is to make its appearance on Thursday next. It is originally Italian composed by three different Masters Bononcini having done one act of it. It was first designed for a private Entertainment at Cardinal Ottoboni's, and is translated into English after the manner of Camilla. The new Eunuch has bin Hisst so severely that he does not intend to Act any more.

It would appear that Valentini did not carry out his threat.

He was not, however, the first-rate singer his successor Nicolini was. Galliard said Valentini was "not so powerful in Voice or Action as *Nicolini,*" but he was "more chaste in his Singing." Colley Cibber called Valentini "a true sensible Singer at that time, but of a Throat too weak to sustain those melodious Warblings for which the fairer Sex have since idoliz'd his Successors." Cibber thought him in "every way inferior to Nicolini, yet he had the Advantage of giving us our first Impression of a good Opera Singer; he had still his Admirers, and was of great Service in being so skilful a Second to his Superior." Indeed, Valentini helped bring Nicolini to England. Vanbrugh wrote to the Earl of Manchester on 24 February 1708, saying in a postscript, "Valentini is mighty earnest with me to get Nicolini over tho' he knows he so much exceeds him; but he wou'd fain See Opera flourish here, and is mightely pleas'd with the Civill Treatment he meets with."

In 1708–9 Nicolini was at the Queen's with Valentini, the former taking the leading roles. They were in *Pirro e Demetrio* on 14 December 1708, Valentini singing the role of Demetrio. For his benefit on 16 February 1709 he chose *Camilla.* He was Fernando in *Clotilda* on 2 March. The next season he sang Almanzor in *Almahide* and Dario in *Idaspe,* and in 1710–11, for £537 for the season, he appeared as Eustachio in *Rinaldo* and repeated some of his earlier parts. He did not sing in 1711–12. In 1712–13 he was Silvio in *Il pastor fido,* Thirsis in *Dorinda,* Egeo in *Teseo,* Ricimero in *Ernelinda,* and Eustachio in *Rinaldo.* The opera manager Owen Swiney left in midseason, owing Valentini 100 guineas. In February 1713 Baron Price offered a legal opinion

on Valentini's situation which is now among the Coke papers at Harvard:

Signore Valentino having informd Mr Baron Price of the tenure of his Articles signed by Mr Swiny and of the first payment made to him upon them and also of the manner of Mr Swinyes going off, & absenting him self from his Creditors, among which Signore Valentino is also one for one hundred guineas more, due for the Second payment on his articles, some time before Mr Swiny absconded twas his opinion that the said Mr Swiny is a Banckrupt, and his Creditors have their remedy against him as such, and where as the new agreement made among the singers had no retrospection to Mr Swinys debts, made by him when in possession of the Theatre, therefore it cannot in Justice be urged that the first payment made by Mr Swiny to Signore Valentino so long before he became Banckrupt, should be urged to hinder him, from coming in, as a divider of the proffitts now arising on their new settlement.

The "new settlement" was an agreement by the singers to perform on a cooperative basis; Valentini had evidently been excluded because he had received partial pay. The Lord Chamberlain ruled that Valentini should be allowed to join the sharing arrangement but should not receive a share until the other singers received their portions.

At the Queen's in 1713–14 Valentini sang in *Dorinda,* was Ciro in *Creso,* and appeared as Segestes in *Arminio.* He joined other singers on 16 March 1714 to petition for the better regulation of their benefits, but for him the matter was moot, for he did not rejoin the opera company in 1714–15. He was still in London, however, for he had a benefit concert at Hickford's Music Room on 31 March 1715. Grove says Valentini sang in five operas in Venice between 1717 and 1719.

A pen and brown ink drawing by an anonymous artist of Valentini in an extravagant pose, wearing an oriental costume, is in the collection of A. R. Gellman, Toronto. Other versions are in the Royal Library, Windsor (attributed to Ricci), and the Cini Foundation Library, Venice (attributed to Zanetti).

"Valeriano," stage name of Valeriano Pellegrini *fl. 1690–1729], singer, composer.*

The *New Grove* reports that the *castrato* Valeriano Pellegrini, called "Valeriano," was a native of Verona. He probably was the Valeriano who sang in Rome from 1690 to 1693. From about 1705 to 1716 he was attached to the court of the Elector Palatine in Düsseldorf. On 9 April 1712 at the Great House in Old Spring Garden, Valeriano made his first London appearance singing at a benefit concert for Giacomo Courti. For the 1712–13 opera season at the Queen's Theatre, Valeriano was paid a total of £645, the highest amount received by any of the singers. He sang Mirtillo in *Il pastor fido* on 22 November 1712, Silvius in *Dorinda* on 10 December, the title part in *Teseo* on 10 January 1713, and Vitige in *Ernelinda* on 26 February. At his benefit on 2 May he received almost £74. In addition to singing in *Ernelinda* that night, Valeriano sang several new songs, including one in English. Valeriano returned to Italy and was a priest in Rome in 1729.

Valerius, John   *1667–1705, freak.*

John Valerius, according to Caulfield's *Remarkable Persons,* was born in 1667 in the upper palatinate of Germany, without arms. After the death of his parents he earned a living by putting himself on display, showing skills he had taught himself, using his feet and toes. Valerius traveled widely on the Con-

Courtesy of Atlas van Stolk, Historisch Museum Rotterdam

JOHN VALERIUS
artist unknown

Courtesy of Atlas van Stolk, Historisch Museum Rotterdam

JOHN VALERIUS
artist unknown

tinent, coming finally to England in 1698–99. Caulfield cites a "very rare book of Valerius's postures" containing 16 prints showing him beating a drum, playing cards and dice, shaving himself, balancing a glass of liquor on his forehead, writing with his toes, and so on. A copy of that volume of plates is in the Atlas van Stolk, Historisch Museum Rotterdam. Though Valerius developed several skills, he was not to be compared with the remarkable Matthew Buckinger. Caulfield observed that Valerius had a thumb where one of his arms should have been, a feminine face, and the breasts of a woman. Valerius put himself on exhibition in London until 1703. He died in 1705.

Valesecchi. *See* VOLSECCHI.

Vallois, Miss   *fl. 1746–1749₁,   dancer.*
See VALLOIS, MME WILLIAM JOVAN DE, CATHERINE.

Vallois, Catherine *b. c. 1746, dancer, actress, singer.*

Catherine Vallois (or, frequently, Valois), the daughter of William Jovan de Vallois and his wife Catherine, made her first appearance on any stage on 15 April 1757, dancing at Covent Garden Theatre. Possibly she was born about 1746, when Catherine de Vallois was not named in the bills. Miss Vallois offered a *Dutch Dance* on 22 April and *Country Lass* along with the *Dutch Dance* on 12 May. She participated in two benefits at the Haymarket Theatre in September 1757, and the bill for 14 September identified her as a "scholar to Mr La Cointe." She danced at Covent Garden again from 31 March 1758.

Miss Vallois's first named part seems to have been Robin in *The Merry Wives of Windsor* at Covent Garden on 25 September 1758, and during the 1758–59 season she was also seen as the Page in *The Orphan*, the Page in *Love Makes a Man*, and the Duke of York in *Richard III*—parts assigned to children. Catherine also danced that season, and at the Haymarket for her benefit with Miss Burn on 18 April 1759 she acted the title role in *Cleone* and danced in a minuet. The occasion was a performance by "children not above thirteen years of age."

In the following season at Covent Garden Catherine served as a dancer between the acts and in pantomimes and appeared as Blouze in *Phebe*, Prince John in *1 Henry IV*, a Grace in *Perseus and Andromeda*, Prince Arthur in *King John*, Prince Edward in *Richard III*, an Aerial Spirit in *The Royal Chace*, Patty in *The Maid of the Mill*, a Nymph in *Orpheus and Eurydice*, Margery in *Love in a Village*, Daphne in *Apollo and Daphne*, Harriet in *The Upholsterer*, Sally in *Thomas and Sally*, Kitty in *The Brothers*, Ceres in *The Rape of Proserpine*, Betty in *The Court of Alexander*, Betty in *Flora*, Amie in *The Jovial Crew*, a Sprite in *Harlequin's Jubilee*, Fanny in *Tom Jones*, Nysa in *Midas*, a Chambermaid in *The Clandestine Marriage*, Cherry in *The Stratagem*, Iris in *The Golden Pippin*, Jessica in *The Merchant of Venice*, Charlotte in *Man and Wife*, Echo in *The Duellist*, a colombine in *The Sylphs*, *Harlequin's Frolicks*, and *The Royal Chace*, Margaret in *Much Ado about Nothing*, Mignionet in *The Way to Keep Him*, Mademoiselle in *The Funeral*, and Ceres in *The Tempest*. Her last appearance at Covent Garden seems

to have been on 9 May 1781, when she sang in the chorus of *Macbeth* (her first attempt at a singing character was Anne in *The Spanish Lady* on 2 May 1765). Her salary as of 22 September 1760 was 2s. 6d. daily; by September 1767 she was earning 6s. 8d. daily.

Miss Vallois made occasional appearances at other theatres: at the Haymarket as Cleone in the spring of 1759, as a dancer between the acts at the Haymarket in the summer of 1765, as a dancer and an actress (often a colombine) at Bristol from 1768 to 1772, as Theodosia in *The Maid of the Mill* at Drury Lane on 5 April 1769 and subsequent dates, and as a dancer at Sadler's Wells from 1773 to 1776 (and probably others years). She was with the Norwich company from 1782 to 1785. With them at "Stirbitch-Fair" at Cambridge on 3 October 1782 she is known to have acted Miss Ogle in *The Belle's Stratagem* and Colombine in *Harlequin Triumphant*, and at Norwich on 12 February 1783 she played Charlotte in *The Fair American*. She was earning a guinea a week at Norwich in 1783; the Committee books there noted that she declined to perform figure dances (because, as we shall see, she was putting on weight).

Catherine Vallois appeared on the York circuit for Tate Wilkinson in 1785 and 1786 at Leeds, York, Wakefield, Doncaster, and Hull as Fanny in *The Mogul Tale*, Maud in *Peeping Tom*, Jenny in *Lionel and Clarissa*, Annette and Clorinda in *Robin Hood*, Nannette in *Fontainebleau*, Phoebe in *Rosina*, Miss Winterbottom in *Hunt the Slipper*, Miss Mummery in *A Beggar on Horseback*, Madge in *Love in a Village*, Lucy in *The Beggar's Opera* (for Mrs Powell), Miss Plumb in *Gretna Green*, Flora in *The Wonder*, Kitty in *High Life below Stairs*, Comfit in *The Dead Alive*, Minette in *A Bold Stroke for a Husband*, Bloom in *I'll Tell You What!*, Princess Huncamunca in *Tom Thumb*, the Second Constantia and the Mother of the Second Constantia in *The Chances*, Cherry in *The Stratagem*, the Third Wife in *A Word to Wives*, Audrey in *As You Like It*, Mrs Meddle in *The Humorist*, Betty in *The Clandestine Marriage*, Mrs Fulmer in *The West Indian*, and a colombine in *Harlequin Salamander*, *The Birth and Adventures of Harlequin*, *The Rural Rumpus*, *The Frolic*, and *The Touchstone*.

Her first appearance in Manchester was as an Orange Girl in *The Wapping Landlady* on 1

March 1790. She was acting in Manchester at least through June 1794 and also performed in Birmingham, remarkably, as a dancer, from 1790 to 1792.

By 1793 Miss Vallois had gained so much weight that *The Thespian Mirror . . . of the Theatres Royal, Manchester, Liverpool, and Chester* commented:

> To the temple of Fortune she never can jump,
> For the noble dimensions and weight of her R—p.
> Besides, other causes too obvious to mention.
> Have laid an embargo upon her ascension.

She was a member of Ward's troupe in Manchester in January 1796. The last notice we have found for Catherine Vallois dates from 1798, when she played Emmeline, Mother to Constantia, in *The Knights of Malta* at the Royal Circus in London. The *Monthly Mirror* in April 1799 indicated that she was then still alive and unmarried.

Of her personal life we know very little. In the will of Charles Atkins, dated 29 July 1775, Catherine "Valois," identified as of Covent Garden Theatre and a spinster, was named residuary legatee.

The *Index to The London Stage* gives to Catherine Vallois some of the citations that belong to her mother, Mme Jovan de Vallois.

Vallois, William Jovan de *fl.* 1732–1738₁, *dancer, choreographer.*

At Lincoln's Inn Fields Theatre on 13 April 1732 a *Pastoral* was danced by Vallois, "lately arrived from the Opera at Paris, the first Time of his dancing in England; [with?] a Scholar to M. Marcelle." Vallois was, as Portuguese Embassy Chapel records show, William Jovan de Vallois (or D'Vallois, but the usual citation in the bills was simply Vallois). He danced a louvre on 1 May and then returned to Paris. On 28 July he was back, dancing an untitled turn at Drury Lane Theatre. He continued appearing at Drury Lane through 22 August. At the Portuguese Embassy Chapel on 16 September 1732 Vallois married Catherine Roger ("Rogers" in the register), the widow of the dancer Anthony Francis Roger. Among the witnesses was the actress Hannah Pritchard of Drury Lane.

Vallois was associated chiefly with Henry Giffard's company at Goodman's Fields The-

atre from 1732–33 to 1735–36 and at Lincoln's Inn Fields Theatre in 1736–37, regularly offering entr'acte dances and playing in pantomimes. On 4 October 1732 Vallois and "Mlle" Vallois "from the Theatre in Paris" made their first appearance together at Goodman's Fields. It seems pretty certain that the several references to a Mlle Vallois in the 1730s and 1740s are to Vallois and his wife and not to a daughter. During the rest of his first season at Goodman's Fields Vallois was cited frequently as an entr'acte dancer, played Harlequin in *The Tavern Bilkers,* was Le Petit Maître in a *Masquerade Dance,* and was given a solo benefit on 20 April 1733. His benefit bill indicated that his house was opposite the Theatre Tavern. Mme Vallois was featured in two dances (one with Vallois), but she did not share the benefit with him. At the benefit, at least one of the dances, *"La Provansalle,"* was choreographed by Vallois. He and his wife shared a benefit at the Haymarket Theatre on 28 May. Vallois was also a teacher; one of his scholars had appeared at Goodman's Fields in October 1732. Vallois danced at Covent Garden Theatre in mid-summer 1733, and on 23 August at Bartholomew Fair he was the Deity of Pleasure in *The Gardens of Venus.*

Vallois continued appearing frequently at Goodman's Fields through the spring of 1736, dancing between the acts and playing such pantomime characters as a Fury, Miller, and Demon in *The Necromancer,* a Follower and Pierrot in *Jupiter and Io,* Victory and a Waterman in *Britannia,* and a Swain and Triton in *Harlequin Shipwrecked.* With the Giffard company at Lincoln's Inn Fields in 1736–37 Vallois continued in his old parts and added a Follower and Sylvan in *Hymen's Triumph.* His last season in London, 1737–38, was spent at Drury Lane Theatre, where he appeared as a Mandarin Gormogon in *Harlequin Grand Volgi* and served as an entr'acte dancer. He shared a benefit on 22 May 1738 with the two Misses Scot, his scholars.

Vallois, Mme William Jovan de, Catherine, formerly Mrs Anthony Francis Roger *fl.* 1724?–1757₁, *dancer, actress, candlewoman?*

The Lincoln's Inn Fields Theatre accounts contain a payment of 7s. on 5 October 1724 to "Cath. Rogers Candlewoman" for six days' work. Possibly the candlewoman was our subject, Catherine Roger (Mme Anthony Francis Roger). A Mrs "Rogers," presumably our subject, was Betty Doxy in *The Beggar's Opera* on 29 January 1728 at Lincoln's Inn Fields. On 18 October 1728 "Mrs Roger" was a Bridemaid in *Harlequin Happy* at Drury Lane Theatre. Her next notice in *The London Stage* has her dancing a Follower in *Diana and Acteon* at Drury Lane on 23 April 1730. On 15 May she was a Shepherdess in *The Fairy Queen.* She danced at Drury Lane in the spring of 1732 and was an Hour of Sleep and a Bridemaid in *Perseus and Andromeda* and Molly in *The Beggar's Opera.* At Tottenham Court on 4 August (just three days after her appearance in *The Beggar's Opera*) Mrs Roger acted Colombine in *The Metamorphosis of Harlequin,* and on 23 August at Bartholomew Fair Mrs "Rogers" was Jenny in *Henry VIII.*

Anthony Francis Roger died in 1731; administration of his estate was granted to Catherine Roger on 22 February 1732. On 16 September 1732 Catherine married the dancer William Jovan de Vallois. In the years that followed Catherine was cited variously as Mlle Vallois (or Valois), Madam D'Vallois, Mrs Vallois, Miss Vallois—but we believe all citations are to the same dancer-actress. Most references call her Mrs Vallois.

With her new husband she was at Goodman's Fields Theatre from 1732–33 through 1735–36 with Henry Giffard's troupe. The pair was heralded as "from the Theatre in Paris" on occasion, and Mrs Vallois was at least once identified as the widow of Monsieur Roger, who had been a pierrot at Drury Lane Theatre. Mrs Vallois danced entr'acte turns regularly with her husband (*Pierrot and Pairayte, French Peasant,* and *Amorous Couple* were examples), and she appeared as an Attendant in *The Amorous Sportsman,* Sukey in *The Beggar's Opera,* Mary Licklips in *The Decoy,* a Grace and a Nymph in *Britannia,* a Companion of Diana in *Diana and Acteon,* a Haymaker in *The Necromancer,* a Nymph in *Jupiter and Io,* and Trusty in *The Provok'd Husband.*

During her tenure at Goodman's Fields Mrs Vallois was seen elsewhere. She and her husband shared a benefit at the Haymarket Theatre on 28 May 1733, when she danced between the acts and played Trusty in *The Provok'd Husband.* In the summer of that year she danced at Covent Garden, and on 23 August she was a Grace in *The Gardens of Venus* at Bartholomew Fair. A year later at that fair she danced in a piece called *The Force of Inclination,* and on 12 August 1735 at the Haymarket she played Dolly in *The Beggar's Opera.*

Her husband moved with the Giffards to Lincoln's Inn Fields in 1736–37, but Catherine's name disappeared from the London bills that season.

On 6 May 1738 Mrs Vallois was in a *Scots Dance* at Drury Lane Theatre, and on 22 May at her husband's shared benefit with two of his students she danced in *French Peasant.* How long she may have been at Drury Lane is not known; there was no indication in the bills that she was making her first Drury Lane appearances. (After 1738 her husband's name disappeared from the London bills.) She danced at Drury Lane in 1738–39 and 1739–40, appearing as a Wife and a Gardener in *Harlequin Grand Volgi,* Mrs Spinnage in *Robin Goodfellow,* a Maid in *Columbine Courtezan,* Dolly in *The Beggar's Opera,* a Haymaker in *Harlequin Shipwrecked,* and a Gipsy in *The Fortune Tellers,* among other assignments. She also appeared in dances between the acts and in *Comus* and *The Harlot's Progress.*

In 1740–41 she was back at Goodman's Fields, though the only mention of her in the bills was on 19 February 1741 when she danced in *King Arthur.* On 22 August of that year she danced in *The Triumph of Britannia over the Four Parts of the World* at Bartholomew Fair. In 1741–42 Mrs Vallois performed at Goodman's Fields, dancing in *The Imprisonment, Release, Stratagems, and Marriage of Harlequin* and appearing as Rachel in *Pamela,* Betty in *The Old Bachelor,* Peg in *The Way of the World,* and Patty in *The Lying Valet.* At Bartholomew Fair in August 1742 she played Medlar in *Scaramouch Scapin* and danced a *Fingalian Dance* with David. In 1742–43 she performed at Lincoln's Inn Fields, appearing as Lucy in *The Devil to Pay* and Dolly in *The Beggar's Opera* and dancing between the acts.

According to the Lord Chamberlain's accounts (LC 5/204, studied by Judy Milhous and Robert Hume) Mrs Vallois was an occasional performer at Drury Lane under Fleetwood in 1743. On 27 September she complained in support of the actors' rebellion against the patentee:

Catherine Vallois late of the Theatre Royal in Drury Lane voluntarily maketh Oath before me [James Fraser] one of his Majesty's Justices of the Peace for the City & Liberty of Westminster that she this Deponent hath owing to her 2*s* 6*d* per Night the Summ of £10 14*s* 6*d* from Chas Fletewood Esqr Patentee of ye said Theatre & that the said Ch Fletewood discharged the Deponent without paying her, tho' she this Deponent had been on the Stage from her Infancy & her Father & Mother, as she has heard her Mother say (who is now living) belong'd to the Theatre in ye time of K. Charles the 2*d* she having perform'd before that Prince but had from her great Age no other support than from ye sallary of this Deponent her Daughter & that for want of her sallary above mentioned she has been drove to so great a distress that she & her aged mother had not more for a whole week than one Quart of Oatmeal to support Nature.

Fleetwood claimed not to have known of her distress, otherwise "he had certainly relieved her." Unfortunately, the information in Catherine's testimony is too general to allow us to identify the name of her parents.

The next notice we have found of Mrs Vallois comes from Bristol. On 3 September 1746 she shared a benefit with two others at the Jacob's Wells summer theatre. The account books show that she had an engagement that ran from 2 June to 5 September. *The London Stage* lists a Miss Vallois at Covent Garden Theatre in 1746–47. That notice would appear to be an error for Mrs Vallois; in any case, no female Vallois was mentioned in the bills that season, and we would guess she had only minor assignments. Mrs Vallois was in Bristol again from 10 June to 31 August 1747, performing for 4*s*. nightly.

Mrs Vallois (again sometimes listed in *The London Stage* as Miss Vallois) performed at Covent Garden from 1748–49 through 1756–57, though she may have missed the 1751–52 season. In 1749–50 she was earning 15*s*. weekly. Her assignments were similar or the same as before: Sukey, Betty, and Dolly in *The Beggar's Opera*, a Follower in *Apollo and Daphne*, a part in a masque in *The Muses Looking Glass*, and the like. On 22 September 1756 Mrs Vallois began the season at Covent Garden playing Betty Doxey in *The Beggar's*

Opera, but that may have been her last stage appearance. The following April Miss "Valois" made her stage debut. Our guess is that this was Catherine, the daughter of William Jovan de Vallois and his wife Catherine. The younger performer continued active to the end of the century.

Vallouis, Simonin   *fl.* 1769–1777], dancer, choreographer.

References in the bills to Siminon or Simonin we take to concern the dancer-choreographer Simonin Vallouis (or Vallouy), who was active at the King's Theatre in the 1770s. We have supposed that references to Mme and Mlle Vallouis are to Vallouis's wife, Mme Niel Vallouis, and that their son was the Vallouis cadet named in several bills.

On 5 September 1769 the *Public Advertiser* reported that "Signor Siminon" (according to *The London Stage*) had been engaged to dance at the King's Theatre in the 1769–70 season. On 10 March 1770 one of the new dances in the opera *Ezio* was composed by "Simonin." Simonin Vallouis was advertised as dancing at the King's on 8 November 1774 with his wife in a grand ballet, *Pirhame et Thisbe,* and in *Le Baillet de Fleur.* On 13 December they appeared in *La Bal Masquer,* on 7 February 1775 in *Les Mexicains* and a *Grand Heroic Historic Ballet,* on 7 March in a *New Ballet,* on 4 April in *La Mascherata* (Mme Vallouis was called Mlle, but it seems clear that there was not a second female Vallouis in the company), on 22 April in a *Grand Chaconne* and *Champêtre Comique* (in which Vallouis le cadet danced), on 25 April in a pas de deux, and on 25 May in a minuet, a *Ballet Pastorale et Pantomime,* and a tragic ballet called *Oreste et Electre* (in which the couple danced the title roles) for their benefit; two of the new dances were composed by Vallouis. During the season Vallouis appeared occasionally in dance works with other partners.

Vallouis and his wife continued at the King's Theatre through the 1776–77 season, appearing in such new pieces as a *Ballet Pastorale, La Fête du Village, Les Maissoneurs Distresse, a Minuet de la Cour, Les Amans Heureux* (with Vallouis cadet), and *Les Chasseurs.* On 8 May 1777 the performance was for the benefit of Monsieur and Madame Valloui; their address was given as No 2, Berkeley Square. During the 1776–77 season Mme Vallouis danced less and less frequently, while Vallouis cadet appeared more frequently and in more important dancing assignments. Though the younger Vallouis continued appearing in London, Vallouis and his wife either retired or left the country.

Vallouis, Mme Simonin, Niel *fl.* *1774–1777*₁, *dancer. See* VALLOUIS, SIMONIN *fl. 1769–1777*₁

Vallouis, Simonin *fl. 1775–1778*₁, *dancer.*

Simonin cadet, presumably the son of Simonin and Niel Vallouis, made his first appearance on 7 January 1775 at the King's Theatre dancing an *Entrée*. Monsieur and Madame Vallouis were also on the program that night. On 22 April Vallouis cadet danced in a new ballet, *Champêtre Comique,* with his parents. He continued dancing in entr'acte pieces to the end of the season in June. In 1775–76 his name did not appear in any bills, but on 2 November 1776 he danced with his parents in *Les Amans Heureux* and continued active at the King's throughout the 1776–77 season. He danced in such works as *La Force de l'Amour, L'Épouse Persane, Provençal* (a solo within a new *Masquerade Dance), La Clochette, Le Culte d'Amour* (composed by his father), and *La Paysanne Distraite.*

Though his parents seem to have left the London stage after the 1776–77 season, the younger Vallouis continued at the King's Theatre for one more season, appearing in *La Polonaise Favourite, La Clochette,* a *Serious Ballet,* a *Divertisement, La Sérénade Interrompuée,* and *Les Amans unis par l'Hymen.* His last appearance seems to have been on 4 April 1778.

Vallouy. *See* VALLOUIS.

Valsecchi. *See* VOLSECCHI.

Van, William *fl. 1794*₁, *instrumentalist.*

Doane's *Musical Directory* of 1794 lists William Van, of Lyon's Inn, as an oboist and a bass (player, probably, not singer) who performed for the Cecilian Society and the Surrey Chapel Society. He also participated in the oratorios at Drury Lane Theatre and Westminster Abbey.

Van Batom, Bernard *fl. 1689–1699*₁, *trumpeter.*

Bernard Van Batom (or Vanbarten) was sworn a trumpeter in the King's Musick on 12 September 1689 at an annual salary of £91 5s. He was last mentioned in the Lord Chamberlain's accounts in 1699.

Van Beck, Mrs Michael, Barbara, née Ursler, called Ursula Dyan *b. 1629, bearded lady, harpsichordist.*

Ursula Dyan, exhibited in London in 1668, was probably Barbara Ursler (or Urslerin), the bearded lady who was born in Augsburg, Germany, on 18 February 1629, the daughter of Balshazzar and Ann Ursler. John Evelyn saw her and told his diary on 15 September 1657,

I also saw the hairy Maid, or Woman, wh[om] 20 years before I had also seene when a child: her very Eyebrowes were combed upward, & all her forehead as thick & even as growes on any womans head, neately dress'd: There come also tw[o] lock[s] very long out of Each Eare: she had also a most prolix beard, & *mustachios,* with long locks of haire growing on the very middle of her nose, exactly like an Island [i.e., Iceland] Dog; the rest of her body not so hairy, yet exceeding long in comparison, armes, neck, breast & back; the Coluur of a bright browne, & fine as well dressed flax: She was now married, & told me had one Child, that was not hairy, nor were any of her parents or relations: she was borne at *Ausburg* in *Germanie,* & for the rest very well shaped, plaied well on the Harpsichord &c: . . .

De Beer's notes to that passage state that she was the wife of Michael Van Beck and that she was born near Kempten, about 50 miles from Augsburg. Brackenhoffer saw her in Paris in 1645. De Beer thought that the bearded lady seen by Pepys in 1668 was a different women, but the most recent editors of Pepys's *Diary* think she was probably the same.

Pepys told of his visit to her on 21 December 1668:

[We] first went into Holborne and there saw the woman that is to be seen with a Beard; she is a little plain woman, a Dane, her name, Ursula Dyan, about forty years old, her voice like a little girl's, with a beard as much as any man I ever saw, as black almost, and grizzly. They offered [to]

BARBARA VAN BECK
engraving by Gaywood

show my wife further satisfaction if she desired it, refusing it to men that desired it there. But there is no doubt but by her voice she is a woman; it begun to grow at about seven years old—and was shaved not above seven months ago, and is now so big as any man almost that ever I saw, I say, bushy and thick. It was a strange sight to me, I confess, and what pleased me mightily. Thence to the Duke's playhouse and saw *Mackbeth*. . . .

Engravings of the bearded lady were made by H. Winze in 1638, Isaac Brunnin in 1653, and R. Gaywood about 1658. Winze's engraving shows her standing, full-length, holding a handkerchief and gloves. Gaywood's picture shows her standing, three-quarter length, with her left hand on an organ; an inscription below in Latin and English contains information about Mrs Van Beck's birth, parentage, and marriage. A copy by G. Scott, half-length, was published by Woodburn, 1816. In an anonymous engraving, published by W. Richardson, she is shown playing a harpsichord.

Vanbracken, Mr *fl.* 1702–1710₁, *actor.*
Our subject's name seems never to have been spelled the same way twice; we have found it as Vanbracken, Van Broken, Van Brockin, Verbrachen, and Verbraken, and our choice for the headnote is arbitrary. He appears to have been a minor actor and not to be confused with the major player, John Verbruggen (d. 1708). Our subject was one of five actors brought before the King's Bench on 16 February 1702 and charged with using "abominable" language in performances of *Love for Love* and *The Sham Doctor* (*The Anatomist*). The players were found guilty and fined £5 each.

Our man was named on a paylist for the Queen's Theatre, dated 8 March 1708, for 5*s*. daily, but his duties were not specified. At William Pinkethman's theatre in Greenwich in 1710 Vanbracken acted Cogdie in *The Gamester* on 21 August, the Boatswain in *The Sea Voyage* on 24 August, and Felix in *The Mistake* on 1 September. He was cited as one of the troupe members from outside London, so he may have spent the 1708–9 and 1709–10 seasons in the provinces.

Van Bright, Walter   *c. 1626–1682, drummer.*

Judging by information we have concerning his marriages, Walter Van Bright was born about 1626. By 22 June 1666, when he was mentioned in the Lord Chamberlain's accounts, he was a kettledrummer in the King's Musick. On that date a warrant was issued to pay him £10 and provide him with sea livery, for he was to attend Prince Rupert and the Duke of Albemarle on a voyage. Similarly, on 3 May 1669 he received £20 in advance for accompanying Lord Henry Howard, the Ambassador to Morocco, to Morocco from 10 June 1669 to 25 August 1670. The total amount paid to five court musicians who made that trip was over £551.

Van Bright played his kettledrums in the band that played for the court masque *Calisto* on 15 February 1675. He seems to have again gone abroad, for he died at sea on board the *Gloucester,* shortly before 8 June 1682, when he was replaced as kettledrummer by Robert Mawgridge.

The Westminster Abbey registers reveal three marriages for Walter Van Bright. On 2 November 1675 he ("widower") married Rebecca Cooper ("spinster"); both were from the parish of St Margaret, Westminster. Of his previous marriage we know nothing. By 1680 Rebecca Cooper Van Bright had died. Van Bright on 22 April received a license to marry Elizabeth Cotter of St Margaret, Westminster; he was 54 and she, a widow, 42. Administration of Walter Van Bright's estate was granted to Elizabeth in June 1682. She died, apparently in Stepney, in 1687, and on 27 September of that year administration of both Walter and Elizabeth Van Bright's estates was granted to Elizabeth Cotter, Mrs Van Bright's daughter.

Van Brockin. *See* VANBRACKEN.

Vanbrugh, John   *1664–1726, proprietor, playwright, architect.*

National Portrait Gallery, London

JOHN VANBRUGH
by Kneller

John Vanbrugh, the son of Giles and Elizabeth Vanbrugh, was born in the parish of St Nicholas Acons, London, in January 1664. He was christened on the twenty-fourth at his parents' home. John's father was of Flemish descent, his mother the daughter of Sir Dudley Carleton of Imber Court, Surrey. The Vanbrugh family fled London in 1665 because of the plague, eventually settling in Chester, where Giles Vanbrugh prospered as a sugar baker. John grew up in a strongly Protestant atmosphere, apparently went to the King's School in Chester, and may have studied architecture in France in 1683 (though Jonathan Swift later hinted that Vanbrugh had received no formal architectural training).

On 30 January 1686 Vanbrugh received a commission in Owen MacCarthy's company of the Earl of Huntingdon's regiment of foot. He remained in the service only seven months and by September 1688 was on the Continent. That month he was imprisoned, apparently at Calais, for speaking in favor of the plans of

William of Orange to invade England. In October 1691 he was moved to Vincennes, and within a year he was confined in the Bastille. There, perhaps, he wrote an early version of *The Provok'd Wife*. Near the end of 1692 Vanbrugh was released by the French, only to be put in jail again by the English upon his arrival home. The mayors of Folkestone and Dover took him for a spy. He was soon given his freedom, thanks to the Earl of Nottingham, and before the end of 1692 he was auditor for the southern division of the Duchy of Lancaster.

By that time Vanbrugh's father had died (in July 1689), leaving John a double share in his estate. In 1694 or 1695 Vanbrugh again went into the military service, terminating his service on 31 December 1695 as a captain in Lord Berkeley's marine regiment of foot. In January 1696 he was in London and within a few months completed *The Relapse; or Virtue in Danger*. He offered it to his acquaintance Sir Thomas Skipwith, one of the two proprietors of Drury Lane Theatre, and it was produced on 21 November. Colley Cibber, then a rising young actor-playwright who had inspired Vanbrugh with *Love's Last Shift* in January 1696, played Lord Foppington in *The Relapse*.

The work was well-received, despite the actor George Powell's drunkenness, which Vanbrugh described in the printed edition in 1697:

One word more about the Bawdy, and I have done. I own the first Night this thing was acted, some indecencies had like to have happen'd, but 'twas not my Fault. The fine Gentleman of the Play [Worthy, played by Powell], drinking his Mistress's Health in Nants Brandy, from six in the Morning, to the time he wadled upon the Stage in the Evening, had toasted himself up, to such a pitch of Vigor, I confess I once gave Amanda [played by Jane Rogers] for gone, and am since (with all due Respect to Mrs Rogers) very sorry she scap'd; for I am confident a certain Lady (let no one take it to herself that is handsome) who highly blames the Play, for the bareness of the conclusion, wou'd then have allow'd it, a very natural Close.

The Relapse remained a favorite with playgoers throughout the following century and is still ranked as one of the best comedies of the Restoration period. The achievement was all the more remarkable because, so far as is known, Vanbrugh had no practical experience in the theatre and learned playwriting only through reading while in prison.

Fluent in French, Vanbrugh next adapted Boursault's *Les Fables d'Esope; Aesop* opened in December 1696, and though it did not catch the public fancy at first, it became a staple at Drury Lane for decades. The work was published in 1697 (with a Part 2, which had been acted at Drury Lane in March 1697), as was Vanbrugh's next produced work, *The Provok'd Wife*, which he gave to Betterton's company at the Lincoln's Inn Fields Theatre. *The Provok'd Wife*, written, it seems, during his incarceration in France, was first performed in mid-April 1697 to much applause. In about one year Vanbrugh had turned out three plays, two of them original works.

The rest of his dramatic output consisted of adaptations: *The Country House*, from the French (January 1698 at Drury Lane; published in 1715); *The Pilgrim*, from Fletcher (29 April 1700 at Drury Lane; published that year); *The False Friend*, from Lesage (February 1702 at Drury Lane; 1702); *Squire Trelooby*, with Congreve and Walsh, from Molière (30 March 1704 at Lincoln's Inn Fields; 1704); *The Confederacy*, from the French (30 October 1705 at the new Queen's Theatre; 1705); *The Mistake*, from Molière (27 December 1705 at the Queen's; 1706); and probably *The Cuckold in Conceit*, from Molière (22 March 1707 at the Queen's; not published). Vanbrugh never completed *A Journey to London;* it was finished by Cibber as *The Provok'd Husband* in 1728.

Lord Berkeley's regiment was disbanded in April 1698, and Vanbrugh found himself with no income and debts of £128. His architectural career appears not to have begun until 1699, when he discussed Castle Howard with the Earl of Carlisle. Vanbrugh seems to have had many friends of rank and influence as well as close relationships with people in literature and the arts, and they may have aided him financially. Nicholas Rowe called Vanbrugh "A most SWEET-NATURED gentleman, and pleasant. . . ." At some point Vanbrugh became a member of the Kit Cat Club, that convivial and influential group that grew increasingly political with the years. If he was not actually a member by 1700, he was certainly on close terms with many who were—Congreve, Dryden, Lord Dorset (the Lord Chamberlain), the Earl of Manchester, and others. Vanbrugh

National Portrait Gallery, London

JOHN VANBRUGH

attributed to Murray

picked up another captaincy, for he is known to have resigned it in 1702 to accept the post of comptroller of the Board of Works, a position that made him a subordinate crown architect under Sir Christopher Wren. The post paid 8s. 8d. daily.

In 1703 Vanbrugh began plans for the Queen's Theatre in the Haymarket. It was to be the first really new theatre in London since 1674, and it became a pet project of the Kit Cat Club. Vanbrugh wrote the publisher Tonson on 15 June that the plot of ground had been purchased with £2000, apparently out of Vanbrugh's pocket. On 13 July Vanbrugh wrote again to Tonson:

Mr Wms has finish'd all the writings for the ground for the Playhouse they will be engross'd and I believe Sign'd on friday or Satterday; wch done, I have all things ready to fall to work on Munday. The ground is the second Stable Yard going up the Haymarket. I give 2000. for it, but have lay'd such a Scheme of matters, that I shall be reimburs'd every penny of it, by the Spare ground; but this is a Secret lest they shou'd lay hold on't, to lower the Rent. I have drawn a design for the whole disposition of the inside, very different from any Other House in being but I have the good fortune to have it absolutely approv'd by all that have seen it.

He had high expectations of recovering his investment. Indeed, the rent from buildings on the site—some houses—provided him with a lifetime income.

Though Vanbrugh had thought the theatre could be built and opened by Christmas 1703, he encountered numerous difficulties— legal problems and protests by the Society for the Reformation of Manners particularly— that prevented completion until the spring of 1705. (The cornerstone was laid by Lady Sunderland and the Duke of Somerset on 18 April 1704.) He had other responsibilities, too, which kept him from completing the theatre: work on Castle Howard (which was not finished until 1714), appointment to the posts of Carlisle Herald Extraordinary in 1703 and Clarenceux in 1704, and commission to design a house for Sir Godfrey Kneller in 1703.

Colley Cibber in his Apology said that to finance the Queen's Theatre Vanbrugh raised £3,000 by subscription from 30 persons at £100 each. Subscribers were to be admitted free for life to all performances at the theatre. Details of the financing of the Queen's may be found in Judith Milhous's article in Theatre Survey in November 1976. The playhouse officially opened on 9 April 1705, before it was completely finished, with the company headed by Thomas Betterton from the old Lincoln's Inn Fields playhouse and with Vanbrugh (with some silent help from Congreve) as manager. The prompter Downes described the event in his Roscius Anglicanus:

About the end of 1704, Mr. Betterton Assign'd his License, and his whole Company over to Captain Vantbrugg to Act under HIS, at the Theatre in the Hay Market. And upon the 9th, of April 1705. Captain Vantbrugg open'd his new Theatre in the Hay-Market, with a Foreign Opera, Perform'd by a new set of Singers, Arriv'd from Italy; (the worst that e're came from thence) for it lasted but 5 Days, and they being lik'd but indifferently by the Gentry; they in a little time marcht back to their own Country.

The Rehearsal of Observator for 5–12 May 1705 contained a notice:

The KIT-KAT Clubb is now grown Famous and Notorious all over the Kingdom. And they have Built [sic] a Temple for their Dagon, the new Play-House in the Hay-Market. The Foundation was laid with great Solemnity, by a Noble Babe of Grace. And over or under the Foundation Stone is a Plate of Silver, on which is Graven Kit Cat on the one side; and Little Whigg on the other.

(Milhous shows that the involvement of Kit Cat members was not as great as has been supposed.) The spring of 1705 saw not only the opening of the Queen's Theatre but the beginning of Vanbrugh's grandest architectural project, Blenheim Palace, for the Duke of Marlborough.

Vanbrugh's theatre was remarkable in several ways. The seating arrangement was based on semicircles, possibly in imitation of the sketches by Sir Christopher Wren made in the 1660s and now preserved at Oxford. The Diverting Post on 14 April 1705, five days after the opening, noted:

When I their Boxes, Pit and Stage did see
Their Musick Rooms, and middle Gallery
In Semi-circles all of them to be;
I well perceiv'd they took peculiar Care
Nothing to make, or do, Upon the Square.

The capacity was something over 700, yet the auditorium was, as Cibber noted, vast. The acoustics were very poor, especially for spoken dialogue, and modifications had ultimately to be made. Cibber wrote:

Almost every proper Quality, and Convenience of a good Theatre had been sacrificed, or neglected, to shew the Spectator a vast, triumphal Piece of Architecture! And that the best Play, for the Reasons I am going to offer, could not but be under great Disadvantages, and be less capable of delighting the Auditor, here, than it could have been in the plain Theatre they came from. For what could their vast Columns, their gilded Cornices, their immoderate high Roofs avail, when scarce one Word in ten, could be distinctly heard in it? Nor had it, then, the Form, it now stands in, which Necessity, two or three Years after, reduced it to: At the first opening it, the flat Ceiling, that is now over the Orchestre, was then a Semi-oval Arch, that sprung fifteen Feet higher from the Cornice: The Ceiling over the Pit too, was still more raised, being one level Line from the highest back part of the upper Gallery, to the Front of the Stage: The Front-boxes were a continued Semicircle, to the bare Walls of the House on each Side: This extraordinary and superfluous Space occasion'd such an undulation, from the Voice of every Actor, that generally what they said sounded like the Gabbling of so many People, in the lofty Isles in a Cathedral. The Tone of a Trumpet, or the Swell of an Eunuch's holding Note, 'tis true, might be sweeten'd by it; but the articulate Sounds of a speaking voice were drown'd, by the hollow Reverberations of one Word upon another.

The first season was short—from 9 April to 29 June—and the opening production, a pastoral opera, *The Loves of Ergasto,* sung by a poor group of imported Italian singers, was not very successful. Congreve, having gained nothing from his investment (and evidently having done little or nothing as Vanbrugh's partner), withdrew from the venture at the end of the season. Vanbrugh was deeply in debt, and the following season, 1705–6, was not financially successful. With his architectural obligations, Vanbrugh could not have given much of his time and energy to the Queen's Theatre, and on 14 August 1706 he rented the management of it for seven years to Owen Swiney. (Judith Milhous and Robert Hume document the confused state of theatrical affairs in the late summer of 1706 in *Vice*

Chamberlain Coke's Theatrical Papers.) Downes wrote:

Captain Vantbrugg by Agreement with Mr. Swinny, and by the Concurrence of my Lord Chamberlain, Transferr'd and Invested his License and Government of the Theatre to Mr. Swinny; who brought with him from Mr. Rich, Mr. Wilks, Mr. Cyber, Mr. Mills, Mr. Johnson, Mr. Keene, Mr. Norris, Mr. Fairbank, Mrs. Oldfield and others, United them to the Old Company; Mr. Betterton and Mr. Underhill, being the only remains of the Duke of York's Servants, from 1662, till the Union in October 1706.

Vanbrugh was to receive £5 per acting day up to a maximum of £700 for the season.

Congreve wrote to his friend Keally on 10 September 1706:

The playhouses have undergone another revolution; and Swinny, with Wilks, Mrs. Oldfield, Pinkethman, Bullock, and Dicky, are come over to the Hay-Market. Vanbrugh resigns his authority to Swinny, which occasioned the revolt. Mr. Rich complains and rails like Volpone when counterplotted by Mosca. My Lord Chamberlain approves and ratifies the desertion; and the design is, to have plays only at the Hay-Market, and operas only at Covent Garden [i.e., Drury Lane]. I think the design right to restore acting; but the houses are misapplied, which time may change.

On 7 May 1707 Vanbrugh lengthened Swiney's lease to 14 years and turned his full attention to his architectural projects.

In the winter of 1707–8 Vanbrugh did an about-face and plunged again into opera management. To avert financial disaster at the Queen's, he used his influence at court to stop the rivalry with the players at Drury Lane; on 31 December 1707 the Lord Chamberlain ordered that Drury Lane should be used for plays and the Queen's for operas. To recoup his own losses, Vanbrugh bought back Swiney's interest, keeping Swiney on as day-to-day manager of the opera troupe. Negotiations with the singers were made by Vanbrugh, and letters written in January and February 1708 indicate that Vanbrugh had high hopes of making opera succeed. On 24 February he wrote the Earl of Manchester:

I intended to trouble y^r L^{d}ship with a Long Letter About Our Opera Affaire, But I have not time to Night, and yet I am engag'd by promise not to let Slip this Post. I'll therfore only Acquaint y^r L^{d}ship, that at last I got the Duke of Marlbo^r: to put an end to the Playhouse Factions, by engaging the Queen to exert her Authority, by the means of which, the Actors are all put under the Patent at Covent-garden House, And the Operas are Establish'd at the Haymarket, to the generall likeing of the whole Towne; And both go on in a very Successfull manner; without disturbing one an Other. This Settlement pleases so well, that people are now eager to See Operas carry'd to a greater perfection, And in Order to it the Towne crys out for A Man and Woman of the First Rate to be got against Next Winter from Italy. But at the Same time they declare for the future against Subscriptions, and have not come into any this Winter. I have therfore (with Severall to back me) laid before my Ld Marlborough the Necessity there is for the Queen to be at Some Expense, And have such an Answer both from him and my Ld Treasurer, as makes me write this Letter to y^r L^{d}ship, to Acquaint you, that if Nicolini and Santini will come Over (my Ld Hallifax telling me this morning y^r L^{d}ship very much desired they shou'd) I'll venture as far as A Thousand Pounds between 'em, to be either divided equally, or More to One and less to tother as yr L^{d}ship shall think fitt to adjust it with 'em, if you please to give your Self the trouble of making the Agreement. This Money I propose to give 'em for Singing during the Next Season, which as things are now Regulated begins the Tenth of September, and ends the Tenth of June. The Opera is very rarely perform'd above twice a Week, and in the begining and latter part of the Season, not above Once, so that their Labour won't be great. If y^r L^{d}ship cou'd engage 'em for Pistolls or Louis d'ores instead of Pounds, 'twou'd be so much Saved to two of your humble Servants, Mr Bertie and my Self, We being now the Sole Adventurers and Undertakers of the Opera, for I have Bought Mr Swiney quite out: Only pay him as Manager. My Affairs are all thank God in a much more prosperous state than When y^r L^{d}ship left London.

But by 6 April 1708 the opera house had lost £1146.

About mid-April Vanbrugh wrote in desperation to Vice Chamberlain Coke (in a letter in the British Library transcribed by James Winston):

I found a letter from you last night. I hope you will not doubt of my Entire disposition to comply with whatever you think right in this unhappy affair as far as the stretch of my power will go and I will accordingly make a very hard shift to clear

Valentinos second month; but must beg a little time for . . . the Tother. For really tis not yet in my power. You are Sensible the daily Receipts of the Opera are not near sufficient to answer the Daily and monthly demands and whenever they fail, there will be a full Stop: So that I am forc'd to apply all other money I have, to keep touch in that point and this Distresses me to the last Degree, All kind of income being very backwards. However I hope to receive very suddenly a large arrear out of which I will certainly make good all you have promised I shall: But methinks if ever my Lord Chamberlain will move the Queen, now should be the time, since he can never be furnishd with more pressing arguments: amongst which, that of the [impossibility] the House at present is under, to make good the Bargains made with Foreigners, would move both the Queen and my Lord Treasurer more than one coud plead: Besides, the Venetian Ambassador was by at My Lord Chamberlain when both my Lord Treasurer & Marlborough Declard it would be right, for the Queen to give a Thousand Pounds a year towards the opera support, and Ill lay my life she comes readily into it whenever she is apply'd to which I therefore earnestly beg you will press my Lord Chamberlain to do, And when he has once (as the proper officer) movd the Queen in it I'll take the trouble off of his hands to solicit it. . . .

On 11 May Vanbrugh wrote again to Manchester:

I . . . am (as well as the town) obliged to you for the endeavours you use to improve the Opera here. What your Lordship says of having one or two of the top voices is most certainly right; as to myself, I have parted with my whole concern to Mr Swiny, only reserving my rent; so that he is entire possessor of the Opera, and, most people think, will manage it better than anybody. He has a good deal of money in his pocket, that he got before by the acting company, and is willing to venture it upon the singers. I have been several times with him lately in consultation with the Vice-Chamberlain Coke (who being a great lover of music and promoter of operas, my Lord Chamberlain leaves that matter almost entirely to him). I have acquainted him with what your Lordship writes, and Mr. Swiny has engaged before him to allow a thousand pounds for Nicolini, to stay here two winters: that is, to be here in September, and at liberty to go away again the May come twelvemonth after. A thousand pounds, I think, makes about 1,200 Pistoles, which undoubtedly he may carry away clear in his pocket, for he can't fail of advantages other ways sufficient to defray his expenses over and over. As for Santini, Mr. Swiny offers the same conditions to her, if your Lordship can prevail with her to come; or if she won't, and you think Regiana would do as well, he leaves it to your judgement, and will allow her the same. If neither of these women will come, he would venture at half this allowance—viz. 600 Pistoles (or something more, as your Lordship shall think reasonable) for the two winters, if a young improving woman could be found that had a good person and action, and that might be esteemed as good a singer as Margarita. If your Lordship can get any of these people over, on the terms here mentioned, Mr Swiny desires me to assure you of punctual performance of his part; nor is there any reason to doubt him, for he has behaved himself so as to get great credit in his dealings with the actors, and I know the Vice-Chamberlain does not the least question his making good all he offers on this occasion. Besides, he has power sufficient to oblige him to it, the license being only during the Queen's pleasure. . . .

Vanbrugh wrote on 14 May to Vice Chamberlain Coke, who had evidently asked him for an accounting:

I am forc'd to be gone for Blenheim, without time to wait on you But do in all I can Comply with what your Letter desires. I had before I rec'd it made up the Accounts, and with much difficulty given Mr Swiny money to pay the Ballance to all the Singers & Dancers except Valentini Margarita and Mrs Sagioni: which Account he will wait upon you with and shew you. I believe there is nobody dissatisfy'd with it but she who has the least reason: I mean the Barroness, she never came to any Agreement at all, And she is paid for every time the Opera has been perform'd in Proportion to what you thought was reasonable to Allow her: which has sattisfy'd even Mrs Tofts & every body Else. Mrs Sagioni shall have her Twenty pounds to morrow. Valentini has had half this last month Advanc'd him long ago, tho' his [benefit] day did not produce it, and I have let him know he shall have the other half as soon as Mr Bertie comes to Towne which will be the end of next Week. The rest will be provided for him I hope, by the time twill be due. Mr Dieupart and Seignor Berti will likewise soon be taken care of: But what to do About Cassani I don't well know. Though something shall: not that I really think he has a Claim to almost any thing; for take the two Audiences together and they were a great deal short of what has been rec'd on Common Occasions, And there was an Expence of near £30. for his Cloaths; with a Cruell Clamour & Disgust of the Towne against the House for Imposing such a Singer: which gave the Opera a very mischievous shock. I therfore think Charity is his Chief Plea, which is of full as much force to the Lords who seem'd to Patronize him, as to me who am so Vast a sufferer by this Years Adventure. I shall be out of Towne but about ten days; what I am Able to do, (either by my self or others for him at my return) I will; And Mr Swiny will in the Interim, lend him something to keep him from Distress. I must upon the whole, beg you to believe, That on any of these Occasions, 'tis my nature & principle to overdoe, rather than leave the least pretence for Complaint. But I am so hard run in this unhappy Business, that there is no room left for Generosity; If I can at last comply with what in rigour I ought, 'tis the utmost I can hope for, I therefore beg you will have a favourable opinion of my Intentions in all these struggles; And if in any perticular I come something short of what you think shou'd be; lay it to my want of Power to do better. . . .

By that time Vanbrugh had sold his interest in the opera venture back to Swiney, retaining only his share in the theatre building, which continued to bring him rent. He wrote Manchester again on 27 July 1708:

I lost so much money by the Opera this last winter that I was glad to get quit of it, and yet I don't doubt but operas will settle and thrive in London. The occasion of the loss was three things: one, that half the season was past before the establishment was made, and then my Lord Chamberlain, upon a supposition that there would be immense gain, obliged us to extravagant allowances. Another thing was that the town, having the same notion of the profits, would not come into any subscription. And the third was that, 'tho the pit and boxes did very near as well as usual, the gallery people (who hitherto had only thronged out of curiosity, not taste) were weary of the entertainment. So that, upon the whole, there was barely enough money to pay the performers and other daily charges, and for the clothes and scenes, they fell upon the undertakers. I might add a fourth reason, which is that I never could look after it myself, but was forced to leave it to managers. Mr Swiny has now undertaken it himself, and I believe will go through with it very well; nor will he want subscriptions to help him. I do not doubt but Nicolini will be mightily well received, and find his account; and if once a peace comes. there will be many things to support music which are wanting now. . . .

On 13 October 1720 Vanbrugh assigned his share in the theatre (by then named the King's) to his brother Charles but continued his support of opera in London by serving as a director of the Royal Academy of Music.

Work had commenced on Blenheim Palace on 19 June 1705, and after countless financial problems the building was completed in 1724. As an architect Vanbrugh favored the spectacular, even though he was responsible for a number of small houses. Blenheim was his greatest achievement, but it has had many disapproving critics over the years.

Vanbrugh was knighted by George I on 19 September 1714. The King reappointed him comptroller to the board of works in January 1715, and on 1716 he was given the post of architect to Greenwich Hospital at £200 annually, though he contributed little to the building. He also received a salary from the King as surveyor of the gardens and waterworks. On 14 January 1719 Vanbrugh married Henrietta Maria Yarburgh at York. She was the daughter of Colonel James Yarburgh and his wife Ann, née Hesketh.

Sir John Vanbrugh died of acute tonsillitis at his house in Whitehall on 26 March 1726 and was buried in his family vault at St Stephen, Walbrook, on 31 March. His will, dated 25 August 1725, was proved by his widow on 22 April 1726. Vanbrugh left bequests to his sisters Mary, Victoria, Robina, and Garencieres; to his brothers Charles and Philip; to his nieces Elizabeth and Robina; and to Garencieres's daughter Lucia. To his son Charles he left property in Greenwich and adjoining the King's Theatre in London and £1000. Charles was not yet 21 when the will was made, and Sir John directed that should Charles die before reaching his majority, the Greenwich property was to go to Philip, Victoria, and Robina. Vanbrugh left the rest of the property to Lady Vanbrugh.

Lady Vanbrugh died on 26 April 1776 at 82; her son Charles, born on 12 May 1720, had died in 1745.

Sir John Vanbrugh's career has been studied in several books, including Laurence Whistler's biography of 1939, Arthur Huseboe's 1976 study for the Twayne series, and Kerry Downes's *Vanbrugh* of 1977; Marie-Louise Fluchère's 1980 work concentrates on Vanbrugh's plays. There is a full entry on Vanbrugh in Colvin's *Biographical Dictionary of British Architects* (1978).

Portraits of John Vanbrugh include:

1. By Geoffrey Kneller, signed. Pictures Vanbrugh half-length, his right arm and hand resting on a ledge and holding a pair of compasses; the herald's badge (Clarencieux) hangs from a gold chain around his neck. One of the Kit Cat portraits, it was painted for Jacob Tonson and was for years in the possession of Tonson's family at Bayfordbury in Hertfordshire. It was presented by the National Art Collections Fund in June 1945 to the National Portrait Gallery (No 3231). A version, probably after Kneller, by an unknown artist, was reproduced in *Country Life,* 2 January 1964. A drawing after the Kneller is in the Byng albums in the British Museum. Engravings after the Kneller portrait include:

a. By J. Simon (reversed, after 1715). Sold by Tonson. All other engravings are copies of Simon's.

b. By T. Chambars. Published as a plate to Walpole's *Anecdotes,* 1762.

c. By A. Duncan. "G. Clint, del." Published by W. Walker, 1823.

d. By W. C. Edwards. Published by J. Murray, 1830.

e. By J. Faber, Jr, 1733.

f. By S. Freeman. Published by Longman, 1807.

g. By J. Miller. Published as a plate to an edition of Vanbrugh's plays.

h. By J. Smith. No 29 of the Kit Cat Club series.

i. By Woodman, Jr. Published by Mathews & Smith, 1808.

j. By W. Worthington. Published as a plate to an edition of Walpole's *Anecdotes,* 1862.

k. At least three anonymous engravings, including one as a plate to the *Universal Magazine.*

2. Attributed to T. Murray, c. 1718 (formerly attributed to Kneller and then Closterman). Also in the National Portrait Gallery (No 1568). It was sold at Christie's on 26 February 1910 (lot 48), when it was attributed to Kneller and paired with a portrait of Lady Vanbrugh, from the collection of A. R. Hood, The Greys, Eastbourne, and in March 1910 came into the possession of the National Portrait Gallery.

3. By J. Richardson, 1725, showing Vanbrugh holding a groundplan of Blenheim. It is in the College of Arms, bought from Rodd about 1824. Another version was with Messrs Appleby in 1946. An engraving by J. Faber, Jr, after Richardson, was published in 1727.

4. Vanbrugh is shown with Dryden, Garth, and Steele in a set of six plates, each containing four oval portraits, titled "Poets and Philosophers of England," engraved by J. Simon.

Vanbrughe, George ₍*fl. 1710?–1732?*₎, *singer, composer.*

The *Catalogue of Printed Music in the British Museum* lists a number of light musical works, mostly songs, by George Vanbrughe; the dates of the various publications are conjectural, ranging from perhaps 1710 to perhaps 1732. Vanbrughe served as a bass singer and composer at Cannons from about 1717 to 1721 for £7 10s. per quarter. During that period he is known to have made at least two concert appearances in London, on 5 March 1718 at York Buildings and on 18 March 1719 at Coignand's Great Room. Both concerts were for his benefit and featured his singing. Some of Vanbrughe's Music was published in 1732, but by that time he may have been no longer active. Grove notes that Vanbrughe was of Netherlandish descent.

Vancour. *See* VASCOURS.

Vandenand, Cornelius *d. c. 1715, kettledrummer, trumpeter.*

Cornelius Vandenand was appointed a kettledrummer in the King's Musick on 6 May 1686. When a warrant dated 9 March 1690 in the Lord Chamberlain's accounts directed that livery be provided Vandenand, he was identified as in the troop of the Earl of Marlborough, but other warrants of later date make no further mention of a military assignment. Twice he was listed as a trumpeter, the last mention being in 1713–14, after which his name disappeared for the accounts.

Vandenand must have died late in 1714 or early in 1715. His will, written on 26 March 1705, was proved by his son John, also a kettledrummer, on 26 January 1715. To his granddaughters Ann and Penn Vandenand, the daughters of his son Cornelius, he left £50 each, to be given them when they should reach 21 or be married. Five guineas each went to Vandenand's brothers John, Peter, and William. Everything else was left equally to his sons Cornelius and John.

In addition to our subject and his son Cornelius, there were at least two other men sim-

ilarly named. Administration of the estate of one Cornelius Vandenanker was granted on 16 February 1694 to Benjamin Disbrowe, husband and administrator of Sara Disbrowe, alias Vandenanker, deceased, relict, legatee, and executrix of Cornelius Vandenanker. A Cornelius Vandenand's widow Penelope proved her late husband's will on 7 January 1710.

Thus we cannot tell if either of the Cornelius Vandenands mentioned in the registers of St Margaret, Westminster (our subject's parish), was our man. The name was spelled several ways in the registers—Vendenende, Vandananday, Vandenando, and Wandinando—but all references appear to be to a Cornelius Vandenand and his wife, Ann. Their son Cornelius was baptized on 24 November 1667, after whom came Thomas in January 1671, Benjamin in July 1673, Jane in September 1675, John in November 1677, and Anne in March 1680. The son Cornelius of 1667 may have been our subject, but he could as easily have been the Cornelius Vandenanker of 1694 or the Cornelius Vandenand of 1710. Probably they were all related.

Vandenand, John ₍*fl. 1714?–1749?*₎, *kettledrummer.*

John Vandenand (or Vandenande) was the son of Cornelius Vandenand and, like his father, was a kettledrummer in the King's Musick. In the Lord Chamberlain's accounts he was cited several times, but the dating of both his entrance into the royal service and his departure from it are uncertain. He may have been at court as early as 1714, the last year in which his father's name was mentioned. The elder Vandenand died about 1715; John proved his will on 26 January 1715. The *Calendar of Treasury Books* shows a payment to John of £14 for a pair of kettledrums for the year 1716, when he was a member of the third troop of Horse Guards.

He served as a court kettledrummer until at least 1738 and perhaps longer. The accounts indicate that in 1738 he was replaced by Frederick Smith, but not because of death, for Vandenand became one of the original subscribers to the Royal Society of Musicians on 28 August 1739. A musical establishment list dating 1749 again notes Vandenand as being replaced at court by Smith.

Vanderhoff, Mynheer *fl.* 1734–1737₁, tumbler, actor.

Mynheer Vanderhoff was one of the tumblers at the Hippisley-Bullock-Hallam booth at Bartholomew Fair on 24 August 1734. We take it that the same person, advertised as "Vander Huff," was the actor who appeared in *All Alive and Merry* at Bartholomew Fair, at Hallam's booth, on 23 August 1737.

Vandermere, John Byron 1743–1786, actor, dancer, singer, manager, scene painter.

John Byron Vandermere was baptized at St Andrew's, Dublin, on 13 July 1743. Perhaps he was the son of or otherwise related to Halteridge Vandermere and Elizabeth Hicks, who were married at that church on 29 October 1727. Our earliest record of his provincial performances dates from 14 September 1767, when he was with a company at Chester. His first appearance at the Haymarket Theatre in London was on 8 June 1768, as Fribble in *Miss in Her Teens*. His next character was Foigard in *The Stratagem* on 23 June. He was then seen as Blister in *The Virgin Unmask'd* on 6 July, Filch in *The Beggar's Opera* on 27 July (repeated on 1 August when he danced a double hornpipe with Miss Street), Hob in *Hob in the Well* on 8 August, Palaemon in the premiere of Barthélemon's burletta *The Judgment of Paris* on 24 August, and the Gentleman Usher in *The Rehearsal* and Mopsus in *Damon and Phillida* on 19 September 1768.

In a specially licensed performance at the Haymarket on 28 February 1769, for the benefit of Phillips, Vandermere acted Roderigo in *Othello*. The next summer at the Haymarket he was playing such roles as Simon in *The Commissary,* Sir Roger in *The What D'Ye Call It,* the Player King in *Hamlet,* the Bailiff in *Tom Thumb,* Setter in *The Old Bachelor,* Mungo in *The Padlock,* and Pindarus in *Julius Caesar.* Engaged again by Foote for the following two summers, Vandermere added to his Haymarket repertoire in 1770 the First Gravedigger in *Hamlet,* Robin in *The Patron,* Circuit in *The Lame Lover,* the title role in *Midas,* and Townley in *Taste.* After the summer season he played there as Foigard in *The Beaux' Stratagem* on 27 September 1770, and, for his benefit, Marplot in *The Wonder* and Fribble in *Miss in Her Teens* on 5 October.

At the Haymarket in the summer of 1771

his new roles included Sancho in *The Wrangling Lovers,* Vamp in *The Author,* Periwinkle in *A Bold Stroke for a Wife,* Marquis in *The Englishman in Paris,* Taylor in *Catherine and Petruchio,* Razor in *The Provok'd Wife,* Sir Benjamin Dove in *The Brothers,* the Irishman in *The Apprentice,* Jack in the premiere of *The Maid of Bath* on 26 June 1771, Jobson in *The Devil to Pay,* Sharp in *The Lying Valet,* the title role in *The Mock Doctor,* Headlong in *The Tobacconist,* Vulcan in the premiere of Hook's comic opera *Dido* on 24 July 1771, Monsieur in *Love Makes a Man,* Woodcock in *Love in a Village* and Sir Ambrose Lafoole in *The Coxcomb* (for his benefit on 16 September), Sir Francis Gripe in *The Busy Body,* Squire Richard in *The Provok'd Husband,* and Gratiano in *The Merchant of Venice.*

Prior to his last summer at the Haymarket in 1771, Vandermere had acted in Foote's company at the Theatre Royal in Shakespeare Square, Edinburgh, in 1770–71, appearing in some of his Haymarket roles and also as Captain O'Clobber in *The Reprisal,* Captain O'Cutter in *The Jealous Wife,* Petit in *The Inconstant,* Ralph in *The Maid of the Mill,* Trim in *The Funeral,* and MacShuffle in *The Oxonion in Town.* That season he also acted at the Crow Street Theatre in Dublin.

After leaving the Haymarket, Vandermere passed the remainder of his career in Ireland. He was at Crow Street in 1771–72, at Limerick and Cork in 1772 and 1773, at Cork in 1775, at Kilkenny in 1776, at Waterford in 1778 (as deputy manager), at Kilkenny again from 1779 to 1781 (as manager), and back at Waterford in 1784. From 1777 to 1779 he was a manager (with Waddy and Sparks) of the Fishamble Street Theatre in Dublin.

While in the Irish county towns Vandermere also served as a scene painter. With Heaphy's company at Cork in 1773 he provided a view of Cork with the harbor's mouth and Haulbowline island and castle for *The Humours of Cork.* In 1775 at that city he painted scenes of a view near Cork and the Lake of Killarney for *Harlequin Restored; or, A Trip to Killarney.*

Vandermere's death date is given in different press clippings as 3 and 12 February 1786. But the register of St Andrew's, Dublin, shows that he was buried there on 1 February 1786. Mrs Vandermere, who acted with him at Edinburgh in 1770–71, was alive in

November 1786, when on the twenty-ninth she shared benefit tickets. Neither she nor their daughter, Miss Vandermere, who performed at Dublin in 1767 and 1770–71, was on the London stage.

The *Thespian Dictionary* (1805) praised Vandermere's acting of Skirmish in *The Deserter* as "unequalled" and claimed that as Lord Ogleby he was second only to King, that his Midas was superior to Edwin's, and that his Lord Froth in *The Double Dealer* was "irresistibly comic." In his later years, however, Vandermere became so deaf he was obliged "to watch the motion of the lips for his *cue.*"

Vandernan, Thomas   *d. 1778, singer, publisher, composer.*

Thomas Vandernan was sworn a Gentleman of the Chapel Royal on 12 November 1743. By about 1750 he had set himself up as a music publisher and engraver. *Splenetick Pills or Mirth Alamode* (c. 1750) was "a collection of humorous songs adapted to the modern taste of the choice spirits. The words by the celebrated poet John Rumfish Esq. Set to music by Dr. Merriwag [Thomas Vandernan]. . . . Printed for Thos. Vandernan, and sold at Mr. Bright at the Blue Peruke in Spring garden Passage. . . ." Vandernan published some ariettas by Alessandro Scarlatti about 1755 and, in 1770, *Divine Harmony. Being a collection of two hundred and seven double and single chants in score . . . sung at His Majesty's Chapels Royal. . . .*"

As a member of the Chapel Royal, Vandernan sang in the *Messiah* at the Foundling Hospital in May 1754 for a fee of 10s. 6d. In 1763 he was appointed copyist to Westminster Abbey, and on 1 March 1767 he joined the Royal Society of Musicians. He died on 2 October 1778. His will, written at Windsor Castle on 7 March 1772, was proved by his widow, Margaret, on 8 October 1778. He left everything, including any money due him from the Chapel Royal, Westminster Abbey, Windsor, Eton, or anywhere else, to his wife. Should she die before he did, the estate was to go to "my beloved Wife's Daughter Margaret Howard spinster."

Vanderpool, F. ₁*fl. 1781*₁,   *house servant.*

Mr F. Vanderpool wrote to Richard Brinsley Sheridan on 22 March 1781 from "Mr. Yewds

Lyon Inn" thanking Sheridan "for your very kind present by M^r. Field to my two girls & I feel myself under great Obligations for the concern you was pleased to express on acc.^t of my unfortunate situation, especially for your benevolent Intention . . . to place me in some little Employ in the House." Vanderpool deprecated his own "mean abilities" but promised to do his grateful best working at Drury Lane.

Vandersluys, Mr ₁*fl. 1746–1751*₁, *dancer.*

On 17 April 1746 at Covent Garden Theatre Mr Vandersluys danced a Follower in *The Loves of Mars and Venus.* Also dancing that night was Miss Vandersluys, later Mrs Joseph Granier; she was our subject's daughter. Though Vandersluys was probably dancing at Covent Garden regularly in the months that followed, he was not named in a bill again until 26 December 1747, when he danced Pan ("Scaramouch") in *The Royal Chace.* On 3 March 1748 he was Scaramouch and a Huntsman in *Apollo and Daphne.* He danced at Smock Alley Theatre in Dublin in 1749–50 and at the New Concert Hall in Edinburgh on 29 October 1751. Mrs Vandersluys, presumably his wife, also danced in Edinburgh and was in Durravan's troupe in Derby in the fall of 1761. She seems not to have performed in London.

Vandersluys, Aleda. *See* **GRANIER, MRS JOSEPH.**

Vandervelt, Mrs. *See* **FRYER, MARGARET.**

Vandinand. *See* **VANDENAND.**

Vanehoor, Mr ₁*fl. 1775–1778*₁,   *house servant?*

Mr and Mrs Vanehoor—house servants probably—subscribed 10s. 6d. each to the Drury Lane Fund in 1775 but left the theatre in 1778.

Vanehoor, Mrs ₁*fl. 1775–1778*₁,   *house servant? See* **VANEHOOR, MR.**

Vanfleet, Mynheer ₁*fl. 1733*₁,   *dancer.*

Mynheer Vanfleet—if that was not a pseudonym—made his first appearance on any stage at Goodman's Fields Theatre on 8 May 1733 dancing the *Dutch Skipper.*

Vangable, Mons ₁*fl. 1745*₁,   *acrobat.*
Monsieur Vangable performed tumbling at Goodman's Fields Theatre on 15, 16, and 20 April 1745.

Vangable, Miss ₁*fl. 1772–1790*₁,   *equestrienne, dancer, acrobat.*
From 1772 to 1788 Miss Vangable (or Vangabel, Vangabell, Vangalla) worked as an equestrian and tumbler at Astley's Amphitheatre. In 1789–90 she danced at the Crow Street Theatre in Dublin.

Vangalla. *See* VANGABLE.

Vangaville, Master ₁*fl. 1746*₁,   *performer.*
A Sadler's Wells bill from April 1746 in the Percival Collection at the British Library names Master Vangaville as a performer. Because others on the bill were called singers or dancers, Vangaville presumably belonged to neither of those categories.

Van Heemskirk, Egbert ₁*fl. 1734–1751*₁, *singer, actor, dancer, painter.*
Egbert van Heemskirk, the second of that name, was the son of a painter and became an artist himself. According to Paulson's *Hogarth,* van Heemskirk (or just Heemskirk) published a series of drolls and poems in 1734 titled *Nothing Irregular in Nature.* Some satiric plates with animal-head figures were done by Heemskirk, but no date has been attached to them. Almost no other information has come down to us about his work as an artist, but there is some detail about his career in London as a performer.
Mr Heemskirk (or Hemskirk, Hemskerk; the bills never called him van Heemskirk) sang "In Praise of English Plumb Pudding" before act V of *The Careless Husband* at the Haymarket Theatre on 16 February 1736, and on 31 March at Lincoln's Inn Fields he played Constant in *The Happy Lovers.* His name disappeared from London bills for a few years, but he turned up at Bartholomew Fair on 27 August 1739 to play a Spaniard in *Columbine Courtezan* at the Lee-Phillips booth. He repeated that role at Southwark Fair on 8 September.

Heemskirk joined the Goodman's Fields troupe for the 1740–41 season and remained there in 1741–42 as well. His roles, some of which required talent as a dancer and singer, included Quaver in *The Virgin Unmask'd* (on 22 November 1740, his first appearance at that playhouse), Butler in *The Devil to Pay,* a Priest and Dr Tackem in *The Imprisonment, Release, Adventures, and Marriage of Harlequin,* Lockit in *The Beggar's Opera,* Alguazil in *The Wonder,* Gaylove in *The Honest Yorkshireman,* and Sol in *The Rehearsal.* In the summer of 1742 he appeared at Sadler's Wells as a singer and dancer, receiving a benefit there on 20 September 1742.
In 1742–43 Heemskirk performed at Lincoln's Inn Fields, repeating roles he had offered at Goodman's Fields and adding such others as Loverule in *The Devil to Pay* and Snap in *Love for Love.* After that season under Henry Giffard, Heemskirk may have left London. In the late 1740s he appeared only sporadically there. On 30 December 1745, for example, "J. Hemskirk" (our subject?) played either Peachum or Macheath in *The Beggar's Opera* at the New Wells, Clerkenwell; on 14 March 1748 he sang at Sadler's Wells, and he was apparently there into the summer; and on 22 April 1751 at the Wells he sang in a concert.
Several songs were published from 1740 to 1750 with Heemskirk named as the singer; in most cases it was stated that he had sung the songs at Sadler's Wells.

Van Heisel, Sebastian ₁*fl. 1686*₁,   *trumpeter.*
Sebastian Van Heisel was evidently a member of the King's Musick, for on 12 October 1686 the Lord Chamberlain ordered that he be delivered a silver trumpet.

Vanhout, Mr ₁*fl. 1753*₁,   *performer.*
Mr Vanhout performed at Bartholomew Fair on 4 September 1753.

Vanini,   Francesca.   *See*   BOSCHI, FRANCESCA VANINI.

Van Moritz, Mons ₁*fl. 1799*₁,   *equilibrist.*
At Sadler's Wells on 17 April 1799 feats of agility were performed by "M. Van Moritz" (the initial we take to stand for Monsieur); it was his first appearance at that theatre. He

Satire of Musical Party

by Van Heemskirk

was cited again in May, and the bill of 8 July has him performing "Equilibres."

Vann, Mrs Thomas. *See* WEWITZER, MISS, LATER MRS THOMAS VANN.

Vanneschi, Francesco ,*fl. 1732–1759*₁, *manager, director, librettist.*

It is not known when Francesco Vanneschi, who had been a librettist in Florence by 1732, came to London. He must have enjoyed some reputation, for when Lord Middlesex reestablished the opera at the King's Theatre in 1741–42 he appointed Vanneschi as his poet and assistant manager. On 5 November 1741 Horace Walpole wrote to Mann that Vanneschi was to have 300 guineas at the opera. Vanneschi prepared the libretto for *Alessandro in Persia,* a *pasticcio* by Galuppi, who was resident composer at the King's that year. On 19 January 1742 *Polidoro* and on 2 March *Scipione in Cartagine* were produced, both with texts by Vanneschi and music by Galuppi.

At the King's Theatre on 1 January 1743 Galuppi's *Enrico* was sung with Vanneschi's text (originally written for a production at Florence in 1732) and was, according to Burney, performed under the author's direction. His function otherwise at the opera that season is uncertain. Indeed, on 14 April 1743 Walpole wrote to Mann, "I really don't know whether Vanneschi be dead; he married some low English woman, who is kept by Amorevoli." The tenor Angelo Amorevoli was engaged at the King's Theatre from October 1741 to May 1743. Nothing is known of his mistress, the new Mrs Vanneschi.

For several years Vanneschi was either out of London or was inactive professionally. On 9 February 1745 his *L'incostanza delusa* was produced with music by St Germain at the Haymarket Theatre. He then provided the text for *La caduta dei giganti,* commissioned by Lord Middlesex from Christoph von Gluck, who was then in London. The opera was produced at the King's Theatre on 7 January 1746 in the presence of the Duke of Cumberland, whose recent victory at Culloden the piece celebrated. Gluck's second opera in London, *Artamene,* was given on 4 March 1746 with a text revised by Vanneschi.

The following season Vanneschi provided the libretti for Paradies's *Phaeton* on 17 Janu-

ary and Terradellas's *Bellerephon* on 24 March 1747. In the printed edition of *Phaeton,* which was dedicated to Lord Middlesex, was prefixed *A Discourse on Operas,* in which the author, presumably Vanneschi, defends musical drama against the objections of critics. Burney wrote that the "best apologies for the absurdities of an Italian opera in a country where the language is little understood, are good Music and exquisite singing." Unfortunately Burney found neither in the performance of *Phaeton.*

In 1748–49 Vanneschi was involved in an awkward situation at the King's Theatre. He was, it seems, Lord Middlesex's appointed director of the opera that season, but the theatre was also made available to a burletta company from Italy headed by John Francis Croza. On 8 November 1748 Croza's company presented a piece called *La commedia in commedia,* the libretto supposedly by Vanneschi and the music by Rinaldo da Capua, "Being the first of this Species of Musical Drama ever exhibited in England." Croza's company survived 43 performances, but by the spring he was having problems with Vanneschi, some of which he explained in a statement to the *General Advertiser* on 20 May 1749. Croza informed the public that he was not "the Undertaker of the Operas" but had come to London in consequence of articles agreed upon with Lord Middlesex, "who employ'd Mr. V—i as a Director." Vanneschi's job was to engage the dancers and other salaried personnel. Croza took exception to Vanneschi's claiming payments for his work as librettist of *La commedia in commedia* in addition to his taking payment of three percent of the receipts every night "as a Gratuity for his Trouble."

Croza remained at the King's Theatre (and sometimes at the Haymarket) until he ran from creditors and the bailiff in May 1750. But Vanneschi's role at the opera for the next several years remains obscure, until in 1753–54 when there was a return to *opera seria,* and he was reappointed manager. As such he took a benefit on 11 May 1754. He tried to meet the competition of Carmine Giordani's small traveling company, hosted by John Rich at Covent Garden, by engaging Regina Mingotti and Colomba Mattei, leading sopranos, and Felice di Giardini as bandleader. But soon Vanneschi found himself bankrupt in the Fleet. Sga Mingotti, with whom he often had quarreled, managed the opera for several seasons. Vanneschi recouped sufficiently to wrest control from her at the end of 1756–57. On 16 May 1757 a license was issued to "Mons. Francesco Vanneschi to perform Italian Operas at the King's Theatre . . . for one whole Year commencing from 1ˢᵗ July 1757 & no longer, without further lease obtained." Though Mingotti had already advertised for subscriptions for the next season, in the *Daily Advertiser* on 31 May 1757 Vanneschi announced that he had secured the license for the coming season.

He managed for two seasons (again advertising for subscriptions on 22 April 1758). After 1758–59 he was replaced by Sga Mattei, who brought back comic operas.

Van Rymsdyck, Mr ₁*fl. 1772–1807?*₁, *performer?*

Mr Van Rymsdyck shared a benefit at the Haymarket Theatre on 18 September 1772. Perhaps he was the "Rymsdick" who worked at Covent Garden Theatre in 1806–7 for £1 10s. weekly.

Vantbrugg. *See* VANBRUGH..

Vanture, Y. ₁*fl. 1728*₁,   *actor.*

Y. Vanture (Young Vanture? or a pseudonym?) played Genius in *The Rivals* in a production by Signora Violante's troupe at the Haymarket Theatre on 21 February 1728.

Varley, Mr ₁*fl. 1771–1792*₁,   *plumber.*

The benefit tickets of Mr Varley were accepted at spring benefits at Covent Garden from 23 May 1776 to 1 June 1792. In the accounts from as early as 18 November 1771 Varley was identified as a plumber. He was evidently a regular theatre employee. The Mrs Varley who worked at the King's Theatre as a dresser from 1783 to 1785 and at the Haymarket Theatre in the same capacity in the summer of 1804 was probably his wife.

Varley, Mrs ₁*fl. 1783–1804*₁,   *dresser.* *See* VARLEY, MR.

Varley, Thomas ₁*fl. 1682*₁,   *mountebank.*

Morley in his *Memoirs of Bartholomew Fair* cites a warrant dated April 1682 ordering the silencing of Thomas Varley, a mountebank, for performing without a license.

Varney. *See also* VERNEY.

Varney, Mr ₁*fl. 1752–1761*₁,   *housekeeper.*

Mr. Varney (or Verney) received annual solo benefits as housekeeper at Drury Lane Theatre from 5 May 1752 to 16 May 1761. As housekeeper or stage doorkeeper he was posted at the stage door, where tickets for the boxes were available.

Vascours,   Mons ₁*fl.   1774–1776*₁, *dancer.*

Mons Vascours (or Voscore, Vascor) and his wife danced at Drury Lane in 1774–75 at a (combined?) salary of £1 10s. weekly. In the summer of 1775 they appeared at Bristol, and, according to Cape Everard's *Memoirs,* Mons Vascours had danced there in 1774 as well. Everard said that the dancer's benefit at Bristol the first summer lost him money, but when Vascours returned to London after his second summer he reported happily. "Oh, grand!—capital benefice!—L'Eté passè, last somere, I lose at Bristol ten pounds by my benefit, and now dis time, I only lose two pounds six!" The dancer "thought he always was to lose what others hope to gain by. . . ." Everard said "Voscore" "was much approved of in his professional capacity" and was "always practising in the theatre or at home. . . ."

The Monsieur Vancour who was named as a dancer on a Sadler's Wells bill of 25 April 1776 was surely our subject.

Vascours, Mme ₁*fl. 1774–1775*₁,   *dancer.* *See* VASCOURS, MONS.

Vaucanson, Jacques de   *1709–1782, machinist.*

According to Campardon's *Les Spectacles de la Foire,* Jacques de Vaucanson was born in 1709. He exhibited a mechanical flute player in Paris in 1736 (says Altick in *Shows of London;* 1738 says Campardon) and disarmed skeptical critics by letting them examine the mechanism. An "automaton" harpsichord player shown earlier in Paris had turned out to be operated within by a little girl, so the critics were justified in their concern.

In 1742, Altick reports, Vaucanson displayed at the Long Room in the King's Theatre in London a mechanical duck, a flute player (probably the same one he had shown in Paris), and a performer on the drum and pipe. The duck drew special attention and was described by the inventor in Diderot's *Encyclopédie:*

I represent the Mechanism of the Intestines which are employed in the operations of Eating, Drinking, and Digestion: Wherein the working of all the Parts necessary for those Actions is exactly imitated. The Duck stretches out its Neck to take Corn out of your Hand; it swallows it, digests it, and discharges it digested by the usual Passage. You see all the Actions of a Duck that swallows greedily, and doubles the Swiftness in the Motion of its Neck and Throat or Gullet to drive the Food into its Stomach, copied from Nature: The Food is digested as in real Animals, by Dissolution, not trituration, as some natural Philosophers will have it.

In 1753 William Hogarth in his *Analysis of Beauty* remembered Vaucanson's duck:

There was brought from France some years ago, a little clock-work machine, with a duck's head and legs fixed to it, which was so contrived as to have some resemblance to that fowl standing upon one foot, and stretching back its leg, turning its head, opening and shutting its bill, moving its wings, and shaking its tail; all of them the plainest and easiest directions in living movements, yet for the poorly performing of these few motions, this silly, but much extolled machine, being uncovered, appeared a most complicated, confused, and disagreeable object: nor would its being covered with a skin closely adhering to its parts, as that of a real duck does, have much mended its figure; at best, a bag of hob-nails, broken hinges, and patten-rings, would have looked as well, unless by other means it had been stuffed out to bring it into form.

Campardon reports that Vaucanson died in 1782.

Vaughan, Mr ₁*fl. 1743*₁, *servant.*

Mr Vaughan, a house servant, is listed as being owed £8 (at 1*s.* 6*d.* per night) in the "Players Petition agt the Patentee of the Theatre Royal in Drury Lane 1743. September" in the papers of the Lord Chamberlain in the Public Record Office (LC 5/204).

Vaughan, Mr ₁*fl. 1765–1772*₁, *actor.*

The Mr Vaughan who was a member of the summer company at Richmond, Surrey, in 1765 and 1766 was perhaps the actor of that name who was in Roger Kemble's company that toured Coventry, Worcester, Droitwych, Bromgrove, and Bath between January 1767 and May 1768. At Worcester on 12 February 1767 Vaughan played Oliver Cromwell in *Charles I.*

On 15 April 1771 a Vaughan acted Stockwell in *The West Indian* in a specially licensed performance at the Haymarket Theatre. A Vaughan performed at the St Mary's Gate Theatre in Derby between 29 November 1771 and 22 February 1772. In Kemble's company and at Derby, Vaughan was accompanied by a Mrs Vaughan. She may have been Ann Standen, who acted at Covent Garden as Mrs Lewis and was for a brief time James Boswell's mistress; she is noticed in this dictionary as Mrs Charles Standen the first.

Vaughan, Mr ₁*fl. 1794–1795*₁,   *watchman.*

A Mr Vaughan was a summer watchman at Drury Lane Theatre in 1794 and 1795. The theatre paid him 12*s.* per week both years. On 17 October 1795 Gell, Branman, and Vaughan, all watchmen, were paid a total of £18 "in full for their summer attendance."

Vaughan, Miss, later Mrs Christian ₁*fl. 1730–1733*₁,   *actress.*

In volume 3 of this *Dictionary* we stated that Mrs Christian (fl. 1730–1733) was the sister of the actor Henry Vaughan and the actress Hannah Pritchard (née Vaughan). We now find some evidence to contradict that assertion. It does seem that Mrs Christian, who, when Miss Vaughan, made her debut at Goodman's Fields Theatre on 1 June 1730 as Araminta in *The Old Bachelor,* was probably the sister of Miss Martha Vaughan, who performed at the same theatre at that time. Martha Vaughan became Mrs Nelson in 1733. In *Born to Please,* a biography of Mrs Pritchard (1979), Anthony Vaughan identifies her as the Martha Nelson who died in Paddington in 1755. The letters of administration of her estate granted to her creditor Esther Jesse (widow) clearly describe her as "Martha Nelson, formerly Vaughan," and state that her only next of kin was a sister, Christian Leeke, wife of Nicholas Leeke. She therefore could not have been related to the performers Henry,

William, or Hannah, all of whom were alive in 1755, as was a non-acting brother Edward.

It is curious that the sister mentioned in Mrs Nelson's will should have been named Mrs Christian Leeke. That person may well have been the sister, Miss Vaughan, who later acted as "Mrs Christian." Possibly she adopted later her first name for the stage.

The stage career of the Miss Vaughan who became Mrs Christian by 1732–33 is given in volume 3 of this *Dictionary*.

Vaughan, Anne *fl.* 1767–1772₁. *See* STANDEN, MRS CHARLES THE FIRST.

Vaughan, Hannah *See* PRITCHARD, MRS WILLIAM.

Vaughan, Henry 1713–1779, *actor, dancer, booth proprietor.*

Henry Vaughan was born in London in 1713, probably in July, for the parish registers of St Giles in the Fields record his baptism on 2 August 1713. He was the third child of Edward Vaughan, a staymaker, and his wife Judith, née Dun. Edward Vaughan, who kept a shop in Holford's Alley, near Drury Lane, may well have provided stays and other accessories to the theatres. His wife Judith was the daughter of one Hannah Dun, who was cousin to Thomas Lennard (1684–1766), an eminent and wealthy lawyer.

Henry Vaughan's elder brother Edward Vaughan (c. 1705–1766) was a fanmaker who kept a shop in Playhouse Yard, Drury Lane, from 1726 to 1733 and thereafter at the Golden Fan at the Royal Exchange, St Michael's Alley, Cornhill; his name and that of his wife Amie Ann, née Vanderman, recur in the Drury Lane Theatre account books for supplying costume fans. Henry's elder sister was Hannah Vaughan (1711–1768), who became the famous actress Mrs Pritchard. His younger brother was William Vaughan (1715–1763), who acted at Drury Lane between 1750 and 1756 and died at Madras while serving as a marine. More detailed information on the Vaughan family and its genealogy may be found in the notice of Mrs William (Hannah) Pritchard in volume 12 of this *Dictionary*.

Of the three Vaughan siblings who took up stage careers, Henry was possibly the first, preceding his sister Hannah, whose first recorded appearance was at Drury Lane on 5 May 1733. Perhaps Henry was the Vaughan who acted Zama in *Tamerlane* at Goodman's Fields Theatre on 4 November 1731 and Ned in *The Beggar's Opera* at Drury Lane on 1 August 1732. He acted Ned again on 8, 11, and 19 August. On 2 September 1734 a Vaughan played the Farrier in a production of *The Farrier Nick'd* in a Bartholomew Fair booth operated by Ryan, Laguerre, Chapman, and Hall.

Henry may have been the player of those earlier roles; nevertheless, when he acted Falstaff in *1 Henry IV* at Covent Garden Theatre on 14 November 1734, it was announced that he had "never appear'd on any Stage before." He repeated Falstaff on 20 January 1735 but was not otherwise recorded in the bills that season.

Perhaps Henry Vaughan served in a very modest supernumerary capacity in London for several years, for when a Mr Vaughan performed at the Aungier Street Theatre in Dublin in 1737–38 he was described as lately arrived from Drury Lane. That Vaughan was a Harlequin in *The Hussar* on 11 October 1737, in *The Necromancer* on 19 January 1738, and in an unknown piece on 26 January 1738, when he also played Roger in *Wit Without Money*. We assume that Henry was indeed a dancer and, as such, later appeared at summer fair booths in London.

By 8 January 1739 Vaughan was back in London, for on that night at Drury Lane he replaced Phillips as Harlequin in *Columbine Courtezan* and performed that role several other times that season. At the same theatre in 1739–40 he danced as one of the Gipsies in *The Fortune Teller,* a popular pantomime that opened on 15 January 1740. On 17 April 1740 he played Deadset in *The Tragedy of Tragedies.* He shared a benefit with Cole and Ray on 23 May 1740.

The bills for 1740–41, however, present us with confusion and uncertainty. At Drury Lane throughout that season a Mr Vaughan danced a specialty hornpipe about a dozen times, the first instance being on 20 October 1740. On several nights, specifically 24 October and 7, 15, and 24 November 1740, when a Vaughan was in the Drury Lane bills for dancing, a Vaughan was in the bills of Goodman's Fields Theatre for acting. On 9 December 1740 a Vaughan acted the Surgeon in *The Relapse* at Goodman's Fields while a Vaughan acted Whisper in *The Busy Body* at Drury Lane. The same situation prevailed on 3 February 1741 with Whisper in *The Busy Body* at Drury Lane and Henry Paddington in *The Beggar's Opera* at Goodman's Fields. The theatres were very far apart and it would have been impossible for the same person to have appeared in both mainpieces. And to complicate the situation further, according to the manuscript notes of William S. Clark a Vaughan acted Falstaff at Smock Alley Theatre in Dublin on 17 November 1740, at a time when the other Vaughans were having a busy week in London. There is always the possibility that one of these Vaughans was either William Vaughan, Henry's younger brother, or yet another performer, unrelated. We feel confident in placing the beginning of William Vaughan's stage career at Drury Lane in 1744–45, though he could well have been the Dublin and London dancer.

It can be suggested with some confidence, we believe, that the Vaughan performing at Goodman's Fields Theatre in 1740–41 was Henry. The Vaughan who danced a hornpipe and acted a few roles that season at Drury Lane was possibly William Vaughan, and so we have arbitrarily decided to distinguish them in the 1740s when their careers seem to have been much interwoven. Henry Vaughan, then, was first seen at Goodman's Fields that season on 24 October 1740, as Sackbut in *A Bold Stroke for a Wife,* and subsequently he acted the Uncle in *George Barnwell,* Slender in *The Merry Wives of Windsor* (the same actor who earlier played Falstaff?), Jeremy in *Love for Love,* Wormwood in *The Virgin Unmask'd,* Wat Dreary in *The Beggar's Opera,* Abel in *The Committee,* the Dropsical Man in *The Chymical Counterfeits,* a Recruit in *The Recruiting Officer,* a Witch in *Macbeth,* Brush in *Love in a Bottle,* a Follower of Hymen in *The Imprisonment, Release, Adventures, and Marriage of Harlequin,* Bagshot in *The Stratagem,* Slur in *The Wife's Relief,* Jaques in *Love Makes a Man,* Ratcliffe in *Jane Shore,* Oxford in *Richard III,* a dancer in *King Arthur,* a dancer in *Harlequin Student,* and the Upholsterer in *The Miser.* It was not an impressive repertoire in terms of status,

but the number of roles do suggest competence and experience.

In the summer of 1741 Henry joined his Goodman's Fields manager, Henry Giffard, at the Tankard Street playhouse in Ipswich; in the company, playing under the pseudonym of "Lyddall," was the young David Garrick. Later that summer Vaughan was back in London for the fairs, playing Doodle in *The Generous Freemason* in Lee and Woodward's booth at Tottenham Court Fair on 4 August 1741. During Bartholomew Fair he played Forge in *Thomas Kouli Kan* at Turbutt and Yates's booth on 22 August and Fearful in *Darius, King of Persia* at Lee and Woodward's booth on the same day, and probably other days, through 26 August.

Again with Giffard at Goodman's Fields in 1741–42, Vaughan added to his repertoire Poundage in *The Provok'd Husband* and Gibbet in *The Stratagem.* When Garrick made his debut on 19 October 1741 as Richard III, Vaughan acted Oxford. On 9 November, with Garrick as Jack Smatter, Vaughan played Isaac in the premiere of Dance's adaptation of *Pamela.* Later that season he appeared as Tyrrel in *Richard III,* Appletree in *The Recruiting Officer,* John in *The Way of the World,* Dulman the Clown in *Harlequin Englishman,* and the Jeweller in *The Miser.* Acting that season at Covent Garden Theatre was another Mr Vaughan, perhaps Henry's brother William.

In the summer of 1742 Henry joined his sister Hannah and her husband William Pritchard in the company that played at the Jacob's Wells Theatre in Bristol from 16 June to 27 August. He returned to London to perform at Lee and Woodward's Bartholomew Fair booth in September and then followed Garrick to Drury Lane Theatre, where on 13 October 1742 Henry acted Tyrrel. It is unclear from the bills whether or not Vaughan appeared in subsequent performances of *Richard III* that season or in other parts, but he seems to have been in the company the entire season. He was listed as being owed £13 17s. 6d. In the "Players Petition agt the Patentee of the Theatre Royal in Drury Lane 1743. September" in the papers of the Lord Chamberlain in the Public Record Office (LC 5/204). Probably he was the Vaughan who acted a few nights during February 1743 at Southwark, playing Jeremy in *Love for Love,* Whisper in *The Busy*

Body, and Dick in *Felora.* He also performed Harlequin at Sadler's Wells during Easter week beginning 4 April 1743.

Henry Vaughan's movements for the next several years were tied closely to those of his sister Hannah. They were together again at Bristol in the summer of 1743 and at Covent Garden in 1743–44. He may have been the Vaughan who acted Bonniface in *The Stratagem* on 16 May and a Gravedigger in *Hamlet* on 29 June and 3 and 6 July 1744 at the Haymarket, though on 16 May he presumably acted Pistol in *The Merry Wives of Windsor* at Covent Garden.

When Vaughan returned to Bristol for the summer of 1744 he had a new bride, with whom he shared a benefit. She had been a Miss Woodley, and, though there is no evidence, perhaps she had acted in the provinces under her maiden name. She did, however, become a member of the Covent Garden company when her husband returned to that theatre for 1744–45. On 13 November 1744 Henry Vaughan signed a three-year lease at a rent of £20 per annum, commencing on 25 December 1744, to rent from the Duke of Bedford a town house on the south side of Duke's Court in the parish of St Martin-in-the-Fields. The agreement provided an option to extend the lease for seven years at £18 per year. In February 1745 the William Pritchards leased the next-door property on the east side for seven years.

The Vaughans returned to the provinces, as was their habit, in the summer of 1745. *The Kentish Post* of 21 August 1745 places them at Canterbury that week. For his benefit Henry offered "a Pantomime Entertainment in Grotesque Characters" called *The Cheats of Harlequin,* evidently put together by Vaughan himself. When the Vaughans were at Salisbury the following season he acted Gobbo in *The Merchant of Venice,* and his pantomime was revived with the title *The Wedding; or, The Cheats of Harlequin,* with Mrs Vaughan as Columbine.

The winter seasons 1745–46 and 1746–47 were again passed at Covent Garden. On 12 February 1747 Henry acted Tester in the premiere of Dr Hoadly's *The Suspicious Husband.* After another summer at Bristol, in which his pantomime was again revived, Henry and his sister joined Garrick at Drury Lane, though Mrs Vaughan seems not to have been engaged

by the new manager. On 17 September 1747 Henry danced a hornpipe, but his name did not appear for a role until 5 December, when he acted Tester. He was not used extensively by Garrick that first season; his only other known role was the Clerk in *The Tempest.* In the summer of 1748 Vaughan joined with Bridges, Cross, and Burton in operating a booth during Bartholomew Fair in the George Inn Yard and during Southwark Fair on the Bowling Green. One of their main attractions was *The Volunteers,* a new comic interlude in which Vaughan played Janny and Mrs Vaughan appeared as Moll. At Drury Lane again in 1748–49 Henry filled a variety of modest roles, including a Gravedigger in *Hamlet,* Daniel in *The Conscious Lovers,* Dapper in *The Alchemist,* the First Watchman in *Much Ado about Nothing,* Peter in *Romeo and Juliet,* and Abhorson in *Measure for Measure,* all parts he again played in 1749–50.

In the season 1750–51 Henry Vaughan's brother William also joined the Drury Lane company, and his name was usually distinguished on the bills by the inclusion of his first initial. Both brothers continued together at that theatre until May 1757, at which time William gave up the stage for the marines. Henry, however, remained with Garrick at Drury Lane through 1765–66. A selection of his roles from 1750–51 to his retirement describes the undistinguished but serviceable journeyman actor: Lopez in *The Pilgrim,* the Lawyer in *Love's Last Shift,* and Master Matthew in *Every Man in His Humour* in 1750–51; Catchpole in *The Apprentice* and the Tailor in *Catherine and Petruchio* in 1755–56; Galloon in *The Gamester* and an unspecified role in *The Author* in 1756–57 (on 27 May 1757 he went over to Covent Garden to play Twitcher in *The Beggar's Opera* for Morgan's benefit); Dwindle in *The Gamesters* in 1757–58; unspecified roles in *The Diversions of a Morning* and *Aesop* in 1758–59; Trapland in *Love for Love* and Tom in *The Funeral* in 1759–60; and an unspecified role in *The Genii* in 1761–62. Vaughan's salary in 1764–65 was a modest 5s. per night, or £1 10s. per week. (His sister's was £14 per week.) In the summers of 1752 and 1753 Vaughan was with the company playing at Richmond and Twickenham; the extant bills reveal that at Richmond he acted Master Matthew on 18 July 1752 and Sir Jealous Traffick in *The Busy Body* on 8 September 1753. During Bartholomew Fair, in the month of September 1759, with Dunstall and Warner, he kept a booth in the George Inn Yard. He was again at Richmond in 1760.

At the end of the 1765–66 season at Drury Lane, Vaughan retired. It was said that this premature retirement (at age 53) was prompted by some shady transactions that were intended to bring Vaughan money to which he was not entitled. In 1758 Henry and his brother Edward Vaughan, the fan maker in the Royal Exchange, had been named co-executors in the will of their wealthy cousin, the attorney Thomas Lennard. Edward, however, died three months prior to Lennard's death on 21 July 1766, thereby leaving Henry as sole executor. Hannah Pritchard seemed to believe that she would receive great advantage from the estate, but Henry tried to manipulate funds into his own hands. According to Tom Davies in his *Dramatic Miscellanies,* Henry, "by fancying himself co-heir with his sister . . . to large property, which was contested by other claimants, (the heirs at law) exchanged a life of innocence and ease of mind for much disappointment and vexation of mind. He died rich, but neither happy nor respected." Henry believed "he had a right to that of which he had acquired possession," but a legal dispute over the will was yet unresolved at Henry's death. In *Notes and Queries* for 12 February 1876, Edward Solly recorded his belief that Henry's "attempts to retain the property from the heirs-at-law, and to apply it to the part benefit of Mrs Pritchard and himself, [were] not any attempt to claim half of his sister's legacy." In any event, Hannah Pritchard left him her best diamond ring in 1768.

Henry had also been named as primary beneficiary in the will that his brother William had drawn on 21 November 1759. William married a month later on 17 December 1759 and added a codicil to his will on 18 April 1762 that authorized a naval surgeon at Madras to receive his prize money and wages and forward these funds to Henry and not to William's widow. The will was proved on 17 August 1764, when administration was granted to Henry Vaughan, brother of the deceased. There is no suggestion, however, that Henry took advantage of his widowed sister-in-law.

Henry Vaughan died on the morning of 13 January 1779, in his sixty-sixth year, according to the *Morning Chronicle* of 15 January. He had outlived his brothers and his sister, and his death occurred a week before that of Garrick on 20 January. He was buried at St Paul, Covent Garden, on 21 January 1779.

It is not known when Henry Vaughan's wife died. Her name disappeared, so far as we can determine, from bills and advertisements after 1749, and she presumably died before her husband. Henry Vaughan died intestate and without completing the administration of the estate of his cousin Thomas Lennard, as a further limited grant of administration on 31 December 1824 reveals.

In his obituary in the *Morning Chronicle* on 15 January 1779, Vaughan was praised for such portrayals as Master Matthew in *Every Man in His Humour,* the Gravedigger in *Hamlet,* and Abraham in *Harlequin's Invasion,* roles he performed "more naturally than any other actor before or since he quit the stage." He was, as described by Davies, "a man formed by nature for small parts of low humour and busy impertinence," such as Tester in *The Suspicious Husband,* Simple in *The Merry Wives of Windsor,* and Simon in *The Apprentice.*

Henry Vaughan appears as one of the Watchmen, with Garrick as Sir John Brute in Johann Zoffany's painting of a scene from *The Provok'd Wife.* The canvas was exhibited at the Society of Artists in 1765 and is now owned by the Wolverhampton Art Gallery. For details about this painting and another version, and about the engraving, see the notice for David Garrick in this *Dictionary* (6:100, item No 232).

Vaughan, Mrs Henry, née Woodley *fl. 1744–1756?*₁,   *actress, dancer.*
Perhaps Miss Woodley had experience acting in the provinces before she joined her new husband Henry Vaughan in the company at the Jacob's Wells Theatre, Bristol, in the summer of 1744. She was engaged with her husband in 1744–45 at Covent Garden Theatre, where she made her debut on 3 October 1744 as Charlotte in *The Mock Doctor.* She played Araminta in *The Old Bachelor* on 7 November and subsequently appeared as one of the Country Lasses in *The Rape of Proserpine* on 8 December, Charlotte again on 2 and 26 April 1745, and Betty in *The Old Bachelor* on 3 May.

Courtesy of Ascott, the National Trust, and the Courtauld Institute of Art

MRS HENRY VAUGHAN, when Miss Woodley
by Hogarth

During the next two seasons at Covent Garden she was also seen as Molly Brazen in *The Beggar's Opera*, Lightning in *The Rehearsal*, Mopsey in *Phebe*, Ursula in *Much Ado about Nothing*, a Grace in *The Loves of Mars and Venus*, a Country Lass in *Orpheus and Eurydice*, and Situp in *The Double Gallant*. Her salary in 1746–47 was 13s. 4d. per week.

Mrs. Vaughan probably returned to Bristol in the summer of 1745; she did perform with her husband at Canterbury that August, appearing as Columbine in his pantomime *The Cheats of Harlequin*. They were again in Canterbury in 1746 and at Bristol in 1747 and 1748. At the end of the latter summer she played Moll Trotfutter in a comic interlude called *The Volunteers* in booths that Henry Vaughan co-managed during the Bartholomew and Southwark fairs.

When her husband went over to Drury Lane in 1747–48, Mrs Vaughan seems not to have been engaged by Garrick. But in the fol-

lowing season, 1748–49, she made her Drury Lane debut on 15 October 1748 as Molly Brazen in *The Beggar's Opera*. That role, which she played a total of four times, was her only part of the season. She made her last known London appearance, as Molly Brazen, on 16 May 1749.

Perhaps Mrs Vaughan was with her husband when he appeared at Richmond, Surrey, in the summers of 1752 and 1753, but the extant bills do not yield her name. The Mrs Vaughan who acted Dorinda in *The Beaux' Stratagem* at Canterbury on 27 July 1756 was probably our subject. After that date, we lose track of her. She was not named in her husband's will in January 1779. No issue of their marriage is known, though an adopted son, Henry Vaughan, was named principal legatee of Vaughan's estate.

A portrait by Hogarth of Mrs Vaughan, when Miss Woodley, several years before her marriage, is in the Ascott Collection (A. Rothschild), the National Trust, at Wing, Bedfordshire. Until recently it was thought to be a portrait of Jane Hogarth, the artist's wife, and it was formerly in the collections of Benjamin West, H. R. Willett, and Baron Lionel de Rothschild.

Vaughan, M. *fl. 1726–1767]*, *boxkeeper.*

M. Vaughan served as boxkeeper at Lincoln's Inn Fields Theatre from 1726 to 1732 and then at Covent Garden from 1732 through 1766–67, a total of 41 years. We first notice him in the bills on 17 May 1726 when he shared benefit tickets with Norris and Houghton. On 17 November 1726 Vaughan was paid 6s. 8d. for two days in full, and on 9 June 1727 he was paid 10s. By 1746–47 his salary was 10s. per week, and by 1760–61 it had been raised to 12s. Each season he shared benefit tickets with other house servants, as on 16 May 1760 when he, Condell, and Green divided £238 9s., not a small sum.

On 16 April 1751 Vaughan, signing his first initial, announced in the *Public Advertiser* that he had been ill for some time and was still too weak to wait on his public for his benefit on 13 May; tickets, however, could be obtained at his lodgings at Mr Bicknell's in Brownlow Street, near Longacre.

Vaughan, Mrs [M.?] *fl. 1728–29], office keeper?*

A Mrs Vaughan is cited on the free list for 1728–29 in an account book for Lincoln's Inn Fields Theatre (in the Harvard Theatre Collection). There is an additional notation: "[Office] by M.[rs] Vaughan 2." Perhaps she worked in the theatre office. She may well have been the wife of M. Vaughan, who served as boxkeeper at that theatre from 1726 to 1732 and then at Covent Garden from 1732 through 1766–67.

Vaughan, Martha ("Patty"), later Mrs Nelson *d. 1755, actress, singer, dancer.*

When Martha Vaughan, sometimes called Patty, played Betty in *Flora* at Goodman's Fields Theatre on 27 May 1730, she was advertised as making her first appearance on that stage, an indication that she had acted elsewhere. Her sister, Miss Vaughan (later Mrs Christian), made her debut at the same theatre a few days later on 1 June 1730.

In our notice of Mrs Christian in this *Dictionary* we incorrectly identified these Vaughan sisters as siblings of the performers Henry, William, and Hannah (later Mrs Pritchard) Vaughan. For our correction see the notice of Miss Vaughan (fl. 1730–1733).

After playing Betty in *Flora,* Martha Vaughan was seen at Goodman's Fields that summer as a dancer in *Lads and Lasses,* Columbine in *Harlequin Turn'd Dancing Master,* Clarissa in *The Temple Beau,* Jenny in *The Fair Quaker,* Mrs Trusty in *The Provok'd Husband* (on 6 July 1730, when her sister acted Myrtilla), and Mrs Favorite in *The Gamester* (on 17 July, when her sister acted Mrs Topknot).

The following season the Vaughan sisters were engaged at Drury Lane Theatre, where on 25 November 1730 Martha played Jenny in *Patie and Peggy.* On 8 February 1731 (called Miss P. Vaughan) she served as one of the Beggarwomen in the comic opera *The Jovial Crew* and on 26 April 1731 played Clara in *The Lover's Opera.* Back at Goodman's Fields Theatre in 1732–33 Martha Vaughan appeared only one time, it seems, and by then she was married. On 30 April 1733, called Mrs Nelson, formerly Miss M. Vaughan, she played Clara in *The Lover's Opera.* That night she also danced a minuet with Jovan de Vallois, who was her teacher. The evening was for the ben-

efit of the other Miss Vaughan, who since October had been acting that season as Mrs Christian.

Martha seems to have made no further appearances in London as Mrs Nelson. She died in Paddington in 1755. Administration of her estate was granted to her creditor Esther Jesse, and in those documents she was described as Martha Nelson "formerly Vaughan," and her sister Christian Leeke, wife of Nicholas Leeke was named as next of kin.

Vaughan, Mrs Thomas. *See* TENNANT, MISS.

Vaughan, William *1715–1763, actor, dancer.*

William Vaughan was baptized on 23 November 1715 at St Giles in the Fields. He was the youngest child of Edward Vaughan, a staymaker, and his wife Judith, née Dun. William's elder brother Henry Vaughan (1713–1779) made his debut at Drury Lane Theatre in May 1733 and served the London theatres as a journeyman actor and harlequin for 32 years. His elder sister Hannah Vaughan became the famous actress Mrs Pritchard. Detailed information on the Vaughan family and its genealogy can be found in the notice of Mrs William (Hannah) Pritchard.

Probably at the usual age of 14, William became an apprentice to his eldest brother Edward Vaughan (c. 1704–1766), a fanmaker who kept a shop in Playhouse Yard, Drury Lane. The names of Edward Vaughan and his wife Amie Ann, née Vanderman, appear in the Drury Lane account books over the years for supplying fans.

Just when William followed his brother Henry upon the stage is uncertain. We have assumed, perhaps incorrectly, that the Vaughan whose name appeared in London bills and advertisements between 1733 and 1740 was Henry. Distinguishing the careers of the brothers thereafter is a matter of some difficulty, since they seem to have had similar repertoires and the contemporary reviewers sometimes confused them. In 1740–41 Henry Vaughan was a busy performer at Goodman's Fields Theatre, playing often on the same nights that another Vaughan was listed in the bills for dancing and acting at Drury Lane. The Vaughan at Drury Lane perhaps was William, and we have arbitrarily decided he was, though that actor may have been unrelated to the family.

The first notice that we believe refers to William Vaughan was the Drury Lane bill for 20 October 1740, when he danced a hornpipe, a specialty he performed about a dozen times that season. He acted Whisper in *The Busy Body* on 9 December 1740 (that night his brother Henry acted the Surgeon in *The Relapse* at Goodman's Fields), and he repeated that role several times. His other parts in 1740–41 included the Mad Taylor in *The Pilgrim*, a Citizen in *Julius Caesar*, and Jeremy in *The Strollers*.

In 1741–42, while his brother Henry Vaughan continued at Goodman's Fields, where the young David Garrick was causing a great sensation, William was in the Covent Garden company. He acted Forrest in *Richard III* on 13 October 1741 and was also seen that season as William in *As You Like It*, Sancho in *Love Makes a Man*, and Fruitful and the Jeweller in *Aesop*.

Both William and Henry Vaughan followed Garrick to Drury Lane in 1742–43. Although the bills reveal no roles for William that season, the "Players Petition agt the Patentee of the Theatre Royal in Drury Lane 1743. September " (in the Lord Chamberlain's papers at the Public Record Office, LC 5/204), reveal that Fleetwood had discharged William Vaughan, his brother, and other personnel who had insisted on being paid money owed to them. William Vaughan was owed £10.

We believe that William's brother Henry was the Vaughan who was with his sister at Covent Garden from 1743–44 through 1746–47. Possibly William was the Vaughan who acted in *Hamlet* at the Haymarket Theatre in the summer of 1744, since Henry was at Bristol that year between 15 June and 27 August. The Haymarket Vaughan played Bonniface in *The Stratagem* on 16 May 1744 and a Gravedigger in *Hamlet* on 29 June and 3 and 7 July.

While Henry Vaughan was regularly engaged at Covent Garden, another Vaughan— perhaps William—appeared occasionally at other London theatres in 1744–45 and was engaged at Drury Lane in 1745–46. According to a story told by Joseph Moser in the *Hibernian Magazine* for October 1804, at that

time William was a volunteer in the Guards and was stationed at the Savoy barracks. Moser's tale of William's drunken escapades is repeated in Anthony Vaughan's biography of Hannah Pritchard, *Born to Please* (1979). Anthony Vaughan presumes that William remained in the army until he went to Ireland in 1748, but we believe that there is a strong likelihood he was the other Vaughan acting in London in the mid-1740s. If so, then he played the Farmer in *The Amorous Sportsman* at Goodman's Fields on 26 December 1744 and the Constable in *The Recruiting Officer* at Drury Lane on 4 April 1745. At the latter house he performed Tubal in *The Merchant of Venice* on 30 April 1745 and danced a hornpipe in *The Beggar's Opera* on 29 May. The following season, 1745–46, at Drury Lane he appeared as Galoon in *The Gamester*, Corin in *As You Like It*, James in *The Miser*, the Landlord in *The Stage Coach*, and Ned in *The Beggar's Opera*.

We find no record of William in 1746–47 and 1747–48, so perhaps that was the period of his duty in the Guards. In 1748–49, however, he was a member of Tom Sheridan's company at the Smock Alley Theatre in Dublin, where he perhaps made his first appearance on 17 October 1748 as Obadiah in *The Committee* (his name appeared for that role in the bill for 4 January 1749, but the cast for the earlier performance is not known). That season he also played the First Planter in *Oroonoko*. For 1749–50 only one of his roles is known— Touchstone in *As You Like It* on 4 May 1750.

Clearly William Vaughan's talents were not thrusting him into theatrical prominence, so it was probably his relationship to Mrs Pritchard and Henry Vaughan that persuaded Garrick to bring him to join the family at Drury Lane in 1750–51. He appeared there as the Host in *The Merry Wives of Windsor* on 22 September 1750 and then acted Gregory in *Romeo and Juliet*, Kate Matchlock in *The Funeral*, the Porter in *The Pilgrim*, Bullock in *The Recruiting Officer*, Gripe in *The Confederacy*, Gibbett in *The Stratagem*, and the Second Gravedigger in *Hamlet*.

The task of distinguishing his roles from those of his brother becomes simplified during the 1750s by the fact that William's first initial was usually given. William remained an actor of inferior status at Drury Lane through 1756–57, playing such roles as the Tailor in

The Relapse, Waitwell in *The Way of the World,* Scapethrift in *Eastward Hoe,* Gobbo in *The Merchant of Venice,* a Witch in *Macbeth,* and John Moody in *The Provok'd Husband* in 1751–52; Old Thrifty in *Scapin,* Charon in *Lethe,* the Town Clerk in *Much Ado about Nothing,* Tyrell in *Richard III,* and the Host in *The Merry Wives of Windsor* in 1752–53; Dicky in *The Constant Couple,* Trapland in *Love for Love,* Gurney in *King John,* and Mouldy in *The Humourists* in 1753–54; a Citizen in *Coriolanus* and Francisco in *The Chances* in 1754–55; a Sailor in *The Fair Quaker,* Cob in *Every Man in His Humour,* and Nathaniel in *Catherine and Petruchio* in 1755–56; and the Uncle in *The London Merchant* and Vasquez in *The Wonder* in 1756–57. On 23 May 1757 he danced the Clown in *The Drunken Peasant* and shared benefit tickets with Palmer and Morris.

According to Moser, "indolence" and "inattention" diminished Vaughan's effectiveness. Having lost interest in acting, he left the theatre after 1756–57 and went to sea. For a time he served aboard the *Britannia* and held the rank of acting captain of Marines. On 29 September 1759 he was commissioned a second lieutenant in the Marines 73rd Company, Portsmouth Division, and on 21 November 1761 he was recommissioned a first lieutenant in the 135th Company in the same division.

William Vaughan died on active duty on 9 August 1763, aboard the *Norfolk* moored in Madras Road, and was buried at St Mary's Church, Fort St George, Madras, on 10 August. In his will, drawn on 21 November 1759 before leaving England, Vaughan described himself as "late belonging to the Theatre Royal, Drury Lane," and he bequeathed his entire estate, wages, prize money, allowances, and pensions to his brother Henry Vaughan. Only a month after writing his will, on 17 December 1759, William had married by license Martha Gilbert, who is described in the registers of St Giles in the Fields as a widow. After experiencing naval action in India, William added a codicil to his will on 18 September 1762 by which in event of his death he empowered Charles Lynd, a surgeon at the naval hospital in Madras, to receive all the prize money and wages due to him and deliver the funds to his brother Henry Vaughan. No mention of his wife was made in the codicil. The will was proved at London on 17 August 1764, when administration was granted to Henry Vaughan, brother of the deceased.

Martha Vaughan, "Widow of the late 1st lieutenant William Vaughan . . . who died on or about the 9th August 1763," was granted a widow's pension of £20 per annum. Presumably she also benefited from her husband's will through her brother-in-law's administration. She died in October 1764 and was buried on the tenth of that month; she was described in the burial register of St Giles in the Fields as of Nottingham Gate in that parish. Administration of her will was granted on 4 January 1765 to Ann Gilbert, her spinster daughter by her previous marriage. No issue of the marriage of William Vaughan and Martha Gilbert is known. The Thomas Lennard Vaughan (1743–1778), a first lieutenant in the Royal Artillery who was killed at Monmouth, New Jersey, during the American Revolution, was the son of the fanmaker Edward Vaughan and the nephew of William Vaughan.

Vaul, De. *See* Duval.

Vaurentile or Vaurenville, Mlle. *See* Deschalliez, Louise.

Vaux. *See also* Faux *and* Fawkes.

Vaux, Mrs   *[fl. 1755–1756],*   actress, singer.

At Southwark on 20 January 1755 Mrs Vaux played Columbine in *Harlequin Restored* for Phillips's benefit. On 18 September that year she was one of the performers in Phillips's troupe at Southwark Fair, and on 27 July 1756, according to the *Kentish Post,* she acted Gipsy in *The Beaux' Stratagem* at Canterbury.

Vaux, Miss   *[fl. 1746],*   singer, actress, dancer.

Miss Vaux sang at the Goodman's Fields Theatre on 24 January and 13 February 1746 and at Sadler's Wells in April sang and danced and played the Genius of England in *Britannia Rediviva.* Perhaps she was related to—or, indeed, was—the Mrs Vaux who performed in London a decade later.

Vaux, Richard ,*fl. 1662–1663*₁, *fifer.*
On 23 June 1662 Richard Vaux, fifer, was appointed to the King's Musick. He was last named in the Lord Chamberlain's accounts on 12 November 1663.

"Vauxhall Syren, The." *See* PINTO, MRS THOMAS THE SECOND.

Veal, ₁**William?**₁ *d. 1771, doorkeeper.*
Mr Veal (or Veil) received partial benefits at Drury Lane Theatre annually from 16 May 1753 to 29 May 1771. He was usually cited as the first galley doorkeeper, but on the bill for 18 May 1763 he was called a lobby door-keeper. Veal earned 9*s.* weekly. He died in 1771, and his widow received a benefit on 10 June 1772. He was probably the William Veal of St Andrew, Holborn, who made his will on 15 August 1771, leaving everything to his wife, Margaret. She proved the will on 31 August. She may have been the Veal who worked as a dresser at 9*s.* weekly in 1776–77 and was cited in the Drury Lane accounts as late as 1789–90 at the same salary.

Veal, Mrs ₁**William?**₁ *fl. 1771–1790?*₁, *dresser? See* VEAL, ₁WILLIAM?₁.

Veale, George *1757–1833, instrumentalist.*
George Veale (or Veal, Vial) was born in 1757. He played viola in the Handel Memorial Concerts at Westminster Abbey and the Pantheon in May and June 1784, and on 6 July 1788 he was admitted to the Royal Society of Musicians. He was at that time single, 31 years old, proficient on the violin and viola, a teacher of guitar, and a participant in the oratorio performances at Drury Lane Theatre. He held a permanent position as violist in the Covent Garden Theatre band. In the 1790s he played in the annual St Paul's concerts sponsored by the Royal Society of Musicians, sometimes serving as a violinist and sometimes as a violist. Veale played viola in the oratories at Covent Garden in February 1800, and he played in the band at Drury Lane at £1 16*s.* weekly from 1812–13 through 1816–17.

By 1832 he was receiving medical aid and an annual pension of £50 from the Royal Society of Musicians. On 6 January 1833 his sister was given £12 by the Society to cover Veale's funeral expenses.

Van der Straeten in his *History of the Violin* states that Veale played in the opera orchestra at the King's Theatre in the second half of the eighteenth century and that he was not the author of the pamphlet against Burney, as stated in the catalogue of the Royal College of Music.

Védie, Mme ,*fl. 1787–1822?*₁, *dancer.*
When the King's Theatre opened for the opera season on 8 December 1787, Mme (but then called Mlle) Védie danced in *Les Offrandes à l'amour,* a new ballet by Noverre. She appeared in that piece throughout the season and also danced in performances of *L'Amour et Psiché* beginning 29 January 1788 and *Euthyme et Eucharis* beginning 13 March 1788.

Her name was absent from London bills until the opera season of 1791, during which she danced at the Pantheon, appearing as a Nymph in *Amphion et Thalie* on 17 February, a Nymph again in *Telemachus in the Island of Calypso* on 22 March, and a role (the mother?) in *La Fille mal gardée* on 2 June. She had been hired in Paris at £70, with £10 travel allowance, according to information provided by Judith Milhous. Her next engagement seems to have been back at the King's Theatre in 1793, where one of her roles that season was a Grace in *Venus and Adonis* on 26 February.

She returned to the King's Theatre in 1795–96. The bills announced her—Mme Vidi—as a dancer in *Little Peggy's Love* and *L'Amant Statue* on 21 April 1796 and in *L'Heureux naufrage* on 7 July and subsequent dates. On 25 May she performed with dancers from the opera in *Little Peggy's Love* at Drury Lane Theatre, for the benefit of Stephan Storace's widow and child.

The name "Vedy" appears 20 years later in the Drury Lane account books; a female dancer of that name was paid £1 10*s.* per week in 1816. A Mme Vedie was in the ballet company at the King's Theatre in 1818; and a male dancer of that name also was employed there then. At Drury Lane in 1821–22, there seems to have been a female and a male dancer named Vidi performing, each earning £1 10s. per week.

Vegelini, The Signors ₁*fl. 1714*₁, *instrumentalists.*

At Stationers' Hall on 27 May 1714, for the benefit of Mrs Orme, "Gli Signori Vegelini (two select Musicians lately arriv'd)" played on instruments never heard in England before. The bill did not say what the instruments were.

Veigel, Eva Maria. *See* GARRICK, MRS DAVID.

Veil. *See* VEALE.

Venables, Mr ₁*fl. 1755–1779?*₁, *actor.*

As a member of Theophilus Cibber's short-lived summer company, a Mr Venables acted the Constable in *The Recruiting Officer* and the Coachman in *The Devil To Pay* at the Haymarket Theatre on 9 September 1755. He also played Cordelio in *The Rehearsal* on 11 and 15 September.

Probably this person was the Venables who, with his wife, was a member of Roger Kemble's company at Worcester in 1767 and who played at the White Hart, Launceston, in May and June 1772. At the latter place Mrs Venables and their son Master Venables also performed. This same Venables was perhaps the actor who played second leads at Bristol in 1778–79 and acted at Birmingham in the summer of 1779, though that person may have been his son.

Venables and his wife were perhaps the parents of Ann Venables, a singer who made her first appearance in London at Drury Lane Theatre on 12 November 1772 and who became the third wife of the musician Michael Arne on 1 May 1773. On 20 January 1759 at St Paul, Covent Garden, the dramatist Dr Thomas Francklin married Mary Venables, the daughter of a wine merchant in the Great Piazza, Covent Garden. Perhaps she was related to our subject.

Venables, Mr ₁*fl. 1772–1799*₁, *actor.*

The Mr Venables who acted Young Freeman in *The Artifice* at the Haymarket Theatre on 16 October 1781 was perhaps the Master Vena-bles, son of the provincial actors Mr and Mrs Venables, who had performed with his parents in a company at the White Hart, Launceston, in May and June 1772. In those provincial appearances Master Venables was Prince John in *Henry IV*, a page in *The Orphan*, and a character in *Midas*.

That Venables, or his father, was a regular member of Pero's company at Derby between 1783–84 and 1789–90. Mr Venables played at Bury and Southport in November and December 1796, at Lancaster in the fall of 1798, and at Edinburgh in the summer of 1799. At Edinburgh he acted Duncan in *Macbeth* on 25 July 1799.

Venables, Miss. *See* ARNE, MRS MICHAEL THE THIRD, ANN.

Vener, Mr ₁*fl. 1673–1675?*₁, *actor.*

Mr Vener (or Venner) played the Eunuch in Duffett's *The Empress of Morocco* at Lincoln's Inn Fields Theatre with the King's Company in December 1673. About 1673–75 he was in the cast of *Brennoralt*, possibly playing Trocke or Mensecke.

"Venetian, The." *See* COLPI, SIGNOR.

Venner. *See* VENER.

Vento, Matthias Friedrich *1735–1775, composer, conductor, opera director.*

Born in 1735 at Naples and educated there at the Conservatio di Santa Maria di Loreto, Mattia Vento (later Matthias Friedrich) had his first opera, *Le deluse acortezze*, performed at Rome in 1756. His *La finta semplice* was produced at Rome in 1759, and his *L'egiziana* was performed at Venice and Milan in 1763. (The latter was revived at Vienna in 1769 and at Florence in 1771.)

Late in 1763, at the invitation of Felice Giardini, who was then conductor at the King's Theatre, Vento came to London. There he contributed to several *pasticcio* works—*Leucippe* on 10 January 1764, *Zenocrita* on 21 February 1764, and *Berenice* on 1 January 1765—before *Demofoonte* was produced on 2 March 1765, with new music entirely composed by him. Burney called the airs "natural, graceful, and pleasing; always free from vulgarity, but never very new or learned." The next season *Sofonisba* was sung on 21 January 1766, with music arranged and composed, in part, by Vento; in that opera Sga Aguilar made her first London appearance. Vento's new serious opera *La conquista del Messico* was given on 4 April 1767. *La musica e la poesia*, a new cantata by Vento, was sung at Almack's in 1768.

Vento busied himself with teaching for several years. In 1771 his *Artaserse* was performed at the Harmonical Meeting, in Soho Square, under Giardini's direction. Excerpts from that opera were sung at Hickford's Room in 1772. Vento contributed to the "Threnodia augustalis" that was given at Mrs Cornelys's Great Room in Soho Square on 20 February 1772 in memory of the Dowager Princess Augusta. A libretto written for the event by Oliver Goldsmith was published anonymously and is now a rare item. Vento was granted a license in 1773 for a concert at any theatre or concert room in the liberty of Westminster, to be performed on 26 April between 8 AM and 4 PM, but no record of such a performance seems to have survived. According to an announcement of 10 January 1774 he was joint conductor with Dr Arnold of the concerts given at the Pantheon that month.

On 13 September 1775 the *Public Advertiser* listed Vento as "Director" of the operas at the King's Theatre, under the management of Mrs Yates and Mrs Brook. That season Vento's *Il bacio* was performed on 9 January 1776 and his *La vestale* on 6 February 1776.

Vento also supplied music for a number of English pastiches, such as *Daphne and Amintor* at Drury Lane on 8 October 1765, *Love in the City* at Covent Garden on 21 February 1767, *Lionel and Clarissa* at Covent Garden on 25 February 1768, and *The Captive* at the Haymarket on 21 June 1769, all written by Isaac Bickerstaffe. Some of Vento's airs were heard in O'Keeffe's *The Castle of Andalusia* at Covent Garden on 2 November 1782, seven years after Vento's death.

He died in London on 22 November 1776. Sainsbury wrote in his *Dictionary* that Vento "had a great number of scholars," and it would have been supposed that he was "very rich . . . from his industry, his general parsimonious manner of living, and his avarice." But "by some strange disposition of his property and affairs," none of his wealth could be found

after his death. Therefore his mother and widow were left destitute and had to rely on charity and "the lowest menial labour." On 7 December 1776 Maria Vento, "widow of Matthias Friedrich, late of the parish of St George, Hanover Square," was granted administration of his unspecified estate.

A list of Vento's music is given in the *Catalogue of Printed Music in the British Museum*. It includes 11 collections of keyboard lessons and sonatas, his opera scores, and some songs from the operas and other theatrical productions. Burney found his harpsichord pieces to be "flimsy, and so much alike, that the invention, with respect to melody and modulation . . . may be compressed into two or three movements." In his sonatas and songs "he avoids vulgar passages, and has a graceful, easy, and flowing melody." His duos for voices, wrote Burney, are "alike trivial and uninteresting." The *New Grove* reports Torrefranca's view that Vento brought from Naples the latest operatic style and that "the subtle changes in the sonatas suggest that Vento also responded to the pre-Classical synthesis of German, Italian, and English elements taking place around him."

Veracini, Francesco Maria 1690–1768, *violinist, composer.*

Francesco Maria Veracini, the nephew of Antonio Veracini, was born in Florence on 1 February 1690. Our subject's father, Agostino Veracini, was not musical but worked as an apothecary and undertaker. Francesco studied with his uncle and the organist of the Florence Cathedral, Giovanni Maria Casini, but left Florence for Venice in 1711. He performed at St Mark's in 1711 and 1712 before coming to London.

His first appearance in London was at the Queen's Theatre on 23 January 1714, when he played a "symphony" at a performance of the opera *Dorinda*. On 17 March he performed sonatas at Hickford's Music Room for the benefit of "The Baroness" (Joanna Maria Lindelheim). He appeared at the Queen's again on 3 April and at Hickford's on 22 April; on the latter occasion he played music of his own composing.

In 1715 Veracini was in Düsseldorf, and the following year he was again in Venice, composing and performing. By 1717 he was in

FRANCESCO MARIA VERACINI
by Richter

Dresden, where he remained until 1722, with occasional trips to Italy. On 13 August he tried to commit suicide—or, according to his account, an attempt was made on his life. In any case, he survived a fall from a third-story (or, by some accounts, second-story) window to return to Italy and eventually to London.

On 27 April 1733 he played a concerto of his own at Hickford's Music Room, and he appeared there again on 25 May. A benefit for him was held at Hickford's on 18 March 1734; that concert was repeated, with some additions, on 25 March. "Verachini" performed again at Hickford's on 11 April and 12 May 1735. "Francis Verachini" played "first Fiddle" at the King's Theatre on 25 November 1735, when his opera *Adriano* was performed. Dr Burney reported that "there was no concert now without a solo on the violin by Veracini." The musician's *La clemenza di Tito* was performed beginning on 12 April 1737 and his *Partenio* opened on 14 March 1738.

Veracini returned to Florence in 1738–39 but was back in London by 28 February 1741, when he played a concerto on the violin between the acts of *Acis and Galatea* at the Lincoln's Inn Fields Theatre. On 9 March *A New Ecologue* and other poems set to music by Veracini were played at the Haymarket Theatre, and he played a violin concerto there on the thirteenth. He performed at Hickford's on 28 April. Veracini played regularly at Drury Lane Theatre from 23 September 1742 to mid-November. He became a member of the Royal Society of Musicians on 1 January 1744, and on 31 January his opera *Rosalinda* (which Dr Burney found "wild, aukward, and unpleasant") opened at the King's Theatre. The *New Grove Dictionary of Music and Musicians* notes that Veracini was shipwrecked in 1745 while crossing the English channel and lost manuscripts of some of his music.

By May 1750 Veracini was back in Florence, where he spent his last years. He died there on 31 October 1768. Dr Burney was impressed with Veracini's violin playing and conducting but not with his arrogant manner.

A portrait of Veracini by F. F. Richter, 1730, is owned by Sir Francis Dashwood at West Wycombe Park, Buckinghamshire. A drawing of the picture by Richter, from the collection of J. F. Gigoux, is in the Gerald Coke Handel Collection; it was engraved by J. June. Probably the engraving by June is the bust-length of Veracini reported to be in the collection of the Hoftheater, Vienna. Veracini is one of the musical artists shown in a large group picture designed by Luigi Scotti and engraved by Bettelini, published at Florence about 1805.

Verbrachen or **Verbraken.** *See* VANBRACKEN.

Verbruggen, John Baptista *d. 1708, actor.*

John Verbruggen was named as a member of the United Company in a Lord Chamberlain's warrant dated 12 January 1688. Thomas Davies in his *Dramatic Miscellanies* in 1784 wrote that

Verbruggen was so passionately fond of Alexander the Great [in *The Rival Queens*], at that time the hero of the actors, that the players and the public knew him for some years, by no other name. I have seen the name of Mr. Alexander to several parts of Dryden's plays; to Ptolemy in *Cleomenes, King of Sparta*, to Aurelius in *King Arthur* and Ramirez in *Love Triumphant, or Nature will prevail*. Verbruggen, I believe did not assume his own name in the playhouse-bills, till the secession of Betterton and others from Drury-lane, in 1695.

That statement was accepted by some writers in later years, but George Thorn-Drury in a letter to Montague Summers argued that Alexander must have been a different person— one who played major parts in the late 1680s and early 1690s and whose name disappeared from cast lists after 1694.

The evidence is confusing. If "Mr Alexander" was named after the character of Alexander the Great, one must certainly ask why, since he is not known to have played the role. Since Davies was writing a century later, he may well have picked up an anecdote that had little basis in fact. Verbruggen's name is not known to have been attached to the role of Alexander until the early years of the eighteenth century. Our guess is that Verbruggen did indeed sometimes use the name Alexander at the beginning of his career (and the name may have had nothing to do with the role in *The Rival Queens*; he may have chosen it because his own name was spelled incorrectly so often—Verbrugen, Verbroggell, Verkruggan, Verbrugger).

The Lord Chamberlain's warrant of 1688 makes it clear that Verbruggen was a member of the United Company that year. His name does not appear in cast lists until late October 1690, when he was listed as one of three Persian Magi in *Distress'd Innocence* at Drury Lane Theatre. Alexander's name appeared in several casts between 1688 and 1690: Termagant in *The Squire of Alsatia* on 2 May 1688 (not 3 May, as in *The London Stage*; that work contains a whole series of dates one day off in May 1688), Licinius in *Valentinian* sometime between 1688 and 1690, Langoiran in *The Massacre of Paris* on 7 November 1689, Hazard in *The Widow Ranter* on 20 November, Meleander in *The Treacherous Brothers* in January 1690, Finardo in *The Amorous Bigotte* in late March, and Gray in *Richard III*, Bellamore and Manley in *Madam Fickle*, and Frank Jerningham in *The Merry Devils of Edmonton* probably in 1690–91. In 1690–91 the names of both Verbruggen and Alexander appeared in cast lists—though never both in the same play. Verbruggen was a Magi in *Distress'd Innocence* in late October 1690; Alexander was Antonio in *The Mistakes* in mid-December; Verbruggen was Captain Bariser in *Bussy D'Ambois* in March 1691; and Alexander was Aurelius in *King Arthur* in early June (not May, argues Robert Hume).

In 1691–92 and 1692–93, however, only Alexander's name appeared: as Nym in *The Merry Wives of Windsor* on 31 December 1691, Florio in *The Traytor* in March 1692, Ptolomy in *Cleomenes* in mid-April, Nickum in *The Volunteers* in mid-November, Garnish in *The Maid's Last Prayer* at the end of February 1693, Sharper in *The Old Bachelor* in March, and Bonavent in *A Very Good Wife* in late April. Twice more cast lists included Alexander: Careless in *The Double Dealer* in October 1693 and Ramirez in *Love Triumphant* in mid-January 1694.

In mid-January 1694 "Alexander" played in *Love Triumphant*; in February Verbruggen was named as Frederick in *The Fatal Marriage*. Quite apart from the quaint juxtaposition of the titles, perhaps there is significance in the name change; on 31 January 1694 at St Clement Danes John "Verbuggin," bachelor, and Susanna Mountfort, widow of the actor William Mountfort (who *was* famous for his Alexander), were married. Thereafter the name of Alexander disappeared from the bills.

Verbruggen is known for three other roles before the United Company split: Tygranes in *The Ambitious Slave* on 21 March 1694, Ambrosio in parts one and two of *Don Quixote* in May, and Lovell in *The Canterbury Guests* in late September. Betterton and many of the older players in the United Company seceded, leaving Christopher Rich at Drury Lane with less experienced and younger performers. Verbruggen remained at Drury Lane, but by 10 April 1695, when Verbruggen and his wife signed new articles, Rich and his partner Skipwith were so fearful of losing Verbruggen to the rival company that they raised him from £2 to £4 weekly. The contract required Verbruggen "with his best care and skill [to] Sing Dance Act Rehearse and Reprsent." He was to receive £4 out of every £20 to be divided among the "adventurers." Both Skipwith and Verbruggen posted bonds of £300. The arrangement ranked Verbruggen with George Powell, the leading actor in the Drury Lane troupe.

Verbruggen's first role with the new Drury Lane company was Belfont in *The Mock Marriage* in September 1695 at the troupe's second theatre in Dorset Garden (not Drury Lane, according to the title page of the 1696 edition). Between then and his departure for the rival Lincoln's Inn Fields company in January 1697 Verbruggen played—usually at Drury Lane but occasionally at Dorset Garden—the following parts: Suetonius in *Bonduca*, Sebastian in *The Rival Sisters*, Carrasco in *3 Don Quixote*, Oroonoko, Alvaro in *Agnes de Castro*, Loveless in *Love's Last Shift*, Prince Frederick in *The Younger Brother*, Wilmore in *The Lost Lover*, Pausanius, Ibrahim, Alphonso in *The Unhappy Kindness*, probably the Governor in *The Spanish Wives*, Lord Whimsical in *The Female Wits*, Loveless in *The Relapse*, and possibly Othello.

A quarrel brought on Verbruggen's break with the Drury Lane company. According to a report in the *Post Boy* of 26–29 September 1696 and a manuscript addition to the copy at the Clark Library, Verbruggen "abused Sr Tho. Skipwith and thereupon occasioned a quarrel between him & Mr Boile." Verbruggen violently assaulted Boile (or Boyle) and "Broke him" and the peace; his abuse of Skipwith consisted of reproachful and scandalous words, and for his behaviour Verbruggen was discharged from acting. The Lord Chamberlain ordered Verbruggen to stay with the Drury Lane troupe until 1 January 1697 to give Rich and Skipwith time to find a replacement, after which he was free to act at whichever theatre he chose. The tone of the order suggests that Verbruggen may have been in the right in the squabble. His last known part at Drury Lane was Loveless in *The Relapse* from 21 to 27 November 1696, though an undated complaint of about December 1696 names a performance of *Othello* in which he may have acted the title role. Verbruggen complained about shares, benefits, and shabby treatment.

Verbruggen's first known role with Betterton and his players at the Lincoln's Inn Fields Theatre was Manuel in *The Mourning Bride* on 20 February 1697 and subsequent dates. During the remainder of the season he was seen as Constant in *The Provok'd Wife*, Guillamour in *The Intrigues at Versailles*, and Sir Francis Wildlove in *The Innocent Mistress*. As at Drury Lane, Verbruggen was given prologue-speaking assignments—an indication of his appeal to audiences. Mrs Verbruggen did not join her husband at Lincoln's Inn Fields but continued acting for Rich and Skipwith.

From the fall of 1697 to the opening of the new Queen's Theatre in 1705 Verbruggen appeared at Lincoln's Inn Fields in such new parts as Frederico in *The Italian Husband*, Fidelio in *The Deceiver Deceived* (later called *The French Beau*), Achilles in *Heroick Love*, Ricardo in *Beauty in Distress*, Castalio in *The Fatal Friendship*, the Duke of Clarence in *Queen Catherine*, possibly King Barnagasso in *Victorious Love*, Xerxes, Barbarelli in *The Princess of Parma*, Emilius in *The False Friend*, Maherbal in *Friendship Improved*, Cuningham in *The Amorous Widow*, Hotspur in *Henry IV*, Claudio in *Measure for Measure*, Mirabel in *The Way of the World*, the younger Clerimont in *The Beau Defeated*, Junius in *The Fate of Capua*, Cassius in *Julius Caesar*, Artaxerxes in *The Ambitious Stepmother*, Polidore in *The Ladies Visiting Day*, Antonio in *The Jew of Venice*, Cyraxes in *The Double Distress*, Censor in *The Gentleman Cully*, Bajazet in *Tamerlane*, Moreno in *Love Betray'd*, Hartley in *As You Find It*, Altamont in *The Fair Penitent*, Edgar in *King Lear*, Apemantus in *Timon of Athens*, Alexander in *The Rival*

Queens (on 29 January 1703, the earliest known appearance for him in that role), Iago in *Othello*, Pierre in *Venice Preserv'd*, Pyrrhus in *Abra Mule*, Page in *The Merry Wives of Windsor*, Caesar Borgia, Amphialus in *Zelmayne*, Clerimont in *The Biter*, and Young Valere in *The Gamester*.

Verbruggen now began receiving some critical comment, both negative and positive. In his dedicatory epistle to Aphra Behn's *The Younger Brother* (1696), Charles Gildon noted that the play "suffer'd not, I'm sure, in the Action, nor in Mr. *Verbruggen's* reading of some of his Part, since he lost nothing of the Force of Elocution, nor Gracefulness of Action. . . ." Gildon did not explain why Verbruggen did not have all of his role of Prince Frederick memorized, but perhaps he was substituting for another actor. Verbruggen was, according to Anthony Aston, recommended by the Duke of Newcastle for the part of Oroonoko. Newcastle "order'd *Oroonoko* to be taken from *George Powel*, saying to Mr. *Southern*, the Author,—That *Jack* was the upolish'd Hero, and wou'd do it best." Southerne praised Verbruggen's portrayal in his dedication in 1696. But the author of *A Comparison Between the Two Stages* in 1702 had one of his characters speak of Verbruggen as "A fellow with a crackt Voice: He clangs his words as if he spoke out of a broken Drum," yet Verbruggen was suggested by *A Comparison* as a young successor to Betterton.

Verbruggen was a sharing actor in the Lincoln's Inn Fields company. He held one share and earned £1 weekly salary. But by 1703 he had been deceived by Betterton, Mrs Bracegirdle, and Mrs Barry—the leaders of the troupe. They pretended that debts had not been paid and stopped Verbruggen's salary, according to Verbruggen's complaint to the Lord Chamberlain. The matter must have been settled satisfactorily, for Verbruggen continued with the troupe, serving as one of the leading players. A document among the Lord Chamberlain's accounts dating from 1703 shows Verbruggen at a maximum of £150 annually, equal to Betterton, Powell, and Wilks and well above Cibber and Booth; that was a proposed salary for a new troupe but may have been close to what Verbruggen actually received as a member of the Lincoln's Inn Fields company.

Verbruggen's first recorded role at the Queen's Theatre (with the old Betterton troupe) was Eurymachus in *Ulysses* on 23 November 1705. After that at the Queen's some of his new characters were Theodorus in *The Faithful General*, Amadis in *The British Enchanters*, the title role in *Valentinian*, Surly in *Sir Courtly Nice*, Horatio in *Hamlet*, Colonel Bruce in *The Comical Revenge*, Ramble in *The London Cuckolds*, the title part in *The Rover*, Lorenzo in *The Spanish Fryar*, Cardinal Wolsey in *Henry VIII*, Chamont in *The Orphan*, the title role in *Don Sebastian*, Sullen in *The Stratagem*, Ranger in *The Fond Husband*, the Lieutenant in *The Old Troop,* and Hannibal in *Sophonisba*. His last known role at the Queen's was Caesar Borgia on 19 August 1707.

By 31 December 1707, according to a Lord Chamberlain's warrant, Verbruggen, Pack, Mrs Porter, and Mrs Bradshaw had left the Queen's without permission and were performing at Drury Lane (though no roles are recorded for Verbruggen there). We know that in 1707–8 Verbruggen was in the Smock Alley troupe in Dublin; a manuscript cast has him down for the Governor of Barcelona in *The Spanish Wives*. That is the last role known for him, but he may have been too ill to play it. The promptbook (at Harvard) shows that Henry Goddard took over the role.

The Verbruggens had a child as early as 1703, according to the registers of St Martin-in-the-Fields, into which parish they must have moved sometime after their marriage in 1694. A son, "Lewis Vanbrugen," was born to them on 17 May 1703 and baptized on 27 May. Mrs Verbruggen died between July and August; the infant was buried the following 2 October. John Baptista Verbruggen was buried on 12 March 1708 at St Martin's. On 26 April at Drury Lane Theatre (where the actors were then performing, while the singers held forth at the Queen's Theatre) a benefit was held for "a Young Orphan-Child of the late Mr Verbruggen and Mrs Verbruggen." That child's birth record has not yet been located, but we know that on 23 November 1708 John George Verbruggen, son of John and Susanna, was baptized at St Clement Danes. Presumably he was the orphan child spoken of in the benefit bill.

Much-esteemed in his day, John Verbruggen was evidently best at rough-hewn charac-

ters. Colley Cibber barely mentioned him in his *Apology*, but Tony Aston's *Supplement* provided a fairly detailed picture of his talents. Aston found Verbruggen a diamond in the rough, a fast study with splendid action and a good voice. He was well built and clean but "a little In-kneed, which gave him a shambling Gate, which was a Carelessness, and became him." Where Betterton was artful, Verbruggen was wild and untaught and consequently good as Edgar in the mad scenes in *King Lear* or as the unpolished hero Oroonoko. Verbruggen was "Nature, without Extravagance—Freedom, without Licentiousness—and vociferous, without bellowing."

The Laureat in 1740 chided Colley Cibber for not saying more of Verbruggen,

who was in many Characters an excellent Actor, as we remember him in *Cassius, Oroonoko, Ventidius, Chamont, Pierre, Cethegus*, as well as in several Parts in Comedy, as the *Rover*, &c. He was an Original, and had a Roughness in his Manner, and a negligent agreeable Wildness in his Action and his Mein, which became him well. The Part of *Bajazet* in Tamerlane, was originally his; and it has never been acted well since the first three or four Nights of his playing it, when he was taken ill: He continued some Years in high and merited Reputation, tho' when he appear'd on the Stage at first, for some Time, he, as well as our Friend *Colley*, were commonly received with a Hiss, and both of them were so inconsiderable, as not to be known by their Sirnames. Mr. *Verbruggen* was called Mr. *Alexander*, from a Passion he had to act that Part, and *Cibber* only known by his Christian name, *Colley*.

It should be noted that *The Laureat* did not say Verbruggen acted Alexander in *The Rival Queens* but that he wanted to play the part; the role was William Mountfort's until his death in 1692.

Verbruggen's name was joined with George Powell's on the dedication of *Brutus of Alba*, published in 1697, but Verbruggen's contribution to the work is not clear.

Verbruggen, Mrs John Baptista, Susanna, née Percival, formerly Mrs William Mountfort   *c. 1667–1703, actress.*

Born about 1667, Susanna Percival was the daughter of the minor actor Thomas Percival of the Duke's Company. Her first known appearance was perhaps as early as the summer of 1681 as Winifred in *Sir Barnaby Whigg* at

Drury Lane Theatre with the King's Company. In February or March 1682 "Sue" was an Attendant in *The Injured Princess*. With the United Company at the Dorset Garden Theatre on 31 May 1683 Mrs Percival (as she was styled, despite her age) played Mrs Jenkins—a breeches part—and Mrs Susan in *Dame Dobson*. She acted Phillis in *The Atheist* in May or June (earlier than *The London Stage* dates the opening).

Before her marriage to the promising actor William Mountfort in 1686 Susanna Percival was seen—usually at Drury Lane, sometimes at Dorset Garden—as Rachel in *The Jovial Crew*, Prudentia in *A Duke and No Duke*, possibly Benzayda in *The Conquest of Granada* (Dryden wrote Jacob Tonson about August 1684 that he did not think she would do the part well, being a comedienne), Matilda in *The Bloody Brother*, Gertrude (or Girtred, as *The London Stage* has it) in *Cuckold's Haven*, Julietta in *The Commonwealth of Women*, Lucia in *The Banditti*, Nell in *The Devil of a Wife* (and she spoke the epilogue), and Diana in *The Lucky Chance*. Susanna Percival married William Mountfort on 2 July 1686 at St Giles in the Fields. She was from that parish and declared herself a spinster 19 years old, marrying with the consent of her parents.

As Mrs Mountfort she continued to gain in popularity and was frequently called upon to speak prologues and epilogues and play important comic roles, occasionally in breeches. Before her husband's death in 1692 she was seen as Carolina and the title role in *Madam Fickle*, Lucia in *Epsom Wells*, Maria in *The Libertine*, Clarinda in *The Virtuoso*, probably Bayes in *The Rehearsal*, Bellemante in *The Emperor of the Moon*, Panura in *The Island Princess*, Isabella in *The Squire of Alsatia*, Lycias in *Valentinian*, Maria in *The Fortune Hunters*, Gertrude in *Bury Fair*, Sylvano in *Pastor Fido*, Elvira in *The Spanish Fryar*, Morayma in *Don Sebastian*, Feliciana in *The Successful Stranger*, Harriet in *The Man of Mode*, the title role in *Sir Anthony Love* (which Southerne wrote for her), Phaedra in *Amphitryon*, Florella in *Greenwich Park*, Lucia in *Cutter of Coleman Street*, Mrs Wittwoud in *The Wives' Excuse*, and Eugenia in *The Volunteers*.

Susanna and William Mountfort had at least four children. Their first daughter, Susanna, was born on 27 April 1690 and was christened on 11 May at St Giles in the Fields. She became an actress in the early eighteenth century and died, insane, in 1720. Their son Edward was born on 1 April 1691 but died in infancy and was buried on 3 May. A second daughter, Elizabeth, was born on 22 March 1692 but died eight days later. William Mountfort was murdered on the night of 9–10 December by Captain Richard Hill, urged on by Lord Mohun. Susanna was pregnant at the time, and their child, Mary, was christened at St Clement Danes on 27 April 1693.

When the House of Lords found Lord Mohun not guilty (on 4 February 1693), Mrs Mountfort was about to appeal, but she was apparently persuaded to drop the appeal in order to save her father, who had been sentenced to death for clipping. There is no evidence to show that William Mountfort had been unfaithful to his wife, though Richard Hill was madly jealous of Mountfort, thinking that the actor was Anne Bracegirdle's lover. Details of the murder can be found in the entries of William Mountfort and Mrs Bracegirdle. Mountfort dictated his will as he was dying, leaving all debts due him to his "Deare Wife Susanna," making her his executrix. All else was to be equally divided between his wife, his daughter Susanna, and "to the child which my s^d wife is now wth Child of, Share & Share alike. . . ."

The date of Mrs Mountfort's daughter's christening, 27 April 1693, makes one question some of the performance dates for Mrs Mountfort in *The London Stage*. Following her husband's death in December 1692 she acted Lady Susan Malepart in *The Maid's Last Prayer* at the end of February 1693, Belinda in *The Old Bachelor* in March, Annabelle (a breeches part) in *A Very Good Wife* in late April, and Catchat in *The Female Vertuosos* in May. Though actresses of the Restoration and eighteenth century are known to have continued performing late in their pregnancies, one wonders if the late April dating of *A Very Good Wife* is correct; in *All the King's Ladies* John Harold Wilson dates the performance March, which is perhaps more likely. Since the casting derives from the 1693 edition of the play (published in June) Mrs Mountfort certainly played the part of Annabelle at some point, but she may have done so after the birth of her daughter.

Mrs Mountfort acted Lady Froth in *The Double Dealer* in October 1693 and Dalinda in *Love Triumphant* in mid-January 1694. On 31 January at St Clement Danes she married the promising young actor John Verbruggen, and it was as Mrs Verbruggen that she played her finest roles and established herself as one of London's best comediennes. Her first known appearance as Mrs Verbruggen was in February 1694, when she spoke the epilogue to *The Fatal Marriage*. Her husband began acting regularly under his own name at that point, giving up the stage name Alexander.

As Mrs Verbruggen, our subject went on to play Lionell in *The Married Beau*, Mary the Buxom in *1 and 2 Don Quixote* ("the extraordinary well acting of Mrs Verbruggen," wrote the author D'Urfey), and Hillaria in *The Canterbury Guests* before joining Thomas Betterton in his break with the United Company. In the complaints that were lodged by the Betterton group about December 1694 and the answers given by the United Company managers Rich and Skipwith we find evidence of Mrs Verbruggen's salary. She was evidently paid 50s. weekly and complained that she deserved 5s. more. As it turned out, both Verbruggens decided to stay with Rich and Skipwith, realizing, perhaps, that they stood a far better chance of playing leading roles than if they went with Betterton, Mrs Barry, and Mrs Bracegirdle. On 10 April 1695 separate articles were drawn up for Susanna and John Verbruggen. She was to have £4 out of every £20 to be divided among the "adventurers"; if that did not come to £105 per year (that is, £3 weekly for 35 acting weeks) the sum would be made up to her. If her share came to more than £105 for the season, she was to keep the overage.

At Drury Lane (or sometimes at the company's second theatre in Dorset Garden) from September 1695 to her death in 1703 Mrs Verbruggen was seen in such new roles as Clarinda in *The Mock Marriage*, Ansilva in *The Rival Sisters*, Mary the Buxom in *3 Don Quixote*, Charlot Welldon in *Oroonoko*, Narcissa in *Love's Last Shift*, Olivia in *The Younger Brother*, Olivia in *The Lost Lover*, Demetria in *Pausanius*, Achmet in *Ibrahim*, the Governor's Wife in *The Spanish Wives*, Marsillia (a satire on the playwright and novelist Mrs Manley) in *The Female Wits*, Berinthia in *The Relapse*, Doris in

1 and 2 Aesop, Jacintha in *The World in the Moon*, Celia in *The Humorous Lieutenant*, Margaret in *Sauny the Scot*, Margaretta in *The Fatal Discovery*, Madam la Marquise in *The Campaigners*, Letitia in *Love Without Interest*, Lady Lurewell in *The Constant Couple*, Lady Dainty in *The Reform'd Wife*, Abigail in *The Scornful Lady* (noted by Colley Cibber in his *Apology*; not cited in *The London Stage*), Miranda in *Love at a Loss*, Louisa in *Love Makes the Man*, Lucia in *The Humours of the Age*, Gillian in *The Bath* (*The Western Lass*), Lady Lurewell in *Sir Harry Wildair*, Lady Brumpton in *The Funeral*, Lady Cringe in *The Modish Husband*, Bisarre in *The Inconstant*, Hypolita in *She Wou'd and She Wou'd Not*, Helena in *The Rover*, Madame Barnard in *The Country House*, Hillaria in *Tunbridge Walks*, and Mrs Whimsey in *The Fair Example*. Her part in *The Fair Example* was acted on 10 April 1703. The troupe went to Bath for the summer, but Mrs Verbruggen pleaded illness and remained behind. She died in childbirth, according to Thomas Davies (writing years later). Mrs Verbruggen was buried at St Martin-in-the-Fields on 2 September 1703.

Susanna Percival Mountfort Verbruggen's contemporaries showered her with praise, though, as one might expect, the vicious *Satyr on the Players* about 1684 accused her of lewdness:

> *Sue Percival so long has known the Stage,*
> *She grows in Lewdness faster than ye Age:*
> *From Eight or Nine she there has Fr——ing been*
> *So calls that Nature, which is truly Sin.*
> *Her Coffee Father too's so basely poor*
> *And such a hireling, that he'l hold the Door*
> *Be Pimp himself, that she may play ye Whore.*

A much more reliable report of her personal behavior can be found in a letter from Sir George Etherege to Mrs Jepson dating from February-March 1688: "Mrs. Percivall had only her youth and a maidenhead to recommend her, which makes me think you do not take it to heart that Mrs. Mumford [i.e., Mountfort] is so discreet." Even *A Comparison Between the Two Stages* of 1702, which berated most performers, found Mrs Verbruggen "a Miracle" and classed her far beyond Jane Rogers and Anne Oldfield—acresses who were "mere Rubbish that ought to be swept off the Stage with the Filth and Dust."

Considering how popular Mrs Verbruggen

was in breeches roles one is surprised to read Tony Aston's description of her person in his *Brief Supplement* to Cibber's *Apology*: she was a "fine, fair Woman, plump, full-featured; her Face of a fine, smooth Oval, full of beautiful, well-dispos'd Moles on it, and on her Neck and Breast . . ." But she had, Aston said, "thick legs and thighs, corpulent and large posteriours . . ." What she did with what she had captivated the town. Aston called her acting all acquired, all designed, but dressed so nicely that it looked like nature. She was consistent in her portrayals, varying hardly at all from one performance of a character to the next. Her "greatest, and usual, Position was Laughing, Flirting her Fan, and,—*je ne scay quois*,—with a Kind of affected Twitter."

Aston also commended her character:

She was the best conversation possible; never captious, or displeas'd at any thing but what was gross or indecent; for she was cautious, lest fiery Jack [Verbruggen] should so resent it, as to breed a quarrel;—for he wou'd often say—"Dammee! tho' I don't much value my wife, yet no body shall affront her"—and his sword was drawn on the least occasion, which was much in fashion at the latter end of King William's reign.

Colley Cibber was so extravagant in his praise of Mrs Verbruggen that one wonders if he had, as he called it, a *tendre* for her: she was

Mistress of more variety of Humour than I ever knew in any one Woman Actress. This variety, too, was attended with an equal Vivacity, which made her excellent in Characters extremely different. As she was naturally a pleasant Mimick, she had the Skill to make that Talent useful on the Stage, a Talent which may be surprising in a Conversation and yet be lost when brought to the Theatre, which was the Case of *Estcourt*. . . . But where the Elocution is round, distinct, voluble, and various, as Mrs. *Montfort's* was, the Mimick there is a great Assistant to the Actor. Nothing, tho' ever so barren, if within the Bounds of Nature, could be flat in her Hands. She gave many heightening Touches to Characters but coldly written, and often made an Author vain of his Work that in it self had but little Merit. She was so fond of Humour, in what low Part soever to be found, that she would make no scruple of defacing her fair Form to come heartily into it; for when she was eminent in several desirable Characters of Wit and Humour in higher Life, she would be in as much Fancy when descending into the antiquated *Abigail* [in *The Scornful Lady*] of *Fletcher*, as when triumph-

ing in all the Airs and vain Graces of a fine Lady; a Merit that few Actresses care for. In a Play of D'urfey's, now forgotton, call'd *The Western Lass*, which Part she acted, she transform'd her whole Being, Body, Shape, Voice, Language, Look and Features, into almost another Animal, with a strong *Devonshire* Dialect, a broad laughing Voice, a poking Head, round Shoulders, an unconceiving Eye, and the most bediz'ning dowdy Dress that ever cover'd the untrain'd Limbs of a *Joan Trot*. To have seen her here you would have thought it impossible the same Creature could ever have been recover'd to what was as easy to her, the Gay, the Lively, and the Desirable. Nor was her Humour limited to her Sex; for, while her Shape permitted, she was a more adroit pretty Fellow than is usually seen upon the Stage: Her easy Air, Action, Mien, and Gesture quite chang'd from the Quoif to the cock'd Hat and Cavalier in fashion. People were so fond of seeing her a Man, that when the Part of *Bays* in the *Rehearsal* had for some time lain dormant, she was desired to take it up, which I have seen her act with all the true coxcombly Spirit and Humour that the Sufficiency of the Character required. But what found most Employment for her whole various Excellence at once, was the Part of *Melantha* in *Marriage-A-lamode*. *Melantha* is as finish'd an Impertinent as ever flutter'd in a Drawing-Room, and seems to contain the most compleat System of Female Foppery that could possibly be crowded into the tortured Form of a Fine Lady. Her Language, Dress, Motion, Manners, Soul, and Body, are in a continual Hurry to be something more than is necessary or commendable. . . . The first ridiculous Airs that break from her are upon a Gallant never seen before, who delivers her a Letter from her Father recommending him to her good Graces as an honourable Lover. Here now, one would think, she might naturally shew a little of the Sexe's decent Reserve, tho' never so slightly cover'd! No, Sir; not a Tittle of it; Modesty is the Virtue of a poor-soul'd Country Gentlewoman; she is too much a court lady to be under so vulgar a Confusion; she reads the Letter, therefore, with a careless, dropping Lip and an erected Brow, humming it hastily over as if she were impatient to outgo her Father's Commands by making a compleat Conquest of him at once; and that the Letter might not embarass her Attack, crack! she crumbles it at once into her Palm and pours upon him her whole Artillery of Airs, Eyes, and Motion; down goes her dainty, diving Body to the Ground, as if she were sinking under the conscious Load of her own Attractions; then launches into a Flood of fine language and Compliment, still playing her Chest forward in fifty Falls and Risings, like a Swan upon waving Water; and, to complete her Impertinence, she is so rapidly fond of her own

Wit that she will not give her Lover Leave to praise it: Silent assenting Bows and vain Endeavours to speak are all the share of the Conversation he is admitted to, which at last he is relieved from by her Engagement to half a Score Visits, which she *swims* from him to make, with a Promise to return in a Twinkling.

Susanna Verbruggen probably deserved the praise. In *An Essay on the Theatres* in the *Harleian Miscellany* (1745) there is praise for the rising comic star of Kitty Clive, and she is called the true successor of Mrs Verbruggen. Since Kitty Clive was demonstrably one of the finest comic talents of the eighteenth century, Mrs Verbruggen's talent must have been great indeed.

Vercany, Signor   *fl. 1735₁*,   *violinist.*

At a concert at Hickford's Great Room on 1 May 1735 Signor Vercany played the violin.

Verhuyck, Mr   *fl. 1724–1729₁*,   *house servant.*

The Lincoln's Inn Fields Theatre accounts name Mr Verhuyck as a gallery boxkeeper on 16 March 1724 at 1s. 8d. daily. He seems to have served in several capacities: as office keeper, pitkeeper, and boxkeeper. The accounts named him regularly through February 1729, by which time young John Verhuyck, probably his son, had begun a stage career and would eventually work as a house servant.

Verhuyck, John   *fl. 1729–1749?₁*, *actor, house servant.*

As a member of the "Lilliputian" troupe at John Rich's Lincoln's Inn Fields Theatre, young John Verhuyck played Mat in *The Beggar's Opera* on 1 January 1729. On 24 March 1731 Master Verhuyck was Tom Thumb in *The Tragedy of Tragedies* when it was first presented. He appears to have given up acting after that and followed in the steps of an elder Verhuyck—probably his father—who had been a house servant at Lincoln's Inn Fields in the 1720s. Latreille identified Verhuyck (presumably the younger one) as a boxkeeper at Covent Garden Theatre in 1735–36 at 2s. nightly. Verhuyck shared in benefits regularly in the years that followed, and from 1742 onward he was identified as a pit doorkeeper. He was last mentioned in the bills on 5 May

1748. It is possible that he was the Verhuyck who sold tickets for the boxes for a Haymarket Theatre benefit on 28 March 1749 from his shop in Piccadilly. He was identified as a printseller.

Verjuice, Mrs   *fl. 1668–1670?₁*,   *performer?*

John Downes in his *Roscius Anglicanus* in 1708 remembered a Mrs Verjuice as a member of the King's Company at the Bridges Street Theatre from 1668 to perhaps 1670. She is not listed in *The London Stage.*

Vermeil, Mlle   *fl. 1748₁*,   *dancer.*

Mlle Vermeil danced a minuet with Signor "Nicholini" at the Haymarket Theatre on 14 April 1748.

Vermigli,   Mons   *fl. 1785–1791₁*, *dancer.*

The name of Mons Vermigli is on the lists of dancers at Astley's Amphitheatre in 1785, 1786, and 1788. Probably he was the Mr Vermilly who danced at the King's Theatre in 1790–91; Vermilly's name was first noticed on the King's Theatre bills on 26 March 1791 when he appeared in *Orpheus and Eurydice* with Vestris, Mlle Hillisberg, and Mlle Mozon. On 12 April he danced Philotête in *La Mort d'Hercule*, and his other assignments that season were Fauline in *L'Amadriade* on 5 May and parts in *Les Folies d'Espagne* on 10 June and *La Fête du Seigneur* on 25 June.

Vermilly. *See* VERMIGLI.

Vernat. *See* VERNET.

Vernell, The Misses   *fl. 1785₁*,   *reciters.*

At the Haymarket Theatre on 2 August 1785, announced as making their first appearances on any stage, the two Misses Vernell recited a duologue, "New Lecture on Heads," at the end of *Rosina.* About six weeks later, on 15 September, they delivered the same recitation at Sadler's Wells. At least one of them was at the Theatre Royal, Norwich, sometime that year. Possibly they were related to John Vernel (1741–1771), who acted in the Dublin theatres between 1759–60 and 1769–70.

Verner, Mr *fl. 1713–1734?*], *violinist?*

A concert was held for Mr Verner's benefit at Stationers' Hall on 3 December 1713. Perhaps he was the Verner who played violin at the Earl of Egmont's concert on 15 February 1734.

Vernet, Le Sieur *fl. 1792*], *musician, posturer.*

Le Sieur and Madame Vernet (sometimes Vernat) were performers at Astley's Amphitheatre, Westminster Bridge, in the summer of 1792. Advertisements in August announced a musical piece, *The Haunted Village*, by Le Sieur and Madame Vernet, "whose performances on the Violin, Tambour di Bass &c. are beyond conception & need only to be seen to be believed. They execute the most difficult pieces of music to various & astonishing attitudes."

Vernet, Mme [*1792*], *musician, posturer*
See VERNET, LE SIEUR.

Verneuil. *See* DE VERNEUIL.

Verney. *See also* VARNEY.

Verney, Mr *fl. 1738–1739*], *dancer.*
The London Stage lists Mr Verney as a dancer at Drury Lane Theatre in 1738–39, but we have not found his name in any bills.

Vernon, Mr *fl. 1743*], *dancer.*
Max Fuchs in his *Lexique* cites a *Daily Post* notice on 19 September 1743 identifying a Mr Vernon as a dancer at Drury Lane Theatre. *The London Stage* makes no mention of Vernon.

Vernon, Mrs *fl. 1791*], *actress, singer.*
"A Lady" made her stage debut playing Rosetta in *Love in a Village* at Covent Garden Theatre on 27 January 1791; the *Oracle* identified her as a Mrs Vernon. The *European Magazine* said:

As it is imagined this lady's success will hardly establish her on the London stage, we shall only observe, that she exhibited marks of care and attention in her study of the character. Her voice was not very extraordinary, but her skill in Music, far from inconsiderable. . . . We judge that she had

begun her theatrical efforts too late to hope for much improvement.

Indeed, she did not appear in London again after the second performance of *Love in a Village* on 29 January.

Vernon, Miss *fl. 1784*], *actress.*
On 8 March 1784 Miss Vernon played Maria in *The Man's Bewitch'd* at the Haymarket Theatre, according to the *Morning Chronical*; the *Gazetteer* gave the role of Maria to Mrs Green.

Vernon, Joseph *c. 1731?–1782, singer, actor, composer.*
Joseph Vernon was born illegitimate in Coventry (about 1739 say most sources; but see below) and grew up in the Coventry Charity School. In his *Memoirs* Charles Lee Lewes said that in 1752 Richard Yates and John Palmer, stopping at the Bull Inn in Coventry on their way to Birmingham, discovered the young Vernon singing for pennies to help his widowed mother. Vernon was apprenticed to Yates and later to Garrick. That story may be true, but the date is certainly wrong, for Master Vernon made his debut singing ("very well" said the prompter Cross) in *Queen Mab* at Drury Lane Theatre in London on 26 December 1750. During the remainder of the 1750–51 season Joseph sang in the masque *Alfred* as well as in *Queen Mab*. At some point he became a chorister at St Paul's Cathedral.

In 1751–52 he sang in the chorus in *Romeo and Juliet*, in *Queen Mab*, a solo, "Haughty Strephon," as an entr'acte entertainment, and a song (no title given in the bills) by Handel. After that season he was usually (but not consistently) called Vernon rather than Master Vernon, which casts some suspicion on the approximate birth year given in most sources. If he was just coming of age in 1752, a birth date of about 1731 would seem more correct. Vernon's roles in plays beginning in 1752–53 would also suggest a young man about 21: Loveless in *The Double Disappointment*, the Second Bacchanal in *Comus*, Thyrsis in *The Shepherd's Lottery*, and, in 1753–54, Donalbain in *Macbeth*, the Valet in *The Suspicious Husband*, Squire Richard in *The Provok'd Husband*, Clincher Junior in *The Constant Couple*, Strut in *The Double Gallant*, Fabian in *Twelfth*

JOSEPH VERNON, as Thurio

by Roberts

Night, Petit in *The Inconstant*, Master Stephen in *Every Man in His Humour*, Verges in *Much Ado about Nothing*, and Launcelot in *The Merchant of Venice*. Similarly, at Richmond in the summer of 1753 "Master" Vernon played Sir John Loverule in *The Lady's Last Stake* and "Vernon" acted Damon in *The Chaplet*, Squire Richard in *The Provok'd Husband*, Malcolm in *Macbeth*, Lord Rake in *The Provok'd Wife*, Quaver in *The Virgin Unmask'd*, Cimberton in *The Conscious Lovers*, Oberon in *The Oracle*, Friendly in *Hob in the Well*, a Bravo in *The Inconstant*, and Mercury in *Lethe*.

From 1753–54 through 1780–81 at Drury Lane Vernon amassed a great number of acting and singing roles, among them Denny in *Henry VIII*, Bernardo in *Hamlet*, a Servant in *Coriolanus*, the Gentleman Usher in *King Lear*, Vizir in *The London Prentice*, Meggot in *The Suspicious Husband*, a Triton in *Britannia*, Palemon and Damon in *The Chaplet*, Garcia in *The Mourning Bride*, The Genius of England in *Eliza*, Sellaway in *The Gamester*, Stephano and Ferdinand in *The Tempest*, Brisk in *The Upholsterer*, Amiens in *As You Like It*, Macheath in *The Beggar's Opera*, Sharp in *The Lying Valet*,

Colonel Bully in *The Provok'd Wife*, Sir John Loverule in *The Devil to Pay*, Rovewell in *The Contrivances*, a Witch in *The Witches*, Thurio in *Two Gentlemen of Verona*, Hunter in *Phoebe*, Balthasar in *Much Ado about Nothing*, Thomas in *Thomas and Sally*, Sir Harry in *The Jealous Wife*, Ramilie in *The Miser*, Young Gilbert in *Love at First Sight*, Feste in *Twelfth Night*, Damon in *The Spring*, Amintas in *The Royal Shepherd*, Roderigo in *Othello*, Mahomed in *Almena*, the title role in *Pharnaces*, Palamede in *The Frenchified Lady Never in Paris*, Hamet in *The Orphan of China*, King Henry in *Rosamond*, Amintor in *Daphne and Amintor*, Chatillon in *King John*, Patie in *The Gentle Shepherd*, the title role in *Cymon*, Friendly in *Flora*, Lorenzo in *The Merchant of Venice*, Atticus in *Theodosius*, Artabanes in *Artaxerxes*, Hawthorn in *Love in a Village*, Leander in *The Padlock*, Apollo in *The Jubilee*, Orpheus in *A Peep behind the Curtain*, William in *May Day*, Floridor in *A Christmas Tale*, Vainlove in *The Old Bachelor*, Azor in *Selima and Azor*, Byron in *The Rival Candidates*, Henry in *The Deserter*, Belfield in *The Milesian*, Lubin in *The Quaker*, Zerbino in *The Wedding Ring*, Lionel in *The School for Fathers*, Henry in *Amelia*, Booze in *Belphegor*, Morley in *Second Thought Is Best*, Edwin in *The Lucky Escape*, Autolycus in *The Winter's Tale*, Ben in *Love for Love*, Bevil in *The Artifice*, a Sailor in *Fortunatus*, Richard in *The Election*, Trimbush in *The Generous Impostor*, Trumore in *The Lord of the Manor*, Lionel in *A School for Fathers*, and Honour in *King Arthur*.

On occasion Vernon strayed from Drury Lane. He sang in *Acis and Galatea* at the Haymarket Theatre on 13 November 1764, in *Manasseh* at the Chapel of the Lock Hospital on 30 May 1766, in *The Cure for Saul* at the King's Theatre on 5 February 1768, in *Ruth* at the Chapel of the Lock Hospital on 25 May 1768, the lead in *The Busy Body* at the Haymarket on 7 October 1768, in *Ruth* at the King's on 5 April 1769, Artabanes in *Artaxerxes* at the King's on 1 June 1769, in *Judith* at the Stratford jubilee in 1769, and in *Judas Maccabaeus* at the Haymarket on 4 May 1770. In the late 1770s Vernon frequently went across the street from Drury Lane to sing at Covent Garden. Examples are on 6 March 1778, when he sang in *Acis and Galatea* (and, ironically, *Acis and Galatea* was also performed that evening at Drury Lane); on 23 and 29

JOSEPH VERNON, as Macheath

artist unknown

October 1778 and later dates, when he sang Antonio in *The Duenna*; and several dates in November and December 1778, when he sang Young Wildman in *The Lady of the Manor*. He also sang in the *Messiah* and *A Miscellaneous Act* at the Haymarket in March 1779, Ben in *Plymouth in an Uproar* at Covent Garden in October 1779, Lorenzo in *The Merchant of Venice* and Young Ballemine in *The Shepherdess of the Alps* at Covent Garden in January 1780, and some songs for Reinhold's benefit at Covent Garden on 18 April 1780 (when he also sang in *The Padlock* at Drury Lane).

Though a popular performer in London, Joseph Vernon incurred the wrath of audiences when, on 27 September 1755, according to the Drury Lane prompter Richard Cross, he

was hiss'd off: in the part of Palemon in yᵉ Chaplet—the anger of the audience proceeded from this—towards the end of last Season he married Miss Potier [Jane Poitier] at the Savoy, without friends consent, & afterwards was drawn in to inform against Mr. Grieston [Grierson], the Parson, who was immediately seiz'd & thrown into Newgate; where he was remov'd to yᵉ King's bench on account of his Sickness, where he now lies for his Tryal. He publish'd his Case, and beg'd the Charity of the Town to keep his Family from starving.

The young couple had been married on 27 June 1755, when Jane Poitier was 19 years old; if we have judged correctly, Vernon was about 24, but if he was born about 1739, as most early sources suppose, he was underage in 1755.

The *Theatrical Biography* (1772) gave the following version of the marriage and resulting uproar:

Having formed an affection for Miss Poitier (since Mrs. Thompson, now Mrs. [*sic*; they did not marry] Bannister) which grew from their intimacy on the stage, he made proposals of marriage to her parents. Though the father's consent became absolutely necessary to this union from the late marriage act [of 1754], the young couple, desirous of being united, for, (to use the more emphatical word of the lady, as appeared upon the trial, 'I will not go home till I am married') prevailed upon Mr. Grierson, at that time a clergyman in the Savoy, to perform that office on the mother's consent. The consequence of this marriage was a warm prosecution, during which, though much interest was made for the offending clergyman, and though he challenged the whole of the jury, he, after a long trial, fell sacrifice to what the lawyers call the *maidenhead* of the act, and he was sent to be transported for fourteen years; which operated so strongly on his mind, that he died on the passage, leaving behind him a disconsolate wife and large family.

The prompter Cross noted in his diary on 18 October that Vernon "was not suffer'd to sing in the Chaplet, but hiss'd as before." On the following 3 January 1756 Vernon as Garcia in *The Mourning Bride*, "tho not meddled with in the 1ˢᵗ Act, was in the 5 hiss'd off, on account of the old affair of his Marriage." Vernon had given evidence against the officiating chaplain and curate.

Most sources (the *New Grove* and Roger Fiske in *English Theatre Music*, among others, following Tate Wilkinson's *Memoirs*) say that the marriage was annulled and that Vernon, suddenly unpopular, spent a year in Ireland. Indeed, the next notice of Vernon in London dates 28 January 1757, when Cross noted that "Mr Vernon play'd his Wife's part [the Genius of England in *Eliza*] & was well receiv'd." Vernon's next appearance was as Stephano in *The Tempest* on 7 November 1757. Separated or not, Mrs Vernon continued performing under her married name until 1762.

Vernon left with Woodward to perform at Smock Alley and at Crow Street in Dublin in

1758–59, making his first appearance at Crow Street on 24 October 1758.

Both *Theatrical Biography* and Lewes in his *Memoirs* note that in Dublin in 1759 at the Brown Bear, Vernon witnessed a drunken murder; Vernon was bought off by the murderer's father, and the brawlers were acquitted. He was back at Drury Lane on 12 October 1759, but only for that performance, at which he sang in *Macbeth*. The *Theatric Tourist* has him singing at Plymouth in 1759. He was in Ireland again in 1760–61 and 1761–62. The *Theatrical Review* of 1763 contained a report from Dublin:

Mr. *Vernon* having been so long absent, claims some notice in this place. We know not in his singing which to admire most, his peculiar delicacy, exquisite taste, or sensible expression; all which it is certain he possesses to a most eminent degree. As an actor too, he may be justly proclaimed a lively and pleasing comedian; a specimen of which he has give us in Sharp [in *The Lying Valet*] and several other parts.

When Vernon sang Macheath in *The Beggar's Opera* at Drury Lane on 21 September 1762 he was hailed as making his first appearance on the English stage in five years. He was earning £5 weekly by 1765, £6 weekly by 1767, and £8 weekly by 1775, augmenting his income by appearing (in 1765) at the Theatre Royal, Norwich, and regularly at Vauxhall Gardens in London in the 1760s and 1770s. He may also have gained extra income racing a colt he owned in 1769. Vernon sang in Chester in 1779, at Bristol from 1780 to 1782, and at Bath in 1781–82.

The prompter Hopkins noted in his diary on 6 November 1776 that "Vernon was so very drunk in the Farce [*A Christmas Tale*] that he could scarcely stand up—a Man in the Gallery cryed out—Hold him up. . . ."

Vernon's last appearance at Drury Lane was on 9 October 1781, when he sang "Here's to the maiden of bashful fifteen" in *The School for Scandal*. The *Morning Post* on 20 March 1782 reported that Joseph Vernon had died at Lambeth on 19 March after a lingering illness. Vernon was buried at St Martin-in-the-Fields. On 15 April administration of his estate was granted to his widow Margaret, née Richardson (Fiske says Wilkinson); they had married on 8 January 1773, according to the *London Magazine*. Vernon was described as late of the parish of St Mary, Lambeth. Vernon was known as a womanizer, and in addition to his illegal marriage to Jane Poitier and his marriage in 1773 to Margaret Richardson, rumor had it that he married a Miss Macartney (according to Tate Wilkinson's *Memoirs*), but the marriage was denied. It was also rumored that in 1768 Vernon the singer had married Lady Caroline Hewey.

Wilkes in *A General View of the Stage* commented favorably on Vernon in the early part of his career: "Instinct sets Mr. Vernon right in Dramatic exhibitions; he has certainly judgment in singing. In acting he shews a proper assurance, and he seems ignorant of it. I have seen him, young as he is, stand well in some part of Mr. Woodward's cast." But William Hawkins in his *Miscellanies in Prose and Verse* in 1775 saw many faults:

Though as the principal vocal performer of Drury-Lane Theatre, I must confess I can find but little entertainment from his singing; . . . there appears to me to be such an affected stiffness in his manner, as if he enjoyed more pleasure from his own harmony than his audience does. Vernon without doubt, has a very good knowledge of music, though in point of voice, I think him by no means in competition with your Mattock's, DuBellamy's, &c. at the other house [i.e., Convent Garden Theatre]; notwithstanding there are many may wantonly contradict what I have here set down; yet were they to hear him sing in private company without the help of music, they'd be as conscious of this as myself, who have been ear witness of this assertion. As an actor, Mr. Vernon undoubtedly has merit in many parts of comedy; and did not too apparent a coxcomb eternally settle itself on his features, there would be no doubt of his acquiring much more applause in his profession than he has yet attained.

The "Alphabetical Character" of actors at Drury Lane in 1777 said:

V—is a Vernon, who still keeps his taste,
But his powers are running to dryness and waste.

Francis Gentleman, usually censorious, liked Vernon:

Vernon, in music, gains unbounded praise,
We to his acting yield applausive lays . . .

Gentlemen thought Garrick used Vernon far too little. Boaden in his biography of Mrs Sid-

JOSEPH VERNON, as Hawthorn

artist unknown

dons said Vernon's "look was an invitation to be happy, and his voice, though weak, sufficed to convey the effect of both words and music. . . . His style was full of meaning."

Vernon's tenor voice was heard in many songs at Drury Lane and Vauxhall: "The Return," "The Albion Song," "Ode to Masonry" (with Dodd and Bannister), "When Damon met Phillis first," "No anxious Care my Heart can know" (with Miss Young), "The Fields now are looking so gay," "Among the fond Shepherds," "Farewell ye green fields," "The Invitation," "Young Arabella, mamma's care," "When Fanny to Woman is growing apace," "When first I gaz'd on Kitty's Face," "By the side of a stream," "The silver moon's enamour'd beam," "Dear Chloe, how blubber'd is thy pretty face," "Ralph's Ramble to London," "You may do as you will," "Without any envy, without any foes," "Fanny of the Hill," "Let fusty old Greybeards of Apathy boast," "The goodness of women some men will dispute," "'Twas underneath a May blown Bush,"

"Now's the time for Mirth and Glee," "Aurora beams bright," "Believe my sighs," "Under the greenwood Tree,""The Hogshead of Port," "Forsaken my Pipe & my Crook," "My Peggy is a young thing," "Ye Sluggards," "Ye Virgins of Britain," "Yes I'll give my Heart away," "Oh where shall I wander," "From College I came," "I sigh for a Damsel that's charming and fair," "Thrice welcome sweet May," "When I drain the rosy Bowl," "Shall I wasting in despair," "Now May her charms discloses," and "Whilst a Captive to your Charms."

Vernon also composed songs: "Some cry up Gennersby," songs in Linco's Travels (with Michael Arne), songs in The Witches, and a setting for Feste's "When that I was and a little tiny boy" in Twelfth Night. Vernon edited The New London and Country Songster about 1780. He offered audiences at Drury Lane "Cries of London & Tombs of Westminster" and "A Whimsical Description of the Antients and Moderns" in the 1760s.

Portraits of Joseph Vernon include:

1. As Cymon in Cymon. Pencil and watercolor by unknown artist. In the Garrick Club (not listed in the printed catalogue).

2. As Cymon. By unknown engraver. Published as a plate to Vocal Magazine, by J. Bew, 1778.

3. As Hawthorn in Love in a Village. By unknown engraver.

4. As Macheath in The Beggar's Opera. Engraving by James Roberts. Published as a plate to Bell's British Theatre, 1777. Roberts's drawing of Vernon as Macheath was in the sale of the collection of original drawings ("which have distinguished Bell's various editions") at Christie's on 27 March 1793 (lot 14); the drawings by Roberts were described as the "Origin of the present improved State of Character Drawings."

5. As Macheath. Engraving by Thornthwaite, after Roberts, a copy of the preceding.

6. As Macheath. Indian ink and wash drawing by unknown artist. In the British Museum (Burney, x, No 7). Published by Wenman as a plate to an edition of the play, 1777.

7. As Macheath. By unknown engraver. Published by J. Harrison, 1776.

8. As Thurio in The Two Gentlemen of Verona. Colored drawing on vellum by James Roberts.

In the British Museum (Burney, x, No 5). Engraving by unknown artist, published as a plate to *Bell's British Theatre*, 1777. Roberts drawing of Vernon as Thurio was in the sale of the Bell collection of original drawings at Christie's on 27 March 1793 (lot 40). See above No 4.

9. In character, half-length, tye wig. Pencil drawing by James Roberts. In the Harvard Theatre Collection, acquired from Thomas Agnew, London, in 1976 with a collection of other drawings by Roberts.

10. "The Apotheosis of Garrick." By George Carter, c. 1782. Vernon appears in this large canvas with many contemporary actors in various attitudes and characters bidding farewell to Garrick who is being wafted up to Mount Parnassus by the Muses. In the Art Galley of the Royal Shakespeare Theatre, Stratford-upon-Avon. An engraving by J. Caldwell and S. Smith was published, with a key plate to the figures, by G. Carter, 1783.

Vernon, Mrs Joseph *b. 1736. See* POITIER, JANE.

Vernsburgh, Charles *d. c. 1780, musician.*

On 28 August 1739 Charles Vernsburgh (or Vernsberg) became one of the original subscribers to the Royal Society of Musicians. He was active to at least 1755 and died before 3 December 1780, according to *The Royal Society of Musicians* (1985).

Vesey, John *ₗfl. 1670–1671,ₗ, scenekeeper.*

The London Stage lists John Vesey as a scenekeeper at the King's Company theatre in Bridges Street in 1670–71. He was cited in the Lord Chamberlain's accounts on 7 March 1671.

Vestment, Nathaniel *d. 1702, singer.*

On 28 June 1683 Nathaniel Vestment was sworn a Gentleman of the Chapel Royal at Windsor, and on 23 July he was admitted to a salaried post. He was one of the bass singers who marched in the coronation procession of James II on 23 April 1685 and attended at the coronation of Willam and Mary on 11 March 1689. He spent 49 days serving the Queen at Windsor and Hampton Court in 1702. That may have been his last service as a court singer. He died on 23 August 1702.

"Vestris à Cheval." *See* DUCROW, ANDREW.

Vestris, Auguste. *See* VESTRIS, MARIE JEAN AUGUSTIN.

Vestris, Gaëtan Appoline Balthazar *1729?-1808, dancer, choreographer.*

Gaëtan Appoline Balthazar (or Appolino Baldassare) Vestris was born, according to Grove, on 18 April 1729 in Florence. An engraving of his tombstone gives the year 1728. He was the son of Tommaso Maria Ippolito Vestris (Italian: Vestri) and his wife Violante-Beatrix de Dominique Bruscagli. Gaëtan had at least six brothers and sisters: Giovanni Battista (1725–1801), Maddalena, Francesco, Maria Teresa Francesca (1726–1808), Angiolo Maria Gasparo (1730–1809), and Maria Caterina Violante (c. 1732–1791). The elder Vestris was employed as a pawnbroker in Florence, but after running into trouble with his employer, Vestris fled with his family to Naples. The family lived there for a while and then began wandering around Europe: Palermo (Gaëtan, with Maria Teresa and Violante, danced at the opera house, according to Lillian Moore in *Artists of the Dance*; that was his first engagement), Bologna, Venice, Genoa, Vienna, Dresden, Milan, and finally, in 1747, Paris.

Most of the family arrived in Paris on 3 October 1747. Maria Teresa had gone there earlier in the year and established herself quickly as a courtesan; Violante arrived later in the year, after finishing a singing engagement at the opera house in Turin. In 1748 Gaëtan was placed in the dancing school of the Paris Opéra to study under the eminent Louis Dupré. By 1749 Gaëtan was a member of the corps de ballet, and when Dupré retired in 1751 young Vestris was appointed a soloist. He and his sister Maria Teresa made a joint debut in a pas de deux that met with great applause.

Vestris became a member of the Académie Royale de Danse in 1753. The following year he quarreled with the ballet master Lany, his sister Maria Teresa's lover. Teresa had hoped to gain advancement in the company through her relationship with Lany, and when she did not receive it, Gaëtan Vestris challenged Lany to a duel. Lany refused to fight, and on 17 February 1754 Vestris was dropped from the company and imprisoned (rather grandly) at St Germain l'Auxerrois.

By 6 September 1754 Vestris was out of prison. On that day he, his mother, his sister Maria Teresa, and his brother Angiolo headed for Berlin, where Vestris had an engagement worth 16,000 livres and travel expenses. After a season in Berlin Vestris went to Turin, where he made his first attempt as a choreographer (an art for which he had no great skill; his forte was dancing). In 1755 he returned to Paris, where the management re-engaged him (having no other premier danseur) and his brother and sister. They danced in *Roland* on 9 December 1755.

In 1757 Vestris began an affair with the young dancer Marie Allard (1742–1802) which, for all intents and purposes, was a marriage. Their son Marie Jean Augustin (called Auguste) was born on 27 March 1760.

Vestris danced for Noverre at Stuttgart in 1760. On 25 April 1761 Vestris joined Noverre's troupe at Stuttgart as the company's first serious dancer. His engagement was for six years at a yearly salary of 2,200 florins plus 130 florins shoe money and money for travel. Vestris took a three-month leave each year from the Opéra in order to work with Noverre. A year later Vestris was made ballet master at the Opéra, a post he held until 1776; he was named choreographer in 1770. That year he broke the convention of dancing masked, in *Medée et Jason*. But Vestris was not always in Paris. A quarrel with the directors at the Opéra led him to accept an engagement in Vienna in 1767, where he danced in Noverre's *Medée et Jason*. He danced in Warsaw before returning to Paris for a performance of *Dardanus* on 14 December 1767. His reappearance in Paris brought ecstatic praise from his adoring audiences.

Imperious and vain, "The French Rose" was nevertheless recognized as a brilliant dancer. He was regularly praised for his noble style, ease, lightness, and precision. He was called the "God of the Dance" by his brother Giovanni Battista, and the nickname was picked up by his followers.

Some of his roles at the Opéra over the years were a Matelot in *Le Carnaval et la folie*, a Turk

Civica Raccolta Stampe A. Bertarelli, Milan

GAËTAN APPOLINE BALTHAZAR VESTRIS
engraving by Focosi

in *Almasis*, a Masque Galant in *Les Fêtes vénitiennes*, a Faun in *Ismène*, a Roman in *Léandre et Héro,* two roles in *Tancrède*, a Triton and Scythe in *Thétys et Pélée*, two parts in *Acanthe et Céphise*, a Shepherd in *Les Sens*, a Follower of Fortune in *Églé*, a Shepherd in *La Guirlande*, Borée in *Les Indes galantes*, a Follower of Polyphème in *Acis et Galatée*, a Shadow in *Les Amours de tempé*, three parts in *Omphale*, a role in *Le Devin du village*, two roles in *Les Fêtes de Polymnie*, three roles in *Les Fêtes greques et romaines*, a Gardener in *La Gouvernante rusée*, two roles in *Titon et l'Aurore*, a Gladiator and a Genie in *Castor et Pollux*, a Satyr in Platée, a Sybarite in *Les Sybarites*, Endymion in *Les Surprises de l'Amour*, and parts in *Alceste, Proserpine, Amadis de Gaule, Canente, Le Prince de Noisy, Armide, Zaïs, Iphigénie en Tauride, Les Fêtes d'Hébé, Nais, Les Fêtes de l'Hymen et de l'Amour, Hypermnestre, Sylvie, Ernelinde, Ajax, Zorastre, Zaïde, Alcyone, Pyrame et Thisbé, Aline, L'Amour et Psyché, Endymion* (his own work, in which he danced the title part), *Zélindor, Orphée* (by Gluck), *Cythère assiégée,*

Apelles et Campaspe, *Les Horaces*, and *Mirza*. In addition to *Endymion*, Vestris choreographed *Le Nid d'oiseau*. Neither ballet was a success. Vestris was paid 4,500 livres annually from 1776 until he left the Opéra.

Gennaro Magri in his *Trattato teorico-prattico di ballo* in 1779 stated that Vestris "during the same turn changes foot two or three times, which really deserves eternal admiration; but the most surprising thing is that while he is turning at the highest possible speed he stops in à-plomb, with such perfection that he remains perfectly immobile in that balancing position." Marian Hannah Winter in her *Pre-Romantic Ballet* quotes from Magri's treatise.

Vestris came to England to dance at the King's Theatre in 1780–81. The *Public Advertiser* referred to him on 25 December 1780: "The spirit of Vestris seems to diffuse itself throughout the whole Body of Dancers at [the King's] Theatre; even the Figurants acquit themselves in a manner that deserves the encouragement of the Public." On 22 February 1781 Vestris's ballet *Ninette à la cour* was presented, with Vestris dancing the Prince and his son Auguste dancing Colas. The evening was a benefit, according to *The London Stage*, for the younger Vestris. Walpole wrote on 26 February that the benefit was for both father and son; "the house could not receive and contain the multitudes that presented themselves. Their oblations amounted to fourteen hundred pounds." That evening marked Gaëtan Vestris's first appearance in England. The younger and elder Vestris were living at No 5, Leicester Street, Leicester Fields.

On 15 March 1781 Gaëtan danced a pas solo and, with Mme Simonet, a pas de deux; it may have been that performance to which Dr Burney referred:

while the elder Vestris was on the stage, if during a *pas seul*, any of his admirers forgot themselves so much as to applaud him with their hands, there was an instant check put to his rapture by a choral—sh! For those lovers of music who talked the loudest when Pacchierotti was singing a pathetic air, or making an exquisite close, were now thrown into agonies of displeasure, lest the graceful movements *du dieu de la danse*, or the attention of his votaries, should be disturbed by audible approbation.

On 29 March Vestris received a benefit at which two of his ballets were performed: *Les*

GAËTEN APPOLINE BALTHAZAR VESTRIS, as the Prince

engraving by Thornthwaite, after Roberts

Caprices de Galatée and *Medée et Jason* (stolen from Noverre, evidently). The latter work was published, as *Medée and Jason*, in 1781. The *London Magazine* in April said that Vestris's "forcible manner of characterizing the passions in the part of Jason distinguished him as an actor superior to all his contemporaries." Edward Pigott saw *Medée et Jason* on 3 April and made a note in his diary (now at Yale): ". . . by the Vestris's, Slingsby, Baccelli &c it is perfectly entertaining; the dance performed by Vestris the Father is not of the capring kind, every action is the most graceful, therefore undescribable. . . . [T]his famous Vestris teaches some of our Ladies of the first rank to dance, his price is 6 Guineas entry & one per Lesson; most of them assemble at the Dutchess of Devonshires." During the season Vestris also danced *The Devonshire Minuet* with Mme Simonet. Near the end of the season, on 5

June, Vestris produced the opera *L'omaggio*, with ballets of his own composition. The *Public Advertiser* two days later claimed that "The Vestris' gave incontrovertible proof of the variety of their powers. . . . They did more, they shewed what this country had never seen—the possibility of presenting to the eye a large and extensive stage filled with dancers all in motion at the same time."

Vestris evidently returned to Paris for the 1781–82 season, but on 12 May 1782 he (and his mistress, the German dancer Anne Heinel) retired from the stage, he with a pension of 4,700 livres. Campardon in his *Académie Royale* quotes the grant, which contains information (given above) relating to the birth of Vestris and his parentage. Vestris suffered financial losses during the French Revolution and was forced to return to the stage. He and his son Auguste were again in London in the spring of 1791, performing at the King's Theatre. (In February 1791, according to Smith's *The Italian Opera in London*, Vestris served as ballet master for the production of *Pirro*; but that identification may be an error for Auguste Vestris, who is known to have danced when the opera was given its first public performance on 10 March.) The elder Vestris made his initial appearance at his benefit on 11 April, dancing Hercule in *La mort d'Hercule, and his Apotheosis*, a spectacle which, according to Vestris in a letter to the *Morning Chronicle* on 15 April, was not produced as elaborately as he had been promised. On 2 June a new dance by Vestris, *La Capricieuse*, was presented, and on 6 June his *Ninette à la cour* was revived. Later that month another new dance of his, *La Fête due seigneur*, was performed, with Vestris in the title role.

On 9 May 1791 Vestris and Mlle Heinel had a son, Adolphe Apollon Marie Angiolo. To legitimatize the child, the couple married on 16 June 1792. Vestris danced again in 1795, 1799, and 1800 at the debuts of his grandsons. Gaëtan Vestris died in 1808. The engraving of his tombstone gives his death as 23 September in Paris; other sources say 23 or 27 September.

Though Gaëtan, his wife Anne, and his son Auguste were the only members of the Vestris clan to appear in London in the eighteenth century, there were others who had continental stage careers, detailed in the fourth edition

Civica Raccolta Stampe A. Bertarelli, Milan

Gravestone for GAËTEN APPOLINE BALTHAZAR VESTRIS

artist unknown

of Grove. Angiolo Vestris, Gaëtan's brother, was an actor, dancer, and flutist in Paris and Stuttgart. He married Françoise Rose Gourgaud (1734–1804), who was a celebrated actress in Paris. Gaëtan's sister Violante was a singer and dancer; she married the musician Felice de' Giardini in 1752, and though she was in London for some time, she did not perform. Gaëtan's sister Teresa was a dancer. Auguste, Gaëtan's natural son, is separately noticed in this *Dictionary*. Auguste Armand Vestris (1788–1825) was the son of Auguste Vestris; he had a dancing career in London in the nineteenth century and married Lucia Elizabeth Bartolozzi, who became a celebrated singer. Charles Vestris (b. 1797) was either the brother or cousin of Auguste Armand; Charles, too, was a dancer and appeared in London from 1814 to 1819.

Emilio Vestris, whose relationship to the other members of the family is not clear, danced in Trieste from 1803 to 1813. Bernardo Vestris danced in London in the 1830s. Emilie Vestris, born in 1804, became Mme Hoguet, according to the *Damen Lexikon*. Stephano Vestris was a poet and served at the King's Theatre in London in 1816.

Portraits of Gaëtan Appoline Balthazar Vestris include:

1. By Thomas Gainsborough. Oil on canvas (30" × 25"). Owned by Sir Robert Peele, 1856; in the Broderip sale, 11 June 1859 (lot 83), bought by Heathcote. In an anonymous (Mitchell) sale on 22 June 1867 (lot 156), bought by Cox. In the Lewis Huth sale at Christie's on 20 May 1905 (lot 98), bought by Asher Wertheimer for 4550 guineas, and illustrated in the *Burlington Magazine*, July 1905 (as frontispiece). In May 1954 the *Burlington Magazine* reported that the portrait was owned by R. A. Lee, of London. A small version (12" × 10"), perhaps by Gainsborough Dupont, was in an anonymous sale on 21 February 1919 (lot 93), and was bought by Croal Thompson; in 1920 it was with J. Levy, New York.

2. Engraved portrait by Focosi, Milan. In the Civica Raccolta Stampe A. Bertarelli, Milan.

3. Engraved portrait by J. Miller. Published as a plate to *London Magazine*, April 1781.

4. As Jason, with Mme Simonet and another woman (probably Mlle Baccelli) in *Medée et Jason*. Engraving by F. Bartolozzi, after Nathaniel Dance, 1781. A copy by an unknown engraver was published by Boydell, 1781.

5. As the Prince in *Ninette à la Cour*. Engraving by Thornthwaite, after James Roberts. Published as a plate to *Bell's British Theatre*, 1781. The drawing by Roberts was in the sale of the Bell collection of original drawings ("which have distinguished Bell's various editions") at Christie's on 27 March 1793 (lot 16).

6. Standing, with a goose, and a man seated playing a violin; with title, "Six Guineas entrance and a Guinea a Lesson." By un-

known engraver. Published by P. Sandby, 20 June 1781. According to the *Catalogue of Engraved Dramatic Portraits* in the Harvard Theatre Collection the dancer in this picture is Gaëtan, but we believe him to be Marie Jean Augustin Vestris.

Vestris, Mme Gaëtan Appoline Balthazar, Anne. *See* HEINEL, ANNE FRÉDÉRIQUE.

Vestris, Marie Jean Augustin, called Auguste Vestris or Vestr'Allard *1760– 1842, dancer, choreographer.*

Marie Jean Augustin Vestris was born in Paris on 27 March 1760, the illegitimate son of the dancers Gaëtan Vestris and Marie Allard. Auguste, as he was called, made his stage debut at the Opéra on 18 September 1772 in a divertissement called *La Cinquantaine*. In his *Correspondance littéraire* Grimm wrote that the youth "danced with the same precision, the same aplomb, and almost the same force as the grand Vestris."

In 1773 Auguste danced Eros in *Endymion* (his father's ballet). He then entered the school of the Académie Royale de Musique, danced minor roles for some years, and gradually rose to the level of premier danseur. His specialty was the *demi-caractère comique*, and he was especially admired for his elevation. Baron Grimm recorded Gaëtan Vestris's evaluation of his son. Up to his chest Auguste "leaves nothing to be desired, but as to the upper part of the body, that still needs years of work. I myself spent a whole year in learning how to make my arms appear shorter; I will give him ten years to learn to dance the menuet, and it will not be too many."

Auguste Vestris came to England for the 1780–81 season at the King's Theatre. On 16 December 1780 he made his first English appearance, dancing in a serious ballet (in which he was featured in a chaconne) and *Les Amans surpris*. Henry Angelo in his *Reminiscences* remembered that "Young Vestris astonished John Bull more by his agility than his grace, and some have been known to count the number of times he turned round like a tee-totum. This may be called *les tours des jambes*—not dancing." Horace Walpole in a letter of 17 December wrote:

The theatre was brimful in expectation of Vestris. At the end of the second act [of the opera *Ricimero*] he appeared; but with so much grace, agility, and strength, that the whole audience fell into convulsions of applause; the men thundered; the ladies, forgetting their delicacy and weakness, clapped with such vehemence, that seventeen broke their arms, sixty-nine sprained their wrists, and three cried bravo! bravissimo! so rashly, that they have not been able to utter so much as *no* since, any more than both Houses of Parliament.

On 23 January 1781 Vestris danced in the ballets *The Nymphs of Diana* and *The Rural Sports*, the first serious and the second "half-character." On 22 February he was given a benefit, tickets for which were available from him at No 5, Leicester Street, Leicester Fields. He danced in *The Country Diversions* and took the role of Colas in his father's ballet *Ninette à la cour*. It was the elder Vestris's first appearance in England. Walpole wrote that "the house could not receive and contain the multitudes the presented themselves. Their oblations amounted to fourteen hundred pounds." Dr Burney was thrilled by the "light fantastic toe of the younger Vestris." On 29 March, at Gaëtan's benefit, Auguste danced in *Les Caprices de Galatée* and was a Prince in his father's *Medée et Jason*. Edward Pigott saw *Medée et Jason* on 3 April and commented in his diary (now at Yale): "the Son, is not yet in his meridian of perfection; tho very Capital, he dances more in the high stile, but still in a very different manner from our nimble elegant Slingsby. . . ." The *Public Advertiser* on 7 June declared that "The Vestris' gave incontrovertible proof of the variety of their powers."

At the Opéra in Paris from 1772 to 1790 the younger Vestris was seen in dozens of ballets that were presented within operas or as separate works. He was Love in his father's *Endymion* in 1773, a Shepherd in *Echo et Narcisse* in 1779, Acis in *Les Caprices de Galatée* in 1780, Zéphyr in *L'Embarras des richesses* in 1782, Éveillé in *La Chercheuse d'esprit* in 1783, a Shepherd in *Renaud* in 1783, Daphnis in *Le Premier navigateur* in 1785, and a Garçon in *Le Coq du village* in 1787. He also had roles in such other ballets as *Sabinus*, *Céphale et Procris*, *Philémon et Baucis*, *Alceste*, *Thésée*, *Atys*, *Iphigénie en Aulide*, *Pénélope*, *Pizarre*, *Phèdre*, *Alcindor*, *OEdipe à Colonne*, *Amphitryon*, *Aspasie*, and *Les Pommiers et le moulin*. His annual salary was 4800 livres. He was imprisoned on 16 July 1784 for refusing to perform at the Paris Opéra before the King of Sweden.

Auguste Vestris returned to the King's Theatre in London for the 1783–84 season. His first appearance was on 6 December 1783 in *The Pastimes of Terpsycore* and *Friendship Leads to Love*. The *Public Advertiser* was ecstatic:

As to the Dances, such exquisite perfection was never seen in England before, because there certainly never was before seen such a band of transcendent Dancers simultaneously subsisting on the same Stage. . . . They were almost equally admirable. Thus, if Vestris and Theodore were most surprising, Lepicq and Rosse were more touching, Slingsby more exhibiting.

During the season Vestris danced a pas de deux with Mme Théodore and appeared in *Le Réveil du bonheur*, a divertissement, *L'Amitié conduite à l'Amour*, *Le Cocq du village* (at his benefit on 26 February), *Le Magnifique*, a *Dance of Shepherds*, *The Four Ages of Man*, *Pygmalion*, *Le Tuteur trompé*, *Le Déserteur*, and *Sémiramis*. On 8 May at Covent Garden Theatre a piece called *Marlborough*, choreographed by Auguste Vestris, was presented. During the season Vestris was living at No 37, Great Pulteney Street, Golden Square.

Vestris was at the King's Theatre again in 1785–86, dancing Acis in *Acis and Galatea* and Daphnis in *Le Premier navigateur* (at his benefit on 23 March 1786); he was also in *L'Amour jardinier*, *Les Deux Solitaires*, *Les Amans surpris*, *Ninette à la cour*, and other entr'acte dances. Vestris was serving as a choreographer, too, producing numbers from the Paris repertoire. But the *Public Advertiser* on 25 March 1786 indicated that Vestris was no longer such a favorite: "Vestris and Baccelli, tho' incomparable in some parts of the art, are far inferior as *actors* to Lepicq and Rossi. . . ." He was living at the time at No 8, Great Suffolk Street, Charing Cross.

Vestris returned in 1787–88, appearing first on 8 December 1787 in a new divertissement and *Les Offrandes à l'Amour*. During the rest of the season he danced in *The Military Dance*, *L'Amour et Psiché* (he played Cupid), a *pas de Russe* with Mlle Hilligsberg, *Les Fêtes de tempe*, *Euthyme et Eucharis* (he danced Eu-

Courtesy of the Fitzwilliam Museum, Cambridge

MARIE JEAN AUGUSTIN VESTRIS, and the Goose
by Nathaniel Dance

thyme), *Adela de Ponthieu*, and *La Bonté du Sei-gneur*. His benefit bill of 13 March 1788 noted that he was still living in Great Suffolk Street. The *General Advertiser* on 5 April praised the performance of two days before: "The Dance between Gardel and Vestris on Thursday is everywhere talked of, in the highest terms of admiration. Such excellence no audience ever before witnessed."

A news clipping in the Daly Collection at the Huntington Library, hand-dated 1789 but probably belonging to 1788, tells of an accident that befell Auguste:

Vestris, the dancer, has had a very narrow escape for his life: this charming dancer, on Sunday [sic], the 11th instant, while performing [rehearsing?] at the opera, experienced a fatal disaster; on his alighting after a surprizing vault, one of the traps gave way, and he fell seventeen feet and a half: fortunately a board, which accidentally lay across the machinery, stopped the further progress of the trap, or the fall would have been at least fifty feet. We are happy to add, he has received no other hurt than what may [be] supposed from the shock.

(There were never performances on Sundays, of course; during the 1787–88 season the eleventh fell on a Sunday in November 1787 and May 1788.)

Vestris danced at Lyon in February 1790. A letter written by Frederic Matthison, now among the Dixon Extracts at the Folger Shakespeare Library, is lavish in its praise for Vestris:

Lyons Feby 1790. A young man a perfect deity in his art, has lately by means of the magic powers with which the graces have endowed his feet, drawn an enchanted circle round the inhabitants of this place, in which he exercises a sway so absolute and undivided that the National Assembly is no longer mentioned, or, at least is only made the subject of conversation in obscure coffee-houses, & the workshops of mechanics; while Vestris the dancer is the exclusive object of attention in all the higher circles. Every night that he performed the concourse to the theatre was so great, that it was impossible to get a place without being there at least two hours before the commencement of the performance. I was present on the last night, and have actually in a great measure fallen in with the general enthusiasm.

It is indeed impossible not to be transported at the ease, the ability & harmony of all his motions: they are so exquisite, that he scarcely appears a mortal but rather a sylph, formed of etherial mould, and destined to skim aloft in higher regions. On that night, as being his last, he seemed emulous even to surpass himself, & scarcely was the performance ended, before wreaths of flowers of poetical, *morceaux* addressed to him, were thrown in abundance upon the stage, accompanied with the most incessant clapping, & earnest entreaties from the pit that he would not leave Lyons at the time he had fixed but if possible stay, and appear before the public at least once more. Upon this he came forward himself, & in the most graceful manner returned thanks for the undeserved applause with which he had been honoured by an audience so highly respectable and so distinguished for its refined and exalted taste; but he was penetrated with the deepest despair at the utter impossibility of complying with so flattering an invitation since the court had refused to prolong his leave of absence.

Vestris' figure is slender & elegant, his countenance is not handsome, but possesses a je ne sçai quoi extremely interesting and fascinating. The simplicity & modesty of his manners, form a striking contrast with the self conceited & supercilious manners of his father, who during the time of Voltaire's last stay at Paris, said, in a public company, "There are only three great men, now existing in the world, Vestris, Voltaire, & the King of Prussia." It is said, that while he was a boy, he would

Hirshhorn Museum and Sculpture Garden, Smithsonian Institution

MARIE JEAN AUGUSTIN VESTRIS
by Jean-Pierre Danton

not unfrequently hold out his foot to him, saying, "Kiss this immortal foot which enchants heaven & earth."

Auguste Vestris danced again at the King's Theatre in 1790–91, not appearing until 26 March 1791, in *Orpheus and Eurydice*. He then danced Hilus in *La Mort d'Hercule and his Apotheosis*, a role in *La Fête des Matelots et des Provençaux*, "Hilas Berger Thesalien, Amant d'Amadriade" in *L'Amadriade*, a pas de deux with Mlle Hilligsberg, *Les Folies d'Espagne* (his work), a pas de trois with Mlle Hilligsberg and Mlle Mozon, and Colin in *La Fête du seigneur*. His benefit tickets for 5 May 1791 were available from him at No 2, Haymarket.

A clipping at the Folger dated 1793 may refer to Auguste: "Among a fresh Transport of Fr. Prisoners of War recently arrived at Cologne is said to be the celebrated Vestres Jr first Dancer of the Opera of Paris who was obliged to take up Arms and march to the Frontiers."

In 1795 Vestris married the dancer Anne Catherine Augier, called Aimée (1777–1809); she had made her debut at the Opéra in 1793. Their son, Auguste Armand, was born in Paris in 1795, according to the *Enciclopedia dello spettacolo*; Grove dates his birth 1788 and does not name the mother. Anne Catherine died in 1809. Auguste Vestris married Jeanne Marie Tuillière in 1823.

Vestris retired from the Opéra on 27 September 1816 and spent his later years teaching such students as Fanny Elssler, Pauline Duvernay, Jules Perrot, and Marie Taglioni. He may have appeared at the King's Theatre in London in 1815; his son Auguste Armand had been there since 1809, serving as a dancer and ballet master. On 22 July 1819 the elder Vestris was imprisoned in France for debt. From 1821 to about 1826 Auguste was a professor at the École "de Perfectionment" and at the École "de grace" at the Opéra. According to Grove, Vestris danced in *Paul et Virginie* at the Opéra in 1826, and Lillian Moore in *Artists of the Dance* notes that at the age of 75 Vestris danced with Marie Taglioni on 8 April 1835. Marie Jean Augustin Vestris died in Montmartre, Paris, on 5 December 1842. His second wife, Jeanne, had died the previous 4 May.

Portraits of Marie Jean Augustin Vestris include:

1. Engraved portrait by C. Bretherton, Jr. Published on 15 August 1781.

2. Engraved portrait by H. Meyer, after J. E. Godolet. Published by Mathews & Leigh, 1809.

3. By unknown engraver. Published as a plate to *London Magazine*, May 1781.

4. In *Les Amans surpris*, standing, arms extended, wreath in right hand. Engraving by J. Thornthwaite, after J. Roberts. Published as a plate to *Bell's British Theatre*, 1781, 20 July 1782.

5. In *Ninette à la Cour*. By James Roberts, who also drew Gaëtan Vestris in this ballet. Both drawings by Roberts were in the sale of the Bell collection of drawings ("which have distinguished Bell's various editions") at Christie's on 27 March 1793 (lot 16).

6. As Colas in *Ninette à la Cour*. Engraving by C. Route, after G. Scorodoomoff. Published by the engraver, 1781.

7. In "Role de l'Enfant prodigue." Full-length, standing, right hand on breast. Engraving by Prud'hom, after Coeuré. Published as a plate to *Galérie Théatrale*, No 46.

8. By Nathaniel Dance. Caricature, pencil, black chalk, and watercolor (24.1 cm × 26 cm). Dancing, on right foot, arms spread, with goose at his right. Stage wings in background. In the Fitzwilliam Museum, Cambridge, acquired in 1963 from the executors of Bruce Ingram. An engraving, a front view, with geese in the lower spandrils, by F. Bartolozzi, was published on 2 April 1781. An engraving by Benedetto Pastorini, after Dance and Bartolozzi, shows the same pose but with a back view. A copy engraved by Gillray was published by A. Buengo on 18 January 1806.

9. By unknown engraver. A variation of the Dance caricature, above. Vestris dances on his right foot, back to front, with monkeys substituted for the geese; with quotation, "He Danc'd like a Monkey, his Pockets well cram'd." Published by W. Humphrey, 1781.

10. Drawing called "Vestris & the Goose." By Paul Sandby. At Christie's on 26 May 1959 (lot 101), from the William Sandby collection of drawings. See also No 6 in the list of pictures of Gaëtan Appoline Balthazar Vestris in this *Dictionary* and W. Sandby, *Thomas & Paul Sandby* (1892), pp. 40–41.

11. Caricature sculpture (11 1/2″ × 3 7/8 × 6½″). By Jean-Pierre Dantan, the younger. Dancing figure, in bronze. In the Hirshhorn Museum, Smithsonian Institution, Washington, D. C. Although sculpted in 1834, the statue was not cast until 1961.

12. Sculpture by Jean-Pierre Dantan, the younger, 1834. Bronze statue of Vestris as Zephir in *Psyché*. In the Musée Carnavalet, Paris.

A portrait in the Tate Gallery (No 1271), called "The Unknown Man" (and given by J. R. Swinton in 1888), had been identified as a portrait of Marie Jean Augustin Vestris by Gainsborough, but E. K. Waterhouse in *Checklist of Portraits by Thomas Gainsborough* rejects the identification of the sitter and suggests that the painting is by Gainsborough Dupont. C. M. Mount in *Gilbert Stuart* seems to suggest that the painting is a self-portrait by Stuart, with assistance from Dupont.

"Vestris, The Flying" *fl. 1786*₁, *equestrian.*

A young equestrian trained by the younger Astley performed at Astley's Amphitheatre in May and June 1786 as "The Flying Vestris."

Vetch. *See* VIETCH.

Vezein, Francis ₁Augustin?₁ *fl. 1720– 1780*₁, *violinist, dancing master.*

On 28 August 1739 Francis Vezein (or Vezin) became one of the original subscribers to the Royal Society of Musicians. He was probably the Augustin Vizin who in February 1720 had been one of the lower-ranking violinists in the Academy of Music opera orchestra, and he was surely the Mr "Vezan" spoken of by Dr Burney in his *General History of Music.* Burney called him a dancing master and an "excellent concert-player on the violin, and constantly employed whenever Carbonelli or Festing was the leader." *The Royal Society of Musicians* (1985) lists Vezein as working at the King's Theatre in the 1730s and as active in the Society to at least 1755 and states that he died "after 3 December 1780."

Vial. *See* VEAL *and* VEALE.

Vials, Mr *fl. 1797–1822*₁, *dancer.*

A Mr Vials was a dancer at Sadler's Wells Theatre by 1797; his name was published as a male dancer in the cast of *Sadak and Kalasrade* that year. He was also employed as a chorus dancer at Covent Garden Theatre from 1798–99 to 1801–2 and then at Drury Lane from 19 January 1802 through 1811–12 (when the company was at the Lyceum). At Drury Lane his salary was £1 5s. per week. He also performed in pantomimes at Sadler's Wells in 1803 and 1808 and probably during interim years.

Theatre account books show him at Covent Garden in 1815–16 and 1816–17 (at £1 5s. per week) and at Drury Lane in 1821–22 (at £1 10s. per week). A female dancer named Vials was at Drury Lane in 1808–9, at Covent Garden from 1810–11 through 1814–15, and

again at Drury Lane between 1815–16 and 1821–22, at a constant salary of £1 10s. per week.

Viblett, Mr *fl. 1675*₁, *violinist.*

Mr Viblett (or Violett) played French violin in the court masque *Calisto* on 15 February 1675.

Vico, Diana *fl. 1707–1726*₁, *singer.*

The Venetian contralto Diana Vico first sang in her native city in 1707, and she performed there off and on through 1726, appearing in 16 operas. In 1714 she came to London. She was later described by Dr Burney as a singer of secondary opera characters but a creditable member of the company at the King's Theatre; she was first mentioned as Ricimero in *Ernelinda* on 16 November 1714. During the rest of the 1714–15 season she was heard in the title role in *Rinaldo*, Vologeso in *Lucio Vero*, Segestes in *Arminio*, Dardanus in *Amadigi di Guala*, and Dario in *Idaspe*. The performance of *Lucio Vero* on 30 April 1715 was for her benefit. In February and March 1716 she repeated her role of Vologeso and also sang Mario in *Pirro and Demetrio*. On 26 May she received a benefit.

In the years that followed Signora Vico sang regularly in various towns in Italy: Bologna, Padua, Genoa, Florence, Turin, Reggio, and Modena. In 1720 she was in the service of the Elector of Bavaria, but by 1724 she was again in Italy, singing in Genoa and Naples. Her specialty was male roles.

She was caricatured by A. M. Zanetti in a drawing now in the Cini Foundation Library, Venice.

Victor, Mr *fl. 1791*₁, *dancer.*

On 26 March 1791, *Entertainments of Music and Dancing*, advertised for the Hanover Square Rooms, were given instead at the King's Theatre, where the right to perform operas was then in suspension. A dancer named Victor took part in a divertissement and in the ballet *Orpheus and Euridice*. Forty similar "entertainments," in most of which Victor was a participant, were given at the King's through 9 July.

Victor, Benjamin *d. 1778, actor, manager, treasurer, playwright, theatre historian.*

Benjamin Victor apprenticed as a barber and peruke maker, "within the liberties of Drury Lane," according to the *Biographica Dramatica* (1812), but he early evinced a strong attraction to the theatre. The *Survey of London* shows that he lived in Catherine Street, Covent Garden, from 1721 through 1724, and perhaps it was there that he established his trade in Norwich stuffs.

In 1722, having been introduced to Steele by Aaron Hill, Victor published *An Epistle to Sir Richard Steele*, countering John Dennis's attack on *The Conscious Lovers*. Victor continued to ply his trade as merchant, but he explored other avenues to fortune as well. In his *Original Letters* (1776), he printed one to Charles Mellish, dated 1730, which describes how Victor's friend Dr Younge brought him to the acquaintance of Lord Malpas, Master of the Horse to the Prince of Wales. Malpas procured Victor an audience, during which he presented a flattering poem to the Prince. But many days' "haunting of levées with unremitting assiduity," he remembered, produced only his satirical poem "The Levée Haunter" and not the position in the royal entourage for which he had angled.

In 1728, Victor was introduced to Booth the actor and began an acquaintance that resulted, in 1733, in *Memoirs of the Life of Barton Booth*. Victor himself experimented very briefly with acting, joining a company of casuals at the Lincoln's Inn Fields Theatre on 18 April 1734. Polydore in *The Orphan* was played by "Victor, who never performed before." Nor did he ever perform again, so far as the records reveal.

Victor reported in his letter to Mellish that he was advised by his city friends to branch out into the Irish linen trade. Accordingly, he made an exploratory trip to Dublin. Returning, "I took a large house in the middle of Pall Mall, over which you may now see your friend's name, in golden capitals, as the importer, and proprietor of Irish linens." In a letter of 1737, Victor spoke of his "House in St. James's Square, at the back of the Irish Linen Warehouse, Pall-Mall." Between 1734 and late 1745 he made two more trips to Ireland on business, but his affairs did not prosper. (He and his wife were living at "Mr. Woodifield's in Maiden-lane, Southampton-street, Covent Garden" on 16 November 1743, ac-

cording to a letter in Boaden's *Private Correspondence of David Garrick* [1831–32]).

On 11 October 1746, Victor settled with his family in Dublin as treasurer and deputy manager to Thomas Sheridan at Smock Alley Theatre. Victor quickly ingratiated himself with the Duke of Dorset when the Duke returned to Ireland as Lord Lieutenant in 1750, and began writing birthday odes for the ducal court at Dublin Castle. When Dorset was forced to resign his position in 1755, he placed Victor on the viceregal establishment as poet laureate of Ireland, with a stipend.

Victor had also made himself indispensable to Thomas Sheridan. But Sheridan was forced out of the Smock Alley management temporarily by the "Patriotic" rioting in 1753. Though Sheridan's troubles had been brought on largely by the public's perception of his closeness to Dorset, Victor, curiously, escaped the odium. Victor and the actor John Sowdon took over the theatre's management for two years. In a letter to Dorset, dated only September 1754, Victor furnished some details of the arrangement:

the late manager's affairs demanded the loan of two thousand pounds which I was to raise for him— for which his wardrobe, and the leases of both theatres were to be mortgaged—and by another deed he set them to me for two years, paying him five pounds every night of performance. Mr. Sowdon (an actor who came hither with the hopes of being a joint manager with Mr. Sheridan) having one thousand pounds for that purpose, I have taken him as my colleague—and thus, my lord, this affair was compleated on the first day of June last— Mr. Sowdon went off to London immediately to engage actors for the approaching season, and left me to repair and direct the theatre, which was greatly wanted.

(LaTourette Stockwell, in *Dublin Theatres and Theatre Customs*, cites three documents from the Dublin Office of the Register of Deeds confirming those transactions. She also records a mortgage of the theatre from Victor to John Tickell on 20 December 1755 and an assignment of Victor's one-half interest to Georges Edmund Howard on 26 June 1756.)

Sheridan returned to the Smock Alley management on 15 July 1755, and Victor reverted to his *status quo ante*. He later testified that he was "well contented to return to my former Station . . . and by that means to a *Certainty*."

But there was no "certainty." For Sheridan's old Dublin enemies among the "Patriots" still attacked him; creditors were clamorous; and there were several fractious actors in the company. There also was an acrimonious exchange of pamphlets over Sheridan's attempt to prevent Spranger Barry from building the Crow Street Theatre, which nevertheless opened on 23 October 1758 and provided difficult competition. Victor had signed on at Smock Alley for £100 a season and a benefit, but it is not clear that he always collected; and much of the increasingly onerous business of the house fell on Victor because of Sheridan's absences. Victor returned to England in 1759, not rich but at least not in debt. His first wife had died sometime in 1757. By June of 1759 he had married again. (The maiden name of neither lady is known; neither one acted.)

From the season of 1759–60 until his death in 1778 Victor was treasurer of Drury Lane Theatre, an office he seems to have discharged with honesty and efficiency. In 1761, he published in two volumes *The history of the theatres of London and Dublin, from the year 1730 to the present time. To which is added, An annual register of all the plays, &c. performed at the Theatres-Royal in London, from the year 1712. With occasional notes and anecdotes*. A second edition, with a third volume, came out later that year, and a "continuation" of the annual register was issued in 1771. The work is discursive, greatly incomplete, and marred by Victor's obtrusive ego, but useful, especially for its anecdotes of actors.

Victor also had ambitions as dramatist and poet. On 22 November 1762, Garrick kindly produced Victor's alteration of *The Two Gentlemen of Verona*, which achieved five scattered performances before 25 January 1763. On that night a "Benefit for the author of the Alterations" was attempted but was canceled after a riot by the audience, which demanded admission at half price after the third act. (Victor furnishes a full account of the riot in the third volume of his *History*.) The alteration was published in 1763.

In 1766 Victor urgently attempted to induce Garrick to stage his tragedy *Altamira* but was not successful. It and another tragedy, *The Fatal Error*, a comedy, *The Fortunate Peasant; or, Nature Will Prevail*, and *The Sacrifice; or, Cupid's Vagaries: a Musical Mask*, were all pub-

lished in Victor's three-volume *Original Letters, dramatic pieces, and poems*, 1776. His only other known publication was the anonymous *The Widow of the Wood*, scandalous gossip about the Wolseley family, so offensive to them that they bought up and destroyed every copy they could find. It was published in 1755 at Dublin and republished at Glasgow in 1769.

Francis Gentleman the actor-critic treated Victor with derision in *The Theatres* (1772)— a "laurel-crowned *Esquire*" who "was a barber, attempted to be an actor, became a treasurer, then a manager in Dublin; where, in fortune's frolics, though not able to write a dying speech, he was appointed *Birth-day Ode Man*, and—oh poor Ireland!—his wife complimented with a pension." The "blockhead" was guilty of "barb'rous rhime" and of "grinning assent" to Garrick's poor management "with consequence and snuff." But Gentleman was at odds with Garrick in 1772 and was writing anonymously as "Sir Nicholas Nipclose."

Isaac Reed treated Victor only a little more gently in *Biographia Dramatica* (1812):

This gentleman's singularities (for some he had) were of quite an innocent nature. He regarded the proper arrangement of a playhouse as the greatest and most important task proposed to human abilities. He was therefore solemnly and tediously circumstantial in his accounts of entrances and exits P.S. and O.P.; described to an inch the height of every plume, and the length of every train . . . ; and dwelt much on the advantages received by many authors, as well as actors, from his experience and admonitions. He likewise contrived to prolong these his narratives by repeated summonses to attention, such as "Sir, sir, sir; observe, observe, observe;" and was the most faithful chronologer of a jest, a riot, or any other incident. . . . The disgusting pronoun *I* being . . . too lavishly employed in his *History of the Stage*, our late satirist, Mr. Churchill, observed that Victor ego should have been its motto.

The aged actress Hester Santlow Booth, remembering his early biography of her husband Barton Booth, left Victor 50 guineas in her will, proved 3 March 1773. He was then living in Maiden Lane, Covent Garden. Benjamin Victor died at his lodgings in Charles Street, Covent Garden, on 3 December 1778, "at an advanced age, and without previous sickness or pain," according to Isaac Reed.

Victoria, Signora. *See* VITTORIA, [ARGENTINA?].

Vida. *See* VEDIE.

Vidale, Robert [fl. c. 1673–1676], actor.

Robert "Vudale" is listed in a Lord Chamberlain's warrant, dated around 1673–74 and cited by Milhous and Hume in the *Register of English Theatrical Documents*. He was probably the actor Robert "Visdale" named in a similar warrant dated 11 September 1674 and the Robert "Vidale" listed in *The London Stage* as a member of the King's Company in 1675–76.

Vidanay. *See* VIDINI.

Vidi. *See* VÉDIE.

Vidini, John Baptist [fl. 1768–1785], violinist.

Upon the recommendation of Joseph Yorke, the violinist John Baptist (Giovanni Battista) Vidini and his wife Sga Victoria Vidini, a dancer, were engaged by Garrick at Drury Lane in 1768–69. Sga Vidini's name began to appear in the bills in the autumn of 1768, but Vidini's employment there is known only by a letter from Yorke, written from the Hague, to Garrick on 22 March 1774:

Constant in my attachments you will think me so too in my importunities, but the attention with which you received my former application in favor of Madlle. Vidini & Mr Jean Baptiste Vidini, encourages me to trouble you once more—I understand that in May last [1773], having other engagements, you had dismist the abovementioned, assuring them that you were satisfied with their behaviour, but could not keep them any longer. . . .

Yorke's solicitation was unsuccessful and the Vidinis did not return to Drury Lane. She soon went over to Covent Garden and he was engaged in the band of the opera at the King's Theatre by 1779. In that year, on 7 February, Vidini was recommended for membership in the Royal Society of Musicians. At that time, in addition to the opera, he was engaged at the Pantheon and in Bach's concerts. He was described as a married man, without children.

Vidini was admitted to the Society on 4 April 1779, but was expelled in 1787 for nonpayment of his subscription.

Vidini was listed by Dr Burney as a second violinist in the Handel Memorial Concerts at Westminster Abbey and the Pantheon in May and June 1784. Manuscripts in the Public Record Office place him still at the opera in 1785.

Vidini's wife performed in London until 1782. When she corresponded with the committee of the Drury Lane Fund in 1808 her husband evidently was already dead. She died in 1822.

Vidini, Signora John Baptist, Victoria *d. 1822, dancer.*

With her husband, the violinist John Baptist Vidini, the dancer Sga Victoria Vidini arrived in London from the Continent in the autumn of 1768. Upon the recommendation of Joseph Yorke, they were engaged by Garrick at Drury Lane in 1768–69. Sga Vidini's name was first noticed in the bills on 16 November 1768 when she performed a new pantomime dance and a *Turkish Dance* with D'Egville. On 5 December she danced a new allemande with D'Egville. With that dancer as her partner she appeared in a variety of specialty dances throughout that season and the following four, until at the end of 1772–73 (when her salary was £5 per week) Sga Vidini and her husband were discharged. In a letter to Garrick on 22 March 1774 (quoted in Signor Vidini's notice) Joseph Yorke tried, to no avail, to persuade the Drury Lane manager to reengage the Vidinis.

She danced at the King's Theatre in the spring of 1774, her name first appearing in that theatre's bills on 24 March for performing with Mlle Heinel, Fierville, and Asselin in a chaconne, a provençale, and a *Polish Ballet*. In October 1774 she began an engagement at Covent Garden Theatre that lasted two seasons. In 1776–77 she was back at Drury Lane, no longer under Garrick's management, but in 1777–78 she returned to Covent Garden for a brief engagement. She also danced at the Theatre Royal, Bristol, in summers from 1774 through 1776.

In 1779 Sga Vidini returned to the King's Theatre to perform a new ballet, *Les Oiseleurs,* with Signor and Sga Zuchelli on 23 January. She appeared in *Hippomène et Atalante* with Mlle Baccelli on 25 March.

Her name next appeared in London bills on 11 July 1782, when she danced at the Haymarket Theatre as Medea in *Medea and Jason*. There on 17 August she appeared in a grand ballet. In 1783 she was still listed as a "Figure dancer" at the Opera, though it is not known whether she performed there that season or anywhere else thereafter.

According to James Winston's records of the Drury Lane Theatrical Fund (at the Folger Shakespeare Library), Victoria Vidini claimed on the fund in March 1786. In the summer of 1808 she had some problem with the Fund Committee. On 21 May 1808 "Madam Vidanay was wrote to attend . . . they not thinking well of her Certificate." On 19 June was recorded "A Frank ans^r from Vidany." On 8 July Moody gave Maddocks her latest letters with "an English translation of the last." Finally, on 12 July the committee gave Maddocks the authority "to pay Madam Vidining's arrears." Thereafter she received a quarterly annuity of £10. She died, according to Winston's notation, in 1822.

Her husband, who was in the band at the King's Theatre until at least 1785, does not seem to have been alive in 1808 when Sga Vidini was corresponding with the trustees of the Drury Lane Fund.

Vidining. *See* VIDINI.

Viebar, Signor *fl. 1722₁,* *lutanist.*
At a concert at Drury Lane Theatre on 14 March 1722 Signor Viebar played a solo of his own composition on the arch lute.

Vietch, Mr *fl. 1780–1781₁,* *manager.*
Benefit tickets delivered by Mr Vietch (or Vetch) were accepted at the Haymarket Theatre on 5 April 1780. On 26 March 1781 Vietch presented a licensed entertainment at the Haymarket.

Viganò, Mons *fl. 1791₁,* *dancer.*
A Monsieur Viganò was with D'Auberval's troupe of leading European dancers that performed at the remodeled Pantheon in London during 1791. Probably he was related to Salvatore and Maria Viganò, who were members of the same company, and had performed with them in Paris and Bordeaux in recent seasons. In London Mons Viganò was paid £70 for the engagement, plus a travel allowance of £10, according to information provided to us by Judith Milhous. His name did not appear in any of the bills, but no doubt he danced in the chorus of *The Deserter* and other ballets requiring a large number of dancers.

Vigano, Pietro *fl. 1784–1785₁,* *opera performer, music copyright?*
Pietro Vigano was paid a salary of £50 as an opera performer in 1784–85 at the King's theatre, according to a document in the Public Record Office. Such a low salary would suggest he was a singer in the chorus. The Drury Lane treasurer paid a Mr Vigano, perhaps Pietro, £3 3s. on 17 December 1796 for copying music.

Viganò, Salvatore *1769–1821,* *dancer, choreographer, composer.*
Born at Naples on 25 March 1769, Salvatore Viganò was the son of the choreographer and ballet director Onorato Viganò and his wife Maria Ester Boccherini, ballerina sister of the composer Luigi Boccherini. Salvatore's brother Guilio Viganò and his sister Celestina (later Mme D'Rossi) were also dancers on the Continent, as were his paternal uncles Antonio and Giovanni Viganò.

Salvatore was early trained in music, studying composition with Boccherini. He composed music for one of his father's ballets, *Cefalo e Procri,* at Venice in 1786. Subsequently he composed for others of his father's works and some of his own. But by 1783 Salvatore had danced, in female roles, at the Teatro Argentina in Rome, where his father was ballet director. In 1788 he went with his uncle Giovanni to perform at the coronation celebrations for Charles VI at Madrid. There he met and married the beautiful dancer Maria Medina. Also at Madrid he met Jean D'Auberval, who took him on as a pupil and engaged the couple at the Grand Théâtre in Bordeaux. Viganò was signed for the Paris Opéra season of 1789–90, but the outbreak of the Revolution

Civica Raccolta Stampe A. Bertarelli, Milan

SALVATORE VIGANÒ
engraving after Bertotti

Harvard Theatre Collection

SALVATORE VIGANÒ
engraving by Altini, after Corporali

persuaded him to stay at Bordeaux for another season.

Early in 1791 D'Auberval led a group of leading European dancers to join Robert O'Reilly's new opera venture at the remodeled Pantheon in London. With the troupe were Salvatore and Maria Viganò, Duquesney, Mme Didelot, D'Egville and his wife, and Mlles Léonore and Rosine Simonet. The Viganòs, hired at a salary of £500, made their debut at the Pantheon on 17 February 1791, dancing in D'Auberval's *Amphion et Thalie*, a ballet that was performed a total of 19 times that season. Horace Walpole was there and found the whole evening "ill-conducted," including the dances, which were "long and bad." On 30 April they danced in D'Auberval's *La Fille mal gardée*. On 9 May *La Siège de Cythère*, another ballet by D'Auberval, was premiered; in that ballet the Viganòs danced Lucanians for 13 performances.

The Pantheon ended its season, after 55 nights of operas and ballets, on 19 *July 1791, and Viganò* returned to Venice to assist his father, who was dance director at the Teatro San Samuele. Salvatore and his wife became popular successes in Venice, where that year he made his debut as a choreographer with two new ballets, *I Divertimenti di Amore* and *Raul, Signore di Crechi*. In the latter, a *Ballo tragicom-*

ica, almost the entire cast consisted of Viganòs, including Salvatore as the Gaoler's Son, his wife as the Gaoler's Daughter, and other roles filled by his mother, father, brother Guilio, and uncle Giovanni. He also staged D'Auberval's *La Fille mal gardée*. The company moved to their new theatre, Le Fenice, in 1792.

In 1793 the Viganòs were contracted to Vienna. There, on 13 May, Salvatore and Maria made their first appearances and soon triumphed in their pas de deux pantomime, in which Maria's fine figure was emphasized in flimsy, revealing costumes.

(According to the *Oracle* of 5 April 1796, the musician Charles Weichsel "lately" in Italy had married a Signora Vigano, a dancer, but it is unlikely she would have been Salvatore's wife Maria, for the Viganòs continued to perform together until at least 1799.)

The Viganòs appeared together at the Teatro S. Bernadetto in Venice during Carnival 1799, but soon afterward they separated, because Maria was unfaithful. All but one of

Courtesy of the Derra de Moroda Dance Archives, Salzburg University, and the Harvard Theatre Collection

Studies of SALVATORE and MARIA VIGANÒ
by Schadow

their children died in infancy, reports Winter, in whose book information on others of the Viganò clan may be found.

Salvatore became ballet master at Vienna in 1799. The company that he directed there until 1803 was, in the judgment of M. H. Winter in *The Pre-Romantic Ballet*, "in its own way as brilliant as that of the Paris Opéra, if a company which becomes a perfect instrument for executing the choreographer's intentions is a criterion." During that period the Viganòs also toured Germany and Austria and returned to Venice on occasion. At Vienna on 16 February 1801 his *Die Geschöpfe des Prometheus* was first danced to Beethoven's music, but it was received without enthusiasm.

In 1812 Viganò joined La Scala, and at Milan he created his most celebrated ballets, *Gli Strelitzi, Riccardo Cuor di Leone, Il Noce di Benevento, Ippotoo Vendicato*, and *Clotilda, Duchessa di Salerno*. In such ballets as *Prometeo, Dadalo*, and *I titani* (described by Winter as "epic studies of mankind's evolution with the developing, endless, unresolved struggle between his good and evil impulses") Viganò was preoccupied with the treatment of moral and ethical questions. In *La vestale, La Spada di Kenneth*, and *Giovanna d'Arco*, he explored themes of individual confrontation. His ballets were termed "choreodramas" by C. Ritorni in *Commentarii della vita e delle opere coreodrammatiche di Salvatore Viganò* (Milan, 1838). His success made him very prosperous; according to a letter by Henri Beyli he earned 44,000 francs "in 1819 alone," when 4,000 francs would be considered the usual income for a ballet composer.

Viganò died at Milan on 10 August 1821 at the age of 52, perhaps having been exhausted by intensive working habits, in which he often consumed many months to achieve his "grandiose conceptions." He had been, in Winter's words, "the towering figure in Austria and Italy."

Portraits of Salvatore Viganò include:

1. Engraving by A. Altini, after F. Caporali (after Bettoni).

2. Engraving of a bust in marble by Bertotti. Published at Milan, 1838.

3. Engraving by G. Bignami, after Bertotti. Published at Milan, 1838.

4. Engraving by G. Gallina, after Ricordi.

5. Drawing by G. Lancedelli, of Salvatore

and his wife Maria dancing at Vienna in 1793. In the possession of Gilberte Cournand. Reproduced by M. H. Winter in *Pre-Romantic Ballet*, p. 186.

6. Engraving by C. Pfeiffer, after Dorffmeister. Published at Vienna, 1794.

7. Engraving by Rados. Published at Milan, 1821.

8. Engraving by N. Rhein, after P. C. Stroely. Published 1793.

9. Drawings by Johann G. Schadow, four studies of Salvatore and his wife Maria in a pas de deux. In the Derra de Moroda Dance Archives, Salzburg University.

10. Engraving by G. Scotto.

11. In a painting by G. de Araciel of the choreographer Guiseppe Rota, the sitter is shown holding in his hands a bust of Salvatore Viganò. In the Museo Teatrale alla Scala, Milan.

In addition to Nos 5 and 9 above, portraits of Maria Viganò include an engraving by C. Pfeiffer, after J. Dorffmeister, published at Vienna, 1794, showing her dancing in the clouds; and an engraving by N. Rheim, after P. C. Stroely, published in 1793, showing her in a dancing attitude.

Viganò, Signora Salvatore, Maria, née Medina ₍*fl. 1788–1799*₎, *dancer. See* VIGANÒ, SALVATORE.

Viganoni, Giuseppe   *d. 1823, singer.*

The tenor Giuseppe Viganoni, engaged as first buffo for the opera, made his debut in London at the King's Theatre on 11 December 1781 as Giannetto in *I viaggiatori felici*. He sang in *La buona figliuola* on 10 January 1782, and on 28 February illness prevented him from repeating that role. He recovered by 2 March to sing Berto in *La contadina in corte*, and he performed Fidamente in *Il bacio* on 9 April 1782. Burney called him a "feeble" singer, not much in favor with the public that season.

The following season at the King's Theatre he appeared as Il Cavalier del Lampo in *Il convito*, Giorgio in *Il trionfo della costanza*, Ali in *Zemira e Azore*, Buonatutto in *Il vecchi burlati*, and Stafanello in *L'Avaro*.

Over the next decade Viganoni sang on the Continent. Michael Kelly visited him at Lucca and heard him sing Sandrino in *Il re Teodoro* at

MARIA VIGANÒ

engraving by Pfeiffer, after Dorffmeister

Vienna on 23 August 1784. During the late 1780s he also sang with the Italian Opera in the Faubourg St Germain, Paris.

In 1795 Viganoni returned to London. At the King's Theatre in 1795–96 he received £1,000 and a benefit, reappearing on 15 March 1796 singing a principal role in *I due gobbi* and then Oreste in *Ifigenia in Tauride* on 7 April, Gianferante in *La modista raggiratrice* on 16 April, in *La buona figliuola* on 5 May, Creonte in *Antigona* on 24 May, Buonafede in *Il Tesoro* on 14 June, and Ali in *Zemira e Azore* on 23 July 1796. The last-mentioned performance was for his benefit, and tickets were available from him at No 13, Pall Mall. The *Morning Chronicle* of 16 March 1796 reported that Viganoni had a "small but a very pleasing voice," and he sang with passion and sentiment; his "science is perfect; and he manages his powers with very polished skill." The *Monthly Mirror* of February 1796 was also very positive: "Viganoni, the new singer, has great taste and uncommon flexibility; as an actor he stands first on the Italian stage; and on the English there are not many before him. He is one of the very few public performers in the

kingdom, that can look and walk like a *gentleman*."

Viganoni's other roles at the King's Theatre included Capitano in *L'amor fra le vendemmie*, Lindoro in *Il consiglio imprudente*, Arviro in *Evelina*, Admeto in *Alceste*, Tamigi in *Le nozze del Tamigi e Bellona*, a role in *Gli schiavi per amore*, Endimione in *L'albero di Diana*, Lindoro in *Nina*, Il Marchese in *Le gelosie villane* for his benefit on 8 June 1797, when tickets were available from him at No 8, Panton Street, Haymarket, and Egisto in *Merope* in 1796–97; Linceo in *Ipermestra*, Arsace in *Semiramide*, Conte Lelio in *La scola dei maritati*, Cinna in *Cinna*, Milord Fideling in *La Cifra*, Conte Ciacinto in *La sposa in equivoco*, Aldelvoto in *Elfrida*, and a principal character in *Il barbiere di Siviglia* in 1797–98; Arsace in *Medonte*, Don Pietro in *Ines de Castro*, a role in *La Frascatana*, Brunello in *I due Svizzeri*, and Enea in *Didone* in 1798–99; and a role in *I zingari in fiera*, Silvio in *I due fratelli rivali*, Timoteo in *Alessandro e Timoteo* (first time on 6 May 1800), Gelindo Scagliozzi in *Il capriccio drammatico*, and Tiridate in *Zenobia of Armenia* in 1799–1800.

Viganoni sang for Salomon's concert at Willis's Rooms in King Street on 7 April 1798. Burney wrote to his daughter Fanny about

GIUSEPPE VIGANONI

engraving by Piaggio

VIGANONI

Civica Raccolta Stampe A. Bertarelli, Milan

GIUSEPPE VIGANONI

engraving by Cardon, after Villiers

hearing him at Mr Walker's concert and supper one evening in May 1799.

His friend Kelly, with whom he often traveled, heard Viganoni sing in *Nina* at the Italian Opera in Paris, before Napoleon. Viganoni
continued at the King's Theatre, London,
through 1804–5. According to Roger Fiske,
editor of Michael Kelly's *Reminiscences* (1975),
Viganoni died in 1823.

A portrait of Viganoni engraved by D.
Piaggio was published in 1793. His portrait
by H. Villiers was engraved by A. Cardon and
was published in 1804; a copy was engraved
by Sasso. Viganoni was pictured in one of 25
medallion miniatures of singers and musicians
by H. de Janvry published on one plate at
London in 1801; the layout of the plate was
designed by P. J. De Loutherbourg, and the
engraving was by Landseer.

Villars, Mons *fl.* 1748–1750,
dancer, actor.

A Monsieur Villars was a member of the
company of French players brought over by
Jean Louis Monnet to perform in London in
1748–49. Villars played Squire in performances of *Harlequin Captive* in Phillips's booth
at Southwark Fair in August 1748, and he
was a member of the French cast of *Les amans
réunis*, the performance of which was disturbed at the Haymarket Theatre on 14 November 1749. Anti-French demonstrations
plagued the company's efforts to perform that
season, and Monnet was thrown into deep financial trouble. According to an account of
disbursements, printed in *The London Stage*,
for 22 May 1750 (the night Drury Lane gave
a benefit for the bankrupt Monnet) Villars
was to receive £32 15s. for his engagement in
London.

For an account of the problems experienced
by Monnet and his company, see his notice in
this *Dictionary*, vol. 10.

Villars, Mr *fl.* 1786–1812?,, *actor,
singer, scene painter?*

A Mr Villars sang the song "Nobody" at the
end of a performance of *She Stoops to Conquer* at
the Windsor Castle Inn, King Street, Hammersmith, on 5 June 1786. That night Mrs
Villars acted Miss Hardcastle in Goldsmith's
comedy. There on 7 June Villars played Old
Norval in *Douglas* and Major Sturgeon in *The
Mayor of Garratt.*

He was probably the Villars who acted at
Edinburgh in 1787 and 1788, his known
roles being the Prompter in *The Critic* on 21
February 1787 and an unspecified part in *A
Peep behind the Curtain* on 16 April 1788. According to T. J. Dibdin's *Reminiscences*, in 1789
Villars was a pompous, corpulent actor at
Dover, who boasted that he had written a
comedy in five acts; Villars found fault with
everything and everybody, but his wife was
the best actress in the company.

Advertised as from Norwich, Villars played
Lord Glenmore in *The Chapter of Accidents* at
the Haymarket Theatre on 2 June 1794. In
September 1795 he and his wife acted at Cheltenham. Possibly he was the Villars who was
acting with the Edinburgh company from
1809–10 through 1811–12, though that person may have been the "Villars Jr" (probably
his son), who with his wife acted in Ireland
from 1797 to 1798. A Villars painted scenery
at the Arthur Street Theatre in Belfast in
1806.

Our subject perhaps was the son of the actress Mrs Villars, a widow who married William Pero, a provincial manager, at Belfast on 24 March 1778. She died at Retford on 14 September 1804 at age 73. She had never appeared on the London stage.

Villars, Mrs _fl._ 1780–1795₁, _actress, singer._

A Mrs Villars acted Mrs Hardcastle in a performance of _She Stoops to Conquer_ at the Windsor Castle Inn, King Street, Hammersmith, on 5 June 1786. That night Mr Villars sang at the end of the play. Two nights later, on 7 June, she played Mrs Sneak in _The Mayor of Garratt_, and Mr Villars acted Major Sturgeon in that afterpiece and also Old Norval in _Douglas_, the mainpiece.

This Mrs Villars was not the provincial actress of that name who as a widow married William Pero, a provincial manager, at Belfast on 24 March 1778 and died at Retford on 14 September 1804 at age 73. Our subject, however, may well have been that Mrs Villars's daughter-in-law.

With her husband, Mrs Villars had acted with the companies at York in 1780 and probably in other seasons in that decade. In 1787–88 at the Theatre Royal, Shakespeare Square, Edinburgh, she appeared in some 40 roles, among them Beatrice in _The Anatomist_, the Chambermaid in _The Jealous Wife_, Jacintha in _The Suspicious Husband_, Midas in _Juno_, Kitty Pry in _The Lying Valet_, Lucy in _The Rivals_, Maria in _Twelfth Night_, Nerissa in _The Merchant of Venice_, a Singing Witch in _Macbeth_, Ursula in _Much Ado about Nothing_, and Wheedle in _The Miser_. That repertoire suggests that Mrs Villars was young-looking and probably pretty. She also acted at Cheltenham with her husband in September 1795.

The Miss and Miss C. Villars, sisters, who acted at Gloucester and Weymouth in 1802, were probably her daughters. The "Villars Jr" who toured Ireland with his wife from 1797 to 1799 was perhaps her son.

Villars, Miss _fl._ 1793–1802?₁, _actress._

"A Young Lady," who was said to be making her first appearance on any stage, played the title role in the farce _Polly Honeycombe_ at the Haymarket Theatre on 26 August 1793. A manuscript list in the Haymarket bills in the Harvard Theatre Collection identifies her as Miss "Villers." The _European Magazine_ of August 1793, however, reported that "A young Lady, whose name is said to be COOPER, made an unsuccessful attempt at the Haymarket, in the character of Polly Honeycomb."

Perhaps she was one of the daughters of the provincial actors Mr and Mrs Villars, who appeared at Hammersmith in 1786. A Miss Villars and her sister Miss C. Villars acted at Gloucester and Weymouth in 1802; the _Monthly Mirror_ of July 1802 claimed that Miss C. Villars had more merit than her sister and, considering her youth, had acquitted herself respectably as Cowslip in _The Agreeable Surprise._

Ville, Mons de'Ferrou. _See_ D'FERROU VILLE, MONS.

Villeneuve, Mr _fl._ 1734–1763₁, _dancer._

The dancer Villeneuve was first mentioned in London playbills on 21 October 1734, when he was Mezzetin in _The Harlot's Progress_ at Drury Lane Theatre. He was seen regularly there during the rest of the 1734–35 season, appearing as a Wind in _The Tempest_, a Triton and Mandarin Gormogon in _Cephalus and Procris_, a Masquerader and one of Les Capricieux in _Columbine Courtezan_, a Fury in _Merlin_, and an Attendant on Apollo in _Harlequin Orpheus_. During the season he also served as an entr'acte dancer. He danced Punch in a new "Chocone" at the Haymarket Theatre on 27 December (a night when he was also dancing at Drury Lane), and on 12 June 1735 he shared a benefit with Miss Oates at Lincoln's Inn Fields Theatre.

Villeneuve remained at Drury Lane through the 1736–37 season, dancing between the acts and appearing in such new parts as a Country Lad in _Harlequin Restored_, a Moor and a Season in _The Fall of Phaeton_, and a Country Lad in _The Burgomaster Trick'd_. In July and August 1737 he danced between the acts at Lincoln's Inn Fields.

From 1737–38 through 1755–56 Villeneuve was a member of John Rich's company at Covent Garden Theatre. His first appearance there was on 3 October 1737, when he danced in _Je ne scai quoi_ with Tench and Miss

Oates. Thereafter he appeared as an entr'acte dancer and as a Mezzetin Man and Fury in *The Necromancer*, a Zephyr, Pluto, and Apollo in *The Royal Chace*, Air and a Fury in *The Rape of Proserpine*, an Infernal in *Perseus and Andromeda*, a Huntsman, Apollo, and a Frenchman in *Apollo and Daphne*, a Swain, Demon, and Country Lad in *Orpheus and Eurydice*, and an Aerial Spirit and Apollo in *Merlin's Cave*. By 1746–47 he was earning £1 weekly for his work, but by then his name appeared with less frequency in the bills. Perhaps by the 1750s Villeneuve was also serving the theatre as a ballet master, for he received solo benefits even though his dancing appearances were few. His last benefit (and the last mention of him in London bills) was on 27 April 1756. His wife's dancing career ran parallel to his for a number of years.

Our subject was probably related to some of the performers in France named Villeneuve. Max Fuchs in his *Lexique* identified our subject as the Villeneuve at the Hague in 1762–63.

Villeneuve, Mrs   *fl.* 1735–1752₁, dancer, actress, singer.

On 15 September 1735 Mrs Villeneuve danced a Gardener's Wife in *Harlequin Grand Volgi*; performing that night was Mr Villeneuve, also a dancer. The careers of the pair ran parallel for several years. During the rest of the 1735–36 season at Drury Lane Mrs Villeneuve danced between the acts and was seen as a Milkmaid in *Harlequin Restored*, Clara in *Rule a Wife and Have a Wife*, a Lady of Pleasure in *The Harlot's Progress*, a Lady of Pleasure in *Columbine Courtezan*, Betty in *The Twin Rivals*, a Follower of Adonis and an Hour in *The Fall of Phaeton*, Myrtilla in *The Provok'd Husband*, and Lucy in *The Livery Rake and Country Lass*. She remained at Drury Lane in 1736–37 adding Margaret in *The Squire of Alsatia*, Mrs Coaxer in *The Beggar's Opera*, and Bellinda in *The Eunuch*.

Villeneuve moved to Covent Garden Theatre in the fall of 1737, but Mrs Villeneuve seems to have left the stage for two seasons. She joined her husband at Covent Garden on 10 August 1739, when she played Lucy in *The Beggar's Opera*. Between then and December 1752 she danced in entr'acte entertainments and was seen in such parts as a Peasant, a Follower of Daphne, and a Polonese in *Apollo and Daphne*, an Amazon and a Country Lass in *Perseus and Andromeda*, a Follower of Eurydice, a Nymph, a Villager, and a Country Lass in *Orpheus and Eurydice*, a Scaramouch Woman in *The Necromancer*, Lightning in *The Rehearsal*, Air and a Sylvan in *The Rape of Proserpine*, a Follower of Comus in *Comus*, an Aerial Spirit in *The Royal Chace*, Betty Doxy in *The Beggar's Opera*, and an Aerial Spirit in *Merlin's Cave*. By 1746–47 she was earning 10s. weekly. Only once did she perform elsewhere during her tenure at Covent Garden: on 23 August 1740 she played Nancy in *The Parting Lovers* at Bartholomew Fair. Her last appearance was on 7 December 1752 at Covent Garden, when she played a Demon in *The Necromancer*.

Villeneuve, Miss   *fl.* 1739₁,   dancer.

Miss Villeneuve, presumably a relative of the dancers Mr and Mrs Villeneuve (their daughter?), danced a *Tambourine* on 17 and 19 September and 2 October 1739 at Covent Garden Theatre. Curiously, the bills said she was "not lately arrived from Paris," according to *The London Stage*.

Villeneuve, George   *fl.* 1784–1915₁, violist, double-bass player.

Dr Burney's list of participants in the Handel Memorial Concerts at Westminster Abbey and the Pantheon in May and June 1784 includes a Mr "Villenieu" among the tenor (viola) players. He was, we believe, George Villeneuve the younger, listed in Doane's *Musical Directory* of 1794 as a double-bass player and violist. George was a member of the New Musical Fund and the Academy of Ancient Music; Doane said that Villeneuve had participated in the Handel performances in Westminster Abbey. He lived at No 6, Newman Street, Oxford Street, and served on the Court of Assistants for the New Musical Fund in 1794 and (again or still?) in 1815.

Villeneuve, George   *fl.* 1794₁,   musician?

George Villeneuve the elder was an honorary subscriber to the New Musical Fund in 1794. We cannot be certain that he was a musician.

Villepierre, Mlle *fl. 1734–1735₁, dancer.*

Mlle (sometimes Mme) Villepierre danced a Sylvan in *The Rape of Proserpine* at Convent Garden Theatre on 30 December 1734. She danced in *The Faithful Shepherd* on 22 February and 17 April 1735, and on 23 April for her benefit she appeared as Lisette in *La Double inconstance* at the Haymarket Theatre, her first appearance on that stage.

Villers, Miss. *See* VILLARS, MISS.

Villiers, Miss *fl. 1773?-1781₁, actress.*

Miss Villiers was advertised for an unspecified role in *The Spendthrift*, an anonymous comedy (dubiously attributed to Samuel Foote) that was performed by special license at the Haymarket Theatre on 12 November 1781. Perhaps she was the "Young Lady" who had made her stage debut as Lucia in *Cato* at the Smock Alley Theatre, Dublin, on 26 February 1773, for Miss Villiers was assigned that role on 12 March 1773, when the *Dublin Mercury* announced she was making "her 2nd app. on any stage."

Villiers, Densengencracolas *fl. 1734–1736₁, dancer.*

A dancer called "Mons Densengencracolas," advertised as making his first appearance on the English stage, performed a French peasant dance and *Le Rostand sabotier* at Lincoln's Inn Fields Theatre on 3 May 1734. He was one of the Drury Lane company after the seceders returned to that theatre on 10 March 1734. Probably he was "Mr De Villiers" who had a benefit at the Haymarket Theatre on 11 February 1736, though no record of his having danced that night survives.

Vincent, Mr *fl. 1750₁, actor.*

A Mr Vincent acted Brindavoine in performances of *L'Avare* at the Haymarket Theatre on 26 February and 1 and 7 March 1750. The company was English but they acted in French, playing also French translations of *The Recruiting Officer* and *The Beggar's Opera*. Vincent's name did not appear in the bills for the latter two pieces.

Vincent, Mr *fl. 1760₁, actor.*

A Mr Vincent acted the role of Nottingham in *The Earl of Essex* at Covent Garden Theatre on 15 October 1760.

Vincent, Mr *fl. 1761–1763₁, dancer.*

A Mr Vincent was a member of the dancing ensemble at Drury Lane Theater in 1761–62 and 1762–63. He regularly performed in such ballets and pantomimes as *Arcadia, The Genii, Fortunatus, The Witches, The Magician of the Mountain,* and in the dancing numbers in *Cymbeline, The Tempest, Much Ado about Nothing,* and *Romeo and Juliet.*

Vincent, The Messrs *fl. 1784₁, singers.*

Mr Vincent, a countertenor, and Mr Vincent "Jr," a tenor, were among the vocalists listed by Dr Burney in the Handel Memorial Concerts at Westminster Abbey and the Pantheon in May and June 1784.

Vincent, Mr *fl. 1789–1795₁, singer, actor.*

A Mr Vincent was first noticed among the chorus singers at the Haymarket on 11 August 1789 and a few nights thereafter in the musical drama *The Battle of Hexham.* On 13 November following he was heard at Drury Lane in the chorus of the ballad opera *The Island of St Marguerite.* He returned to sing twice in the chorus at the Haymarket the following summer and then was recorded no more at the patent theatres.

Vincent sang specialty songs at Sadler's Wells performances of *The Savages* in 1791 and the musical *Queen Dido* on 9 April 1792, and he played Thames in *The Hall of Augusta,* an Officer in *Sans Culottes,* and an Austrian Officer in *The Honours of War* in 1793, and Time in *Pandora's Box* and a Wool Stapler in *Momus's Gift* in 1795. After that, he dropped out of sight.

Vincent, Mrs *fl. 1677₁, actress.*

A Mrs Vincent played Aurelia in *Scaramouch* at Drury Lane Theatre on 5 May 1677.

Vincent, Mrs *fl. 1715–1716₁, actress.*

Mrs Vincent—possibly related to the Mrs Vincent who acted in 1677—played a number of roles at Lincoln's Inn Fields theatre from 11 January 1715 to 4 July 1716: Rutland in *The Unhappy Favorite*, Olivia in *Love in a Sack*, Clara in *The False Count*, Honoria in *Love Makes a Man*, Teraminta in *The Wife's Relief*, Lucinda in *2 Don Quixote*, Lucinda in *The Lucky Prodigal*, Celia in *The Woman's Revenge*, Eliza in *The Plain Dealer*, and Chloris in *The Woman Captain*. She shared a benefit with Coker on 18 May 1716; receipts came to over £65.

Vincent, Mrs *fl. 1723–1735*], actress, dancer.

The Mrs Vincent who acted at Lincoln's Inn Fields Theatre from 1723 to 1735 may have been the Mrs Vincent who appeared there in 1715 and 1716, but certain identification is not possible. Our subject received her first notice on 7 October 1723, when she acted Isabinda in *The Busy Body*. That role, and others she acted in the 1723–24 season, suggest an experienced actress. She played Bellemante in *The Emperor of the Moon*, Lady Anne in *Richard III*, Lady Truman in *The Drummer*, Kate in *1 Henry IV*, Lady No in *The London Cuckolds*, Aurelia in *Cutter of Coleman Street*, Imoinda in *Oroonoko*, Lady Dunce in *The Soldier's Fortune*, Angelina in *Like to Like*, and Matilda in *Edwin*. She shared a benefit with Cross the numberer on 10 April 1724; receipts came to about £105. In the summer of 1724 she performed at both Lincoln's Inn Fields and the Richmond Theatre, playing Belinda in *The Fair Quaker of Deal*, Leanthe in *Love and a Bottle*, and Belliza in *Love's Contrivance* at the former and Scentwell in *The Busy Body* and Teresa in *The Spanish Fryar* at the latter. On 2 September she appeared at Southwark Fair as Lucy in *Merlin*.

In the seasons that followed, Mrs Vincent added such new parts as Isabella in *The Squire of Alsatia*, Clara in *The Cheats of Scapin*, Ophelia in *Hamlet*, Honoria in *Bath Unmask'd*, Dorinda in *The Stratagem*, Biancha in *The Taming of the Shrew*, Hour in *Mars and Venus*, Mrs Apwigeon in *The Female Fortune Teller*, a Peasant Woman in *Apollo and Daphne*, Emilia in *The Fond Husband*, Mrs Woodly in *Epsom Wells*, Lady Ample in *The Wits*, a Country Lass in

The Rape of Proserpine, Scaramouch's Wife in *The Loves of Damon and Clemene*, Araminta in *The Confederacy*, Belinda in *Tunbridge Walks*, Mrs Ford in *The Merry Wives of Windsor*, Eugenia in *The London Cuckolds*, Paraba in *Sesostris*, Arabella in *The Wife's Relief*, Isabella in *The False Friend*, Lettice in *Sylvia*, Casana in *The Prophetess*, Angelina in *Love Makes a Man*, and (at the new Covent Garden Theatre) an Amazon in *Perseus and Andromeda*. Her last known appearance was in that last role on 13 February 1735. From 1732 on Mrs Vincent performed infrequently.

Her salary in September 1724 was 10s. daily. Her benefits, always shared with one other person, sometimes brought in almost £150 and rarely dropped below £100. The *Index to The London Stage* conflates the Mrs Vincent of 1715 and 1716 and our subject, calling the conflation "Mary Vincent." But Mary Vincent played only one character: Mrs Vixen in *The Beggar's Opera* on 1 January 1729 and throughout the month. She was one of a number of "Lilliputians" (children) in the cast and may have been our subject's relative.

Vincent, Miss. See also FERGUSON, MRS.

Vincent, Miss *fl. 1762–1771*], actress, dancer.

A Miss Vincent, announced anonymously as a young gentlewoman who had never appeared before, acted Miss Sprightly in *The Counterfeit Heiress* and danced a minuet with Signor Sodi at Covent Garden Theatre on 16 April 1762. The young gentlewoman is identified as Miss Vincent in Reed's "Notitia Dramatica" in the British Library. That night's performance was for the benefit of Mrs Elizabeth Vincent (née Bircks), who acted Myrtilla in the same comedy, so no doubt the neophyte was her daughter. Miss Vincent's father, then, was Richard Vincent the elder (1701–1783), a musician in the Covent Garden band. About 19 months later, Miss Vincent's name appeared in the Covent Garden bills for Miss Biddy Bellair in *Miss in Her Teens* on 15 November 1763, when it was stated that she was making her second appearance on any stage. Her mother acted Tag that night.

Among the other roles Miss Vincent acted at Covent Garden in 1763–64, her first full season, were Isabella in *The Squire of Alsatia,* Corinna in *The City Wives Confederacy,* Rose in *The Recruiting Officer,* Parisatis in *The Rival Queens,* and Serina in *The Orphan.* In 1764–65 she added to her repertoire Cherry in *The Stratagem,* Rosara in *She Wou'd and She Wou'd Not,* Anne Page in *The Merry Wives of Windsor,* Lady Blanch in *King John,* Arabella in *The Male Coquette,* Miss Prue in *Love for Love,* Bridge in *Every Man in His Humour,* and Miss Hoyden in *The Relapse.* She played some of the above roles in 1765–66 and added Mincing in *The Way of the World,* Miss Jenny in *The Provok'd Husband,* and Miranda in *The Busy Body.* She played Harriet in *The Miser* for the first time on 1 January 1767. The *Rational Rosciad* wrote of her that year:

> *Attention, junior Vincent must attract*
> *Who on our hearts so sensibly does act;*
> *A bud, in execution now she glows,*
> *For favour to expand her to a rose.*

After the 1767–68 season Miss Vincent was not reengaged at Covent Garden and perhaps went to perform in the provinces. She did appear again in London occasionally in 1770–71, at the Haymarket out of season, acting Scentwell in *The Busy Body* on 5 October 1770, Margery in *The Miller of Mansfield* on 21 November, Isabella in *The Mistake* on 14 December, and Leonora in *The Mourning Bride* on 4 March 1771.

Miss Vincent's brother Richard Vincent the younger (d. 1766) was a London musician. Another brother, Charles Vincent, acted at Drury Lane briefly in 1777.

Vincent, Charles *fl.* 1777–1795], *actor.*

The "Young Gentleman" who made his first appearance on the stage at Drury Lane Theatre on 22 January 1777 as Dorilas in *Merope* was identified in a notation by J. P. Kemble on a playbill as Mr Vincent. The *Monthly Mirror* some years later (November 1801) also identified him as such and as the son of the Covent Garden musician Richard Vincent the elder (1701–1783). His mother, then, presumably was the actress Elizabeth Vincent (née Bincks). Charles's sister, Miss Vincent, had made her debut at Covent Garden on 16 April 1762, some 15 years before his. Their brother Richard Vincent the younger (d. 1766) was a musician who married the Drury Lane actress Isabella Burchell.

Charles Vincent's debut as Dorilas was witnessed by Tate Wilkinson, who in his *Wandering Patentee* reported that "taken for all in all, it was one of the best first performances I thought I ever witnessed." Vincent's second appearance at Drury Lane was as George Barnwell in *The London Merchant* on 6 June 1777, when his name appeared in the bills. Less than a fortnight later he was acting in the summer company at Richmond, Surrey; a clipping in the Richmond Reference Library, dated 17 June 1777, reports that "Mr Vincent in Florizel [*Florizel and Perdita*] convinced us that with a strict attention to the Stage, and assiduity to his business, we may pronounce him, without flattery, if not a capital, a very promising young man." While visiting Jefferson at Richmond that summer Wilkinson met Vincent and found him "the very pink of courtesy; pocket was seldom consulted, so elegance and ease could be purchased." Vincent then kept a gondola "for his health" and took daily traverses on the Thames.

Wilkinson was so impressed with Vincent's style that he hired him for his northern circuit: "I, on my part, never entered into any one engagement more eagerly," he wrote. Vincent acted Romeo at Wakefield on 10 September 1777, but to Wilkinson's surprise and dismay "he could not be heard in any part of that Theatre distinctly." Moreover, he was imperfect in his lines, a fault Wilkinson conjectured he had been led into by "his love of ease," for he was in that respect "a second David Ross, who was the Prince of negligence." Next he failed as Tyrrel in *The Fashionable Lover,* and while playing Hamlet at Doncaster on 22 September 1777 "the same fault of the deficiency of lungs appeared again," and he had little success in "adhering to the text," so Wilkinson dismissed him.

Subsequently Vincent, according to Wilkinson, suffered "various adventures, good fortunes, and misfortunes." He was twice married, and "got a decent fortune with both his partners," and also had a family. After taking orders, Vincent kept a school near Wakefield where he was respected as a teacher and orator, and by 1795 he was also curate of St

Civica Raccolta Stampe A. Bertarelli, Milan

CHARLES VINCENT, as Dorilas

engraving by Reading, after Roberts

John's in Leeds. The actor Tom King recorded in his journal on 14 May 1789 taking tea with Wilkinson and Vincent ("formerly on the Stage, now in orders") and then being brought by Vincent to Leeds.

In the Borthwick Institute at York University are papers relating to one Charles Vincent, who was ordained and nominated assistant curate at the Chapel of Ofset in the parish of Dewsbury on 15 July 1787, but that person, according to an extract of the baptismal register at St Faith the Virgin, London, for 13 January 1754, was the son of William and Mary Vincent.

A picture of Vincent as Dorilas in *Merope* by an anonymous engraver, after J. Roberts, was published as a plate to *Bell's British Theatre,* 12 February 1777. A copy engraved by B. Reading was published by Bell in November 1777.

Vincent, J. ₍*fl. 1793–1794*₎, *singer.*
J. Vincent, of Silver Street, Bloomsbury Market, was listed in Doane's *Musical Directory* for 1794 as an alto who performed in the Ox-

ford Meeting in 1793 and in the Handel Memorial Concerts at Westminster Abbey; he also sang in the concerts of the Academy of Ancient Music.

Vincent, James *d. 1749, organist.*
James Vincent was one of the original subscribers to the Declaration of Trust that established the Royal Society of Musicians in August 1739. Also signatories were his father Thomas Vincent the elder (d. 1751?), a bassoonist in the Guards; the oboist Thomas Vincent the younger (c. 1720–1783); and Richard Vincent the elder (1701–1783), an instrumentalist and composer.

James died on 6 October 1749. His obituary in that month's *London Magazine* described him as "James Vincent, joint organist of the Inner Temple Church with Mr. Stanley, also organist of St. Luke's in Old Street." Dr Burney identified him as the brother of the younger Thomas Vincent and son of the elder Thomas Vincent and called him "a brilliant performer."

Compositions by him listed in the *Catalogue of Printed Music in the British Museum* include *Advice to Cupid* (1735?), *Delia Constant* (1740?), *Love's Bacchanal* (1745), *On a Lady Stung by a Bee* (1754), and *Strephon Charm'd, or the Surpriz'd Fair* (1735?).

Vincent, Mary ₍*fl. 1729*₎, *actress.*
Mary Vincent played Mrs Vixen in *The Beggar's Opera* from 1 through 27 January 1729 at Lincoln's Inn Fields Theatre. She was evidently a child, for the production was advertised as being by a company of Lilliputians.

Vincent, Pasqual ₍*fl. 1784–1788*₎, *tumbler.*
A Mr Vincent was a member of a company of tumblers and dancers (including Scaglioni's dancing dogs) advertised as from Sadler's Wells, which came to Coopers' Hall, Bristol, for an engagement beginning 11 December 1784. A Chester playbill of 29 October 1787 advertised "A Select Troop (Engaged for Four Nights) from SADLER'S WELLS," one member of which was "The Famous Venetian Pasqual Vincent," who would

perform several most surprising Feats of Activity, consisting of Ground and Lofty tumbling &c.

without Batule, Spring Board, or any other Assistance . . . , exhibit in a surprising Manner the
Grand Rondado D'Arriva with a Variety of Surprising Performances, with Tables, Chairs, &c.
and turn Eight Somersets at once, with other Feats
not to be equalled by any in the Kingdom.

Pasqual Vincent's London appearances have
not been recorded. He performed at the Theatre Royal, Norwich, at some time in 1788.

Vincent, Richard   *1701–1783, instru-
mentalist, composer.*

The August 1783 issue of the *Gentleman's
Magazine* announced the death in Tottenham
Court Road on 10 August of Richard Vincent,
aged 82, and described him as "the oldest
Musician belonging to Covent-garden playhouse and to Vauxhall-gardens, who enjoyed,
till the last year of his life, a remarkable flow
of spirits."

Vincent's musical career had begun by
1720, for about 15 February of that year his
name was placed on a list of members of the
opera band at the Academy of Music, as a
fourth-rank bassoonist earning £40 per year.
He was a member of the King's Musick by 1
April 1724, on which date he was paid for
"playing in the *Te Deum* at St James's."

He was one of the original subscribers to
the Declaration of Trust that established the
Royal Society of Musicians in August 1739.
Also charter members were his brother, the
bassoonist Thomas Vincent the elder (d.
1751?); and the latter's sons Thomas Vincent
the younger (c. 1720–1783) and James Vincent (d. 1749).

Richard Vincent played harpsichord in a
concerto given for Collett's benefit at Hickford's Room on 24 March 1737. He also
played harpsichord in a subscription concert
in the Great Room, Dean Street, Soho, on 11
January 1752, among the many other concerts
he doubtless assisted in during his long career.
He was probably the Mr Vincent who was
paid 5s. per night as a member of the Covent
Garden orchestra in 1767–68. The *Monthly
Mirror* of November 1801 described him as a
"good musician" in the Covent Garden orchestra, particularly on the oboe. In 1769 he
lived in the Little Piazza, Covent Garden.

At St Benet, Paul's Wharf, on 12 December
1737 Richard Vincent had married Elizabeth
Bincks (sometimes Binks), a young actress

and probably the daughter of the Mrs Bincks
who was a dresser at Covent Garden Theatre
from 1735 to 1740. Elizabeth Bincks made
her debut at Lincoln's Inn Fields Theatre in
1729 and acted there and at the new Covent
Garden Theatre in the 1730s. She was billed
as Mrs Vincent beginning 12 January 1738.
Elizabeth Vincent maintained an active career
on the London stage into the 1770s, though,
as Francis Gentleman put it in his *Dramatic
Censor* (1770), "much advanced in years."

At least three of Richard and Elizabeth's
children became members of the profession.
Their son Richard Vincent the younger (d.
1766), also a musician, who lived in the area
of Covent Garden, married the Drury Lane actress Isabella Burchell, later Mrs John Mills
(1735–1802). Another son, Charles Vincent
(fl. 1777–1795), acted at Drury Lane for a
short while in 1777 and joined Wilkinson's
company at Wakefield in September 1777; he
proved unsuccessful as an actor and by 1795
was curate of St John's in Leeds. The *Monthly
Mirror* of November 1801 called him the
youngest son of Mrs Vincent of Covent Garden Theatre. A Miss Vincent (1762–1771),
no doubt a daughter of Richard and Elizabeth
Vincent, made her debut at Covent Garden
Theatre at the latter's benefit on 16 April
1762 and performed at that house through
1767–68. The St Paul, Covent Garden, registers record the baptism on 30 April 1758 of
Sarah, the illegitimate daughter of "Richard
Vincent, Sr."

The will of a Richard Vincent that was
proved at London on 2 August 1783 could not
have been our subject's, as he did not die until
10 August. That person's wife was named Isabella, and they had five children baptized at
St Paul, Covent Garden, in the 1740s. Perhaps the families were related.

The original *Catalogue of Printed Music in the
British Museum* credited the elder Richard Vincent with *A Sett of Familiar Lessons for the Harpsichord . . . Opera 2d*, printed by John Cox, at
Simpson's, for the author (1748), but the later
edition credits that work to Thomas Vincent
(c. 1720–1783).

Vincent, Mrs Richard, Elizabeth, née
Bincks   *b. c. 1708, actress.*

Elizabeth Bincks, when a child, made her
appearance on the stage of Lincoln's Inn Fields

Theatre on 1 January 1729 as Macheath in a production of *The Beggar's Opera* performed by a Lilliputian company that also included the young Henry Woodward, who had three roles in the production. Probably Elizabeth was the daughter of the Mrs Bincks who was a dresser at Covent Garden Theatre from 1735 to 1740; Mrs Bincks perhaps had been a house servant at Rich's Lincoln's Inn Fields Theatre by the time of Elizabeth's debut.

Two years after her debut as Macheath, Miss Bincks, now a young woman, acted Jenny in *The Provok'd Husband* at Lincoln's Inn Fields on 2 November 1731. On 18 April 1732 she played an unspecified role in *The Maggot,* and on 3 May 1732 she appeared as Ophelia to Ryan's Hamlet. In 1732–33 she was a regular member of Rich's company, playing Ophelia, Jenny, and Penelope in *Tunbridge Walks* at Lincoln's Inn Fields during the first half of the season. Then at the new Covent Garden Theatre she acted Lesbia in *Achilles* on 10 February 1733, followed by Lucy in *The Beggar's Opera,* the Young Duke of Malfy in *The Fatal Secret,* Lady Loverule in *The Devil to Pay,* Betty in *The Mock Lawyer,* Lucy in *Oroonoko,* Helen in *The Rape of Helen,* Eliza in *The Plain Dealer,* and Lucia in *A Cure for Covetousness.* Sometimes her name appeared in the bills spelled "Binks."

At Covent Garden over the next four seasons Miss Bincks continued to act the roles noted above and added such parts as Valeria in *The Rover,* Alinda in *The Pilgrim,* Isabella in *The Squire of Alsatia,* Sylvia in *The Recruiting Officer,* Margery in *The Country Wife,* Angelica in *The Gamester,* Phillis in *The Conscious Lovers,* Hoyden in *The Relapse,* Cephisa in *The Distrest Mother,* and Miranda in *The Busy Body.* In the summer of 1735 she performed with the company at Richmond, Surrey, and also was seen as Silvia in *The Constant Couple* in Fielding and Oates's booth at Bartholomew Fair on 24 August 1734.

On 12 December 1737 Miss Bincks married the Covent Garden musician Richard Vincent the elder (1701–1783) at St Benet, Paul's Wharf. When Elizabeth returned to Covent Garden on 2 January 1738 to act Arabella in *The Fair Quaker of Deal* she was advertised as Mrs Vincent. She then enjoyed an uninterrupted engagement at Covent Garden through 1747–48, playing a familiar reper-

toire of young ladies in comedies. Her salary in 1746–47 was £3 per week. She also performed summers at Richmond, Surrey, in 1743 and regularly from 1746 through 1750.

In 1748–49 Mrs Vincent took up an engagement with Sheridan at the Smock Alley Theatre in Dublin, where she first appeared on 3 October 1748 as Rosalind in *As You Like It.* Chetwood, who had seen her act in London some seven years earlier, found her a "greatly improved" performer. Among her numerous other roles in Dublin that season were Portia to Macklin's Shylock, Desdemona to Sheridan's Othello, Lucy in *The Beggar's Opera,* Lady Froth in *The Double Dealer,* Ophelia in *Hamlet,* Imoinda in *Oroonoko,* Amanda in *The Relapse,* and Millamant in *The Way of the World.*

Mrs Vincent returned to Covent Garden Theatre in 1749–50 to resume her accustomed line. Her address for benefit tickets between 1750 and 1752 was at the Cock and Turk's Head in Bedford Street. In the 23 seasons from 1749–50 to 1772–73 she remained regularly at Covent Garden, playing dozens of parts. Many of her youthful roles she clung to for some years. Toward the end of her career she did assume such parts as Mrs Peachum in *The Beggar's Opera,* the Duchess of York in *Richard III,* the Queen in *Cymbeline,* Sysigambis in *The Rival Queens,* Calphurnia in *Julius Caesar,* and the Duchess of Suffolk in *Lady Jane Gray.* She also acted Goneril in *King Lear,* Isabel in *Henry V,* Queen Elinor in *King John,* and Nerissa in *The Merchant of Venice.* She introduced Anna in the original London cast of *Douglas* on 14 March 1757. Her salary in 1760–61 was 13s. 4d. per day, a figure that remained constant at least through 1767–68.

The *Rational Rosciad* in 1767 condemned her:

Vincent, still disagreeably the same,
Without a spark of vivifying flame,
Blunders continually in all she plays,
Merits much censure, and deserves no praise.

Five years earlier *The Rosciad of C--v--nt G--rd--n* (1762) had described her faults:

NEXT V--NC--NT comes, in robes of purple clad;
Who simpers, tho' her part be e'er so sad;
Whose scrieching voice one's very brain distracts,
Whose action makes one grieve she ever acts.
When sounding MARTIAN's steady soul she's seen,
And as PULCHERIA strives to ape a queen,

We plainly see, with no great stretch of art,
She minds her person much more than her part;—
Better to show her airs, and affectation,
She walks a peeress at the Coronation;
Of borrow'd robes seems not a little proud,
*And struts, like *******, thro' the gazing croud.*

In *The Theatres* (1771) Francis Gentleman criticized Colman for keeping her on:

Make harass'd Vincent, verg'd on sixty-three,
Smirk, cant and trip thro' girls in tragedy.

Though she was a wonderfully worthy "mother, friend, and wife," Gentleman declared her unworthy for the stage; her "age cries loudly for the fund."

At the end of the 1772–73 season she was discharged from Covent Garden, perhaps unfairly, according to a letter by Kitty Clive dated 6 October 1773:

. . . I have been greatly shocked to hear the Managers of Covent Garden Theatre have behaved so famously [*sic*] to Mrs Vincent as to discharge her after her long services and amiable behaviour and after her having been received by the publick in some of the most principal parts. I had an opportunity of saying a great deal to Mr Coleman. I was quite angry; he lays it on the others. . . .

According to Richard J. Smith's manuscript "History of the Stage" in the British Library (11826.r.), Elizabeth Vincent was still alive in 1777. It is possible that she was the Mrs Vincent who earned £1 11s. 6d. per day at Liverpool in the summer of 1778, but that person more likely was the provincial actress of that name who had acted at Edinburgh with her husband in March 1777.

Elizabeth Vincent's husband Richard, described as the old musician at Covent Garden Theatre, died on 10 August 1783 at the age of 82. His obituary notice in that month's *Gentleman's Magazine* did not mention a widow. At least three of their children became performers. A son, Richard Vincent the younger (d. 1766), a musician, married the actress Isabella Burchell; another son, Charles Vincent (fl. 1777–1795), acted briefly in London in 1777 but then became a schoolmaster and churchman; and a daughter, Miss Vincent (fl. 1762–1771), made her debut at Covent Garden on 16 April 1762 and performed at that theatre through 1767–68. The *Gentleman's Magazine* of August 1792 reported the death on 4 August at Kentish Town, after a long illness, of "Mrs Binks, of King-str. Covent-garden."

Vincent, Richard   *d. 1766, instrumentalist, composer.*

Richard Vincent was the son of the musician Richard Vincent the elder (1701–1783), a bassoonist who at his death in 1783 at the age of 82 was the oldest musician belonging to Covent Garden Theatre and Vauxhall Gardens. His mother was Elizabeth, née Bincks, who acted in London for many years under both her maiden and married names. He was the nephew of Thomas Vincent the elder and the cousin of Thomas Vincent the younger (c. 1720–1783) and James Vincent (d. 1749), both musicians.

Though we find no contemporary bills placing Richard Vincent as an employee at any theatre or pleasure garden, it is not unlikely that he joined others in his family, including his father, in employment in those places. *Mortimer's London Directory* of 1763 called him a player on the violin and kettledrum but cited no specific engagements. He lived at that time in King Street, Covent Garden, near the patent houses. The *Monthly Mirror* of November 1801, however, referred to him as a leader of the band at Vauxhall at the time of his marriage in 1755. Dr Burney wrote that Richard Vincent "for more than thirty years the principal hautbois at Covent-garden, was, *ab origine,* in the Vauxhall band." He had become a member of the Royal Society of Musicians on 5 January 1752.

On 25 August 1755 at St Paul, Covent Garden, Richard Vincent married Isabella Burchell, of the parish of St Mary Lambeth, an actress and singer at Vauxhall Gardens who thereafter performed as Mrs Vincent for some years at Marylebone Gardens and Drury Lane Theatre.

Richard Vincent died in London on 28 August 1766 and was buried at St Paul, Covent Garden, on 31 August. On 25 August 1766, three days before his death, he had made his will, which he signed "Rich. Vincent Junr." Describing himself as of the parish of St Marylebone, Vincent bequeathed all of his estate, unspecified, to his "loving Wife Isabella," to whom administration was granted on 10 December 1766. His widow married Captain

John Mills in October 1767 and went with him to India until 1771, when she returned to act a few times over the next two years. She died in 1802.

Our subject's brother Charles Vincent made his debut at Drury Lane on 22 January 1777 and had a brief stage career before taking orders. Their sister, Miss Vincent, made her debut at Covent Garden on 16 April 1762 and acted in London several seasons.

Richard Vincent and his wife Isabella had at least three children, at least one of whom went on the stage. They are named in the notice of Isabella Vincent.

Vincent, Mrs Richard, Isabella, née Burchell, later Mrs John Mills *1735– 1802, singer, actress.*

Isabella Burchell was born in Surrey in 1735, and as a girl, it is said, she worked as a milkmaid on the Surrey estate of Jonathan Tyers, the Vauxhall proprietor. He discovered her talents, gave her a musical education, and in 1751, when she was 16, introduced her as a singer at his pleasure gardens. The song *Young Colin was the bonniest Swain* was published that year as sung by her at Vauxhall. For nine years she entertained there as a popular singer. On 25 May 1754 Arthur Murphy wrote in his *Gray's Inn Journal* that her "Voice is improved to a great Degree of Perfection." Several collections of songs sung by her, Lowe, and Miss Stevenson were published in the 1750s.

On 25 August 1755 at St Paul, Covent Garden, she married the oboist Richard Vincent the younger, who was at that time a musician in the Vauxhall band. Isabella was described in the marriage register as "of St Mary Lambeth," and the marriage, allowed "by license," was witnessed by the actress Elizabeth Vincent, Richard Vincent's mother. Isabella continued at Vauxhall as Mrs Vincent, and after several years and pregnancies, she was engaged by Garrick, who introduced her at Drury Lane Theatre on 23 September 1760 in the role of Polly in *The Beggar's Opera.* On 20 October she sang in the procession in *Romeo and Juliet,* and on 17 November she had a vocal part in *The Tears and Triumphs of Parnassus,* an elegy on the death of George II. On 13 December she was Zaida in *The Enchanter,* and

By permission of the Trustees of the British Museum

Said to be ISABELLA VINCENT (but doubtful)

engraving by Smith, after Engleheart

on 30 March 1761 she sang with Lowe and Champness in a *New Coronation Ode.* For her benefit on 9 April 1761 she acted her first and one of her very few tragic roles, Ophelia in *Hamlet.* On 29 April she was in the chorus for *Macbeth.*

At Drury Lane in 1761–62 Mrs Vincent's assignments included singing in the masque in *Cymbeline,* a vocal part in *Florizel and Perdita,* and many appearances to sing such specialty numbers as "The Lark's Shrill Note," "Hearts of Oak," and "The Camp Alarm'd." Tickets for her benefit on 20 April 1762 could be had from her at the "Norwich Stuff Warehouse" in King Street, Covent Garden. In 1762–63 she performed a vocal part in *The Musical Lady,* Amaryllis in *The Spring* (for which she was praised in the *Public Advertiser*), and Arethusa in *The Contrivance.* In *The Battle of the Players* (1762), she was said to be "not yet completely versed in all the Arts and Strategems of War" but "a great support of the Garrickeans; and . . . in Time, she will be found capable of supporting the highest Poets, with Honour and Dignity."

Her portrayal of Helena in the Garrick-Colman version of *A Midsummer Night's Dream,* which opened on 23 November 1763, was damned along with nearly all else connected with the production. The prompter Hopkins wrote in his diary, "Upon the whole, never was anything so murder'd in the speaking. Mr W. Palmer and Mrs Vincent were beyond description bad. . . ." On 2 November 1764 she played Zara in Rolt's new serious opera *Almana,* and on 13 November she sang in *The Genii.* She went over to the Haymarket Theatre on 14 November 1764 to perform in *Acis and Galatea* for the benefit of the family of a fire victim. Back at Drury Lane she sang in *The Winter's Tale* on 26 March 1765 and also offered a number of specialty songs during the season, for which she was paid 16s. 8d. per day, or £5 per week.

By the summer of 1765 she had become a leading vocalist at Marylebone Gardens, where she offered songs by Arne and Handel, often accompanied by a new instrument called the "Tintinnabula." For her benefit there on 3 July 1766, tickets were available "at her Lodgings, at Mr More's, Grocers, next to the Savoy Gate in the Strand."

In *The Rosciad,* Charles Churchill praised her Polly in *The Beggar's Opera* for her simplicity and naturalness and favored her portrayal over Charlotte Brent's. On 21 January 1766, however, Hopkins noted in his diary that she was "imperfect" in Polly (i.e., she did not have her lines under control). When Sylas Neville saw her as Arethusa on 1 May 1767 he told his diary that "Widow Vincent's voice pleases me much." Her husband had died on 28 August 1766. In his will made three days before his death, Richard Vincent left his entire estate, value unknown, to his "loving wife Isabella," to whom administration was granted on 10 December 1766.

In her last season at Drury Lane, 1766–67, still earning £5 per week, she sang in *The Hermit, Romeo and Juliet, Cymbeline, Macbeth,* and *Marriage à la Mode* and played Ceres in *The Tempest* and Polly in *The Beggar's Opera.*

After appearing at Marylebone Gardens in the summer of 1767 (on the last night of the season, 18 September, singing in *Solomon*), she "quitted the Stage" to marry at the Chapel Royal, the Savoy, on 24 October 1767 Capt John Mills (1727–1811), then a civil servant,

one of the survivors of the Black Hole of Calcutta. After her marriage she reportedly spent several years in India. The *New Grove* incorrectly states that she returned to London to act Mrs Peachum at Covent Garden in 1771, 1772, and 1773; that actress was Elizabeth Vincent (née Bincks).

The *Monthly Mirror* of June 1802 announced that on 9 June "Mrs. Mills, wife of Captain Mills, of Hampstead Road," had died, and identified her as the former performer Mrs Vincent. She was buried in the Old St Pancras churchyard. The inscription on her tombstone, now obliterated, read: "In Memory of Mrs. Isabella Mills / Wife of John Mills, Esq. / Of this Parish / Who departed this life June 9, 1802. / Aged 67 Years." There followed several verses in her praise.

(Some confusion surrounds the Christian name of Captain Mills, for it seems that Lysons in his *Environs* mistranscribed it as James. A notation in the British Library copy of the *Environs* corrects it to John. The *European Magazine* of September 1802 called him John; but the same journal, in August 1811, reported his death at the age of 89 and called him Jacob Mills, of Camden Town. No doubt John was his name, and it was entered in the register of the Savoy Chapel Royal when he married Mrs Vincent in 1767 and on his tombstone in Old St Pancras churchyard: "John Mills, Esq. / Who departed this Life 29th July, 1811, / Aged 90 years."

The registers of St Paul, Covent Garden, record the baptisms of three girls, the daughters of Richard Vincent by his wife Isabella: Elizabeth, baptized on 26 September 1757; Sophia, baptized on 20 February 1760 and buried on 3 March; and Penelope Louisa, baptized on 24 May 1763 and buried on 27 September of that year.

The surviving child Elizabeth may have become the adult actress who made her debut anonymously at Covent Garden as Polly in *The Beggar's Opera* on 29 March 1788. The *Gazetteer* gave her married name as Mrs Ferguson and stated she was making her second appearance on any stage. Her first probably had been at Richmond, Surrey, for the *European Magazine* of 1790 stated that about 1788 a Mrs Ferguson, who was the daughter of the Drury Lane actress Mrs Vincent, had performed at

Richmond. If Mrs Ferguson was Isabella Vincent's daughter Elizabeth who was born in 1757 and fathered by Richard Vincent, then she would have been 30 at the time of her London debut, a somewhat late introduction to the stage, especially in the youthful role of Polly. More likely, Mrs Ferguson was Mrs Vincent's child by John Mills. (Mrs Vincent was 32 at the time of her second marriage.) By John Mills Isabella also had at least three sons: John Wedderburn Mills, Samuel Thomas Mills, baptized at the Mission Church on 15 March 1769, and Alfred Mills (1776–1833), a painter and engraver who died at Walworth on 7 December 1833, leaving a widow and six children. Alfred Mills is noticed in *The Dictionary of National Biography* and Bryan's *Dictionary of Painters and Engravers*. Manuscript biographical sketches of Captain John Mills and Isabella Mills written by Percy Rudolph Broemel, a descendant, are in the Marylebone Public Library.

(It should be noted that the registers of St Paul, Covent Garden, also record the baptism of six children of a Richard Vincent by his wife Isabella between 18 August 1740 and 24 January 1747, some years before our subject married the musician Richard Vincent and during a period when she was still a child. We are unable to connect these Vincents with any of our subjects and take the names to be coincidental.)

The *Catalogue of Engraved British Portraits in the British Museum* lists a portrait of Mrs Mills, an actress, who is identified as Isabella, née Burchell. Isabella Vincent seems never to have acted as Mrs Mills, and the portrait, engraved by J. R. Smith after G. Engleheart and published in 1786, shows a youthful person, when Isabella Mills was already about 51. Broemel's manuscript reports that Mrs Mills was painted by Engleheart in 1780, and the Smith engraving was published in *George Engleheart* (1902) with the statement that it was a portrait of the singer Mrs Mills, noted for her portrayal of Polly. Possibly the portrait is of Susan Moore, a young actress who lived with the actor John Mills (d. 1787) in the 1780s and was called Mrs Mills; she then married the younger John Fawcett at York in April 1788. A portrait attributed to William Beechey and called "Priscilla [*sic*] Vincent The Singer" was at the Godfrey Phillip Galleries,

London, in 1930; a photograph of it appeared in an advertisement in the *Pantheon,* January 1930.

Vincent, [S.?] [*fl.* 1733–1753], *dancer.*

A Mr Vincent's name appeared in the Covent Garden bills as a dancer from 1733–34 through 1738–39, in 1741–42, and from 1748–49 through 1752–53. It is possible that more than one Vincent was involved, but the dancing roles over the years were similar and in some instances the same, such as Mercury in *Perseus and Andromeda* in 1734–35, 1741–42, and 1750–51. Other roles for Vincent were a Chasseur in *The Royal Chace* and Slumber and Pan in *Apollo and Daphne* (in which he appeared numerous times). The account books for Covent Garden show that on 29 September 1749 "S." Vincent was paid 13*s.* 4*d.* for two days; his name was taken off the list on 21 April 1750, but he was employed at that theatre for the next two seasons. "Mrs" S. Vincent was paid £1 per week at Covent Garden in 1746–47, perhaps also as a dancer, but possibly that notation is a transcription error for "Mr" S. Vincent.

Vincent, Mrs [S?] [*fl.* 1746–1747], *dancer? See* VINCENT, [S?].

Vincent, Thomas *c. 1720–1783, oboist, composer, manager.*

Thomas Vincent was the son of the bassoonist Thomas Vincent the elder (d. 1751?) and the brother of the organist James Vincent (d. 1749). His uncle Richard Vincent (1701–1783) and cousin of the same name (d. 1766) were also London musicians. Young Thomas was taught by Giuseppe Sammartini. Our subject, his father, brother James, and uncle Richard were all original subscribers to the Declaration of Trust that established the Royal Society of Musicians in August 1739. By 1743 the younger Thomas was playing oboe in the annual spring concerts given at the King's Theatre for the benefit of the Musicians' Fund. He performed regularly in those concerts through at least 1761. In May 1754 he was paid 10*s.* for playing in the annual benefit concert of the *Messiah* at the Chapel of the Foundling Hospital; he received 10*s.* 6*d.*

for similar service on 27 April 1758 and probably participated in performances there in other years. He played for a concert performance of *Acis and Galatea* in Dean Street, Soho, on 1 April 1758. During the 1750s he also joined his colleagues in the oratorios at Covent Garden and Drury Lane. And on 29 February 1764 he played on oboe concerto in a performance of *Judith* in the Chapel of the Lock Hospital, Hyde Park Corner. In his *Musical Memoirs* (1826) William Parke recorded that Vincent and Simpson were "the two principal oboe players" still using the English oboe in the 1760s.

Mortimer's London Directory of 1763 listed him as "one of his Majesty's and of the Queen's Band," with an address at Brook Green, Hammersmith. Just when he entered the royal music establishment is not clear, though the name of Thomas Vincent appears in the livery lists regularly from 1727 to 1760. The earlier references are probably to his father, who was also in the royal musical service, in the Guards, until his death in late 1751.

In 1764–65 Vincent joined Peter Crawford and John Gordon in the proprietorship of the opera at the King's Theatre. Crawford soon withdrew to be replaced by a banker named Drummond, and the new trio managed opera affairs until 1769, losing a considerable sum of money in the venture. Burney wrote that

Mr. T. Vincent, the impresario, had been in great favour with the prince of Wales, father to his present Majesty; had acquired a considerable sum of money in his profession, which he augmented by marriage. However, the ambition of being at the head of so froward a family as an opera vocal and instrumental band, turned his head and his purse inside out; in short, he soon became a bankrupt, and his colleagues, though they escaped utter ruin, were not enriched by the connexion.

Possibly Thomas was the "Mr Vincent" who performed at the Rotunda in Dublin in 1770. He participated in the spring oratorios at Drury Lane in 1775, first appearing on 3 March, when he played a concerto on the oboe and it was announced he had "not performed in Public for several Years."

Thomas Vincent died in 1783. From an extract of the will of one John Gowland (PRO LC 5-106) we learn something of the financial affairs of Vincent and the name of his wife. In his will, which was proved on 23 August 1776, Gowland mentioned that he was the "Assignee of Thomas Vincent, Barber and Musician to the King." On 28 September 1774, obviously deep in debt, Vincent had assigned to Gowland "all of his Salary of £40 per annum of his Place of Musician Ordinary," plus all other allowances and fees paid to him "by virtue of his Place of Barber to His Majesty." Gowland passed along his right in Vincent's emoluments to James Robson, a bookseller in New Bond Street and his executor in trust with instructions that after taking his necessary costs Robson should give the rest to Penelope Vincent, Thomas's wife, for as long as she should live, "for her sole and separate use," and not subject to her husband's control or debts. Only after her death was Vincent to receive back his assignments and then only on the condition that he "not Sell or otherwise incumber the same."

The Thomas Vincent who was listed as a member of the King's Musick in 1793 and 1795 was perhaps his son.

Our subject composed music for the songs *The Maiden's Resolution* (1760?), *Chloe sat sheltered,* and *The Happy Lover* (1760?). His *Six Solos for a Hautboy, German Flute, Violin, or Harpsichord with a Thorough Bass . . . Opera prima* was published in 1748. Also published that year was his *Sett of Familiar Lessons for the Harpsichord . . . Opera 2d* (printed by John Cox, at Simpson's, for the Author), a work sometimes ascribed to Richard Vincent (1701–1783). On 20 December at Covent Garden Theatre the pantomime *Harlequin's Museum* was premiered with music compiled by Thomas Goodwin from various English composers, including Vincent.

Vincent, Thomas   *d. 1751?, bassoonist, composer.*

The elder Thomas Vincent was, according to Dr Burney, for many years a bassoon player in the Guards. One of his sons, James Vincent (d. 1749), was an organist and composer, and another son, Thomas Vincent the younger (c. 1720–1783), was for a long time an oboist at the King's Theatre and a sometime opera impresario. The elder Thomas's brother Richard Vincent (1701–1783) was also a London musician and the father of the musician Richard Vincent the younger (d. 1766), who was the husband of the singer and actress Isabella Vincent (née Burchell).

Vincent was providing some music to the Lincoln's Inn Fields Theatre by 1727, for on 19 December of that year he was cited on the free list and received a small fee "for Mr. Vincent's Musick." He was probably the Vincent who with some other composers had provided music for some dances published in 1721.

Thomas Vincent was an original subscriber to the Declaration of Trust that established the Royal Society of Musicians in August 1739, and he served on the first Board of Governors. Also original subscribers were his sons Thomas and James and his brother Richard. The name of Thomas Vincent was on the list of the King's Musick regularly from 1727 to 1750, but some of those notices were probably for his son Thomas, who was, it seems, also a member of the King's Band for some time.

His will was proved on 13 January 1752 when sole administration was granted to his son and sole executor, Thomas Vincent. So the elder Vincent probably died late in 1751.

Vincent, Thomas   *fl. 1784?–1795₁, oboist.*

The Mr Vincent who was listed by Dr Burney as an oboist in the Handel Memorial Concerts at Westminster Abbey and the Pantheon in May and June 1784 was perhaps the Thomas Vincent who was a member of the King's Musick in 1793 and 1795.

Probably that Thomas Vincent was the son of the more famous oboist Thomas Vincent (c. 1720–1783).

Vincent, Zelophead Wyeth   *fl. 1794₁, singer.*

Zelophead Wyeth Vincent, of Bow Lane, Cheapside, was listed in Doane's *Musical Directory* (1794) as an alto who was a member of the Choral Fund, the Cecilian Society, and the Longacre Society; he sang in the chorus of the Drury Lane oratorios and in the Handel Memorial Concerts at Westminster Abbey.

Vincentio. *See also* ALBRICI, VINCENZO.

Vincentio, Mr   *fl. 1783–1785₁,* house servant.

The Lord Chamberlain's accounts name Mr Vincentio as a box- and lobby keeper at the King's Theatre from 1783 to 1785.

Vincenzo. *See* ALBRICI, VINCENZO.

Viner, William   *d. 1716, violinist, composer.*

Mr Viner played a solo in a concert at York Buildings on 23 May 1707 and was given a benefit concert there on 31 March 1710. He may have been the Mr "Vinum" playing at the Queen's Theatre in 1708–9 (according to a document in the Coke papers at Harvard). He was surely the English violinist and composer William Viner, who was Master of State Music in Ireland from 1703 to his death in 1716. He composed some solos for violin and bass. He was praised in Pilkington's *The Progress of Musick* in Ireland:

> *The Muses now from Albion's Isle retreat,*
> *And here, with kind indulgence, fix their seat;*
> *Then Viner rose, with all their warmth inspired,*
> *A Bard caress'd by all, by all admir'd.*
> . . . .
> *While round in crowds the fair creation stand*
> *The polish'd Viol trembling in his hand,*
> *While swift as thought, from note to note he*
> *   springs,*
> *Flies o'er the unerring Tones, and sweeps the*
> *   sounding strings.*

Grove (fifth edition) notes that Viner died in November 1716. His will was proved on the thirtieth.

Vinicombe, Richard   *fl. 1759–1786₁, trumpeter.*

Richard Vinicombe (or Vinicomb) was a trumpeter in the King's Musick in 1759 and joined the Royal Society of Musicians on 4 August 1771. He played trumpet in the Handel Memorial Concerts at Westminster Abbey and the Pantheon in May and June 1784 and again in 1785 and 1786.

Vining, Miss E.   *fl. 1798–1806₁, dancer, singer.*

Miss Vining's name was first noted in the Drury Lane bills on 16 January 1798 when she was listed as one of the Female Slaves dancing in the chorus of *Blue-Beard*, a music drama by Colman the younger that had its

premiere on that night and received 64 performances before the season ended. Her salary
that season was £1 5s. per week, and it seems
to have remained at that level during the nine
years she was engaged at Drury Lane. In
1798–99 Miss Vining danced in numerous
performances of *Blue-Beard,* and on 14 November 1798 she danced in the premiere of
Prince Hoare's *The Captive of Spilburg.* On 6
December she was one of the Villagers in a
revival of the ballet *The Scotch Ghost.* Other
assignments for Miss Vining included dancing
in the premiere of Colman's *Feudal Times* on
19 January 1798 and in the ballet *Moggy and
Jemmy* on 5 February 1799. The following season, 1799–1800, she filled similar roles and
danced in the chorus for *The Egyptian Festival,*
Franklin's comic opera that premiered on 11
March 1800 and played a total of ten times.

The account books, which recorded her first
initial "E," indicate that she continued in her
modest capacity at Drury Lane at least
through 1804–5. She also began an engagement at the Haymarket Theatre on 2 July
1800, when she was a dancing Negress in the
premiere of Fawcett's pantomime, *Obi; or,
Three-Finger'd Jack;* she was seen there each
summer through 1806. The Haymarket accounts record that on 12 June 1806, "Miss
Vining being ill, [she] employ'd a Chorus
Singer and Dancer, at her own expence, to
supply her place," a practice to which Miss
Vining had to resort 14 successive nights that
summer. Yet notations of performers paying
their own substitutes are very rare. She seems
to have been the only performer required to
do so in 1806, though in that season at the
Haymarket absenteeism among stars, chorus,
and band was frequent.

Possibly Miss E. Vining was related (perhaps as sister) to Frederick Vining (1790?–
1871), who appeared at Bath in 1809 and
made his debut at Covent Garden Theatre on
17 September 1813 and who is noted in *The
Dictionary of National Biography.* If so, then she
was also related to the actor James Vining
(1795–1870), who is also noted in the *DNB.*
Other Vinings helped populate the London
stage in the nineteenth century, including
Henry Vining and William Vining. The latter's wife was the Mrs Vining who acted at
Covent Garden in the 1820s. Frederick Vining married the actress Jemima Bow in 1814,

and their daughter Fanny Vining (later Mrs C.
Gill) acted with Kean and Macready. According to a clipping dated "Sep 1847" in the Garrick Club, the actor Charles Taylor (who died
that month at the age of 71) had survived his
wife, a former Miss Vining. She must have
been his second wife, for on 26 July 1796 Taylor had married the Bath actress Miss S. T.
Herbert.

Vinnecotio. *See* ALBRICI, VINCENZO.

Vinson, William Sunderland *fl.*
1794₁, *singer.*
Doane's *Musical Directory* of 1794 listed
William Sutherland Vinson, of Park Lane, as
a bass who sang for the Choral Fund.

Vinum. *See* VINER.

Violante, Mlle *fl. 1726–1734₁. See*
VIOLANTE, ROSINA.

Violante, Signor ₁Larini?₁ *fl. 1727–
1733₁, rope slider.*
Probably Signor Violante had previously
given exhibitions on his travels throughout
England with his wife, but the first notice we
find for this "famous Italian Flyer" was on 31
May 1727 when he slid down a rope, head
first, from the top of the newly completed
steeple of St Martin-in-the-Fields to the west
side of the Royal Mews, opposite. He covered
the distance of 300 yards in half a minute, in
the presence of the royal princesses. A week
later, on 3 June, *Read's Weekly Journal* reported
another of his descents, "head foremost, his
legs and arms extended, from the top of the
steeple, *over the houses* in St Martin's Lane."
The *Craftsman* reported on 10 June 1727 that
when Violante planned a similar feat at Bel-
size House a few days later the vicar took
down the scaffold.

In the summer of 1728, while his wife Sga
Violante was performing at Bristol, the press
reported that the "Famous Signor Larini, who
lately flew from Vincent's Rocks, near the
Hotwell, Bristol," would fly from a conve-
nient height erected on the castle wall; other
preparations were made "to divert the Spectators, by Vaulting, Walking the Slack Rope,
and by ascending and descending on the Slope

Rope." The *Craftsman* of 6 July 1728 reported the flyer's name as Violante. Almost a century later, the *Bristol Mirror* of 27 May 1826 also credited Violante with the descent from St Vincent's Rocks to the other side of the river: "It is said that he was not made fast to the rope, but merely held on, with one hand and one foot, to loops, hanging to the running blocks on which he flew."

Notices are scanty, but probably Violante entertained at the various London fairs and perhaps appeared in some of the exhibitions sponsored by his wife. He is reputed to have been the rope vaulter pictured swinging above the heads of the crowd in Hogarth's painting of Southwark Fair. An engraving by Hogarth was published in 1733 in several editions.

The *Bristol Mirror* of 27 May 1826 suggested that Violante had hanged himself while performing, at a time unstated: "This Violante was no doubt a wonderfully clever fellow; but in risking his life a hundred times in *descending* by ropes, he ultimately lost it, by being accidentally compelled to perform the experiment in a contrary direction!" His wife settled in Edinburgh, where she died in 1741. His daughter Rosina, who danced as a child at the Haymarket, married the dancer George Richard Estcourt Luppino. The Mlle Larini Violante who performed at Goodman's Fields in April 1734 may have been Rosina but perhaps was another daughter.

Violante, Signora [Larini?] 1682–1741, *rope dancer, tumbler, actress, manager.*

In a genealogy of the Luppino family provided in *Who's Who in the Theatre*, Signora Violante's year of birth is given, without documentation, as 1682. Some early accounts of theatrical activities at Edinburgh suggest that Signora Violante performed feats of strength and dexterity in that city in 1716, but the date of her first visit to that northern capital is a matter of conjecture and probably, we believe, did not occur until at least a decade later.

The first visit to London, however, by this Italian gymnast seems to have been in the spring of 1720, when she was with a French company under the direction of De Grimbergue. The foreigners performed a repertory of pantomimes, *commedia dell'arte* pieces, and miscellaneous entertainments at the King's

Theatre three nights a week between 5 March and 21 June and also appeared several times at Lincoln's Inn Fields Theatre. The casts for these performances were not listed in the advertisements, but probably Sga Violante danced some pantomime characters. On 26 April 1720 the bills announced that "Signora Violenta will perform several Extraordinary Things, with a Pair of Colours," in *La Fille Capitaine*. Her rope dancing with flags, sometimes advertised as "The Flourishing of the Colours," was repeated several times during the engagement. One scheduled performance was canceled on 29 April when Sga Violante became ill.

Advertisements for Lincoln's Inn Fields on 6 June 1720 promised "a surprising Entertainment of Rope-Dancing" by Sga Violante, who, despite her earlier appearances at the King's, was announced as "lately arriv'd from Italy; and who never yet perform'd in England." She repeated her act at Lincoln's Inn Fields on 7 and 9 June. At the Folger Library is a manuscript transcription from *Oxoniensis* of 6 June 1720 of a poem on rope dancers that describes the adept Sga Violante:

> . . . In shirt and hose of snowy hue,
> That the sleek limbs expose to view
> Mounts the steep ladder undismay'd
> And boldly leaps the Lempen jade
> In equilibrium pois'd astride
> Now swings erect from side to side:
> Now to the yielding rope she bends,
> And swiftly to the roof ascends
>
> . . . .
>
> Her motions with the music chime
> And follow to its nimble time
> Now unconcern'd for neck or brains
> An artificial fall she feigns,
> Drops her slight hold, her body bends,
> And by a single limb suspends
> But now, she gives her genius scope,
> And vent'rous treads the tighten'd rope
> A lengthen'd pole with ends of lead
> Her body poses on the thread:
> New wonders here her art displays,
> Intently fix'd on pence and praise
> That while she vaults on airy wing,
> Help'd by the cord's elastic spring
> Rises by turns, by turns descends,
> While with her weight the cable bends.
> In rows aloft, the shouting tars,
> Whom fate to upper seats prefers
> Like golden Jove on Danae's tower,
> Of halfpence reign a copper shower.

In the spring of 1726 Sga Violante was once again in London with a "famous Italian Company of Comedians" that offered *commedia dell'arte* performances at the Haymarket Theatre from 24 March through 11 May. She shared colombine characters with Mlle Le Brun and appeared regularly in specialty dances.

After the Italian players left she stayed on to perform entertainments of tumbling and rope dancing at the Haymarket, beginning on 1 June 1726 and extending through the summer. On the first night, for her own benefit, she displayed her flags and also walked "upright forwards & backwards on the Rope, the lower end fixed to the Footmen's Gallery," according to transcriptions of advertisements found in the Latreille manuscripts at the British Library. On 8 June she performed rope dancing "so famous that the like was never seen in this kingdom," and the advertisements proclaimed her "the wonder of the world for dancing on the Stiff Rope with two Flags one in each hand. . . . She dances with a person standing upright on her shoulders; she likewise dances with a man tied to each foot." For another benefit, on 29 June, in the presence of his Excellency Mahomet Ben Ali Abgali, Ambassador from the Emperor of Morocco, she presented the same program, but with the addition of a minuet dance on the rope by a five-year-old child, who probably was her daughter. That night, however, Sga Violante "by her fall from the Gallery Box . . . broke the little toe of her left foot." Confined to her bed, she apologized in the press for not being able to perform on 1 July. By 28 August she had recovered sufficiently from the accident to resume her entertainments through 5 September. On 7 September she began similar diversions in a booth she shared with Gibbon at Southwark Fair.

Evidently encouraged by the response to her exhibitions, Sga Violante took over the Haymarket in 1726–27 for a season of pantomimes, dancing, and acrobatics. Her company, most of whom were foreigners, performed about 70 nights between 2 November 1726 and 28 April 1727. On opening night two youngsters, ages six and ten, perhaps her children, danced a minuet "to perfection on the Rope." On 8 November Sga Violante danced on the rope with swords tied to her legs, one child on her shoulders, and two on

her feet. On that night, moreover, her sister—unnamed—vaulted on the slack rope "in defiance to any one that ever appeared on a public stage" and concluded her act by turning "round the Rope like a windmill." Sga Violante rope-danced on 11 November with pails of water on her legs. On 14 April 1727 her daughter, age 11, danced on the rope "with Napkins tied to her ancles without touching the rope with her feet." The same night on which the 11-year-old daughter appeared at the Haymarket a Miss Violante, identified as Sallé's scholar, performed a harlequin dance at Lincoln's Inn Fields Theatre.

According to John Williams in *A Pin Basket to the Children of Thespis,* Sga Violante was in Dublin in 1727 and then traveled to Edinburgh, where the magistrates prohibited her company from performing. Hitchcock, the Irish prompter, wrote that in 1727 she took possession of premises in Fownes's Court, Dublin, to set up a tumbling booth. We find no specific evidence for her appearance in either city that year, but one "Mlle Violente . . . danseuse de corde italienne," perhaps our subject, was engaged by Restier at the Saint Laurent Fair in Paris in the same year.

By the autumn of 1727 Sga Violante was back in London, opening on 23 October "with a new Company She has formed in her travels through France & Italy of the most enterprizing performers that ever appeared in this Kingdom." Latreille's notes record at least 48 performances at the Haymarket between that date and 6 May 1728. On 28 February 1728 the company began to perform *The Rivals; or, The Happy Despair,* a pantomime in which Sga Violante played Columbine.

In July 1728 Sga Violante took her company to Bristol, where they presented *The Rivals* at the theatre on St Augustine's Back. In August and September Sga Violante often entertained on the rope and danced with her child. During that visit to Bristol, her husband, a rope slider who had performed some daring feats in London the previous year, descended by a rope from the top of St Vincent's Rocks to the other side of the river and also flew from the castle walls.

The following year Sga Violante received a benefit, by command of the Prince of Wales, at the Haymarket Theatre in London 28 April 1729; that is the only extant notice of a performance by her that season in London, though she may have given others. On 23 December 1729 the *Old Dublin Intelligencer* reported that, "A few days past the celebrated Madam Violante, the most famous rope-dancer now living, arrived here from England after a tedious and dangerous passage of six weeks. Her Company performed in our Theatre Royal [Smock Alley] five times to the great satisfaction of our Nobility, Gentry and Citizens." Her entertainments continued in Dublin until March 1730, when she went to Cork. Back in Dublin the next fall she performed again at Smock Alley. According to Gratton Flood, she had opened a new booth in George Lane on 20 November 1729, though other sources state the year as 1731. Sometime during that period she had a booth at Fownes's Court. Among the entertainments she concocted at one of these booths was a Lilliputian production of a pirated version of *The Beggar's Opera,* in which the teenaged Peg Woffington appeared. It has sometimes been said that Peg had made her stage debut hanging from the rope dancer's feet, but there is no evidence for Peg's participation in those feats.

In 1730, Jonathan Swift, Dean of St Patrick's, wrote satirically in his *Vindications of Lord Carteret:*

I have not heard whether any care has hitherto been given to discover whether the Italian rope-dancer, Violante, be a whig or tory in her principles, or even that she has ever been offered the oath by the Government: on the contrary I am told that she openly professes herself to be a highflyer and it is not improbable that by her outlandish name she may also be a Papist at heart: yet we see this illustrious and dangerous female openly preferred by principal persons of both parties.

During 1731–32 the performances offered by Sga Violante's company in Dame Street, Dublin, especially those given by the children, drew large numbers from the Theatre Royal. William Chetwood in his *General History* (1749) found her "shockingly indecent" and described her limbs as "masculinely indelicate, and were of a Piece with the Features of her Face." Chetwood reported that she had not enjoyed the same success in Ireland as she had in England and, "finding her Tumbling tiresome, fell into playing and Pantomime." She played "several Dramatic Pieces with Gro-

tesque Entertainments" but soon was stopped by the Lord Mayor.

In 1732 Sga Violante brought her troupe to London, where the *Daily Post* announced that at the Haymarket on 4 September would be presented "the most surprizing Performances that ever were shown in the English Theatre," for the benefit of "the famous Signora Violante, who is just arrived with a new extraordinary fine Company." Also on the bill was *The Beggar's Opera,* "after the Irish manner, which was perform'd 96 times in Dublin with great applause." The part of Macheath was played "by the celebrated Miss Woffington." A harlequin dance was performed by Master La Fevre and Miss Violante, and the latter also offered a louvre in boy's clothes. During that September engagement, which concluded on the twentieth, Sga Violante danced on the rope each night, though she had given up her Columbine parts in the pantomimes to her daughter. The bills for 11 September announced a busy night for Sga Violante who would

perform several new and surprizing Performances on the Strait Rope, never perform'd by anyone besides herself: [1] She dances a Minuet as Neatly as a Dancing Master on a Floor. [2] She Dances with a Board, ten Foot in length, loose upon the rope. [3] She Dances with two Boys fastened to her feet; which Occasions great Mirth. [4] She Dances with two heavy Men ty'd to her Feet. [5] She performs the Exercise of the Colours. After this surprising Performance, Miss Violante will Dance a Louvre in Boys Cloaths.

The next night, 12 September, the company performed *The Beggar's Opera* and their entertainments of dancing and acrobatics at the Great Assembly Room in Richmond Wells for the benefit of the manager.

No London appearances are recorded for Sga Violante during the 1733–34 season, though probably she made some. In the winter she toured in the north, performing at the Angel in Norwich, among other places. In November 1734 she gave her exhibitions of rope dancing at the Great Booth in Griffin Yard, Cornhill, in Ipswich.

Late in 1735 she performed in Edinburgh, where she finally settled. On 2 February 1736, in a performance given for the benefit of the poor of the city, the "famous Italian rope dancer" danced on the straight rope and exhibited "other surprising performances which have justly received the applause of the Publick these several months back." On 9 February she was advertised to perform on the slack rope at the "new theatre" in Carubber's Close. That building was remodeled by the poet Allan Ramsey and reopened in November 1736 with a prologue that dedicated the establishment to elevated taste, so Sga Violante was obliged, it seems, to seek another stage. On 17 December she began a run of six performances at the Old Assembly Hall, offering her standard repertoire of rope dancing.

Madame Violante also opened a dancing school at Edinburgh that reputedly enjoyed great success. It was attended by the young Dr Carlyle of Inveresk, who in his autobiography noted that it was "much frequented by young ladies." On 14 February 1740 the press carried notice of the postponement of the ball scheduled for 18 February at "Mrs Violante's dancing-school" because of slow ticket sales. On 10 June 1740 she was obliged to issue in the papers a denial of the false report that she had stolen a diamond ring from one of her pupils.

Notice of Sga Violante's death "lately," evidently in Edinburgh, appeared in the *Scot's Magazine* in June 1741. Her husband, who seems sometimes to have been called Larini, was reported to have accidentally hanged himself while performing. Their daughter Rosina Violante was probably the child who danced at the Haymarket between 1727 and 1732; she married the dancer George Richard Estcourt Luppino (son of the dancers George Charles Luppino and Charlotte Mary Estcourt). The Mlle Larini Violante who danced at Goodman's Fields in April 1734 may have been Rosina, though she was perhaps a second daughter.

Violante, Larini. *See* VIOLANTE, ROSINA.

Violante, Rosina, later Mrs George Richard Estcourt Luppino   *d. 1789, dancer.*
Rosina Violante was one of the daughters of the Italian rope dancers Signor and Signora [Larini?] Violante. Possibly she was the five-year-old child who danced a minuet on the

rope at the Haymarket Theatre on 29 June 1726 for the benefit of Sga Violante. At that theater on 2 November 1726 two youngsters, ages six and ten, probably Sga Violante's children, danced a minuet on the rope "to perfection." And there on 14 April 1727 a child identified as Sga Violante's daughter, age 11, danced on the rope "with Napkins tied to her ancles without touching the rope with her feet." On that same night, a Miss Violante, described as Sallé's scholar, performed a harlequin dance at Lincoln's Inn Fields Theatre.

One of Sga Violante's daughters played Gypsey in performances of *The Rivals; or, The Happy Despair,* a pantomime presented at the Haymarket by her mother's company beginning 28 February 1728. That 20 March the daughter shared a benefit with La Fevre, "being the only reward allowed them for performing the whole season."

In the summer of 1728 Sga Violante and one of her children danced at the theatre on St Augustine's Back in Bristol. A Mlle Violante performed with her mother's company at the Dame Street Theatre in Dublin in 1731–32. When the company returned to London to perform at the Haymarket in the autumn of 1732, Miss Violante danced a louvre, in boy's clothes, on 4 September and several other nights and also acted Columbine in *The Jealous Husband* on 11 September. And, finally, on 27 April 1734 at Goodman's Fields Theatre the dance of *Harlequin and Harlequinette* was performed "by Mons Leblanche and Mlle Larini Violante, the first time of their Performances since their arrival in this Kingdom," and a louvre was danced by the latter in boy's clothes. (The name of Larini was also associated with Signor Violante.)

We cannot determine which of the Violante girls, if indeed there was more than one, was Rosina. According to a genealogy provided in *Who's Who in the Theatre* (eleventh edition), Rosina married the dancer George Richard Estcourt Luppino. She is reputed to have died in 1789 and to have been buried at St John's Church in Hertford beside her husband, who had died two years earlier, but the burial register does not record these events. Their son Thomas Frederick Luppino (1749–1845) became a scenographer and dancer; he married the dancer Rosine Simonet.

Violenta *or* Violenti *See* VIOLANTE.

Violett. *See* VIBLETT.

Violette, Mlle. *See* GARRICK, MRS DAVID.

Viotti, Giovanni Battista   *1753–1824,*
violinist, composer, band leader, manager.
In an autobiographical manuscript entitled
"Précis de la vie de J. B. Viotti, depuis son
entrée dans le monde jusqu'au 6 mars 1798.
Donné à Hambourg à Mons. Coleman Macgregor, Consul Brittannique à Teneriffe," Giovanni Battista Viotti gave the date of his birth
as 23 May 1753. According to *Grove's Diction-*
ary of Music and Musicians (fifth edition), he
was born at Fontanetto da Po and was baptized on 25 June 1753, the legitimate son of
Antonio Viotti, a blacksmith, and his wife
Maria Magdalena Milano. Having been
taught the fundamentals of music by his father, an amateur horn player, at the age of 11
he was instructed for a year by Giovanni, a
lutist of Fontanetto, who soon became professor at the Irvée Academy of Music. When
playing at a church festival at Strambino in
1766, young Viotti sufficiently impressed the
Bishop that he recommended the boy as a
companion to the 18-year-old Alfonso del
Pozzo, Prince of Cisterna. Viotti, it is said,
astonished the royal musician Colgnetti by
playing at sight a difficult sonata by Ferrari;
Colgnetti persuaded the Prince's father, the
Marchese di Vogliera, to take the lad into his
palace at Turin and assume responsibility for
his further education. Viotti studied at first
with Antonio Celoniat but upon Pugnani's return from London in 1770 became his pupil.

At the age of 14 Viotti composed his first
violin concerto, which he later published as
No 3. He joined the orchestra of the royal
chapel at Turin on 27 December 1775. In
1780 he toured with Pugnani, playing at Geneva, Dresden, and Berlin, where Frederick
the Great frequently joined Viotti in playing
concerted music. From Berlin that year Viotti
and his master went to Warsaw and then on
to St Petersburg, where the Empress Catherine tried, with many presents, to persuade
him to remain at her court. But Viotti left
with Pugnani in 1781, visiting Berlin and
other northern German cities. In his *History of*

the Violin, van der Straeten next places Viotti
in London, where he "created a profound impression, eclipsing even the fame of Geminiani." We find, however, no record of Viotti in
London in 1781 or 1782.

Early in 1782 he went to Paris, and after
giving a small private concert he had a very
successful debut at the Concert Spirituel on
15 March. One critic immediately ranked
him "among the greatest masters." He was, at
one period, leader of Prince Gueménée's orchestra and then first violinist to the Prince of
Soubise. By 1783 he was regarded in France
as the greatest violinist of his day, but after an
appearance for the last time at the Concert
Spirituel on 8 September 1783 he abruptly retired from public performances, for reasons
not clearly understood. In 1784 he was appointed as Queen Marie Antoinette's accompanist, with a life pension of £150. When he
was living with his friend Cherubini in 1785
he held private academies on Sunday morn-
ings for musicians of note, at which he often
played solos and concertos and his latest compositions were performed.

In 1788 Viotti joined Léonard Antié, the
Queen's hairdresser, in the management of the
Théâtre de Monsieur, under the patronage of
the King's brother, the Comte de Provence.
There he began to produce Italian operas with
an exceptional company of singers, but that
enterprise was aborted by the Revolution.
When the court removed from Versailles to
the Tuilleries in 1790 Viotti had to transfer to
the Théâtre de la Foire Saint-Germain, which
proved unsatisfactory for opera. With the help
of some wealthy nobles and the intendant Feydeau de Brou he built the Théâtre Feydeau,
which he occupied in 1791.

But turbulent conditions finally forced
Viotti to leave Paris on the eve of the arrest of
the monarchs. He arrived on 21 or 22 July
1792 at London, where Salomon engaged him
for his concerts in the Hanover Square Room.
Viotti soon established himself as a teacher.
He returned to Paris in July 1793 on the
death of his mother to handle the affairs of his
brothers, who were still minors, and then returned to England by way of Switzerland,
Germany, and Flanders, arriving at London in
December.

In 1794 and 1795 Viotti was a regular performer at Salomon's concerts. In 1794 he was engaged as a violinist at the King's Theatre. On 6 March he and Salomon played a violin concertante at the King's and he accompanied Mme Banti on 26 April 1794. At the Haymarket Theatre on 22 May 1794 Master Julian Baux, age 6, performed one of Viotti's concertos. That year Doane's *Musical Directory* listed Viotti as a violinist in Salomon's concerts, living at No 34, Wells Street, Oxford Street. In 1794–95 he became acting manager at the King's Theatre, where on 3 January 1795 it was announced that "The Whole [opera was] under the direction of Viotti."

Viotti continued as director of music and also as leader of the orchestra at the King's Theatre for another two and a half seasons. His salary in 1795–96 was £300. He composed the music for the new ballet *Apollon Berger* on 27 December 1796. His happy situation was shattered on 20 February 1798 when he was replaced as orchestra leader by Salomon, and in March 1798 he was arrested by the king's officers and expelled from the country as a "suspected alien," one who sympathized with the French revolutionaries. Among the public charges made against him was employing "heinous and sanguinary expressions against the king." Viotti proclaimed his innocence in a statement to the *Times* and in the autobiographical "Précis" of his life, which several months later he presented to Coleman Macgregor, British Consul at Tenerife. Both *Grove's Dictionary* (fifth edition) and van der Straeten find the accusations unfounded slander, suspicions brought on by some innocent letters Viotti had written to France. Spiteful Jacobins were enraged at his escape from Paris. But in his *Reminiscences* Michael Kelly related dining one day in 1796 at the Crown and Anchor in the Strand with Viotti and meeting three of Viotti's friends whom the musician convened once a month as a "little dinner-club." Kelly found the friends "three of the greatest revolutionists": Charles Lameth, former president of the National Assembly; Dupont, a popular orator and also a member of the National Assembly; and the Duke D'Aiguillon, formerly one of the twelve peers of France and a great patron of the arts. Kelly lamented "that men possessing such amiable manners, should, from strong repub-

Civica Raccolta Stampe A. Bertarelli, Milan

GIOVANNI BATTISTA VIOTTI
engraving by Lambert, after Guerin

lican principles, bring themselves into misfortune," and he assured his readers, "I had nothing to do with their politics."

Van der Straeten states that Viotti was arrested while in the company of friends on 6 March 1798. The *Times,* however, reported on 5 March 1798 that on 3 March 1798 "Salomon led the band for the first time these two years, in place of Viotti, who has been sent out of the country, under the authority of the Alien Bill. He left town yesterday." He went in exile to an estate owned by his friend George Smith at Schönefeld, on the Elbe near Hamburg, where he occupied three years of enforced leisure in composition and correspondence, much of the latter to the William Chinery family back in London. They were, in the words of the *New Grove,* "the most beneficial influence that ever affected his life." While at Schönefeld he wrote a number of violin duets, a book of which was dedicated to William Chinery. In the preface to that work, *Six Duets for Violins,* he wrote, "This book is the fruit of the leisure afforded me by misfortune. Some of the pieces were dictated by trouble, others by hope." He also did some teaching, one of his pupils being Friedrich Wilhelm Pixis, the talented younger brother of the famous musician Johann Peter Pixis.

Viotti was allowed to come back to London in 1801, but he was unable to reestablish his musical connections. With the assistance of Chinery he ventured into the wine trade with George Smith. He visited Paris in 1802, where he played some of his latest compositions for artistic friends, who admired them greatly. Baillot praised his playing especially.

Late in 1803 Viotti returned to London to enjoy the cordial hospitality of the musical Chinery family. Mme Anne Vignée-Lebrun relates her fortnight's visit to Gilwell, the Chinery country house near Stewardstone (Epping Forest), during which she enjoyed regular nightly concerts given by Viotti, Mrs Chinery, and Mrs Chinery's 14-year-old daughter Caroline.

Viotti's business undertaking occupied him for about a decade and ended with disastrous losses. In 1813, however, he made tentative gestures at returning to his musical career, and he was actively involved in the formation of the Philharmonic Society, playing with the orchestra at the opening concert on 8 May 1813, under Salomon's leadership. He conducted the orchestra occasionally, and in a concert that first year led one of his own quartets.

During a visit to Paris in 1818 Viotti played one of his concerti at an emotional reception in his honor, during which many of the auditors wept. Remaining in Paris, Viotti in 1819, through the influence of his old patron the Comte de Provence, who was now King Louis XVIII, was appointed director of the Opéra at a salary of 12,000 francs per year. While Viotti was on a visit to London, the French king's nephew, the Duc de Berry, was assassinated in the theatre, causing the house to be shut down. The company moved to the Théâtre Favart and, after two months, to the Théâtre Louvois in May 1821. When the latter theatre also proved unsatisfactory the enterprise was taken to the rue Le Peletier on 16 August 1821. On 27 January 1821 Viotti had been obliged to write to the Baron de Ferté requesting some furniture, since after an absence of 29 years he possessed no household

effects and lacked the means to buy them. The Opéra suffered adversities for which Viotti was blamed in some quarters, so he soon resigned its directorship, again disenchanted by intrigues. For a short time he managed the Théâtre Italienne, but he retired by the autumn of 1821; on 31 October of that year Le Miroir regretted his resignation for "Never has the Théâtre Italienne appeared to us better managed."

Viotti was still in Paris on 13 March 1822, the day he made his will. But he returned to London soon after, despondent and in poor health, to live in Mrs Chinery's home, first at No 17, Montague Street, Portman Square, until the end of 1823 and then at No 5, Upper Berkeley Street. He died at the latter address on the morning of 3 March 1824. His place of burial is unknown, though van der Straeten speculates that it may be at Stewardstone, where several of the Chinery children were buried.

In his will Viotti expressed deep torment because he was so deeply indebted to Mrs Chinery:

That good and excellent creature placed the sum of 80,000 francs at my disposal to assist me in my business. The house failed, and I was forced to relinquish not only my own capital but also the 80,000 francs lent to me with such disinterested magnanimity. That sacred debt is the misfortune of my life, and it will disturb the peace of my ashes, if I should have the misfortune to be unable to discharge it.

He asked that "If I die before I can pay off this debt, I pray that everything I have in the world may be sold off, realized, and sent to Madame Chinery, or her heirs, praying only that they shall pay to my brother, André Viotti, the sum of 800 francs, that I owe him."

E. Heron-Allen, in Grove's Dictionary (fifth edition), had described Viotti as a man to whom nature had been bountiful in physical and mental attributes: "His head was grand and powerful, his face—though lacking in perfect regularity of feature—was expressive, amiable and radiant; his figure was well-proportioned and graceful, his manners were distinguished, his conversation animated and polished." He was also kind hearted and gentle.

GIOVANNI BATTISTA VIOTTI
by Trossarelli

Viotti is characterized by van der Straeten as "the father of the modern school of violin playing." He was "the greatest virtuoso of his time but he never debased his extraordinary technical powers by using them for any but the noblest and highest purposes of his art." He possessed great fullness of tone, and he was unequalled in the beauty of his poetical expression. Though he performed before the public for less than ten years, as the *New Grove* points out, "the impression he left was so strong that he dominated an entire generation of violinists." His compositions are distinguished by "nobility of thought and charm of thematic invention." His later works in London were influenced by Haydn's symphonic form. But they proved to be too restrained for the new romantic flamboyancy and fell from favor.

A prolific composer, Viotti wrote 29 concertos for the violin, two symphonies concertante for two violins, strings, and wind, 54 violin duets, 36 trios for two violins and bass, and numerous trios, string quartets, and sonatas. A list of his compositions is given in the *New Grove* and the *Catalogue of Printed Music in the British Museum*. He left two violins—a fine Stradivarius in the possession of Messrs W. E. Hill & Son about 1911—and a Klotz that once belonged to Mrs Chinery.

Additional information on Viotti's life and works can be found in notices by Heron-Allen in *Grove's Dictionary* and by Chappell White in the *New Grove*. At the time Heron-Allen wrote his piece on Viotti he was in possession of the musician's will, some of his letters, and his "Précis." A number of articles on Viotti have been published, including important ones by E. van der Straeten in *Die Musik* (Berlin, vol I, Nos 18 and 19) and *The Connoisseur* (November 1911). C. White has written a dissertation, "G. B. Viotti and his Violin Concertos" (Princeton University, 1957). Portraits of Viotti include:

1. By George Chinery. Drawing, reproduced in *The Connoisseur* (November 1911, p. 160). Similar to a drawing in the Royal College of Music, perhaps by Chinery.

2. By Anne Vigée Lebrun. Life-size portrait, once believed lost, discovered in possession of Viotti's lineal descendants, the Greene family, in 1911. Reproduced in *The Connoisseur* (November 1911, p. 152).

3. By J. Trossarelli. In the possession of Viotti's lineal descendants, the Greene family, in 1911. Reproduced in *The Connoisseur* (November 1911, p. 157). Engraving by Mayer. Also lithographed by Peyre and published by Mme Veuve Lanner, 1834.

4. By unknown artist. Six miniature portraits, drawn from life by a member of Viotti's orchestra in Paris. Owned in 1911 by E. Heron-Allen, who obtained them from Julian Marshall. These were reproduced in *The Connoisseur* (November 1911, p. 156).

5. By unknown artist. Pen and ink wash portrait, full-length, holding book and bow. In the British Museum. Reproduced in the *New Grove*.

6. Engraved portrait by W. Arndt. Published by Breitkopf & Härtel, Leipzig. Similar to No 1, above.

7. Engraved portrait by Lambert, after an original design by P. Guérin. Title page of Fayolle's *Notices sur Tartini*. Similar to No 1, above.

8. By unknown engraver. Published with his *Six Duets for Violins*, by Buchanan at Hamburg.

9. Bust, sculptured by Flatters, 1813. Location unknown.

10. Portrait on bronze medal, by Peuvrier, 1824. In the Royal College of Music.

Vipont, Mr   *fl. 1735₁,*   *impresario.*
On 1 October 1735 a concert of instrumental music was given at Mr Vipont's New Long Room in Hampstead.

Visconti, Caterina   *fl. 1741–1766₁,* *singer.*
Caterina Visconti sang the prima-donna roles in operas at the King's Theatre in 1741–42 for 1,000 guineas. She sang an unspecified role in *Alessandro in Persia* on 31 October 1741, in *Penelope* on 12 December, Ilione in *Polidoro* on 19 January 1742, Arsinoe in *Scipione in Cartagine* on 2 March, in a benefit concert for indigent musicians on 13 April, and in *Meraspe o l'olimpiade* on 20 April. In 1742–43 she sang Alinda in *Gianguir,* the title role in *Mandane,* a role in *Enrico,* Aspasia in *Temistocle,* in a benefit concert, and Eurene in *Sirbace.* In 1743–44 Signora Visconti added the lead in *Rossane,* Ermesenda in *Alphonso,* the

lead in *Rosalinda,* Senocrita in *Aristodemo,* and Rosmira in *Alceste.*

She was heard again in London in January and February 1754 singing Mandana in *Artaserse* and songs in a benefit concert. On 10 April 1766 she turned up again at the King's Theatre, singing in a benefit concert. The Duchess of Northumberland heard her and told her diary that "Visconti is tolerably pretty but has not the least Idea of Music." Dr Burney wrote in his *General History of Music:*

The Visconti had a shrill flexible voice, and pleased more in rapid songs than in those that required high colouring and pathos. She was so fat, that her age being the subject of conversation in a company where Lord Chesterfield was present: when a gentleman, who supposed her to be much younger than the rest, said she was but two and twenty; his lordship, interrupting him, said "you mean *stone,* Sir, not years."

Visconti, Gasparo. *See* GASPARINI.

Visdale. *See* VIDALE.

Vitalba, Mr   ₁*fl. 1775*₁,   *dancer.*
Mr Vitalba made his first appearance at the King's Theatre on 22 April 1775 dancing a pas de deux with Mlle Sophie Louille. He danced with her again on 25 April and 16 May. On 27 May Vitalba was replaced by Vallouis.

Vittoria, Signora, or Argentina, Signora, stage names of Gabriella Gardellini or Teodora Areliari?   ₁*fl. 1716–1727*₁, *dancer.*
An Italian troupe arrived in London on 21 September 1726 for an engagement at the King's Theatre that began on 28 September and lasted until April 1727. In the troupe was a dancer variously identified as Signora Vittoria (or Victoria) and Signora (or Mrs) Argentina. We are guessing that these were stage names used by one of the dancers; at Victoria's shared benefit on 23 March 1727 *Argentina Ortolana* was presented, and perhaps the performer borrowed the character's name. The woman may have been Gabriella Gardellini or Teodora Areliari, former members of the troupe of the Duke of Modena, according to Professor Anya Peterson Royce. Or perhaps

her real name was Argentina Vittoria or Vittoria Argentina.

Our dancer seems to have made her first London appearance in *Il matrimonio disturbato* on 26 November 1726 as Signora Vittoria. She danced on 17 December and had a benefit on 16 February 1727 as Argentina, was given another on 23 March as Vitoria, and as Argentina played the Maid Devil in *La dama demonio* on 8 April, and was either Amarillis or Asparillis in a dance on 25 April.

Viviani, Elena Croce   ₁*fl. 1716*₁, *singer.*
Elena Croce Viviani was advertised as "lately arriv'd" when she sang Lucilla in *Lucio Vero* at the King's Theatre on 1 February 1716. She appeared as Deidamia in *Pirro e Demetrio* on 10 March and Climene in *Cleartes* on 18 April. She had benefits on 6 and 13 June.

Vivier. *See* VIVIEZ.

Viviez, Mrs   ₁*fl. 1755–1768*₁,   *dancer.*
Mrs Viviez (called Vivier earlier in her career) was a member of the corps de ballet at Covent Garden Theatre from 1755 through at least 1767–68. Her name was first noticed on the bills of 30 April 1755, when she shared benefit tickets with Jona, Jarvis, and Miss Condell. Similarly, she shared tickets with other minor personnel on 19 May 1756, 30 April 1757, 8 April 1758, 28 April 1759, 12 April 1760, 22 May 1764, 22 May 1765, 9 May 1766, and 20 May 1767. Her salary in 1760–61 was £1 10s. per week. A salary list for Covent Garden as of 26 November 1761 has her down for £35 per season and places her relatively low in the classifications of employees. Arthur Murphy reported her salary as 4s. 2d. per day in 1767–68, the last season she seems to have been at Covent Garden.

Among Mrs Viviez's known assignments at Covent Garden were Juno in *The Judgment of Paris,* chorus dancing in *The Prophetess,* a new dance with Gallini and Mrs Granier, and a *Comic Ballet* in 1757–58; in *The Threshers* and a Bacchant in *The Feast of Bacchus* in 1758–59; in *The Fair* and in the choruses of *The Rape of Proserpine* and *Comus* in 1759–60; in *The Hungarian Gambols* in 1760–61; in *Apollo and*

Daphne in 1761–62; and in *The Wapping Land-lady* in 1766–67.

In the summer of 1757 she danced at the Haymarket Theatre, making her first known appearance there on 17 June in *The Marine Boys Marching to Portsmouth.* She danced in a medley concert on 5 July 1757.

On 8 April 1758 a "Viviez Jr" received £7 7*s.* for benefit tickets at Covent Garden. That person's name appears in no other records, but he, or she, was no doubt related to Mrs Viviez and probably was a performer.

Viviez Jr.   [*fl.* 1783], *performer?* *See* VI-VIEZ, MRS.

Vizin. *See* VEZEIN.

Vogler, Georg Joseph, called "Abbé Vogler" *1749–1814, pianist, organist, composer.*

Georg Joseph Vogler was born at Pleichach, near Würzburg, on 15 June 1749, the son of a violinist and instrument maker at the court of the Prince-Bishop of Würzburg. His step-father, Wenceslaus Stantinger, was also a violin maker.

The studies, travels, teaching, and performances of this outstanding German musician are covered in detail in the *New Grove Dictionary.* Therefore this notice is limited to his professional activities in London, which were only a minor part of his long career.

Vogler visited London in 1783 when the Royal Society gave its approval of his musical system, which involved chord studies and a progressive theory of modulation. Perhaps he also performed in concerts at that time, though no notices to that effect have survived. He returned to London early in 1790 (a visit not mentioned in the *New Grove,* though recorded in the fifth edition) and at the Pantheon gave a series of concerts, the last of which occurred on 31 May. His performances on the "Orchestrion," his invention, were much applauded. The instrument, which Sainsbury likened to the "Panharmonicon," is described in the *New Grove* as "9 feet square, 6 feet high on each side and 9 in the centre," and containing 900 pipes and shutters. The engagement at the Pantheon brought Vogler

between £1,000 and £1,200 and an assignment to reconstruct the Pantheon's organ.

Vogler died at Darmstadt on 6 May 1814. A long list of his compositions and theoretical writings is given in the *New Grove,* where Margaret H. Grave concludes that "Vogler stands out as a remarkably dedicated intellect, who through incessant writing, teaching and performing added a colourful and progressive voice to the musical activity of his time." Vogler had invented the octochord, "an eight-string device with which he measured anew the mathematical relations between intervals." He had great influence as a teacher of composition and singing, counting among his pupils Ritter, Kraus, B. A. Weber, Meyerbeer, and Sterkel.

Joseph and Gerhard Vogler, German music publishers, possibly were Georg Joseph Vogler's brothers, though no connection is known. About 1777 they established themselves at London, in Glasshouse Street, near Swallow Street, in premises previously occupied by Robert Worman. There they published and sold music until 1785.

Vogler is the subject of Robert Browning's poem "Abt Vogler (After He Has Been Extemporizing upon the Musical Instrument of His Invention)" in *Dramatis Personae,* 1864. A portrait by Friedrich Oelenhainz of Georg Joseph Vogler, with his octochord, is in the Städtisches Reiss-Museum, Mannheim.

Volage, Mr   [*fl.* 1741], *dancer.*
Mr Volage danced at the James Street Theatre on 6 October 1741.

Volange, stage name of Maurice-François Rochet *1756–1810, actor.*
Born at Nantes on 25 March 1756, Maurice-François Rochet, called Volange, after gaining some acting experience in the Antilles, returned to France to play in the provinces before he joined Lecluze's troupe at the St Laurent Fair about 1778 and was successful in the role of Janot in *Janot, ou les Battus payent l'amende.* On 22 February 1780 he appeared for the first time at the Comédie-Italienne in *Les Trois Jumeaux vénitiens,* in which he earned extraordinary acclaim.

Most of what is known of Volange's career

derives from an article by Dumeran Lavedan in *Monte Dramatique*, 5 August 1837. But much of the information provided therein is challenged by Max Fuchs in his *Léxique*. In 1780 Volange joined the Variétés-Amusantes, where he remained until 1785. According to Dumeran, between engagements at the Variétés-Amusantes Volange toured the provinces and foreign lands, playing at Melun and Geneva, and at London in April and May 1786. We have found no record of performances by Volange in London.

In 1790 he acted at Bordeaux and Nimes. He was in Stockholm in 1792. In the 1790s he also continued to appear in Paris, at the Variétés, and, it is said, at the Palais Royal.

Volange died in 1810. Some additional information about him is given by Fuchs and by Campardon in *Les Spectacles de la Foire* and in *Les Comédiens du Roi*. Perhaps the Mme Volange who was engaged as a dancer at the Orchard Street Theatre, Bath, in 1803–4 and at the King's Theatre, London, in 1804 was related.

Volar, Mrs *fl. 1728₁*, *actress.*
Mrs Volar played a Countrywoman in *The Rivals* at Lincoln's Inn Fields Theatre on 21 February 1728. Playing the Devil was Mr Vollan, and it is possible that either his name or hers was misspelled and that they were husband and wife.

Volee, John *fl. 1661–1663₁*, *musician.*
John Volee was appointed to the King's private music on 18 October 1661. A Lord Chamberlain's list for autumn 1663 included John Vole and Jean de la Volle, and our guess is that these were one and the same person, though the proper spelling remains a question.

Vollan, Mr *fl. 1728₁*, *actor. See* VOLAR, MRS.

Volsecchi, Marianna *fl. 1762–1763₁*, *singer.*
Marianna Volsecchi (or Valesecchi, Valsecchi) sang at the King's Theatre in 1762–63, but most of the bills supplied no casts. The

only role known for her is Diana in *Orione*, which she sang on 19 February 1763. At the Haymarket Theatre on 9 June she sang in a concert.

"Voltore." *See* "DE VOLTORE."

Volumner, Mr *fl. 1701₁*, *musician.*
Instrumental music was played by Mr Volumner at York Buildings on 24 March 1701.

Von, Mr *fl. 1771₁*, *dancer.*
Mr Von made his "first appearance in England" dancing "in demi-character" at the Haymarket Theatre on 24 April 1771.

Von Ducrow. *See* DUCROW.

Von Esser. *See* ESSER.

Von Holberg. *See* HOLBERG.

"Von Poop-Poop Broomstickado." *See* "BROOMSTICKADO" and SKEGGS.

Vowell, Mr *fl. 1770–1780₁*, *actor.*
In 1770–71 Mr Vowell was a member of the company at the Theatre Royal, Shakespeare Square, Edinburgh, which was under the management of Samuel Foote that season. Vowell appeared as Mr Butler in *The Busy Body* on 19 November 1770; his other known roles that season were the Cook in *The Devil to Pay*, Dr Hellebore in *The Mock Doctor*, a Waiter in *The Oxonian in Town*, the Doctor in *Macbeth*, Le Beau in *As You Like It*, and a Servant and William in *The Jealous Wife*.

When Foote returned to London to direct his summer season at the Haymarket Theatre in 1771, Vowell was among the northern actors engaged by him. Vowell made his London debut on 20 May 1771 as one of the Mob in *The Minor*. He acted a Watchman in *The Upholsterer* on 22 May, and during the remainder of the summer appeared in other modest roles: Bridoun in *The Commissary*, Pedro in *Catherine and Petruchio*, Dapper in *The Citizen*, Thomas in *The Virgin Unmask'd*, a Scholar in *The Padlock*, the Cook in *The Devil to Pay*, Hellebore in *The Mock Doctor*, one of the Mob in *The Contrivances*, a Servant in *The West Indian*, a Servant in *The Busy Body*, Jasper in *Miss in Her Teens*, Salanio in *The Merchant of Venice* and a role in *Madrigal and Truletta*.

Vowell returned to the Haymarket in the summer of 1772 to fill a similar journeyman function, but among his roles that season was the more important one of Trippet in *The Lying Valet* on 1 June 1772. On 19 September he played a Lieutenant in *Richard III*. His name did not appear again in the London bills until 21 September 1774, when he acted an unspecified role in *The Duellist* at the Haymarket. He was again in London in the summer of 1777, when as a member of the company acting at China Hall, Rotherhithe, he played a more important repertoire of parts: Captain Loveit in *Miss in Her Teens*, Charles in *The Busy Body*, Bellamy in *The Suspicious Husband*, Bellmour in *Jane Shore*, Frederick in *The Wonder*, Truman in *George Barnwell*, Hastings in *She Stoops to Conquer*, Lodovico in *Othello*, and Tradelove in *A Bold Stroke for a Wife*.

Vowell's last known London appearance was as Colonel Parapet in a revival of King's *The Modish Wife*, in a specially licensed performance at the Haymarket on 3 January 1780.

Voyer, Miss *[fl. 1798–1801]*, *house servant?*

A Miss Voyer was employed by Drury Lane Theatre from as early as 24 February 1798 (when her name appeared as Voyle) through at least 1800–1801. She was paid the low sum of 3*s*. 4*d*. per day, probably as a house servant. Her name did not appear in any bills. In the Huntington Library is a manuscript order dated 1799, from Sheridan to Peake, for the reinstatement of Miss Voyer.

Voyle. *See* VOYER.

Vudale. *See* VIDALE.

= W =

Wabor, Mr *fl. 1795₁, house servant?*

The accounts for Drury Lane Theatre cite a Mr Wabor on 25 April 1795 as being paid 4s., but for what services we do not know. He was apparently one of the house servants.

Wacklin. *See* WAKELIN.

Wadderburn, Mrs *fl. 1723₁, actress.*

Mrs Wadderburn played Hearty in *The Female Fop* at the Haymarket Theatre on 12 December 1723.

Waddy, John *1751–1814, actor, manager, singer.*

The Irishman John Waddy was born in 1751. He was originally intended for the law, but he was acting in Dublin by 1774, when he was a member of the summer company at the Smock Alley Theatre. Again at Smock Alley in 1774–75, at Cork in July and September 1775, and at Kilkenny in June and August 1776, he then joined Tate Wilkinson's company on the York circuit in 1777–78, acting Romeo at Doncaster as his first appearance. Waddy studied Mosca in Jonson's *Volpone* for about a week, and he acted it "with such propriety and knowledge of that difficult author," wrote Wilkinson in his *Wandering Patentee* (1795), that the performance seemed "an astonishing work, when the shortness of time was considered for so arduous and difficult an undertaking." Wilkinson regarded Waddy as being "one of the greatest utility of any actor I almost know."

In 1779 Waddy joined John Vandermere in the management of the Fishamble Street Theatre in Dublin and then became a country manager. He acted at King's Lynn in 1781 and in August of that year was with Herbert's company at Peterboro, where the managers of the Norwich Theatre wrote to him their offer for an engagement. The terms proposed were

a guinea and a half per week during the Norwich season, with benefit, and "in the Circuit a share & a Benefit." Nothing was offered to Mrs Waddy. Waddy was requested to join them at the Bury Fair.

He evidently accepted the terms and in 1782 was at Norwich, where he remained a regular until 1796. On 12 August 1782 with that company at Colchester he acted Captain O'Cutter in *The Jealous Wife,* and at "Stirbich" (Stourbridge) Fair on 30 October 1782 he played Saville in *The Belle's Stratagem.* At Norwich on 28 February 1783 he acted Carbine in *The Fair American.* The Norwich Committee Books record transactions with Waddy. On 30 May 1783 Waddy was ordered to pay Mr Starkey, the treasurer, "ten Guineas in part of his Note for £19.19.0," and that same day the treasurer was ordered to pay "Mr Waddy's Bill for three Suits of Clothes the Sum of—5.5.0."

In the autumn of 1793 a fall from his horse incapacitated Waddy, and he was unable to perform with the Norwich company at the Stourbridge Fair. Later his peregrinations took him to Ipswich in December 1794, when he was called "much too conceited an actor." In August 1796 the *Monthly Mirror* reported that Waddy, from Norwich, would be joining Covent Garden Theatre for the ensuing season, and in October the magazine stated that he had been articled for five years.

Engaged at a salary of £3 per week, Waddy made his debut at Covent Garden on 5 October 1796 as Conolly in *The School for Wives.* The critic for the *Monthly Mirror* was not impressed:

He is a tall heavy figure, with a rotund and inexpressive countenance; and voice that reminds us of the famous *Greek herald's,* which Homer tells us was as loud as that of *fifty* men. We thought he gave the *brogue* of *Conolly* with tolerable readiness and humour; but there was an awkwardness in his deportment and action that surprised us, considering his long acquaintance with the stage. . . .

That critic wondered what use Mr Waddy could be to Covent Garden and could not see "how he is to be employed." But the reviewer in the *How Do You Do?* for 8 October 1796 was more sanguine, claiming that though the part of Conolly had insufficient "pith and marrow" to afford a performer a fair display of his comic powers, Waddy, "without descending to any unworthy means of extorting applause, made as much of it as the character will bear." In the latter's opinion Waddy appeared likely "to prove a respectable and useful performer. His figure is stout and manly, his voice strong and audible, and his deportment easy and unembarrassed."

On 10 October 1796 Waddy played his second role, Kent in *King Lear,* and his performance did not improve the *Monthly Mirror*'s critic's opinion of him. His subsequent roles that season included Father Luke in *Love in a Camp,* Snare in the premiere of Holman's *Abroad and at Home* on 19 November 1796, Father Frank in *The Prisoner at Large,* Major Sturgeon in *The Mayor of Garratt,* Compass in *The Poor Sailor,* Foigard in *The Beaux' Stratagem,* Vernon in *1 Henry IV,* Farmer Oatland in the premiere of Morton's *A Cure for the Heart Ache* on 10 January 1797, O'Shea in the premiere of Reynolds's *Bantry Bay* on 18 February, Mr Norberry in the premiere of Mrs Inchbald's *Wives As They Were, and Maids As They Are* on 4 March, and Counsellor Plausible in *The Man of the World.* On 26 May 1797 Waddy shared benefit tickets with several other performers.

After acting at Birmingham in the summer of 1797, Waddy returned to Covent Garden, still at £3 per week, to add to his London repertoire in 1797–98 Claudius in *Hamlet,* Father Luke in *The Poor Soldier,* a Lieutenant in *Richard III,* Don John in *Much Ado about Nothing,* Cacafogo in *Rule a Wife and Have a Wife,* Colloony in *An Irishman in London,* Asman in *The Sultan,* M'Query in *The Way to Get Married,* the Earl of Lincoln in *England Preserv'd,* the Mayor of Coventry in *Peeping Tom,* Chip in the premiere of J. C. Cross's musical interlude *The Raft* on 31 March 1798, Sir Carroll O'Donovan in *The Life of the Day,* Patrick in *British Fortitude,* Father Paul in *The Duenna,* Ostrich in the premiere of Cumberland's *The Eccentric Lover* on 30 April 1798, Daniel Dowlas in *The Heir at Law,* Downright in *Every*

Man in His Humour, the Irishman in *Voluntary Contributions,* Solus in *Every One Has His Faults,* Sir John Bull in *Fontainebleau,* M'Gilpin in *The Highland Reel,* and Vortex in *A Cure for the Heartache.* On 5 June 1798 he replaced Quick as Lord Vibrate in Holcroft's *He's Much to Blame.* On 30 May 1798 he shared tickets with Hull and Mrs Litchfield, and tickets (from which he received £69 and 12*s.* 6*d.*) could be had from him at No 214, opposite Southampton Street at High Holborn.

Waddy continued at Covent Garden for 14 seasons; by 1801–2 he was earning £4 10*s.* per week, a level he retained through 1809–10, his last season. Among his original or important roles in 1798–99 were the Duke in *Othello,* Major Sturgeon in *The Mayor of Garratt,* Subtle in The *Tobacconist,* Medium in *Inkle and Yarico,* Daniel Dowlas in *The Heir at Law,* Truepenny in the premiere of T. S. Dibdin's *Five Thousand a Year* on 16 March 1799, Melton in the premiere of Holcroft's *The Old Cloathsman* on 2 April, Frank in *The Prisoner at Large,* Lawyer Circuit in the premiere of T. J. Dibdin's *The Birth Day* on 8 April, Aristander in *Alexander the Great,* Capulet in *Romeo and Juliet,* the Duke of Suffolk in *Henry VIII,* and Lord Torrendale in *Life's Vagaries.* For his benefit on 5 June 1799, shared with Hull, total receipts were £348 8*s.* 6*d.* (less house charges), and tickets were available from Waddy at M'Knowl's, No 8, Great Wild Street, Lincoln's Inn Fields.

In the summer of 1799 he joined the Haymarket company, making his first appearance there on 19 June as the Baron in *The Purse.* That summer he also acted Peery in *Ways and Means,* Doctor Specific in *The Jew and the Doctor,* Hosier in *The Road to Ruin,* an Irishman in *Rosina,* and John d'Aire in *The Surrender of Calais.* After 2 July 1799 Waddy left the Haymarket to act the rest of the summer at Brighton.

At Covent Garden in 1799–1800 Waddy added the Doctor in *Macbeth,* the Chaplain in *The Orphan,* Sullen in *The Beaux' Stratagem,* Lawley in the premiere of Mrs Inchbald's *The Wise Man of the East* on 30 November 1799, Wensel in the premiere of Cumberland's *Joanna* on 16 January 1800, Stukely in *The West Indian,* Gerald in the premiere of Morton's *Speed the Plough* on 8 February 1800, the Governor in *The Critic,* the title role in *Cymbe-*

line on 13 May, and Sir George Thunder in *Wild Oats.* At the Haymarket in the summer of 1800 he played Daniel Dowlas in *The Heir at Law* on 13 June and Amalekite in *Zorinski* on 17 June, and then he went to play at Birmingham, where on 27 June he was announced as making his first appearance in three years.

In his *Monody on the Death of Palmer* (1798), T. Harral called Waddy a "heavy somnific actor." In the *Authentic Memoirs of the Green Rooms* (1799 and 1801) Waddy was acknowledged as "a most excellent vulgar comedian," but his country authority had deluded him into believing he could act kings and great figures. As a provincial manager, it was said, he had monopolized all the principal characters: "Tragedy—Comedy—Opera—Farce—Dance, or singing—minuets, or hornpipes—cotillions, or country reels—a pas de seul, or a hop in a sack—all come alike to him—he blunders with equal facility and happiness through all." Waddy specialized in Irish characters, but all his roles were seasoned "with a most delightful smack of the brogue." Roach wagged in the *Authentic Memoirs* that Harris, the Covent Garden manager and a man of democratic leanings, deliberately would cast Waddy in regal roles with a view to caricaturing sovereignty and "turning the kingly office into ridicule and burlesque." When Quick seceded from Covent Garden at the turn of the century, Waddy took over many of his parts, and he was successful as Lord Duberly in *The Heir at Law,* Vortex in *A Cure for the Heart Ache,* and Sir George Thunder in *Wild Oats.* On 28 May 1801 he played Falstaff in *1 Henry IV* for the first time (benefit tickets were available from him at No 28, Upper King Street, Bloomsbury).

After leaving Covent Garden at the end of 1809–10, Waddy acted for a while at the Surrey Theatre. In April 1814 the *European Magazine* reported John Waddy's death at Oakingham, Berkshire, on 12 April 1814, at the age of 63. In his will, dated 13 October 1810 and proved at London on 27 May 1814, he stated that he then resided at No 15, Abingdon Street, Westminster, and was a performer in the Surrey Theatre. He left £10 per year to his daughter Elizabeth Crisk, wife of John Crisk (a mariner then a prisoner in France), and to his other daughter, Mary Waddy, he

left the lands and property bequeathed to him by his father, "Cadwr Waddy," to be held at lease, at Drineagh, County Wexford, in Ireland.

Waddy had married Mary Lamb at Dublin in 1774, according to public records in that city. On 15 March 1778 their daughter Mary was baptized at St Michael le Belfry in York. The *Monthly Mirror* of June 1802 reported the death "lately" of Mrs Waddy, who had been a minor player in the provinces. Waddy, however, seems to have remarried, for a Mrs Waddy was on the Covent Garden paylist for £1 10s. per week from 1803–4 through 1807–8. The second Mrs Waddy may have died soon after, for she was not mentioned in his will. Waddy's daughter, Mary Waddy, made her debut at Covent Gardens on 8 October 1802 as Julia Faulkner in *The Way to Get Married,* was well received, and was engaged for the season. Her portrait, engraved by T. Cheesman, after Buck, was published by W. Holland in 1804.

Wade, Mr   *fl.* 1726₁,   *dresser.*
On 6 March 1726 Mr Wade was paid £1 1s. as a dresser at Lincoln's Inn Fields Theatre. Those were his arrears, but the account books do not indicate how long he had been working at the theatre.

Wade, John   *fl.* 1712–1732₁,   *dancer.*
For his first stage appearance John Wade danced a turn called *Skipper* with Thurmond at Drury Lane Theatre on 9 June 1712. On 12 June 1713 he danced a *Dutch Skipper,* and thereafter he appeared at Drury Lane fairly regularly through the 1718–19 season. Often the entr'acte dances in which he performed had no titles, but a few did: *Four French Peasants,* a *Pastoral Dance of Myrtillo,* and the like. Wade also took some pantomime roles on occasion, such as a Follower of Mars in *The Loves of Mars and Venus* (his first one, on 2 March 1717), the Monster Crocodile in *The Shipwreck,* and Punch in *The Dumb Farce.*

After 1718–19 Wade seems to have left the stage to teach. John Waver listed him in 1721 among the prominent dancing masters in England. John Wade returned to the stage for a single appearance at Goodman's Fields Theatre, dancing *Two Pierrots* with Burney for Burney's benefit, on 21 April 1732.

Waghorne, Mr *(fl. 1731₁),* *musician?*
Benefit concerts were held for a Mr Wag-
horne, probably a musician, on 4 June and 7
July 1731 at the Devil Tavern.

Wagner, Mr *(fl. 1792–1794₁),* *actor.*
Mr Wagner's name appeared several times
in the Sadler's Wells casts in the 1790s. Sometime in 1792 he was a Lieutenant in *The Savages,* the Second Officer in *La Forêt Noire,* a
Monkey Lover in *Medea's Kettle,* and an Officer
in *The Honours of War;* he was a Sans Coulottes
Officer in *Sans Coulottes* in 1793, and he had a
part in *Penmaenmawr* in 1794.

Wagner, [Frederic?] *(fl. 1770?–1794₁),*
violinist, composer?
Frederic Wagner, the composer of *Twelve
New English Songs* (1770?), may have been the
Mr Wagner who played second violin in the
Handel Memorial Concerts at Westminster
Abbey and the Pantheon in May and June
1784. Doane's *Musical Directory* of 1794 lists
Wagner as having performed in the Concert of
Ancient Music and in the Queen's band. He
had lodgings in Buckingham House.

Waightly. *See* WHEATLEY.

Wainwright, Mr *(fl. 1794₁),* *violinist.*
In 1794 Doane's *Musical Directory* listed Mr
Wainwright, a violinist who performed the
Handelian concerts at Westminster Abbey and
was resident at Liverpool. Probably he was related (perhaps he was a son) to Robert Wainwright, who in midcentury was organist at
the Collegiate Church in Manchester and who
died at Liverpool on 16 July 1782. One John
Wainwright published at London *A Collection
of Psalm Tunes, Anthems, Hymns, and Chants* in
1776, and the anthem *Christians awake, salute
the happy Morn* about 1795. A Richard Wainwright published a favorite sea song called *Our
Topsails atrip* at Liverpool about 1790.

Wainwright, Miss *(fl. 1794₁),* *singer.*
A Miss Wainwright, soprano, of No 28,
Pall Mall, was listed in Doane's *Musical Direc-
tory* in 1794.

**Wainwright, Sarah, later Mrs Edward
Allen** *(fl. 1764–1784₁),* *singer, actress.*

Sarah Wainwright, said to have been a pupil of Dr Arne, was announced as a young
gentlewoman making her first appearance on
any stage when she acted Maukin in *The
Guardian Outwitted* at Covent Garden Theatre
on 12 December 1764. She was identified as
Miss Wainwright in a notation on Larpent MS
No 243 in the Huntington Library. On 2 January 1765, with her name now in the bills,
she played Margery in *Love in a Village* for her
second and evidently last appearance in a London theatre.

Sometime in 1765 Miss Wainwright became one of the English performers whom David Douglass recruited for his American Company. She made her first recorded appearance
in America in Charleston, next to the Queen
Street Theatre, on 13 November 1765 when
she and Nancy Hallam sang in a concert produced by Peter Valton, organist of St Philip's. In January 1766 she made her debut at
the Queen Street Theatre, where she seems
to have remained employed through the
summer.

In the autumn she was with the American
Company when it opened the Southwark Theatre in Philadelphia. Seilhamer and Pollock
both wrote that she made her first appearance
in that city on 26 November 1766 as Polly in
The Beggar's Opera. But Sonneck in *Early Opera
in America* lists Miss Wainwright as Sally in
the original American cast of the comic opera
Thomas and Sally, which was performed at
Philadelphia on 14 November 1766. On 12
December 1766 she acted the nonmusical role
of Jessica in *The Merchant of Venice.* Sometime
prior to 19 March 1767 *Love in a Village* was
performed for the first time, for that date was
announced as the fourth night. Sonneck lists
the cast for the surviving bill of that fourth
performance, but does not include the role of
Rosetta. That character certainly was filled by
Miss Wainwright, for in January 1767 the
critic in the *Pennsylvania Gazette,* without
specifying her role, wrote that "Miss Wainwright is a very good singer, and her action
exceeds the famous Miss Brent." (Charlotte
Brent—later Mrs Pinto—was the regular Rosetta at Covent Garden in the mid-sixties.)
For her benefit on 4 June 1767, when *The
Chaplet* was performed for the first time, Miss
Wainwright and Woolls sang "God Save the
King" at the end of Act I; she sang "The Spin-

ning Wheel" after Act II and "Lovely Nancy" after Act IV.

When Douglas opened his new John Street Theatre in New York on 7 December 1767 Miss Wainwright acted Cherry in *The Beaux' Stratagem* and Mrs Riot in *Lethe.* On 21 December she appeared as Sally and on 11 January 1768 as Rosetta. She took on the serious role of Goneril in *King Lear* on 25 January and then again acted Jessica in *The Merchant of Venice* on 28 January. That season she also sang specialty numbers and participated in concerts given by the company. Her other roles in New York in 1767–68 included Lucetta in *The Suspicious Husband,* Nell in *The Devil to Pay,* Lady Bab in *High Life below Stairs,* Rose in *The Recruiting Officer,* Maria in *The Citizen,* Mrs Sealand in *The Conscious Lovers,* Charmion in *All for Love,* and Lady Wronghead in *The Provok'd Husband.*

After another season at the John Street Theatre, for some reason she retired from the stage, an intention that was announced on the bills for 27 April 1769. She went to live in Philadelphia, and, according to Seilhamer, she accommodated her old manager by appearing a few times when the company played in the Southwark Theatre before the Revolution. Those appearances occurred between 1 and 15 November 1773.

Circumstances must have forced Miss Wainwright from retirement, for she was acting again at Charleston in the spring of 1774, appearing as Lucy in *The West Indian* and Mysis in *A Picture of a Play House* on 25 April and as Betty in *A Bold Stroke for a Wife* and Jenny in *Neck or Nothing* on 2 May. When Douglass took the American Company to Jamaica to sit out the Revolution, she was with them at their opening in Kingston on 1 July 1775. She was playing with the company at Montego Bay from 17 March through 15 May 1777 and there again from February to December 1782. Meanwhile she was a regular at Kingston, with her name in the bills from 1779 through 1782.

In her *Charleston Stage,* Willis states, without source, that soon after 1779 Miss Wainwright married a Mr Page and retired. In his *Revels in Jamaica,* Richardson Wright advises, "Some coyly hint that in Jamaica she married a Mr. Miranda and on his death gave her heart and hand to a fellow Jamaican actor, Isaac Mo-

rales." Morales was with the Kingston company between 1779 and 1782. On 4 September 1779 he advertised in the *Mercury* his availability as a teacher of the Spanish language. He did not accompany the American Company back to the mainland in July 1785, and neither did Miss Wainwright. It is unlikely they were married, however, for a notice in the *South Carolina Weekly Gazette* of 30 January 1784 seems to settle the question of the actress's spouse about that time with intelligence from Kingston that Edward Allen and Miss Sarah Wainwright, "late of the American Company," had been married recently. Her husband perhaps was the Mr Allen, announced as from the Theatre Royal in Edinburgh, who collaborated with Richard Goodman in giving the "Lecture upon Heads" and other entertainments at Charleston and Philadelphia in 1775.

Waistkum, Mr   *fl. 1749₁,*   *actor.*
On 10 April 1749, when Mr Waistkum played Crack in *Sir Courtly Nice* at Covent Garden Theatre, he was advertised as never having appeared on that stage before. Of his previous experience we know nothing. On 12 April he acted Don Cholerick in *Love Makes a Man* for his second and last appearance in London.

Waite, Mrs   *fl. 1782₁,*   *actress.*
Mrs Waite played an unspecified principal character in a specially licensed performance of *Love at a Venture* at the Haymarket Theatre on 21 April 1782. The performers were described as "engaged from different Theatres."

Waite, George   *fl. 1749?–1794₁,* *singer, musician.*
According to the notes left by William S. Clark, a musician named George Waite was employed at the Smock Alley Theatre in Dublin in 1749–50. Possibly he was the Mr Waite listed 35 years later by Dr Burney as a bass singer in the Handel Memorial Concerts at Westminster Abbey and the Pantheon in May and June 1784. George Waite was noticed in Doane's *Musical Directory* of 1794 as a bass singer, of No 11, Lower Lambeth Marsh, who sang in the Titchfield Chapel Society, the Drury Lane oratorios, and the Handelian performances at Westminster Abbey.

Wakefield, Robert   *fl. 1784–1794*, violinist.

Robert Wakefield played first violin in the Handel Memorial Concerts at Westminster Abbey and the Pantheon in May and June 1784. Doane's *Musical Directory* of 1794 noted that Wakefield also played in the oratorios at Covent Garden Theatre and at Ranelagh Gardens. He lived at Mr Betts's in the Royal Exchange.

Wakelin, James   *fl. 1749–c. 1779*, actor, manager.

James Wakelin, who was the husband of the Sadler's Wells dancer and provincial manager Ann Wakelin, received a benefit at the Haymarket Theatre on 16 May 1749. That night *The Revenge* and *The Country Wedding* were performed, but the casts are not known. Wakelin must have assisted his wife in the management of the Kent circuit until it was taken over, about 1772, by their daughter Sarah Baker. In 1771 he managed a strolling company that played in Norwich and was ordered to leave that city by 7 December. He also was at Bartholomew Fair about 1779, with his daughter Sarah.

Wakelin's death date is unknown to us. His wife died at Rochester in June 1787 at an advanced age. She and their daughters Mary Wakelin and Sarah Baker are noticed separately.

A 38-page pamphlet entitled *The Squabble of the Richmond Players,* written by "Don Buskinsocko," a member of that company, was published in London, undated, and was sold by J. Wakelin, who perhaps was related to our subject.

Wakelin, Mrs James, Ann, née Clark   d. 1787, manager, acrobat, dancer, puppeteer.

The marriage of James Wakelin to Ann Clark, a minor, on 10 June 1738 at St Luke's Finsbury has been called to our attention by Ian Templeton. Ann Wakelin (or Wakelyn, Wacklin) was an acrobatic dancer who had a long career as a provincial manager. She often described herself in her advertisements as "of Sadler's Wells." The date of her first association with that Islington house is not known. The Mr Wakelin who received a benefit at the Haymarket Theatre on 16 May 1749 was

probably her husband. Ann and Wakelin traveled the countryside for some years. She managed a company based in Tunbridge Wells that was taken over about 1769 by her daughter Sarah, who on 6 January 1760 had married a stroller named Thomas Baker.

Mrs Wakelin had her company in Yarmouth in 1769. On 23 February of that year the proprietors of the Norwich Theatre, who also owned the Yarmouth playhouse, consented that "Mr Crouse do agree with Mrs Wacklin for her having the use of the playhouse at Yarmouth [this] Season in case she will undertake to pay Mr. Crouse for the use of the proprietors the Sum of Twenty Guineas out of which we do agree that two Guineas shall be paid to the Mayor of Yarmouth for the Town dues." Several years later, on 28 November 1771, the Norwich Committee requested the Norwich mayor "to give His orders that Mr Wakelyns Company [which Ann was probably with] now performing in this City may not continue performing here longer than Saturday the 7th of December."

In her article "The Players in Cambridge" in *Studies in English Theatre History* (1952), Sybil Rosenfeld recounts the various visits made regularly by Mrs Wakelin and her company to the Stourbridge Fair in Cambridge between 1762 and 1777 when they offered acrobatic dancing, tumbling, and puppet shows.

Mrs Wakelin was no longer in her daughter Sarah Baker's company, nor did she come to Stourbridge Fair, after 1777. Another daughter, Mary Wakelin, who performed in her mother's company about 1774, is noticed separately, as are James Wakelin and Sarah Baker.

Wakelin, Mary   *fl. 1763–1800*, dancer, acrobat, actress, wardrobe mistress.

Mary Wakelin was the daughter of the provincial managers Ann Wakelin and her husband James Wakelin and the sister of the actress and manager Sarah Baker. Probably she had been performing on the Kent circuit, which her mother managed, before we first notice her as a member of the Norwich company in 1763. She appeared at Bristol in the summer of 1766, offering "amazing Performances" of stiff-rope dancing in the old Assembly Room on St Augustine's Back, and by

1770 was a slack-wire dancer in the troupes brought occasionally to Sadler's Wells by her mother. About 1774 she and her sister Sarah (by then manager of the Kent company) played at Bartholomew Fair.

No doubt Mary was also a performer in her mother's companies that visited Stourbridge Fair in Cambridge regularly between 1762 and 1777. In her sister Sarah Baker's company that was based in Tunbridge Wells and toured Kent, Mary was dancer, actress, wardrobe mistress, and cook. The Tunbridge Wells bills show her in her sister's company regularly between 1794 and 1800.

Wakelin, Sarah. *See* BAKER, SARAH.

Wakelyn. *See* WAKELIN.

Walcot, Mrs, later Mrs Chambers [*fl.* 1782–1810], *actress, singer.*

Mrs Walcot probably had some provincial experience before she was engaged in 1782 at the Theatre Royal, Shakespeare Square, in Edinburgh, where her first appearance seems to have been on 8 June as Belinda in *All in the Wrong.* She acted Julia Faulkland in *The Rivals* on 15 June, Mrs Vixen in *The Beggar's Opera* on 29 June, and Cecilia in *The Chapter of Accidents* on 3 August. At Edinburgh in 1783 she had a number of important roles, including Alicia in *Jane Shore,* Angelina in *Love Makes a Man,* Clarinda in *The Suspicious Husband,* Emily in *The Deuce Is in Him,* and Lady Randolph in *Douglas.*

Leaving Edinburgh after 1783, Mrs Walcot engaged at Brighton for the season of 1784, which ran from 28 July through 13 October. On 26 April 1785 she made an appearance at the Haymarket Theatre for the benefit of Mrs Greville. Announced as from Edinburgh, Mrs Walcot acted Mrs Strickland in *The Suspicious Husband.* She then returned to Brighton to begin the season there on 27 June 1785. She was also a member of the Brighton company in 1786 and perhaps for several years thereafter. Between February and June 1790 she was with a company at Coventry managed by Stephen Kemble. She returned to Edinburgh on 21 January 1793. Said to be making "her first appearance for ten years," she acted the Mayoress in *Peeping Tom of Coventry.* She was also

seen there that season as Curtis in *Catherine and Petruchio,* Goody Rheum in *The Old Woman Weatherwise,* Lady Acid in *Notoriety,* Lady Diana Dupely in *Cross Partners,* Lady Dunder in *Ways and Means,* Mrs Manly in *The Fugitive,* Mrs Quickly in *The Merry Wives of Windsor,* Mysis in *Apollo,* and a singing Witch in *Hodge Podge.* That was a repertoire decidedly inferior to the one she had appeared in at Edinburgh ten years earlier. Over the next four years in that company it hardly improved in status and included such roles as Mrs Drugget in *Three Weeks after Marriage,* the Mother in *The Recruiting Serjeant,* and Lady Alton in *The English Merchant.* Among her more interesting roles were the Nurse in *Romeo and Juliet,* Sysigambes in *The Rival Queens,* and Mrs Malaprop in *The Rivals.* On 18 January 1794 she acted Gertrude in *Hamlet* and on 16 April 1796 the Queen in *Cymbeline.* On 4 December 1795 Mrs Walcot and her daughter, Miss Walcot, appeared together in a performance of *Richard III* at Newcastle.

In the autumn of 1797 Mrs Walcot, who the previous season at Edinburgh had still been serving as a utility actress of mature females, was engaged at Drury Lane Theatre to supply the place of Mrs Elizabeth Hopkins, a declining actress of advancing age and increasing girth who had been discharged from that theatre at the end of 1795–96. Mrs Walcot made her debut at Drury Lane on 21 September 1797 as Mrs Rigid in *The Will.* Her next role was Mrs Matadore in *The Humourist* on 28 September, followed by Mrs Heidelberg in *The Clandestine Marriage* on 3 October. The *Monthly Mirror* judged that she did not "exactly hit our idea of what *Mrs. Heidelberg,* and of course all parts of a similar cast, require from the performer." The critic found her "manner is too polished and *lady-like,* her speech too indicative of good-breeding, her powers too confined, and her colouring too faint, to give the necessary effect to a representation, of which vulgarity, turbulence, and extravagance are the leading and essential features." On the other hand, the *Monthly Mirror* critic greatly admired her Mrs Rigid, which demanded a "very different treatment."

Other roles acted by Mrs Walcot in her first season at Drury Lane were the Nurse in *Isabella* (with Mrs Siddons in the title role), Mrs Cockney in *A Trip to the Nore* (at its premiere on 9 November 1797), Mrs Quickly in *1 Henry IV,* Alice in the premiere of Lewis's *The Castle Spectre* on 14 December 1797, the Nurse in *A Trip to Scarborough,* Mrs Clack in the premiere of Holcroft's *Knave or Not* on 25 January 1798, Mrs Ratcliffe in *The Jew,* Gradisca in *The Italian Monk,* Juliana in *The Prisoner,* Nell Trot in the premiere of Iliff's *The Ugly Club* on 6 June 1798, and Lady Dunder in *Ways and Means.*

In 1798–99 Mrs Walcot's salary was raised from the £4 per week she had received the previous season to £5. Her new roles included Lady Rounceval in *The Young Quaker,* Miss Pickle in *The Spoil'd Child,* Mrs Peachum in *The Beggar's Opera,* Mrs Lofty in the premiere of Cumberland's *A Word for Nature* on 5 December 1798, Mrs Hamford in *The Wedding Day,* Lady Freelove in *The Jealous Wife,* Tabitha in the premiere of Lewis's *The Twins* on 8 April 1799, Mrs Scout in *The Village Lawyer,* an unspecified role in the anonymous *Trials of the Heart* on 24 April, Mrs Sanderson in Maria Theresa De Camp's *First Faults* on 3 May, and Mrs Pattypan in *The First Floor.*

At Drury Lane in 1799–1800 Mrs Walcot's new roles included Lady Brumback in Bannister's farce *Of Age Tomorrow,* which opened on 1 February 1800 and ran 35 nights, and Mrs Goodly in Prince Hoare's *Indiscretion* on 10 May 1800. On 21 May 1800 she acted Mrs Hardcastle in *She Stoops to Conquer.* In his *Dramatic Censor,* Dutton praised her performance of Lady Brumback, stating that she "personated the half-expectant, half-desponding Old Maid with considerable judgment." He also noted that she excelled in characters like Mrs Heidelberg. The *Authentic Memoirs of the Green Room* (1799) called her "no inadequate representative" of the characters once played by Mrs Hopkins, since she was "possessed of much good sense and feeling." But after 1799–1800 Mrs Walcot was relegated to the provinces.

According to the *True Briton* of 25 September 1797, Mrs Walcot's husband was a physician. The Miss Walcot who appeared in children's roles at Drury Lane in 1797–98 was no doubt her daughter. Perhaps the Mr Walcot who began his career at the Fishamble Street Theatre in Dublin on 22 December 1797 was related.

By 1810, Mrs Walcot had become Mrs

Chambers. (Perhaps she was the Mrs Chambers who had acted at Worcester in June 1805.) That January the *Monthly Mirror* reported that she had been acting in Crisp's company at Shrewsbury the previous season until 24 November 1809; the correspondent was of the opinion that "Mrs Chambers (late Mrs. Walcot, of Drury Lane) in her line, is far before any person out of London, or I think I should not speak too highly in saying equal to any there." A Mr Chambers, no doubt her husband, was also in the Shrewsbury company in late 1809. Possibly he was the Chambers (noticed in this *Dictionary* 3:143) who had been at Drury Lane for two seasons, 1777–78 and 1778–79; we speculate that the London Chambers may have been the actor of that name who died at Shrewsbury about 1820, "the oldest provincial comedian in the kingdom."

Walcot, Miss *fl. 1795–1807?₁,* actress.

Miss Walcot appeared, probably as the young Duke of York, in *Richard III* at the Theatre Royal, Newcastle, on 4 December 1795. She was no doubt the daughter of the actress Mrs Walcot, who also performed in that production at Newcastle. The mother was engaged at Edinburgh a number of seasons in the 1790s. There Miss Walcot also appeared in such characters as Miss Biddy in *Miss in Her Teens* in 1794–95; a Child in *The Bank Note,* a Child in *The Children in the Wood,* the Duke of York in *Richard III,* Edward in *Every One Has His Fault,* and the Page in *The Fall of David Rizzio* in 1795–96.

Miss Walcot came with her mother to Drury Lane in 1797–98, making her first appearance there as a Boy in *The Adopted Child* on 7 November 1797. On 22 March and 28 April 1798 she played the First Child in *The Children of the Wood.* She appeared in an unspecified role in *The Eleventh of June* on 5, 7, and 13 June 1798. The next season her name appeared in the bills only on 7 May 1799 when she acted Juliana in *The Prisoner,* but she probably helped fill the stage as an extra on occasion. Indeed, the following season, 1800–1801, her name was listed in the theatre's account book on 3 January 1801 for having been paid 15s. as a "super [numerary]."

Probably our subject was the Miss Walcot

who played Mrs Malfort in *The Soldier's Daughter* at Edinburgh on 26 March 1807.

According to the *True Briton* of 25 September 1797 Miss Walcot's father was a doctor. Perhaps she was also related to the Mr Walcot who made his Irish debut at the Fishamble Street Theatre in Dublin on December 1797.

Walcup, Miss *fl.* 1795–1799₁, *actress, singer.*

On 23 January 1795 "A Young Lady" made her stage debut playing Marianne in *The Dramatist* at Covent Garden Theatre; the *London Chronicle* identified her as Miss Walcup, and the *European Magazine* said she was from Greenwich. "Her figure and manner were impressive in her favor," the magazine reported, "but she seemed to act under the disadvantage of indisposition. Her voice was almost inaudible at any distance." During the rest of the season she was in the chorus of Country Girls in *The Mysteries of the Castle* and a Villager in *The Battle of Hexham.* She was paid £1 weekly for her services. In 1795–96 Miss Walcup was Nancy in *The Poor Sailor,* Molly Brazen in *The Beggar's Opera,* an English Amazon in *Lord Mayor's Day,* a Bacchant in *Comus,* a chorus member in *The Lad of the Hills* (also in the cast was Miss E. Walcup, probably her sister), and a Bard in *Oscar and Malvina.* She also sang in *Macbeth, Romeo and Juliet, Hamlet,* and *Zorinski.*

Miss Walcup continued at Covent Garden through the 1798–99 season, appearing in chorus parts in *Bantry Bay, Italian Villagers, Harlequin and Oberon, Joan of Arc, The Mouth of the Nile,* and *Albert and Adelaide.* She played Zorayda in *The Mountaineers* and also sang in choruses of plays, as before; new ones included *The Village Fête.* Miss Walcup was named in the Richmond Theatre bills on 23 September 1796 and 7 July 1797. She was surely the Walcup named in the Covent Garden benefit bill of 17 May 1799.

Walcup, Miss E. *fl.* 1796–1797₁, *singer.*

Miss E. Walcup, probably a sister of the Miss Walcup who began acting at Covent Garden in 1795, sang in the chorus of *The Lad of the Hills* on 9 April 1796 at that house. She was again there from 7 October 1796 to 4 March 1797, earning £1 weekly for singing in

The Wicklow Mountains, an alteration of *The Lad of the Hills.*

Walcup, Grace, later Mrs Sydney *fl.* 1795–1801₁, *singer, actress.*

On 24 October 1795 Miss Grace Walcup (sister to Miss Walcup and Miss E. Walcup, probably) appeared at Covent Garden Theatre as Betty Doxey in *The Beggar's Opera.* She continued through 4 December for £1 weekly. She and the Miss Walcup who also began appearing at Covent Garden in 1795 were probably the two Misses Walcup who were in the company at Richmond in July 1797. Grace returned to Covent Garden to be a Countrywoman in *The Raft* on 31 March 1798; on 9 April she sang in *Harlequin's Return.*

The *Morning Chronicle* on 10 September 1799 reported that Grace Walcup had lately married a Mr Sydney. She was in *The Beggar's Opera* again at Covent Garden beginning on 18 September 1799 as Mrs Sydney, and she continued the whole season, now at £2 weekly. Her chores included singing in *Macbeth, Romeo and Juliet,* and *Joanna,* and between the acts on 8 March 1800 she and two others sang "Come every jovial fellow." Mrs Sydney was seen as Jenny in *The Highland Reel,* Louisa in *The Farmer,* Jane in *The Naval Pillar,* an Islander in *The Death of Captain Cook,* a Woman of Zenana in *Ramah Droog,* Adela in *The Death of the Nile,* an Attendant in *The Volcano,* a Nun in *Raymond and Agnes,* Ellen Woodbine in *Netley Abbey,* a Welsh Woman in *St David's Day,* a character in *Paul and Virginia,* and Fanny in *Marian.* Her benefit tickets were accepted on 23 May. Mrs Sydney continued at Covent Garden Theatre through the 1800–1801 season at £2 weekly.

Waldré, Vincent *c. 1742–1814, scene painter.*

Vincent Waldré was born in Vicenza about 1742 and came to London in 1774, according to the Rosenfeld and Croft-Murray "Checklist" in *Theatre Notebook,* 20. He worked as a scene painter and machinist at the King's Theatre in 1777–78 on *Creso, La clemenza di Scipione, L'amore soldato,* and *L'amore artigiano.* He went to Dublin with the Marquis of Buckingham where he decorated St Patrick's Hall and, in 1793, painted the ceiling and proscenium of the private theatre that had been made out of the Fishamble Street Music Hall. In January 1798 Waldré was in charge of the scenery, decorations, and machinery at the Crow Street Theatre. He was later appointed architect to the Board of Works. He married an English woman, settled in Dublin, and died there in August 1814 at the age of 72.

Waldron, Boys   *d. c. 1760, musician.*
Boys (or Boyce) Waldron (or Waldren) was an original subscriber to the Royal Society of Musicians on 28 August 1739. He remained active to at least 1755 and bequeathed £50 to the Society in 1760. *The Royal Society of Musicians* (1985) asserts that Waldron died about that year.

Waldron, Francis Godolphin   *1744–1818, actor, manager, singer, prompter, author.*
Francis Godolphin Waldron (or Waldren) was born in 1744, probably in London. According to notations written in an early nineteenth-century hand made on the Folger Library's copy of Waldron's *Shakespearean Miscellany* (1804), he served as an apprentice to the eminent wood carver Hayworth, "who lived in the house now No 8 in Denmark St." (Hayworth was uncle to Samuel De Wilde, who also served his time with him as an apprentice wood carver and became a successful theatrical portraitist.)

Waldron, however, seems to have abandoned early any thoughts of becoming a wood carver, for by 1766, at the age of 22, he was with a company acting at the New Concert Hall in Edinburgh. That year he appeared in a performance of *The Clandestine Marriage* on 21 April, but in which role we do not know. He was still there (or had returned) in 1769, when his roles included Beau Clincher in *The Constant Couple* and Robin in *The Absent Man* on 23 March and the title role in the burletta *Amintas* on 15 April.

Drawing closer to London, in the summer of 1769 Waldron acted with the company at Richmond, Surrey. In the autumn he was engaged by Garrick at Drury Lane Theatre, where he made his first appearance on 6 October 1769 as Scrub in *The Beaux' Stratagem.* William Hopkins wrote in his prompter's diary that night: "Mr Waldron from Edinburgh . . . is a mean figure a small Impediment in his speaking and wants power he met

with some applause." When Garrick's very successful production of *The Jubilee* was premiered on 14 October 1769, Waldron was to be found walking in the procession, a service he performed throughout the season. His next role was Marall in *A New Way to Pay Old Debts* on 21 October, followed by Francis in *1 Henry IV* on 23 October, Daniel in *The Conscious Lovers* on 8 November, and Matthew in *Every Man in His Humour* on 29 November. His other roles in his first season at Drury Lane included Gripus in *Amphitryon* on 1 February 1770, the Maid in *Rule a Wife and Have a Wife* (a production in which many female roles were taken by men) on 1 March, Tom in *The Funeral* on 3 April, Canton in *The Clandestine Marriage* on 16 April, the Apothecary in *Romeo and Juliet* on 8 May, Paris in *The Jealous Wife* on 10 May, Ragout in *The Brave Irishman* on 14 May, and Philip in *High Life below Stairs* on 16 May. During March, when Drury Lane was accommodating oratorios and other productions in which he had no parts, Waldron traveled back up to Edinburgh to act at the new Theatre Royal in Shakespeare Square; one of his roles there was Old Philpot in *The Citizen* on 26 March 1770.

After passing the summer again at Richmond, where he had a benefit on 22 September 1770 in *Love in a Village,* he returned to Drury Lane to begin his second season on 29 September as Abram in *Harlequin's Invasion.* On 3 October he played the Second Gravedigger in *Hamlet.* A performance in that character a year later prompted *The Theatrical Review* to censure his ambitions: "This lisping Gentleman, unfortunately, for himself, and to the mortification of the Audience, steps into Characters far beyond the reach, either of his ideas or power of execution." But Waldron continued to add to his repertoire Maw-worm in *The Hypocrite,* a Beggar in *The Ladies' Frolick,* Dicky in *The Constant Couple,* the poet in *The Author,* Old Gerald in *The Anatomist,* and an unspecified role in the premiere of Mrs Pye's unsuccessful farce, *The Capricious Lady,* on 10 May 1770. On 20 May, when he shared a benefit with W. Palmer and Atkins, he acted Philip in *High Life below Stairs.* In 1771–72 roles new to him included Lint in *The Mayor of Garratt,* Varland in *The West Indian,* Fabian in *Twelfth Night,* Napthalie in *The Fashionable Lover,* Steve in *The What D'Ye Call It,* the original Sir Samuel in *The Humours of the Turf* (on 25 April 1772), and a Sailor in *The Fair Quaker of Deal.*

Waldron's only new roles in 1772–73 were the Beggar in *The Beggar's Opera*, Dwindle in *The Gamesters*, Robert in *All in the Wrong*, and an unspecified part in the popular pantomime *The Pigmy Revels*. The season for Waldron, however, was distinguished by the appearance of the first of his many theatrical compositions, *The Maid of Kent*, a comedy that premiered at Drury Lane on 17 May 1773 and in which Waldron acted Metre. The story is based on *The Spectator*, No 123. The occasion was his benefit, which brought modest profits to Waldron of £34 19s. 6d.; total house receipts were only £99. According to the prompter Hopkins the new comedy was received "with some applause." The *Covent Garden Magazine* that month noted the thin house and called the play "the hasty production of an unskilful writer." *The Maid of Kent* had only that single performance that season; it was played twice the next season, for Waldron's shared benefit on 7 May 1774 and for Bannister and Griffiths's benefit on 19 May, and it was revived at the Haymarket Theatre on 21 September 1795 in a revision by Waldron called *'Tis a Wise Child Knows Its Father*, again for his benefit. The original comedy was published in 1778 (it is also in Larpent MS 13.M.); the revision, never published, survives in Larpent MS 14.S. at the Huntington Library.

Continuing at Drury Lane for a total of 27 seasons, through 1795–96, he played numerous subordinate roles, mostly in comedy, like Whittle in *The Irish Widow*, Hurry in *The Maid of the Oaks*, Trapland in *Love for Love*, and a variety of servants, Irishmen, and characters in pantomimes. Some of his many other roles over the years included Justice Shallow in *The Merry Wives of Windsor*, Lucianus in *Hamlet*, Justice Woodcock in *Love in a Village*, Antonio in *The Chances*, Corin in *As You Like It*, and Alphonso in *The Spanish Fryar*. On 15 May 1783 he played Sir Peter Teazle in *The School for Scandal* for Tom King at very short notice. Occasionally he went to help out at Covent Garden, playing there Justice Shallow on 21 May 1782, Governor Harcourt in *The Chapter of Accidents* two nights later, and Cockletop in *Modern Antiques* on 6 January 1792. Waldron's

Folger Shakespeare Library

FRANCIS GODOLPHIN WALDRON, at age 20
artist unknown

salary at Drury Lane was £2 10s. per week in 1775–76 and had risen to £4 by 1790–91. The accounts of the theatre record loans made to him from time to time—£60 on 20 May 1783 and £30 on 5 July 1787, for example.

Waldron was one of the committee appointed on 18 May 1774 to draw up the procedures for establishing the Drury Lane Fund for the benefit of theatrical personnel, and he served the fund for many years. In the *Authentic Memoirs of the Green Room* (1799) a story is told of how he received that responsibility:

One day, while Mr. Garrick and his friends were settling some important matters relative to the theatrical fund, they were considering who they should employ to take an active part in its management. During the time of deliberation, Waldron, very fortunately for himself, was walking behind the scenes, and caught the eye of Garrick, who, for the want of a better, immediately proposed him, and the rest unwilling there should be any delay, readily consented.

After playing at Birmingham in the summer of 1774, he returned to Drury Lane for his regular round of modest roles. On 12 May 1775 for his benefit shared with Mrs Greville, Waldron played an unspecified supporting part in his own two-act farce *The Contrast; or, The Jew and Married Courtezan,* acted only once in London and never printed. (A play called *The Contrast,* perhaps Waldron's, had been acted at Manchester on 17 January 1774.)

Our first notice of Waldron's connection with the theatre at Richmond, Surrey, dates from 1769, though he may have been a member of that summer company in earlier years. At the close of the 1776 season the lease of the theatre held by the incumbent managers Simon Slingsby and Thomas Jefferson was relinquished at the request of the proprietors, Messrs Horne and Hubbard, who wished to sell the property. When the theatre was auctioned at Skinner's, Waldron took it with the highest bid, £3,610, and paid a deposit of £722. But he had difficulty raising the rest of the money. He tried to borrow £1,800 from Garrick, who wrote to Colman on 23 August 1776 that had he "not disposed of my Money, I should assist him," for Waldron was "a very honest Man & will perform Every promise he makes." Garrick suggested that if Colman had some money he might help Waldron, but evidently Colman did not. In desperation, Waldron published on 2 September 1776 an appeal for subscriptions in an eight-page pamphlet, *To the Nobility, Gentry, and Others, Inhabitants of Richmond, and the adjacent Villas and Villages.* He described himself as "a performer at said Theatre for several Seasons" and in danger of forfeiting his deposit "in Case of a Failure in making his Purchase good." He offered interest and a scale of privileges for investors of £100, £50, or £25 but acknowledged that his plea was "made more to the Heart than to the Head." That appeal failed, Waldron lost his £722, and the property reverted to the proprietors. In 1777 and 1778 a tallow-chandler of Richmond named Wheble and one other person, according to Gilliland's *Dramatic Mirror,* acquired the lease.

In the summer of 1777 Waldron returned to Richmond to act. In 1778 he acted for Joseph Fox at Brighton in June, and he was again at Richmond that summer. About that time he finally acquired the lease of the Richmond Theatre and Assembly Rooms at an unknown fee (though his predecessors Slingsby

and Jefferson had paid a total of £250 per annum, according to a letter dated 27 January 1804 from William Smith to James Winston, now in the Birmingham Public Library). In the Huntington Library is Waldron's manuscript titled "The Dramatic Chronicle. An Occasional address. to be spoken at the opening of the Theatre-Royal on Richmond Green. 1779." In 1779 Waldron's comedy *The Richmond Heiress* was performed there; an alteration from Thomas D'Urfey, it was not printed, nor does it survive in the Larpent collection.

Though both Gilliland and Winston (in his *Theatric Tourist*) state that Waldron held the management only in 1779 and 1780 and that in 1781 and 1782 the lease was rented by twelve tradesmen called by the townsfolk The Twelve Apostles, documents in the Public Record Office record licenses granted to Waldron for theatre performances at Richmond in 1782 and 1783. Gilliland put the theatre under William Palmer between 1783 and 1785. Though Waldron gave up the Richmond management after 1783, he continued there as a summer performer from time to time; the surviving bills record his presence in 1785 and 1790. During the period of his management at Richmond, on off nights Waldron took some of his players to act at Windsor. Manuscripts in the Public Record Office specify the granting of licenses to Waldron and his company in 1781, 1782, and 1783 for performances at the Windsor Theatre "During Eton Vacation at Whitsuntide. His Majesty being resident."

In the summer of 1785 Waldron brought a company to play 14 nights between 17 June and 27 July at the Windsor Castle Inn, King Street, Hammersmith. On the 25th of July Waldron's benefit tickets were available at the Cock and Magpie. Among his Hammersmith roles during that engagement were Gibby in *A Woman Keeps a Secret,* Old Norval in *Douglas,* Solomon in *The Quaker,* Justice Woodcock in *Love in a Village,* Hardcastle in *She Stoops to Conquer,* and Sciolto in *The Fair Penitent,* most of these being a notch or two above his usual responsibilities at Drury Lane. At Hammersmith again the following summer his company performed at least 17 nights between 5 June and 8 August 1786, and Waldron ventured higher, acting Shylock in *The Merchant of Venice* on 9 June, Polonius in *Hamlet* on 30

FRANCIS GODOLPHIN WALDRON, as Sir
Christopher Hatton

engraving by Gardiner, after Harding

June, Lingo in *The Agreeable Surprise* on 5 July,
and Sir Francis Wronghead in *The Provok'd
Husband,* among other roles. Waldron also
sold tickets for the boxes at his lodgings, No
17, Dorville's Row. Waldron was one of the
members of Fox's company at Brighton in the
summer of 1791, and no doubt he appeared
at other provincial theatres in other summers
until 1794, when he joined Colman's opera-
tion at the Haymarket Theatre.

During those years of managerial adventures at Richmond, Windsor, Hammersmith,
and elsewhere, Waldron remained engaged at
Drury Lane during winters. From 1777 to
1779 he lived at No 16, Glanville Street,
Rathbone Place. In May 1783 benefit tickets
were available from him at No 19, Martlet
Court, Bow Street. He worked eight years
under Garrick's management, though he
seems not to have been accounted one of "The
School of Garrick." Waldron had cause to
complain in February 1779 that some of the
members of the Fund Committee had attended Garrick's funeral "as part of the Com-

mittee," but without him, and he threatened
to resign. In an answer to him on 5 February
1779 (now in the Lilly Library, Indiana University) Thomas Holcroft claimed that the
members had gone to the funeral as individu-
als and asked Waldron "to postpone Your Resignation till after the next monthly meeting
and do them the honour once more to sit in a
Committee with them they being resolved
that if this business does not end amicably it
shall not be for want of their endeavours." Evidently Waldron's wounded pride was
soothed.

Among Waldron's original roles at Drury
Lane, in addition to those specified above,
were Sir Veritas Vision in Heard's *Valentine's
Day* on 23 March 1776, Dyer's Daughter (a
skirts role) in Portal's comic opera *The Cady of
Bagdad* on 19 February 1778, Sir Christopher
Hatton in Sheridan's *The Critic* on 30 October
1779, and Pestle in Dent's musical farce *Too
Civil by Half* on 5 November 1782. He also
performed leading roles in new pantomimes,
like Columbine in the popular and anonymous *The Caldron; or, Pantomimical Olio,* which
opened on 20 January 1785.

Waldron's *The Imitation; or, The Female Fortune Hunters* was brought on for his benefit on
12 May 1783. This five-act comedy had first
been acted at Richmond as *The Belle's Stratagem* in August 1782. It was played at Hammersmith on 26 July 1786 and then again at
the Haymarket on 14 January 1794 as *Heigho
for a Husband,* at which time the author's son
George Waldron appeared as William. The
last-named version was printed in 1794 and
also survives in Larpent MS 599. T. J. Dibdin
later altered it yet once more to *Love in Full
Gallop* in 1816. Waldron's interlude *The King
in the Country,* based on Heywood's *Edward IV,*
was played at Richmond and Windsor in
1788 after King George III's return from
Cheltenham. It was published in 1789.

Waldron is credited as author of *Candid and
Impartial Strictures on the Performers Belonging to
Drury-Lane, Covent Garden, and the Haymarket
Theatres.* The first edition appeared in 1796,
and in it Waldron the actor is described suc-
cinctly (presumably with tongue in cheek?) as
a player of "Respectable old men, where no
humour is necessary, not one atom of which
has he in his whole composition." At the end
of the 1795–1796 season, after 27 years of

service there, Waldron was discharged from Drury Lane along with many others. One newspaper reported that Waldron "who is often useful and always intelligent is among those who depart from the Regions of Old Drury."

By that time, however, Waldron had become engaged at the younger Colman's summer enterprise at the Haymarket Theatre. He had acted there during 1792–93, when the Drury Lane company used that house while its new theatre was being built. Waldron joined Colman in the summer of 1793, making his first appearance on 17 June as an Old Man in *The Surrender of Calais.* That season he acted also the Mayor of Coventry in *Peeping Tom* and Barebones in *The London Hermit.* His roles were few and minor, for he was also serving the Haymarket as prompter. When Colman extended his activities into the regular season 1793–94, Waldron acted a character in *The Mountaineers,* Erpingham in *Henry V,* Sir Gilbert Pumpkin in *All the World's a Stage,* Sir Jasper in *The Mock Doctor,* and Perriwinkle in *A Bold Stroke for a Wife.* He was the original Sir Matthew Medley in Hoare's *My Grandmother* on 16 December 1793. On 2 December 1793 he introduced his *The Prodigal,* an interlude altered from *The Fatal Extravagance* and published in 1794 (also in Larpent MS 25.S.). In the summer of 1794 he acted Don Manuel in *She Wou'd and She Wou'd Not.*

On 9 June 1795 he was the original Prompter in Colman's *New Way at the Old Market.* For his benefit on 21 September 1795, Waldron had two of his own works played—*Love and Madness* (Larpent MS 68.M.) based on *The Two Noble Kinsmen,* and a three-act comedy, *'Tis a Wise Child Knows Its Father* (Larpent MS 14.S.), a revision of his *The Maid of Kent.* Tickets were available from his house at No 54, Drury Lane (where he had also lived in 1794). Acting in both pieces was George Waldron, his son, who had first appeared at the Haymarket the previous season.

In the summer of 1796 Waldron added to his Haymarket repertoire Tubal in *The Merchant of Venice* and Lucianus in *Hamlet.* In 1797 he published *The Virgin Queen,* a very bad attempt at a sequel to *The Tempest* that remained unacted.

Waldron continued as prompter and sometime actor at the Haymarket through the summer of 1805, living between 1796 and 1800 at No 4, Cross Court, Bow Street. On 15 June 1799 he played the Jew in the premiere of Henry Neuman's *Family Distress.*

He appeared at Birmingham in the summers of 1797, 1799, and 1800. According to Allardyce Nicoll, Waldron's burlesque *The Man with two Wives; or, Wigs for Ever,* published in 1798, was performed on 24 March of that year at the Royalty Theatre in London. His comic opera *The Miller's Maid* (with music by Davy) was brought out successfully at the Haymarket on 25 August 1804; it was founded on Robert Bloomfield's *Rural Tale.* The songs of the opera were printed with the cast lists. Waldron's last theatrical contribution, *A Trip to Marseilles; or, The Labyrinth of Love,* which survives in Larpent MS L.1487, was played in May 1806 at the Sans Souci in Leicester Place (earlier called the Academical Theatre). That year Waldron was granted a license for one year from 15 June 1806 for plays and entertainments of music and dancing by children under 17 years of age, but the theatre was unspecified.

Waldron's first wife was with him as a member of the summer company at Richmond in 1775 and 1777 (and probably in 1776 and after 1778). Her first appearance at the Haymarket Theatre was on 31 March 1778 as Betty in *A Bold Stroke for a Wife.* She acted in several performances at the Haymarket in March and April 1785 and with Waldron at Hammersmith in July 1786. The last performances we have noted for Mrs Waldron were at the Haymarket on 30 September as Tag in *Miss in Her Teens* and Damaris in *Barnaby Brittle.* By then, however, she was estranged from her husband, who had taken up with the young actress Sarah Harlowe.

It is not possible to state with certainty just when Waldron's relationship with Sarah Harlowe began. She was a Londoner, 21 years younger than Waldron, and her maiden name may have been Wilson. She had assumed the stage name of Mrs Harlowe because she thought it would look good on a playbill. Perhaps she was acting with Waldron's Richmond company in the early 1780s. She performed twice at the Haymarket in December 1786 and January 1787 and was with the Richmond company in the summer of 1788. Probably about that time she began living with

Waldron, whom she never married and whose name she never assumed, despite a liaison that lasted until his death in 1818. Their theatrical careers were closely allied, but she achieved considerably more acclaim as a performer. At the beginning of the nineteenth century they were together at the Haymarket and at Drury Lane. Waldron returned to the latter house in a very modest capacity in 1800–1801 at 6s. 8d. per day (£2 per week), and by 1805–6, his last season, it was the same. Mrs Harlowe's at that time was £6 per week, and the account books show that Waldron nearly always signed for Mrs Harlowe's wages. According to the *Authentic Memoirs of the Green Room* (1799), in the earlier period of their "matrimonial" life Sarah Harlowe and Waldron suffered some temporary separations, but the union was kept firm by their four children.

On 27 December 1806 Waldron's claim on the Drury Lane Fund, of which he was still a trustee, was granted, and he retired after 40 years on the stage at the age of 62. He did make several subsequent appearances at the Haymarket and at Brighton with his son in 1807.

Francis Godolphin Waldron died in March 1818 at his home in Orange Street, Red Lion Square. In his will, made on 12 December 1805, he described himself as of Duke Street, Lincoln's Inn Fields, and "apprehensive of death from age and bodily weakness" (he lived another 12 years). He left all his property to Mrs Sarah Harlowe of the Theatre Royal, Drury Lane, in trust for his four younger children, evidently by Sarah, namely Sarah Elizabeth, Frances Anne, Francis, and William Waldron. To his "foster son" George Rusdon and his oldest son George Waldron he left sums of £5. On 28 July 1818 Sarah Harlowe, "widow," of Seymour Crescent, Eustace Square, and Robert Jones, bookseller of Paternoster Row, appeared to swear to Waldron's handwriting, and on the following day Sarah was granted administration.

Waldron's son George, the issue of his earlier marriage, was baptized at the Richmond Parish Church on 18 August 1771. (A son Francis Waldron baptized there on 18 September 1770 seems not to have survived.) As "Waldron Junior" George played at the Haymarket as early as 1793. The elder son of Sarah and Waldron, perhaps Francis, was 16 in 1809, when on 26 June of that year his father wrote to Field at Brighton to recommend the lad (whom he did not name) for the position of messenger or other minor servant. The boy, Waldron said, had performed Douglas "with much approbation, for my last Benefit, at the Haymarket Theatre." The Mrs Hale who acted with her husband at Lynn in Norfolk in 1815 was identified by John Brunton in a letter to Winston in March 1815 as "a Daughter [probably Sarah Elizabeth] of Mrs Harlowes."

Despite his long service to the stage Waldron never rose much above the rank of utility player. In his *Miscellanies in Prose and Verse* (1775), William Hawkins labeled him an "inferior" actor. Several critics called attention to his speech impediment, described in the *Authentic Memoirs of the Green Room* (1799) as "such a disagreeable lisp, as must always give offence to a delicate ear." Toward the end of his career his line was confined almost entirely to old men in comedy. He too much imitated the manner of Parsons and, especially, Shuter and indulged in "such an overflow of colouring, grimace, and gesture, that in London, where there is much chaste and excellent acting, it fails of its aim and becomes disgusting."

The *Monthly Mirror* of August 1798 referred to Waldron as "a very worthy and ingenious man." In addition to his plays, which are in the words of Joseph Knight (in *The Dictionary of National Biography*) "without originality or value," Waldron was an editor and bookseller and a worthy and well-read antiquarian. In 1783 he published a completion of Ben Jonson's pastoral *The Sad Shepherd* (reprinted by W. Greg with his edition of the play, 1805). He edited Downes's *Roscius Anglicanus* with additions by T. Davies, 1789. His other literary works included *The Literary Museum; or, Ancient and Modern Repository* (1792) and *The Biographical Mirrour. Comprising a Series of Ancient and Modern English Portraits* (1795–98), a semi-scholarly attempt to elucidate British history (treating some musicians but few actors). *Free Reflections on Miscellaneous Papers and Legal Instruments under the hand and seal of William Shakespeare; in the possession of Samuel Ireland* he brought out in 1796; at Ireland's sale in 1801 Waldron purchased for £5 the manuscript of "Mr. Malone's able inquiry into the authenticity of the papers attributed to Shakespeare, in consequence of the late Mr. Ireland's marginal remarks."

Waldron also edited Chaucer's *The Loves of Troilus and Cresid, with a Commentary by Sir Francis Kinaston* (1796). In 1796 he assisted Charles Dibdin with the editing of the *How Do You Do?*, a periodical that appeared in eight numbers from 30 July to 5 November. In 1800 he brought out with Dibdin *A Compendious History of the English Stage*, followed by *A Collection of Miscellaneous Poetry* (1802); *The Shakespearean Miscellany*, in four parts (1802); and *The Celebrated Romance . . . Rosalynde. Euphues Golden Legacie* (1802). He also contributed a biographical notice of Thomas Davies, the actor and bookseller, to Nichols's *Literary Anecdotes*.

Soon after Waldron's death his library was put up for auction. The *Gentleman's Magazine* (1818) reported that the library "abounds in curious articles relative to the Drama and History of the Stage. The works of our eminent Dramatic Writers are enriched by him with ample MS notes and illustrations." A catalogue of the sale on 21 May 1818 of Waldron's books, priced, is in the British Library.

A pencil sketch portrait of Waldron, at age 20, by an unknown artist is in the Folger Shakespeare Library. A portrait of him as Sir Christopher Hatton in *The Critic* was engraved by W. N. Gardiner, after S. Harding, and was published by E. Harding, 1788. He appeared as Fabian with others in a scene from *Twelfth Night* painted by Francis Wheatley. The painting, which is in the Manchester City Art Gallery, is reproduced in this *Dictionary*, 6:435, with the notice of James Dodd. Waldron also is the central figure pictured, with other actors, as Sir Gilbert Pumpkin in a scene from *All the World's a Stage* painted by Samuel De Wilde. Now in the possession of the National Theatre, this painting is described in detail and its provenance is given by Messrs Mander and Mitchenson in *The Artist and the Theatre;* it is reproduced in this *Dictionary* (5: 284) with the notice of Joshua Bridges Fisher. De Wilde's picture of Waldron as Sir Gilbert Pumpkin and Mrs Henry as Kitty Sprightly, without the other characters, was sold at Christie's on 5 June 1953 (lot 85), from the

collection of Sir H. Hughes Stanton, and was bought by Lawson.

Waldron, Mrs Francis Godolphin the first   *fl. 1770–1788*[1],   *actress, singer.*
Francis Godolphin Waldron's first wife, whose name before her marriage is unknown to us, was presumably Mrs Waldron by 1770; their son Francis was baptized at the Richmond Parish Church on 18 September of that year. (That child seems not to have survived, and Waldron later had another son named Francis, by Sarah Harlowe.) Another son, George, was baptized there 11 months later, on 18 August 1771.

Mrs Waldron was acting with her husband at Richmond in 1775 and 1777. At the Haymarket Theatre on 31 March 1778 she played Betty in *A Bold Stroke for a Wife*. She returned to the Haymarket in 1785 to act Jenny Diver in *The Beggar's Opera* and Jenny in *All the World's a Stage* on 15 March and Lucetta in *The Suspicious Husband* on 26 April. With her husband's company, playing at the Windsor Castle Inn, Hammersmith, in the summer of 1786, she appeared as Cowslip in *The Agreeable Surprise*, Fanny in *The Maid of the Mill*, Kathleen in *The Poor Soldier*, Miss Alscrip in *The Heiress*, and Maud in *Peeping Tom of Coventry*. That summer Mrs Waldron was also with the company that William Palmer took to play at the Stourbridge Fair in Cambridge.

Again at the Haymarket, on 12 March 1787, this time without her husband, Mrs Waldron acted Mrs Fulmer in *The West Indian*, for Griffith's benefit. In 1788 she returned to the Haymarket to play Toilet in *The Jealous Wife* on 9 April for Mrs Greville's benefit and Tag in *Miss in Her Teens* and Damaris in *Barnaby Brittle* on 30 September.

By 1788, Mrs Waldron was estranged from her husband, who had begun a relationship with the young actress Sarah Harlowe that would last until his death in 1818. What happened to Mrs Waldron after 1788 is not known.

Waldron, George   *b. 1771, actor.*
George Waldron was baptized at Richmond Parish Church on 18 August 1771, the son of the actor Francis Godolphin Waldron and his

first wife, an actress whose first name is unknown. By the time George Waldron took to
the stage his parents were estranged, and his
father was living with the actress Sarah Harlowe.

At the Haymarket Theatre, where his father was prompter and utility actor, George
Waldron appeared on 11 June 1793 as Idle in
The Son-In-Law, distinguished in the bills as
"Waldron Jun." In his first season at the Haymarket, which Colman extended from the
summer throughout the winter season 1793–
94, young Waldron, at 22, played a variety of
anonymous roles in crowds of peasants, ruffi-
ans, and servants. Among his named characters, all inconsequential, were Putty in *The
Flitch of Bacon,* Quildrive in *The Citizen,* John
Grum in *The London Hermit,* Roger in *The
Mayor of Garratt,* Vasquez in *The Wonder,* John
in *The Suicide,* and Cudden in *An Agreeable
Surprise.*

Waldron remained engaged at the Haymarket every summer through 1798, playing the
same sort of utility roles by the dozen, adding
robbers, grave diggers, and French waiters to
his repertoire. In 1798 he played a few parts
of a slightly more ambitious line, like Male-
vole in *False and True,* Jacob in *The Road to
Ruin,* Don Sancho in *Two Strings to Your Bow,*
and Gobbo in *The Merchant of Venice.* The author of the *Authentic Memoirs of the Green Room*
(1799) wondered why the manager would
hazard the success of the pieces and the dignity of the theatre by allowing Waldron even
those slightly better roles: "Though this
gentleman will certainly make a better player
than his father, he must be conscious . . . that
his puerile void face wants expression," and
probably, the critic predicted, would "always
be a bar to eminence."

After 1798 we lose track of George Waldron until 1804. In the summer of 1804 he was
acting at the Haymarket Theatre. Also acting
there that summer was "Mrs Waldron Jun."
She made her first appearance on the Haymarket stage on 26 June 1804 and is noted in the
account books (Folger Library MS w.b.7) as
"Mrs G. Waldron."

George Waldron's name was gone from the
Haymarket list in 1805, though his wife continued with that summer company through
1810 at least. George Waldron was acting at

Brighton, with his father, between August
and October 1809; notice of that engagement
is the last evidence we have of him.

Walford, Mr *fl. 1723–1724₁,* *actor.*
Mr Walford shared a benefit with Mrs Pur-
den at the Lincoln's Inn Fields Theatre on 13
May 1723 when *Love's Last Shift* was pre-
sented. Gross receipts came to about £70. On
18 May 1724 at his shared benefit he acted
Sancho in *Love Makes a Man* and split gross
receipts of almost £106 with the widow
White. The following 2 September he acted
Mrs Hermit in *Merlin* at Southwark Fair.

Walgrave, Mr *fl. 1797₁,* *actor.*
A Mr Walgrave acted Belville in a specially
licensed performance of *The Country Girl* at
the Haymarket Theatre on 18 September
1797.

Walker, Mr *fl. 1732–1740₁,* *actor.*
At the Haymarket Theatre Mr Walker
played Octavian in *The Cheats of Scapin* on 16
February and Squib in *Tunbridge Walks* on 8
March 1732. On 7 April 1735 at Southwark
he acted Balance in *The Recruiting Officer.* At
Lincoln's Inn Fields Theatre between 11 July
and 29 August 1735 Walker acted a number
of characters: Trueman in *The London Merchant,* Manly in *The Provok'd Husband,* Jack
Comic in *The Stage Mutineers,* Lord Belmont
in *Squire Basinghall,* the Parson in *The Tragedy
of Tragedies,* Sylla in *Caius Marius,* and Manuel
in *Love Makes a Man.* On 26 April 1736 at
York Buildings he played Sir John in *The Devil
to Pay.* At Drury Lane on 27 October 1740 he
was a Follower in *The Rural Sports.* Those citations seem not to concern the popular actor
Thomas Walker.

Walker, Mr *fl. 1737–1755₁,* *house
servant.*
Along with other house servants at Drury
Lane Theatre, Mr Walker distributed benefit
tickets on 27 May 1737, 25 May 1739, 19
May 1740, and 25 May 1741. He was identified on 24 May 1742 as a doorkeeper. He
was called a numberer when he took a joint
benefit with three other functionaries on 23
May 1743, but not when he shared a benefit
with four others on 15 May 1744.

Walker shared with five people on 9 May 1745 and on 16 May 1746, when he was again called a numberer. Then occurred a seven-year break in the record. He shared benefits on 17 May 1753, 21 May 1754, and 5 May 1755. After the last date the name Walker was not associated with Drury Lane Theatre for a decade.

Walker, Mr *fl. 1749₁*, *actor.*

When *The Tempest* was performed at Phillips's Great Theatrical Booth opposite Cow Lane on 23 August 1749 during Bartholomew Fair, a Mr Walker played Ferdinand. That night the gallery of the booth fell, killing two and injuring several.

Perhaps he was the Walker who was on the bill as Chatillion in *The Life and Death of King John* at Cushing's Booth, facing the King's Head, 23 through 27 August 1749.

Walker, Mr *fl. 1765–1795₁*, *doorkeeper.*

A Mr Walker, identified as a doorkeeper being paid 9s. per week at Drury Lane Theatre, is on a pay list dated 9 February 1765, supposedly in the hand of David Garrick, given to H. H. Furness by Fanny Kemble.

At some point Walker switched theatres, if, as we believe, he was the Mr Walker who is always listed among ten or a dozen minor house servants who were allowed to share in benefit tickets at Covent Garden Theatre in May of 1771, 1775, 1776, 1777, 1781 through 1784, 1786 through 1788, and 1790 through 1792. The Covent Garden accounts in the Folger Library report a 1793–94 salary for Walker, a house servant, of 12s. per week. British Library Add. MS 29949 assigns the same salary for the 1794–95 season and calls him a doorkeeper. This Walker's relationship, if any, to the house servant of earlier years is not known.

Walker, Mrs *fl. 1750s?₁*. HORSINGTON, MARGARETTA..

Walker, Miss *fl. 1779₁*, *actress.*

When the Lord Chamberlain gave permission for a group of casuals to act *Falstaff's Wedding* ("The Characters entirely dressed in the Habits of the Times") at the Haymarket The-atre on 27 December 1779, a Miss Walker, otherwise unknown, acted Bridget.

Walker, Adam *1731?-1821, inventor, exhibitor, lecturer.*

Adam Walker was born about 1731 at Patterdale in Westmoreland, the son of a "woolen manufacturer," according to *The Dictionary of National Biography.* He was taken from school early but taught himself from borrowed books, making remarkable progress in theoretical study and constructing practical models of corn mills and paper mills, which were operated by water wheels on small streams near his home.

At 15 Adam was so far advanced in learning as to obtain a post as usher at Ledsham School in Yorkshire. At 18 he became writing master of a school in Macclefield, where he also studied mathematics. He lectured on astronomy at Manchester, set up his own seminary there, and quickly gave that up to travel as a lecturer in "philosophy." About 1764, according to the *Monthly Mirror* (1798), he "married his first and only wife from *Lancaster.* Happy in an union to a very suitable mind, he purchased the most complete travelling apparatus for illustrating the principles of EXPERIMENTAL PHILOSOPHY, which was then in the kingdom. . . ."

After successful lecture tours all over Great Britain and Ireland, Walker met Joseph Priestley, who persuaded him in 1778 to bring his talks to the Haymarket Theatre in London. He had, it seems, already invented his large and improved version of the orrery, which he called the Eidouranian. After removing his "philosophical" lectures to a house in George Street, Hanover Square, where he gave a series every winter, he concentrated attention on his orrery, which by 1782 was at the Lyceum "or GREAT EXHIBITION ROOM near EXETER 'CHANGE in the STRAND." As the advertisement of 23 October put it:

This instructive and splendid machine has now arrived at its ultimate state of improvement and exhibits the diurnal and annual motions of every planet and satellite in the solar system, without any cause of support.

Day, Night, Twilight, Winter, Summer, Long and Short Days; the Waxing and Waning of the Moon; Solar and Lunar Eclipses; the Cause of the

National Portrait Gallery, London

ADAM WALKER and his Family: Seated: Mrs Walker, Eliza Walker (daughter), and ADAM WALKER Standing: (sons) WILLIAM WALKER, Adam John Walker, and Deane Franklin Walker

by Romney

Tides; the Transit of Venus and Mercury; and the Descent of a Comet, are so like Nature that a bare inspection of the machines gives the clearest idea of these Phenomena.

Admission was 3s. to the pit, 2s. to the gallery.

Evidently either Adam Walker had constructed two Eidouranians, or very shortly after the date of that advertisement he turned the enterprise over to his son William, for *Samuel Farley's Bristol Journal* of 16 November 1782 advertised that "Walker Junior's Astronomical Lecture" would be exhibited at Bris-

tol on 19 November and following. The apparatus remained in Bristol until 31 January 1783, and it returned there from 1 until 15 March.

Adam Walker was a considerable inventor and engineer, devising many engines: for raising water, for automation, for watering land, and for ploughing. He planned and oversaw the erection of the rotatory lights to warn navigation off the Scilly Isles. His lectures, called collectively *An Epitome of Astronomy,* were published, as were several other studies in experimental philosophy.

National Gallery of Scotland

ADAM WALKER

medallion by Tassie

The *Monthly Mirror* gave Walker liberal praise as a man: "it may be allowable to say, that, perhaps, there is not any character in the metropolis better known for information, philanthropy, liberality of sentiment and conduct; for ease of address, good nature, good spirits, persevering exertion, and all the more solid qualities, that give value to the character of the philosopher and the man."

Adam Walker lectured at Westminster School, Winchester School, and other academies on astronomy, chemistry, hydrostatics, and magnetism. At Syon House Academy and at Eton he engaged the fascinated attention of young Percy Bysshe Shelley, who later incorporated some of Walker's ideas in his poetry, according to Desmond King-Hele in *Shelley: His Thought and Work* (2nd ed., 1971), cited by R. D. Altick in *The Shows of London* (1978).

Adam Walker died at Richmond, Surrey, on 11 February 1821. In addition to his eldest son, William (1766–1816), his successor as lecturer and exhibitor, Adam Walker and his wife had three other children: Adam John, rector of Bedston in Shropshire; Deane Franklin (1778–1865), who succeeded to the lectures after his brother William's death, continuing them at London and also at Harrow and Rugby; and a daughter, Eliza (d. 1856), who married Benjamin Gibson of Gosport, Hampshire.

Portraits of Adam Walker include:

1. Drawing by S. Drummond. Location unknown. Anonymous engraving published as a plate to the *European Magazine,* 1792.

2. By George Romney. Half-length, perhaps cut down from full-length. A photograph of the portrait in the Witt Library places it in the collection of Lord Wavertree.

3. By George Romney. Canvas (53¼" × 65¼"). Adam Walker and his family: he and his wife and his daughter Eliza (d. 1856 as Mrs Benjamin Gibson) seated at a table, and, standing in the background, his three sons, William (1767–1816); Adam John, Rector of Bedston, Shropshire; and Deane Franklin (1778–1865). The picture was given to Adam Walker by the artist about 1801, and it descended to the sitter's granddaughter, Miss E. E. Gibson, who bequeathed it to the National Portrait Gallery (No 1106) in 1897.

4. By George Romney. Romney with his wife, Adam Walker (standing in the boat), and others about to embark in a ferryboat at Bowness, Lake Windermere. Canvas (32½" × 48½"). The painting was in the Miss Elizabeth Romney sale at Christie's on 25 May 1894 (lot 169) and was bought by Day. It was sold by Mrs Ronald Baynes at Christie's on 10 December 1954 (lot 45) and was bought by Frost and Reed, who eventually sold it to Mrs Robert O'Brien in 1960. It was shown in the exhibition of Romney's work at Kenwood in 1961. The painting was again at Christie's on 18 June 1971 (lot 50, illustrated in the sale catalogue) and was bought for £4,500 by Plowden.

5. Medallion portrait, by Tassie. In the National Gallery of Scotland.

Walker, D. *,fl. 1784₁, violinist.*

Among the performers listed by Charles Burney as assisting at the Handel Memorial

Concerts at Westminster Abbey and the Pantheon in May and June 1784 was a Mr D. Walker, second violin.

Walker, Hannah, née Fox   *fl. 1791?-1794*, *singer.*

Doane's *Musical Directory* (1794) lists Mrs Hannah Walker, "late Miss Fox," of No 5, Angel Court, Snow Hill, "canto," who belonged to the Longacre Society, a musical group. She sang in the "Grand Performances" at Westminster Abbey, that is, the spring Handelian celebrations, the latest of which had been in 1791. She had also sung at some time in the oratorios at Drury Lane.

Walker, Jarvis   *b. 1666?, trumpeter.*

Our subject was probably the Jarvis Walker who was christened at St Margaret, Westminster, on 16 August 1666. His parents were Joseph and Mary Walker. Perhaps he was named after the Serjeant Trumpeter Jarvice (or Gervase) Price, whose will he witnessed on 5 June 1686. On 18 May 1685 Walker was sworn a trumpeter in the King's Musick, a position he still held in 1749. His annual salary was £91 5s.

Walker, John   *fl. 1685*, *singer.*

At the coronation of James II on 23 April 1685 John Walker was one of the Children of the Choir of Westminster.

Walker, John   1732–1807, *actor, lexicographer.*

John Walker was born at Colney Hatch in the parish of Friern Barnet, Middlesex, on 18 March 1732, according to *The Dictionary of National Biography.* Nothing is known of his father, who died when John was a small child. Of his mother it is known only that she was from Nottingham and was the sister of the Rev James Morley, a dissenting minister at Painswick, Gloucestershire.

Walker's schooling was probably brief. He was apprenticed to a trade but after his mother's death absconded to a provincial acting troupe. In the summer of 1754 he joined the company at the Jacob's Wells Theatre in Bristol, to which he was to return periodically for the rest of his career. Garrick hired him at Drury Lane Theatre, where he performed a

number of tertiary and secondary parts in the winter seasons 1754–55 through 1757–58, spending his summers in Bristol.

At Drury Lane in 1754–55 Walker played a Senator in *Coriolanus,* a Slave in *Barbarossa,* Friar Peter in *Measure for Measure,* Darby in *Jane Shore,* and Doodle in *The Tragedy of Tragedies.* (The presence in the theatre in that and subsequent seasons of the dancer Walker has caused the *Index to The London Stage 1660–1800* to confuse their performances seriously.) In 1755–56 John Walker played some unspecified part in *The Rehearsal,* Perez in *The Mourning Bride,* the Lieutenant in *The Earl of Essex,* Stratocles in *Tamerlane,* Rogero in *The Winter's Tale,* Melidor in *Zara,* and a Lord in *All's Well that Ends Well.*

In 1756–57 Walker added to his repertoire a Mutineer and Lucius in *Cato,* Polidas in *Amphytrion,* the original Poet in Foote's farce *The Author,* Selim in *The Mourning Bride,* Alphonso in *The Spanish Fryar,* Angus in *Macbeth,* Antonio in *Much Ado about Nothing,* Spinner in *The Modern Fine Gentleman,* a Gentleman in *Richard III,* and the Player in *The Beggar's Opera;* and in 1757–58, the Beggar in *The Beggar's Opera,* Spinoza in *Venice Preserv'd,* Acreless in *The Gamesters,* Waitwell in *The Way of the World,* and Hackum in *The Squire of Alsatia.*

In May 1758 Walker married a young actress, Sybilla Minors (or Myners). On 16 September, the Drury Lane prompter Cross noted in his diary: "Mr Woodward has enter'd into partnership with Mr Barry in a new Theatre [Crow Street, Dublin,] & has taken from us Mr Walker & Wife (Miss Minors that was)" and some others from the theatre. Mr and Mrs Walker acted at Crow Street during the next four seasons, but they apparently returned to Bristol as usual in the summers of 1759, 1760, and 1761.

In June 1762 the couple set sail again for England, acting at Birmingham on 14 June, then moving on to Bristol. In October they returned to London and signed on with John Beard at Covent Garden Theatre. John Walker had of course to adjust to a new company where some of his old roles were already "owned" by others. At Covent Garden in 1762–63 he added to his repertoire Aesop in *Lethe,* Downright in *Every Man in His Humour,*

JOHN WALKER
engraving by Hicks, after Barry

Duke Senior in *As You Like It*, the King of France in *All's Well that Ends Well*, Burleigh in *The Earl of Essex*, and Claudius in *Hamlet;* and in 1763–64, Lord Brumpton in *The Funeral*, Lord Belguard in *Sir Courtly Nice*, and Sir John Buck in *The Englishman in Paris*.

In 1764–65 he added Kent in *King Lear*, Seofrid in *The Royal Convert*, Volusius in the altered *Coriolanus*, and Gloster in *Jane Shore;* in 1765–66, Banquo in *Macbeth*, Sealand in *The Conscious Lovers*, Don Alvarez in *The Mistake*, Northumberland in *Virtue Betrayed*, Crab in *The Englishman Returned from Paris*, the title role in *Cato*, Cecil in *The Albion Queens*, and Pandulph in *King John;* and in 1766–67, the Archbishop of Canterbury in *Henry V,* Sciolto in *The Fair Penitent*, Dervise in *Tamerlane*, Sullen in *The Stratagem*, Sir Theodore Brumpton in *The School for Guardians*, the King in *The Humourous Lieutenant*, Don Bernhard in *The Double Falsehood*, and Brutus in *Julius Caesar*.

Walker and his wife had been at Bristol in the summers of 1762, 1763, 1764, 1766, and 1767. They returned to Dublin and the Crow Street Theatre—now under Henry Mossop's management—in the winter season of 1767–68. An undated letter (but of about March 1768), now in the Forster Collection in the Victoria and Albert Museum, from Walker in Dublin to Garrick in London, suggests that Garrick had offered a new engagement at Drury Lane. But after one last summer season in Bristol in 1768, John Walker turned his back on the theatre to engage in the intellectual pursuits by which posterity has more generally known him.

Walker was a member of the debating club known as the Robinhood Society and was praised by Francis Gentleman, the anonymous author of its *History* (1764), himself an actor, critic, and teacher of elocution, as

a Man of extreme good Sense, Erudition, and Candor. He greatly excells as an Orator, having a full, round, and strong Voice, a Facility of Utterance, a graceful Pronunciation, and a beautiful Action. . . . We have been much surprized at the low Estimation this Gentleman is held in here [at Covent Garden], as an Actor. We have seen him perform very capital Characters at the Theatre-Royal in *Crow-Street, Dublin*, with great Judgment and Execution, and with universal Applause; and must own we are at a Loss to impute his being placed on *Covent-Garden* stage in a different and inferior Walk.

When Gentleman wrote his *Dramatic Censor* (1770) he remembered Walker especially as Cato, in which part he "discovered a very considerable share of merit," though he had some shortcomings, and as Brutus—he "made a decent shift with the part."

In January 1769 Walker joined the eccentric Roman Catholic controversialist James Usher (1720–1772) in the establishment of a private school at Kensington Gravel-Pits. After two years the partnership dissolved, and Walker began a peripatetic career of lecturing on elocution. He toured England, Scotland, and Ireland with success, being invited by the heads of Oxford colleges to give private lectures. He met Edmund Burke, and Dr Johnson developed a liking for him and a respect for his studious habits. Boswell records part of a conversation Walker and Johnson had about the teaching of oratory. The association with

Usher had converted Walker to the Roman Church and he became a close friend of John Milner, Bishop of Castabala.

In 1791 Walker published the fruit of many years of lexicographical research, his remarkable *Critical Pronouncing Dictionary and Exposition of the English Language,* a work which was to achieve 28 editions by 1826. It became, in the words of Thompson Cooper,"long regarded as the statute-book of English ortheopy." Walker produced at least eight other scholarly works—guides to rhyming, the pronunciation of classical and biblical names, and the teaching of elocution. (See the *Cambridge Bibliography of English Literature.*)

On 29 April 1802 Walker's wife Sybilla died. He died at his house in Tottenham Court Road on 1 August 1807 and was buried beside his wife in St Pancras Church. By his lecturing and writing he had gained a comfortable fortune, which he distributed by his will, made on 13 June 1805. He described himself as a "Teacher of Elocution" who was then "in the same state of health in which I have been for some years past and of sound and disposing memory." He hoped for salvation, "tho I have been not only an unprofitable but a wicked servant," and directed that his body be "frugally interred." The will made numerous and generous bequests. Mary Barry, a niece of his late wife, received £1,500; the children of his Uncle Joseph Morley of Radford near Nottingham, £1,500; the grandchildren of his Uncle James Morley of Gloucester, £1,500; and Richard Berry, "alias Turner, shoemaker," £1,000. Much smaller sums went to a variety of servants, tradesmen, kinsmen, and friends, including 20 guineas to "Mrs. Mynors now in Saint Margaret's workhouse," presumably a relative of his late wife. The grand total of his specific bequests was £6,300, and there was a residue, of unstated value, for the enjoyment of his executors, Francis Dudley Fitzmaurice, Dr Richard Atkinson, Robert Barnwell, and Daniel Wright.

A miniature portrait of John Walker by John Barry is in the Victoria and Albert Museum. An engraving of it, three-quarter-length, by R. Hicks was issued; a copy by J. Heath, bust only, in oval, was also published. A portrait in the Garrick Club (No 491A) by J. D. Herbert, drawn in pencil and sepia ink,

once said to be of John Walker, is actually of the Dublin actor Joseph Waker.

Walker, Mrs John. *See* MINORS, SYBILLA.

Walker, Joseph   *d. c. 1682, trumpeter.*
Joseph Walker was appointed a trumpeter extraordinary (without fee) in the King's Musick on 27 January 1662. On 1 February 1664 he was given a salaried position at £60 annually. It seems very likely that he was the Joseph Walker who was cited in the baptismal registers of St Margaret, Westminster, in the 1660s. He and his wife Mary had a daughter Martha, who was baptized on 6 July 1665, a son Jarvis on 16 August 1666, a son John on 25 August 1667, and a second Martha (the first must have died in infancy) on 23 October 1668. Jarvis was probably the Jarvis Walker who joined the King's Musick as a trumpeter in 1685. Joseph Walker was replaced on 5 January 1682; he was cited as deceased, and replacements were sometimes made within days of a musician's death.

Walker, Thomas   *1698–1744, actor, singer, booth operator, playwright.*
Thomas Walker, the son of Francis Walker of St Anne, Soho, was christened on 5 June 1698 and was schooled at a private academy run by a Mr Midon. He acted with Shepherd's company in 1714, playing Paris in *The Siege of Troy,* a droll. Barton Booth saw him in that part and was responsible for engaging him at Drury Lane. Walker's first mention in the bills there was on 2 June 1715, when Walker played the third Whore in *The City Ramble.* The following 2 November he was mentioned in a bill for properties. *The Dictionary of National Biography* has him playing Tyrrel in *Richard III,* probably on 6 December 1715. On 12 December he acted his first important part, Young Fashion in *The Relapse.* After that he was seen as Captain Jolly in *The Cobler of Preston* on 3 February 1716 and the King in *The Duke of Guise* on 9 August. Walker received a solo benefit on 21 May when *Cato* was given; the cast was not listed in the bill.

Walker remained at Drury Lane through the 1720–21 season, appearing as Cardono in *The Cruel Gift,* Axalla in *Tamerlane,* the first

Player in *Three Hours after Marriage*, Portius in *Cato*, Granius in *Caius Marius*, Bassanius and Aaron in *Titus Andronicus*, Beaupré in *The Little French Lawyer*, Charles in *The Non-Juror*, Bellmour in *Jane Shore*, Carbine in *The Play Is the Plot*, Valentine in *Love in a Wood*, Cornwall in *King Lear*, Hilliard in *The Jovial Crew*, Octavius in *Julius Caesar*, Rameses in *Busiris*, Pisander in *The Bondman*, Lord Douglas in *The Earl of Warwick*, Vernon in *1 Henry IV*, Duart in *Love Makes a Man*, Brutus in *The Invader of His Country*, Dollabella in *All for Love*, Laertes in *Hamlet*, Cassio in *Othello*, Daran in *The Siege of Damascus*, Alcibiades in *Timon of Athens*, Prince John in *2 Henry IV*, Pharnaces in *Mithridates*, Garcia in *The Mourning Bride*, Edmund in *King Lear*, and Sir Charles in *The Fair Quaker*.

Walker began his association with the late summer fairs on 5 September 1720 when he and Lee operated a booth at Southwark Fair, producing *The Siege of Bethulia*, a droll. In August 1721, at Lee's booth at Bartholomew Fair, Walker played Achier in that work, and at Lee's Southwark Fair booth in September Walker acted the Englishman in *The Noble Englishman*, another droll. Very little is known of Walker's personal life during that period, but the *Evening Post* of 4–7 May 1717 said that he was indicted with Thomas Ash for the murder of an abbot and a bailiff near the playhouse; he was found guilty, but since his acting schedule that spring seems to have been undisturbed, Walker might not even have been imprisoned.

In the fall of 1721 Walker defected to the Lincoln's Inn Fields company, causing Sir Richard Steele to complain to the Lord Chamberlain on 21 September:

I presum'd to trouble your Grace some time since concerning Mr. Walker who had engag'd Himself to the other House, tho He is a Sworn Servant to His Majesty in the King's Theatre [Drury Lane, the Theatre Royal], and is in Debt to the Company, as well as having very particular obligations at a very well known Circumstance of distresse in His Life.

Your Grace has two methods practis'd in the Office, either to order the offender to return, or Silence Him. What you will please to do in it, your Grace, at your Leisure, will determine; but indeed our affairs are in a doubtfull way, for a want of Your Influence and Protection.

By permission of the Trustees of the British Museum

THOMAS WALKER, as Macheath

engraving by Faber, after Ellys

Evidently the Lord Chamberlain decided not to take either of the courses urged by Steele. Two days later Walker began acting at Lincoln's Inn Fields.

His first part under John Rich's management was Edmund in *King Lear* on 23 September 1721, after which he was seen in some of his other old roles (Cassio, Axalla, Sir Charles) and a number of new ones: Charles in *Love Makes a Man*, Polydore in *The Orphan*, Richmond in *Richard III*, Worthy in *The Recruiting Officer*, Bassanio in *The Merchant of Venice*, Southampton in *The Unhappy Favorite*, Hotspur in *1 Henry IV*, the title parts in *Don Sebastian* and *Oroonoko*, Osmyn in *The Fair Captive*, Aimwell in *The Stratagem*, Horatio in *Hamlet*, Charles in *The Busy Body*, Young Worthy in *Love's Last Shift*, Bedamar in *Venice Preserv'd*, Townly in *The London Cuckolds*, Mellefont in *The Double Dealer*, Cruize in *Injured Love*, Bellmour in *The Old Bachelor*, Fantome in *The Drummer*, Erric in *Hibernia Freed*, Lorenzo in *The Spanish Fryar*, Ambrosio in *Don Quixote*, Belfond Jr in *The Squire of Alsatia*,

Bevil in *The Woman's Revenge*, and Paris in *Domitian*.

Beginning on 5 September 1722 at Southwark Fair Walker produced *The Royal Revenge*, a droll, with "All the Habits entirely new." On 25 September, using actors from Drury Lane, he presented *Valentine and Orson*, another droll, at his Great Booth in Bird Cage Alley in Southwark; on 3 October, after the season had begun at Lincoln's Inn Fields, he may have produced *The Busy Body* at Southwark.

At Lincoln's Inn Fields during the next ten years Walker essayed such new roles as Antony in *Julius Caesar*, Lenox in *Macbeth*, Adrastus in *Oedipus*, Constant in *The Provok'd Wife*, Leandro in *The Spanish Curate*, Hephestion and Cassander in *The Rival Queens*, Cheatly in *The Squire of Alsatia*, Woolfort in *The Royal Merchant*, Plume in *The Recruiting Officer*, Pheroras in *Mariamne*, Ulysses in *Troilus and Cressida*, Tigranes in *A King and No King*, Roebuck in *Love and a Bottle*, Massinissa in *Sophonisba*, Cortez in *The Indian Emperor*, the title character in *Massaniello*, Lovemore in *The Amorous Widow*, Octavian in *The Cheats of Scapin*, Wellbred in *Every Man in His Humour*, Frederick in *The Rover*, Tranio in *The Taming of the Shrew*, Harcourt in *The Country Wife*, Oronces in *Aesop*, Dick in *The Confederacy*, Freeman in *She Wou'd If She Cou'd*, Cromwell in *Henry VIII*, Pierre in *Venice Preserv'd*, Loveworth in *Tunbridge Walks*, Young Valere in *The Gamester*, Macheath in *The Beggar's Opera* (his most famous role; the long run began on 29 January 1728), Corvino in *Volpone*, the Governor in *The Island Princess*, Friendly in *Hob's Opera*, Juba in *Cato*, Myrtle in *The Conscious Lovers*, Pylades in *Orestes*, Paris in *The Judgment of Paris*, Blunt in *The Committee*, Alexander in *The Rival Queens*, and Wronglove in *The Lady's Last Stake*.

Thomas Walker seems to have been in debt constantly. A special benefit was given for "a Gentleman under misfortunes" on 22 November 1722; a bill transcribed by Reed in his "Notitia Dramatica" in the British Library identified as Walker the man who acted Paris in *Domitian or the Roman Actor* that night. Perhaps the misfortune was the same as the one referred to in Steele's letter of a year before.

In the summer of 1723 Walker apparently went to Ireland, but we have found no record of what he did there. Latreille transcribed a newspaper notice asserting that the report that Quin and Walker had been drowned in Ireland was false.

For his labors at Lincoln's Inn Fields in the 1720s Walker was paid £1 6s. 8d. daily. His benefits, at least before the remarkably successful *Beggar's Opera*, did not bring in large sums—sometimes as little as £20 after house charges were subtracted—but on occasion he attracted over £150 in gross receipts.

Walker was not originally intended for the role of Macheath in *The Beggar's Opera*, but James Quin refused the part. The choice fell on Tom Walker, despite the fact that (according to Genest) he was not a trained singer. His success was immediate. A poem accompanied an engraving of Walker made by Ellys and Faber in 1728:

> If Wit can please, or Gallantry engage,
> Mackheath may boast he justly charms the Age,
> A second Dorimant, like him in Fame,
> The Fop's Example, and the Ladies Flame.
> The Fair in Troops attend his sprightly Call,
> Nor longer doat upon an Eunuch's Squall;
> Well pleas'd they blush, and own behind the Fan,
> His Voice, his Looks, his Actions speak the Man.

A benefit ticket for Walker as Macheath has survived, and, of course, the prison scene was painted by Hogarth, with Walker as the central figure.

Walker went over to the Haymarket Theatre on 16 February 1732 to play Octavian in *The Cheats of Scapin*, and he returned there on 8 March to act Squib in *Tunbridge Walks*. On 17 August 1732 he and Rayner had a booth at Tottenham Court and produced *A Wife Well Manag'd* and *The Humours of Harlequin*, but that seems to have been the extent of Walker's activity outside Rich's troupe during the 1730s.

He made his first appearance at Rich's new Covent Garden Theatre on 14 December 1732 as Sir Charles in *The Fair Quaker of Deal*. He acted there through 1738–39, adding to his repertoire such new characters as Periphas in *Achilles*, Hubert in *The Royal Merchant*, the King in *The Maid's Tragedy*, Bajazet in *Tamerlane*, Angelo in *Measure for Measure*, the Mad Scholar in *The Pilgrim*, Hector in *Troilus and Cressida*, Sempronius in *Cato*, Morelove in *The*

Courtesy of the Tate Gallery

Scene of *The Beggar's Opera*, by Hogarth

(see key to figures)

Careless Husband, the title role in *Timon of Athens*, Clerimont in *The Double Gallant*, Solyman in *Abra Mule*, Fainall in *The Way of the World*, Banquo in *Macbeth*, Horatio in *The Fair Penitent*, Kite in *The Recruiting Officer*, Young Rakish in *The School Boy*, Marcian in *Theodosius*, Chatilion in *Cymbeline*, Faulconbridge in *King John*, the King in *Hamlet*, Norfolk in *Richard II*, Burgundy in *Henry V*, Suffolk in *1 Henry VI*, and Scandal in *Love for Love*.

During that period Walker appeared occasionally at the old Lincoln's Inn Fields playhouse, playing some of his standard parts, but surely he was not the Walker who acted a number of roles there in the summer of 1735, since none of the characters were in Thomas Walker's repertoire. Nor was our man the Walker who acted Balance in *The Recruiting*

Officer at Southwark in April 1735 and Sir John in *The Devil to Pay* at York Buildings in April 1736.

In the 1730s Walker was being paid 16*s.* 8*d.* daily and his value to Rich appears to have declined with the years. Walker was becoming negligent, as a notice in the *Daily Journal* of 29 April 1735 shows:

We hear . . . the Double Deceit . . . was not acted last Night, on account of a Letter sent by Mr Walker, who had a principal Part in it [Young Courtlove], acquainting Mr Rich, that he had study'd his Part, but could not make himself Master of it, and therfore desir'd he would provide some body else to do it. N. B. The Part is about Eight Lengths [i.e., sides], and was above eight Weeks in Mr Walker's Hands.

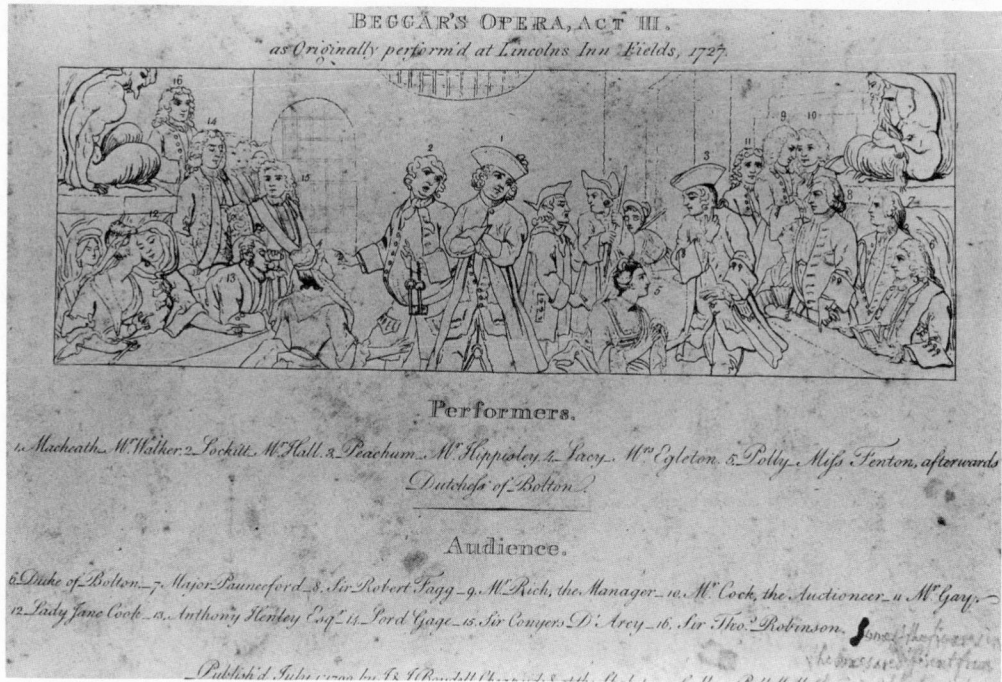

BEGGAR'S OPERA, ACT III.
as Originally perform'd at Lincolns Inn Fields, 1727.

Performers.

1. Macheath. Mr Walker. 2 Lockitt. Mr Hall. 3 Peachum. Mr Hippisley. 4 Lucy. Mrs Egleton. 5 Polly. Miss Fenton, afterwards Dutchess of Bolton.

Audience.

6 Duke of Bolton. 7 Major Pauncefort. 8 Sir Robert Fagg. 9 Mr Rich, the Manager. 10 Mr Cock, the Auctioneer. 11 Mr Gay. 12 Lady Jane Cook. a. Anthony Henley Esq. 13 Lord Gage. 14 Sir Conyers D'Arcy. 15 Sir Tho. Robinson.

From the Collection of Edward A. Langhans

Key to the figures in Hogarth's scene of
The Beggar's Opera

(*The London Stage* records Walker as having played the part on 25 April.) Walker at the time had lodgings in Bedford Court, Covent Garden.

The *Daily Post and General Advertiser* on 20 February 1739 said that Walker, "who had the Misfortune of burning his Foot very severely some Time since . . . hopes in a short Time to be able to appear on the Stage again." The calendar shows that his appearances in February were well-spaced; he acted only twice that month, and not until May was he performing with his usual regularity. The following season, 1739–40, he had no permanent engagement at a London Theatre, though he made two appearances at Drury Lane: on 14 September 1739 as Pierre in *Venice Preserv'd* and on 17 May 1740 as Macheath. Both benefits were for himself, which suggests that he was again in financial difficulty. On the September bill he stated mysteriously: "Significant reasons will be given hereafter for this undertak-

ing; & in the mean time I cannot omit acknowledging my gratitude to the Master of this Company, who has behaved on this occasion in the most gentlemanlike manner. To my very good masters the Town. T. Walker." At the spring benefit he said he was living at Gay's Head in the Strand.

In 1740–41 Walker acted at Goodman's Fields with Giffard's troupe, appearing first on 18 October 1740 as Pierre in *Venice Preserv'd.* He then acted a number of his standard parts, such as Oroonoko, Kite, Bajazet, Polydore, Hotspur, Young Fashion, Macheath, Aimwell, and Richmond and brought out such new ones as Othello, Torrismond in *The Spanish Fryar,* Hastings in *Jane Shore,* Pembroke in *Lady Jane Gray,* the Ghost in *Hamlet,* and Antigonus in *The Winter's Tale.* (He was not the Walker who appeared at Drury Lane on 27 October 1740, for he acted that night at Goodman's Fields.) The following season he seems not to have been engaged anywhere, but Goodman's Fields gave him a benefit on 27 May 1742, at which he played Macheath.

Evidently unable to find employment in London, Walker went to Dublin. On 9 August 1742 he appeared at the Smock Alley Theatre as Oroonoko; on the nineteenth he played Kite in *The Recruiting Officer;* and on the twenty-first he was Macheath in *The Beggar's Opera*. During the 1742–43 season at Aungier Street and at Smock Alley he played Bajazet, Macheath, Cassius in *Julius Caesar,* and Orestes in *The Distrest Mother*. In 1743–44 he acted Othello and played Sebastian in his own *Love and Loyalty*. The first performance of his *Love and Loyalty* met with much applause, according to a note by Kemble, but Walker, destitute as usual, could not pay the house charges for the second night, which was to be for his benefit. The management locked the doors of the theatre. Chetwood felt that the disappointment hastened Walker's death and noted that the actor died a martyr to drink. "He follow'd Bacchus too ardently, insomuch that his credit was often drown'd upon the Stage, and, by Degrees, almost render's him useless." His last performance may have been in *Love and Loyalty* on 24 May 1744 at Aungier Street. Thomas Walker died the following 5 June at the age of 46.

Critics of the eighteenth century found Thomas Walker splendid in some characters, but not an actor of the first rank, despite his fame. Davies said of Walker's Polydore in *The Orphan,* "His look, deportment and action gave a distinguished glare to tyrannic rage, and uncommon force to the vehemence of anger." Walker patterned his Polydore after Booth's—a "gay libertine air." Davies thought Walker a "more than . . . tolerable copy of his master." Davies described Walker as having a manly, expressive face, his voice strong and pleasing until he spoiled it by intemperance. He liked Walker as Bajazet and Hotspur, Bellmour in *The Old Bachelor,* and especially as the bastard Faulconbridge in *King John*—he played that part with "such native humour, spirited action, and vigorous deportment, that, I think, no actor has, since his time, given an equal idea of the part." And "though Garrick, Sheridan, Delane, and Barry, have attempted it, they all fell short of Tom Walker." His other famous bastard, Edmund in *King Lear,* was taught him by Booth—easy,

natural, manly and commanding, but disengaged.

John Hill in *The Actor* tried to describe Walker's chief failing, his lack of control: "his ruin was, that his sensibility continually ran away with him; and when he had a passion to express that would have moved an audience, the blood was in his face before the time, his whole person was disordered, and unless people knew the part, they could not find out for what; for the vehemence of his feeling took away his utterance, and he could not speak articulately." *The Comedian* in 1732 agreed that Walker needed to use moderation.

His Macheath was evidently a triumph. Davies noted that Walker "knew no more of music than barely singing in tune," but his singing was "supported by his inimitable action, by his speaking to the eye, not charming the ear." "Gentleman" Smith, who had seen virtually all the Macheaths of the eighteenth century, called "Walker the *only* Macheath we have ever seen."

Thomas Walker's playwriting career was modest. A venture in which Walker was involved was alluded to in the Lincoln's Inn Fields accounts on 5 January 1724: "To Mr. Miars bookseller in considerason of his damage in buying & printing the Farce of Shephard written & sold by Mr. Walker & Mr. Leigh but never acted. 10—10—10." Nothing more seems to be known of this work. On 31 July 1724 Walker's *Massaniello* came out; it was a compression of the two parts of D'Urfey's original. Of it John Leigh wrote,

Tom Walker his creditors meaning to chouse,
Like an honest, good-natured young fellow,
Resolv'd all the summer to stay in the house
And rehearse by himself Massaniello.

The Quaker's Opera, his imitation of *The Beggar's Opera,* was performed at Southwark Fair in September 1728 and the following month at the Haymarket. At Goodman's Field Theatre on 24 February 1730 Walker's *The Fate of Villainy* was presented, but it did not succeed. *Love and Loyalty,* a reworking of *The Fate of Villainy,* was presented in Dublin just before Walker died.

Thomas Walker's wife Mary died on 20 March 1737, according to the *Daily Advertiser*. She was buried at St Paul, Covent Garden, on 23 March.

Harvard Theatre Collection

Benefit ticket for THOMAS WALKER

engraving by Sympson, after Hogarth

A portrait of Thomas Walker, oil on canvas (25″ × 19½″), by an unknown artist is in the National Portrait Gallery (No 2202). It was purchased from P. Morley Horder of No 5, Arlington Street, London, in 1928 by Spinks; later that year it was given by Walter Horace, second Viscount Bearsted, to the NPG. The portrait sometimes has been attributed to Hogarth. John Ellys's portrait of Walker (1728) as Macheath is known by the engraving by Faber, Jr. Walker is the central figure in Hogarth's famous scene of *The Beggar's Opera,* with Lavinia Fenton as Polly Peachum, and other actors. There are at least six versions of the painting, and a chalk drawing by Hogarth is a sketch for the one in the Tate Gallery.

Those versions are listed in this *Dictionary* 5:225. See also Ronald Paulson, *Hogarth: His Life and Times* (1:180–93), and sales catalogues for Sotheby's on 14 June 1961 (lot 10) and Christie's on 15 July 1983 (lot 48) and 16 March 1984 (lot 69). Hogarth's sketch of Walker as Macheath in prison was engraved by J. Sympson, Jr, about 1735 as a ticket for Walker's benefit at Covent Garden. Sympson may have used as a model a sketch by Hogarth, which is now in the Royal Library, Windsor Castle.

Walker, ₍Thomas?₎ ₍*fl.* 1750–1790?₎, *dancer.*

At a benefit performance at Drury Lane

Theatre on 6 May 1751, dancers named Walker and Harrison performed a hornpipe. Walker's performance was the first for a dancer whose name was to appear in many London notices for 40 years or more. C. B. Hogan in *The London Stage 1660–1800* calls him Thomas Walker, a baptismal name that is withdrawn by the *Index to The London Stage 1660–1800*. That compilation badly confuses the dancer Walker with the actor John Walker at several points.

Though the subject of this entry ranged widely, he was most frequently employed by Drury Lane Theatre, where he was sometimes on the roster as dancing master. When he danced elsewhere he was billed as "from Drury Lane." As early as 3 May 1755 he was identified on a benefit playbill as "Mr Walker (the Dancing Master)," doubtless to distinguish him not only from the actor John Walker but from the house servant named Walker who shared in a benefit two nights later. Though he was seen sometimes dancing hornpipes, Walker got his first named role, so far as we can determine, on 8 September 1753 in the summer theatre at Richmond, Surrey, when he played Rinker in the pantomime *Harlequin Skeleton*. (He had danced in *Harlequin Enchanted* at Drury Lane in April, but no roles were then advertised.)

In the summer of 1755 Walker, with Mrs Walker, also a dancer, joined Theophilus Cibber's group, "Bayes's New-Raised Company of Comedians," at the Haymarket. Walker did hornpipes and joined with the veterans Settree and Signora Fiorentina in ensembles like *La Dance du village*. Mrs Walker danced only the hornpipe. The couple took time off on 6 September to go over to Bartholomew Fair and appear at Bence's Room in Swan Yard, he to play Harlequin, she Columbine, in *The Fairy; or, Harlequin in the Shades*. Waker was not noticed in the Fair bills after that date.

In November 1755 Walker was one of the unfortunate British dancers who were rejected along with the foreigners in the debacle of Garrick's *Chinese Festival*. Sometimes, in the manner of the day, Walker introduced his pupils to Drury Lane's stage—"Master Cape (scholar to Walker)," and "Master Wallace, . . . student to Walker," and "Double-hornpipe by Walker and a young gentleman, his Scholar." On at least one occasion, that of

the benefit of Costollo, Stede, and Mrs Pitt at Covent Garden on 1 May 1764, he went to the rival house to dance with Mrs Pitt's young daughter, "his scholar."

By 1765 Walker was earning £1 per week; by 1767, £1 5s., a salary he still owned in 1775, as recorded in the Folger account books. In his later years one of Walker's staples was the hornpipe, which he danced in Act III of *The Beggar's Opera*. The last sure notice of his performance of that, or of anything, was on 21 May 1783 (though the 1790 edition of *Don Juan* adds a Walker to the playbill's list of dancers in that "Grand Pantomimical Ballet.") A Walker, "dancing master," probably our Walker, advertised in the *British Journal* of 2 January 1779 his intention of opening a dancing school in Bristol. But our Walker—we believe it was he—shared a Drury Lane benefit with three other dancers on 6 June 1786.

Walker, Mrs ₁Thomas?₁ ₁*fl.* 1755₁, *dancer. See* WALKER, THOMAS?₁ ₁*fl.* 1750–1790₁

Walker, Thomas ₁*fl.* 1780?–1815₁, *singer, actor, music copyist.*

The alto (countertenor) singer Thomas Walker is as difficult as the other performing Walkers to distinguish from his numerous namesakes. He is particularly liable to confusion with a dancer, several house servants, and an actor named Walker who were often in London and sometimes in the same theatre with him.

Thomas Walker joined the Drury Lane chorus at some indeterminate time in the 1780s. He may be the Walker referred to cryptically on the Drury Lane accounts as early as 1780–81 (Folger MS W.b.283–294), who shared benefits and suffered financial deficiencies therefrom in 1786 and 1787 and borrowed and repaid money in 1789. But that is more likely to have been the dancer.

Thomas Walker was named as an "Alto Voice" in a surviving account of money paid the band and singers employed by the Academy of Ancient Music in its concerts of the 1787–88 season. Doane's *Musical Directory* of 1794, citing his residence as No 5, Angel Court, Snow Hill, testified to his participation in several of the annual Handelian performances at Westminster Abbey, in meetings of the Surrey Chapel Society, the Oxford Music Meeting, the Cecilian Society, and the Longacre Society, and to his membership in the New Musical Fund.

But Walker's mainstay seems to have been his chorus job at Drury Lane, which he kept until well into the nineteenth century, occasionally earning extra sums copying music. In the summers of 1795 to 1799, he also appeared at the Haymarket.

Walker was the quintessential spear-carrier, being employed, from 1792 to 1800, as a Vintager in *The Pirates,* a Moor in *The Mountaineers,* a Robber in *The Battle of Hexham,* an Indian in *The Cherokee,* a Sailor in *Lock and Key,* a "Janizary" in *Blue-Beard,* a Soldier in *The Captive of Spilburg,* and so on, always surrounded by other Moors, pirates, soldiers, or robbers. He was one of those hordes of assistants demanded by the huge spectacles and enormous theatres of the end of the century. He exercised his voice in the concert settings mentioned and several times—for instance at the Haymarket on 15 January 1798 and on 24 January 1799—in the *Messiah.* He still belonged to the Musical Fund in 1815 and was then on its Court of Assistants.

Walker, William   *1766–1816, exhibitor, lecturer.*

William Walker, born 23 June 1766 at Kendal, in Westmoreland, was the son of Adam Walker the inventor, exhibitor of the orrery known as the Eidouranian, and lecturer on astronomy and natural science. His birthplace and date, along with a portrait, are given in the *Monthly Mirror* for December 1798 in what purports to be a biographical sketch but is really a discourse on the history of orrery-like instruments.

Not much is known about William Walker. He was evidently exhibiting the Eidouranian as early as 1782, when he advertised a series of lectures in Bristol. By the time of the *Monthly Mirror* sketch, "The very popular and instructive lectures of Mr. WM. WALKER [had] engaged the attention of large and respectable audiences, in various parts of the island, for several years. . . ." He had exhibited and lectured at York in 1784 and again in 1796, according to information furnished us

By permission of the Trustees of the British Museum

WILLIAM WALKER

engraving by Ridley, after Barratt

by Miss Sybil Rosenfeld. The Lord Chamberlain's records in the Public Record Office show that William Walker was granted licenses for his astronomical lectures at the Haymarket Theatre on Wednesdays and Fridays during Lent each year, 1794 through 1814.

The *Biographical and Imperial Magazine* for April 1789 gave a description of the proceedings when Walker lectured at Covent Garden Theatre:

To exhibit it the house is darkened, and the machine occupies the place of the curtain. By means of lights behind, the planets are shewn transparent in their proper colours, and move regularly in their orbits, exhibiting thus to view the heavenly bodies in motion. Mr. Walker lectures during this revolution, and stands on the stage, explaining the various phenomena.

The *Gentleman's Magazine* for April 1816 reported the death of William Walker at the manor house, Hayes, Middlesex, on 14 March 1816. He left a widow and children.

A portrait of William Walker engraved by Ridley, after a miniature by Miss E. Barratt, was published as frontispiece to the *Monthly*

Harvard Theatre Collection

View of WILLIAM WALKER on stage at a performance of his *Eidouranian*
engraving after Burney

Mirror, December 1798. A view of the proscenium of the English Opera as it appeared on
the evening of 21 March 1817 shows Walker
and his Eidouranian exhibition on the stage.
A similar picture appeared in Horace Wellbe-
loved's *London Lions,* c. 1826. William Walker
also appears in a painting, by George Romney, of the Walker family. Also in the group
are William Walker's father, mother, sister,

and two brothers. See the picture list for
Adam Walker, No 3.

Walker, William *fl.* 1768–1792₁,
actor, tailor, manager.

A performer identified by Lord Chamberlain's documents in the Public Record Office
as William Walker was a member of Samuel
Foote's company at the Haymarket Theatre in

the summer of 1768, appearing for the first time in London, so far as is known, as Bagshot in *The Stratagem* on 23 June.

He appears also to have been the Walker who was (at least from 1777 through 1784) the tailor at No 4, New Round Court, the Strand. His address at benefit times in October 1781 and 9 February 1784 was the Globe, Pall Mall. (He was also the Haymarket Theatre's tailor. When a burlesque *Ballet Tragi-Comique* afterpiece was given in 1784 and those concerned were given satirical mock-Italianate names, the "tailor" was identified as "Walkerino.")

Meanwhile, Walker pursued an acting career of a sporadic and rather specialized nature at the Haymarket. It involved no more than 40 performances in about a dozen parts between 1768 and 1792. Plainly, Walker was a Scot. His favorite roles were Bauldy and Roger in Allan Ramsay's *Patie and Roger; or, The Gentle Shepherd* and Old Norval in John Homes's *Douglas,* performed by a group of Caledonians year by year at times when the Haymarket was normally dark.

Most of those performances were for Walker's benefit, and all fell outside the season or the interest of the summer Haymarket where he was employed. That he was the moving spirit in their production is shown by the fact that he always applied to the Lord Chamberlain for the license, up to 1793.

On 13 October 1777, when the Lord Chamberlain licensed a Haymarket performance for the benefit of Walker and an actor named Stewart, the bill gave interesting evidence of the thickness of the Scottish burr of Walker and his companions. *The Gentle Shepherd* was "Done into English, from the Original of Allan Ramsay, by Cornelius Vanderstop, Esq. As it has long been the Desire of the Nobility and Gentry to have this celebrated Piece performed in English, the Gentleman who has undertaken this ardent [*sic*] Task hopes it will give Satisfaction to the Public in General." Presumably Walker and others had to practice hard to master pronunciation of Vanderstop's English equivalents to the Scottish dialect words.

Walker's other roles, most at the summer Haymarket and all of them repeated over the years, were: in 1768, a Constable in *The Beggar's Opera,* and some unspecified part in *The*

Orators; in 1772, some part in *The Rehearsal;* in 1774, Macpherson in *The Devil upon Two Sticks* and a part in *The Duelist;* in 1776, the original Colonel Ancient in *The Prejudice of Fashion* "by a Gentleman from Edinburgh"; in 1777, the original MacLocust in *The Advertisement,* a comedy by Sarah Gardner; in 1778, Zacharides in *The Tailors* and the Scotchman in *The Apprentice;* and in 1781, Beaufort in *The Citizen.* Walker's last recorded performance was as Old Norval on 26 December 1792. But for several years before that he had performed only once or twice for others' benefits. (The *Index to The London Stage 1660–1800* incorrectly conflates the careers of William Walker and Walker the Covent Garden doorkeeper and shows Walker the tailor as a separate person.)

Walkerino. *See* WALKER, WILLIAM [*fl.* 1768–1792].

Walkup. *See* WALCUP.

Wall, Mrs [*fl. c. 1672–1690?*], actress.

Mrs Wall was named in two promptbooks: *The Comedy of Errors,* which was probably performed about 1672 at the Nursery in the Barbican or, less likely, on tour, and *Belphegor,* which was presented in Dublin about 1677–78 or, less likely, 1682–83 and in London in late June 1690. She played the Lady Abbess in *The Comedy of Errors* and a Woman in *Belphegor.* J. Wall and William Wall were named in the Shakespeare promptbook, and one of them was probably her husband. J. Wall played Dromio of Syracuse, and William Wall acted the Duke of Ephesus, the Gaoler, and an Officer.

Wall, Mrs [*fl. 1723–1727*], dancer.

Mrs Wall was a dancer at Lincoln's Inn Fields Theatre from 1723–24 through 1726–27. She was first noticed in the playbills for dancing in *The Busy Body* on 7 October 1723. She appeared in that assignment numerous other times that season, during which she also danced in *The Necromancer,* as Oriana in *Amadia,* and in many specialty dances. In 1724–25 she was paid 6*s.* 8*d.* per day for dancing such roles as Europa in *Jupiter and Europa,* Lachesis in *Harlequin Sorcerer,* and one of the

Graces in *Mars and Venus*. During 1725–26 she was prominent in the ensemble dancing at Lincoln's Inn Fields and frequently performed as Lally's partner. Her known roles in ballets in 1726–27 were a Nymph and a Polonese Woman in *Apollo and Daphne*.

Wall, Anne *fl. 1735–1741₁,* *sweeper.*

"Anne Wall, Sweeper," was allowed payment for 179 days at 1s. 6d. per day at Covent Garden Theatre during the 1735–36 season, according to British Library MS 11791dd18. Evidently she continued to practice her humble specialty. Folger Library MS W.a.94 shows weekly payments to her of 6s. during the 1740–41 season.

Wall, J. *fl. c. 1672₁,* *actor.* *See* WALL, MRS *fl. c. 1672–1690?₁.*

Wall, William *fl. c. 1672₁,* *actor.* *See* WALL, MRS *fl. c. 1672–1690?₁.*

Wallace, Thomas Wogan *fl. 1754?–1778?₁,* *actor, dancer.*

A Wallace was at the Jacob's Wells Theatre in Bristol in 1754. Perhaps he was the Master Wallace who played Puff in *Miss in Her Teens* at Drury Lane Theatre in London on 28 April 1755. On 5 May 1756 he and other children acted in *Lethe*. On 15 May 1760 a Master Wallace danced a hornpipe; he was described in the bill as a student of Walker, making his first appearance (as a dancer?). On 5 July 1760 at Jacob's Wells a Wallace danced a hornpipe. In July 1761 and again in July 1763 Wallace played Lady Freelove in *The Jealous Wife* at Jacob's Wells. In 1766 Thomas Wogan Wallace, "comedian," probably our subject, subscribed to John Cunningham's *Poems*. Wallace was still active in Bristol, playing small parts, in 1767 and 1768. Perhaps he was the Mr Wallace, comedian, who subscribed for two copies of Hitchcock's *The Macaroni* in York in 1773. On 9 February 1778 at the Haymarket Theatre in London a Wallace played Bates in *The Irish Widow*. We are guessing that all of these citations concern the same person.

Wallace, William *fl. 1775–1776₁,* *performer?*

The Drury Lane Fund Book shows that William Wallace subscribed 10s. 6d. to the fund in 1775 but neglected payment the following year. He may have been a minor performer.

Wallack, William *c. 1760–1850, actor, dancer, singer.*

William Wallack was born about 1760 (his age at the time of his death in 1850 was said to be 90). Neither his parentage nor the circumstances of his early life are known. He was certainly the Wallack on the company list at Astley's Amphitheatre, Westminster Bridge, in 1785. On 8 July 1787, William Wallack of St George, Southwark, married Elizabeth Granger, widow, of St Paul, Covent Garden, at the latter church. She was a Drury Lane actress and chorus singer. (The assertion of James Dibdin in *Annals of the Edinburgh Stage* that Wallack had married "an equestrian performer of the name of Mary Johannot" is false.)

Scattered surviving playbills of Astley's Amphitheatre show Wallack and his wife occasionally employed there from the summer of 1787 through August 1795. Wallack played, in September 1787, a Non-commissioned Officer in *The Siege of Quebec; or, The Death of General Wolfe;* on 4 September 1789, a London Fop in *The Royal Naval Review; or, Devonshire and Cornwall Loyalty;* on 6, 17, and 19 May 1791, the Secretary in *The King and the Cobbler;* and in July 1791, Philip in *The Tithe Sheaf; or, Village Plot.*

According to James Dibdin, the Wallacks and their small daughter played at a circus in Leith Street, Edinburgh, early in 1792. From 21 April through 28 May 1792, all three Wallacks performed at Edinburgh's Theatre Royal, Shakespeare Square. Norma Armstrong's manuscript calendar preserves some of their roles. William Wallack played Merlin in *Cymon*, Ali in *Selima and Azor*, the Clown in *The Triumph of Harlequin*, a Knight in *Richard Coeur de Lion*, Muley in *A Day in Turkey*, and the Admiral in *The Fugitive*. (For roles performed by the daughter and by Mrs Wallack, see the latter's entry.)

In the winter season of 1795–96, the elder Wallacks played at the Fishamble Street Theatre in Dublin, but none of their roles are known. They had returned to London by May 1796, and both were probably at Astley's; Mrs Wallack was cited on one bill, that of 16 May.

Harvard Theatre Collection

WILLIAM WALLACK, as Malcolm

anonymous engraving, after T. Roberts

Perhaps he was the "Wallaker" who played Young Marlowe in *She Stoops to Conquer* at Wheatley's Riding School, Greenwich, on 17 May 1799. In 1799 was published Sanderson's song *Pat's Planxty* as sung by Wallack at the Royal Circus. In 1800, the bills at that establishment mentioned him several times: on 21 and 29 May he sang "favorite comic songs," and on 22 September, "In the course of the Evening, but that Night only, [was] introduced an entire New Pathetic Ballad, in character, by Mr Wallack, called THE JEW; or, A Heart to Feel and a Hand to Give." On 6 October, Wallack played a Principal Character in the new burletta *The False Friend*. (His wife appears to have been in Cork early in 1800, according to W. S. Clark, but perhaps she went to Ireland without him.)

On 26 September 1803, at the Royal Circus ("his 7th Appearance there these three Years") Wallack was Oxenham of Plymouth in *Iron Arm and Sir Francis Drake,* and on 28 November he assumed Teddy O'Riley in the new burletta called *Flats and Sharps.*

We have learned little more about William Wallack, though probably he continued to sing and act roles at London's circuses and minor playhouses. Long after the eighteenth century was over he managed to achieve a patent-house situation. Manuscript lists at the Garrick Club show him as a member of the Drury Lane company in 1809 and in every season from 1813–14 through 1817–18. British Library MS Add 29411 contains the notation for 25 November 1814: "Ag Sal Wm Wallack 3 years 8—9—9 [per week]." That is the latest professional news we have of him.

William Wallack's principal importance was as progenitor of a family of performers who, with their marital connections, were heavy contributors of talent to the British and, particularly, the American stages in the nineteenth century. Wallack was the father of at least four children (all actors) with Elizbeth Field Granger Wallack. The eldest, Henry John Wallack (1790–1870), married, first, the actress Fanny Jones, and they were the parents of four performing children: James W. Wallack (1818–1873), who married the actress Ann Duff Mary Sefton (1815–1879); Julia Wallack Hoskins; George Wallack; and Fanny Wallack Moorhouse. On 7 July 1837, Henry John Wallack married the actress Marie Turpin (d. 1860). There were no children by that marriage.

William and Elizabeth Wallack's second son, James William Wallack (1795?–1864), married the actress Susan Johnstone, a daughter of the Irish comedian and singer Jack Johnstone (1749–1828). Their son, the American actor Lester Wallack (1820–1888), married Emily Millais (d. 1909), sister of the eminent pre-Raphaelite painter Sir John Millais.

The William Wallacks' first daughter, Mary (d. 1834), was an actress who became Mrs Stanley, then Mrs Hill. She evidently died without issue. The second daughter, the actress Elizabeth Wallack, married a showman named Pincott. Their daughter, the actress Leonora Pincott (1805–1884), married the actor Alfred Wigan (1814–1878).

William Wallack was also stepfather to his wife's child by Dr Granger, Julia Granger (she, however, was brought up by her grandmother, Mrs Booth). Julia acted in England as Miss Granger, then under the assumed name Mrs Edward, and finally (in the United States) as Mrs Robert Jones. Her success was considerable, and she became known as "the Jordan of America." Julia Granger Jones died on 11 November 1806 at the age of 24. Her daughter the actress Julia Elizabeth Jones (1800–1870) married the New York actor-manager Edmund Simpson (whose real name was

Shaw). A second Jones daughter, Mary Ann, also acted. She married a Mr Bancker and died in 1825.

There are outdated and often untrustworthy notices of both Henry John Wallack and James William Wallack in *The Dictionary of National Biography* and the *Dictionary of American Biography*. The rumor, retailed in both dictionaries, that as a four-year-old child James William appeared on a London circus stage with his family has not been confirmed.

A portrait of William Wallack as Malcolm in *Hallowe'en,* by an anonymous engraver after T. T. Roberts, was published by C. Beauclerc in 1799 with the title, "Mr. Wallack as Malcolm discovering himself at the Wedding in the Spectacle of Hallowe'en at the Royal Circus."

Wallack, Mrs William, Elizabeth, née Field, formerly Mrs Granger   1760?-1850, *actress, singer.*

Elizabeth Field, born in London, perhaps in 1760, was the daughter of Ursula Agnes Booth (1740–1803), actress at Drury Lane Theatre, whose husband John Booth was a tailor there. Almost certainly John Booth was stepfather to Elizabeth Field and to the younger actress Ann Field, for whom Booth is recorded in Drury Lane treasury accounts at the Folger Library as having received payment for board allowance in 1778 and 1779.

At some point before Elizabeth Field's first appearance on the stage, in 1778, she married a Dr Granger, about whom nothing is now known. She was serving as a chorus singer by 3 Oct 1778 when a payment, 13*s.* 4*d.* "for last week," was made to Mrs Granger. She sang as Mrs Granger at Sadler's Wells at least once, on 15 April 1779, according to a surviving bill in the Percival Collection in the British Library.

The assertion in J. W. Wallack's notice in the *Dictionary of American Biography* that Mrs Granger "had for a time been David Garrick's leading woman" is absurd. She did not come on the stage until Garrick had retired, and her roles were few and modest. She did, however, act and sing at Drury Lane Theatre occasionally from 1779 to 1783. She was named in a playbill for the first time on 3 November 1779 when she was one of a numerous Chorus of Spirits in *The Tempest*, a service she per-

formed several times also the following season. On 1 May 1781, she, her mother Mrs Booth, and Ann Field her sister were in the chorus accompanying the funeral procession in *Romeo and Juliet.* On 4 January 1783 she had an unspecified "principal part" in *Lun's Ghost; or, The New Year's Gift,* a new pantomime. On 12 April Mrs Granger was given her final named role, Mrs Trippit in *The Lying Valet;* on 17 April she sang a principal character in the anonymous comic opera *The True Briton;* and on 25 April she resumed her vocal assistance to *Romeo and Juliet.*

Mrs Granger's only contributions to Drury Lane's 1782–83 season were 30 performances, from 26 December through 3 March, as a character in Tom King's new pantomime *The Triumph of Mirth; or, Harlequin's Wedding.* After she sang on 12 May 1783—again along with her mother and sister—as a Beggar in *The Ladies' Frolick,* she disappeared from Drury Lane. Where she went or what she did for the next four years is a mystery.

On 8 July 1787, at St Paul, Covent Garden, "Elizabeth Granger, widow," of that parish married the actor and singer William Wallack, and from then on her career, like her husband's, lay principally away from the London patent theatres. Fugitive playbills of Astley's Amphitheatre at Westminster Bridge for the five years following Mrs Wallack's marriage show her and her husband in occasional productions of melodrama, spectacle, and pantomime. She was on Astley's company list in 1788; on 4 September 1789 she was one of six Female Rowers in *The Royal Naval Review at Plymouth;* on some date in July and on 19 September 1791 she played the Widow in *The Tithe Sheaf; or, Village Plot.*

At least three members of the William Wallack family were in Edinburgh in the spring of 1792. James Dibdin, in the *Annals of the Edinburgh Stage,* testified that the Wallacks' small daughter, "with her father and mother, had previously been performing at the Circus in Leith Street," Edinburgh; they came to the Theatre Royal, Shakespeare Square, in April. Mrs Wallack played only three roles there: Lesbia in *Selima and Azor* and Mrs Rachel Cleaveland in *The Fugitive* on 23 May and Tiffany in *Which Is the Man?* on 30 May, according to Norma Armstrong's manuscript calendar. Young Miss Wallack played

Harvard Theatre Collection

ELIZABETH WALLACK

artist unknown

Julie in *Richard Coeur de Lion* on 7 April (according to Dibdin), and Armstrong added two other roles, a Fairy in *Selima and Azor* on 23 May and the First Fairy in *The Triumph of Harlequin* on 28 May. William Wallack was given six small supporting roles (see his entry). Mrs Wallack, apparently alone, returned to Edinburgh on 21 January 1793, when she was listed for the Maid in *The Rivals.*

The record of Elizabeth Wallack's career becomes increasingly attenuated after 1793. She was on a vagrant bill for Astley's Amphitheatre on 22 August 1795 as Mrs Vulcan in *The Reasonable Wife; or, A New Way to Cure Tipsy Husbands.* In the 1795–96 season she and her husband crossed to Dublin to play at the Fishamble Street Theatre, but for that sojourn no playbills survive. The couple had returned to London by 16 May 1796, when Mrs Wallack had a role unspecified in *The Magician of the Rocks* at Astley's.

According to Clark in *The Irish Stage in the County Towns,* Mrs Wallack appeared once at Cork in the spring of 1800. On 28 November

1803, at the Royal Circus, she was Bridget in Charles Dibdin's new burletta *Flats and Sharps,* in which her husband also appeared. A Mrs (possibly Miss) Wallack is shown in the Drury Lane accounts (Folger MS W.B. 312) as receiving six-day weekly salaries of £1 5s. for "Chorus" in the seasons of 1808–9, 1812–13, and 1813–14. William Wallack was also in the company during those seasons.

The entry for 1 January 1824 in James Winston's diary (edited by Alfred L. Nelson and Gilbert B. Cross as *Drury Lane Journal*) reads: "Wallack's mother is now on the Drury Lane Fund. She was a Mrs. Grainger and before a Miss Field." She died on 6 March 1850, according to the *Era Almanac* (1868), which ads that her age was then 100—surely incorrect.

Mrs Wallack's importance to the theatre far transcended her own theatrical performances. She was the mother, by her first husband, of Julia Granger (1782–1806), who as Miss Granger played successfully in London and then as Mrs Robert Jones acted briefly but brilliantly in the United States, becoming known as "the Jordan of America." Julia Jones's two daughters were actresses. The younger, Julia Elizabeth Jones (1800–1870), married the American actor-manager Edmund Simpson (1783–1848).

Elizabeth Field Granger Wallack also had five children with William Wallack, and all were performers, including the distinguished nineteenth-century British-American actors James William and Henry Wallack.

A portrait of Elizabeth Wallack by an anonymous engraver shows her nearly three-quarter-length, to front, seated, full face, and looking elderly. The example in the Harvard Theatre Collection is a process print without inscription.

Wallaker, Mr *fl. 1799₁,* *actor.*
Mr Wallaker played Young Marlow in *She Stoops to Conquer* on 17 May 1799 at Wheatley's Riding School in Greenwich.

Waller, Mr *fl. 1707₁,* *actor.*
At Drury Lane Mr Waller acted Brazen in *The Recruiting Officer* on 18 October 1707, Loveworth in *Tunbridge Walks* on 23 October, and Carlos in *Love Makes a Man* on 25 October.

Waller, Mr *fl. 1765*]*,   actor.*

At the Haymarket Theatre in the summer of 1765, with Samuel Foote's troupe, Mr Waller played Beaufort in *The Citizen* on 8 July, an unspecified part in *The Lyar* and Lint in *The Mayor of Garratt* on 15 July, an unspecified part in *The Orators* on 31 July, and an unspecified part in *The Patron* on 21 August.

Waller, Mr *fl. 1785?–1800?*]*,   house servant?*

The Drury Lane account books cite a Mr Waller on 16 May 1785, 22 October 1799, and 30 September 1800. On 17 June 1795 a Mr Waller, possibly the same person, shared in benefit tickets at Covent Garden Theatre. Waller may have been a house servant.

Wallinger, Samuel *fl. 1792–1793*]*, musician.*

The records of the Worshipfull Company of Musicians show that Samuel Wallinger, of No 3, Rose Court, Addle Hill, became a freeman on 20 March 1792. He was probably the son of the Samuel Wallinger who was apprenticed to John Ward on 26 April 1760 and became a freeman on 21 March 1767. The elder Wallinger was living in Golden Lane in 1767, and though he had been apprenticed to a musician, he became a coal merchant. Similarly, William Wallinger, who was doubtless related to Samuel and his son, was bound apprentice to John Ward on 28 February 1758, became a freeman on 21 February 1765, and became a chandler. The younger Samuel Wallinger followed music as a career and was admitted to livery on 7 June 1793.

Wallis, Mr *fl. 1736–1742*]*,   actor.*

A Mr Wallis appeared in the London bills for the first time, as Dugard in *The Inconstant,* at the Haymarket Theatre on 19 February 1736. He seems to have found occasional employment with two of the fugitive companies that inhabited that theatre during the following six months, filling small roles like a Messenger and a Rake in *Pasquin* and Lord Sugarcane in *The Deposing and Death of Queen Gin.* He turned up in the Hallam-Chapman booth at Bartholomew Fair on 23 August playing Cardinal Aquinas in *Fair Rosamond.*

Few casts are listed in the bills for the Haymarket in 1736–37. But Wallis was there

some of the time. He shared a benefit with Noble and Mrs Pattison on 7 March 1737. He dropped out of sight, or at least out of print, until the season of 1740–41, when he joined the Giffards at Goodman's Fields. There he played Kite in *The Recruiting Officer.* Gratiano in *Othello,* Oronces in *Aesop,* Thorowgood in *George Barnwell,* Poundage in *The Provok'd Husband,* Ratcliff in *Jane Shore,* a Dropsical Man in *The Chymical Counterfeits.* Alphonso in *The Spanish Fryar,* and Glendower in *I Henry IV.*

In the summer of 1741 Wallis was occupied at some of the fairs: on 4 August as one of the Witches in *Harlequin Sorcerer* at "Lee and Woodwards Great Til'd Booth near the Turnpike" at Tottenham Court; on 22 August as Cardinal Aquinas again at Hallam's Booth at Bartholomew Fair; and as a Countryman in *Harlequin the Man in the Moon* at "Lee and Woodward's Booth on the Bowling Green" on 14 September during Southwark Fair.

The last reflection we have of Wallis's pale career is from the bill of "Phillips and Yeates' Booth opposite Hospital Gate, West Smithfield," on 5 August 1742 during Bartholomew Fair, when he played Valentine in *The Indian Merchant.*

Wallis, Mr *fl. 1762*]*,   house servant?*

A Mr Wallis was allowed benefit tickets at Drury Lane Theatre on 20 May 1762.

Wallis, Mr *fl. 1762?–1763*]*,   actor.*

On 24 July 1762, one Wallis played Darby Tatter in *The Funeral* at Bristol in a company with some London actors. Perhaps he was the Wallis who was at the Haymarket Theatre in London toward the end of the summer season of 1763, acting Sir Charles Freeman in *The Beaux' Stratagem* on 5 September and, two days later, Jaques in *Love Makes a Man.*

Wallis, Mr *fl. 1794–1801*]*,   drummer.*

The Folger Library's Drury Lane accounts reflect scattered payments ranging in amount from £1 16s. 6d. to £6 15s., from 8 July 1794 through 3 January 1801, to a Mr Wallis "for Side Drums" (cf. modern "snare drum"). Evidently Mr Wallis was not a regular member of the band but was called upon whenever the special effects possible to the side drum were required. The side drum was used primarily in military bands; perhaps Wallis was a musician in a regimental band, as several other contemporary Wallises were.

Wallis, Mrs *fl. 1748₁,* *house servant.*
A Mrs Wallis, probably a house servant, shared benefit tickets with the widow Johnson at Covent Garden Theatre on 29 March 1748.

Wallis, Mrs *fl. 1756₁,* *exhibitor.*
On 14 February 1756 *Felix Farley's Bristol Journal* announced that on display in Bristol was a collection of 13 life-size figures from Germany. The proprietor of the exhibition was a "Mrs Wallis from London."

Wallis, Mrs *fl. 1760₁,* *dresser.*
A Mrs Wallis is on the list of "Women Dressers" at Covent Garden Theatre in September 1760 preserved in the British Library's Egerton MS 2271.

Wallis, Mrs *fl. 1794–1795₁,* *dresser.*
The name of a Mrs Wallis is found in the Covent Garden Theatre account books for 1794–95 as a dresser earning 9s. per week.

Wallis, [D.?] *fl. 1765–1777?₁,* *dancer.*
Mr Wallis, a dancer, whose salary was 15s. per week, is cited in a surviving Drury Lane pay list purportedly in David Garrick's hand and dated 9 February 1765. According to the Drury Lane account book in the Folger Library, his pay was the same on 24 January 1767.

He may have been the D. Wallis, "male dancer," who was paid £1 per week at Drury Lane during the 1776–77 season.

Wallis, Elizabeth *b. 1777, actress.*
Miss Elizabeth Wallis, at the age of eight, appeared as young William in a performance of *The Countess of Salisbury* at Kendal, on 25 February 1785. She was one of the daughters of the provincial actors Fielding and Jane Wallis (née Miller), who that night played Gray and the Countess, respectively. Elizabeth's sister Tryphosa Jane Wallis and her father played the famous Hubert-Arthur scene from *King John* after the mainpiece. The family had strong ties to the theatre at Richmond, York-

shire, where they were connected with the Wrights, Butlers, and Tayleures, who formed a large network of related performers on the minor Yorkshire circuit that included Beverley, Harrogate, Kendal, Northallerton, Ulverston, and Whitby. The somewhat complex details of her parents' backgrounds are given in the notice of Tryphosa Jane Wallis, a beauty who enjoyed some success on the London and Bath stages in the late 1780s and 1790s.

Of the extensive family, only Elizabeth and Tryphosa Jane made it to the London stage in the eighteenth century. And Elizabeth appeared there only once, when she acted the Page in *The Follies of Day* for her sister's benefit at Covent Garden on 22 April 1795. She was announced as making her first appearance on that stage, "and her Third on Any Stage." The *European Magazine* reported that she performed her little role "with a portion of spirit and archness that deserved applause." Elizabeth acted again at the Crow Street Theatre in Dublin during the summer of 1795. After that time we lose track of her.

Wallis, Thomas *1778–1840, instrumentalist.*
Doane's *Musical Directory* of 1794 noticed "Thomas Wallis, Junr," then of No 24, New Peter Street (his father's address), and declared that he played clarinet and horn in the band of the third regiment of Guards. He was said to be then just 16 years old. Documentary evidence submitted to the Royal Society of Musicians on 3 May 1801 showed him to have been baptized on 9 June 1778 at St Margaret, Westminster, the son of Thomas and Jane Wallis. He had married Elizabeth Percifull of that parish at St John the Evangelist, Westminster, on 15 September 1796. By 1808 they had four children: Elizabeth, age 10; Mary, six; Sarah, five; and Matilda, 10 months. Thomas had been in the band at Sadler's Wells and had assisted in the oratorios at Covent Garden Theatre, apparently before 1800.

The influential Ashleys—Charles, General, and Richard—were Wallis's sponsors for membership in the Royal Society of Musicians on 3 May 1801, 5 September 1802, and in June 1804. Each time the membership committee rejected him by large majorities. Finally, on 3 April 1808, "with 9 yeas & 3 Nays he was declared a fit person to be recommended to a General meeting." At that time, he was said to be engaged as first trumpet in the pit bands at Covent Garden and the Haymarket and as first horn for the Covent Garden oratorios.

Despite the discouraging rejections, Thomas Wallis became a diligent and useful member of the Society, playing trumpet in its annual charity concerts at St Paul's and rising by 1812 to be a Governor. He was again a Governor in 1834. He died in 1840, and his widow claimed a pension from the Society.

To the 1808 list of four daughters the Wallises had added a son in 1809. Thomas Samuel Wallis, trumpeter, pianist at the Haymarket and Adelphi Theatres, and organist of St Mary Chapel of Ease, Lambeth, was elected a member of the Society on 2 January 1831. On 28 December 1836 he married the sixteen-year-old Eliza Mary Reneman Jackson at St Andrew, Holborn. Curiously, the only child of that union recorded by the Society arrived 15 years after the marriage: Lydia Sophia, born 10 December 1851 at the Wallises' residence, No 3, Melbourne Square, North Brixton. Thomas was by then Doctor of Music. He died in 1864 and was buried on 22 October at South Metropolitan Cemetery. Mrs Wallis applied for relief, for she had "No property or cash—scarcely any household furniture."

Wallis, Thomas *fl. 1791–1794*, bassoonist.

Thomas Wallis of No 24, New Peter Street, Westminster, is noticed in Doane's *Musical Directory* of 1794 as a subscriber to the New Musical Fund (confirmed by the fund's official list for 1794) and a participant in one or several of the Handel Memorial Concerts in Westminster Abbey, the one most recent to Doane's date having been in 1791. He had a son Thomas, also a musician, noticed above. Perhaps both Wallis the drummer (fl. 1794–1801) and the John Wallis of Earl Street, Seven Dials, a horn player with the band of the first regiment of Guards, cited by Doane, were also kin.

Wallis, Tryphosa Jane, later Mrs James Elijah Campbell *1774–1848, actress, singer.*

Tryphosa Jane Wallis was born on 11 January 1774 at Richmond, Yorkshire, the daughter of two provincial performers who had a long and important connection to the theatre in that city. Her mother was Jane Wallis (1750–1785), the daughter of the strollers Henry Miller and Tryphosa Miller. Her father, Fielding Wallis (1754–1817), was the son of the Rev Thomas Wallis, rector of Boho and Templecarne in County Fermagh, Ireland.

Our subject's maternal grandmother, Tryphosa Miller (1727–1797), was the daughter of the Rev Christopher Brockell, granddaughter of the Rev William Brockell, and great-granddaughter of the Rev John Brockell. In 1749, at the age of 22, Tryphosa Brockell married Henry Miller. The Miller's second daughter (our subject's aunt), Katherine, married the actor William Tayleure (d. 1782), the son of a Norfolk clergyman. After Henry Miller's death sometime before 1771, Tryphosa Miller married her second husband, J. Wright, who was involved with the company's management, and had by him a son, John Brockell Wright, who also became a member of the deeply inbred troupe. J. Wright soon died and by 1773 Tryphosa Miller Wright had married her third husband, Samuel Butler (1750–1812), a former staymaker at York turned actor, and 23 years her junior. The complexity of the various family relationships is detailed in Sybil Rosenfeld's *The Georgian Theatre of Richmond Yorkshire* (1984).

When our subject's father, Fielding Wallis, joined the circuit at Ripon in 1771, he was acting under the assumed name Stuart. His future mother-in-law, Tryphosa Miller Wright, by then the widow of J. Wright, was the manager, and his future wife, Jane Miller, was acting in the troupe. Wallis married Jane Miller in 1773. After the birth of their daughter Tryphosa Jane at Richmond in 1774, they had seven additional children, at least two of whom also went on the stage. Margaret Wallis acted at Bristol in the early 1780s without success and in July 1796 married the Rev James Tate. Another sister, Elizabeth Wallis, also acted at Bristol and Kendal and appeared once in London, as the Page in *The Follies of the Day,* for her sister Tryphosa Jane's benefit at Covent Garden on 22 April 1795; but her career soon ended, it seems, after an engagement in Dublin in the summer of 1795.

According to the *Thespian Dictionary* and *The Secret History of the Green Room,* Tryphosa Jane performed several roles when she was very young. On 17 December 1778, when she was not quite five, she appeared at the Crow Street Theatre in Dublin. She continued to play children's roles at the Crow Street and Smock Alley theatres for several seasons, and at the latter house in 1783 for her father's benefit she caricatured the Fine Lady in *Lethe.* She also performed with the family at Kilkenny in February 1783 and May 1784.

The Wallis family returned to England late in 1784 to join Butler's company, playing at Pontefract, Kendal, and other northern towns on the circuit. A playbill for Kendal on 25 February shows the family at work in *The Countess of Salisbury,* with Wallis as Grey, Mrs Wallis as the Countess (for her benefit night), and Miss Elizabeth Wallis as William. Following the tragedy, Wallis and his daughter Tryphosa Jane played the famous Hubert-Arthur scene in *King John.* In the afterpiece, *The Flitch of Bacon,* Wallis acted Justice Benbow. A note on the back of the playbill records that receipts were £28 7s., and £3 was shared. In the summer of 1785 Tryphosa Jane acted for Wilkinson at Leeds, appearing as the Fine Lady, a role in which Wilkinson found her "very clever."

While the family was acting at Harrogate in the summer of 1785, Tryphosa Jane enjoyed the kind patronage of Lord and Lady Loughborough, and when Mrs Wallis died in childbirth on 18 December 1785 at the age of 35, leaving Fielding Wallis with eight children under the age of 12, the Loughboroughs took in the eldest, Tryphosa Jane. In a long letter to the Rev William Leigh Wilkinson of Guisborough (cited by Rosenfeld), Wallis described his daughter's fortunate circumstances:

My Eldest Girl's amiable manners has establish'd her so much in her angel Benefactresses esteem, that the dear Woman has condescended to declare, 'that she never long'd for life so much, as since their acquaintance' and my Lord told me last York assizes, that he believed my daughter to be everything I would wish; she is treated in every particular as one of their own, and is I fancy highly accomplished. The consequence of all this Sir, you might tremble for, if I did not inform you, that she is supposed to be the greatest Theatrical Genius in the World, and in truth when she left me, she was a prodigy—but she is not yet quite 14.— In the course of last Spring Lady Loughborough ask'd and obtain'd from her Brother Ld. Courtney a Living he had in his Gift, on his Estate in Ireland, with £160 a year which she directly presented to my Girl, for her Grand Father, who has just got to his own home again, after taking possession of it, for it does not oblige him to relinquish his other Living.

It was during that period that she was painted by Romney in the characters of "Mirth and Melancholy."

Through the influence of her benefactors, Miss Wallis made her first appearance at Covent Garden Theatre on 10 January 1789, one day shy of her sixteenth birthday. Her debut role was Sigismunda in *Tancred and Sigismunda,* and the veteran Alexander Pope acted the other title role. She was much puffed in the press as a prodigy, who had appeared with her parents in many of the provincial theatres. She was received with applause and exhibited "great marks of feeling and sensibility," according to that month's *European Magazine,* where she was described as of middle size, not inelegant, with expressive features, but somewhat deficient in dignity. Though she seemed better suited for comedy than tragedy, her voice was "pathetic and interesting," but it lacked power because of her extreme youth and embarrassment The press found her carriage and deportment particularly easy and graceful.

After acting Sigismunda again on 16 January 1789, she appeared as Belvidera—a most demanding role—in *Venice Preserv'd* on 21 January. Her performance encouraged the critic in the *Biographical and Imperial Magazine* of January 1789 to believe she would prove "a considerable acquisition to the manager." For her benefit on 11 February 1789 she played Rosalind (and sang the "Cuckoo Song") in *As You Like It.* Tickets were available from her at Alden's, No 15, Caroline Street, Bedford Square, and gross receipts amounted to £297 10s.

Miss Wallis's final role that season at Covent Garden was Roxalana in *The Sultan.* Despite her talent, her youth and lack of experience and her bouts of stage fright made it evident that she was not sufficiently ready for an engagement at a major patent house. Her failure

Norton Gallery and School of Art, West Palm Beach

TRYPHOSA JANE WALLIS, as Imogen
by Dupont

in London, as Tate Wilkinson explained, "was not a matter of surprise, when we consider a child armed against the Colossus of Tragedy, Mrs. Siddons."

Miss Wallis returned to reside with the Loughboroughs at Harrogate, and in the summer of 1789 she played four nights with her grandmother's company when they visited that town. Samuel Butler, her grandmother's new husband and co-manager, put up a notice in the green room, in deference to Lady Loughborough: "The gentlemen of the theatre are requested not to wear their hats while Miss Wallis is in the house." As Harriot Mellon told the story, each actor then found a reason to wear his hat, in opposition to Butler's obsequiousness.

On 17 October 1789 Miss Wallis made her first appearance at the Orchard Street Theatre in Bath, as Rosalind in As You Like It, and thus began a five-year engagement with that theatre during which she played many characters of importance and became a great favorite of the town. On 21 January 1790 she acted Amanthis in The Child of Nature. She was also seen that season as Lucille in False Appearances, Indiana in The Conscious Lovers, Calista in The Fair Penitent, Maria in The Citizen, and Beatrice in Much Ado about Nothing, among other roles. In the summer of 1790 she acted at Leeds, York, and Harrogate. She appeared at Beverley on 2 June, and John Courtney entered in his diary (cited by Rosenfeld) that she played Amanthis "amazingly well and was a very pretty girl." On 5 June, when she acted Sigismunda, she impressed Courtney by wearing "the richest dress . . . I think I ever saw on the Stage." Given to her by Lady Loughborough, it was reputed to have cost £100, and it "was the same she had on in London when she first performed there." When she acted Indiana and Roxalana on 9 June, the house was jammed with patrons, bringing her the amazing sum of £44. That night she wore "a most superb Turkish dress made by herself by Mrs. Otley's Directions." She acted, among other places, at Weymouth in September 1791, playing Rosalind for a command performance.

Among her many roles at Bath (and at Bristol, the sister theatre) over the subsequent seasons were Violante in The Wonder, Imogen in Cymbeline, the title role in Julia de Roubigné (an

original part on 23 December 1790), Portia in The Merchant of Venice, Lady Amaranth in Wild Oats, Juliet in Romeo and Juliet, Isabella in Measure for Measure, Cordelia in King Lear, the title role in Jane Shore, Euphrasia in The Garden Daughter, Perdita in The Winter's Tale, Catherine in Catherine and Petruchio, and Lady Macbeth—an impressive array of capital roles for one not yet 20.

Having seen her at Bath, Thomas Harris engaged her at Covent Garden at £18 per week. At an emotional farewell benefit at Bath on 4 March 1794, Miss Wallis delivered an effusive farewell speech in which she thanked Bath audiences for having raised her up, the manager Keasberry for having been a second father to her, and the actor Dimond for having been a true friend. But since she was very much responsible for her seven motherless siblings, she was obliged to take advantage of the liberal financial terms and opportunities awaiting her in London. (According to The Secret History of the Green Room, one of her brothers was lost in the naval service.) Before her departure from Bath she was presented by "a large and polite circle" with a costly medallion, described by Penley in The Bath Stage as "representing Shakespeare inviting timid genius from the shade, and holding to her view a sprig of laurel." On the reverse was the inscription, "Presented to Miss Wallis, by the ladies and gentlemen of Bath, as a small tribute to private virtue and public merit." On 28 July 1794 Miss Wallis enjoyed a benefit at Bristol, when she again delivered her farewell address.

Announced as from the Theatre Royal, Bath, she made her first appearance at Covent Garden in five years on 7 October 1794 as Imogen in Cymbeline. The London Chronicle on 9 October observed that she "does not seem to have chosen any particular model to govern her acting, like most of the female candidates of later years, who have generally founded their manner upon the style of Mrs. Siddons." The critic in that month's European Magazine thought she gave "a most accomplished representing of the part," and he was happy to see the vast improvements she had made; she was, he believed, better suited for comedy than serious drama. Universal applause accompanied her debut throughout. After repeating Imogen on 10 October, she acted that season Lady

Townly in *The Provok'd Husband*, Juliet in *Romeo and Juliet*, Amanthis in *The Child of Nature*, Calista in *The Fair Penitent*, Beatrice in *Much Ado about Nothing*, Indiana in *The Conscious Lovers*, Euphrasia in *The Grecian Daughter*, Cordelia in *King Lear*, Adelaide in *The Count of Narbonne*, Susan in *The Follies of a Day*, and Olivia in *A Bold Stroke for a Wife*. Her original roles were Georgina in Mrs Cowley's *The Town before You* on 6 December 1794, Julia in M. P. Andrews's *The Mysteries of the Castle* on 31 January 1795, Lady Surrey in Watson's *England Preserv'd* on 21 February, Augusta Woodbine in O'Keeffe's *Life's Vagaries* on 19 March, Miss Russel in Macready's *Bank Note* on 1 May, Joanna in Holcroft's *The Deserted Daughters* on 2 May, and Ida in Boaden's *Secret Tribunal* on 3 June 1795. For her benefit on 22 April 1795 she acted Mrs Oakly in *The Jealous Wife* and Susan in *The Follies of a Day;* tickets were available from her at No 76, Gower Street, Bedford Square. Gross receipts were £33 5s. 6d. That night her sister Elizabeth Wallis made her first and only appearance on the London stage, as the Page in the afterpiece.

That year *The Secret History of the Green Room* described Tryphosa as having a pallid countenance and regular features, with a clear and "marking" eye. Her figure was delicate; her genteel and graceful manners attested to her good breeding. Her voice, however, tended to become hoarse and unmusical when she spoke with energy. "She injures her declamation by one repeated cadence, seemingly caught from a Scottish preceptor, as it is utterly unlike either the English or the Irish. She begins high, and gradually descends. The first words have in course an improper evaluation, and the last are lost in a gutteral gulph." But the author had much good to write about her:

But if her recitation be thus defective, her action is easy, firm, and picturesque; her arms oftener repose than is now usual; and she seeks little after practised starts and constrained attitudes. In comedy she is a perfect gentlewoman, and exhibits no sign that she has changed the drawing-room for the stage. . . . Her Juliet is in some scenes excellent, so is her Imogen. Deserted love, plaintive melancholy, and soft friendship, she can delineate justly; all beyond these nature has denied, and art will scarcely supply them.

TRYPHOSA JANE WALLIS
engraving by Bartolozzi

The author of *The Secret History* thought that if she were wise enough to limit her efforts, Miss Wallis might "become a star of considerable magnitude." But her father had pushed her along too fast, and his extravagant notions of her powers had done her damage. If she had been less praised she would have received less money from the London management, but she would have been in a more comfortable situation, one in which "her powers would have had the leisure to matriculate, and her influence on the public be progressive."

That same year in his *Candid and Impartial Strictures on the Performers* (1795), F. G. Waldron put Miss Wallis in a proper perspective. She had been so overpuffed that after a few nights the town felt cheated—"at least, com-

paratively to what we were at first taught to
believe." When placed against a more modest
standard, her talents could be more appro-
priately measured:

Her person is elegantly formed, and her manners
pleasing. Her voice clear and articulate, as her face
is handsome; but there is something of the *vixen,*
expressed in her eyes, which are otherwise good,
that is by no means pleasing to us. She speaks dialogue tolerably well, and may be considered a useful second rate actress; but to place her in the same
rank of elegance as the inimitable *Farren,* is not
only to injure her, but to insult the good sense of
a British audience.

In the summer of 1795 Miss Wallis went to
act for Daly at the Crow Street Theatre, but
Dublin audiences did not flock to her. In July
1795 the elder Charles Mathews wrote that
Daly had offered £30 per night but she had
refused, wishing to share the house. She was a
loser by that arrangement, as on some nights
she did not share £10. "People all say she is a
charming actress, but not fit to come as a star
after Miss Farren and Mrs. Siddons."

On 11 September 1795, she acted at Cork
and then returned to London to reappear for
her second season at Covent Garden on 18
September as Miss Russel in *The Bank Note.*
To her London repertoire she added Cecilia in
The Chapter of Accidents, Julia in *The Rivals,*
Augusta in *Life's Vagaries,* Perdita in *The Winter's Tale,* and Rosolia in *Zorinski.* Her original
roles were Emmeline in Reynold's *Speculation*
on 7 November 1795 and Julia Faulkner in
Morton's *The Way to Get Married* on 23 January
1796. She acted Lady Eleanor Erwin in *Every
One Has His Faults* and Lady Bab Lardoon in
The Maid of the Oaks for her benefit on 20
April 1796, when gross receipts were £377
15s. 6d. She still lived in Gower Street, according to the playbill. On 25 May 1796 she
went over to Drury Lane to act Roxalana in
The Sultan in a special benefit for the family of
the late Stephen Storace. Her critical reception did not improve. In his *Pin Basket to the
Children of Thespis* (1796), Anthony Pasquin
(John Williams) found her still pretty, but her
manner seemed weepy, making her voice "monotonous" and "incapable of giving any great
effect" to the speech of her Shakespearean
characters. The manager Harris, it was said,

TRYPHOSA JANE WALLIS, as Juliet
engraving by Grozer, after Graham

was sorry that he had her for "three years certain at sixteen pounds a week." (Actually her
salary was £18.)

In the summer of 1796 Miss Wallis acted at
Edinburgh and Glasgow. On her way back to
London she appeared one night in Birmingham, 5 September, for Middleton's benefit,
acting Juliet and Roxalana. That summer the
press had reported the marriage of Miss Wallis
and the Rev James Tate, but the *How Do You
Do?* of 18 October 1796 published a clarifi-
cation to the effect that it had not been Tryphosa Jane but her sister Margaret who had
married. The former's marriage, however, that
journal reported, would occur soon after the
expiration of her articles: "She is a good girl,
and her anxiety and care to her family deserves

every attention which can contribute toward her felicity."

At Covent Garden in 1796–97 she acted Eliza Ratcliffe in *The Jew,* Lady Sadlife in *The Double Gallant,* Catherine in *Catherine and Petruchio,* Cordelia in *King Lear,* Arethusa in *Philaster,* and Harriet in *The Guardian,* among other roles. She was the original Lady Danvers in Reynold's *Fortune's Fool* on 29 October 1796, Jessy in Morton's *A Cure for the Heart Ache* on 10 January 1797, and Miss Dorillon in Mrs Inchbald's *Wives as They Were, and Maids as They Are* on 4 March 1797. In December 1796, with Harris's consent, she had returned to Bath and Bristol to play a round of her characters, including Jane Shore, Beatrice, Roxalana, and Lady Townly. The *Monthly Mirror* reported her intention to quit Covent Garden at the close of the season and to resume her situation at Bath.

On 26 April 1787 Miss Wallis took her final benefit at Covent Garden, playing Adriana in *The Comedy of Errors* and Harriet in *The Guardian.* Ticket receipts were again healthy—£376 9s. 6d. The playbill showed that Miss Wallis's address was still in Gower Street. On 6 May she acted, for the first time, Lenora in *Lover's Quarrels,* for Mrs Mattock's benefit. She played Mrs Belville in *The School for Wives* for the prompter Wild's benefit on 22 May, and she repeated Leonora for Mrs Clendining's benefit on 25 May, the latter being her final performance in London until she returned as Mrs Campbell in 1813.

The *Monthly Mirror* of May 1797 announced that Miss Wallis, "who has left Covent-Garden for good [is] performing at Glasgow and some other theatres in the North, and then—heigho, for a husband!" In June she acted at Newcastle, opening on the nineteenth as Lady Teazle in *The School for Scandal.* Her engagement at Glasgow, scheduled for six nights, was reduced to four because of her "indifferent success." At the Theatre Royal in Shakespeare Square, Edinburgh, she acted Julia Faulkner in *The Way to Get Married* on 8 July 1797, and, indeed, soon after that month, at Gladsmuir, Haddingtonshire, in Scotland she married James Elijah Campbell, of the third regiment of Foot Guards. He was of an ancient Scottish family of Kingancleugh, and had been commissioned ensign on 9 December 1795.

Upon her marriage to Campbell, Miss Wallis left the stage. The local Bath press reported that she was living in Bath in September 1804 and that Campbell had volunteered for the Navy, "having in his earlier years circumnavigated the globe with Capts. Portlock and Bligh." (By 1833 Campbell had become a captain in the Royal Navy.)

On 20 February 1813, as Mrs Campbell late Miss Wallis, she returned to Covent Garden to act the title role in Garrick's *Isabella.* But she suffered stage fright and failed. She repeated the character one more time but then retreated. That April she tried again, this time at Bath, in the new Theatre Royal in Beaufort Square, where she excited considerable interest and acted for six nights to crowded houses, as Lady Townly and Hermione. She was engaged at Bath the following season and was seen as Rutland in *The Earl of Essex.* Lady Gentle in *The Lady's Last Stake,* Zaphira in *Barbarossa,* and the Marchioness in *The Doubtful Son,* but she never recaptured the favor she had enjoyed from Bath audiences in the 1790s, and after that engagement she retired permanently, about the age of 30.

She died on 29 December 1848 and was buried at All Saints, Edmonton. The inscription on her tombstone reads:

> Beneath this Stone
> lie the remains of
> TRYPHOSA JANE CAMPBELL
> widow of
> James Elijah Campbell
> late a Captain
> of the Royal Navy
> She died Dec. 29th 1848,
> Aged 74 years,
> with humble confidence in the
> Meritorious death of her Redeemer
> for pardon and acceptance
> She gently fell asleep
> in faith resigning her Spirit
> to him who gave it.
> This tomb was erected
> by her son

Buried in the same vault were the remains of her late sister, Margaret Tate (widow of James Tate, vicar of Edmonton), who died on 6 March 1851, in her 76th year, and five of the Tate children.

By James Campbell, Tryphosa Jane Wallis had at least seven children. The deaths of two

TRYPHOSA JANE WALLIS, as "Mirth and Melancholy"

engraving by Keating, after Romney

of these were announced in the *Gentleman's Magazine* for April 1833: "*March* 25. Jane, aged 20, and on the 26th, Mary, aged 17, daughters of Capt Campbell, R. N. of King's Terrace, Southsea. The young ladies were the daughters of Mrs. Campbell, formerly Miss Wallis, of the Theatre-Royal, Covent-Garden." The will of her daughter Charlotte Eliza Jane Campbell, spinster, made on 5 August 1826 at Hamphire Terrace, Southsea, Portsmouth, provides some information about the family. Charlotte bequeathed to her father £100; she left £20 to each of her brothers: James, John, Fielding, and Hugh. Her sisters, unnamed, were to receive "the remainder of the sum vested by the Countess Dowager of Rosalyn [Lady Loughborough] in the funds on the account of my Mother and myself." Charlotte Campbell's will was proved on 4 August 1848, when administration was granted to the Rev Charles Hardy, who had been one of the executors of Capt Campbell's will. Capt Campbell had survived his daughter Charlotte, but barely; he died before he could take upon him the letters of administration for his daughter Charlotte's will, apparently not too long a time before his wife had died.

An unflattering anatomization of Tryphosa Jane Wallis's talents was performed in the *Monthly Mirror* for September 1797, shortly after she left her London engagement, in which it is inferred that any status she had enjoyed as an actress was due to the patronage of the Lord Chancellor. She was condemned as an "entirely artificial actress" who never revealed "a trait of genius":

her tragedy was light and frivolous, and her comedy cold, formal, and austere. Of her *action* we cannot speak, since she never used any . . . [T]he character of her face was indeed equivocal; her expression of sadness was mingled with gaiety, and that of joy blended with sorrow. Thus . . . we hardly knew whether we were to laugh or cry. . . . There was great vivacity, however, in her *eye,* which communicated an occasional interest to her countenance. Yet, at best, it could only be called pretty, and PRETTINESS is the characteristic by which posterity must distinguish Miss Wallis. Her figure was *pretty;* her face was *pretty;* the public thought her a *pretty* woman; and, in our opinion, she was only a *pretty* actress.

Her best characters were Miss Dorillon, Julia Faulkner, and Jessy Oatland. She was also successful as Joanna in *The Deserted Daughter.* She was admired in characters of sweetness, simplicity, and modesty, these being her own attributes, reportedly.

No one regretted her retirement, claimed the *Monthly Mirror.* But she was admired for being "a virtuous woman, preserving her character amid temptations . . . and supporting a father and several sisters by the exertions of her industry."

Her father, the old provincial trouper Fielding Wallis, had died, according to the *Gentleman's Magazine* of April 1817, on 15 March of that year.

Portraits of Tryphosa Jane Wallis include:

1. Engraved portrait by F. Bartolozzi, standing under a tree, hands crossed, 1795.

2. Engraved portrait by D. Gibson, after a miniature. Published by A. Molteno, 1795.

3. As Amanthis in *The Child of Nature.* Engraving by J. R. Smith, published by the artist, 1797.

4. As Aspasia in *Irene.* Engraving by P. Audinet, after J. Roberts. Published as a plate to *Bell's British Theatre,* 1796. A portrait by James Roberts called Miss Wallis as Irene in *Irene* was one of the original paintings sold at Leigh and Sotheby's on 25 May 1805 (lot 265). No doubt in the sale catalogue's description Irene was a mistake for Aspasia.

5. As Imogene in *Cymbeline.* By Gainsbor-

ough Dupont. Oil on canvas (30" × 25"). Exhibited at the Royal Academy, 1795. In the Norton Art Gallery, West Palm Beach, Florida (originally mistakenly identified in that gallery as Mrs Baddeley).

6. As Irene (?) in *Irene.* See above, No 4.

7. As Juliet in *Romeo and Juliet.* By J. Graham. Probably the portrait of her exhibited by Graham at the Royal Academy in 1796 and owned by Robert Walters of Ware Priory, Hertfordshire, when *The Dictionary of National Biography* was written. Engraving by J. Grozzier, published by Atkins, 1796.

8. As Palmira in *Mahomet the Imposter.* The original painting by S. De Wilde was sold at Leigh & Sotheby's on 25 May 1805 (lot 274). It was engraved by W. Leney for *Bell's British Theatre,* 1795.

9. As "Mirth and; Melamcholy" in George Romney's painting "L'Allegro e Penseroso," 1788. At Petworth House. Engraving by J. Jones, 1798, and G. Keating, 1799. Jennifer Watson calls our attention to two preparatory drawings by Romney in the Fitzwilliam Museum and an oil sketch identified as a "Sketch of the Head of Comedy" in the Fine Arts Museum of San Francisco. In their *Catalogue Raisonée of the Works of George Romney,* Humphrey Ward and W. Roberts note another portrait by Romney which may have been of Miss Wallis. That picture was at Christie's on 7 May 1898 (lot 89), and was bought by Leggatt.

Walls. *See* WALL.

Walmisley. *See also* WAMSLEY.

Walmisley, Edward *fl.* 1787–1794₁, *singer.*

Master Edward Walmisley was listed in Doane's *Musical Directory* in 1794 as a tenor in St Peter's choir, in Westminster Abbey Handelian performances, and in the Covent Garden oratorios. His address was No 14, North Street, Westminster, the same as that of his younger brother Master Thomas Forbes Walmisley, who was also listed by Doane. Edward was the first or second of the four sons of William Walmisley, Clerk of the Papers to the House of Lords. Like all his brothers, Edward was sent to Westminster School, where he was admitted as a chorister in 24 April 1787; and like all his brothers, except Thomas Forbes, he became a parliamentary clerk.

Walmisley, Thomas Forbes *1783–1866, singer, organist, composer.*

Thomas Forbes Walmisley was born in Union Street (now St Margaret), Westminster, on 22 May 1783, the third son of William Walmisley, Clerk of the Papers to the House of Lords. He was a chorister at Westminster Abbey, and, like his three brothers, he attended Westminster School, from 1793 to 1798. But he was the only one of William Walmisley's offspring to become a professional musician, the other three obtaining parliamentary clerkships. (Thomas's elder brother Edward did sing, as a child, in the Covent Garden oratorios and in the Abbey Handelian concerts.)

In the spring of 1796 Thomas sang in the oratorios at Covent Garden Theatre when he was not quite 13 years old. Master Walmisley's name appeared in the bills as a principal performer in *L'allegro ed il penseroso* on 17 February 1796. Doane's *Musical Directory* that year described Master Thomas Walmisley Junior as a singer in the Westminster choir and the Covent Garden oratorios; his address was No 14, North Street, Westminster, the same as his brother Edward's and presumably the family residence.

Walmisley began teaching piano and singing in 1803 and was composing vocal scores in 1805. From 1810 to 1814 he served as assistant organist at the Female Orphan Asylum, and in 1814 he succeeded Robert Cooke as organist of St Martin-in-the-Fields, in which position he remained until 1854. He was also secretary of the Cencentores Sodales from 1817 to 1847, when at its dissolution the society gave him its stock of wine. Walmisley was elected to the Catch Club in 1827.

He died on 23 July 1866 and was buried in the family plot at Brompton cemetery. In 1810 Walmisley had married the eldest daughter of the scene designer William Capon. They had a total of 12 children; six sons and four daughters survived infancy. The eldest son, the musician Thomas Attwood Walmisley (1814–1856), who is noticed in Grove, died before his father, who edited his

By permission of the Board of the British Library

THOMAS FORBES WALMISLEY
by F. M. Walmisley

son's *Cathedral Music* in 1857. Our subject's son Henry Walmisley (1830–1857) became organist of Holy Trinity, Bessborough Gardens, and another son, Frederick Walmisley (1815–1875), was an artist. The following persons listed in the *Westminster School Register* were, no doubt, also Thomas Forbes Walmisley's children (or those of his brothers): John Richard Lambert Walmisley, born 6 April 1818 and admitted 3 July 1827; George Augustus Walmisley, born 3 January 1820 and admitted 26 January 1830; and Philip Moss Walmisley, born 19 November 1821 and admitted 17 January 1831.

Walmisley was distinguished as an organist and teacher. Though he composed church music, he was better known for his glees, some 59, four of which won prizes. Among his published works are *A Collection of Glees, Trios, Rounds, and Canons* (1826), *Three Canons*

"View of Gobray Fall"

by THOMAS WALMSLEY

(1840), *Sacred Songs* (1841), and a number of songs, listed in the *Catalogue of Engraved Printed Music in the British Museum* and the *New Grove*.

A portrait of Thomas Forbes Walmisley by Mac Caul was in the possession of his son Arthur Walmisley when the notice in *The Dictionary of National Biography* was written. Also in the possession of that son was a portrait of his father from F. W. Walmisley (another son); it was reproduced in Myles B. Foster's *Anthems and Anthem Composers*, 1901.

Walmsley, Sarah. *See* EDWIN, MRS JOHN.

Walmsley, Thomas *1763–1805, scene painter.*

The painter Thomas Walmsley was born in 1763 at Dublin, where his father, Thomas Walmsley, the captain-lieutenant of the 18th

Dragoons, was quartered with his regiment. He was descended from a well-connected family of Rochdale, Lancashire. After some disagreement with his family, Walmsley came to London and is said to have studied under Giovanni Colomba, who was a scene painter at the King's Theatre from 1773–74 through 1779–80. Walmsley was paid £8 by Covent Garden Theatre on 18 February 1782 (perhaps for work on Bates's *Which Is the Man?*, which premiered on 9 February).

Returning to Dublin, he painted some scenery at the Crow Street Theatre, including scenes for Gluck's *Orfeo* in January 1784. His scenery for *The Campaign* was described in the *Hibernian Journal* 30 January 1784: "the first scene being a happy contrivance of giving the distant Perspective of a Fort, a beautiful View of a Sea, Shipping, rural Scenery and a terminating Sky, comprehended a Series of Paintings in the Manner of Loutherbourg, executed by *Mr. Warmsley,* one of his Pupils, which does infinite Credit to Mr. Daly's Judgment, in his Choice of such an Artist." Back in England he was employed at Liverpool at £2 per week in 1786 and took £23 8*s.* at his benefit there on 16 October. At York in 1788 he executed a new landscape scene for *Henry VIII,* shown at Wilkinson's benefit on 25 March. When the Crow Street Theatre was reopened in 1788 Walmsley again painted scenery there.

By 1790 Walmsley was living at No 2, Surrey Road, Westminster Bridge, and was exhibiting landscapes in London. That year at the Society of Artists he exhibited a "Welsh view" at the Spring Gardens Rooms and another view of Wales, near Knighton. In 1791–92 he was employed as a scene painter at Covent Garden, his first payment of which we have a record being 10 guineas on 5 December 1791. He earned £5 5*s.* per week. With Richards, Hodgins, and Pugh he contributed scenes to *Blue-Beard* on 21 December 1791. Other productions on which he worked were *Columbus, Harlequin Museum,* and *The Governor* in 1792–93; *Harlequin Chaplet, Harlequin and Faustus* (landscape and water mill), and *The Travellers in Switzerland* in 1793–94; and *Hercules and Omphale, Mago and Dago,* and *Windsor Castle* in 1794–95. He also executed scenery designed by Hamilton for *Aci e Galatea* at the King's Theatre on 21 March 1795. At the new Theatre Royal, Liverpool, Walmsley, Waitmore, and Wilkins contributed scenes in 1803.

Between 1790 and 1796 Walmsley sent a number of pictures to the Royal Academy, contributing three views of Killarney in the last year; these were engraved by Francis Juker. According to Redgrave, "He painted, chiefly in body-color, some small landscapes of merit. His works were remarkable for the great luminousness of his skies."

Walmsley retired in ill health to Bath. He died there in 1805. Publications of his landscapes before and after his death included views of the Dee and North Wales, 1792–94; larger views of North Wales, 1800; views of Killarney and Kenmare, 1800–2; miscellaneous British scenery, 1801; views in Bohemia, 1801; views of the Isle of Wight, 1802–3; miscellaneous Irish scenery, 1806; and views in Scotland, 1810.

Walpole. *See also* TOMKINS, MR.

Walpole, Charlotte, later Mrs Edward Atkyns *c. 1758–1836, actress, singer, dancer.*

Charlotte Walpole was the daughter of William Walpole of Athlone, County Roscommon, according to information given in *Notes and Queries* in 1903 by H. S. Vade-Walpole. W. J. Lawrence recorded that she made her acting debut at Crow Street Theatre in Dublin as Leonora in *The Padlock* in January 1776. According to information collected by W. S. Clark, she then went over to Smock Alley Theatre in April, returning to Crow Street from May until the end of that season. Clark found her name on the bills of the Cork theatre for 7 October and 10 December 1776. In 1776–77, she played at the Fishamble Street Theatre in Dublin, then again at Crow Street.

Miss Walpole's first London appearance was at Drury Lane Theatre on 2 October 1777 as Rosetta in *Love in a Village.* Other roles that season were Gillian in *The Quaker,* Jessica ("with a song") in *The Merchant of Venice,* Polly in *The Beggar's Opera,* Wilhelmina in *The Waterman,* Euphrosyne in *Comus,* and the Widow Brady ("with an *Epilogue Song*") in *The Irish Widow.* Her pay was £4 per week. Her address at benefit time, 1 May 1778, was No 150, Drury Lane. She cleared £48 5*s.* on that occasion.

Miss Walpole went to Bristol after the 1777–78 season, and Kathleen Barker in *The Theatre Royal, Bristol,* reports the puff that the managers there inserted in the newspapers calling attention to her success in breeches parts: "She is a good Singer, and excellent Actress, and it is a matter of dispute with the young Londoners in which characters she appears to most advantage, *male* or *female.*" Among those characters at Bristol were Sir Harry Wildair in *The Constant Couple,* of course, but also Macheath in *The Beggar's Opera* and Lord Foppington in *A Trip to Scarborough.*

Charlotte came back to Drury Lane for the 1778–79 season, adding to her repertoire Nancy in *The Camp,* Sylvia in *Cymon,* an unspecified character in *The Contract,* and Clarinda in *The Double Gallant.* When she played Sir Harry Wildair on 16 April 1779 for her benefit, the presented a dance at the end of the

CHARLOTTE WALPOLE, as Nancy
engraving after Bunbury

mainpiece. She lived then at No 15, Henrietta Street, Covent Garden.

Charlotte Walpole had attracted the admiration of Edward Atkyns, Esq, of Ketteringham Hall, near Wymondham in Norfolk, a great-grandson of a Lord Chief Justice, according to Vade-Walpole. On 18 May 1779, they were married at St James's. Mrs Atkyns did not return to the stage. A son, Wright Edward Atkyns (later a captain in the First Royals) was born in 1780. The elder Edward Atkyns died on 27 March 1794 at age 36.

Mr and Mrs Atkyns had evidently spent some time abroad because of financial difficulties. Vade-Walpole quotes a letter from Lady Jerningham dated from Lille in 1784: "A great many people have taken refuge here, to fly from their creditors in England; among the rest a Norwich family and a Mrs. Atkins of Ketringham. She was a player, a friend of Miss Younger. You may remember to have heard of her, and *he* was always a great simpleton or else he would not have married her."

Charlotte seems to have continued to attract admiration. A note among Winston's theatrical jottings at the Folger Library, dated only 1790, reads: "Mrs. Atkins late Miss Walpole of DL Theat., is perhaps the most ent^g [enterprising? entertaining?] Female Equestrian. This Lady whose resd^ce is at Lisle in Flanders frequently rides for an airing . . . to Calais wh. is 74 miles and returns the follg Day with the greatest ease."

Charlotte Walpole Atkyns died in 1836. She has frequently been confused with one of Horace Walpole's nieces, the Charlotte Walpole who married Lionel, Lord Huntingtower, in 1760.

A portrait of Charlotte Walpole as Nancy in *The Camp* was engraved by an unknown artist, after H. W. Bunbury, and published by Watson & Dickinson, 1780. She is shown as Gillian in a scene from *The Quaker,* with William Parsons as Solomon, John Bannister as Steady, and Mrs Wrighten as Floretta, in a drawing by Thomas Rowlandson which is in the British Museum. An engraving of the scene was published in 1781.

Walsh. *See also* WELSH.

Walsh, Mr   *fl.* 1736₁,   *harpsichordist.*
At Covent Garden Theatre on 19 February

1736 Mr. Walsh played the harpsichord in a performance of Handel's *The Feast of Alexander.* He may have been a relative of the younger John Walsh (music publisher) and his brother Samuel. The *Index to The London Stage* mistakenly calls Mr Walsh an actor.

Walsh ₁Henry Green?₁ ₁*fl.* 1770s-1809₁, *singer, musician.*
A Mr Walsh from Dublin was listed in Doane's *Musical Directory* in 1794 as a participant in the Handelian performances at Westminster Abbey. He was described as a "Bass," though it is not clear if he was a singer or string player.

We suggest the likelihood that this Dublin musician was Henry Green Walsh, who was a chorister in the Chapel Royal in the 1770s. In the Public Record Office is a petition from about that decade from Henry Green Walsh to the Earl of Salisbury, the Lord Chamberlain, for his clothing allowance as a Chapel Royal child. Henry Green Walsh seems to have passed most of his adult career in Dublin. On 2 April 1804 he was elected a professional member of the Irish Musical Fund. On 7 May 1809 he was ousted for not having paid either his subscription or his fine for not attending the Handel commemoration concert in Dublin. He was apparently reinstated by 1809, and on 6 March of that year he was appointed to play in the orchestra of the annual concert, but on 10 April 1809 he was fined £1 14*s.* 1*d.* for having been absent from the event.

Walter. *See also* WALTHER.

Walter, Mr   ₁*fl.* 1788–1801?₁,   *singer, actor.*
The Mr Walter who shared a benefit at Drury Lane Theatre with three others on 3 June 1788 was probably the Walter who was advanced £52 10*s.* by John Philip Kemble on 22 January 1793. He may also have been the chorus singer Walter who was at Drury Lane in 1800–1801 in walk-on parts.

Walter, Mrs   ₁*fl.* 1742–1746₁. *See* BELLAMY, MRS, LATER MRS WALTER.

Walter, Master   ₁*fl.* 1798–1800₁,   *actor.*
At Drury Lane Theatre on 5 June 1798

Master Walter played an unspecified role in *The Eleventh of June*. There on 22 December 1800 he was named among the pantomime players.

Walter, Elizabeth *fl.* 1725–1747₁, *dancer, actress.*

On 22 February 1725 at Drury Lane Theatre, Mrs. Elizabeth Walter was Daphne's Follower in *Apollo and Daphne*. During the remainder of the season Mrs Walter danced regularly between the acts—as she did for many seasons thereafter—and she shared a benefit with the younger Topham on 6 May. Mrs Walter performed at Drury Lane through 1743–44, serving as an entr'acte dancer and playing such parts as Flora in the masque in *Harlequin Doctor Faustus*, a Countrywoman and a Spirit in *The Miser*, a Countrywoman in *Harlequin's Triumph*, a Bridesmaid in *Harlequin Happy and Poor Pierrot Married*, a Nymph in *Acis and Galatea*, and Attendant, an Hour of Sleep, Colombine, and Mopsophil in *Perseus and Andromeda*, Mincing in *The Way of the World*, Mrs Fidget in *The Country Wife*, Colombine in *The Fairy Queen*, a Follower, a Syren, and Colombine in *Cephalus and Procris*, Scentwell in *The Busy Body*, Miranda in *The Tempest*, Flavia in *Don John*, Flora in *Hob*, Lovewell in *The Provok'd Wife*, Gypsy in *The Stratagem*, Mrs Coaxer in *The Beggar's Opera*, Jenny in *The Tender Husband*, Busy in *The Man of Mode*, Colombine in *Harlequin Restored*, Juno in *The Judgment of Paris*, Juno and a Hungarian in *The Harlot's Progress*, Rose in *The Recruiting Officer*, Lucy in *Oroonoko*, Pomona in *Cupid and Psyche*, a Countrywoman in *Harlequin Orpheus*, a Season in *The Fall of Phaeton*, Colombine in *Harlequin Grand Volgi*, and Venus in *A Voyage to the Island of Cytherea*.

After 1733–34 Mrs Walter appeared in fewer pantomime roles and parts in plays but continued as a favorite entr'acte dancer. Her last appearance at Drury Lane was on 5 May 1744 when she and Desse appeared in an untitled dance. As of May 1738 she was living in a house behind Mr Acton's, a fishmonger in Bridges Street. A year later her lodging (the same house, evidently) was described in her benefit bill as next to the baker's in Bridges Street. In April 1742 her benefit bill said only that tickets could be had of her at the "Three

Queens, a Hosier, in New-street, Covent Garden."

In 1746–47 Mrs Walter was at the Smock Alley Theatre in Dublin. She signed her full name, Elizabeth Walter, on a petition by the players to the Lord Lieutenant.

Walters, Mr *fl.* 1743₁, *house servant.*

In the players' petition to the Lord Chamberlain against the Drury Lane patentee Charles Fleetwood in September 1743 (LC 5/204), one Walters is listed as a house servant whose salary was 1s. per night and to whom Fleetwood was said to owe arrears amounting to £3 19s. 6d.

Walters, Mr *fl.* 1756–1777₁, *actor.*

On 3 September 1756 at the Swan Inn in West Smithfield Mr Walters played Aminidab in *Adventures of Half an Hour*. He was probably the Walters who served as an extra in Bristol in 1769. Walters was at Covent Garden Theatre in London by 20 May 1769, when he was mentioned in the accounts. The benefit bill of 18 May 1770 cited him as Aminadab in *A Bold Stroke for a Wife*, and he was named in the accounts on 23 May. On 29 December 1770 he was added to the cast of *Mother Shipton*, and in May 1771 he shared a benefit with several other minor members of the company. Walters stayed at Covent Garden through the 1772–73 season, the unnamed role in *Mother Shipton* being the only acting assignment known for him. In the summer of 1772 he had acted a Coachman in *The Commissary*, had an unnamed part in *The Devil upon Two Sticks*, and played Blunt in *Richard III* at the Haymarket Theatre for Samuel Foote.

Perhaps Walters remained at Covent Garden in 1773–74, but he was not mentioned in the bills or accounts. On 8 May 1775 he was cited in a Covent Garden benefit bill, and in the summer of 1775 he acted again at the Haymarket, playing in *The Nabob, The Commissary, The Rehearsal, The Orators,* and *A Trip to Portsmouth* and as Claussen in *The Dutchman* and Hounslow in *The Beaux' Stratagem*. The pattern continued through the spring of 1777. At Covent Garden he played a Fish Woman in *Orpheus and Eurydice* and a Coachman in *The Commissary*, and at the Haymarket he was seen as James in *The Mock Doctor*, the

Printer's Devil in *The Author,* a Coachman in *The Commissary,* Zacharyades in *The Taylors,* Sparkle in *The Miser,* and Ned in *The Beggar's Opera.*

From 20 June through 23 July 1777 Mr Walters acted at China Hall, Rotherhithe, appearing as one of the Mob in *The Mayor of Garratt,* Buckle in *The Suspicious Husband,* James in *The Mock Doctor,* Cook in *The Lying Valet,* a Coachman in *The Devil to Pay,* an unspecified character in *All the World's a Stage,* and Obadiah Prim in *A Bold Stroke for a Wife.*

Walters, Miss *fl. 1778₁, actress.*
At the Haymarket Theatre on 28 December 1778 Miss Walters played Nonparel in *The Covent Garden Tragedy.*

Walthen. See WATHEN, GEORGE.

Walther, Caroline Friderike. See MÜLLER, FRAU CHRISTIAN FRIEDRICH.

Walther, John *fl. 1677–1720₁, singer, violinist.*
John Walther (or Walter, Walters) was one of the Children of the Chapel Royal, but his voice had changed by 19 June 1677 and he left the Chapel. About 1708 he petitioned to play violin in the band at the Queen's Theatre for £1 nightly, but paylists among the Coke papers at Harvard show that he had to settle for 8s. He played second violin at least through 23 June 1712, when he signed a receipt for his pay, and perhaps as late as 1713. He was presumably the John Walters who was a member of the opera orchestra of the Academy of Music in February 1720.

Walton, Mr *fl. 1773–1777₁, house servant.*
A Mr Walton was granted benefit tickets at Drury Lane Theatre on 28 May 1773. On 23 May 1775 he shared a benefit with Tomlinson, Mortimer, and Carlton Senior, as he did on 18 May 1776 and 30 May 1777. He had been identified as a first-gallery cheque taker on 5 October 1775, in the Drury Lane accounts at the Folger Library (W.b. 319), but during the 1776–77 season he was called a doorkeeper. No salary was cited.

Walton, Mr *fl. 1784₁, singer.*
Mr Walton from Lichfield, a countertenor, was listed by Burney among the vocal performers in the Handel Memorial Concerts at Westminster Abbey and the Pantheon in May and June 1784.

Walton, Mr *fl. 1785–1804?₁, actor, singer.*
A Mr Walton played Frankly in *The Suspicious Husband* at the Haymarket Theatre on 26 April 1785, a benefit for the unemployed actress Susan Greville. Walton was probably from some provincial theatre, like the actress who was being benefited that night. He did not appear again in a London patent theatre, so far as we know. But perhaps he was the Walton whom Sybil Rosenfeld, in *The Theatre of the London Fairs,* cited as acting in the summer of 1789 at a small theatre near Hosier Lane. That Walton had some part unspecified in a musical interlude, *The Recruiting Sergeant,* and played a Clown in *The Enchanted Urn; or, Harlequin's Release.*

Walton was next seen as Sattin in *The Miser* and as a Clown in the pantomime *The Drunken Peasant,* along with some London actors—including Ned Shuter—and elements of the Norwich company at Gloucester on 26 March 1788. Mrs Walton was also in the company (playing Wheedle in *The Miser* and Frizalta in *Tom Thumb the Great*) as was one of their daughters, a juvenile, playing Tom Thumb. The Waltons returned to Gloucester with some of these performers the following year. A surviving bill shows Walton there as a Janissary in *A Mogul Tale* and a Country Lad in *The Maid of the Oaks* on 18 September 1789. Mrs Walton was a Lassy in the afterpiece. Also at Gloucester on 21 October following, two Misses Walton—juveniles and daughters of our subject—walked in *The Triumph of Liberty.* Evidently they were the Miss Walton and Miss S. Walton whom the *Monthly Mirror* reported at St Mary's Hall, Coventry, with the manager Watson in December 1796. Miss S. and Master Walton played some parts at that theatre from 24 February through 22 May 1797.

The only other probable notice we have found for our Mr Walton is that of 4 June 1804, at the Leigh Theatre, when he played Scrub in *The Beaux' Stratagem* and the Coachman in *High Life below Stairs.* But one of the Walton girls was probably that Miss Walton who assumed a number of leading comedy roles at Edinburgh in the seasons 1806 through 1809.

Walton, Miss   ₁fl. 1776–1779₁,   actress.

The Miss Walton of this entry acted at Doncaster and Hull in 1776 and at York in 1777. Her first London appearance was announced on the Haymarket playbill of 18 September 1777. That night she acted Mademoiselle in *The Provok'd Wife* in a specially licensed performance after the summer season ended. Her appeal was evidently considerable, for when she was given unspecified parts in *The Coquettes* and *The True-Born Irishman* in another Haymarket performance on 9 October, the bill boasted the return of "the young Lady who performed in *The Provok'd Wife.*"

She was on the roster of the York company again in the winter season of 1778.

Miss Walton played Mademoiselle in *The Female Chevalier* on 18 May 1778, the opening night of the Haymarket summer season. She repeated the part several times through 5 June, then she was cited no more until 27 August when she played Charlotte in *The Apprentice.* Both that play and *The Provok'd Wife* were repeated on 2 September. Miss Walton was advertised only once more in London—at the Haymarket as Mademoiselle in *The Provok'd Wife* on 18 August 1779.

Waltz, Gustavus   ₁fl. 1732–1759₁, singer, actor.

The German bass Gustavus Waltz made what may have been his first appearance, as Osmyn in *Amelia,* at the Haymarket Theatre on 13 March 1732. He shared a benefit with Snider on 24 April when *Amelia* was repeated, and on 17 May he was Polyphemus in *Acis and Galatea.* In his second season at the Haymarket he added to his repertoire Mars and Honour in *Britannia* and either Grizzle or the Ghost in *The Opera of Operas.* He went over to the Lincoln's Inn Fields Theatre (called "Walz") on 16 April 1733 to sing Antinous in *Ulysses.* He was with Handel in Oxford in July 1733 and later years. In 1733–34 Waltz was at Drury Lane Theatre, though he made some appearances at the King's Theatre. At the for-

mer he was seen as both Grizzle and the Ghost in *The Opera of Operas,* an Earthly Spirit in *The Tempest,* Bacchus and Mynheer Bassoon in *Cupid and Psyche,* a Follower of Mars in *Love and Glory,* and Mars in *Britannia,* while at the King's he sang Emireno in *Ottone,* Minos in *Arianna in Creto,* Proteo in *Il Parnasso in festa* (the *New Grove* says he sang Mars in that opera on 13 April 1734, but there was no performance at the King's on that date), the Chief Priest in *Deborah,* Altomaro in *Sosarme,* the title role in *Caio Fabricio,* and Tireno in *Il pastor fido.* Dean in *Handel's Dramatic Oratorios and Masques* speculates on Waltz's participation in Handel's oratorios.

The 1734–35 season found Waltz in Handel's company at Covent Garden Theatre in such new roles as the King of Scotland in *Ariodante,* Haman in *Esther,* Melisso in *Alcina,* and Abner in *Athalia.* Waltz was given a benefit at Hickford's Music Room on 21 February 1735. In 1735–36 Waltz was still with Handel at Covent Garden, but he seems to have appeared only as Nicandro in *Atalanta.* In April 1736 he sang in *A Grand Epithalamium* at Drury Lane. In 1737 his only appearance we have found was at a benefit for him at Hickford's on 7 April; one of his scholars, Master Cook, also performed. In 1738–39 at Covent Garden he sang Orlando in *Angelica e Medoro* and at the King's Theatre the title part in *Saul,* a bass part in *Israel in Egypt,* and probably a bass part in *Jupiter in Argos.* In 1739–40 he was at Covent Garden singing a Bachanal in *Cupid and Bacchus,* Grizzle in *The Opera of Operas,* and a Villager in *Orpheus and Eurydice.* The accounts indicate that in the fall of 1740 Covent Garden was paying Waltz by the performance, his fee varying according to his role. For Gubbins in *The Dragon of Wantley* he received £1 1s. each performance; for being a Villager in *Orpheus and Eurydice* or in the *Macbeth* chorus he made 10s. 6d; and for a part in *Pan and Syrinx* he earned £1 1s. In 1741–42 at Covent Garden he was named only as participating in *Orpheus and Eurydice.*

Waltz was at Drury Lane in 1742–43 to play Gubbins in *The Dragon of Wantley.* On 1 January 1744 he joined the Royal Society of Musicians. He sang the King in *The Queen of Spain* at the Haymarket in January, and on 16 April he was Colin in *The Kiss Accepted and Returned.* He sang in *Solomon* and *Alexander's*

GUSTAVUS WALTZ

engraving by Müller, after Hauck

Courtesy of the Royal College of Music

GUSTAVUS WALTZ
by Williams

Since we know he worked for a nightly fee in 1740 at Covent Garden, perhaps he spent the bulk of his career jobbing in.

The names of most of Waltz's students are not known, but he was the teacher of Isabella Young (later Mrs Scott) as well as Master Cook. Hawkins may have begun the story that Waltz had been Handel's cook. The tale may have been true, though, as the *New Grove* points out, it cannot be verified. Dr Burney did not hear Waltz in his prime and described him as having "a coarse figure, and a still coarser voice." But Burney thought he "had a great deal of humour" as an actor.

A portrait (16¼" × 13½") of Gustavus Waltz, signed by J. M. Hauck, shows him seated at a violoncello (an instrument he is not known to have played professionally), with a pipe and pot of beer on a table beside him. The picture at one time belonged to J. W. Taphouse of Oxford and was exhibited in the Loan Collection of the Inventors Exhibition in 1885. It was sold at Christie's on 11 November 1983 (lot 155) for £3000 and now is in the fine Handel collection owned by Gerald Coke. The picture was engraved by Müller. A portrait of Waltz by John Michael Williams is in the Royal College of Music.

Wamsley. *See* **WALMISLEY.**

"Wandering Melodist, The." *See* **INCLEDON, CHARLES BENJAMIN.**

Wane, Mrs *fl. 1739₁, actress.*
Mrs Wane, advertised as "A Gentlewoman, who never appeared on any stage before," played Calista in *The Fair Penitent* at Drury Lane on 3 November 1739.

Wapshott, Thomas *fl. 1787₁, carpenter.*
In *The World* for 12 October 1787 Thomas Wapshott was listed as a carpenter at Drury Lane Theatre.

Warboys, Thomas *1748–1785, actor, playwright.*
Thomas Warboys, advertised as a young gentleman making his first appearance on any stage, acted Posthumus in *Cymbeline* at Covent Garden Theatre on 19 January 1770. The *Whitehall Evening Post* next day identified him.

Feast at Ruckholt House in June. At Drury Lane in January 1745 he appeared as Capochio in *The Temple of Dulness* and Sir Trusty in *Rosamund;* in February at the Haymarket he sang in *The Queen of Spain* again and at Drury Lane appeared in *The Dragon of Wantley;* and in April he was Puff (a "Degraded Field Marshall") in *King Pepin's Campaign.* In 1748 Waltz sang at the Haymarket in January and December; in 1749–50 he sang at Covent Garden in *Macbeth* and as an Infernal in many performances of *Perseus and Andromeda;* he was Cepheus in *Perseus and Andromeda* in 1750–51 and repeated some of his earlier assignments.

Waltz sang in the *Messiah* at the Chapel of the Foundling Hospital on 15 May 1754 for 10s. 6d. On 27 April 1758 and in May 1759 he sang there in the *Messiah* again for the same fee. The records do not show any further activity for Waltz, and his death date is not known. He appears to have spent almost all of his career flitting from one theatre to another, rarely serving as a regular company member.

Warboys was decidedly unsuccessful in his debut, and the review in the *Town and Country Magazine* that month (where his name was also given) suggested that the novice would probably be deterred from following the profession, "as he possesses scarce any of those talents the stage requires; and is not happy either in his person, or physiognomy." Indeed, as Gilliland put it in his *Dramatic Mirror* (later copied into the *Biographia Dramatica*), Warboys "had the prudence to relinquish a profession in which he was not qualified to excel."

Warboys had been brought up in the counting house of Sir Robert Ladbroke and was contemporary there with William Powell, who then became a very successful but short-lived actor, dying in 1769 shortly before Warboys made his undistinguished debut.

In 1777 Warboys published in a quarto edition two plays: *The Preceptor,* a comedy and an adaptation of D'Ancourt's *Le Besoin de l'Amour,* and *The Rival Lovers,* a farce and an adaptation of Regnard's *La Sérénade.* Neither piece was performed in London.

In his *History . . . of St Mary, Islington* (1811), John Nelson reported that Thomas Warboys was buried at that church on 7 April 1785, having died at the age of 37.

Warburton, Master   *fl.* 1787₁, *dancer.*

Master Warburton made a single appearance on the London stage at Drury Lane Theatre on 4 June 1787 in a minuet and cotillion with Miss Taylor and others.

Ward, Mr   *fl.* 1724–1736?₁,   *house servant.*

A Mr Ward was a pit doorkeeper at Lincoln's Inn Fields Theatre in 1724–25, and shared in benefit tickets on 12 May 1725. Perhaps he continued in John Rich's employ and was the Mr Ward who earned 2s. per week as a boxkeeper at Covent Garden Theatre in 1735–36.

Ward, Mr   *fl.* 1737₁,   *house servant.*

A Mr Ward shared benefit tickets with other house servants at Drury Lane Theatre on 21 May 1737.

Ward, Mr   *fl.* 1741₁,   *office keeper.*

On 28 April 1741, a Mr Ward, who lived at the corner of Rupert Street in Goodman's Fields and was an office keeper at the Goodman's Fields Theatre, received a benefit at that theatre.

Ward, Mr   *fl.* 1760₁,   *musician.*

A Mr Ward's name was on a Covent Garden Theatre paylist dated 22 September 1760 as a musician earning 6s. 8d. per night.

Ward, Mr   *fl.* 1765–1766₁,   *dresser.*

The names of Mr and Mrs Ward, dressers, are on a Drury Lane Theatre paylist dated 9 February 1765, each earning 1s. 6d. per day. On 8 November 1766 Mr Ward was paid 10s. by the Drury Lane treasurer for two weeks' "additional salary."

Ward, Mrs   *fl.* 1765₁,   *dresser. See* **WARD, MR** *fl.* 1765–1766₁.

Ward, Mr   *fl.* 1767₁,   *singer*

A Mr Ward sang in *Lycidas* at Covent Garden Theatre on 4 November 1767.

Ward, Mr   *fl.* 1770–1775₁,   *actor.*

An actor named Ward appeared as Young Philpot in *The Citizen* on 16 November and as Grizzle in *Tom Thumb the Great* on 19 December 1770 in specially licensed performances at the Haymarket Theatre. That actor (or another of the same name) was a member of Foote's summer company at the Haymarket from 1772 to 1775. He acted unspecified roles in *The Nabob* on 29 June 1772 and *The Rehearsal* on 10 August 1772. In the summer of 1773 he played an unspecified role in *The Devil upon Two Sticks,* Le Brush in *The Register Office,* Headlong in *The Tobacconist,* Hearty in *A Trip to Portsmouth,* and Sir Francis in *The Pantheonites.* His other known roles there included Tressel in *Richard III* on 30 September 1774 and, again, Headlong in *The Tobacconist* on 19 September 1775.

Ward, Mr   *fl.* 1776₁,   *actor.*

A Mr Ward acted Dr Butts in a performance of *Henry VIII* at China Hall, Rotherhithe, on 25 September 1776. His name was not in the advertisements for any other productions by the company at China Hall that autumn. (Possibly he was Thomas Achurch Ward, who was about to make his debut at Covent Garden Theatre on 7 October 1776. In his manuscript notes C. Beecher Hogan speculated that the China Hall actor was the same person who played at Perth in 1785 and that he may have been the William Ward who acted Shylock at Doncaster in October 1772.)

Ward, Mr   *fl. 1783₁,*   *color man.*
The name of Mr Ward is listed on a document in the Public Record Office (LC 7/3) as a "color man" as the King's Theatre in 1783. Perhaps he was a paint mixer in the scene shop or a tradesman who provided pigment.

Ward, Mr   *fl. 1794–1795₁,*   *dresser.*
A Mr Ward was paid 6s. per week as a men's dresser at Covent Garden Theatre in 1794–95.

Ward, Mrs   *fl. 1725–1729₁,*   *actress.*
See WARD, MRS JOHN *1711–1786.*

Ward, Mrs   *fl. 1776–1779₁,*   *dancer.*
Mrs Ward is named in a Folger Library manuscript (W. b. 319) as a dancer at Drury Lane Theatre in 1776–77, earning £1 per week. She was probably the "Miss" Ward found in another Folger manuscript (W. b. 282) as having been paid £1 1s. on 9 October 1779 for six days' salary. The Mrs Ward of this entry is not noted in *The London Stage* bills.

Ward, Mrs   *fl. 1783–1785₁,*   *dresser.*
The name of Mrs Ward is listed on a document in the Public Record Office (LC 7/3) as a women's dresser at the King's Theatre from 1783 to 1785.

Ward, Mrs   *fl. 1792–1793?₁,*   *actress, dancer?*
A Mrs Ward acted Mrs Watchly in a specially licensed performance of *Wit's Last Stake* at the Haymarket Theatre on 22 October 1792. She (or another Mrs Ward) performed at Sadler's Wells Theatre, probably as a dancer, in *The Witch of the Lakes* on 15 April 1793 and as Harmony in a production of *The Hall of Augusta,* published as performed there that season.

Ward, Mrs   *fl. 1798–1799₁,*   *dancer.*
A Mrs Ward was a member of the corps de ballet at Covent Garden Theatre by 12 February 1798, when she appeared in the premiere of J. C. Cross's *Joan of Arc,* a ballet-pantomime that ran for 14 nights that season. In 1798–99 she danced in *The Genoese Pirate* on 15 October 1798, *Albert and Adelaide* on 11 December, *The Magic Oak* on 25 March 1799, and *Raymond and Agnes* on 13 April.

Ward, Master   *fl. 1744₁,*   *violinist.*
In his *History of Clerkenwell,* W. Pinks reported that in 1744 concerts of vocal and instrumental music were given throughout the year at the Cobham's Head, a public house in Cold Bath Square. One of the musicians in these concerts was a violinist named Master Ward. Whether or not he was related to the family of musicians headed by John Ward (fl. 1744–1763?) is not known.

Ward, Master   *fl. 1749–1750₁,* *dancer.*
Master Ward danced as Eo, one of the Infernals, in *A Duke and No Duke* at Drury Lane Theatre on 26 December 1749. That afterpiece had a total of some 17 performances that season. It is possible that he was one of the sons of Sarah Ward (1727–1771), who that season began an engagement at Drury Lane, but we have no evidence to connect them.

Ward, Miss   *fl. 1769–1770₁,*   *dancer.*
Miss Ward danced a double hornpipe with Walker at Drury Lane Theatre on 25 April 1769. She and Walker repeated the dance on 16 and 20 May. In the following year their names appeared and the bills for the same entertainment on 4 May 1770, so Miss Ward probably had appeared at other times that season.

Ward, Miss *fl. 1779₁. See* WARD, MRS *fl. 1776–1779₁.*

Ward, Henry   *fl. 1734–1758₁,*   *actor, playwright.*
The Mr Ward who acted Syphax in *Cato* at the James Street Theatre on 23 May 1734 was probably Henry Ward, a minor actor and playwright and later the husband of the prominent actress Sarah Ward (d. 1771). The Ward who played Axalla and spoke a new prologue to *Tamerlane,* for his benefit at York Buildings on 8 July 1734, was also probably Henry.

That night he spoke the prologue to and acted Don Pedro in the afterpiece, *The Disappointment*, a farce that he probably also wrote. At Lincoln's Inn Fields Theatre on 31 March 1736 for the benefit of William Pritchard, Henry Ward's new ballad opera, *The Happy Lovers; or, The Beau Metamorphos'd*, was performed, with the author acting the Beau. That night he also played Abel in *The Committee*. *The Happy Lovers* was published that year.

Ward continued his occasional activities in London's minor theatres when he acted Lord Dapper in the premiere of Fielding's *The Historical Register* at the Haymarket on 21 March 1737. On 13 April 1737, when he acted Dapper again in *The Historical Register*, he also played Lord Dapper in Fielding's *Eurydice Hiss'd*.

By 1744 Ward was a member of the company at York, where he must have met Sarah Achurch, whose family was acting in that city at that time. By the summer of 1745 they had married and were in Scotland together. At Edinburgh the young Mrs Ward was instrumental in forwarding the building of the first permanent theatre in the Canongate. Among Henry Ward's roles at Edinburgh were the Priest of Hymen in *The Amours of Harlequin and Columbine* on 26 August 1746, the Ghost in *Hamlet* on 16 November 1747, Jack Stocks in *The Lottery* on 25 February 1748, and Captain Macheath in *The Beggar's Opera* on 26 April 1748.

Henry Ward's farce *The Vintner Trick'd* was acted at Drury Lane Theatre in London on 9 April 1746 for the benefit of Luke Sparks; the piece was published in London that year. He may still have been in London at the time, for a Mr Ward, announced as making his first appearance on that stage, had acted Wildair in *The Constant Couple* at Goodman's Fields Theatre on 27 February 1746. That year was published *The Works of Henry Ward, Comedian*, containing three farces: *The Happy Lovers; or, The Beau Metamorphos'd* (Lincoln's Inn Fields, 31 March 1736); *The Petticoat-Plotter; or, More Ways than One for a Wife;* and *The Widow's Wish; or, An Equipage of Lovers*. No productions of the last two are known.

When Mrs. Ward was engaged at Covent Garden Theatre for the 1748–49 season, Ward accompanied her to London, and he made his first appearance on the stage of Cov-

ent Garden on 7 October 1748 as Jack Stocks in *The Lottery*. On 28 October he acted Roderigo in *Othello* (his wife played Desdemona) and on the next night Roger in *The London Cuckolds*. Ward seems not to have appeared again on the London stage. Probably he was still living with Sarah Ward in 1752 when on 20 January she gave birth to a son. Sometime in the summer of that year, however, Sarah Ward began her relationship with West Digges and lived on and off with Digges until 1758. At Dublin in October 1752 she gave birth to a daughter who was perhaps Henry Ward's child.

From time to time Henry Ward resurfaced in Sarah's life. He was a member of the same company with her at Belfast from November 1754 to March 1755. When Sarah returned to London (without Digges) to take up an engagement at Covent Garden in the autumn of 1758, Henry Ward was with her. In her *Apology*, George Anne Bellamy wrote that Sarah was "accompanied by a frightful being, to whom she gave the title of husband." That is the last notice we have of him. His estranged wife Sarah died in London in 1771. How many of Sarah Ward's children were by Henry Ward is not known. Their son Thomas Achurch Ward, who became an actor and manager, was born in 1747. Their daughter, Margaretta Priscilla Ward, an actress, married the actor Thomas Kniveton and later became Mrs John Banks.

Ward, Mrs Henry, Sarah, née Achurch, sometimes called Mrs West Digges

1727?–1771, actress, manager.

The announcement of Sarah Ward's death on 9 March 1771, in the *Public Advertiser* of 11 March, stated her age as 44, so she was probably born in 1727. She was the daughter of the York actor Thomas Achurch (d. 1771), who acted occasionally in London, and his wife, who made only one appearance of record in London, as Harriet in *The Miser* at the James Street Theatre on 31 May 1734. Sarah had at least three sisters. One, whose first name is not known, married the actor Robert Mahon (1734–1799)—a marriage we failed to mention in Mahon's notice in volume 10 of this *Dictionary*. A Miss Henrietta Achurch was acting at York in 1763, and she and a Miss Anne Achurch were subscribers to the *Works* of Henry Ward (their brother-in-law), published in 1746. (In an item in *Notes and Queries*, 9 November 1940 [p. 332], Cecil Brooking states that Sarah Achurch was the niece of the actress Esther Hamilton [d. 1786], who ended her days as an object of pity and charity by her fellow players, but he cites no evidence to establish that relationship and we find none.)

Sarah seems to have begun her theatrical career at York, with her family, in the mid-1740s. When she first appeared at Edinburgh in 1745, she was already married (at about the age of 17 or 18) to the minor playwright and actor Henry Ward, who had performed in London in the 1730s. In his article "The Original Lady Randolph," *Theatre Notebook*, 8 (1959), George H. Bushnell detailed young Mrs Ward's leadership of a project to erect the first regular theatre in Edinburgh. Mrs Ward and the company she seems to have headed, having been denied permission by the Aberdeen clergy and authorities to play in that city in 1745, went to Edinburgh. She managed to obtain subscriptions and credit from tradesmen sufficient to lay the cornerstone of a new theatre in a cul-de-sac on the south side of the Canongate in 1746, and while they awaited its completion the company acted at the Merchant Taylors' Hall, nearby, until early 1747. Sarah's husband was also with the company at that time. When the new Canongate Theatre opened early in 1747 under Ryan's management, Mrs Ward and West Digges—who was to figure prominently in her life—were leading members of the company. Among Mrs Ward's characters at Edinburgh in 1748 were the title role in *Zara* on 25 February, Queen Elizabeth in *The Albion Queens* on 30 March, Miss Lucy in *The Virgin Unmask'd* on 5 May and 25 July, Imoinda in *Oroonoko* on 4 July, and Alicia in *Jane Shore* on 2 August.

When Dennis Delane went to act at Edinburgh in the summer of 1748, he was sufficiently impressed with Sarah Ward to recommend her to John Rich, manager of Covent Garden Theatre, who engaged her for the ensuing season. Delane's sending her to Rich cost him his warm relationship with David Garrick, who afterwards would not even return a greeting in the street; and thereafter Delane took to the bottle heavily and died in

1750—all according to Tom Davies in his *Dramatic Miscellanies*.

Mrs Ward made her debut at Covent Garden on 3 October 1748 as Cordelia to Quin's King Lear. Her husband Henry Ward also was in the company and appeared on 7 October as Jack Stocks in the afterpiece *The Lottery;* he acted Roderigo in *Othello* on 28 October and Roger in *The London Cuckold* the next night but was named in no other roles that season. During the remainder of the 1748–49 season, however, Sarah Ward acted an impressive list of major roles, quite extraordinary, in fact, for a 21-year-old in her first London season: Calista in *The Fair Penitent*, Alicia in *Jane Shore*, Lucia in *Cato*, Miranda in *The Busy Body*, Desdemona in *Othello*, Arpasia in *Tamerlane*, Hermione in *The Distrest Mother*, Lady Lurewell in *The Constant Couple*, Lady Brute in *The Provok'd Wife*, Roxana in *The Rival Queens*, Belinda in *The Man of Mode*, Marwood in *The Way of the World*, and Amanda in *Love's Last Shift*. When she took her benefit on 3 April 1749, as Almeyda in *Don Sebastian* and Kitty Pry in *The Lying Valet*, her father, Mr Achurch from York, acted Sharp in the latter piece.

Illness forced Mrs Cibber, the great tragedienne at Drury Lane, to refrain from acting in 1749–50, so Garrick lured Mrs Ward across the road to join his company. She made her first appearance at Drury Lane on 13 October 1749 as Cordelia, this time to the great Garrick's King Lear. On 21 October she acted Calista and followed that role with Monimia in *The Orphan*, Amanda, Lady Lurewell, Andromache in *The Distrest Mother*, Valeria in *The Roman Father*, Lady Easy in *The Careless Husband*, and Mariana in *Edward the Black Prince*. When she acted Monimia for her benefit on 20 March 1749, tickets were available from Mrs Ward, next door to the chapel in Little Wild Street, and the profit to her was £95 19s. 6d. In *The Actor* (1750), John Hill allowed that Mrs Ward was capable of "great expression, and even of great tenderness in many cases," but that she did not equal Mrs Cibber in "passionate declarations" because she did not feel them from the heart.

In the summer of 1750 Mrs Ward was with Linnett's company at Bath and Bristol. In her second season at Drury Lane, 1750–51, she added to her repertoire Maria in *The London*

Merchant, Mrs Strickland in *The Suspicious Husband,* Lady Sharlot in *The Funeral,* Lady Easy in *The Careless Husband,* Arabella in *The London Cuckold,* and Selima in *Tamerlane.* The *General Advertiser* on 24 January 1751 announced that "Mrs Ward, last Sunday Morning [20 January], belonging to Drury Lane, was safely deliver'd of a son, at her lodgings in little Wild St., and is in a fair way of recovery." She returned to work on 11 March 1751, when she acted Valeria in *The Roman Father* for Mrs Pritchard's benefit. For her own benefit on 19 March she acted Oriana in *The Inconstant,* and total receipts were £210 (less house charges). At Drury Lane in 1751–52 she added to her repertoire Lady Anne in *Richard III,* Dame Kitely in *Every Man in His Humour,* Lavinia in *The Fair Penitent,* Emelia in *Eugenia,* and Hero in *Much Ado about Nothing.* At the time of her benefit on 19 March 1752, she still lived next door to the chapel in Little Wild Street, near Drury Lane.

During the summer of 1751 Mrs Ward had gone north in hopes of setting up a theatre in Aberdeen with a group of actors gathered from Edinburgh. But once more they were refused permission to act in Aberdeen and were obliged to play in a booth they erected outside the jurisdiction of the magistrats; the venture failed for lack of audiences. After the 1751–52 season at Drury Lane, Mrs Ward once more traveled north, to act for a while with Lee's company at Edinburgh. Then Lee took his troupe, which included West Digges, to Glasgow, where they set up a booth in Castle Yard, but Whitfield's religious zealots tore it down.

It must have been during that summer of 1752 that Sarah Ward began her relationship with the troublesome and troubled actor West Digges. An intimate record of their common-law marriage is provided in a series of letters that passed between them from 1752 until their final separation in 1758. That liaison is related in some detail in our notice of West Digges.

From Glasgow, Sarah and Digges sailed to Ireland by way of Liverpool, and after playing at Cork until September they joined Tom Sheridan's Smock Alley company in Dublin for the 1752–53 season. Evidently Mrs Ward's failure to return to Drury Lane had not

been anticipated, and she had been lured away by her devotion to Digges. Garrick wrote to Samuel Richardson sometime after 29 November 1752 that he was sorry he could not oblige with a performance of *Every Man in His Humour:* "Mrs Ward who play'd ye Part of Mrs Kitely has left Us & We have Nobody ready in That Character." On 30 November 1752 the play was performed at Drury Lane with Mrs Davies filling Dame Kitely.

Mrs Ward's debut at Smock Alley in the autumn of 1752 had to be delayed because she was pregnant, but by whom is not clear. If she had begun her relationship with Digges that summer, he was not the father, for the *Dublin Journal* for 24–28 October 1752 announced that "Last Wednesday Morning Mrs Ward, who is engaged to perform this season, at the Theatre Royal in Smock-Alley, was safely delivered of a Daughter, and is in a fair Way of Recovery." It is not known when and for how long Mrs Ward became estranged from her husband Henry Ward. He perhaps was the father of the daughter born in Dublin that October. We do know that Mr and Mrs Henry Ward afterwards were together, acting at Belfast, from November 1754 to March 1755.

She made her debut at Smock Alley on 24 November 1752, acting Monimia in *The Orphan.* On 6 December she played Fribble in *Miss in Her Teens,* announced as making her first appearance in "Boy's Cloathes." During her three-year engagement at Smock Alley, according to the author of *The Present State of the Stage* (1753), Mrs Ward received great applause in such roles as Juliet and Monimia, and the enthusiasm of Irish audiences dispelled her "Coldness" and gave her more fire. But her consort Digges was constantly being harrassed for debt, and in 1753–54 he became a key actor in a political riot at Smock Alley, caused by Sheridan's forbidding Digges to repeat an inflammatory passage in *Mahomet* which had been applauded at an earlier performance by one of the warring factions. When Sheridan refused to apologize for the omission the audience demolished his theatre, and next morning the disgusted Sheridan left Ireland for London. Digges also left the country, to escape his debtors, leaving Sarah behind.

Resuming her professional travels, Sarah

was acting at Newcastle from 12 September to 12 December 1753, in Edinburgh until May 1754, and then at Chester until late June. She returned to Dublin in October 1754 and then settled in the Belfast company from November 1754 to March 1755. Also in that company was a Mr Ward, presumably the estranged husband Henry. In April and May 1754 Mrs Ward traveled to Waltham Abbey, Essex, and Birmingham, then Glasgow, and in November she finally reached Edinburgh, where within a few months she was rejoined by Digges. Sarah acted Mrs Sullen in *The Stratagem* on 25 November 1755. In addition to her usual roles—Calista, Andromache, Lady Lurewell, Imoinda, and others—in 1756 she was seen at Edinburgh as Angelina in *Love Makes a Man*, Beatrice in *Much Ado about Nothing*, Clarinda in *The Suspicious Husband*, Cynthia in *The Oracle*, Dorinda in *The Tempest*, and Millamant in *The Way of the World*, roles that suggest she had developed a successful touch for comedy. On 28 September 1756 she and Digges were reunited on stage as Romeo and Juliet.

By October of 1756 Digges replaced James Callender as manager of the Canongate Theatre. On 14 December 1756 he produced the premiere of Home's *Douglas*, in which he acted Douglas and Mrs Ward played Lady Randolph. This celebrated production, which ran for about seven consecutive nights, was a sensation in Presbyterian Edinburgh and spawned law suits and a schism in the church establishment and also resulted in the disciplining of several clerics who saw *Douglas* at the Canongate Theatre and dared to praise it.

In April 1758 debts obliged Digges to relinquish his management—which had been marked with squabbles—back to Callender and several associates. Sarah moved on to Newcastle, where she assumed the name "Mrs Digges" for a brief time. She acted in Liverpool in the summer of 1758, and in November she and Digges arrived together in Dublin for another engagement at Smock Alley, for the 1758–59 season.

During the summer of 1759, perhaps while the couple were at Newcastle, their relationship came to an abrupt end. It seems that Sarah finally had had enough of Digges's infidelities, indifference, and extravagance. He had brought one of his intrigues, with a Mrs Betty, into the house; Sarah wrote him that he "was killing *poor forsaken Mrs Ward* by inches, a person whose whole soul was wrapt up in Mr Digges." Though he had called her his "Dear Sally" and his "Dearest Life," and though they had at least six children, he had tired of the association that Sarah had regarded as a true marriage. In one of her last surviving letters to him (undated), she wrote: "I am doom'd to be wretched without you. . . . The love I bear Mr Digges will I cherish in my breast and give to his child, if it shall please God to let it see the light." The fact that Mrs Ward had received an engagement at Covent Garden for 1759–60 may have caused the separation. According to George Anne Bellamy's *Apology,* Mrs Ward arrived in London "accompanied by a frightful being, to whom she gave the title of husband." Henry Ward, it seems, had returned once more to Sarah. Mrs Bellamy, a member of the Covent Garden company at that time and perhaps threatened because her own physical attractions were declining, described Mrs Ward:

This lady had one of the most beautiful faces I ever beheld. But her figure was vulgar to a degree. By the stoop and magnitude of her shoulders it might be imagined that she had formerly carried milk pails. Her beauty would have been much more conspicuous in that line . . . than in the character of a queen or young princess. Yet . . . being pregnant into the bargain, it was determined that she should appear as Cordelia. . . .

Cordelia was one of Mrs Bellamy's leading roles. It should also be noted that in 1761 George Anne began an affair with West Digges in Dublin that continued at Edinburgh and lasted for several years.

It was not as Cordelia but as Lady Randolph that Sarah Ward made her return to Covent Garden, on 23 November 1759. She was to remain engaged at that theatre for 12 seasons, until her death. In 1761–62, when she lived at Mr Trouton's in Surrey Street in the Strand, her salary was £8 per week, or £272 for the season. In March 1762 benefit tickets could be had from her at Mr Dean's in Queen Street, Soho. According to a paylist for the Covent Garden company, as of 14 September 1767, provided by Arthur Murphy (in Jesse Foote's *Life of Murphy*), her salary in 1767–68 seems to have been reduced to £1 per day.

In that final period of her career at Covent Garden, Sarah Ward acted a great number of capital roles, a selection of which includes Indiana in *The Conscious Lovers,* Zara in *Zara,* Sigismunda in *Tancred and Sigismunda,* Mrs Partlet in *The Spirit of Contradiction,* Statira in *The Rival Queens,* and Juliet in *Romeo and Juliet* in 1759–60; Constance in *King John,* Eudocia in *The Siege of Damascus,* the title role in *Cleone,* and Athenais in *Theodosius* in 1760–61; and Mariana in *The Miser,* Violante in *The Wonder,* Portia in *The Merchant of Venice,* Mrs Ford in *The Merry Wives of Windsor,* Mrs Oakly in *The Jealous Wife,* Laetitia in *The Old Batchelor,* and Belvidera in *Venice Preserv'd* in 1761–62. The anonymous author of *The Rosciad of C—v—t G—rd—n* wrote of her in 1762:

> *Thrice happy actress! form'd by Nature's hand,*
> *To rule the heart, the passions to command,—*
> *To make us weep poor CONSTANCE's wretched*
>   *fate,—*
> *To raise 'gainst tyrant JOHN our utmost hate.*
> *When in the virtuous VIOLANTE's part,*
> *Thou speaks the real feelings of thy heart,*
> *We cease to wonder!—thou hast not disclos'd*
> *A secret in thy faithful breast repos'd.*

Her roles in 1762–63 included the Queen in *Richard III,* Estifania in *Rule a Wife and Have a Wife,* Dame Kitely in *Every Man in His Humour,* Rodogune in *The Royal Convert,* the Countess of Roussillion in *All's Well that Ends Well,* Amanda in *Love's Last Shift,* and the Queen in *The Earl of Essex.* She added to her repertoire in 1763–64 Zara in *The Mourning Bride,* Lady Capulet in *Romeo and Juliet,* and Lady Macbeth in *Macbeth* (on 21 May 1764). Other roles included Clarissa in *The City Wives Confederacy* and Octavia in *All for Love* in 1764–65; Queen Elizabeth in *The Albion Queens* in 1765–66; Mrs Goodman in *The English Merchant* and Theano in *Medea* in 1767–68; Lady Autumn in *The Sister* in 1768–69; and Lady Wrangle in *The Refusal* and Queen Elizabeth in *The Unhappy Favorite* in 1769–70. On 4 May 1763, Mrs Yates being ill, Sarah Ward went over to Drury Lane to play Belvidera in *Venice Preserv'd.*

In 1770–71 Mrs Ward acted little, appearing as the Queen in *The Earl of Essex* on 10 October and 12 November 1770 and Gertrude in *Hamlet* on 3 December 1770. She was suffering a severe illness, and on 11 March 1771 the *Public Advertiser* announced that Mrs Ward, of Covent Garden Theatre, had died on 9 March, at the age of 44. Sarah Ward, "from St Martin in ye Fields," was buried at St Paul, Covent Garden, on 15 March 1771.

Sarah Ward may have had as many as six children by West Digges. Information concerning their names and possible times of birth are given in the notice of Digges. She seems to have had at least three children by her husband Henry Ward: Thomas Achurch Ward born probably in 1747 at Edinburgh, another son born in London on 24 January 1751, nd a daughter born in Dublin on 25 October 1752. At least two of her children became actors. On 5 October 1767, when Mrs Ward played Mrs Goodman in *The English Merchant* at Covent Garden, her daughter, Miss Ward, acted Amelia ("pretty well," according to Sylas Neville's *Diary,* but she had "a stiffness and an indifferent voice"). That Miss Ward was probably Margaretta Priscilla Ward (d. 1793), who was regularly engaged at Covent Garden until she married the actor Thomas Kniveton in September 1771 and continued to act there as Mrs Kniveton; she later became Mrs Banks. She is noticed separately in this *Dictionary* as Mrs Thomas Kniveton. Henry and Sarah Ward's son Thomas Achurch Ward (1747–1835) acted several seasons in London and then became manager of the theatre in Manchester, in which he was also a chief actor. In 1775 he married the actress Sarah Hoare (1756–1838). Both Thomas Achurch Ward and his wife are also noticed on these pages.

The actor James Quin had described Sarah Ward in her earlier years as a "a flat-baked pancake," but when Sylas Neville saw her at Covent Garden in 1767 she was "a very different figure now from what she was some years ago." In his *Dramatic Miscellanies,* Tom Davies confirms that when she was younger Mrs Ward had an agreeable figure and attractive features; in her mature years, Davies found her more suited to parts of vigor and loftiness, such as the high passion of Hermione (in *The Winter's Tale*). She was, according to Davies, a better Calista (in *The Fair Penitent*) than a Juliet.

The *Catalogue of Dramatic Portraits in the Harvard Theatre Collection* (4:232) confuses Sarah Ward with her daughter-in-law Sarah

Hoare Ward (Mrs T. A. Ward) and wrongly identifies the latter as the grandmother of the Kembles. We believe that our subject, Sarah Ward, is the Mrs Ward who is depicted by an anonymous engraver as Hermione, with her sister Elizabeth Whitlock as Imogene, in *The Winter's Tale.* She is perhaps the subject of an engraving by C. Sherwin, after J. Ramberg, of Mrs Ward as Portia in *Julius Caesar,* published as a plate to *Bell's Shakespeare,* 1785, but we believe that person is Mrs Thomas Achurch Ward; the same plate, with the engraver's name changed to Woodman, after Ramberg, was published by John Cawthorn, 1807.

Ward, John   *1704–1773, actor, manager, singer.*

John Ward was born in 1704, but little is known about his antecedents and early years. Some early stage historians termed him an Irishman, but James G. McManaway in his important article "The Earliest Promptbooks of *Hamlet," Publication of the Bibliographical Society of America,* 43 (1949), finds that many of the stories about John Ward's youth, including those penned by Anne Kemble Hatton (sister of Sarah Siddons) in her manuscript memoirs (in the Folger Library), are tinged with romantic imagination and some malice. She wrote that the family had reason to believe that John Ward was "the offspring of a man of high Rank by a distant relation of his own, who did not outlive the infancy of the child."

The Wards in their itinerant years were active around Leominster and were known during their time in Ireland as "the Wards of Leominster." But if John had been born into an old Leominster family it is curious that there survives no record to that effect. Mrs Hatton also states that Ward was raised "liberally" and that after having received an army commission he was sent to Cork, where he married a milliner who yearned to go upon the stage. Ward's marriage, claimed Anne Hatton, caused the loss of his father's assistance; and thus Ward was forced to take up acting and soon became the manager of an itinerant company. The legend that Ward also acted with Thomas Betterton is untrue, as Ward was only about five years old when Betterton died in 1710.

The first specific notice we have of John Ward comes in a memorandum (in the Folger Library) from John Rich, manager of Lincoln's Inn Fields Theatre, to the Drury Lane managers Booth, Cibber, and Wilkes; dated 19 October 1722, it informs us that Rich had "Entertain'd in my Service as an Actor John Ward. . . ." Ward's first known appearance at Lincoln's Inn Fields came a month later, when, on 17 November 1722, he acted Ascanio in *The Spanish Curate.* He repeated that role on 19 and 20 November, 6 December, and 23 January 1723. On 22 February 1723 he acted Hazeroth, a young lord, in the premiere of Fenton's *Mariamne,* a role in which he reappeared a number of times that season. He shared a benefit with Chapman and Mackenzie on 14 May 1723 when *Julius Caesar* was played, but Ward's first Shakespearean role is not recorded.

Ward remained engaged at Lincoln's Inn Fields for another three seasons, adding to his repertoire Chiron in *Titus Andronicus* and Vernon in *Henry IV* (for his shared benefit on 20 May 1724) in 1723–24. In the summer of 1724 he was acting with Bullock and Spiller's company at Southwark Fair, and he shared a benefit there with Mrs Haughton on 24 September when he played the title role in *Oedipus.* Back at Lincoln's Inn Fields in 1724–25, his salary was six shillings per day. The promptbook of *Money the Mistress,* performed at Lincoln's Inn Fields on 19 February 1726, records Ward as playing a Servant. No other roles for him are recorded in *The London Stage,* but McManaway and others state that during that period Ward also acted in *The Spanish Fryar, The Island Princess, The Royal Merchant, The Old Bachelor, The Beaux' Stratagem, Love's Last Shift,* and *Hamlet.*

During his engagement at the Lincoln's Inn Fields Theatre John Ward met his future wife, Sarah Butcher, the daughter of the provincial actors Mr and Mrs Butcher. On 4 October 1725 a Mrs Ward made her first known appearance at Lincoln's Inn Fields, acting Dainty Fidget in *The Country Wife.* McManaway suggests that she was the bride of John Ward and had been engaged by the company before her marriage. We find no record of a Miss Butcher acting in London about that time, but it should be noted that a Mr and Mrs Butcher, no doubt Sarah's parents, were indeed members of the Lincoln's Inn Fields company in 1724–25.

If the Mrs Ward who acted the part of Dainty Fidget, a lady of pretended virtue, was John Ward's wife, then she would have been only about 14 years of age at the time. (The inscription on Sarah Ward's tombstone indicates that she was 75 when she died in 1786.) Therefore, we caution that the Mrs Ward who performed in London between 1725 and 1729 may have been a different person. In 1724–25, Mrs Ward acted such roles as Hillaria in *Love's Last Shift,* Eugenia in *The London Cuckolds,* and Valeria in *The Rover.* Though John Ward seems not to have remained in the company after the 1725–26 season, Mrs Ward was there through 1728–29 and in the latter season was also engaged at the Haymarket Theatre. It should also be noted that a Miss Butcher, the daughter of the actress Mrs Butcher, was with Dymer's company at Canterbury in January and February 1728; she, of course, could have been another Butcher child.

Ward probably toured the provinces for several years after leaving London before he and Mrs Ward joined Elrington's company at the Smock Alley Theatre, Dublin, in 1730–31. The first notice we have of Ward in Dublin came on 27 April 1730, when he acted Friendly in *Flora.* On 19 March 1730 Mrs Ward had received a benefit; *Hamlet* was performed but neither her role nor Ward's is known. The following season at Smock Alley, Ward played Richard and his wife played Elizabeth in *Richard III* for their benefit on 22 March 1731. He appeared as Perdiccas in *The Rival Queens* on 29 March. In the early summer the Wards set themselves up at "the Great Booth in Dames's Street" where they had a benefit on 5 May, when the first performance in Ireland of *The Double Dealer* was given. Then they took their company on tour during the summer, venturing back to England; the *Dublin Intelligencer* of 22 September 1731 reported them acting at Chester.

The Wards were back in Dublin by 1734–35, in which season they performed at the Ransford Street Theatre. There Ward is known to have acted Macheath in *The Beggar's Opera* on 3 February 1735 and Essex in *The Unhappy Favorite* on 6 March. The following season at Ransford Street his roles included

Courtesy of the Garrick Club

JOHN WARD
artist unknown

Gerrard in *The Royal Merchant* on 13 November 1735 and Don Carlos in *Love Makes a Man,* with Mrs Ward as Louisa, for their benefit on 11 December. Several months earlier, on 2 September 1735 at Clonmel, Mrs Ward had given birth to a daughter Sarah, the future wife of Roger Kemble and matriarch of the Kemble clan.

In 1736–37 the Wards moved to the Aungier Street Theatre, Dublin, where they remained through 1740–41, during which period some of Ward's roles included the title part in *Oroonoko,* the First Manager in *The Rival Theatres,* Richard in *Richard III,* Hamlet (for his benefit on 12 February 1737, when Peg Woffington played Ophelia), the title part in *Henry VIII* (for his benefit on 24 January 1739), Ralph in *Wit without Money,* and the title part in *Aesop.* On 16 March 1738 *Measure for Measure* was acted for Ward's benefit, but Ward's role is not known. (The production was announced as the first of that play on the Irish stage, but a version of *Measure for Measure* seems to have been played at Smock Alley in the 1670s.) At Ward's benefit on 25 April 1740, young Peg Woffington for the first time played Sir Harry Wildair in *The Constant Couple,* a role that greatly advanced her reputation.

It has been believed that Ward's "roughness" and his straitlaced "Methodistical" views drove Woffington from the Aungier Street Theatre, but it seems that either love or greater theatrical opportunity caused her to elope to London, where she was employed at Covent Garden Theatre in November 1740. She soon moved over to Drury Lane Theatre, and when the 1741–42 season began the Wards also were in the company at the latter house.

John Ward made his debut at Drury Lane as Laertes in *Hamlet* on 19 September 1741. He acted Douglas in *Henry IV* on 9 October, Duke Frederick in *As You Like It* on 15 October, the Second Merchant in *The Comedy of Errors* on 11 November, and Trebonius in *Julius Caesar* on 10 December. Probably he was the Ward who acted Melidor in *Zara* at the James Street Theatre on 7 April 1742 (for the benefit of a "Tradesman in Distress").

After the 1741–42 season, John Ward and his wife seem not to have been engaged on a London stage. A Mr Ward acted Harry Wildair in a production of *The Constant Couple* at Goodman's Fields Theatre on 27 February 1746, but we believe that he was Henry Ward. By that time John Ward was the leader of a company strolling throughout Warwickshire and on the Welsh border. The parish register of Owestry records on 5 April 1746 the baptism of Margaret Woffington Ward, "d. of John & Sarah Ward, of the Comedian Band, of St. Austin parish, Mdx."

Gaining in reputation, Ward took his company to Stratford-upon-Avon in May 1746. Information on that important engagement is found in a letter (in the Folger Library) from the Reverend Joseph Greene of Stratford to his brother Richard in Lichfield:

A Company of Strolling-Players (much yᵉ best Set I have seen out of London, & in which opinion I am far from being singular) came here in May last, & continued wth a little intermission till September. . . . Ward, prevail'd with [Greene's] father Bartlett ye present Mayor, to lend him our Spacious Townhall, wherein to erect his Theatre for yᵉ term aforemention'd; on ye previous condition of

depositing in his hands five guineas for ye Use of yᵉ Poor of Stratford. . . . Yᵉ Actors met with much encouragement, even beyond what they themselves cou'd have expected.

Ward enhanced his position in Stratford by giving the total receipts from a performance of *Othello* on 9 September 1746 to restore Shakespeare's memorial bust in Holy Trinity Church. The sum of £17 was taken, and, according to Greene, all the characters (except Brabantio, acted by Woodward) "were well personated, & the whole Conducted with such decorum, & its Consequence, Applause." Ward acted Othello, and his wife played Emilia. The event seems to have been the first recorded production of a Shakespearean play in Stratford (for additional information see the article by Isabel Mann in the *Shakespeare Association Bulletin,* 24 July 1949). After much squabbling among the administrators, the monument was restored in 1749. (At the time of the performance a glazier named William Shakespeare, who claimed to be a descendant of the great dramatist, gave Ward a pair of gloves said to have "oft covered" Shakespeare's hands. Ward cherished them for many years, until in 1769, he sent them to David Garrick, who wore them as part of his costume when he delivered his Jubilee Ode at the celebration in Stratford that year. Supposedly these are the gloves now preserved in the Royal Shakespeare Theatre at Stratford.)

Over the following two decades the Wards led their company throughout much of England and Wales. They played regularly at Ludlow, Leominster, Hereford, Ledbury, and other places. By 1758 they were making regular tours on a circuit that included Brecon, Hay, Presteigne, Newton, and Ludlow. In January 1759 they opened an engagement of 22 weeks at Coventry.

The young Roger Kemble had joined the strollers at Birmingham in 1752. Against Ward's wishes, his daughter—about 16 or 17—married Kemble at Cirencester on 6 June 1753. But the truants were soon back in Ward's company, and Ward, so goes the story, consoled himself with a witty thrust at his new son-in-law: "My daughter Swore she would never marry an *Actor,* and by G—d Sir, she has religiously kept her word."

The Kembles stayed with Ward until 1761,

Courtesy of the Garrick Club

JOHN WARD
attributed to Beach

when they formed their own company. But they rejoined Ward in 1763, and in February 1767 at Worcester the group was billed as "Mr Kemble's Company of Comedians." Ward seems to have retired at Leominster after giving performances of *Richard III* and *The Procession of Their Majesties' Coronation* there in January 1766.

John Ward offered performances of much higher quality than usually found among provincial companies. He provided a wide variety of entertainment, a mixture of the best authors, old favorites, pantomimes, and even some spectacles. The *Gloucester Journal* of 25 August 1747 announced a performance of *Henry VIII* "with the whole ceremony of the coronation of Queen Anne Bullen and the military ceremony of the Champion (on horseback) in Westminster Hall. The Robes, Armour, Canopy and Bishops and Judges'

dresses and all the decorations of the play entirely new." Additional details about Ward's professional activities in the provinces are given by Cecil Price in *The English Theatre in Wales* (1948), where he writes that Ward "made the temporary theatre in barn, hall, or inn the centre of polite provincial life and brought London tastes and diversions to the country towns. Kemble was to continue the tradition."

John Ward died at Leominster on 30 October 1773. The inscription on his tombstone in Leominster churchyard reads:

Here waiting for the Savior's great Assize,
And hoping thro' his merits there to rise
In glorious mode in the dark closet lies
JOHN WARD, Gent.
Who died Oct. 30, 1773, aged 69.
Also SARAH his wife, who died Jan. 30, 1786,
aged 75 years.

Ward became a Methodist and applied stern discipline to his company and his children. John and Sarah had numerous children, but according to Anne Hatton, their granddaughter, only three survived—William and Stephen, who had little theatrical talent, and Sarah, who married Roger Kemble. Sarah Kemble never appeared on the London stage. She died in London on 24 April 1807, at the age of 71, and was buried at St Marylebone on 29 April. According to Anne Hatton, Sarah had "inherited the strong mind and genius of her father," and she had "his dark intelligent eyes, his handsome haughty countenance with the tall and masculine figure of her mother." The Kemble children (most of whom are noticed in volume 8 of this *Dictionary*) received their beauty and talent, it seems, through their mother's line, from the Wards.

Ward, Mrs John, Sarah, née Butcher
1711–1786, actress, singer.

Sarah Butcher was the daughter of the provincial performers Mr and Mrs Butcher, who acted for a brief period in London during the 1720s. The Stephen Butcher who played in the provinces in midcentury and was described as a young man at Coventry in 1749 was probably Sarah's brother. A Mrs Butcher, either Sarah's mother or sister-in-law, was with Roger Kemble's touring company in the 1760s.

Our subject probably was the Mrs Ward who made her first noticed appearance at Lincoln's Inn Fields Theatre on 4 October 1725, acting Dainty Fidget in *The Country Wife*. She was only about 14 years of age and had recently married John Ward, a young actor in the Lincoln's Inn Fields company. (We find no record of a Miss Butcher acting in London at that time, but Mrs and Mrs Butcher were indeed members of the Lincoln's Inn Fields company in 1724–25. A Miss Butcher was with Dymer's company at Canterbury in January and February 1728; she perhaps was Sarah's sister.)

In 1725–26 at Lincoln's Inn Fields, Mrs Ward also acted Hillaria in *Love's Last Shift*, Eugenia in *London Cuckolds*, and Valeria in *The Rover*. Though John Ward seems not to have remained in London after that season, Mrs Ward was at Lincoln's Inn Fields in 1728–29, acting Jenny in *The Cobler's Opera* on 24 April 1729. She (called "Miss" Ward) had appeared as Polly in *The Beggar's Opera* in the Fielding and Reynolds booth during Southwark Fair in August and September 1728. She was again (now as "Mrs" Ward) at Southwark Fair in September 1729, playing Rose in *The Recruiting Officer* on the twenty-third. On 30 September she acted Tippet in *The Beggar's Wedding* at Blackheath. In 1728–29 she also appeared at the Haymarket Theatre as Polly in *The Beggar's Opera* on 8 October 1728 (and 5 March 1729), in an unspecified role in *Love and Revenge* on 15 November, as Aurora in *The Humours of Harlequin* on 25 February 1729, and as Rose in *The Recruiting Officer* on 28 March 1729.

The remainder of Mrs Ward's career was closely aligned with that of her husband, as she toured with him to Dublin in the 1730s and throughout parts of England and Wales until 1766. They operated one of the finest companies of provincial strollers in Britain during the eighteenth century. Those activities are traced in our notice of John Ward. Some of the roles played by Mrs Ward were Lady Elizabeth in *Richard III*, Kitty Carrott in *What D'Ye Call It*, and Roxana in *The Rival Queens* at Smock Alley, Dublin, in 1730–31; Louisa in *Love Makes a Man* at Ransford Street, Dublin, in 1735–36; Lady Hartwell in *Wit without Money* at Aungier Street, Dublin, in

1737–38; and Emilia in *Othello* at Stratford-upon-Avon in 1746.

In 1766 the Wards gave over the management of their company to Roger and Sarah Kemble (their daughter) and retired to Leominster, where John Ward died on 30 October 1773 at the age of 69. According to the inscription on the tombstone in Leominster churchyard, Sarah Ward died on 30 January 1786 at the age of 75. A notation in John Philip Kemble's memorandum book (in the British Library, Add 31973) reads: "Sarah Ward, my mother's mother, died at Birmingham Jany 30th 1786—AEt. 76."

Sarah Ward was the grand matriarch of the distinguished Kemble family of performers. For information about her children see the notice of John Ward; and for information about her grandchildren, see the Kemble notices in volume 8 and Sarah Siddons's notice in volume 14 of this *Dictionary*.

Ward, John   *fl.* 1744–1763?], violinist.

A John Ward of Wych Street was listed in *Mortimer's London Directory* of 1763 as a violinist at Drury Lane Theatre. We assume that he was the John Ward, a member of the Worshipfull Company of Musicians, who had many apprentices bound to him between 1744 and 1763. Possibly he was the John Ward, musician, of Rose and Crown Court in Moorfields, who became a freeman of that company on 6 March 1743 and was admitted to livery on 26 March 1756.

His son, "John Ward Jun," was apprenticed to him on 31 December 1744, as was another son, William Ward, on 10 May 1754. William became a freeman on 8 October 1761.

There are several John Wards recorded in the records of the Worshipfull Company of Musicians at the London Guildhall. A John Ward, son of the late John Ward (not our subject), was apprenticed to Phebe Ward, "Cit & Musician of London," on 6 February 1769. Similarly, a William Ward, son of the late John Ward, was bound to William Burnett, musician, on 23 February 1774. That William Ward, a musician in the "Old Change," became a freeman on 4 December 1782 and was admitted to livery on 14 July 1790. He married Frances Maria Ashley, of the Ashley musical family, at St George, Hanover Square, on 11 July 1799. A John Ward, yet another of that name, of No 9, Cripplegate Buildings, became a freeman on 24 July 1771 and was admitted to livery on 25 July 1771. Several persons named Ward (Aaron, Cornelius, George, and Thomas) published and sold music in London during the eighteenth century and in the first quarter of the nineteenth century. They are listed in Humphries and Smith, *Music Publishing in the British Isles*.

Ward, John   *fl. 1744–1756?*₁,   *violinist*.

"John Ward Jun" was apprenticed to his father, the violinist John Ward (fl. 1744–1763?), on 31 December 1744. His brother William Ward (fl. 1754–1764?) was also apprenticed to his father, on 10 May 1754. The younger John Ward was probably the violinist of that name who was admitted to the Royal Society of Musicians on 4 July 1756.

Ward, Joseph   *fl. 1794–1815*₁,   *violist?*

Joseph Ward was listed in Doane's *Musical Directory* as a "tenor," presumably a violist (but possibly a singer), and a member of the New Musical Fund, with an address at Longman and Brodrip's in Tottenham Court Road. In 1815 he was serving on the Court of Assistants of the New Musical Fund, along with William Ward (fl. 1794–1815), who was probably related.

Ward,   Margaretta   Priscilla.   *See* KNIVETON, MRS THOMAS.

Ward, Peter   *fl. 1663*₁,   *musician*.

The Lord Chamberlain issued a warrant on 11 February 1663 appointing Peter Ward to the King's private music.

Ward, Richard   *d. c. 1777?, organist*.

Richard Ward was one of the original subscribers to the Royal Society of Musicians on 28 August 1739. He was organist of St Antholin, Budge Row, and St Bartholomew the Great. *Mortimer's London Directory* of 1763 lists Wood not only as an organist but as a teacher of the harpsichord and gave his address as

Budge Row, Cheapside. *The Royal Society of Musicians* (1985) says Richard Ward died before 12 February 1777.

Ward, Thomas   *fl. 1771–1795*₁,   *musician*.

Thomas Ward became a member of the Royal Society of Musicians on 2 June 1771, but he was eventually expelled (probably on 20 June 1779) for nonpayment of his subscription. On 6 May 1792 the Governors of the Society considered the petition of a Mr Ward who was formerly a member but had been expelled. After referring to the minutes of 2 June 1779, the Governors rejected the petition. The Minute Books for 1779 are missing from the records of the Society.

We believe that our subject was the Thomas Ward, described as a musician, who married the singing actress Sophia Potts at St Thomas à Becket, Portsmouth, on 17 September 1772. In his *Wandering Patentee*, Tate Wilkinson wrote of him as still alive, and claimed that the musician "behaved as civil to his lady as a gentleman should do, to deserve the name of *good-natured husband*." Ward's wife was still acting with the York company in 1801.

Ward, Mrs Thomas, Sophia, née Potts   *fl. 1766–1801*₁,   *actress, singer*.

According to Tate Wilkinson's *The Wandering Patentee*, Sophia Potts was the niece of the actress Esther Hamilton (Mrs John Hamilton, earlier Mrs George Bland and later Mrs Sweeny). In his "Notitia Dramatica" in the British Library, Reed identified Sophia as a niece of Thomas Hull. (Hull and Mrs Hamilton may well have been related, for it was Hull's influence that allowed that actress to live out her old age as a dresser and wardrobe keeper at the Richmond Theatre.) Reed also identified Miss Potts as the "Young Lady" who was advertised in the Covent Garden bills on 26 April 1766 as making her first attempt on any stage, as Emily ("with *Songs* in character") in *All in the Right*, an afterpiece that was translated and adapted from Detouches by Thomas Hull. Although Miss Potts was not named in the bills, on 10 March 1767 she was paid £4 4s. by Covent Garden for performing eight nights as one of the Fairies in *The Fairy*

Favour, a masque by Hull that premiered on 31 January 1767. On 21 April 1767 she appeared as a Page in *Rosamond.*

Over the next several seasons Miss Potts probably continued to appear at Covent Garden in walk-on roles, or perhaps she was engaged at a provincial theatre. We find her at the Bristol Theatre in the summer of 1769, but she was back at Covent Garden in the 1769–70 season. The latter theatre's treasurer paid her £1 1*s.* on 25 March 1770 for walking 12 nights in *Man and Wife; or, The Shakespeare Jubilee,* a comedy by Colman that had opened on 7 October 1769. On 20 April 1770, for Hull's benefit, she sang "The Blackbirds, a Cantata."

At Covent Garden on 24 April 1771 she played for her first time Leonora in *The Padlock,* again for Hull's benefit. In the following season, 1771–72, advertised as a "Young Gentlewoman," she appeared as Fanny in *The Maid of the Mill.* When she played that role again on 28 February 1772 she was named in the bills as Miss Potts. She was again so identified in the bills when she replaced Mrs Mattocks in the entertainment *True Blue* on 14 December 1771, acted Leonora again on 16 December, and replaced Mrs Woodman as one of the Nymphs in *The Fairy Prince* on 17 January 1772.

On 17 September 1772 Sophia Potts married Thomas Ward, a musician, at St Thomas à Becket, Portsmouth. We believe that her husband was the Thomas Ward who had become a member of the Royal Society of Musicians on 2 June 1771 and was later expelled for failing to pay his subscription. Some years later, the Governors of the Society considered on 6 May 1792 a petition from a Mr Ward, who had formerly been a member but had been expelled. After referring to the minutes of 20 June 1779, the Governors rejected the petition. (The Minute Books for 1779 are missing from the records of the Society.)

Now advertised as Mrs Ward, she returned to London to play Lucy in *The Beggar's Opera* at the Haymarket Theatre on 25 January 1773 (a performance not listed in *The London Stage*). The *Morning Chronicle* of 26 January 1773 identified Mrs Ward as "lately" Miss Potts. A critic calling himself "Theatricus" saw the performance and wrote to the *Morning Chronicle* of 1 February:

An excellent performer in Lucy: a Mrs. Ward, if I am not mistaken, the same person I think to have seen (then a Miss Potts) last season at Coventgarden perform Fanny, in the Maid of the Mill: she then betrayed some rays of genius, but she is now materially improved: her voice is clear, full and constant, her conduct of it was so discreet, that I protest with all attention, I did not catch her once out of time or tune . . . ; nor indeed was her acting inferior; a forcible gleam of character, spirit, in short, so much of the indefinable *Naivete* ran through all her scenes, that except for Mrs. Clive, I never saw the part so well represented . . .

On 6 May 1773 the *Morning Chronicle,* mistakenly calling her Mrs "Ford" but providing her maiden name, reported that she was now engaged at the Bath Theatre Royal. The next day that paper corrected itself, identifying her as Mrs Ward, formerly at Covent Garden and married to a musician.

Mrs Ward remained a regular member of the Bath company through 1781–82, and she was also at Bristol in the spring and summer of 1779 and the 1779–80 season. She returned to London occasionally in summers to sing at Marylebone Gardens. On 30 June 1774 at Marylebone she appeared in Arnold's new burletta *Don Quixote,* and songs written by Hook and sung by her there that season were published that year. She sang at Marylebone Gardens again in 1775. In 1780 she was with the company at Stourbridge Fair, Cambridge, and played in *Fortunatus* on 5 October. Mrs Ward became a member of Tate Wilkinson's company at York in 1781 and remained with him through 1801, though her name is not found on the York bills every season. She also appeared in Liverpool and Hull and other cities on the Yorkshire circuit. When she acted at Hull in November 1783 she was advertised as from Bath. In his *Wandering Patentee,* Wilkinson described her as "well made," though not handsome: "She had a great emulation and pride to sport her legs in small clothes against [Dorothy] Jordan, to whom she had an implacable hatred." Her husband, wrote Wilkinson, "was a musician and behaved as civil to his lady as a gentleman should do, to deserve the name of a *good-natured husband.*"

Ward, Thomas Achurch   *1747–1835, actor, manager.*

Thomas Achurch Ward, according to the *Dramatic Register,* was 88 at the time of his death in November 1835 and thus would have been born in 1747, probably at Edinburgh, where his mother and father were acting that year. Thomas's father, Henry Ward (fl. 1734–1758), was a minor actor and playwright who performed in London in the 1730s. His mother, Sarah Ward (1727–1771), was the daughter of Mr and Mrs Thomas Achurch, actors who performed on several occasions in London but were mainly associated with York. Thomas Achurch Ward was the brother of Margaretta Priscilla Ward, an actress who married the actor Thomas Kniveton in September 1771 and was regularly engaged at Covent Garden Theatre in the 1770s. She later became Mrs John Banks.

Very little is known about Ward's apprenticeship in the theatre, though he must have traveled about with his parents, and he perhaps even made a few appearances on provincial stages when a young boy. When Thomas was about 5, in 1752, his mother and father separated because Sarah Ward began an alliance with the actor West Digges that lasted until the summer of 1759. It is possible, but unlikely, that Thomas was the Ward who acted at the Haymarket Theatre in specially licensed performances on 16 November and 19 December 1770 and in Foote's summer company there from 1772 through 1775. A Mr Ward, possibly young Thomas, acted with a company at Glasgow between 4 February and 25 April 1771, but that person could have been any one of several of that name performing in the provinces at that time. But he seems to have been the Ward who acted at the Theatre Royal in Shakespeare Square, Edinburgh, from 1772 to 1774. His roles during that period included the Captain in *King Lear* on 1 December 1773 and a part (Conolly?) in *The School for Wives* on 28 March 1774.

In the summer and fall of 1775 Ward was with Younger's company at Birmingham. He was announced as making his first appearance on that stage on 24 July 1775 as Hardcastle in *She Stoops to Conquer.* Sometime between 25 August and 1 September 1775 he married the young actress Sarah Hoare (1756–1838). Her parents were probably provincial actors. Two of her sisters went on to stage careers: Katharine Hoare (1762–1807), who married the

actor Sparks Powell, and Letitia Ann Hoare, who was successively Mrs Sage and Mrs Robinson.

At Birmingham on 28 August for Mrs Ward's benefit, tickets could be had at "Mr Gibb's, Baker in the Church Yard," and on 25 September, Ward's benefit tickets could be bought at Mr Munro's in Peck Lane. The separate addresses could be explained by the likelihood that the places where tickets could be had were not really their lodgings, but rather locations of convenience. It is possible, also, that the Mrs Ward who had her benefit on 28 August was not Thomas's wife but another actress of that name, perhaps Sophia Ward (née Potts).

Ward and his new wife were with the Liverpool company in 1776. His name was on the paylist for 10s. per week. On 16 August 1776 he was paid a total of £61 1s. for himself and Mrs Ward. Upon Younger's recommendation, the Wards were engaged at Covent Garden Theatre for the 1776–77 season, each at £3 per week, a considerable increase in their financial status.

On 7 October 1776 Ward made his Covent Garden debut as Romeo to Mrs Jackson's Juliet. (Mrs Ward did not appear until 14 November, when she acted Rodogune in *Ethelinda.*) On 11 November he acted Tressel in *Richard III* and on 25 November Surrey in *Henry VIII.* That season he also appeared as Philotas in *The Grecian Daughter* (on 28 November 1776, the night Spranger Barry, playing Evander, made his last appearance on the stage), Lovell in *High Life below Stairs,* Malcolm in *Macbeth,* and probably Vellinus in the London premiere of Mason's *Caractacus* on 6 December 1776. For a benefit shared with his wife on 6 May 1777, he acted Philotas and she played Euphrasia (for the first time) in *The Grecian Daughter;* tickets could be had of the Wards at Stacy's, No 76, the corner of Longacre, Drury Lane, and receipts were £197 18s. (less house charges of £66 1s.).

Their articles not having been renewed at Covent Garden, the Wards returned to their provincial careers. They rejoined the Manchester company in November 1778; among their roles there that season were Hamlet and Gertrude. They remained at Manchester the next season, and when he acted Charles Surface in *The School for Scandal* at Richmond,

Surrey, on 16 June 1781, he was announced as from the Theatre Royal, Manchester. That summer at Richmond he acted Hamlet, Belcour in *The West Indian,* Romeo, and Orlando in *As You Like It.*

Ward was in Jackson's company at Edinburgh by the 1782 season, where he was to be found through 1787. (His wife, however, after a season at Edinburgh, was engaged at Drury Lane during the 1780s.) Among Ward's characters at Edinburgh were Acres in *The Rivals,* Archer in *The Beaux' Stratagem,* Belcour in *The West Indian,* Captain Brazen in *The Recruiting Officer,* Chamont in *The Orphan,* Charles Surface in *The School for Scandal,* Cloten in *Cymbeline,* George Barnwell in *The London Merchant,* Lord Ogleby in *The Clandestine Marriage,* Lothario in *The Fair Penitent,* Macduff in *Macbeth,* and Ranger in *The Suspicious Husband,* among many others, in a line mainly consisting of serious young men in comedy and tragedy.

Ward also acted in Tate Wilkinson's company at the York spring meeting of 1783. In *The Wandering Patentee,* Wilkinson remembered Ward—who acted Posthumus, Lord Foppington, and other principal characters—as a "good Person" with "a great share of spirit and vivacity" who was well received.

In the autumn of 1783 Ward interrupted his Edinburgh tenure to make another attempt on the London stage, this time at Drury Lane Theatre, where his wife was engaged. He was added to the Drury Lane list on 4 October 1783 at 13s. 4d. per day. On 18 October 1783, announced as from Edinburgh, Ward made his debut at Drury Lane as Ranger in *The Suspicious Husband.* His other roles that season were Slender in *The Merry Wives of Windsor* on 27 January 1784, Martin in *Neck or Nothing* on 10 February, and Frank in *The Absent Man* on 29 March. On 10 May 1784 he shared a benefit with his wife; they acted Clodio and Louisa in *Love Makes a Man,* and tickets could be had of them at their lodgings, the corner of Broad Court and Drury Lane. The receipts were £135 2s., less house charges of £107 12s. 11d., according to *The London Stage* (but a Drury Lane account book [British Library Add 29710] records for that date: "Benefit—Mr. & Mrs. Ward Def[icit] 70.3.11.").

Of Ward's performances that season, J. H. Leigh wrote in *The New Rosciad* (1785):

> WARD next came on, and vainly tried to tread
> A *Royal Stage,* on which he scarce cou'd walk;
> Before we act, we sure shou'd learn to talk. . . .

The Secret History of the Green Rooms (1790), mentioning Ward in his wife's notice, stated that at Drury Lane "Ward and the Public differed so widely in the opinion of his performance [as Ranger], that he was immediately thrown on the shelf, as inadequate to the task he had undertaken . . . [and was] discharged at the conclusion of the season."

Once more Ward returned to the provinces, acting mainly at Edinburgh. He was at Liverpool again in the summer of 1786; at his benefit on 14 August receipts were £96, less £35 charges. After the spring of 1787, he left Edinburgh to join the company at Bath and Bristol for three seasons, 1787–88 through 1789–90, playing mainly straight leads in broad comedy.

When the new Theatre Royal in Manchester opened on 5 February 1790, Ward was joint manager with John Banks (d. 1831), his sister Margaretta's second husband. In the 1790s they also acquired the managership of the theatres at Chester and Liverpool. Mrs Ward joined her husband in Manchester by 1794, and they both continued to play leading roles in their productions.

The anonymous author of *The Thespian Mirror . . . of the Theatres Royal, Manchester, Liverpool, and Chester* (1793) found Ward:

> . . . *affable sprightly and pleasing.*
> *In the walks of light comedy few can excell him,*
> *But to undertake tragedy nought should impel him.*
> . . . .
> *He knows, in despite of his dissonant voice,*
> *The road to the heart, and to make it rejoice.*

The *Monthly Mirror* reporter from Manchester in January 1796 found Ward a very agreeable actor: "with all the disadvantages of voice, person, and years, he possesses a portion of true *vis comica.*" His wife, however, could scarcely "stand firm," and would not, in that reporter's opinion, be engaged if she were not a "near relation" of the manager. The same reporter hoped that Banks—"for in Ward, as a *manager,* no confidence is placed"—would seek reinforcements, especially in the scenic department: "The scenery, in spite of a storm by moonlight, painted for *Zorinski,* still testifies to the antiquarian spirit of its proprietors; its shattered condition threatens a speedy downfall and unless a speedy reformation takes place, the managers will, according to the old phrase, 'bring an old house about their ears.'"

Complaints against Ward's lackadaisical managerial style continued for many years. His acting, for the most part, was praised, though he was criticized for appearing less and less as the seasons rolled on. The author of the anonymous *Letter to Mr. Ward* (Manchester c. 1798) offered "moderate and constructive" criticism, citing Ward's taking over a part played to applause by Jones, his seemingly "expedient" indispositions, his "careless" benefits, and his lack of generosity and good sense as a manager. For his benefits he selected "amusements adapted to the taste of a holiday mob," and some six years back, claimed the correspondent, Ward had spread it about the town that he and his benefits had been threatened because of his political zeal, "which you did by publishing letters to and from yourself, fabricated the Lord knows where," in order to gain public sympathy. In 1798 the *Universal British Directory* listed him as one of the managers of the Manchester theatre and living in Falkner Street.

In September 1800 Ward was joined by a new partner, the singer Thomas Ludford Bellamy, who bought John Banks's shares in the theatres at Manchester, Chester, Shrewsbury, and Lichfield. The 1800–1801 season opened somewhat "inauspiciously" with a weak company, but as the season progressed the addition of actors like Turner, Archer, Lovegrove, Mrs Forbes, and Bellamy and his wife greatly strengthened the productions. And, as the *Monthly Mirror* reported, Ward had long been "deservedly a favourite, as an actor."

During 1803 and 1804 the Manchester *Townsman* and the *Theatrical Inquisitor* levied hard criticism upon the managers, most of it directed at Ward, who was accused of conducting the theatre on a "niggardly plan,"

making frequent changes of personnel, mutilating plays by cuts, ordering repetitive music, and causing low morale. The neglectful management and low salaries led to poor discipline among the performers. It was said that Ward as "master of the vessel was the most lazy hand on board the ship" and would concoct any excuse or illness to avoid playing. "But where shall I find words," wrote the *Townsman* on 13 December 1803, "to describe the wonderful excellencies of the manager, who keeps himself, like Jove on the summit of Olympus, shranded [*sic*] from mortal eyes, lest man, by frequently seeing him, should become too familiar with his presence and cease to adore him?"

Praise was forthcoming, however, for Ward's acting of such roles as Ranger, Mercutio, and Marplot, in which he was described as "really inimitable." As the Copper Captain in *Rule a Wife and Have a Wife* he possessed "a particular vein of sprightliness and gaiety, which accords admirably, with characters of this description." On 2 February 1804 the *Townsman* claimed that he "would never wish to see Faddle [in *The Foundling*] better performed."

In March 1805 Bellamy gave up his interest in the management and his place was taken by the actor Charles Mayne Young. Ward and Young struggled along for another two seasons, but on 23 June 1807 they were obliged to announce the closing of Manchester's first Theatre Royal.

The *Dramatic Register* recorded Thomas Achurch Ward's death as occurring on 30 November 1835 at the age of 88. His wife Sarah Ward probably died in 1838. They had three children—two girls and a boy—who acted at Manchester and other places on the circuit. Some information on them is given in Mrs Ward's notice.

Ward, Mrs Thomas Achurch, Sarah, née Hoare *1756?–1838?, actress.*

Sarah Hoare, born probably in 1756, may have been the child of provincial actors. Two of her sisters also went into the profession. One, Katharine (1762–1807), acted in London by 1779 and by 1782 was married to the actor Sparks Powell; she is noticed in this *Dictionary* under her married name. The other,

Letitia Ann, became the common-law wife of a Cheapside haberdasher named Sage, and after several unsuccessful attempts at acting in London she ventured briefly into ballooning, became Mrs Robinson, and ended her days as a dresser at Drury Lane; she is noticed in these volumes as Mrs Sage. The Hoare sisters were "nearly related to Hoare the banker," according to Gilliland. That banker was Henry Hoare (d. 1828) of Fleet Street and one of the founders of the Church Missionary Society; his son Charles James Hoare (1781–1865) is noticed in *The Dictionary of National Biography.* Probably our subject was also related to Prince Hoare (1755–1834), the dramatist and painter, who was the son of William Hoare (1702?–1792), the Bath artist.

The *Authentic Memoirs of the Green Room* claimed that Sarah Hoare was a young mantua maker at Liverpool when her friends persuaded her that she had talents for the stage. (The assertion that she had been a mantua maker was repeated by the *Thespian Dictionary* [1805] but then was denied in the *Monthly Mirror.*) She procured an introduction to Joseph Younger, the Liverpool manager, who engaged her and, according to *The Secret History of the Green Rooms* (1790), "brought her forward with every advantage it is in the power of the Manager to give." *The Secret History* seemed to hint that Younger, "who always paid great deference to the fair sex," may have developed a special interest in young Sarah. Her debut at Liverpool probably occurred in the summer or autumn of 1774.

The first notice of Miss Hoare's connection with Younger's company, however, was at the King Street Theatre in Birmingham in the summer of 1775, though according to an article about her that appeared in the Birmingham *Campaign* that summer she had been with Younger for almost a year and had

gone through the fatigues of her station with great courage and spirit, altho' she has not been twelve months in the service; she seems possessed of many requisites, tho' entirely destitute of delicacy and sensibility—her feelings being merely mechanical. . . . She has great powers, which she displays upon every occasion, too often improperly: she aims all her power to copy Mrs. Y——s [Yates], and like all copyists, she follows her even in her errors. Her hands are often raised in a very awkward manner, without any meaning in the world;

if she was to rehearse with a 7 lb. weight in each hand, she would find an advantage in it.

Despite her faults Sarah Hoare had "acquired an uncontroulable ascendancy," as the *Secret History* put it, and insisted on choice of parts over Mrs Siddons, then a young actress, who in 1775 was a member of Younger's company when it played at Leicester, Worcester, and Cheltenham.

At Birmingham on 7 August 1775 tickets could be had of "Miss Hoare," and on 25 August her name was still given as Miss Hoare in the playbills. Sometime between that date and 1 September 1775 Sarah married Thomas Achurch Ward, who was an actor in the Birmingham company and the son of the minor actor and playwright Henry Ward (fl. 1734–1758) and Sarah Ward (1727–1771), an actress of some consequence in London and Edinburgh. On 7 September 1775 she was advertised as Mrs Ward, late Miss Hoare. On 25 September benefit tickets could be had from Ward at Mr Munro's in Peck Lane. It should be noted that on 28 August benefit tickets for a "Mrs Ward" could be had at Mr Gibb's, a baker, in the Church Yard. That Mrs Ward may have been the newly wed Sarah Hoare, and the address different from that of her husband could be explained by the possibility that the places where tickets were available were not their lodgings but addresses of convenience. But we think it also highly likely that the Mrs Ward whose benefit was on 28 August 1775 was not Thomas A. Ward's wife but another Mrs Ward, perhaps Sophia Ward (née Potts).

Sarah Ward and her husband were at Liverpool in 1776, where she was on the company list for 10s. 6d. per week. Younger's recommendation obtained them an engagement at Covent Garden Theatre for the 1776–77 season, each at £3 per week. Though Ward made his first appearance at Covent Garden on 7 October 1776 as Romeo, it was not until 14 November 1776 that Sarah Ward made her debut, as Rodogune in *Ethelinda.* On 18 December she acted Zara in *The Mourning Bride* and on 26 December Queen Eleanor in *King Henry the Second; or, The Fall of Rosamond.* On 5 May 1777 she played Roxana in *Alexander the Great;* on 6 May she appeared as Euphrasia and her husband played Philotas in *The Gre-*

cian Daughter for their shared benefit. Tickets could be had of them at Stacy's, No 76, corner of Longacre and Drury Lane.

The Wards were not reengaged at Covent Garden for the next season. We lose trace of them for several years. In the autumn of 1780 Sarah Ward returned to London, this time to Drury Lane Theatre, to play for several months. She first appeared as Alicia in *Jane Shore* on 17 October and then acted Zara in *The Mourning Bride* on 1 November, Octavia in *All for Love* on 13 November, Roxana in *Alexander the Great* on 26 November, and Octavia again on 27 December. Perhaps she was with her husband when he acted at Richmond, Surrey, in June 1781, announced as from the Theatre Royal, Manchester.

In 1781–82 the Wards acted at Edinburgh, where her roles included Alicia in *Jane Shore*, Amanda in *A Trip to Scarborough*, Calista in *The Fair Penitent*, Hermione in *The Distrest Mother*, Hermione in *The Winter's Tale*, Juliet in *Romeo and Juliet*, Lady Frances Touchwood in *The Belle's Stratagem*, Lady Lurewell in *The Constant Couple*, Louisa in *Love Makes a Man*, Millwood in *The London Merchant*, Mrs Belville in *The School for Wives*, Mrs Oakly in *The Jealous Husband*, and Zara in *The Mourning Bride*.

In the autumn of 1782 Sarah Ward returned once more to London, to begin an engagement at Drury Lane Theatre that would last over a decade. She appeared at the theatre on 1 October 1782 as Desdemona in *Othello*. The *Public Advertiser* of 4 October criticized the costumes she and Mrs Hopkins (who acted Emilia) wore: "Mrs Ward and Mrs Hopkins seemed to have forgot their Engagement on the Stage, and dressed themselves for a Card Party . . . frizzed, hooped, and fly-capp'd." On 22 October Mrs Ward acted Lady Sneerwell in *The School for Scandal*. During the remainder of that season she was also seen as Araminta in *The Confederacy*, Alicia to Mrs Siddons's Jane Shore, Lady Dainty in *The Double Gallant*, the First Constantia in *The Chances*, Isabella in *The Wonder*, Millwood in *The London Merchant*, Mrs Clerimont in *The Tender Husband*, Belinda in *The Fair Quaker*, and Mrs Foresight in *Love for Love*. The following season, 1783–84, she added to that repertoire Mariana in *Measure for Measure*, Mrs Strickland in *The Suspicious Husband*, Lady

Courtesy of the Garrick Club

SARAH (Mrs Thomas A.) WARD, as Octavia
by De Wilde

Anne in *Richard III* (on 6 November 1783, when J. P. Kemble acted Richard for his first time in London), Lady Allworth in *A New Way to Pay Old Debts*, Margaretta in *Rule a Wife and Have a Wife*, and Fidelia in *Love in a Veil*. On 10 May 1784 she acted Louisa and her husband (who had returned to Drury Lane that season for a brief engagement) played Clodio in *Love Makes a Man* for their shared benefit, at which they seemed to have incurred a deficit. Tickets could be had of the Wards at their lodgings at the corner of Broad Court and Drury Lane.

In *The New Rosciad* (1785), J. H. Leigh was severely critical of the Wards. After dismissing her husband with "[he] vainly tried to tread/ a *Royal Stage* on which he scarce cou'd walk," Leigh turned to Mrs Ward:

> *She has attempted* Desdemona *too!!!*
> *And really in bombast, she plays as true*
> *As ever Stroller did in country town,*
> *And, without flatt'ry, with as much renown.*

At Drury Lane Mrs Ward's additional roles in 1784–85 included Lady Grace in *The Provok'd Husband*, the Lady in *Comus*, Marcia in *Cato*, Selima in *Zara*, Mrs Kitely in *Every Man in His Humour*, Aurelia in *The Maid of Honour* (an adaptation by Kemble from Massinger, which premiered on 27 January 1785), Caelia in *The Fox*, Clarinda in *The Beau's Duel*, Nottingham in *The Earl of Essex*, Melinda in *The Recruiting Officer*, and Mrs Wilding in *The Gamesters*. For her benefit on 25 April 1785, when she acted Lady Dainty in *The Double Gallant*, tickets were again available from her at No 44, corner of Broad Court and Drury Lane. In 1785–86 she acted Diana in *The Humourist*, Alithea in *The Country Girl*, Hermione in *The Winter's Tale*, Megra in *Philaster*, the Tragic Muse in *The Jubilee*, Birtha in *Percy*, Amanda in *A Trip to Scarborough*, and Marwood in *The Way of the World*.

During the remainder of her tenure at Drury Lane, Mrs Ward added the following roles to her repertoire: in 1786–87, Lavinia in *The Fair Penitent*, Isabella in *Cleone*, Anna in *Douglas*, the Queen in *Hamlet*, the Queen in *Cymbeline*, Jane Shore in *Jane Shore*, Almeria in *The Mourning Bride*, Mrs Lovemore in *The Way to Keep Him*, and Fulvia in the premiere of Jephson's *Julia* on 14 April 1787; in 1787–88, Regan in *King Lear* and Paula in the premiere of Bertie Greatheed's *The Regent* on 29 March 1788; in 1788–89, Lady Loverule in *The Devil to Pay*, the Queen in *Richard III*, Lady Capulet in *Romeo and Juliet*, the Countess in *The Follies of the Day; or, The Marriage of Figaro* (for her benefit on 27 May 1789), and Queen Elizabeth in the premiere of John St John's *Mary Queen of Scots* on 21 March 1789 (and on 1 May 1789 she read the part of the Countess in *False Appearances*, for Miss Farren, who was indisposed); in 1789–90, the Queen of France in *Henry V*, Mrs Bromley in *Know Your Own Mind*, Lady Ralegh in *The Life and Death of Sir Walter Ralegh*, Lady Graveairs in *The Careless Husband*, Marcella in *The Pannel*, Lady Restless in *All in the Wrong*, and Angelica in the premiere of Kemble's *Love in Many Masks* on 8 March 1790; and in 1790–91, Emilia in *Othello*.

In 1791–92 the Drury Lane company moved into the King's Theatre while their new house was being built. There Mrs Ward's new roles were Mrs Blandish in *The Heiress*,

Mrs Oakly in *The Jealous Wife*, and Valeria in *Coriolanus*. That season she also participated in the private theatricals given at Wargrave in December and January. During the summer of 1792 she acted at Liverpool. In 1792–93, when her salary was £5 per week, she acted Mrs Rachel Cleveland in *The Fugitive* and Elinor in *King John* (on 12 February 1793 at the Haymarket, where the Drury Lane company also played); on 29 April 1793 she helped out by reading the part of Charlotte in *The Gamester* for Mrs Kemble, who was ill. Mrs Ward's address in London was No 12, Catherine Street, the Strand, from May 1786 to at least May 1789, and No 6, York Buildings, Covent Garden, from at least May 1791 to May 1793. Her salary in 1792–93 (her last season in London) was £5 per week; for her last benefit on 22 May 1793 she shared £310 16s. 4d. with Whitfield.

In *The Children of Thespis* (1792), Anthony Pasquin (John Williams) wrote of Mrs Ward:

In smart walking ladies and Tragedy queens,
See WARD take the lead, tho' long out of her
*   teens:*
To Nature, for beauty, she's somewhat in debt;
And is perfectly learn'd in stage etiquette.
That Merit smiles on her, it must be confess'd;
And she always takes care that her person's well
*   dress'd.*

Mrs Ward's last performance with the Drury Lane company at the Haymarket Theatre was as Lady Sneerwell in *The School for Scandal* on 4 June 1793. Kemble's alteration of *All's Well That Ends Well*, as published in 1793, assigns the role of the Countess to Mrs Ward; but that role was acted by Mrs Powell when the version was first performed at the new Drury Lane Theatre on 12 December 1794, some 19 months after Mrs Ward had left the company.

After leaving London, Mrs Ward joined the Manchester company, where her husband was joint manager. She remained a mainstay at Manchester until at least 1812 and also acted at Liverpool, Edinburgh, Chester, Hull, and Woodbridge.

Over her years at Manchester the press commented on Mrs Ward in a generally favorable manner but became increasingly critical of her playing roles for which she had become much too mature. The *Monthly Mirror* of February

Act 2   JULIUS CÆSAR.   *Scene 1*

Mᴿˢ WARD in PORTIA.
Dear my Lord,
Make me acquainted with your Cause of Grief.

By permission of the Trustees of the British Museum

SARAH (Mrs Thomas A.) WARD, as Portia
engraving by Woodman, after Ramberg

1797 found her portrayal of Margaret of An-
jou in *The Earl of Warwick* to be excellent. A
large portion of *A Peep into the Theatre* (Manchester c. 1798) is devoted to telling the town
about the talents of Mrs Ward, who always
gave pleasure in every character she assumed.
The author of *Impartial Reflections* (Manchester
c. 1798) agreed, except for those characters
that "are evidently too young for her, and
which nothing but the parsimony of the managers could make it necessary for her to take,"
for surely "her good sense renders it impossible that any thing but necessity could induce her to appear in such characters as Juliet,
Angela, &c."

The Manchester *Townsman* (No 1) in 1803

commented that Mrs Ward was "unquestionably the best actress that had trod the Manchester stage for many years, and in some sentimental parts of genteel comedy, is entitled
to a high degree of praise." She had, however,
taken on a part "considerably above her powers" when she had acted Elvira in *Pizarro*. Her
Gertrude in *Hamlet* was "everything that
could be wished for," and as Belvidera in *Venice
Preserv'd,* in the last act, "she outdid herself;
she was great beyond example." Her acting of
Lady Randolph in *Douglas* was "powerfully expressive and affecting," and she played Calista
in *The Fair Penitent* with "great merit."
Throughout that 1803–4 season the same
journal continued in high praise of her portrayals of such roles as Millwood, Lady Macbeth, the Spectre in *The Castle Spectre,* and Mrs
Beverley in *The Gamester,* calling her acting in
the last play "truly Siddonian." But she was
chastized for playing Miss Rusport in *The West
Indian,* because she was getting too old to act
ingenues. The *Theatrical Inquisitor* (1804)
played the same refrain: ". . . 'tis ridiculous
. . . to suppose a lady, verging on sixty years
of age, can personate the blooming maid of
eighteen."

The *Thespian Review . . . of the Performers on
the Manchester Stage* (1806) wrote of her acting
of Ortilia in *Alfonso* that February:

The cruel, vicious Ortilia, who for the honour of
humanity, let us hope, could only exist in the
poet's brain, was finely given by Mrs. WARD; and
the lengthened faces, the shrinking from the stage,
and the chilled blood of every person who heard
her . . . all bore a silent attestation of the superior
excellence of the horrid picture which was drawn
of female depravity. Though the hearts of the audience bore testimony against *Ortilia,* yet their
hands spoke as loudly and in as much applause of
Mrs. WARD, as the *present fashion of applauding*
would admit.

A clipping in the C. B. Smith collection,
"Dramatic Autographs" (vol 7), in the Garrick Club, reports that Mrs. Ward died "on
the 19th inst. at her house in Chatham-street
[Manchester], in her 85th year." No month or
year is stated, but the notes of the late C.
Beecher Hogan suggest 1838. Her husband,
Thomas Achurch Ward, had died on 30 November 1835, at the age of 88. Their daughter, Miss Ward, had appeared at Manchester
on 4 April 1796 and as Amanthis in *My*

City Art Gallery, Manchester

SARAH (Mrs Thomas A.) WARD, as Rodogune

Delft tile, after Roberts

Grandmother in February 1797. The *Monthly Mirror* reported at that time that she had performed many characters in Shrewsbury and Chester "with applause."

The Wards seem to have had at least two performing daughters, for in 1801 the *Monthly Mirror* reported that the manager's daughter, a Miss Ward, had "commenced" her career at Manchester in a very promising manner, acting—for her third time upon any stage—*Amelia Wildenhaim,* in which she evinced "much discernment, and a cultivated mind." One of these actresses was the Miss Ward who acted at the Theatre Royal, Shakespeare Square, Edinburgh, in 1804 and at Manchester from 1804 to 1806. And one of the daughters, according to J. L. Hodgkinson and R. Pogson's *The Early Manchester Stage,* married "a noted Manchester surgeon." A Master Ward acted at Edinburgh in 1804.

The *Catalogue of Dramatic Portraits in the Harvard Theatre Collection* (4: 232) confuses Mrs Thomas Achurch Ward with her mother-in-law Mrs Henry Ward and incorrectly calls her the grandmother of the Kembles. Portraits of Mrs Thomas Achurch Ward include:

1. A miniature portrait by John Smart, signed and dated 1782, of a Mrs Ward, looks like other known portraits of Sarah Ward. The miniature was reproduced in an advertisement by D. S. Lavender, London, early in the 1980s and was still with him in February 1986.

2. As Lady Lurewell in *The Constant Couple,* "taken from life" by W. Loftis, 1789. In the Folger Library (Art vol C. 16).

3. As Octavia in *All for Love.* By Samuel De Wilde (oil on canvas, 14½" × 10¾"). In the Thomas Harris sale on 12 July 1819 (lot 66). In the Garrick Club (No 269), from the Mathews collection. Engraving by P. Audinet as a plate for *Bell's British Theatre,* 1792.

4. As Portia in *Julius Caesar.* Engraving by C. Sherwin, after J. Ramberg. Published as a plate to *Bell's Shakespeare,* 1785. (But possibly the sitter is Mrs Henry Ward.)

5. As Portia. The same plate as above, with the engraver's name altered to R. Woodman, after Ramberg. Published by John Cawthorn, 1807.

6. As Rodogune in *Ethelinda; or, The Royal Convert.* Pencil drawing by James Roberts, a study for the picture below. In the Harvard Theatre Collection, acquired with many drawings of other actors from Thomas Agnew in 1976.

7. As Rodogune. Engraving by T. Thornthwaite, after James Roberts. Published as a plate to *Bell's British Theatre,* 20 October 1776.

8. As Rodogune. Engraving by R. Godfrey, after James Roberts. Published as a plate to *Bell's British Theatre,* 27 December 1794.

9. As Rodogune. Engraving by unknown artist, after James Roberts. Published as a plate to *Bell's British Theatre,* November 1777.

10. As Rodogune. On a Delftware tile, after James Roberts. In the Thomas Greg Collection, City of Manchester Art Gallery.

Ward, William   *fl.* 1744–1749₁, *trumpeter.*

A William Ward was admitted to the Royal Society of Musicians on 1 January 1744. Probably he was the same William Ward who replaced Richard Collet as a trumpeter in the King's musical establishment that year. In 1749 he was still a member of the King's Musick.

Ward, William   fl. 1754–1764?, musician.

A William Ward was apprenticed to his father, the violinist John Ward (fl. 1744–1763?), on 10 May 1754. He became a freeman of the Worshipfull Company of Musicians on 8 October 1761. Probably he was the William Ward who became a member of the Royal Society of Musicians on 3 June 1764. His brother John Ward (1744–1756?) was also apprenticed to his father, on 31 December 1744.

Ward, William?   fl. 1770–1785?, actor.

An actor named Ward appeared as Young Philpot in *The Citizen* on 16 November and Grizzle in *Tom Thumb the Great* on 19 December 1770 in specially licensed performances at the Haymarket Theatre. That actor (or another of the same name) was a member of Foote's summer company at the Haymarket from 1772 to 1775. He acted unspecified roles in *The Nabob* on 29 June 1772 and *The Rehearsal* on 10 August 1772. In the summer of 1773 he played an unspecified role in *The Devil upon Two Sticks,* Le Brush in *The Register Office,* Headlong in *The Tobacconist,* Hearty in *A Trip to Portsmouth,* and Sir Francis in *The Pantheonites.* His other known roles there included Tressel in *Richard III* on 30 September 1774 and, again, Headlong in *The Tobacconist* on 19 September 1775.

A Mr Ward acted Dr Butts in a performance of *Henry VIII* at China Hall, Rotherhithe, on 25 September 1776. His name was not in the advertisements for any other productions by the company at China Hall that autumn. In his manuscript notes C. Beecher Hogan speculated that the China Hall actor may have been the William Ward who acted Shylock at Doncaster in October 1772 and played at Perth in 1785. A Mr W. Ward was in the Birmingham company during the summer of 1776.

Ward, William   fl. 1774–1799, musician.

A William Ward, son of the late John Ward, was bound apprentice to William Burnett, musician, on 23 February 1774. He became a freeman of the Worshipfull Company of Musicians on 4 December 1782 and was admitted to livery on 14 July 1790. A musician in the "Old Change," he married Frances Maria Ashley, one of a prominent musical family, at St George, Hanover Square, on 11 July 1799.

Ward, William   fl. 1789–1790, pugilist.

At Covent Garden Theatre on 30 December 1788 a sparring match between Humphrys and Death was exhibited in the Irish fair scene of *Aladin,* causing the *Town and Country Magazine* of January 1789 to deplore the degradation of a theatre royal. A similar exhibition was given there on 27 January 1789, this time by the pugilists William Ward and Watson.

Most of the sketchy information concerning William Ward (whose real name was Warr) comes from Pierce Egan's *Boxiana* (1812). He was "Extremely well formed in the breast and arms; and about five feet nine inches, in height; strongly made. . . ." Ward was also an excellent teacher of the "science" of boxing.

In the spring of 1789 Ward was traveling with Watson to see a bout between Humphreys and Mendoza at Stilton, and during a stop at the Bell Inn at Enfield Ward had words with a blacksmith named Swaine, who challenged him. A blow to Swaine's stomach killed him, and Ward was tried at the Old Bailey, convicted of manslaughter, fined one shilling, and imprisoned for three months.

The advertisement for the Royal Circus on 24 July 1790 announced, "For the last time, the art of BOXING will be displayed by Mr. MENDOZA, Mr. WARD, Mr. JACKSON, and Mr. RYAN."

Egan stated that Ward died of consumption and was buried in St Giles churchyard, but he gave no date. Ward had a son, Jack Ward, who was also a pugilist but who made no theatrical appearances.

A match between William Ward and William Wood is depicted in a painting by Reinagle now at Broderick Castle. Ward is shown as a spectator, with Thomas Johnson, John Jackson, and Butcher, all boxers, watching a match between Daniel Mendoza and Richard Humphrey, in an engraving by James Gillray, published by S. W. Fores on 9 October 1790.

Courtesy of Broderick Castle and the National Galleries of Scotland

Match between WILLIAM WARD and William Wood

by Reinagle

Ward, William ₁fl. 1794₁, *musician.*
A William Ward "Junr" was described in Doane's *Musical Directory* of 1794 as a bass (player or singer?), a member of the Handelian Society and participant in their concerts at Westminster Abbey, with an address in Hyde Street, Bloomsbury. The other William Ward listed in Doane's directory that year was probably his father.

Ward, William ₁fl. 1794–1815₁, *musician.*
A William Ward was described in Doane's *Musical Directory* of 1794 as a violinist and horn player and a member of the New Musical Fund, with an address at No 3, Foster Lane, Cheapside. He was still a subscriber to the New Musical Fund in 1805 and probably was the William Ward who served on that fund's Court of Assistants in 1815. The William

Ward "Jun" who was also listed in Doane's directory was probably his son.

Warden, Robert fl. 1672–1673₁, *scenekeeper, doorkeeper.*
The London Stage lists Robert Warden as a scenekeeper in the King's Company at the Lincoln's Inn Fields Theatre in 1672–73. According to Milhous and Hume's *Register of English Theatrical Documents,* Warden was called a "Dorekeeper" in a Lord Chamberlain's warrant of 5 August 1673, but he was grouped with the company's scenekeepers. He could have served in both capacities.

Wardle, Daniel ₁fl. 1749–1759₁, *trumpeter.*
Daniel Wardle was a trumpeter in the King's Musick from 1749 to at least 1759.

Ware, Mr *fl. 1776₁,* *actor.*

On 25 September 1776 a Mr Ware of Deptford played Lord Sand in *Henry VIII* at China Hall, Rotherhithe. He acted Old Philpot in *The Citizen* on 14 October. Presumably Ware was a professional performer, but we cannot be certain.

Ware, Mr *fl. 1788₁,* *dancer.*

On 12 and 16 May 1788 Mr Ware danced Mezzetin in *The Royal Chace* at Covent Garden Theatre.

Ware, Master *b. c. 1787, violoncellist.*

Master Ware, advertised as ten years old, played the violoncello at Drury Lane Theatre on 18 May 1797. He was one of a group of "Lilliputians" about his age who gave a musical entertainment. At the Birmingham Theatre in the summer of 1797 he accompanied Miss Leake on the cello.

Ware, Frederick *b. c. 1775, violinist, violist.*

According to Sainsbury's *Dictionary of Musicians* in 1824, Frederick Ware was born about 1775, served as first tenor player (violist) for many years at Covent Garden Theatre, led concerts in Liverpool and in London at Vauxhall, and about 1824 was first violist at the King's Theatre. In his history of the violin van der Straeten says that Ware was a pupil of Wilhelm Cramer and appeared in public as a violin virtuoso in 1781 (at the age of about six?).

Ware was an instrumental performer in the oratorio at Covent Garden Theatre on 11 March 1791 and was listed in Doane's *Musical Directory* of 1794 as a member of the Professional Concerts and a participant in the Handelian performances in Westmister Abbey. Doane gave Ware's address as No 8, George Court, Princes Street, Soho. Accounts for the Haymarket Theatre at the Folger Shakespeare Library show "Fred" Ware earning 8*s.* 4*d.* nightly at Covent Garden Theatre in 1799–1800. He was in the band at the Haymarket Theatre in the summers from 1807 to 1810. He was presumably the F. Ware who sent the Royal Society of Musicians thanks for donations on 1 June 1834. Frederick was probably related to the other musical Wares of the late eighteenth and early nineteenth century, but

in what way we have not been able to determine.

Ware, George *fl. 1784–c. 1800₁,* *violinist, composer, impresario?*

A Mr Ware, possibly George the violinist, "conducted" concerts of vocal and instrumental music for the poor for the Belfast Charitable Society on 6 May 1784. The band was led by a Mr Byrne, so Ware may have been the organizer. A Mr Ware junior was listed as playing second violin in the Handel Memorial Concerts at Westminster Abbey and the Pantheon in May and June 1784 in London. When he subscribed in 1789 to George Parker's *Life's Painter* he was identified as of the "T. R. London," but which Theatre Royal was meant we do not know. Doane's *Musical Directory* of 1794 lists George Ware junior as a member of the New Musical Fund and a violinist in the Handelian performances at Westminster Abbey; Doane said Ware was a resident of Edinburgh at that time. The *Catalogue of Printed Music in the British Museum* cites a song by George Ware: *Laura,* published about 1800. George Ware's sons, J. Ware and William Henry Ware, both musicians, are noticed below.

Ware, J. *fl. 1788–1800₁,* *violinist.*

Master J. Ware and his brother William Henry Ware, sons of George Ware, played a *concertante* for two violins at Covent Garden Theatre on 28 May 1788. He was, we think, the "younger Master Ware" who composed and compiled the music for *The Giant Defeated,* which was performed on 12 June 1789 at Covent Garden Theatre. J. Ware played in the concert of sacred music at Covent Garden on 28 February 1800.

Ware, [John?]₁ *fl. 1728–1743₁,* *actor.*

A Mr Ware shared a benefit at the Theatre on St Augustine's Back in Bristol on 30 August 1728; *The Provok'd Husband* was performed, but the newspapers did not carry the cast. Ware was in *The Beggar's Opera,* probably about that same time. On 29 March 1729 in London Ware played Temo in *Hurlothrumbo* at the Haymarket Theatre. Between then and 17 June he was seen as Darony in *Hurlothrumbo,* a Shepherd and Sylvan in *The Humours of Harlequin,* and Dash and Cant in *The Beggar's Wed-*

ding. On 10 October 1733 Ware made his first (and evidently last) appearance on the stage of Drury Lane playing George Barnwell in *The London Merchant*. A John Ware acted Axalla in *Tamerlane* in Edinburgh on 5 November 1733. Perhaps the actor we have been following was named John.

On 9 October 1736 Ware appeared as a Dropsical Man in *The Worm Doctor* at Lincoln's Inn Fields under Giffard's management. Between then and 27 November Ware was seen as Andravar in *Mithridates*, Decius in *Cato*, the Prince of Tanais in *Tamerlane*, Scruple in *The Recruiting Officer*, Woodall in *Sauny the Scot*, and Stanmore in *Oroonoko*. Mrs Ware was also in the company.

Ware was at Covent Garden Theatre on 27 June 1738 playing Lodovico in *Othello*, and on 7 July he acted Sir Philip in *A Bold Stroke for a Wife*. He turned up next at Bartholomew Fair on 22 August 1741 playing Prince Brunetto in *The Devil of a Duke*. The last notice of him is at Bartholomew Fair on 23 August 1743, when he played an unspecified role in *The Cruel Uncle*.

Ware, Mrs _[John?_] *fl. 1733–1741_]*, *actress*.

Mrs (John?) Ware played Elvira in *The Spanish Fryar* on 28 September 1733 at Drury Lane, her first appearance on that stage. Where she had acted before is not known. She was on the London stage again on 11 November 1736, playing Lamorce in *The Inconstant* at Lincoln's Inn Fields Theatre. On the thirteenth she was seen as Melinda in *The Recruiting Officer*. On 7 and 17 December Mrs Ware was an Attendant in *Britannia*. She joined John Rich's troupe at Covent Garden Theatre in the 1737–38 season, playing Belinda in *The Fair Quaker of Deal* on 9 November 1737 for her first appearance at that house. That season she also played Margaretta in *Rule a Wife and Have a Wife*, Lady Basset in *The Prodigal Reform'd*, Kate in *1 Henry IV*, Katherine in *Henry V*, Margaret in *1 Henry IV*, Leonora in *The False Friend*, Eurydice in *Oedipus*, and Melinda in *The Recruiting Officer*.

Mrs Ware stayed at Covent Garden through 1740–41 at 3s. 4d. daily, adding to her list such new characters (new at London, at any rate) as Trusty and Myrtilla in *The Provok'd Husband*, Monimia in *Mithridates*, Mademoi-

selle in *The Provok'd Wife*, Mrs Frail in *Love for Love*, and Julia in *The Fatal Marriage*. Her last notice was on 12 May 1741, when she acted Margaretta in *Rule a Wife and Have a Wife*.

Ware, William Henry 1777–1828, *violinist, violist, violoncellist, composer*.

William Henry Ware, the son of George Ware and the brother of J. Ware, was christened at Bromley, Kent, on 20 February 1777, according to information later supplied to the Royal Society of Musicians. As Master Ware he played a *concertante* for two violins with his brother at Covent Garden Theatre on 28 May 1788. On 25 August 1796 at the Birmingham Theatre Ware played a concerto on the violin, and on 3 March 1797 at Covent Garden Theatre in London he was in the orchestra. Ware was back in Birmingham to play a duet with Master Ware (J. Ware, we take it, who was the younger of the two, so far as we can tell) in the summer of 1797.

Ware was recommended for membership in the Royal Society of Musicians on 2 December 1797. He was described as having studied music for upwards of seven years. He was engaged at Covent Garden Theatre but also led the band at the Birmingham Theatre in the summers. Ware had several students, even though he was only 20 years old. He was unanimously elected to the Society on 4 March 1798, after turning 21. He played violin at the Society's St Paul's concert in May and was in the oratorio orchestra at Covent Garden on 8 February 1799. Ware became a Governor of the Royal Society of Musicians on 5 July 1801. He performed at the St Paul's concerts through 1806 and continued active at Covent Garden at least until 1814. At some point he became leader of the band there, and he stated prefatory to one of his compositions that he was the theatre's composer.

During the summers from 1807 on Ware was the leader of the band at the Haymarket Theatre. In 1821–22 he was listed as a member of the band at £5 15s. weekly. The Lord Chamberlain's documents in the Public Record Office reveal that in 1807 Ware was granted a license to perform selections from the *Messiah* at the Haymarket on 30 January, and in 1808 he was given a license to present an oratorio at Covent Garden on 17 February. William Henry may have been the Ware who in 1817 and 1818 played viola in the orchestra at the King's Theatre.

William Henry Ware about 1822 was a music seller and publisher at No 146, Strand. About 1823 he was joined in the business by R. W. Evans.

The Royal Society of Musicians granted Ware ten guineas for medical aid on 7 November 1824, and the Minute Books show a history of physical ailments thereafter. By the summer of 1825 he had temporarily recovered and was engaged at the Haymarket Theatre, but by April 1826 he was again indisposed. Ware was granted funds for medical aid in the years that followed. On 6 July 1828 he was confined to his bed with a "general dropsy," and on 13 October he died. Mrs Ware was granted £12 for his funeral, and she received a widow's allowance from the Society. She lived at least until 1837.

Ware composed or compiled music for a number of light entertainments in the early years of the nineteenth century, mostly for the spectacles at the Royal Circus but some for Covent Garden and the Haymarket. Among his works were music contributed to *The Eclipse; or Harlequin in China, The Golden Farmer, Zamor and Zamora, The Jubilee of 1802, Abellino, Leander and Leonora, The Sorceress of Strozzi, Momus and Mercury, The Magic Sword, Edwin of the Green, Imogen, Werter and Charlotte, King Caesar, Harlequin's Almanac,* and *Harlequin and Mother Goose.* He also composed a trio for two violins and violoncello.

William Henry Ware was probably related to the several other musical Wares of the late eighteenth and early nineteenth centuries. A portrait (23½″ × 19½″) by J. Cawse of W. H. Ware, leader of the band at Covent Garden, in brown coat and yellow vest, was bought at Christie's on 19 February 1954 (lot 130) for three guineas by Hills.

Waring, Mrs *fl. 1732₁, performer?*
Mrs Waring was given benefits at the Haymarket Theatre on 23 March and 10 May 1732. She may have been a performer.

Warmsley. *See* WALMSLEY.

Warneck, Mrs *fl. 1776–1777₁, house servant?*
Widow "Warnuck's" benefit tickets were accepted at Covent Garden Theatre on 11 May 1776. Perhaps she was a house servant or the widow of a house servant. Mrs Warneck shared in benefit tickets again on 15 May 1777.

Warner, Mr *fl. 1748–1749₁, box lobby keeper.*
At Drury Lane Theatre on 16 May 1748 Mr Warner, a box lobby keeper, shared a benefit with four other house servants. The following 17 September the management received £5 14s. from Warner—his arrears after his benefit the previous spring. Warner shared another benefit on 11 May 1749. He may have been related to the Warners who were house servants at the Lincoln's Inn Fields Theatre.

Warner, Mr *fl. 1754₁, violist.*
Mr Warner, identified as Warner junior, played viola in the *Messiah* at the Foundling Hospital in May 1754. He was presumably related to the Warner who also played viola in that performance and in 1758, 1759, and 1760.

Warner, Mr *fl. 1754–1760₁, violist.*
Mr Warner played viola in the *Messiah* at the Foundling Hospital in May 1754, 1758, 1759, and 1760.

Warner, James *fl. 1724₁, lobby doorkeeper.*
The accounts for the Lincoln's Inn Fields Theatre show a payment on account of £3 3s. to James Warner, lobby doorkeeper. He was probably related to John Warner and perhaps to the other theatrical Warners of the period.

Warner, James *d. 1775, actor, singer, manager.*
At Mile End Green, on 30 September 1734, Rako in *Gardener's Wedding* was played by Mr (James) Warner. At Welch Fair in London Spa Fields on 23 August 1735 Warner shared the management of a booth with Yeates and Hind. James Warner may by that time have married Yeates's sister Nancy; they were certainly married by August 1740, when Mrs Warner's performance career as his wife began. She had acted with him in *Gardener's Wedding* in 1734 as Nancy Yeates. At Welch Fair on 31 August 1739 Warner played Gubby in *Merlin,*

By permission of the Board of the British Library

JAMES WARNER

engraving by Delegal, after Parkinson

and at Tottenham Court on 4 August 1740 Warner was Pierrot in *Harlequin Grand Volgi.* On 23 August he was the Clown in *Orpheus and the Death of Eurydice,* and a year later, on 4 August 1741 at Tottenham Court, he acted Slouch in *Harlequin Sorcerer.*

Warner played Vulcan in *The Wrangling Deities* on 22 August at Bartholomew Fair, and he was Addlehead in *Harlequin the Man in the Moon* at Southwark Fair on 14 September. He, Yeates, and Rosoman managed a booth at Mile End Fair in Upper Moorfields on 4 October 1742. On 9 May 1743 at May Fair at a booth he managed with Yeates and Rosoman he played the Clown in *Trick upon Trick.* The booth, located at the upper end of Little Brookfield, was "founded after the Manner of an Amphitheatre, with Boxes on the Stage." Warner, Yeates, and Rosoman managed a booth at Tottenham Court on 4 August 1743, presenting *King Richard III* and *The Harlot's Progress.* On 23 August 1743 at Bartholomew Fair in a booth he managed with Yeates and Rosoman, Warner again acted the Clown in *Trick upon Trick,* and the following 8 Septem-

ber at their Southwark Fair booth he was the Clown in *Harlequin Triumphant.*

On 30 December 1745 at the New Wells, Clerkenwell, Warner played Lockit in *The Beggar's Opera* for his benefit, and on 10 March 1746 at Hickford's Music Room he repeated that role. In April at Sadler's Wells he was the Clown in *The Fortunate Volunteer;* on 25 August at Bartholomew Fair he and Fawkes ran a booth and Warner played Clodpole in *Harlequin Incendiary;* on 8 September at Warner's booth at Southwark Fair he presented *The Fate of Villainy* and *The Imprisonment of Harlequin* (in which he played Clodpole the Clown); and on 20 October at the New Wells, Clerkenwell, Warner was given a benefit. With Yeates and Lee he operated a booth at Bartholomew Fair on 22 August 1747, presenting *The Siege of Troy.* Warner played Trusty in *The Unnatural Parents* at Bartholomew Fair on 24 August 1748 and joined with Lee and the junior and senior Yeateses to present *The Fair Maid of the West* at Southwark Fair on 7 September 1748.

On 16 April 1750 at the New Wells, Clerkenwell, Warner was the Clown in *Harlequin Mountebank,* and at Southwark Fair in September he and Yeates operated a booth and offered *Jephtha's Rash Vow,* with Warner and Bluster. In 1753 Warner was named in Sadler's Wells bills, as he was again in 1755. On 18 September 1755 at Southwark Fair Warner and Yeates's widow presented *The Unnatural Parents* and *The Comical Humours and Adventures of Trusty.* Warner produced *The Intriguing Lover* and *Harlequin's Vagaries* at Southwark Fair in September 1757, and a year later he offered *The Old Widow Bewitched* and *The Taking of Cape Briton.* On 19 and 21 September 1761 at Southwark Fair Warner produced *George for England* and *The Triumphs of Hymen.* On 26 September 1767 Warner was the Clown in *Harlequin Restored* at Sadler's Wells, according to bills in the Percival Collection at the British Library. Disher in *Clowns and Pantomimes* states, "In Garrick's time, the clown of the Wells was Jemmy Warner, notable as Falstaff and Sancho Panza, who kept to the costume of the Merry Andrew." He was named in Sadler's Wells bills through 1772 in such works as *The Harlot's Progress, Cupid's Frolick, The Imprisonment of Harlequin,* and *Trick upon Trick.* Warner died on 10 November 1775, according to the *Morning Chronicle.*

A portrait of James Warner, engraved by J. Delegal after T. Parkinson, was published by the engraver, 1777.

Warner, Mrs James, Nancy, née Yeates
*fl. 1734–1752?*₁,   *actress, singer.*

Miss Nancy Yeates was a Bridesmaid in *Gardener's Wedding* at Mile End Green on 30 October 1734. In the cast as Rako was Mr (James) Warner. The two married not long thereafter. On 4 August 1740 at Tottenham Court at Yeates's booth Mrs Warner was Colombine in *Harlequin Grand Volgi;* Mr Warner was Pierrot. At Yeates's booth at Bartholomew Fair on 23 August Mrs Warner was Colombine in *Orpheus and the Death of Eurydice.* At Bartholomew Fair on 23 August 1743 at the Yeates-Warner-Rosoman booth Mrs Warner was in *The Cruel Uncle.* She sang Lucy in *The Beggar's Opera* at the New Wells, Clerkenwell, on 30 December 1745, and on 16 September 1747 at Southwark Fair she shared a benefit with her brother, "Yeates Jun." On 21 March 1752 at the Haymarket Theatre the bill mentioned a Mrs Warner, but there is no certainty that our subject was the woman named.

Warner, John. *See* WARRINER, JOHN.

Warnuck. *See* WARNECK..

Warr. *See* WARD, WILLIAM   *fl. 1789–1790*₁,

Warrell, A.   *fl. 1784–1824?*₁,   *actor, singer, scene painter?*

Mr Warrell (Warrall, Warwell, Worrell?) sang, along with his wife, at Ranelagh Gardens in the summer of 1784. Mrs Warrell went on to perform at Dublin later in 1784, Doncaster in 1786, York, Bristol, and Bath in 1787, London in 1788, and Brighton in 1789. Warrell presumably accompanied her in those travels, but there is no evidence. He played Vincent in *The Ladies' Frolic* for his wife's benefit at Covent Garden on 1 June 1790. She had been at the theatre since February, but Warrell's name does not appear on any other playbill that season.

Mrs Warrell's contract was renewed for the 1790–91 season. Perhaps Warrell sang in some choruses, for the Covent Garden account shows that on 13 June 1791 he was allowed benefit tickets. In the summer of 1792 both Warrells were acting at Brighton. In January 1793 the fortunes of the family—by then the Warrells had five children—improved somewhat when both the elder Warrells were hired at Edinburgh's Theatre Royal, Shakespeare Square. As was always the case with the Warrells, the wife was more prominent, but the bills that season show her husband in a few respectable tertiary roles: Brabantio in *Othello,* Catalpo in *Columbus,* Don Diego in *The Padlock,* the Duke in *The Merchant of Venice,* Robert in *The Haunted Tower,* Tomlins in *The Man of the World,* and Wolf in *The School for Wives.*

It was at Edinburgh, very likely, that Thomas Wignell recruited the Warrells, with many of their fellows of the 1793 season, for service at the new Chestnut Street Theatre in Philadelphia. But the yellow fever raged in the city, and the theatre could not operate. The company began to play in Annapolis instead.

The new house in Philadelphia finally opened on 17 February 1794, and that season five of the seven Warrells—Mr and Mrs Warrell and the three boys, James, Harry, and Thomas—appeared there either acting or dancing. (James and Thomas opened a dance academy in Richmond, Virginia, in 1800. One of the Warrells—either our subject or one of his sons—may have been the Worrall who painted scenery at the Federal Street Theatre in Boston from 1808 until about 1824.)

Our Mr Warrell (who is given the initial A. for his baptismal name by Alan S. Downer in his edition of *The Memoirs of John Durang*) was constantly employed at the Chestnut Street Theatre in Philadelphia past the end of the eighteenth century, though, as Seilhamer judged, he "had few pretensions as an actor. . . ." His roles, virtually all comic ones, were usually walk-ons or ones in which his lines were few, as the 30 parts he acted in his first season show: one of the Banditti in *The Castle of Andalusia,* an Officer in *Isabella,* a Rustic in *Rosina,* Justice Benbow in *The Flitch of Bacon,* Justice Guttle in *The Lying Valet,* John in *The Jealous Wife,* a Sailor in *The Sailor's Landlady,* Goodwill in *The Virgin Unmask'd,* Sir William Meadows in *Love in a Village,* the Landlord in *The Son-in-Law,* a Coachman in *The Rivals,* Chicane in *The Agreeable Surprise,*

Bernardo in *Hamlet*, Fronte in *La Forêt Noire*, Duke Frederick in *As You Like It*, Friar John in *Romeo and Juliet*, Somerset in *The Battle of Hexham*, Alonzo in *The Mourning Bride*, Stephano in *The Merchant of Venice*, Siward in *Macbeth*, Pantaloon in *Harlequin Shipwrecked*, the Master of Horse in *The Critic*, Formal in *How to Grow Rich*, Alguazil in *The Wonder*, Sir Jasper in *The Citizen*, the Notary in *The Spanish Barber*, Cornelius in *Cymbeline*, Dr Camphire in *The Devil upon Two Sticks*, the Bailiff in *Ways and Means*, and Antonio in *The Tempest*.

Warrell, Mrs A. *fl.* 1769?–1799₁, actress, singer.

The Covent Garden Theatre accounts show a payment of £10 10s. to a Mrs "Warwell" for "walking 12 nights in Man & Wife." *Man and Wife* had been presented frequently between 7 October 1769 and March 1770. Probably she was Mrs (A.) Warrell, who sang with Burton at Finch's Grotto Gardens about 1775 and with her husband at Ranelagh Gardens in the summer of 1784.

Mrs Warrell made her debut at Smock Alley Theatre in Dublin on 13 December 1785, according to information compiled by W. S. Clark. She was there without her husband, so far as available information shows; and she cannot have stayed more than a season. Tate Wilkinson, in *The Wandering Patentee* (1795), recalled that in September 1786 "Mrs. Warrell, a singer from Manchester (since known at Covent Garden) came for a year and piped in Rosetta" in *Love in a Village*. She played at Wakefield, Doncaster, Hull, York, and Leeds on Wilkinson's circuit as Patty in *The Maid of the Mill*, Nora in *The Poor Soldier*, the title role in *Rosina*, Clorinda in *Robin Hood*, Patty in *The Gentle Shepherd*, Jessica in *The Merchant of Venice*, Celia in *Fontainebleau*, Signora Figurante in *Gretna Green*, Leonora in *The Padlock*, Daphne in *Midas*, Lorenza in *The Castle of Andalusia*, Viola in *The Strangers at Home* (for her benefit on 26 December 1786 at Hull), the title role in *Queen Mab*, Actea in *The Maid of the Oaks*, Sylvia in *Cymon*, Juno in *The Golden Pippin*, Eliza Greville in *The Flitch of Bacon*, Celia in *As You Like It* (for her shared benefit at York on 10 May 1787), and Constantia in *The Man of the World*.

Mrs Warrell left York on 25 May 1787 and signed to a split season at the Orchard Street Theatre in Bath (her debut there being on 20 October 1787) and the Jacob's Wells Theatre at Bristol.

But London was attractive, and when Jack Palmer defiantly challenged the patent houses by erecting the Royalty Theatre, Mrs Warrell was one of the country actors who responded to his call for performers. We do not know all of her parts at the Royalty (Seilhamer says that "her first London appearance" was "at the Royalty Theatre, July 15ᵗʰ, 1788, in the title-role of the little piece called 'Poll of Plympton'."). The Royalty enterprise was defeated long before the summer of 1789, when Mrs Warrell joined the company at Brighton. Her husband was also of the Brighton troupe and may have accompanied her on her Dublin, York, Manchester, and Bristol-Bath excursions, though we have no evidence.

Mrs Warrell was hailed in the bills as "from the Theatre Royal, Bath," when she made her first appearance at Covent Garden Theatre singing Rosa in *Fontainebleau* on 18 February 1790. Thereafter that season she represented Eliza in *The Flitch of Bacon*, Lorenza in *The Castle of Andalusia*, Diana in *Lionel and Clarissa*, Rachel in *The Ladies' Frolic* (on 1 June, when her husband appeared as Vincent in that piece), and Rosetta in *Love in a Village*.

Mrs Warrell returned to Covent Garden in the 1790–91 season, adding to her repertoire Angelina in *Robin Hood*, Mrs Tokay in *The Wives Revenged*, Norah in *The Poor Soldier*, unspecified "Vocal Parts" in *The Picture of Paris*, *The Widow of Malabar*, and *The Maid of the Oaks*, and a "Principal Character" in *Primrose Green*. In addition, during both seasons, Mrs Warrell lent her voice to occasional entr'acte entertainments like the curious *Nicketerotion at the Meeting of Antony and Cleopatra* and the "Solemn Dirge" for Juliet Capulet's funeral. At the time of her benefit, 4 June 1791, Mrs Warrell, and presumably her family, lived at No 48, Carey Street, Lincoln's Inn Fields.

Mr and Mrs Warrell and their five children were probably somewhere on a provincial circuit in 1791–92. By the winter of 1792–93, they were at the Edinburgh theatre, where both the elder Warrells acted. In addition to her former roles, Mrs Warrell performed Araminta in *The Young Quaker*, Emily in *The French Invasion*, Jenny in *The Bonny Lass of*

Harvard Theatre Collection

MRS WARRELL

artist unknown

in *The Castle of Andalusia*. She was used very sparingly her first two seasons at Philadelphia but had good roles, many of which she had played at London. In later seasons she played somewhat more frequently. There is no record of her performing after the season of 1799–1800.

Roles that Mrs Warrell added to her repertoire at Chestnut Street were Lucinda in *Love in a Village*, Clarinda in *Robin Hood*, Louisa in *The Farmer*, Cecilia in *The Son-in-Law*, Louisa in *The Duenna*, Lucy in *The Embargo*, a Bacchante in *Comus*, and Zoriana in *Slaves in Algiers* in 1794; Flora in *Hob in the Well* in 1794–95; Molly Maybush in *The Farmer*, Jenny in *The Deserter*, and Alinda in *The Sicilian Romance* in 1795–96; Cowslip in *The Agreeable Surprise*, Donna Isabella in *The Wonder*, Emma in *Peeping Tom of Coventry*, Zorayda in *The Mountaineers*, Eliza in *The Flitch of Bacon*, Mrs Page in *The Merry Wives of Windsor*, Jessica in *The Merchant of Venice*, Ismene in *The Sultan*, Clara in *The Adopted Child* and Caroline in *The Dead Alive* in 1796–97; and Angelica in *The Shipwreck*, Urganda in *Cymon and Sylvia*, Mrs Manners in *The American in London*, Juletta in *The Spectre*, and Josephine in *The Children in the Wood* in 1797–98.

In 1798–99, Mrs Warrell added to her stock of roles Phoebe in *Rosina*, Fanny in *Lock and Key*, Sally in *Thomas and Sally*, Lucy in *The Beggar's Opera*, Janetta in *False and True*, Constantia in *The Mysteries of the Castle*, Lady Priory in *Wives as They Were*, Queen Dollallola in *Tom Thumb the Great*, Sally Shamrock in *The Shipwreck*, and Irene in *Blue Beard*. At the Chestnut Street Theatre on 30 December 1799, with President Adams in attendance, Mrs Warrell was one of four singers assisting in a *Monody on the Death of the much lamented the late Lieutenant General of the Armies of the United States*, George Washington.

A portrait of Mrs Warrell by an unknown engraver is in the Harvard Theatre Collection.

Leith, Jenny in *The Highland Reel*, Lady Eleanor in *The Haunted Tower*, Leonora in *The Padlock*, Polly in *The Beggar's Opera*, Signora Figurante in *Gretna Green*, and a Singing Witch in *Macbeth*.

Probably while the Warrells were at Edinburgh, they were recruited by Thomas Wignell for the new Chestnut Street Theatre in Philadelphia. The elder Warrells and four of their five children—James, Harry, Thomas, and a daughter whose first name is not known—set sail with some 50 other passengers for America. (Their elder daughter Eliza had remained in England, where she would perform as Mrs William Atkins after her marriage in 1796.)

When the travelers' ship arrived in the Delaware River, they learned that Philadelphia had been emptied by an epidemic of yellow fever. The company was diverted to Annapolis and points south until winter weather reduced the incidence of sickness. When the new Chestnut Street Theatre opened on 17 February 1794, Mrs Warrell played Victoria

Warrell, Eliza. *See* ATKINS, MRS WILLIAM.

Warren, Mr *[fl. 1703?]*, dresser, stand-in.

In his *General History* the prompter W. R. Chetwood retailed a story "which I gather'd from that Stage Chronicle, Mr. John Bowman." Boman (or Bowman) was an actor of the

Restoration and early eighteenth century who was especially good in comic parts, so we should perhaps be wary of taking his anecdote too literally. It concerned the dresser Warren in a performance of *The Fair Penitent* during its first season, 1703 (though Chetwood thought the play had been done in 1699):

> *Lothario,* after he is kill'd by *Altamont* in the 4th Act, lies dead by Proxy in the 5th, raised on a Bier Covered with Black by the Property-man, and the Face whitened by the Barber, the Coat and Perriwig generally filled by one of the Dressers. Most of the capital Actors in the establish'd Theatres have generally a dresser to themselves, tho' they are paid by the Manager, to be ready, on all Occasions, for Stage-guards, Attendance, &c.
>
> Mr. [George] *Powell* played Lothario, and one *Warren,* his Dresser, claimed a Right of lying for his Master, and performing the dead Part of *Lothario,* which he proposed to act to the best Advantage; tho' *Powell* was ignorant of the Matter. The Fifth Act began, and went on, as usual, with Applause; but, about the Middle of the distressful Scene, Powell called aloud for his Man *Warren,* who as loudly replied, from the Bier on the Stage, *Here, Sir! Powell* (who, as I said before, was ignorant of the Part his Man was doing) repeated, without Loss of Time, *Come this Moment, you Son of a Whore! or I'll break all the Bones in your Skin. Warren* knew his hasty Temper; therefore, without any Reply, jump'd off, with all his Sables about him, which, unfortunately, were tied fast to the Handles of the Bier, and dragg'd after him. But this was not all; the Laugh and Roar began in the Audience, till it frighten'd poor *Warren* so much, that, with the Bier at his Tail, he threw down *Calista* (Mrs. *Barry*), and overwhelm'd her with the Table, Lamp, Book, Bones, together with all the Lumber of the Charnel-house. He tugg'd, till he broke off his Trammels, and made his Escape; and the Play, at once, ended with immoderate Fits of Laughter: Even the grave Mr. *Betterton*
>
> Smil'd in the Tumult, and enjoy'd the Storm.
>
> But he would not let the *Fair Penitent* be play'd any more that Season, till poor *Warren's* Misconduct was something forgot.

The first known performance date for the play was in May 1703. During the rest of the year it is known to have been presented on 8 June. We have no way of knowing whether Warren was our subject's surname or Christian name.

Warren, Mr *fl.* 1722–1728?[1], *actor.*
A Mr Warren acted Bellmour in *Jane Shore* at the Haymarket Theatre on 28 June 1722.

Perhaps he was the Mr Warren who acted with Lewis's company at St Augustine's Back, Bristol, in August 1728; that Warren played in *The Beggar's Opera* and *The Beaux' Stratagem.*

Warren, Mr *fl.* 1746[1], *actor.*
A Mr Warren played Golindo in *The Fate of Villainy* in Warner's Booth on the Bowling Green at the Southwark Fair on 8 September 1746.

Warren, Mr *fl.* 1759–1771?[1], *singer.*
A Mr Warren was a chorus singer at Covent Garden Theatre from 1759–60 through 1762–63, and perhaps earlier and later. On 10 December 1759 he was listed in the bills as one of the Recruits in *The Fair,* a pantomime that was repeated the next night. On 13 October 1761 and several times thereafter he again appeared in *The Fair,* and he sang as an extra in *Comus* on 11 November and in *The Coronation* on 13 November 1761, receiving 5s. for each appearance. The next season his assignments included one of the Harvester extras in *Harlequin Sorcerer,* revived at Covent Garden on 1 November 1762. His name appeared in no other Covent Garden records after that season.

Possibly he was the Mr Warren who appeared with Miss Ray and Joah Bates at William Bewley's estate at Houghton in September 1771 to sing a large collection of catches and canons they had brought with them. But that person was more likely the composer Edmund Thomas Warren, who edited and published collections of catches, glees, canons, and motets and madrigals between 1763 and 1790. That composer seems not to have performed on the London stage, nor did Thomas Warren, another composer, who in 1763 was secretary to the Kit Cat Club and lived in Great Queen Street, Lincoln's Inn Fields.

Warren, Mr *fl.* 1775–1776[1], *actor.*
A Mr Warren, announced as making his first appearance on that stage, acted Brazen in *The Recruiting Officer* at Richmond, Surrey, on 22 July 1775. His name also appeared in the Richmond bills in August 1776.

Warren, Mr *fl.* 1784[1], *violist.*
A Mr Warren, senior, was listed by Dr Burney as one of the "tenor players" (violists) in

the Handel Memorial Concerts at Westminster Abbey and the Pantheon in May and June 1784. Probably he was related (perhaps the father) to William Warren (d. 1839), a violinist in those concerts who was a musician at Drury Lane Theatre and a member of the Royal Society of Musicians.

Warren, Miss ₁*fl.* 1747₁, *actress.*

A Miss Warren, announced as making her first appearance on any stage, acted Cherry in *The Stratagem* at Drury Lane Theatre on 26 January 1747. Her name did not appear again in the London bills.

Warren, John ₁*fl.* 1744–1745₁, *proprietor.*

After the death of Francis Forcer the younger in April 1743, the next known proprietor of Sadler's Wells was John Warren, whose management of that pleasure garden and spa began in May 1744. Unlike his predecessor, Warren was an unsuccessful entrepreneur. The standards at the Wells were so far lowered by May 1745 that the establishment was included in a list of places condemned by the authorities and soon afterward was closed. When Sadler's Wells reopened in February 1746 it was under the management of Thomas Rosoman.

Warren, Maria, later Mrs King?, Mrs Somers, and Mrs Nicholas ₁*fl.* 1726–1737₁, *actress, singer, dancer.*

Miss (sometimes Mrs) Maria Warren was a member of Rich's company at Lincoln's Inn Fields Theatre by 17 May 1726, when she shared a benefit. She was on that theatre's paylist and free list in 1726–27. On 17 May 1727 she sang in English and Italian and shared a benefit with three other performers. That season she acted Rose in *The Recruiting Officer* on 11 March 1727, offered songs on 13 March, played the Boor's Wife in *The Loves of Damon and Chemene* on 20 March, and performed a Witch in *Harlequin a Sorcerer,* replacing Mrs Chambers on 7 June 1727.

At Lincoln's Inn Fields in 1727–28 Miss Warren sang specialty numbers on occasion and appeared as Jenny Melton in *The Cobler's Opera* on 26 April 1728. When she replaced Miss Fenton as Polly Peachum in *The Beggar's Opera* on 19 June 1728, "To the great Surprize

Henry E. Huntington Library and Art Gallery

MARIA WARREN(?)

artist unknown

of the Audience," reported the *Craftsman* on 22 June, "she was very much applauded." On 2 July 1728 she acted Lucy in *Tunbridge Walks* and also sang "Gentle Sighs." In 1728–29 she again played Polly and Jenny Melton and danced as a Nymph in *Apollo and Daphne* on 23 November 1728. On 25 April 1729, when she performed Polly, she shared a benefit with Mrs Vincent.

Fogg's Journal of 22 February 1729 reported that "Miss Maria Warren who had succeeded Miss Fenton as Polly" had lately married "a Mr King, who possessed an Estate of £1200 a year." Either that paper gave her husband's name incorrectly or Miss Warren had managed another marriage by 12 January 1730, for on that date the *Daily Post,* erroneously reporting her death "a few days since in the country," gave her husband's name as "Nicholas" and described him as a gentleman of fortune but "under age."

Miss Warren, or Mrs Nicholas, was, however, far from dead, though she does seem to have given up the stage. On 15 October 1736 the *Daily Post* reported that she was in trouble: "Yesterday Miss Warren the late Polly Peachum who a few years since married Mr. Nicholas, a Gentleman of Fashion in the West of England, was committed to Newgate for having two husbands." She had been brought to the Sessions House but gained a delay of trial till the next sessions, "when she would produce witnesses of her innocence." She was ordered to find bail, which presumably she did. The trial was set for Thursday, 9 December 1736, when, the *Daily Post* reported two days later, she was tried at the Old Bailey "for marrying Mr. Nicholas, her former husband, Mr. Somers, being living; and after a long trial She was acquitted." The sequence of Miss Warren's mates was evidently Mr King (if he existed), Mr Somers, and then Mr Nicholas. The press reported that Miss Warren was "sister to the famous Mrs Mapp," the "Bone-Setter of Epsom."

On 7 September 1737, she returned to Lincoln's Inn Fields for a special entertainment honoring the Ambassador Extraordinary from the Emperor of Morocco. The mainpiece was *Othello,* evidently considered an appropriate choice. There was also "Singing in Italian and English by Mrs. Nicholas (late Miss Warren) being the first time of her appearance on the stage since her performing the part of Polly in *The Beggar's Opera,* eight years ago."

The song *'Twas down in a Meadow I chanc'd for to pass* was published sometime in the late 1720s as sung by Miss Warren at Lincoln's Inn Fields Theatre.

A portrait by an unknown artist, in the Huntington Library, called in the art files Miss Warren and an actress "at the time of George III," may be of Maria Warren.

Warren, Mrs Thomas, Ann, née Powell, later Mrs John Martindale, *c. 1761– 1821, actress.*

Ann Powell, one of the two daughters of the excellent actor William Powell (d. 1769) and his wife Elizabeth Powell (later Mrs John Abraham Fisher), was born late in 1760 or sometime in 1761. In November 1780, their mother having died earlier that year, Ann and her sister Elizabeth Mary were under the guardianship of John Morgan, the administrator of their father's estate; but in May 1782,

Courtesy of Thomas Agnew

ANN (Mrs Thomas) WARREN

by Romney

both young women having attained the age of 21, administration was granted to them.

Possibly Ann was the Miss Powell who acted at China Hall, Rotherhithe, in the summer of 1777, playing Miss Neville in *She Stoops to Conquer* on 2 July, Desdemona in *Othello* on 21 July, and the Mask'd Lady in *A Bold Stroke for a Wife* on 23 July. But a year later, on 1 July 1778, "A young gentlewoman," announced as making her first appearnace "on any stage," acted Miss Neville; she was identified in the *Morning Chronicle* next day as "Miss Powel."

In October 1780, while still a minor, Ann Powell married Thomas Warren of the Inner Temple. (Her husband was not the actor H. P. Warren, as has often been stated; that Irish performer married at Sligo in 1805 Miss E. Powell, also an Irish player, who was not a daughter of William Powell.) Again advertised as a young lady "who never appeared on any stage," Ann acted Elvira in *Percy* at Covent Garden Theatre on 10 December 1785. A notation on J. P. Kemble's copy of the playbill identifies her as Mrs Warren, and Reed's "Notitia Dramatica" in the British Library confirms that she was William Powell's daughter. On 4 February 1786, now called Mrs Warren, she acted Lady Townly in *The Provok'd Husband,* and on 10 February (for the benefit of Mrs Abington, who played Scrub that night) she acted Mrs Sullen in *The Beaux' Stratagem.* Her other roles that season at Covent Garden included Lady Bell Bloomer in *Which Is the Man?* on 16 February, Lady Gentle in *The Lady's Last Stake* on 4 March, Indiana in *The Conscious Lovers* on 11 March, Rosetta in *The Foundling* on 8 April, Almeria in *The Mourning Bride* on 19 April, Cecilia in *The Chapter of Accidents* on 3 May, Lady Racket in *Three Weeks after Marriage* on 4 May, Mrs Sullen again on 6 May, and Olivia in *A Bold Stroke for a Husband* on 26 May 1786. In the *New Rosciad* (1786), Leigh wrote of her:

Born with one spark of Powell's deathless flame
. . . .
With natural grace, and elegance of mien,
She calls down plaudits in each sprightly scene;
In More's Elvira she superior shone,
And all her father's feelings were her own.

After that season, however, Mrs Warren did not reappear on the boards of a London theatre, though she may have acted in the provinces. She married John Martindale on 8 August 1795 at St George, Hanover Square. He became a proprietor of Covent Garden Theatre through her one-eighth share inherited from her father. Martindale, who it is said kept a clubhouse in St James's Street, made her a widow again. She died in a house in King Street in September 1821. In 1811 she had provided funds to repair and beautify her father's monument in Bristol Cathedral; on the monument she is identified as "Ann Martindale, youngest daughter of the deceased William Powell." Her elder sister Elizabeth Mary Powell married George White, a clerk to the House of Commons. Through her, White also became a one-eighth shareholder in Covent Garden Theatre. The Whites' two daughters married a Mr Willet and a Captain Forbes, respectively.

Mrs Ann Warren was pictured as Helena in *All's Well that Ends Well* in an engraving by Thornthwaite, after M. Brown, published as a plate to *Bell's Shakespeare,* 1786. The original drawing by M. Brown was sold at Christie's

By permission of the Trustees of the British Museum

ANN (Mrs Thomas) WARREN, as Helena
engraving by Thornthwaite, after Brown

on 27 March 1793 (lot 95) and was bought by Gretton; its present location is unknown. An engraving by J. Scott, after T. Stothard, of her as Rosetta and Joseph George Holman as Belmont in *The Foundling* was published as a plate to the *New English Theatre,* 1786. She is not known to have played either Helena or Rosetta in London. When Miss Powell, she was pictured in a family portrait by J. H. Mortimer in 1788; others included are her sister Elizabeth Mary Powell, her father William Powell, and her mother Elizabeth. That painting is in the Garrick Club (No 13), and is reproduced in this *Dictionary,* 12: 132. A portrait of Ann Warren by George Romney (38½" × 30½"), painted about 1786–87, was in the collection of Capt T. A. Tatton in 1928. It was sold at Christie's in the Sulley sale on 1 June 1934 and was bought by Wells. The portrait was with Thomas Agnew in 1969, but its present whereabouts is unknown. It was engraved by C. H. Hodges.

Warren, William   *d. 1839, violinist.*

When William Warren was recommended on 5 January 1777 for membership in the Royal Society of Musicians, he was described as having been a professional musician for seven years (the usual prescription) and a single man. He was admitted on 4 May 1777. He was probably the Mr Warren who was listed by Dr Burney as one of the second violinists in the Handel Memorial Concerts at Westminster Abbey and the Pantheon in May and June 1784. The Mr Warren, senior, who played tenor in those concerts was probably related, perhaps as his father.

Warren's name was on the list to play at the annual concerts given in May by the Royal Society of Musicians at St Paul's for most years between 1785 and 1797. In 1794 Doane's *Musical Directory* gave his address as No 7, Stangate Street, Lambeth, and described him as a violinist, a member of the Royal Society of Musicians, a player in the oratorios and the Handelian concerts at the Abbey, and engaged at Drury Lane Theatre. Warren's name is found on the music list of Drury Lane in 1794 and again in 1801; in the latter year he earned £2 per week. His name appeared in the advertisements for the oratorios at Covent Garden Theatre in March 1794 and February 1795.

The files of the Royal Society of Musicians record that William Warren died in March 1839. Possibly this violinist was related to the William Warren who was organist of Christ Church Cathedral at Dublin from 1805 to 1816 and of St Patrick's Cathedral there in 1827 and 1828. In 1809 that William Warren was reported to be "the best organist in the empire." His name appears frequently in the Minute Books of the Irish Musical Fund between 1795 and 1823, and he served that society as president in 1818.

Warren, Mrs William the second. *See* WIGNELL, MRS THOMAS ANNE.

Warrenbergh. *See* WOREMBERG.

Warriner, John   *fl. 1725–1738₁, house servant.*

The John Warner, gallery boxkeeper, named in the Lincoln's Inn Fields accounts on 7 January 1725 for a payment on account of £55 *s.* was surely the Mr Warriner (sometimes Warrener) of later years. Warriner was named in benefit bills at Lincoln's Inn Fields and (after 1732) Covent Garden as a boxkeeper through the spring of 1738.

Warten, Mr   *fl. 1794₁,   singer.*

Doane's *Musical Directory* of 1794 lists Mr Warten of Lichfield as a bass who sang in the Handel concerts at Westminster Abbey in London.

Warton, Mrs John. *See* MAHON, MISS M.

Warwell, Mr   *fl. 1732–1734₁,   actor, singer.*

Mr Warwell played Macheath in *The Beggar's Opera* on 10 March 1732 at the Haymarket Theatre. On the seventeenth he was Father Aubany in *The Wanton Jesuit.* At Drury Lane Theatre in 1733–34 he played a Countryman in *Harlequin Doctor Faustus,* a Chinese Guard in *Cephalus and Procris,* the Inchanter in *The Country Revels,* and a Satyr in *Cupid and Psyche.* On 5 April 1734 at the Haymarket he acted Fairlove in *Don Quixote in England,* and at Lincoln's Inn Fields on 17 May he was supposed to share a benefit with Hewson, but "a Disturbance . . . entirely hinder'd the Performance of the Play [*The Stratagem*]."

Warwell, Mrs. *See* WARREL, MRS.

Warwhick. *See* WARWICK.

Warwick, Mr   *fl. 1793–1814₁,   doorkeeper.*

The doorkeeper Warwick was named in Covent Garden Theatre accounts from 1793–94 through 1813–14, usually at 12*s.* weekly but occasionally at 15*s.* weekly. He was listed in benefit bills from 14 June 1794 on. *The London Stage* cites him also as Warwhick.

Warwick, Mrs   *fl. 1735–1760₁,   charwoman.*

A female Warwick senior was a charwoman at Covent Garden Theatre in 1735–36 and was paid 12*d.* daily for 179 days, according to the accounts transcribed by R. J. Smith at the British Library. Perhaps the same woman was the Mrs Warwick, charwoman, earning 1*s.*

daily at Covent Garden on 22 September 1760. She may have been Susan Warwick's mother or sister.

Warwick, Francis   *fl. 1794₁,   singer.*
Doane's *Musical Directory* of 1794 lists Francis Warwick, alto, as singing in the oratorios at Drury Lane Theatre and Westminster Abbey. Warwick's address was No 10, Red Lion Court, Fleet Street.

Warwick, Susan   *d. 1736?, charwoman, performer.*
When *The Necromancer* was presented at Covent Garden Theatre on 1 October 1736 there was a terrible accident involving Susan Warwick, one of the house servants (a charwoman) who was also a supernumerary. The *Daily Post and General Advertiser* on 2 October reported the event:

Last Night in the entertainment of Dr Faustus . . . when the Machine wherein were Harlequin, the Miller's Wife, the Miller and his Man, was got up to the full Extent of its flying, one of the Wires which held up the hind part of the Car broke first, and then the other broke, and the Machine, and all the People in it fell down upon the Stage; by which unhappy Accident the young Woman [Susan Warwick] who personated the Miller's Wife had her Thigh broke, and her Kneepan shatter'd, and was otherways very much bruised, the Harlequin had his Head bruised, and his Wrist strained; the Miller broke his Arm; and the Miller's Man had his Scull so fractured that his Life is despaired of.

The *Daily Advertiser* on 4 October reported that James Todd, who had been the Miller's Man, "died in a miserable manner. Susan Warwick, who represented the Miller's Wife, lies at the point of Death at the infirmary at Hyde-Park Corner." The two others "are like to recover." The four were house servants standing in for the actors Rich, Nivelon, Salway, and Mrs Moreau. We do not know if Susan Warwick survived the accident.

Our subject was probably the female "Warwick Junior" cited in the Covent Garden accounts in 1735–36 as a charwoman earning 12*d.* daily for 179 days. She may have been the daughter or sister of a second female Warwick charwoman, called in the accounts Warwick senior.

Warwick, William   *fl. 1794₁,   flutist.*
Doane's *Musical Directory* of 1794 lists William Warwick as a flutist who belonged to the Choral Society and the Cecilian Society. He lived at No 2, Charter House Square.

Wasborough, J.   *fl. 1794₁,   violinist.*
Doane's *Musical Directory* of 1794 lists J. Wasborough of College Green, Bristol, as a violinist who played in the Handel performances at Westminster Abbey in London. Doane also lists Wasborough Jr. a violoncellist, but the younger man did not perform in London. A Mr "Washbrough" had played the harpsichord at the Assembly Room in Bristol on 23 November 1776 and may have been a relative.

Wasell, John   *fl. 1739–1744₁,   musician.*
On 28 August 1739 John Wasell became one of the original subscribers to the Royal Society of Musicians. He was still active in 1744.

Washbourne, William   *fl. 1699–1727₁,   singer?*
The Lord Chamberlain issued a warrant on 20 June 1699 swearing William Washbourne (or Washburn) a Gentleman of the Chapel Royal extraordinary (without fee). Washbourne was named in warrants many times through 2 February 1727, but we do not know when he began his salaried appointment. Most of the warrants citing him concern his attendance on the monarch at Windsor, Hampton Court, or Kensington. The warrants do not give the amount of money Washbourne was paid for such attendance, but the number of days is cited. He was usually away from London from one to four months almost every year. Since his name was regularly grouped with singers, he was probably a member of the choir.

Wass, Robert   *d. 1764, singer.*
Robert Wass may have been the Wass who was in the chorus of the Funeral Anthem for Queen Caroline on 17 December 1737. On 13 March 1744 Robert Wass was sworn a Gentleman of the Chapel Royal in place of Anselm Bailey, who had resigned. Wass was admitted

to the Royal Society of Musicians on 3 April 1748.

During the 1750s, Wass, a bass, made regular appearances in various London concerts and oratorios. His first appearance in Handelian oratorios at Covent Garden Theatre in 1752, according to Winton Dean in the *New Grove*, was as Caleb in *Joshua* on 14 February, though no cast was listed in the advertisements. He sang Lebul in *Jephtha* at Covent Garden on 26 February 1752, a part specifically composed for him by Handel, and he delivered Handel's song "Honour and Arms" at the King's Theatre on 24 March 1752. Other oratorios in which he sang leading bass parts were *Alexander's Feast* on 11 February 1754 and *Acis and Galatea* on 2 February 1758, both at the Haymarket Theatre. Probably he sang in other Handelian pieces at the several theatres: *Hercules* in 1752, *Samson* in 1752 through 1754, *Joshua* and *Deborah and Saul* in 1754, *Athalia* in 1756, and *Solomon and Susannah* in 1759.

He performed in concerts at the Great Room in Dean Street, Soho, and in the *Messiah* at the Foundling Hospital, receiving for the latter £1 11s. 6d. in 1754, £1 1s. 6d. in 1758, and 10s. 6d. in 1759. Wass also sang regularly in the choirs of St Paul's and Westminster Abbey. In 1761–62 he was paid five shillings per week as a chorus singer in performances of *The Coronation* at Covent Garden Theatre.

Provincial appearances by Wass in concerts and oratorios included Oxford in 1754, Bristol in August 1758, Birmingham in October 1759, and the Meetings of the Three Choirs Festivals in 1761 and 1762.

Robert Wass died on 27 March 1764. In his will drawn on 18 March 1764 he described himself as of the parish of St Clement Danes and one of the vicars choral of St Paul's Cathedral. To his second wife Elizabeth Wass he left all his household furniture and goods and his clothes (to be made use of by his son Samuel "as occasion may require"). The rest and residue of his estate he bequeathed to his son Samuel Wass and his daughter Ann Wass, "minors the natural and lawful children by a former wife of the said deceased." Simon Wass, the testator's brother, witnessed the will, in which Henry Wass of Lad Lane, Robert's cousin, was named executor. By the time the will was proved on 8 October 1764, Robert's widow Elizabeth had died, and administration was renounced by Henry Wass, and then also by Samuel Wass, the uncle and guardian of Robert's surviving minor children Samuel and Ann. Administration, therefore, was granted to one Ann Paterson, a widow, and "a creditrix of the said deceased." (Possibly she was Robert Wass's first wife, who after a separation from him may have married a Mr Paterson.)

Waterer, Mr ₍*fl.* 1795–1819₎, *house servant.*

Mr Waterer was first mentioned in the Drury Lane accounts and benefit bills in 1795–96, when he was listed among the house personnel. He was cited regularly through 1818–19, by which time he was earning £1 10s. weekly. He was working as a boxkeeper in 1800, a ticket taker in 1806, in the two-shilling gallery in 1811–12, and as pit money-taker in 1812–13. Mrs Waterer was mentioned in the accounts in June 1802, but her duties were not specified.

Waterhouse, Master ₍*fl.* 1792₎, *actor, singer.*

Master Waterhouse played an unspecified role in *The Enchanted Wood*, a musical entertainment that had its premiere at the Haymarket Theatre on 25 July 1792. Perhaps he was the son of the actor William Waterhouse.

Waterhouse, William ₍*fl.* 1783–1790₎, *actor, singer.*

William Waterhouse made his debut at the Capel Street Theatre in Dublin on 18 December 1783 as an unspecified character in *Gibraltar*, a new comic opera by Giordani. The advertisement in the Dublin *Freeman's Journal* for 16–18 December announced that he was making his first appearance on any stage. In 1784–85 and 1785–86 he acted at the Crow Street Theatre in Dublin and was at Cork in August 1785. During the winter of early 1786 Waterhouse was engaged at Liverpool, where he shared a benefit with Hammerton that failed to make the modest house charges of £35. From 1786–87 through 1788–89 Waterhouse was engaged at the Orchard Street Theatre in Bath and at Bristol playing minor parts. During those years he also acted at Manchester in March 1787 and at Brighton in the summer of 1788.

Announced as from the Crow Street Theatre, Waterhouse made his first appearance at the Haymarket Theatre on 26 June 1790 as Macheath in *The Beggar's Opera*. The *European Magazine* that month reported that his manner and figure were genteel, but "his acting wanted force and animation." He possessed a deep tenor voice, yet "he seemed to have an impediment in his speech." On the whole, he was favorably received. His second role was Don Garcia in the premiere of Scawen's comic opera *New Spain; or, Love in Mexico* on 16 July 1790. The critic in the *Biographical and Imperial Magazine* that month thought he played the character without being "amiss," if allowance were to be made for his "intolerable lisp." The speech mannerism was evidently an impediment and not an affectation. On 6 August 1790 he performed Amintor in *Daphne and Amintor*. His other roles in August were Quaver in *The Virgin Unmask'd* on the eighteenth, a Campley in *Inkle and Yarico* on the nineteenth, and Melvil in *Summer Amusement; or, An Adventure at Margate* on the twentieth, when he sang with others a selection of songs. He acted William in the premiere of O'Keeffe's comic opera *The Basket Maker* on 4 September. On 13 October 1790 he played Arionelli in a special performance of *The Spanish Barber* given at the Haymarket for Palmer.

The *Thespian Dictionary* (1805) stated that Waterhouse "had some knowledge of music, which he taught, but there was an imperfection in his voice, which retarded his progress on the stage." William Waterhouse signed his full name to a letter sent by Smock Alley performers to the *Hibernian Journal* on 30 January 1786. The Master Waterhouse who played an unspecified part in the premiere of *The Enchanted Wood* at the Haymarket on 25 July 1792 was perhaps his son.

Waterhouse, William   *d. 1822, violoncellist.*

William Waterhouse was elected a member of the Royal Society of Musicians on 6 August 1769. That year he played in the *Messiah* at the Foundling Hospital. In 1773 he was in the service of the Duke of Cumberland, and he was participating in the Concerts of An-

cient Music by 1789. Also, on 27 May of that year he was a principal instrumentalist, along with the Ashleys, Ashbridge, Cramer, the Parkes, and others in a concert of Handel's music directed by Dr Cooke at St Margaret, Westminster. He was one of the violoncellists in the band at the Pantheon for the opera season there between February and July 1791. In 1794 he was listed in Doane's *Musical Directory* as a resident of Mount Street, Grosvenor Square, a principal violoncellist, a member of the Royal Society of Musicians, and an instrumentalist in the Concerts of Ancient Music, the Opera, and the Handelian performances in Westminster Abbey.

In 1791 he was put on the list of musicians assigned to play in the annual charity concert by the members of the Royal Society of Musicians for the benefit of the clergy at St Paul's in May. He was similarly assigned in May 1793. He began to serve as a Governor of the Society in 1792, a responsibility he also had the next year. The Society's Minute Books show that he was a member of the Court of Assistants in 1795, 1807, 1813, 1816, and 1822. We know little otherwise about his professional activities in the early nineteenth century. Perhaps he was the Waterhouse who was new to the band at the Haymarket Theatre in the summer of 1810. According to the records of the Royal Society of Musicians, he died on 28 July 1822.

Waters, Mr   *fl. 1739–1749₁,   dancer, actor.*

The Waters who was Harlequin in *The Escapes of Harlequin by Sea and Land* at Bullock's Booth at Bartholomew Fair on 23 August 1739 was very probably the Waters who was listed as a dancer in a Sadler's Wells variety bill of April 1746, who played Harlequin in *As You Like It; or, Harlequin's Whim* at the New Wells, "London Spaw," Clerkenwell, on 15 September 1746, and who played a Committeeman in *The Committee* at the New Wells, Lemon Street, for Lewis Hallam's benefit on 27 February 1749. In the 1739 performance Mrs Waters was Columbine. Those are the only known notices for either performer.

Waters, Mrs.   *fl. 1739₁,   dancer. See* WATERS MR. ₁1739–1749₁.

Waters, Mr *fl. 1743₁,* *performer?*
house servant?

A Mr Waters shared a benefit with Hussey, Brook, and Stevens at Lincoln's Inn Fields Theatre on 3 June 1743. Hussey was a dancer and actor; Stevens was a house servant. The functions of Waters and Brook are not known.

Waters, Mr *fl. 1745₁,* *singer.*

A Mr Waters was one of the small chorus of six singers by which Lewis Hallam sought to camouflage the dramatic performance *Massacre at Paris* as "A Concert of . . . Musick" at Goodman's Fields Theatre on 28 October 1745 and several nights following.

Waters, Mr *fl. 1760–1762₁,* *rope dancer, tumbler, equilibrist.*

In scattered Sadler's Wells bills of 1760 and 1762 a Mr Waters is called a tumbler and a rope dancer. In one he is described as balancing a half-pound weight atop a straw while dancing on the slack rope.

Waters, Mr *fl. 1795₁,* *house servant?*

A Mr Waters was one of 24 people of Drury Lane Theatre, most of whom can be identified as servants of the house, who distributed benefit tickets on 5 June 1795.

Waters, John *fl. 1674–1680₁,* *singer.*

John Waters was one of the Children of the Chapel Royal studying under John Blow. On 18 May 1674 he journeyed with the other boys to Windsor to attend the King there until 3 September at a fee of 3s. daily. On 15 February 1675 Master Waters sang in the court masque *Calisto.* By 26 February 1677 his voice had broken, but Blow was still given money for the boy's maintenance and the usual clothing. Waters was still receiving maintenance at the beginning of 1680.

Waters, Miss M. A. *fl. 1798–1802₁,* *singer, actress.*

A letter signed Miss "M. A. Waters", published in the *Times* of 22 November 1798, asserted that Joseph Mazzinghi was Waters's only teacher. On the twelfth of that month she had been introduced at Covent Garden in Cobb's enormously popular new comic opera (for which Mazzinghi had written the music) as "A Young Lady (first appearance on any

stage)" in the role of Zelma. She continued at Covent Garden until the end of 1801–2 season. The "Theatrical Chit-Chat" column in the *Monthly Mirror* for June 1802 announced that "Miss Waters had quitted the stage."

Her other roles to 1800–1801 were Nainda in *The Princess of Georgia,* Margaretta in *No Song No Supper* (for her benefit on 24 May 1799 when the gross receipts were £461), Mary in *The Turnpike Gate,* the original Page in Richard Cumberland's melodrama *Joanna,* and the title role in *Marian* ("with a New Song [*He has left me—the youth, the dear youth I adore*], written by T[homas] Dutton, the Music by Mazzinghi"). Mazzinghi wrote for her several other occasional songs.

In addition to her dramatic singing roles, Miss Waters sang in the spring oratorios at Covent Garden and participated there in the chorus singing required in *Macbeth* and in the "solemn dirge" for Juliet's funeral procession. In 1799–1800 she was making £2 2s. per week and in 1801–2 £4. At the time of her benefit of 24 May 1799 she was living at No 42, Conduit Street, Hanover Street.

Rather more criticism of her singing and acting survives than one would expect for a career of such brevity and relative modesty. Some of it was due to her excellence, and some was responsive to the current mood of xenophobia around the end of the century. At her debut in 1798 the critic of the *Monthly Mirror* found that she

has been well instructed, and she has considerable taste; but her manner is affectedly Italianized; her voice is sufficiently powerful, but it is not very melodious, nor has her ear the certainty that is so important to a singer's reputation: her execution, however, is scientific and her lower notes . . . astonish by their roundness, articulation, and depth. Her ability as an actress is not much, and there is a *strangeness* in her walk, which we never observed in any other human being. Miss Waters has an expressive countenance, and a figure uncommonly elegant and interesting.

The same (or another) *Monthly Mirror* critic, in October 1799, came down harshly:

Miss Waters does not much improve in her acting, and we are rather apprehensive, that she indulges a higher opinion of her abilities, than seems to be entertained by the public; but if we are right in our conjecture, it might be, suitably enough, whispered in her ear, as Rosalind does to Phoebe,

"I see no more in you, than in the ordinary of nature's sale-work."

We have observed, that whenever this lady appears on the stage, there is a faction of foreigners in the boxes, who make it their business to ejaculate half a dozen *bravo's!* at the end of every verse she sings, and to make a hideous clatter and confusion, greatly to the annoyance of the audience, in order to produce . . . an *encore* of the song. Does this happen because Miss Waters is a pupil of Mr. Mazzinghi . . . ? These persons should be apprised, that *cabals* are foreign to the temper and decorum of an English audience, who know well enough how to distinguish and reward legitimate merit, without taking the queue [*sic*] from any exotic junto whatever.

Thomas Dutton (who had written at least one song for her) scolded her in his *Dramatic Career* in 1800 for "excessive modesty," she having "long stoutly remonstrated against, what many of her sex are too partial to, *wearing the breeches.*" Instead, she wore a nondescript costume "of doubtful gender." But he again and again commended her voice— "sweet, powerful, and of extraordinary compass." To him, she was the "first vocal performer at the [Covent Garden] Theatre." The song "Happy were the days" from *Ramah Droog* was published in 1798 "as sung by" Miss Waters.

Waters, Nicholas   *1755–1788, actor.*
The *World* on 28 May 1788 reported the death at his sister's in Chandos Street, Covent Garden, of "Nick" Waters, aged 33, who had been William Powell's footboy and then acted at Covent Garden Theatre, the Haymarket Theatre, and at Windsor and Richmond. His principal character, according to that brief obituary, was the Coachman in *The Commissary*, but his name does not appear for that role in any London bills. Indeed, the only time we find that surname in the bills during our subject's lifetime was at the Haymarket in the summer of 1772, when Mr Waters acted the Printer's Devil in *The Author,* Jsaper in *Miss in Her Teens*, Robert in *The Mock Doctor*, and an unspecified role in *The Rehearsal.* A Mr Waters played at Cork in the summers of 1778 and 1781, but that person was perhaps the actor who was also there in 1792, after Nicholas Waters's death.

Among the mock epitaphs of actors given

by George Parker in his *Humourous Sketches* (1782) is:

> *Here rests NICKY WATERS, whose heart was a*
> *   mint,*
> *Tho' the owner ne'er knew half the good that was*
> *   in't.*
> *Tho' still fond of fun he for humour was ripe,*
> *To grub on my Alderman [i.e., roast fowl & sau-*
> *   sage] slang'd every ngiht [sic],*
> *Yet still if a friend was disturb'd for the pence,*
> *To his very last dud NICK would readily sense,*
> *Then peace to his spirit, wherever it flies,*
> *If he tides down the Thames, or should act in the*
> *   skies[.]*
> *One [sic] earth ev'ry player will meet him with*
> *   love,*
> *And GARRICK for him shall be RENSHAW*
> *   [i.e., a pawnbroker in Russell St] above.*

Waters, Samuel   *fl. 1723[?], musician.*
Elizabeth, daughter of Samuel Waters, "fidler," was buried 29 September 1723 at St Giles, Cripplegate, according to the register.

Waters, Thomas   *fl. 1702[?], performer.*
A notice in the *Post Man* of 8 September 1702 said that strollers Thomas Waters and others were to pay town constables 2s. daily for the right to perform.

Wathen, Mr   *fl. 1729–1731[?], actor.*
The first notice we have of Mr Wathen is of his appearance in one of several companies that occupied the Haymarket Theatre in the winter season of 1728–29. He played Pearmain in *The Recruiting Officer* on 31 January 1729. During the remainder of that season he added the Second Countryman in *The Humours of Harlequin*, Death in *Hurlothrumbo*, Pigg in *The Smuglers*, Scrip in *The Beggar's Wedding*, and Faithful in *Rape upon Rape.*

Wathen was not named in any other London playbill that we have seen until he joined the actors at Reynolds's booth during the time of Bartholomew Fair, late August 1730, as one of the Foresters in *Harlequin's Contrivance.* In September following he moved on to Southwark Fair and "the Theatrical Booth in Bird-Cage Alley." There he played Doodle in *Tom Thumb.*

In the Haymarket winter season of 1730–31 Wathen added to his repertoire Scarecrow in *The Author's Farce*, Doodle in *The Battle of the Poets,* Sawney MacStaytape in *The Jealous Taylor,* Somebody in *The Author's Farce,* Trapland in *Love for Love,* a role unspecified in *The Spendthrift,* Clerimont in *The Cobler of Preston,* John in *The Letter Writers,* Leicester in *The Fall of Mortimer,* and, on another night, a Citizen in that tragedy. After that season Wathen's name disappeared from the bills.

Wathen, George   *1762–1849, actor, singer, manager.*

George Wathen was born in 1762, one of several children of a London surgeon, Samuel Wathen, and Samuel's wife, the youngest daughter of Sydenham Malthus, an apothecary. The short account in *The Theatric Tourist* (1805) says that George "was bred to the profession of arms, and promoted to a lieutenancy in the 39th regiment, at the memorable Siege of Gibraltar." Gilliland adds that he later transferred to the 14th regiment. He had engaged in amateur theatricals in the army, and on entering on half-pay service at the lull in British-French hostilities he retained this interest. He also clung to the title "Captain," which earned him some derision later among his fellow actors. (The *Authentic Memoirs of the Green Room* [1806], in a slightly different version, says that after Gibraltar he served in Jamaica and "sold out with the brevet rank of Major.")

In December and January 1790, 1791, and 1792 Wathen assisted Lord Barrymore by acting in and directing the amateur Wargrave theatricals. He purchased the lease of the summer theatre at Richmond on 18 June 1792. (A surviving bill, that of 28 July, shows him as Lissardo in *The Wonder* and Lingo in *The Agreeable Surprise.*) He also was involved that summer in a coffee-house fray with the verse satirist John Williams ("Anthony Pasquin"). Wathen alleged that Williams had insulted him and had been caned for it. Williams asserted that he had been assaulted in cowardly fashion by Wathen and the actor Barrymore and that though he, Williams, had lost the use of his right arm, he had cudgeled Wathen heroically. Williams and Wathen blackguarded each other all summer most scurrilously in such papers as *The World,* the *Oracle,* and, in a final burst of vituperation, the *Thespian Magazine* for September 1792. Challenges were issued but no duels ensued.

On 22 February 1793 Wathen joined Daly at Dublin's Crow Street Theatre, assuming the stage name "Mr George." Returning to Richmond in the spring of 1793, Wathen ran immediately into a legal difficulty. He produced a version of John O'Keeffe's musical farce *The Agreeable Surprise.* The piece was a dozen years old—it had been seen first at the Haymarket on 4 September 1781—but the elder George Colman, the Haymarket manager, who had bought it from O'Keeffe, jealously asserted his sole right to its performance. A jury found for Colman, but Mr Justice Buller, on the motion of Mr Law, counsel for Wathen, set aside the verdict. A clipping in the Folger Library (W. a. 110) gives the gist of the proceedings:

> The question for the opinion of the Court was— "Whether the law, respecting literary property, extended to jokes and stories."
> Mr. Law said it was absurd to suppose that literary property imported, or extended to a performance like that in question. He cited the song in this Farce beginning with the words *Horum corum,* &c. which, he said, was meer *gibberish.* . . .
> Mr. Justice Buller said, that those were men whose memories were so retentive as to be able to repeat the whole of a sermon they had heard–but he believed no lawyer could say an action could be maintained for repeating any discourse which a man's memory had carried away. It were still more absurd to say that a man should not repeat or rehearse a joke or story he had heard upon a Stage.

The judge's opinion seems to have done no permanent damage to property in dramatic works. The trial did not do even any immediate harm to the relationship between Wathen and the younger Colman, now manager for that same summer, on 20 August 1793, Wathen made his first public dramatic appearance in London playing Mungo in *The Padlock* at Colman's Haymarket Theatre. (His first appearance in London had been at Lord Barrymore's Theatre in Savile Row on 22 July 1790.)

In the winter of 1793–94 Wathen crossed again to Ireland to play at Crow Street. But he seems to have returned to England early, for in February and March the *Thespian Magazine* reported him at the Theatre Royal, Manchester. The Lord Chamberlain's records in the Public Record Office show that once more, in 1794, he was granted a license for theatrical performances at Richmond, from 19 June to

GEORGE WATHEN

by Condé

30 September, "during His Majesty's residence." But if W. S. Clark, in *The Irish Stage in the County Towns,* is correct, Wathen himself was back in Ireland, acting at Cork, early in September and in October 1794.

On 26 January 1795 Wathen made his first bows from the Drury Lane stage, playing Sadi, a secondary role in *The Mountaineers.* He repeated the part on 2 February and that night also played Lenitive in *The Prize.* But those were tryout performances, and he was not immediately given a contract. He was called upon for Bannister's benefit, on 19 May, to sing Reeve's song "The Cobler."

Wathen was on the Lord Chamberlain's books as a licensee at Richmond again in 1795. (A letter in the Enthoven Collection from Henry Norbury to James Winston, asserts that "Mr Walthen" leased the theatre from 1792 through 1795.) Evidently Wathen managed there that summer, though perhaps principally through his under-manager, Williames. For he was busily performing for Colman at the Haymarket from 10 June through 15 September, adding the following to his repertoire: Toby Thatch in *The London Hermit,*

Tiptoe in *Ways and Means,* the Mayor of Coventry in *Peeping Tom,* Sheepface in *The Village Lawyer,* Doctor Cathartic in *Summer Amusement,* a Recruit in *The Recruiting Officer,* Old Gobbo in *The Merchant of Venice,* Osric in *Hamlet,* Obadiah Prim in *A Bold Stroke for a Wife,* Shadrach in *The Young Quaker,* the original Peter in Robert Benson's musical farce *Love and Money,* and the original Frank in Prince Hoare's musical farce *Three and the Deuce.*

By late 1795 Wathen began to attract some critical notice. The anonymous author of *Candid and Impartial Strictures on the Performers Belonging to Drury-Lane, Covent-Garden, and the Haymarket* (F. G. Waldron, a rival actor in some of the same lines) was peremptory: "An humble follower of [John] Edwin [the younger], but keeps himself at a respectful distance. He is always comical, but strange as it may appear, [he] but seldom makes us laugh. We think it would have been better for himself and family had he retained the cockade." An anonymous newspaper paragrapher (in a Winston transcript dated 1794, in the Folger Library) had heard that "Capt. Wathen is in Treaty with the Proprietor of D.L. to act as the Double of Jack Ban[niste]r in whose Char[acter]s he is perfectly au fait."

Whether or not it had occurred to Sheridan and Kemble to secure Wathen as a backup performer to the immensely popular John Bannister, Wathen did sign on with Drury Lane in the fall of 1795. There he remained in the winter seasons, going to the Haymarket in most summers, until 1806. According to the paylists in the Folger Library, his salary in 1802–3 was £8 per week. The intensification of the conflict with Napoleon then drew him back into military service.

The additions to George Wathen's repertoire, at Drury Lane and the Haymarket, season by season, were as follows: at Drury Lane, in 1795–96, Catchpenny in *The Suicide,* a "Vocal Part" in the chorus of William Linley's new pantomime *Harlequin Captive,* Squire Sturdy in *The Shepherdess of Cheapside,* some part unspecified in John Grubb's new afterpiece *Alive and Merry,* Robin in *No Song No Supper,* a performance of catches and glees with Bannister, Suett, and others in *The Phoenix,* Will Steady in *The Purse,* and songs in *A Musical Olio;* at the Haymarket, summer,

Folger Shakespeare Library

GEORGE WATHEN
by Dighton

1796, the original Jack Hawser in *Banian Day* (George Brewer's musical farce), Lazarillo in *The Spanish Barber*, some character in *The Magick Banner*, Gregory Gubbins in *The Battle of Hexham*, Grumio in *Catherine and Petruchio*, Quirk in *Ways and Means*, Crop in *No Song No Supper*, Obadiah Prim in *A Bold Stroke for a Wife*, a Sergeant in *The Surrender of Calais*, Medium in *Inkle and Yarico*, a character in *Don Pedro*, William in *The Purse*, a Carrier in *1 Henry IV*, Doctor Pedant in *A Mogul Tale*, Sam Surge in *The Married Un-Married*, Sir Toby Fuz in *A Peep behind the Curtain;* and at Drury Lane in 1796–97, Jeremy in *Love for Love*, Jessamy in *Bon Ton*, Tradelove in *A Bold Stroke for a Wife*, Guillot in *Richard Coeur de Lion*, Lory in *A Trip to Scarborough*, the original Chattles in J. C. Cross's musical farce *The Charity Boy*, Friday in *Robinson Crusoe; or, Harlequin Friday*, Tim in *The Honeymoon*, Gibby in *The Wonder*, the original Morado in Prince Hoare's comic opera *A Friend in Need*, a Citizen in *Coriolanus*, Sir Christopher Hatton in *The Critic*, the original Toby in Andrew Franklin's farce *The Wandering Jew*, Roberto in *The Prisoner*, Ruttekin

in *Robin Hood*, Bullock in *The Recruiting Officer*, and Darby in *The Poor Soldier*.

In the summer of 1797, at the Haymarket, Wathen added Cymon in *The Irishman in London*, Jack Connor in *The Prisoner at Large*, Diggory in *She Stoops to Conquer*, and La Gloire in *The Surrender of Calias;* at Drury Lane, 1797–98, Soto in *She Wou'd and She Wou'd Not*, Jenkins in *The Wheel of Fortune*, Snake in *The School for Scandal*, Martin in *The Haunted Tower*, Veritas in *The Will*, the Second Player in *Hamlet*, O'Thunder in *A Trip to the Nore*, Jessamy in *Bon Ton*, the original Edric in Matthew Gregory ("Monk") Lewis's melodrama *The Castle Spectre*, Snuffle in *The Mayor of Garratt*, one of the Spahis in George Colman's new melodrama *Blue-Beard*, the original Cudgo in Charles Dibdin's musical farce *Hannah Hewit; or The Female Crusoe*, an original part (unspecified) in John O'Keeffe's interlude *The Eleventh of June*, the original Crank in Edward Henry Iliff's burlesque *The Ugly Club*, and Martin in *The Haunted Tower;* at the Haymarket, summer, 1798, Johnny in *Throw Physick to the Dogs* and Harry Hawser in *The Shipwreck;* at Drury Lane, 1798–99, Sancho in *Love Makes a Man*, the original Andrew in George Colman's melodrama *Feudal Times*, Vinegar in *The Son-in-Law*, and Sable in *The Funeral;* at the Haymarket in the summer of 1799, Zekeil Homespun in *The Heir at Law*, James in *Blue Devils*, Zarno in *Zorinski*, Lerida in *The Red-Cross Knights*, Walter in *The Children in the Wood*, and an appearance singing sea songs in *Tars at Torbay;* at Drury Lane in 1799–1800, Ralph in *The Maid of the Mill*, Ralph in *The Secret*, Frank in *The East Indian*, Tony Lumpkin in *She Stoops to Conquer*, Thomas in *Indiscretion;* and at the Haymarket in the summer of 1800, Moses in *The School for Scandal* and Cymon in *The Irishman in London*.

Wathen did not stimulate the critics to much observation. F. G. Waldron's early comment, anonymous and biased, we have quoted. Still smarting four years after his drubbing of 1792, Anthony Pasquin (John Williams) in *A Pin Basket to the Children of Thespis* (1796) dismissed Wathen waspishly: "The Captain might do very well as a player among Lords, but the Lord deliver us from seeing him play amongst actors." The anonymous *Druriad* of 1798 was also insulting:

Harvard Theatre Collection

The Earl of Barrymore as Scrub and GEORGE WATHEN as Archer
engraving by Audinet, after De Wilde

With awkward form, and vague quiescent face,
Wretched buffoonery, and low grimace;
Lo! Wathen tumbles in, by folly led,
And quick compulsive gravity of head.
Alas! alas! poor shifting weather-cock!
Why didst thou change the halbert for the sock?

Thomas Dutton, in *The Dramatic Censor* (1800) was kinder but briefer: ". . . in clowns and boorish servants Mr. WATHEN appears to advantage." He played Tony Lumpkin "with considerable success." The *Authentic Memoirs of the Green Room* (1806) summed up his art in praising his rustics and "jolly tars" and deploring his imitation of Jack Bannister, "whose manner he copies even to *minutiae.*" Yet obviously in the estimation of the audience and the judgment of the managers Wathen had considerable value as a low comedian and singer of the hearty sea songs of that jingoistic era. The *Catalogue of Printed Music in the British Museum* contains several songs "as sung by" Wathen.

Wathen's private character is harder to assess. If even a fraction of the charges of ferocity and brutality leveled at him by Williams in 1792 are true, he was at best proud and cruel. He was perhaps also boastful, if not cowardly. Williams addressed him as "the Theatrical Bobadil" and testified:

With those who know this regenerated Bully Dawson, intimately, he is held in derision: he was accustomed to *amuse* us in the country, with the accounts of the wonderful assistance he gave to General Eliot in preserving the Rock of Gibraltar. "Turk Gregory never did such feats in arms!" According to his *own* asseveration, he rowed alone in a boat from the Garrison, and shewed his breech to the Spanish Admiral: on another momentous occasion, he swam several leagues with the Governor's dispatches between his teeth. In short, he became a sort of merry proverb among us, and every thing we heard that was highly marvelous, or boasting, we emphatically called a Wathen.

Yet Wathen seems to have prospered. In the last years of the century he lived at No 2, Frith Street, Soho, a good address. In the Garrick Club is a document that shows that he lent the hard-pressed R. B. Sheridan £2000 at 5% interest on 5 March 1799.

At some time after his retirement from active duty, Wathen became one of the Military Knights of Windsor. According to the *United Service Magazine* for May 1849 he had died at

Windsor Castle on the previous 21 April, aged 87. In *Letters from the Late Lord Chedworth* (1840) it is stated that he had married the daughter of Dr Norford of Bury. She did not live to receive the furniture, money, plate, and other effects—value unspecified—devised to her in his will, signed at Windsor on 30 June 1845. She preceded him in death, on 12 October 1848, according to the *Gentleman's Magazine* of November 1848. His will was proved at London on 3 May 1849 by the oath of Elizabeth Frances Wathen, spinster, his daughter and the residuary legatee.

Portraits of George Wathen include:

1. Engraved portrait by J. Condé. Wathen holding a volume of O'Keeffe's plays. Published as a plate to *Thespian Magazine,* 1792.

2. By Robert Dighton. Pencil drawing in Folger Shakespeare Library.

3. Engraved portrait, after Hobday. Published as a plate to Parsons's *Minor Theatre,* 1794.

4. By George Knapton, 1755. Presumably George Wathen is among the children in a painting by Knapton of Dr Samuel Wathen with his wife and children, now in the City Art Gallery of Birmingham.

5. As Archer, with Richard Barrymore as Scrub, in *The Beaux' Stratagem.* By Samuel De Wilde. In a private collection, New York. An engraving by Audinet was published as a plate to *Bell's British Theatre,* 1791. The same engraving by Audinet, in an octagonal frame, was published by Cooke as a plate to *British Drama,* 1806, and a copy engraved by W. Leney was published as a plate to *Bell's British Theatre,* 1792.

Watkins, Mr *fl. 1743*], *actor.*

On 4 August (and probably every day through 12 August) 1743 during Tottenham Court Fair, Daniel, Malone, and James's Great Theatrical Booth presented *The Glorious Queen of Hungary; or, The British Troops Triumphant,* in which Mr Watkins played the Dragoon. It is possible but not very likely that he was the Watkins who played minor parts at Drury Lane in the 1760s and 1770s.

Watkins, Mr *fl. 1760–1775*], *actor, singer.*

A Mr Watkins shared a benefit at Drury Lane Theatre on 6 May 1760 with the performers Clough, Raftor, and Walker; thus he must have been serving unobtrusively that season, even though he was not noticed in the playbills. He was hardly more obtrusive in the humble parts he filled during the following 15 years.

A list, in order of appearance, would include Gurney in *King John*, Tom in *High Life below Stairs*, and a part unspecified in Richard Bentley's new pantomime *The Wishes; or, Harlequin's Mouth Opened* in 1760–61; a part in *The Rehearsal*, Pearce in *The Minor*, Nym in *The Merry Wives of Windsor*, and Thomas in *The Virgin Unmask'd* in 1761–62; a Servant in *The Musical Lady*, a Planter in *Oroonoko*, a part in

Fortunatus, Fang in 1 *Henry IV*, a Waiter in *The Witches*, a part in *The Magician of the Mountain*, an Outlaw in *The Two Gentlemen of Verona*, and Harry in *The Mock Doctor* in 1762–63; a part in *Philaster*, one of the Mob in *The Mayor of Garratt*, a part in *The Dupe*, and the Landlord in *The Stagecoach* in 1763–64; Alguazile in *She Wou'd and She Wou'd Not* in 1764–65; unspecified parts in *A Fairy Tale* and *The Hermit* in 1765–66; a servant in *The Widow'd Wife* and a Footman in *False Delicacy* in 1767–68; a Coachman in *Harlequin's Invasion* and a Servant in *The Hypocrite* in 1768–69; a Footman in *A Word to the Wise* in 1769–70; a part in *The Pigmy Revels* in 1772–73; a part in *The*

City Art Gallery of Birmingham

ASTLEY BRANSBY as Aesop, WILLIAM PARSONS as the Old Man, and MR WATKINS as the Servant

by Zoffany

Genii and a Jockey in *The Note of Hand* in 1773–74; and a part, now unknown, in *Harlequin's Jacket* in 1774–75.

A surviving Drury Lane paylist for 9 February 1765 gives Watkins 12*s.* per week, among the three lowest salaries in the company of 90. By 24 January 1767 it had been raised to 15*s.*

The dancers Ann and Mary Watkins were probably the daughters of our subject. Despite his obscurity, Watkins is preserved vividly for posterity in Johann Zoffany's painting of the scene from *Lethe,* now in the City Art Gallery of Birmingham. In that painting Watkins appears as the Servant, with Astley Bransby as Aesop and William Parsons as the Old Man. An engraving by J. Young was published by T. Simpson, 1788.

Watkins, Mr ｣*fl. 1774–1802*₁, *house servant.*

A Mr Watkins was on the Drury Lane company list in 1774 and on 5 October 1775 was called a "pit doorkeeper" in the account books in the Folger Library. He surfaces from time to time thereafter in the accounts (curiously, never in the benefit bills): in 1789–90 at 4*s.* 6*d.* per week; in 1790–91, expenses of £23 17*s.* paid at the end of season; on 2 April 1799, as doorkeeper, paid arrears of £2 12*s.* 6*d.*; on 22 January 1800, as pit doorkeeper; and throughout 1801–2 as doorkeeper. His relationship, if any, to Watkins, "scowrer," is not known. On 6 April 1799 a "Watkins ironmonger," perhaps kin, was paid £5 5*s.*

Watkins, Mr ｣*fl. 1792*₁, *scowrer.*

One Watkins, "scowrer," was paid £23 17*s.* 4*d.* on 8 March 1792 "to 4 June," according to the account books of the Drury Lane theatre at the Folger Library.

Watkins, Mrs ｣*fl. 1761*₁, *dresser.*

On 14 November 1761 Mrs Watkins was entered in the Covent Garden manuscript account book, in the Folger Library, as a dresser "from Monday the 9th Inst. Inclusive" at 1*s.* 6*d.* per day.

Watkins, Ann *d. 1795, dancer, actress.*

Ann Watkins was the younger of two sisters, the elder of whom, Mary, became Mrs Pulley. Both were dancers, and until Mary's marriage their careers are hard to differentiate. The girls were in all probability daughters of the Drury Lane actor Watkins, at whose benefit (shared by four others) on 17 May 1764 a Miss Watkins danced a hornpipe "By Desire." That was the first appearance of a Miss Watkins in any known London playbill. She was probably a juvenile, for she (or her sister) did not appear again until 13 May 1766 when again Watkins shared a benefit and the hornpipe was a feature. On 25 May 1767 when benefit time came around again Miss Watkins danced a double hornpipe with Walker, as she did a year later, on 24 May 1768.

On 3 October 1772 was played the first "named" part given a Miss Watkins: Colombine in the pantomime *The Witches; or, A Trip to Naples.* One or both Misses Watkins by then must have been obscurely in the chorus. On 16 December 1773 a Miss Watkins replaced Mrs Sutton as Colombine in *The Genii,* and she replaced her again as Colombine in *The Elopement* on 3 November 1775. At least one of those notices would appear to have belonged to Mary the elder sister who (as Mrs Pulley) stepped into *The Elopement* as a replacement again on 27 December 1777—but one cannot be sure.

Not until 13 November 1780 did the name Miss Watkins again appear in a bill, and that was surely Ann Watkins, since Mary had been billed as Mrs Pulley since 1777. At the Haymarket, Ann played Gauze in the revival (after ten years) of Ned Shuter's comic interlude *The Detection.* Her only other recorded appearance was on 14 May 1782 when, for the sake of Mary Pulley and her sharers—Miss Armstrong, Phillimore, and Spencer—Ann danced "a *Hornpipe* (for that Night only)."

James Winston's transcription of the Drury Lane Fundbook, now in the Folger Library, calls Ann the younger sister and says that she died in November 1795.

Watkins, Mary. *See* PULLEY, MRS MARY.

Watkins, Nathaniel *c. 1630–1702, singer.*

Nathaniel Watkins was born about 1630 and on 9 November 1660 was appointed to the Chapel Royal as a countertenor at an annual salary of £40. When he married Susan Fuller on 23 September 1662, Watkins was described as of St George, New Windsor, a bachelor about 32 years old. Miss Fuller was from the London parish of St Margaret, Westminster, where many musicians lived; she was a spinster about 20 years old, marrying with the consent of her father, a tailor. Though much of Watkins's time must have been spent at the Chapel Royal in London, in the 1670s he was several times chosen to attend the King at Windsor, for which service he received from six to eight shillings daily. Watkins remained active in the royal musical establishment until his death on 8 May 1702.

He had written his will on 16 January 1700 at Windsor Castle, requesting burial in the upper cloister there or in the Chapel of St George. His wife had apparently already died, for he made no mention of her nor of any children. To Mrs Ann Hartwell he left £20, to Thomas Clarke 20s., and to the poor widows of the parish 40s. Everything else he left to his friend Charles Potts of Windsor Castle, who proved the will on 28 May 1702.

Watkins, Ralph *fl. 1673₁, musician.*
The Lord Chamberlain on 17 July 1673 ordered the apprehension of Ralph Watkins and others for performing music in public without licenses.

Watkins, Richard *fl. 1670–1671₁, scenekeeper?*
The London Stage lists Richard Watkins (or Watkyns) as a member of the King's Company at the Bridges Street Theatre in 1670–71. The Lord Chamberlain's accounts cited Watkins, apparently as a scenekeeper, on 25 January 1671.

Watkinson, Mr *fl. 1799–1801?₁, singer.*
A Mr Watkinson sang a song, with Hayden and Master Crisp, between the acts of a performance of *Douglas* at the Old Crown Inn, Highgate, on 15 May 1799. Maybe he was the Watkinson on the bill at the Theatre Royal, Margate, on 31 July 1801.

Watley, Mr *fl. 1784–1794?₁, violinist, organist?*
Mr Watley played second violin in the Handel Memorial Concerts at Westminster Abbey and the Pantheon in May and June 1784. Per-

haps he was the Watley listed in Doane's *Musical Directory* of 1794 as an organist from Cirencester, Gloucestershire.

Wats, Mr *fl. 1675₁, actor.*
The 1676 edition of *Sophonisba* has a Mr Wats (or Watts) playing Maherbal at Drury Lane Theatre on 30 April 1675, though the prompter Downes in his *Roscius Anglicanus* of 1708 said Nicholas Burt played that part. Possibly "Wats" was an error for Watson, but Downes said Marmaduke Watson played Varro in *Sophonisba*. Wats is not otherwise known.

Watson, Mr *fl. 1775₁, house servant?*
Benefit tickets were accepted on 27 May 1775 at Covent Garden Theatre for Mr Watson, probably a house servant.

Watson, Mr *fl. 1792₁, singer.*
The London Stage has a Mr Watson singing in *Orpheus and Eurydice* at Covent Garden Theatre on 28 February 1792.

Watson, Mr *fl. 1799–1822₁, house servant?*
The Drury Lane Theatre accounts list Mr Watson and four others as sharing a benefit on 28 May 1799; *The London Stage* does not show a benefit on that date. Watson was cited again in the accounts in the early years of the nineteenth century and was on the company list in 1821–22 at £3 weekly. He may have been a house servant.

Watson, Mrs *fl. 1776–1809?₁, actress, singer.*
At the Haymarket Theatre on 20 September 1776 Mrs Watson sang Jenny Diver in *The Beggar's Opera*. On 9 April 1782 she was Jenny in *The Gentle Shepherd* there, and on 9 February 1784 she repeated that role. A Mrs Watson—perhaps the same woman—was at Drury Lane Theatre in 1808–9.

Watson, Miss. *See also* BROOKS, MRS, NÉE WATSON.

Watson, The Misses *fl. 1784₁, actresses.*
At the Haymarket Theatre on 23 February 1784 Miss Watson senior and Miss Watson junior had roles in *The Patriot*.

Watson, Miss _fl. 1792–1801₁, singer._

On 19 October 1792 at Covent Garden Theatre Miss Watson sang in the chorus of _The Woodman;_ on 29 October she sang in the chorus of _Macbeth._ In 1793–94, when she was earning £1 5s. weekly for her labors, she sang in _Sprigs of Laurel, Romeo and Juliet, The Woodman, Cymon,_ and _Macbeth_ and played Old Kathlane in _Dermot and Kathlane._ On 9 May 1801 she was at Drury Lane Theatre singing in the chorus of _Adelmorn the Outlaw._

Watson, Edward _b. 1759, violinist, violist, harpsichordist._

According to evidence provided to the Royal Society of Musicians, Edward Watson was born in 1759, and by 6 April 1783, when he was recommended for membership, he had practiced music for seven years, was engaged in the Ancient Music oratorios, played the violin and viola, and taught the harpsichord. At that time he was single and 24 years old. In May and June 1784 he played first violin in the Handel Memorial Concerts at Westminster Abbey and the Pantheon, and in May 1785 he played viola in the Royal Society of Music's St Paul's concert. In 1791 he was playing second violin in the orchestra at the King's Theatre and the Pantheon. Doane's _Musical Directory_ of 1794 listed Edward Watson as living at No 15, Broad Street, Carnaby Market. He played viola that year in the annual St Paul's concert.

Watson, Elizabeth. _See_ BOMAN, MRS JOHN, ELIZABETH.

Watson, Emily _fl. 1800–1809₁, dancer._

Miss Watson danced a Negress in _Obi_ at the Haymarket Theatre on 2 July 1800. The Drury Lane bills from 1801 through 1809 cite Miss Watson, a dancer. In 1807–8 she was called Emily Watson, and her salary was given as £2 5s. weekly; in 1801 it had been £1 weekly, but the accounts show it rising by 1806 to £1 10s. and then to £2 5s. by 1807.

Watson, Marmaduke _fl. 1660–1697₁, actor._

Marmaduke Watson was a member of the King's Company under Thomas Killigrew as of 6 October 1660 and remained with the troupe at its various theatres—Vere Street, Bridges Street, Lincoln's Inn Fields, and Drury Lane—at least until the union of the rival companies in 1682. His first known part was Isabella in _The Royall King_ about 1661–62 at Vere Street, which suggests that when he joined the company he was still a boy and was at first assigned female roles, after the Elizabethan fashion. About 1661–62 he was Lord Bonvile and a Young Gallant in _The Royall King._ Manuscript casts at the University of Leeds show that in the early 1660s Watson played Alphonso in _The Cardinal_ and a Lord in _The Court Secret._ Though Watson was mentioned several times in the Lord Chamberlain's livery warrants, no other parts are known for him until 1668–69, when at the Bridges Street playhouse he acted Lucio in _The Sisters._ On 6 November 1668 he was Bakam in _The Island Princess;_ in August 1670 he played Hostilius in _The Roman Empress;_ and in December 1670 and January 1671 he appeared as Hamet in the two parts of _The Conquest of Granada._

He acted Ebulus in _Marriage à la Mode_ at the Lincoln's Inn Fields Theatre about April 1672, and at that house he was seen also as Don Manuel in _The Spanish Rogue_ in March 1673, Captain Middleton in _Amboyna_ in May, Sforza in _The Maides Revenge_ in 1673–74, apparently the King of Poland in _Brennoralt_ about 1673–75, Crimalhaz in Duffett's _The Empress of Morocco_ in December 1673, and Captain Salteel in _The Mistaken Husband_ about March 1674. Sometime between 1670 and 1676 Watson may have acted a Servant in _The Night Walker._

Lacy's 1673 map of the parish of St Paul, Covent Garden, shows a property measuring 400' by 10' running northwest-southeast, split by Bedford Bury, with the northwest end of the plot fronting on St Martin's Lane. The property belonged to a Mr Watson, and since other property in the parish was marked with such theatrical names as Kynaston, Harris, and Baker, perhaps that Mr Watson was Marmaduke. A second plot was also assigned to Watson: a small L-shaped property on the south side of Russell Street, 20 feet from the Covent Garden Piazza.

Marmaduke Watson's first recorded role at the new Drury Lane Theatre was Silvius in _Nero_ on 16 March 1674, after which he is known to have acted Montano in *Othello*, a Swordsman in *A King and No King*, Varro in *Sophonisba* (but see the entry of Mr Wats), Old Thrashard in *The Country Innocence*, Eumenes in *The Rival Queens*, Arratur in *Wits Led by the Nose*, and the Physitian in *Trick for Trick*. As one of the younger members of the King's Company, Watson signed an agreement on 28 September 1677 for a reconstituted troupe under Charles Killigrew. But that came to nothing, as did another agreement of 30 July 1680 that Charles Killigrew tried to make with some of the players in an attempt to save the foundering King's Company. Under the 1680 agreement Watson would have had a half share in the troupe, and with others Watson sued on 23 February 1681 for a share of the profits. But affairs had become hopeless, and in 1682 the troupe was absorbed by the stronger Duke's players.

Downes claimed that Watson joined the new United Company, but in *The Early Irish Stage*, W. S. Clark shows that Watson was one of the London actors recruited by Joseph Ashbury for service at the Smock Alley Theatre in Dublin. A manuscript cast for *The Night Walker* in 1684–85 shows Watson as a Servant, and Clark places Watson in Dublin from 1682 to about 1688. One wonders, then, who the Marmaduke Watson was who was buried on 7 March 1684 at St Clement Danes in London—a son of the actor, perhaps, or our man's father. The last notices we have of Watson are back in London, with Betterton's troupe at the Lincoln's Inn Fields Theatre in November 1697: Watson acted Fidalbo in *The Italian Husband* and Strechwell in *The Deceiver Deceived*.

Watson, Plesaunce ₁fl. 1715–1740?₁, actor.

The actor Watson performing at Lincoln's Inn Fields Theatre from 1715 on was, according to a Drury Lane company list of 12 April 1722, Plesaunce Watson. It is tempting to suppose that the London Watson was the elder John Watson (1689–1766) who performed in Dublin from 1723–24 to 1759–60 and played at least two roles performed by the London Watson, but a close comparison of performing dates shows that they were two different performers.

Plesaunce Watson in 1715 at Lincoln's Inn

Fields played Cardenio in *2 Don Quixote* on 11 October and Sir Walter Raleigh in *The Unhappy Favorite* on 22 October. Watson was given a benefit at Coignand's Great Room on 20 March 1719, when *The Fair Penitent* was presented. He joined the Drury Lane company in 1720, playing Hastings in *2 Henry IV* on 17 December and subsequent dates, and he shared a benefit with Cross on 24 May 1721. He remained at Drury Lane through December 1732, playing such new parts as Demetrius in *Timon of Athens*, Vainlove in *The Old Bachelor*, Cunningham in *The Rival Fools*, the Duke in *Rule a Wife and Have a Wife*, Farewell and Belguard in *Sir Courtly Nice*, Freeman in *The Plain Dealer*, Worthy in *The Recruiting Officer*, Truman in *The Squire of Alsatia*, William de la Pole in *Humphrey, Duke of Gloucester*, the Duke of Orleans in *Henry V*, Lysimachus in *The Humorus Lieutenant*, Phoebus in *Amphitryon*, Peregrine in *Volpone*, Alonzo in *The Mourning Bride*, Dorilant in *The Country Wife*, Montano in *Othello*, Clerimont in *The Double Gallant*, Louis in *The Comical Revenge*, Octavius Caesar in *Julius Caesar*, Carlos in *The Adventures of Five Hours*, Doubty in *The Lancashire Witches*, Sir John in *Sir Martin Marall*, the Prince of Tanais in *Tamerlane*, Diphilus in *The Maid's Tragedy*, Poins in *1 Henry IV*, Francisco in *Wit without Money*, the Elder Worthy in *Love's Last Shift*, Reynard in *Whig and Tory*, Pizarro in *The Indian Emperor*, Lycander in *Timoleon*, Eugenio in *The Lover*, Stanmore in *Oroonoko*, Cromwell in *Henry VIII*, Winwife in *Bartholomew Fair*, Barnwell senior in *The London Merchant*, Guyomar in *The Indian Emperor*, Alonzo in *Injured Innocence*, Captain Bravemore in *The Modern Husband*, Smith in *The Rehearsal*, Mr Critick in *The Tragedy of Tragedies*, Seyward in *Macbeth*, Loveless in *The Relapse*, Cunningham in *The Amorous Widow*, and Horatio in *Hamlet*. His last known appearance at Drury Lane was at Belguard in *Sir Courtly Nice* on 9 December 1732. During his tenure at Drury Lane he played the Parson in *The Tragedy of Tragedies* at the Haymarket Theatre on 24 March 1731. On 23 August 1740 a Watson played Neptune in *Cephalus*. He was probably our subject, but we cannot be certain.

Watson, Robert ₁fl. 1780s₁, pugilist.

On 27 January 1789 pugilist Robert Watson, who had been fighting since the mid-1780s, participated in a sparring match with Ward at the Covent Garden Theatre.

Watson, Sophia   *fl.* 1791–1792[1], *dancer.*

Sophia Watson of George Street, St Margaret's, Westminster, was hired as a figurante at the Pantheon early in 1791. Her salary for the season was £35, according to the Bedford Opera Papers, cited to us by Judith Milhous. The only service recorded for Miss Watson that season was as the Muse de la Rhétorique in *Amphion et Thalie* on 17 February 1791. But she was evidently useful, for the Pantheon's Wardrobe Book shows the purchase of six costumes for her, and she was rehired in 1792 at the same salary.

Fuchs in his *Lexique* has a Mlle Watson, probably our subject, dancing in *La Foire de Smirne* at the Haymarket Theatre on 14 April 1792, but *The London Stage* does not list her in the cast.

Watson, Thomas   *fl.* 1755–1784[1], *boxkeeper, doorkeeper, box office keeper.*

On 3 May 1755 Mr Watson, boxkeeper (sometimes doorkeeper) at Drury Lane Theatre, shared a benefit with two others. He shared benefits at Drury Lane through 28 May 1783. In the summers he worked at the Richmond theatre from as early as 1765. In the Drury Lane accounts from 1766–67 Watson was cited as the box office keeper at 15*s.* weekly. References in the accounts to Watson continued through 1784. Watson lived in Little Russell Street. Our subject was probably the Watson sharing in a benefit at the Haymarket Theatre on 9 February 1784; tickets could be had of him at "the Fleece, Little Windmill Street (being the original Scotch house)." Fitzgerald in his life of Kitty Clive cited Thomas Watson as for many years boxkeeper at Drury Lane and Richmond and said that Watson kept the Bell Tavern in Church Row, Hounsditch.

Wattle, Charlotte Ann Frances.   *See* TWISLETON, MRS THOMAS JAMES.

Watts, Mr   *fl.* 1786[1], *actor.*

On 7 June 1786 at the Windsor Castle Inn, King Street, Hammersmith, a Watts, Jr was one of the Mob in *The Mayor of Garratt*. He was doubtless a son or other relative of John Watts, who was at that theatre during the season.

Watts, Mr   *fl.* 1794[1],   *scene painter.*

One Watts, a scene painter, was paid 5*s.* to 8*s.* per day for his work at Covent Garden Theatre in 1794, according to records of that theatre's accounts in British Library MS Egerton 2293.

Watts, Charles   *fl.* 1787–1800?[1],   *instrumentalist.*

Charles Watts, a violoncellist and violinist, played bassoon in the band of the first regiment of Guards and lived at No 34, Tufton Street, Westminster, according to Doane's *Musical Directory* of 1794. He may have been the Charles Watts whose wife Mary was buried at St Paul, Covent Garden, on 12 April 1787. According to an entry in the Treasurer's Book at the Folger Library, a musician named Watts—possibly Charles—was a member of the band at Drury Lane Theatre in 1799–1800.

Watts, George   1773–1845,   *violinist, pianoforte manufacturer.*

George Watts, the father of the eminent nineteenth-century painter George Frederic Watts, was born in Hereford on 1773, according to the painter's biography, written by his widow and published in 1910. George Watts worked in his father's shop in Hereford as an instrument maker and, apparently, cabinet-maker. By 1794 he was in London, living at the Exchequer in New Palace Yard according to Doane's *Musical Directory.* He was a violinist for the Choral Fund and played at Astley's Amphitheatre. By 1818 he described himself as a pianoforte manufacturer, but he dabbled in experiments and was a failure in business.

Watts had two girls and a boy by his first wife. On 23 February 1817, by his second wife, Harriet, née Smith, he had a son, George Frederic Watts. The second marriage brought four sons, but only George Frederic survived infancy. The young painter was successful enough to be able to support his father until the elder Watts died in 1845.

A portrait of George Watts painted by his son George Frederic Watts in 1835 was en-

GEORGE WATTS

engraving by Walker, after G. F. Watts

graved by Emory Walker. The engraving was published as a plate to Mary Watts's *Life of G. F. Watts,* 1912. The location of the original is unknown to us.

Watts, John   *fl.* 1778–1795?], *actor, singer.*

The anonymous "Gentleman" said to be making his first appearance when he sang Macheath in *The Beggar's Opera* at the Haymarket Theatre on 12 June 1780 was identified in the *Westminster Magazine* for June as Mr Watts. He was said to be "late an upholsterer in Conduit Street . . . capable of being useful, but the Stage is not an elegible pursuit for him." The *Morning Cronicle* for 13 June was similarly equivocal: he had a "tolerably good figure, and not an inharmonious high tenor voice. He sang several of the airs very agreeably, but the whole undertaking was much above his powers." The critic added charitably that Watts would do well in "a less arduous part than this of Macheath."

Hogan, in *The London Stage,* identifies that actor as John Watts. But there is reason to suspect—as is often the case—that the "first appearance" claim was spurious. It certainly seems that John Watts was the Watts who had twice performed at the China Hall Theatre, Rotherhithe, in 1778—as Priuli in *Venice Preserv'd* on 15 June and Obadiah Prim in *A Bold Stroke for a Wife* on 18 June—for Louisa Cranfield, who was later to become John Watts's mistress and, much later, his second wife, was associated with that house, and those roles were in his line of parts.

At any rate, John Watts and his first wife made their Irish debuts, she at Crow Street Theatre and he at Capel Street Theatre, Dublin, on 11 December 1782, according to the *Hibernian Journal* of that date. John could have been the Watts recorded as a member of the York circuit company in 1783–84. If he was, he came back to London early that spring to play Roger in *The Man's Bewitch'd* in a performance he arranged for his own benefit on 8 March 1784. The playbill stated that tickets could be had of him at No 2, Upper James Street, Golden Square.

When a company of casuals played for Robert Dighton's benefit at the Haymarket on 13 December 1784, Watts acted the Nephew in *The Irish Widow.* He was probably also in the company at Richmond, Surrey, in the summer of 1785, for a Mrs Watts, very likely his first wife, was a member.

After another absence—perhaps acting in the provinces or in Ireland again—Watts returned to the theatrical fringe of the metropolis in the summer of 1786, at Windsor Castle Inn, King Street, Hammersmith, from 5 June through 26 July, acting Dick in *The Lying Valet,* a Countryman in *The Country Girl,* the Miller in *The King and the Miller of Mansfield,* a Gravedigger in *Hamlet,* Pedro in *Catherine and Petruchio,* Farmer Stump in *The Agreeable Surprise,* the Duke in *Venice Preserv'd,* Father Luke in *The Poor Soldier,* Pantaloon in *Robinson Crusoe,* a Servant in *The Heiress,* Dumplin in *Peeping Tom of Coventry,* Watt in *All the World's a Stage,* Vasquez in *A Bold Stroke for a Husband,* John Moody in *The Provok'd Husband,* the Landlord in *The Fool,* and the Porter in *The Belle's Stratagem.* On 7 June a "Watts, Jr" was pressed into service as one of the Mob in *The Mayor of Garratt.* Whether he was a son or some other younger kinsman is not known.

Louisa Cranfield was using Watts's name

professionally as early as 1785, and it is probable that his first wife was by that time dead. Watts married Miss Cranfield at St Paul, Covent Garden, on 31 August 1791. The couple were probably the Mr and Mrs Watts known to have been at "The New Theatre in the Market Place," Ashley, in 1792, and he may have been the Watts who was on a bill at South Shields on 15 July 1795, playing Weasle in *The Wheel of Fortune* and Endless in *No Song No Supper*, both within John Watts's comic capability.

The date of John Watts's death is not known. His second wife, Louisa, had a long, though rather undistinguished, London career after he disappeared from the record.

Watts, Mrs John the first _fl. 1782–1785?_, *actress, dancer?*

The first Mrs John Watts made her Irish debut at the Capel Street Theatre on 11 December 1782, according to a notice in the *Hibernian Journal* of that date. She had accompanied her husband to Ireland, and she probably went back to England with him. She was very likely the Mrs Watts who danced with the Richmond company in the summer of 1785. She may have died before 1787, when Louisa Cranfield began to assume the name "Mrs John Watts".

Watts, Mrs John the second, Louisa, née Cranfield *1763–1838, dancer, singer, actress.*

The relationship of the dancer, singer, and actress Louisa Cranfield, who became the second Mrs John Watts, to the performers Mr Cranfield (fl. 1780–1803), Mrs Cranfield (fl. 1790–1798), T. Cranfield (fl. 1796–1805?), Miss P. Cranfield (fl. 1801–1802), and George Cranfield (fl. 1807–1808) is not certain. But it now appears that the first two cited above were *not* Louisa's parents as they were conjectured to be in Mr Cranfield's entry in volume 4 of this *Dictionary*. He was probably Louisa's brother and Miss P. Cranfield their sister. The *Authentic Memoirs of the Green Room* (1799) was briefly dismissive of Louisa and her family: "This lady was studied in the pantomimical school, and in such capacity is engaged at [Covent Garden Theatre]. Her family have been dancers and skippers in Jones's and other similar companies."

As a 12-year-old, Louisa made her Covent Garden debut dancing a hornpipe on 4 May 1775 when she shared a benefit with two others. Exactly a year later, 4 May 1776, she repeated her hornpipe and did a minuet with Halloway. On 11 May following she danced a minuet and allemande with Rudd. She was at the China Hall Theatre at Rotherhithe in the summer of 1777. A small company there evaded the Licensing Act by presenting dramatic "rehearsals" by "Pupils" between "the several parts of the Concert. . . ." Louisa danced a number of times and also acted, once as the Milliner in *The Suspicious Husband* and once as Lettice in *The Devil to Pay*.

Miss Cranfield was listed as "Principal Performer" in the bill for Messink and Delpini's new pantomime *The Norwood Gypsies*, which had a long run at Covent Garden after its premiere on 11 November 1777. She was probably Colombine, a part she filled when the piece was revived in 1780. That was already her line: the published text of Charles Dibdin's pantomime *The Mirror; or, Harlequin Everywhere*, performed at Covent Garden on 30 December 1779, assigned the Colombine of that piece to her, though the playbill had given it to Miss Brown. Also in 1779–80 Louisa was Colombine in the dance sequences of the musical interlude *The Fête Anticipated*.

She continued to perform at Covent Garden well into the nineteenth century, mostly in anonymous singing and dancing roles—shepherdesses, nymphs, orange wenches, bacchantes, peasants, and aerial spirits—in the spectacles of the time. She had a few secondary and tertiary named parts like Miss Ogle in *The Belle's Stratagem*, Sukey Tawdry in *The Beggar's Opera*, Tattle in *All in the Wrong*, Lucy Waters in *The Brothers*, Nancy in *He Would Be a Soldier*, Mrs Bruin in *The Mayor of Garratt*, the Duchess in *Barataria*, Myrtilla in *The Provok'd Husband*, and the original Commode in Samuel Birch's musical farce *The Packet-Boat*. In 1794–95 her salary was £2 per week, and she was still paid that sum in 1815–16, according to the treasurer's accounts of Covent Garden, from which her name disappeared after 1815–16.

In 1787 Louisa Cranfield had begun to be known as Mrs John Watts, though she did not marry Watts until 31 August 1791, at St Paul, Covent Garden. In addition to her service at Covent Garden Theatre, she danced for John Palmer at the Royalty Theatre in the summer of 1787. She and Watts were at the "New Theatre in the Market Place," Ashby, in the summer of 1792 and the Birmingham Theatre in the summer of 1795.

Louisa Cranfield Watts died in London in 1838 at the age of 75, according to the *Survey of London,* and was buried at St Martin-in-the-Fields on 15 December.

Watts, Richard   *fl.* 1784–1794₁, *singer, organist.*

Charles Burney listed a Watts among the bass singers assisting in the Handel Memorial Concerts in Westminster Abbey and the Pantheon in May and June 1784. Doane's *Musical Directory* of 1794 identified him as Richard Watts, adding that he played the organ and lived in Blackman Street, the Borough.

Watts, Roger   *fl.* 1742–1775₁,   *actor.*

At Covent Garden Theatre on 3 October 1746 the role of Sir Tunbelly Clumsy in *The Relapse* was taken by "Watts, from Bristol, being the 1st time of his appearing on any stage in London." So far as we can see, it was his last London appearance.

He must have been Roger Watts, who was a fixture of the Jacob's Wells Theatre in Bristol from at least 1742 through 1752. Newspaper notices show him playing there such parts as Hothead in *Sir Courtly Nice,* the Duke in *Othello,* Don Pedro in *Much Ado about Nothing,* the Bawd in *The Harlot's Progress,* and Lord Touchwood in *The Double Dealer.* Watts also acted at Bath in 1750.

Arnold Hare, in *Theatre Royal Bath The Orchard Street Calendar,* lists a Watts, probably Roger, who played at Bath in every season but one (1761–62) from 1759–60 to 1774–75.

Waud, Charles   *fl.* 1799–1810₁, *house servant.*

Documents in the Lord Chamberlain's records (W. B. 31157 to W. B. 31293) show that licenses for masquerades and performances were granted to Charles Waud on eight occasions from 4 February 1799 to 30 April 1810, "in Trust for the Pantheon proprietors." Mrs Waud, doubtless his wife, had been granted a license for a "play and entertain-

ment" at the Haymarket Theatre on 3 April 1797, according to WB 31107. (A company of caterers, Waud and Cox, supplied suppers to Ranelagh Gardens in the mid-1790s.)

Waud, Mrs [Charles]   *fl.* 1797₁, *house servant?* See WAUD, CHARLES.

Way, Mr   *fl.* 1792₁,   *house servant?*
The benefit tickets of Mr Way, probably a house servant, were accepted at Covent Garden Theatre on 1 June 1792.

Waylin. *See* WEYLIN.

Wayte, Mr   *fl.* 1731–1737₁,   *office keeper.*
The benefit bills at the Goodman's Fields Theatre show Mr Wayte to have been the office keeper there from 1731–32 through 1735–36. In 1736–37 he served in the same capacity at the Lincoln's Inn Fields Theatre, his benefit being a shared one on 28 April 1737. Perhaps he was related to John Wayte, who on 14 March 1732 was assigned the Aungier Street (Dublin) properties previously held by Thomas Griffith and others.

Wearman, Miss   *fl. c.* 1765–1775₁, *singer*
The *Catalogue of Printed Music in the British Museum* lists songs published about 1765 that were sung at Vauxhall Gardens by Miss Wearman, Vernon, and Gibson. The *Jester's Magazine* in October and December 1764 published songs sung by Miss Wearman at Vauxhall, one being "The Maid's Advice." Songs printed about 1775 indicated that Miss Wearman was still singing at Vauxhall.

Weaver, Mrs James, Elizabeth, née Farley   *fl.* 1660–1678?₁,   *actress.*
The prompter John Downes in the *Roscius Anglicanus* of 1708 listed Mrs (Elizabeth) Weaver as one of the original actresses in the King's Company when it was formed in 1660. She was usually called Mrs Weaver in cast lists, but her maiden name was Farley, and she apparently never married James Weaver of Gray's Inn, whose name she used. Samuel Pepys hinted on 11 January 1668 that Elizabeth Farley was for a brief period after the

Restoration a mistress of Charles II, but by the end of the 1660–61 theatrical season she was being called Mrs Weaver. Flecknoe intended her for the title part in *Erminia* that season at the theatre in Vere Street. The Lord Chamberlain's accounts called her Mrs "Ffarley" in a company list dated 27 March 1661, but the manuscript cast for *The Royall King* (at the Folger Library), dating about 1661–62, has her as Mrs Weaver. Another Folger manuscript cast, for *Love's Sacrifice*, about 1663–64, lists her as Biancha. A manuscript cast at the University of Leeds shows her as Isabella in *The Court Secret* in the early 1660s.

At St Andrew, Holborn, on 20 May 1661, Elizabeth, the (supposed) daughter of James and Elizabeth Weaver, was baptized, according to Roger S. Powell. On 14 January 1662 James Weaver asked permission to sue Elizabeth "ffarloe" on a bond of £30. The details of the matter are obscure, but the *Calendar of State Papers* for 1664–65 shows that in the fall of 1662 Mrs Weaver "brought in all her parts" to the Vere Street Theatre and said she was leaving the stage. After that it was discovered that she was pregnant and not married to Weaver. A petition against her by Henry Dobson dating about 30 September 1662 said that

one Eliz: Farley hath gone by the name of Eliz: Weaver wife to a gent of Grayes Inne to defraud her creditors and now being discovered that she is none of his wife altho she hath had a child by him and having no other shift for the defrauding of her said creditors but merely being sworne one of his Maties servants . . .

She owed Dobson £11 11s. 6d. (the original debt had been over £25). The actress Mrs Knepp told Samuel Pepys on 11 January 1668 that Charles II "first spoiled Mrs Weaver, which is very mean, me thinks, in a prince," but that must have happened much earlier in the 1660s.

Elizabeth was in constant trouble. Miles Lovett sued her on 3 March 1663 and Robert Kerby on the following 13 June; Robert Toplady attached her goods, for which he was arrested in August 1663. David Little went to court against her in March 1664, George Langford and Henry Rooke in 1665, and Francis Poyntz and Anne Hame in 1665.

She continued to act, however. At the Bridges Street Theatre with the King's Company in 1664–65 she was seen as Sylviana in *The Siege of Urbin*, Servlina in *Thomaso*, and Alibech in *The Indian Emperor*. She was probably the "Mrs Farlowe" who acted Mrs Martha in *Love in a Wood* in March 1671 and, at Drury Lane Theatre, Theocrine in *Wits Led by the Nose* in mid-June 1677, Eudoria in *The Rambling Justice* in late February 1678, and Luce in *The Man of Newmarket* and a Whore in *Trick for Trick* in March 1678. She was very likely the woman referred to in a poem in Rochester's *Works* about 1670, the first line of which runs, "Dreaming last night on Mrs. Farley."

Weaver, John *1673–1760, dancer, dancing master, choreographer.*

John Weaver, the son of John and Anne Weaver, was baptized on 21 July 1673 at Holy Cross, Shrewsbury. The elder Weaver taught dancing at Shrewsbury School before moving his family to Oxford, where he again set up as a dancing master. He died in 1701. The younger John Weaver was a dancing master in Shrewsbury for a number of years. Before coming to London, Weaver married a woman whose Christian name was Catherine (or Katherine). By 27 December 1702, when their son John was christened at St Andrew, Holborn, in London, the Weavers were living in Red Lyon Street. Their son died in infancy. On 12 August 1704 a daughter Elizabeth was christened; a second daughter, Katherine, was born in 1705 but died the following year. By then the Weavers were living in Prince's Street, Holborn. In 1707–8 the family returned to Shrewsbury; a daughter Anne Elizabeth was christened at St Julian's on 12 March 1708. On 11 July 1709 at St Chad's a second John was christened. On 2 (?) November 1710 their son Richard was baptized. On 13 September 1712 a daughter, Catherine, was baptized. Weaver's wife was buried the same day. She had died in childbirth.

During these early years of the eighteenth century John Weaver was establishing himself as one of the most important dancers and choreographers of the period. As early as 6 July 1700 he was dancing at Drury Lane Theatre in London in an entr'acte dance inserted into a performance of *The Pilgrim*. He did turns between the acts at Lincoln's Inn Fields Theatre on 21 October 1701, and he danced a *Roger a Coverly*, after the Yorkshire manner, on

29 December 1702. In his *History of the Mimes and Pantomimes* in 1728 Weaver claimed that he produced a piece called *The Tavern Bilkers* at Drury Lane in 1702, "the first entertainment that appeared on the English Stage, where the Representation and Story was carried on by Dancing Action and Motion only." *The London Stage* does not list such a work (*The Cheats; or, The Tavern Bilkers* dates from 1717 at Lincoln's Inn Fields), but perhaps the *Comical Entertainment in a Tavern between Scaramouch, Harlequin and Punchanello,* danced by Sorin and Baxter at Drury Lane on 12 October 1703, was the Weaver piece. In 1703 Weaver danced at York Buildings on 5 February and at Drury Lane on 28 May.

In 1706 he published two important works: *A Small Treatise of Time and Cadence in Dancing* and a translation of Feuillet's *Choréographie,* titled *Orchesography.* In 1707 Weaver wrote down the characters for his patron Isaac's dances for the Queen's birthday (*The Union*). Isaac may well have been the Samuel Isaack who in 1701 was a leaseholder in Red Lyon Street. On 19 March 1712 Weaver wrote from Salop to *The Spectator* (a staunch supporter of Weaver's efforts) announcing his intention to publish an *Essay towards an History of Dancing.* It appeared in print in September, the month Weaver's wife died.

In his *History of the Mimes and Pantomimes* Weaver claims that his *Perseus and Andromeda* was done at Drury Lane in 1716. No work of that title is known to have been performed that year (though a *Perseus and Andromeda* was put on a decade later); perhaps Weaver was remembering his *Loves of Mars and Venus,* which was given at Drury Lane on 2 March 1717 (1716 old style calendar) with Weaver dancing the part of Vulcan. That work was "a New Dramatick Entertainment of Dancing after the Manner of the Antient Pantomimes." Or was he remembering *The Shipwreck,* done at Drury Lane on 2 April 1717 with Weaver playing Perseus (Harlequin) and Mrs Bicknell dancing Andromeda (Colombine)? That work may have been composed by Weaver; he used it for his benefit on 9 April. Weaver continued dancing in pantomimes and between the acts at Drury Lane through 1728–29, though he was absent from the London stage in 1722 and from 1724 to 1728.

Weaver's sons, John and Richard, made their stage debuts at Drury Lane on 31 March 1718 dancing at *Italian Night Scene between Harlequin and Scaramouch* for Weaver's benefit. They appeared twice in May but seem not to have pursued careers in London further. Weaver's entr'acte dances over the years were not usually given titles in the bills, but a few were: *English Clown, The Original Irish Trot, The Sailor and His Lass* (with Mrs Bullock). His dance compositions included *Harlequin Turn'd Judge* (December 1717) and *Orpheus and Eurydice* (March 1718). In 1721 he published his *Anatomical and Mechanical Lectures upon Dancing,* which had been read at the Academy in Chancery Lane.

He played Columbine's Father in *Harlequin Happy and Poor Pierrot Married* (March 1728), Roger in *Acis and Galatea* (March 1728), and the Clown (Squire's Man) in his *Perseus and Andromeda* (November 1728). In the late 1720s Weaver's activity slowed, and between the spring of 1729 and February 1733 he was not named in London bills. *The Dictionary of National Biography* credits Weaver with *The Judgement of Paris,* which opened at Drury Lane on 6 February 1733. On 15 February, when that work was repeated, the performance was for Weaver's benefit and was the last notice of Weaver's activity in London.

Charles Burney was in Shrewsbury from 1742 to 1744 and years later remembered John Weaver (in his manuscript memoirs now at the British Library). Weaver had remarried:

The old friend of my father, Mr. Weaver, now near 90 [*recte* 70], still continued to keep open his boarding school wth. the assistance of the beautiful Mrs. Weaver & daughters; taught to dance, & had an Annual Ball, at wch. his scholars, besides the Minuet, Rigadon, and L'Ouvre, performed figure and pantomime dances such as in the beginning of the century he had invented as Ballet Master in London. In remembrance of my father he gave me lessons; & alotted me a part in a Wooden Shoe dance at one of his balls.

About 1750 at Shrewsbury, in the Great Room over the Market House, Weaver revived his *Judgement of Paris,* according to Owen and Blakeway's *History of Shrewsbury.*

John Weaver died in Shrewsbury on 24 September 1760 and was buried at St Chad's on 28 September. After the death of his first wife in 1712, Weaver had married again. By his second wife, Susanna, he had a daughter "Prissila," who was christened on 31 May 1716. On 20 January 1721 their daughter Dorothy was baptized at St Mary's. A daughter Anne was christened at St Alkmund's on 3 May 1722. A daughter Susannah was born in 1723 and a son William in 1728. The parish registers of St Chad's record the burial of William, son of John Weaver, in 1729 and the baptism and burial of a son Thomas in 1731, but those citations may concern not our subject but his son, born in 1709. Our John Weaver drafted his will on 2 January 1760, leaving each of his children a guinea. His widow Susanna was named residuary legatee and executrix. She died on 5 February 1773.

Dr Burney remembered John Weaver as a man of wit and ingenuity. Owen and Blakeway called Weaver "a little dapper cheerful man, much respected in the town" of Shrewsbury. Only in recent years has Weaver's importance in the development of the *ballet d'action*—scenical dancing, as Weaver called it—been fully appreciated. He predated Marie Sallé and Jean Georges Noverre and was serious in his attempts to tell stories through dance. John Rich, the manager of Covent Garden Theatre (and, before 1732, Lincoln's Inn Fields) and an accomplished harlequin, popularized the pantomime in London, but John Weaver deserves more credit than is usually given him for developing the form, first with his early experiments based on *commedia dell'arte* and then with his attempts to create danced stories after the manner of the ancient Romans. His theoretical writings on dance are important contributions to the literature and show him very much a man of his time in his emphasis on the laws of nature as the basis for ideas on dance. "Nature," he wrote in his preface to *The Loves of Mars and Venus* in 1717, "assign'd each motion of the Mind its proper Gesticulation and Countenance, as well as Tone; whereby it is significantly and decently express'd." In his *Essay towards an History of Dancing* in 1712 he laid out his theory of theatrical dancing:

STAGE DANCING was at first design'd for *Imitation;* to explain Things conceiv'd in the Mind, by the *Gestures* and *Motions* of the Body, and plainly and intelligibly representing *Actions, Manners,* and *Passions;* so that the Spectator might perfectly under-

stand the *Performer* by these his *Motions,* tho' he say not a Word. Thus far the Excellency of the *Art* appears; but its Beauties consist in the regulated *Motion* of all Parts, by forming the Body, Head, Arms and Feet, into such *Positins, Gestures* and *Movements,* as represent the aforesaid *Passions, Manners,* and *Actions;* so that in a skilful Representation of any *Character,* whether *serious* or *grotesque,* the Spectator will not only be pleas'd and diverted with the Beauty of the *Performance* and Symmetry of the *Movements;* but will also be instructed by the *Positions, Steps* and *Attitudes,* so as to be able to judge of the *Design* of the Performer. And without the help of an Interpreter, a Spectator shall at a distance, by the lively Representation of a just Character, be capable of understanding the *Subject* of the Story represented, and able to distinguish the several *Passions, Manners,* or *Actions,* as of *Love, Anger,* or the like.

In his preface to *The Loves of Mars and Venus* Weaver was specific about how various passions and affections were to be expressed:

ADMIRATION

Admiration is discover'd by the raising up of the right Hand, the Palm turn'd upwards, the Fingers clos'd; and in one Motion the Wrist turn'd round and Fingers spread; the Body reclining, and Eyes fix'd on the Object; but when it rises to

ASTONISHMENT

Both Hands are thrown up towards the Skies; the Eyes also lifted up, and the Body cast backwards.

JEALOUSY

Jealousy will appear by the Arms suspended, or a particular pointing the middle Finger to the Eye; by an irresolute Movement throughout the Scene, and a Thoughtfulness of Countenance.

UPBRAIDING

The Arms thrown forwards; the Palm of the Hands turn'd outward; the Fingers open, and the Elbows turn'd inward to the Breast; shew *Upbraiding,* and *Despite.*

ANGER

The left Hand struck suddenly with the right; and sometimes against the Breast; denotes *Anger.*

THREATS

Threatning, is express'd by raising the Hand, and shaking the bended Fist; knitting the Brow; biting the Nails; and catching back the Breath.

. . . and so on.

An admirable discussion of Weaver's contribution is Selma Jean Cohen's "Theory and Practice of Theatrical Dancing" in *Famed for Dance,* by Ifan Kyrle Fletcher, *et al.,* 1960. Richard Ralph's exhaustive study, *The Life and Works of John Weaver* (1985), is an invaluable source.

Weaver, John   *b. 1709, dancer.*
John Weaver the younger was baptized at St Chad's, Shrewsbury, on 11 July 1709. He was the son of the dancer and dancing master John Weaver and his wife Catherine. His brother Richard was christened on 2 (?) November 1710. On 31 March 1718 at Drury Lane Theatre in London John and Richard made their first stage appearances dancing an *Italian Night Scene between Harlequin and Scaramouch* at their father's benefit. They repeated that turn on 13 May and served as entr'acte dancers on 21 May. They seem to have given up London performing after that.

The parish registers of St Chad's in Shrewsbury record the burial of William, son of John Weaver, in 1729 and the baptism and burial of a son Thomas in 1731, but those citations may concern not our subject but his father.

Weaver, Richard   *fl. 1710]*,   *dancer.*
See WEAVER, JOHN. *b.* 1709.

Weaver, Thomas   *fl. 1667–1670]*, *scenekeeper.*
The London Stage lists Thomas Weaver as a member of the King's Company at the Bridges Street Theatre in 1667–68 and 1669–70. The Lord Chamberlain's accounts cited Weaver as a scenekeeper on 9 April 1668.

Web, Mr   *fl. 1739–1741]*,   *house servant?*
On 29 May 1739 and again on 8 May 1741 a Mr Web shared a benefit with several others, all known to be house servants, at Covent Garden Theatre.

Webb. *See also* WEBBE.

Webb, Mr   *fl. 1726–1742]*,   *house servant.*
A Mr Webb was a servant of the Lincoln's Inn Fields Theatre who appears in surviving house accounts in the Harvard Theatre Collection as employed sometimes as a boxkeeper, sometimes as a pitkeeper, and occasionally as an officekeeper. Covent Garden accounts at the British Library call him a billsetter.

He was probably the same Webb listed by Latreille as assistant boxoffice keeper at Covent Garden Theatre in 1735–36, drawing a salary of 6*d.* per night. That theatre's playbill for 27 May 1740 shows him sharing a benefit with the gallery doorkeeper Tyfer. On 18 May 1742 he shared a benefit with the servants Rivers, Sadler, and Trott.

Webb, Mr   *fl. 1776–1780?]*,   *actor.*
The Mr Webb who shared a benefit at Drury Lane Theatre with the minor actor Richard Hurst on 26 April 1776 may have been the Webb who, on 1 May 1777, played Willoughby in *A Word to the Wise* in a benefit performance at the Haymarket Theatre for "a Gentleman" under misfortunes. He may also have been the Webb who acted Frederick in *The Students* at the Haymarket for the benefit of Mr Stewart on 17 January 1780.

Webb, Mr   *fl. 1783–1785]*,   *house servant.*
A Mr Webb, demonstrably not Thomas Webb, was named in documents at the Public Record Office dated 1783, 1784, and 1785 as an assistant to the stage doorkeeper at the King's Theatre "on opera nights."

Webb, Mr   [*1784–1797?]*,*singer. See* WEBBE, SAMUEL.

Webb, Mr   *fl. 1797]*,   *actor, singer.*
A Mr Webb was in the company at the theatre at Richmond, Surrey, as of 1 September 1797, when the bills advertised *The Way to Get Married* and *The Maid of the Mill.* His roles are not known, but "songs" were to be sung by "Mr Webb, from Hungerford."

Webb, Mrs   *fl. 1734]*,   *actress.*
On 26 December 1734 at Drury Lane the afterpiece following the mainpiece *Cato* was the oft-repeated pantomime *Columbine Courtezan,* which contained a *ridotto al'fresco* with a cast of masquers varying from performance to performance. On that night—perhaps as a

special Christmas treat—a new character, Signiora Garagantula, was presented by "Mrs Webb, the Tall woman from Leicestershire." How tall she was or what her other attractions were cannot now be ascertained. There is no evidence that she played again in London.

Webb, Master *fl.* 1791–1799₁, dancer.

Master Webb was one of many dancers who performed in Carlo Delpini's new pantomime *Blue-Beard; or, The Flight of Harlequin* at Covent Garden Theatre on 21 December 1791. Bills on the third night assigned the part of Little Old Man to young Webb. The pantomime ran into February. On 25 July and six nights following Master Webb danced at the Haymarket Theatre in the new masque by W. B. Francis, *The Enchanted Wood.* Master Webb was in one performance of *Blue-Beard* at Covent Garden on 8 October 1792.

On 12 March 1796 a Master Webb, probably the same, appeared as the original Robber's Boy in the younger George Colman's melodrama *The Iron Chest* at Drury Lane Theatre, and he repeated the performance at the Haymarket on 29 August following. He was again at Covent Garden as the Lover's Servant in *Harlequin's Medley* on 9 June 1797, and reappeared on 16 March 1799 as the Boy in T. J. Dibdin's new comedy, *Five Thousand a Year.* Master Webb's last known appearance was as a Robber in a performance of *The Iron Chest* for Johnstone's benefit at Covent Garden on 23 April 1799.

Webb, Miss *fl.* 1770–1782₁, dancer, singer?

A Miss Webb, probably a juvenile, danced and perhaps sang along with Master Mathews and others in the afterpiece *Cupid's Frolic* at Sadler's Wells in September 1770. She was also in the company in the summer of 1771, and one of the rare bills in the Percival Collection in the British Library shows her as performing some part in *The Imprisonment of Harlequin* on 24 September that year.

She remained with the company or returned to it in 1776 and in 1782, unless another Miss Webb was then concerned. On 27 December 1779, a Miss Webb who may well have been the one from Sadler's Wells had joined a company of casuals at the Haymarket Theatre for

a specially licensed performance of *Falstaff's Wedding* "Written in imitation of Shakespeare by the late ingenious Dr [William] Kenrick," in which she represented Doll Tearsheet ("with a *song*"). She also played Molly Wheedle in *The Rival Milliners* that evening.

Webb, Miss *fl.* 1795₁, dancer.

A Miss Webb was one of nine dancers listed as performing in the spectacle called *Lord Mayor's Day* at Covent Garden on 16 November 1795, but she had almost certainly appeared in the three previous performances on 9, 10, and 12 November. She was named again in the playbill of the final presentation on 24 November.

Webb, Miss *fl.* 1798–1799₁, actress.

A Miss Webb was the original Adolphus in Samuel Birch's melodrama *Albert and Adelaide* at Covent Garden Theatre on 11 December 1798. It was billed as her first appearance at that theatre. She performed the breeches role 18 times during the season.

The *Hibernian Journal* of 18 December 1799 said that Miss Webb "of Covent Garden" had made her Irish debut at Crow Street Theatre, Dublin. Evidently, she was not the dancer of 1795.

Webb, Alexander *d.* 1823, actor, singer, dancer.

James Winston in *The Theatric Tourist* (1805) states that Alexander Webb was acting at Liverpool when (apparently in 1788) John Philip Kemble came from London to assume the title role in *King John:*

Webb was to play the Citizen who speaks from the walls; and he recited at morning rehearsal, the very long speech originally written by Shakespeare, but omitted [in London] in representation. Mr. Kemble advised him to conform to the practice in London; and stated the awkward situation of the principal characters in case of refusal. Webb nodded assent: but, in the evening delivered the whole faithful to his Author in every letter, and was rewarded with abundant applause. Kemble who had measured his strides, and his stops, and his starts, with the nicest precision, to eke out the quantity [of time] given in London, was much disconcerted through the rest of the scene.

Nevertheless, according to Winston, the incident brought Webb to Kemble's attention.

After playing in the summer of 1788 at the Haymarket, he was hired the following winter season, 1789–90, at Drury Lane, remaining for nearly every season, according to the records of the Drury Lane Fund, until the spring of 1812. (The Drury Lane company lists at the Garrick Club show him absent in 1801–2. That year, according to surviving Covent Garden accounts, he was at that house. He had made £1 5*s.* a week before his defection. At Covent Garden he was paid only £1.) Webb also acted again at Liverpool in the summer of 1792 and was very likely the Webb reported in the company at Crow Street, Dublin, in 1816–17.

Alexander Webb's repertoire of some 120 roles up to 1800 was confined principally to secondary and tertiary characters and walk-ons—subsidiary Shakespearean lords, comic servants, eccentrics in melodrama, and other underlings, like Hali in *Tamerlane the Great*, Cambridge in *Henry V*, a Slave in *Oroonoko*, Alguazile in *The Pannel*, Bagshot in *The Beaux' Stratagem*, Silvertongue in *The Belle's Stratagem*, Sir Walter in *The Surrender of Calais*, a Goatherd in *The Mountaineers*, Derby in *Jane Shore*, and Bernardo in *Hamlet*. He was the original Hubert in James Cobb's comic opera *The Haunted Tower*, Biskey in John Philip Kemble's comedy *Love in Many Masks*, Stanislaus in Kemble's melodrama *Lodoiska*, Thomas in Thomas Holcroft's comedy *The Man of Ten Thousand*, Memnon in J. H. D'Egville's pantomime *Alexander the Great*, Simon in Colman's melodrama *The Iron Chest*, George in Benjamin Thompson's drama *The Stranger*, as well as nameless henchmen, butlers, hostlers, and huntsmen in many other new plays, operas, and pantomimes.

If Webb was usually well in the background, he was always dependably there. How long past the turn of the century he continued to act we do not know. A manuscript in the Harvard Theatre Collection gives a death date of 17 January 1823 for a Drury Lane actor named Webb, almost certainly our subject, though his first name is not given there. It is furnished by the Winston transcriptions of the records of the Drury Lane Actors' Fund.

Webb, ₁**Edward?**₁   *fl.*   1792–1800₁,
dancer, actor.

Mr Webb was first noticed in the playbills as part of the large dance corps involved in the lavish revival of the pantomime *Harlequin's Invasion* by the Drury Lane company at the King's Theatre on 27 December 1792. There is a good chance that he had been in the company before that date and that he remained during that season, unlisted in any bill. However, no adult dancer named Webb (see Master Webb, separately noticed) appeared in the bills again at any London theatre until 15 October 1798 when a Webb, whom we assume to have been our subject, was one of the "Principal Ballet Characters" in John Cartwright Cross's new pantomime ballet *The Genoese Pirate* at Covent Garden Theatre. Webb next was seen as a Domestic in *Raymond and Agnes* on 13 April 1799. During the rest of the season he walked on as a Waiter in *The Norwood Gypsies* and a "Principal Character" in *Lover's Vows*. He was cited several times also in the bills of Covent Garden during the season of 1799–1800, dancing in Tom Dibdin's new pantomime *The Volcano; or, the Rival Harlequins* and as a Country Lad in *The Deserter of Naples* and repeating his part in *Raymond and Agnes*.

An Edward Webb had applied to the Lord Chamberlain for a license to put on a benefit performance at the Haymarket on 13 May 1796. C. B. Hogan, in *The London Stage*, identifies the dancer and actor we have been following as Edward Webb.

Webb, Henry   ₁*fl.*   1736?–1793₁,
trumpeter.

The Lord Chamberlain's warrants cite the trumpeter Henry Webb as replacing John Seignior in the King's Musick in 1736 or perhaps earlier. Webb is named in Establishment warrants in 1738, 1749, 1759, and 1793, unless there was a sequence of two Henry Webbs.

Webb, John   1611–1672, *scene designer, architect.*

John Webb was born in London in 1611 of a family from Somerset and received part of his education at Merchant Taylors' school from 1625 to 1628. He was a pupil of the eminent architect and scene designer Inigo Jones, and many of Webb's architectural works were either done in conjunction with

Jones or were continuations or executions of his master's designs. From 1633 to 1641 Jones employed Webb as Clerk Engrosser of the old St Paul's works, according to the Works Accounts. Webb was also related to Jones by marriage, but the sources are not in agreement about just what the relationship was. In Walpole's *Anecdotes* is a footnote by Dallaway and Vertue indicating that Webb was a nephew of Jones and married Jones's only daughter, but another note states that Webb married Jones's niece. Jones's will merely indicates that Webb married Ann Jones, Inigo Jones's kinswoman.

From Webb's will we learn the names of seven of his children—James, William, Henry, Katherine, Martha, Elizabeth, and Rebecca, all of whom were alive in 1672—and of Webb's sister (or sister-in-law?), Bridgett Moone (or Mohun?—a relative of the actor Michael Mohun?). In the registers of St Martin-in-the-Fields we have found many references to a John and Ann Webb and their children Elizabeth, William, Henry, Martha, and Rebecca. But other children are also mentioned: Thomas, Sarah, John, and Benjamin. References to these all fall between 1644 and 1654. There were apparently two other couples whose names were John and Ann Webb in the parish, citations of them and their children dating 1640 on the one hand and 1661–1664 on the other.

One cannot be certain that the citations from 1644 to 1654 concern our subject's children but it seems very likely that they do. Elizabeth Webb was christened on 26 August 1644, Thomas on 17 November 1645 (he was buried on 21 July 1647), Sarah on 26 April 1647, William on 11 August 1648, John on 14 September 1649 (he was buried on 29 June 1650), Henry on 14 February 1651, Martha on 2 March 1652, "Rebekah" on 6 September 1653, and Benjamin on 31 December 1654 (the day of his birth).

Though most of Webb's work was architectural, he was involved in theatrical productions as early as 1635, when he appears to have assisted Inigo Jones with the scenery for the court masque *Florimene*. William G. Keith attributed two studies in perspective and an alternate ground plan for that production to Webb. As Jones's pupil, Webb was probably

involved in other court productions in the Caroline period, but the only other drawing attributable to Webb is a double-spread ground plan of the elaborate court production of *Salmacida Spolia* in 1640. Webb's work on Caroline theatrical productions would appear to have been only as an assistant to Jones. Collections of drawings at the British Library, Chatsworth, and Worcester College, Oxford, for pre-Commonwealth projects are mostly the work of Jones. Jones died in 1652, leaving some property to Webb and designating him his executor.

The most important theatrical work of John Webb was the scenery for *The Siege of Rhodes*. The historic production at Rutland House in 1656 by Sir William Davenant marked the renewal of theatrical activity after 14 years of official (but not actual) silence. Webb's plans for the tiny theatre Davenant erected within his house and sketches of the proscenium arch, permanent side wings, and the movable shutters and relieves have survived. By comparison with the work of his master, Webb's talent was modest. If Davenant made use of Webb's services in other productions we have no record of it. Elizabeth Scanlan in her study of the first Lincoln's Inn Fields Theatre assumed that Webb had a hand in its conversion from a tennis court, but there appears to be no clear evidence of that.

The only other examples of Webb's work are some designs for *Mustapha,* which was presented at the Lincoln's Inn Fields playhouse by Davenant on 3 April 1665, shortly before the plague closed the theatres, and at court on 18 October 1666, just as theatrical activity was resuming after the fire of London. The *Mustapha* designs are very like those for *The Siege of Rhodes* and show the same, uninspired design talent. According to Sybil Rosenfeld in her *Short History of Scene Design in Great Britain,* the scenery, though designed by Webb, was painted by Robert Streeter, a much more talented decorative painter than Webb.

Eleanor Boswell in *The Restoration Court Stage* points out that a letter among the State Papers indicates that Webb was responsible for converting the great hall in Whitehall into a permanent court theatre. In his protest against Sir Christopher Wren's being made surveyor of the works, Webb wrote, "At

Design for *The Siege of Rhodes*
by John Webb

Whitehall hee [i.e., Webb] made yor. Theater, and thereby discovered much of the
Scenicall Art, wch. to others then himselfe was
before much unknowne." The petition from
Webb is undated but is calendared with 1668
papers; Wren was appointed surveyor in 1669
at the death of Sir John Denham, even though
Webb held the reversion.

Early in the 1660s Webb had asked to be
appointed surveyor of works to the King, ar-
guing his fidelity to the royal cause, his affili-
ation with Inigo Jones, the intention of
Charles I that Webb be given the post, and
Webb's commission to prepare the royal pal-
aces for residence, a £8140 project. Webb was
given a reversion to the post after Sir John
Denham. From 1661 to 1666 he assisted

Denham in executing part of Inigo Jones's design for Greenwich Palace. His salary, according to *The Dictionary of National Biography,* was
£200 per year. By the mid-1660s he styled
himself as John Webb of Butleigh, Somerset, where he had evidently inherited family
property.

In the 1660s Webb busied himself with a
number of architectural projects, sometimes
with Denham and often following plans originally made by Inigo Jones. Webb did some
repairs at St Paul's Cathedral in 1663, designed Burlington House beginning in 1664,
and worked on such other projects as Lord
Carleton's Amesbury in Wiltshire, Gunners-
bury House near Kew, and perhaps Ashburn-
ham House in Westminster, Bedford House

on Bloomsbury Square, Horseheath Hall in Cambridgeshire, Ramsbury Manor in Wiltshire, and Ashdown Park in Berkshire.

John Webb died on 30 October 1672. He said he wished to be interred in the burying place belonging to his house in Butleigh, which is probably where he died. To his wife Ann (or Anne) he left most of his valuables and household goods, but some also went to his son James. To his daughter Katherine Webb he left all the furniture and paintings in her bedchamber. His son William was given various properties in Butleigh as well as Webb's library of books, prints, "cuts," and architectural drawings. It was Webb's desire that the collection should be kept intact and not subject to selling "or unbezelling," though he noted that any duplicates among his books could be given to his son James. William was to pay a legacy of £200 to his sister Martha Webb within two years of John Webb's death. It was Webb's intent that the bequests to his son William should be full satisfaction "of all legacies given to him by Master Inigo Jones deceased." To his son Henry Webb he left £800, which consisted of £600 to be collected from debtors and £200 to be raised out of fines due, apparently from tenants on Webb property. Henry was also to have all of Webb's household goods at Greenwich, where Webb owned property. Rentals worth £12 annually were to go to his son William. His daughter Elizabeth Webb was to have £800 and all legacies left her by Inigo Jones and others. Daughter Martha was to receive £400 to add to £200, which had evidently been given her earlier. Rebecca Webb was bequeathed £600.

John Webb had grandchildren, but the will did not specify which of his own children were their parents. Grandchild Elizabeth, daughter of Dr Westley, and Frances, the daughter of Mrs Anne Jegowe, were to receive 20s. each for mourning rings. Dr Westley's wife was probably Webb's daughter Martha, since she was not called Martha Webb in the will but merely Martha. Mrs Anne Jegowe was presumably a daughter of John Webb, though she was not otherwise named in the will, nor was there an Anne Webb mentioned in the St Martin's parish registers. John Webb left his grandson John Webb his silver case of mathematical instruments; the boy was presumably

the son of either James, William, or Henry Webb. Only James was mentioned in the will as married, though all three sons may have been.

John Webb's sister (though that term was then sometimes used to refer to a sister-in-law) Bridgett Moone was to receive an annuity of £5. John Webb specified that his wife was to give his daughters proper maintenance until their legacies were raised through leasing pieces of Webb's Butleigh property. Webb named his wife his executrix and made her residuary legatee; among the items not otherwise bequeathed that she would fall heir to were Webb's corn and cattle, so some portion of his property had been farm land.

Either Mrs Webb died before the will was proved or she gave her power to her daughter Elizabeth, for Elizabeth was named executrix in the probate. But Elizabeth was named "relict," so perhaps there was an error in the will; Ann Webb was clearly John Webb's relict.

John Webb edited Inigo Jones's *The Most Noble Antiquity Called Stoneheng* in 1655 and wrote *Vindication of Stoneheng Restored* in 1665. In 1657 he designed the frontispiece to Walton's *Polyglot Bible*. There is an extensive entry on Webb, including a list of his architectural works, in Colvin's *Biographical Dictionary of British Architects*.

Webb, [Lydia?], later Mrs Thomas Marshall the second, then Mrs Wilmot *fl.* 1788–1812,], *actress, singer*.

The subject of this entry was a foundling, if the testimony of the *Thespian Dictionary* (1805) is true: "Mr. Webb, returning home late one night, found in the street a deserted female infant. . . ." Pitying "the poor babe's forlorn situation" and fearing for the child's safety if he entrusted her to the unfeeling workhouse bureaucracy, he adopted her. Mr Webb was an actor, whom John Bernard, long afterward in his *Retrospections,* remembered as "Dicky" Webb.

The dramatic tale of rescue seems possible, for the account adds, "Mrs. Webb introduced to the public, on her benefit at the Haymarket, 1788, her adopted daughter, in the character of Leonora" in *The Padlock,* and the bill for the evening, 30 July 1788, confirms that fact. It was said to be the girl's "first appearance on any stage." Miss Webb's adoptive father did not live to witness her debut; he had died in 1784. The Harvard Theatre Collection contains the signature "Lydia Webb," which, the Collection's files suggest, may be our subject's.

Her adoptive mother was an established comic actress and singer at the Haymarket, at Covent Garden, at Edinburgh, and, indeed, in "nine-tenths of the Companies in the three kingdoms," to quote the exaggeration of *The Secret History of the Green Rooms* (1790). So perhaps Mrs Webb used her wide acquaintance to place her daughter in a country company for seasoning before the young woman's next attempt at the Haymarket. That came exactly two years after the first one, on 30 July 1790—and again on her mother's benefit night—when the girl assumed the starring role of Polly in *The Beggar's Opera*.

But again it was a one-night effort, and after that the record grows uncertain for a period. It would be tempting to believe that our Miss Webb went to Ireland, for W. S. Clark in *The Irish Stage in the County Towns* found a Miss Webb there in 1790. But apparently that actress had been at Waterford in July, as well as Limerick in August and at Ennis in September and October. Unless our Miss Webb came to the Haymarket for one performance, after acting in Ireland in July, and then returned to Ireland immediately, she was not the same person.

It is, however, probable that our Miss Webb was the one reported at Manchester on 11 April 1791 and 29 and 30 May 1792 and at Birmingham for the summer season of 1792. Almost certainly she was the Miss Webb who "generously" offered her services "gratis" in a concert for the benefit of Mr Hobbs (a performer who was ill) at the Bristol Assembly Rooms on 29 October 1792, for by that time she was a success at Bath and Bristol. The *Morning Herald* of 26 September 1792 reported that she had made her debut at Bath on 22 September and identified her as the daughter of the London comedienne. *The Secret History of the Green Room* (1792) asserted that she had

lately acquired considerable laurels as a Singer in the country. She at present leads the Opera in the fashionable town of Bath, which is the last step towards London. Her personal accomplishments,

her powers of voice, her taste and execution, are highly spoken of, and with a good Master, and assiduity, it is expected she will soon be a distinguished favourite amongour vocal performers.

Sometime before 4 January 1793 Miss Webb married—or assumed the name of—the comedian Thomas Marshall, whose first wife had died in January 1791. The Marshalls were recruited shortly thereafter by Thomas Wignell for the Philadelphia theatre. They sailed from London on 15 July 1793 in the *George Barclay*. William Dunlap was doubtless correct in writing that they appeared first (with the Philadelphia company) at Annapolis later in 1793. But the first solid evidence of their acting in America comes from the playbills of the new Chestnut Street Theatre published by T. C. Pollock in *The Philadelphia Theatre in the Eighteenth Century*. Mrs Marshall appeared on the opening night of the Chestnut Street, 17 February 1794, playing Lorenza in *The Castle of Andalusia*, with her husband playing Don Fernando.

The success predicted by *The Secret History* came immediately in America and grew for many seasons. Mrs Marshall became a favorite as ingenue and soubrette with the Philadelphia company for the next six seasons. But she sometimes went, with critical approval, into tragedy, and she also sang very well.

Iola Willis, in *The Charleston Stage in the Eighteenth Century*, says that Mrs Marshall, née Webb, was at Charleston in 1800. She defected from Wignell and sailed secretly from Charleston after a dispute with the manager over his allotment of a coveted part to Mrs Merry. In 1800, according to W. B. Wood in his *Personal Recollections of the Stage*, our subject went back to England briefly, separated from her husband, and "contracted a second marriage with a Mr. Wilmot," by whose name she afterward appeared in New York. There is some doubt that the pair were legally married. (Wood testified that Thomas Marshall went back to England and, totally blind, survived for some years on a pension from the theatrical fund.)

Mary R. Michael, in an unpublished dissertation, "A History of the Professional Theatre in Boston . . . to 1816," reports that Mr and Mrs Wilmot joined Snelling Powell's company at Boston's Federal Street Theatre in the

1802–3 season. At the end of the 1803–4 season the Wilmots appear to have left for Charleston, according to W. B. Wood. Martin Shockley, in *The Richmond Stage 1784–1812,* then locates them in the West and Bignall company at the new theatre in Richmond, Virginia, which opened in January 1806, and they returned there for the season that ran from December 1806 to February 1807. In June 1807 the Wilmots were at Chestnut Street with Thomas A. Cooper. G. C. D. Odell's *Annals of the New York Stage* picked up a New York *Post* advertisement of 16 July for the Vauxhall Theatre in New York, heralding the summer season (through 16 September) in which the Wilmots were prominent. On 23 July Mrs Wilmot had also joined Webster of "the Dublin Theatre," singing at the Assembly Room of the City Hotel.

Mrs Wilmot was at the Chestnut Street Theatre again on 15 March 1809 and returned for several engagements during the 1809–10 season. Reese James, in *Old Drury of Philadelphia,* spots her in the Washington bill of that company on 26 July 1810 and the Baltimore bill of 1 March 1811. Odell says that both the Wilmots were present when Dwyer and McKenzie opened the Circus in Anthony Street, New York, on 20 May 1812. Mrs Wilmot had been with the Olympic Theatre in London in the winter-spring season of 1812. She was said to have come from there when, on 6 August, she joined other singers and some instrumentalists for a concert at Tammany Hall. That is the latest news of either of the Wilmots. It may be that the naval hostilities that flared into the War of 1812 that summer had something to do with her cessation of activity. Perhaps the Wilmots went back to England. Richardson Wright, in *Revels in Jamaica,* cites a Miss Wilmot, of the theatres of Bath and London, who was announced as arriving in M. W. Adamson's company in Barbados in 1813. She may have been a daughter of our Mrs Wilmot.

By general agreement, [Lydia?] Webb Marshall Wilmot was, after Mrs Merry, the favorite American actress of her day. Chief Justice Gibson was one who ranked them thus, and he confided to a friend of W. B. Wood's that "Mrs. Marshall . . . was a great favorite with General Washington." Dunlap's description of her as "a pretty little woman, and a most

charming actress in the pickles and romps of the drama," is insufficient. Her range was enormously wider. Seilhamer's assessment in his *History* seems correct:

She could assume with equal ease, grace and propriety the forward, pouting airs of an awkward country minx; the impertinence of a rude boy . . . ; the staid manners of a well-educated lady, and the softness and tenderness of a *Juliet.* She did not, however, escape adverse comment. When "Tamerlane" was played she was severely censured for her dress as Selima, "which was before midleg high and displeasing alike to males and females."

In view of her importance to the early American stage, we give a complete list of the roles she added in her first season and a half at Philadelphia. In the spring of 1794 she played Lorenza in *The Castle of Andalusia,* Mariamne in *The Dramatist,* Rosetta in *Love in a Village,* Harriet in *The Guardian,* Edward in *Every One Has His Faults,* Annette in *Robin Hood,* Louisa in *The Deserter,* Lucy in *The Virgin Unmask'd,* Moggy in *The Highland Fling,* Lydia in *The Rivals,* Cowslip in *The Agreeable Surprise,* Miss Biddy in *Miss in Her Teens,* Madelon in *The Surrender of Calais,* Charlotte Rusport in *The West Indian,* Hypolita in *She Wou'd and She Wou'd Not,* Rosalind in *As You Like It,* Juliet in *Romeo and Juliet,* Adeline in *The Battle of Hexham,* Rosa in *How to Grow Rich,* Fetnah in *The Slaves of Algiers,* Selima in *Selima and Azor,* Rachel in *The Prisoner at Large,* and Dorinda in the altered *Tempest.*

In 1794–95 she added Clarissa in *Lionel and Clarissa,* Maud in *Peeping Tom of Coventry,* Priscilla Tomboy in *The Romp,* Mrs Grumble in *The Volunteers,* Fanny in *The Clandestine Marriage,* Sophia in *The Road to Ruin,* Miss Peggy in *The Country Girl,* a Pastoral Nymph in *Comus,* Zelide in *The East Indian,* Aurra in *The Farm House,* Josephine in *The Children in the Wood,* Nell in *The Devil to Pay,* Selima in *Tamerlane,* Miss Hardcastle in *She Stoops to Conquer,* Miss Alton in *The Heiress,* Lady Bill in *Know Your Own Mind,* Jenine in *Auld Robin Gray,* Amanthis in *The Child of Nature,* Edwitha in *The Noble Peasant,* Margaretta in *A New Way to Pay Old Debts,* Nancy Buttercup in *Set a Beggar on Horseback,* Gillian in *The Quaker,* Clarinda in *The Suspicious Husband,* the original Rachel Friendly in *Triumphs of Love* (a new comedy by Murdock, "a Citizen of Philadelphia"), and

Hannah in *The Wedding Day.* She continued to add roles at much that rate until 1800.

A portrait of Lydia Webb Wilmot (25" × 30"), painted from a miniature, was begun by the American artist Thomas Sully in July 1805 and was finished the same month. Sully sold the portrait, presumably to Mrs Wilmot, for $3000. The present location of the portrait is unknown.

Webb, [Richard?] *d. 1784, actor, singer.*
The "Young Gentleman" who made his "first appearance on any stage" at Drury Lane Theatre as Aboan in *The Royal Slave* on 27 April 1770 was identified in Isaac Reed's "Notitia Dramatica" in the British Library as a Mr Webb. Very likely he was the "Dicky" Webb spoken of in John Bernard's *Retrospections* as acting later in 1770 in Edinburgh.

"Dicky" Webb was with a strolling company in Glasgow and elsewhere in Scotland from February until April 1771, according to Elbridge Colby's extracts from the *Glasgow Journal.* By 1772 he was again in Edinburgh, where he acted with Joseph and Elizabeth Inchbald and (said James Boaden) carried on a flirtation with Mrs Inchbald that was harmless but which much annoyed her elderly husband. By 1774 Webb had (perhaps) married the widowed Mrs (Lydia?) Child Day, an actress with the Edinburgh company. The Webbs remained at Edinburgh during the winter seasons (usually January to May) until the spring of 1779. Dicky there amassed a repertoire of some 80 important secondary characters—bluff squires, blunt judges, hearty landlords, and wise men of substance, as well as a few eccentrics, braggart soldiers, and comical foreigners: Gonzalo in *The Tempest,* the Bishop of Winchester in *Lady Jane Gray,* Bonniface in *The Beaux' Stratagem,* Drawcansir in *The Rehearsal,* Major Oakly in *The Jealous Wife,* Bardolph in *1 Henry IV,* Justice Guttle in *The Lying Valet,* Sir John Bevil in *The Conscious Lovers,* Justice Ballance in *The Recruiting Officer,* Hardcastle in *She Stoops to Conquer,* Sir Oliver Surface in *The School for Scandal,* Stockwell in *The West Indian,* and so on.

Webb played Willoughby at Colman's Haymarket Theatre on 1 May 1777 in *A Word to the Wise* in a benefit performance for an unnamed person suffering "misfortunes." In the summer of 1778 he returned to the Haymarket as a regular member of the company. With his wife he also accompanied Joseph Glassington to play briefly at Stourbridge Fair that summer. At some time in 1778 he also played at York. At Edinburgh again in the winter-spring season of 1779, he came back to the Haymarket in the summers of 1779 and 1780. He joined the company at Covent Garden in the fall of 1780 and was a regular there until the end of the 1782–83 season, serving again in 1781 and 1782 on the summer programs at the Haymarket.

Dicky Webb's wife had preceded him to the Haymarket and had quickly become a favorite in farce and comic opera. Webb was never nearly so prominent as she. Compared to his list of roles at Edinburgh, his repertoire at London looks meager. Yet he contributed steadily, repeating some of his former parts and adding the following at the Haymarket: in 1778, the original Bounce in George Colman's comedy *The Suicide;* in 1779, Dr Camphire in *The Devil upon Two Sticks;* and in 1780, Parchment in *The Wedding Night* and the original Agreeable Companion in Colman's pantomime *The Genius of Nonsense.*

At Covent Garden in 1780–81 Webb added Charino in *Love Makes a Man,* the original Shrimp in Frederick Pilon's farce *The Humours of an Election,* Corporal Flint in *St Patrick's Day,* and a Witch in *Macbeth;* at the Haymarket in 1781, Robin in *The Author,* the Coachman in *The Dead Alive,* the Mayor in *The Nabob,* the original John Bull in Colman's *A Preludio,* Sukey Tawdry in *The Beggar's Opera,* Gripe in *The Confederacy,* and Capulet in *The School of Shakespeare;* at Covent Garden in 1781–82, the original Jailor in James Messink's pantomime *The Choice of Harlequin* and Don Lopez in *The Wonder;* at the Haymarket in 1782, the original Landlord in Frances Burney's comedy *The East Indian* and Philario in *Cymbeline;* and at Covent Garden in 1782–83, Jemmy Twitcher in *The Beggar's Opera,* Uncle Toby in *Tristram Shandy,* and Charles in *As You Like It.*

Like his wife—who is supposed to have wooed him with her cooking—Webb was very fat: "This worthy couple weighed at least sixteen stone each," according to Oxberry's *Dramatic Biography* (1825). And, like his wife, he was kindly and well-regarded. He was also, perhaps, spendthrift—or maybe just unlucky. The Argosy MS in the Harvard Theatre Collection, apparently citing the *Morning Post* of 27 July 1784, dates his death as "last week" in the rules of the King's Bench, where he had been imprisoned for debt. The year and place are confirmed by Isaac Reed's "Notitia Dramatica" in the British Library.

Webb was survived by his wife, a son, and an adopted daughter. The daughter he had found abandoned as an infant, in a London street. She grew up to achieve success as an actress in Britain and the United States, billed successively as Miss Webb, Mrs Thomas Marshall, and Mrs Wilmot.

Webb, Mrs [Richard?], née Child, formerly Mrs [George?] Day   *d. 1793, actress, singer.*

Mrs Webb was for 15 years one of the most popular comediennes acting on the stages of Covent Garden Theatre and the Haymarket Theatre, and (wrote the author of *The Secret History of the Green Rooms* [1790]) "to enumerate the Companies she had performed in would be to enumerate nine-tenths of the Companies in the three kingdoms."

Yet little is known of her early life beyond what *The Secret History* asserted: "Her maiden name was Child. She married Mr. Day, and was in the Norwich company thirty years ago." (In the index to C. B. Hogan's volumes of *The London Stage*, where no authority is cited, her baptismal name is given as Ludia. But in view of her daughter's probable first name, Lydia, Miss Child's may have been the same.)

Certainly Miss Child made her debut at Norwich on 17 March 1764, according to the *Mercury* of that city. Two recollections of the events of the early career of John ("Plausible Jack") Palmer give us subsequent news of her. Palmer was at Colchester under Hurst's management in 1765. "Here his talents were thought so lightly of, that he would have been discharged but for the interposition of Mrs Webb, who was then in that company, and married to a Mr. Day," testified the author of *A Sketch of . . . the Life of John Palmer* (1798). "From Colchester, the Company went to Ipswich, and, as it was difficult to procure lodgings, six of them took up residence in Bridewell, the remains of the famous college

founded by Cardinal Wolsey," according to "Memoirs of John Palmer, Esq." in the *Thespian Magazine* (1793), which names among the six a "Miss Child."

Whether or not Miss Child was married to Mr Day by 1765, our subject probably did marry him before the end of the sixties. She may have been the Mrs Day who with a Mr Day acted at Smock Alley Theatre in Dublin in 1770–71. Our doubts that they were Mr and Mrs *George* Day, expressed in his entry in volume 4, persist, but the identification is not impossible.

Mrs Day was at the Theatre Royal, Shakespeare Square, in Edinburgh, during the 1772–73 season, acting a series of comedy roles. By the winter-spring season of 1774 she had married (or assumed the name of) "Dicky" Webb of that company. (The assertion of *The Secret History* that "After the death of her first husband" she lived for "many years" with "Mr. Jackson, a Comedian well known in Bath and Bristol" seems false.)

The Webbs acted regularly in Edinburgh in the winter-spring seasons beginning each January through 1779. Mrs Webb's roles there (as Mrs Day), collected by Norma Armstrong, were as follows: Alicia in *Jane Shore*, Cordelia in *King Lear*, Dorcas in *Thomas and Sally*, Lady Rusport in *The West Indian*, Mrs Heidelberg in *The Clandestine Marriage*, Mrs Honeycombe in *Polly Honeycombe*, Queen Catherine in *Henry VIII*, Queen Elizabeth in *The Albion Queens*, Queen Gertrude in *Hamlet*, and Rhodope in *Orpheus*.

As Mrs Webb, at Edinburgh, she repeated some of those roles and added, in 1774, Chloris in *The Rehearsal*, Dame Quickly in *The Merry Wives of Windsor*, the title role in *The Irish Widow*, Filagree in *A Trip to Scotland*, the Hostess in *1 Henry IV*, Kitty Pry in *The Lying Valet*, Lady Brute in *The Provok'd Wife*, unspecified characters in *The Bankrupt*, *The Maid of Bath*, *The Man of Business*, and *The Nabob*, Lady Dove in *The Brothers*, Lady Freelove in *The Jealous Wife*, Mrs Bridgemore in *The Fashionable Lover*, Mrs Snip in *The Invasion of Harlequin*, Tag in *Miss in Her Teens*, Urganda in *Cymon*, the Wife in *The Recruiting Sergeant*, Constance in *King John*, and Hecate in *Macbeth*.

Mrs Webb continued to add to her repertoire. In 1775, she played Margaret in *The

Deserter, Mrs Sneak in *The Mayor of Garratt*, the usually male role of Justice Midas in *Midas*, and Lady Restless in *All in the Wrong*; in 1776, a Bacchanalian in *Comus*, Dorcas in *The Mock Doctor*, Emilia in *Othello*, the Freemason's Wife in *The Clock Case*, Lady Brumpton in *The Funeral*, Lady Mary Oldboy in *Lionel and Clarissa*, Margery in *The Dragon of Wantley*, Mrs Mechlin in *The Commissary*, Pallas in *The Golden Pippin*, Phyllis in *The Conscious Lovers*, Lady Wronghead in *The Provok'd Husband*, and Zara in *The Mourning Bride*.

She added, in 1777, Bridget Bumpkin in *All the World's a Stage*, Mrs Malaprop in *The Rivals*, Mrs Peachum in *The Beggar's Opera*, Mysis in *Midas*, the title role in *The Old Maid*, and the Widow Blackacre in *The Plain Dealer*; in 1778, a part unspecified in *The Ladies' Frolic*, Fanny in *The Maid of the Mill*, Lady Pride in *The Modern Union*, Lucy in *The Recruiting Officer*, Mrs Frail in *Love for Love*, Mrs Hardcastle in *She Stoops to Conquer*, Mrs Magnum in *The Volunteers*, the Mother in *The Chances*, Nell in *The Camp*, and the Nurse in *Isabella*; and in 1779, Mrs Candour in *The School for Scandal*, Lady Catherine Rouge in *The Invasion*, Lady Randolph in *Douglas*, Lucy in *The Guardian*, Mrs Browley in *Know Your Own Mind*, Muslin in *The Way to Keep Him*, Nell in *The Devil to Pay*, and the Queen in *Cymbeline*.

It was an extensive and varied repertoire that commended Mrs Webb to London managers as a useful singer and actress of comic eccentrics. The elder George Colman gave her a summer contract at the Haymarket in 1778 and renewed it in 1779. (She had also accompanied her husband to Stourbridge Fair, near Cambridge, to act briefly in the summer of 1778 at Joseph Glassington's booth, according to Sybil Rosenfeld. At some time in 1778 she also acted at York.) By the fall of 1779 she was also on Colman's list at Covent Garden, where she was an important attraction until the end of her career. Her husband remained, for the time being, in Edinburgh.

By the time Mrs Webb arrived in London in the summer of 1778 (via York, where Tate Wilkinson gave her a few nights' engagement beginning 14 May), she had become very fat. *The Secret History* thought her such an admirer of culinary art that "she studied cooking more than Shakespeare." She had attracted her hus-

Harvard Theatre Collection

MRS R[ICHARD?] WEBB, caricature as Cowslip
by Gillray

band Webb through her culinary ability: "A more jolly couple than Mr. and Mrs. Webb never trod the Stage—their appearance was not at all calculated to excite compassion, and make a lucrative benefit in a country town; they had, however, a good income from the Edinburgh Theatre, which enabled them to indulge their favourite passion."

Mrs Webb made her first appearance at the Haymarket on 1 June 1778, hampered probably by the petite dimensions of the theatre. The *Morning Post*'s critic reported:

Last night a Mrs. *Webb*, from the theatre-royal in Edinburgh, made her first appearance at this theatre in the character of Mrs *Cross* in Mr. Colman's comedy of *Man and Wife.* ———— We think her a *first rate*, in point of bodily size, and *second rate* as to theatrical merit; tho' to do her justice, she marked some of the comic scenes very forcibly, and would have executed the whole in a superior style, had she been less vociferous, or been fortunate enough to have had stage room for her *lungs of leather!*

The *Morning Cronicle* was more charitable:
". . . notwithstanding that she had no great
opportunity of shewing her talents, [she] gave
us reason to hope she will prove an useful
comic actress and that she may be capable of
supplying . . . [Sarah] Gardner's place successfully and creditably." That writer added,
"Report says she possesses a sound musical
voice and is sufficient mistress of the art of
singing to render herself additionally serviceable to the stage on that account. . . ." When
she sang for the first time, in the chorus of
Macbeth on 7 September, the writer for the
Chronicle wrote that she "afforded proof of a
most powerful and harmonious voice" and
chided Colman ("who seems this summer to
have been musically mad") for "never before"
employing her as a singer. Before the end of
the summer season, her partisan, the critic in
the *Chronicle,* even discovered "proof of her
possessing what the town did not imagine she
was blessed with—talents for tragedy, and
those of no mean sort." She had, "at very short
notice, undertook to read the part of Bonduca" in the tragedy *Bonduca* when Katherine
Sherry was indisposed. She "did not dully re-
cite from the *litera scripta,* but delivered the
speeches of the hapless Queen with so much
spirit and propriety that unless the book in
her hand had shewn she was reading, not one
in the audience could have supposed it to be
the case."

But a tragedienne she was never to be, except when she occasionally lent her immense
physique to the part of some Queen in Shakespeare or in pseudoclassic drama. She earned
her modest seasonal increments at Covent
Garden—from £2 per week in 1779–80, increased to £2 10s. the following season, then
to £4 10s. in 1781–82, and to £5 from 1789–
90 to the end of her career—by playing parts
in which her figure ("which is uncommonly
lusty and grotesque," said the author of *The
Secret History*) and her remarkably clear enun-
ciation could best assist her portrayals. That
meant comedy and farce of the broadest sort.
The German visitor Carl Philip Moritz, who
saw her as Mrs Cheshire in *The Agreeable Surprise* in June 1782, wrote: "A Mrs Webb
played the part of a cheesemonger—a common woman—so naturally that I have never
seen its equal. Her massive body and whole
external appearance, however, made her as if

cut out for the part" (Reginald Nettel's translation). By 1788, she was exploiting her size
and her peculiar talent in a manner that made
her an obvious target for one of Anthony Pasquin's (John Williams's) most memorable
broadsides in *The Children of Thespis:*

Like a lusty old Sybil, who rambles elate,
With a raven-ton'd voice to anticipate Fate;
Mark WEBB, like a whale, bear her fatness be-
*   fore her,*
As the sprats of the Drama for mercy implore her;
Her high-garnish'd phiz give young Pleasantries
*   birth,*
And her well-fed abdomen's a mountain of mirth:
See the coarse-hewn old Dowager's mix'd with the
*   rest,*
Like a piece of brown dowlas near lace from Tri-
*   este;*
And darts her huge beak for the prizes and pick-
*   ings,*
As an overgrown hen amidst delicate chickens:
Impertinent Doubts run to measure her size,
While Temperance looks at her frame with sur-
*   prise.*
Her airs are as harsh as a Brighthelmstone dipper,
And loosely assum'd like a pantaloon's slipper;
Tho' base without force, like the oath of a harlot,
Or the impudent grin of a shoulder-deck'd var-
*   let.—*
This mould of the fair sex is true female stuff,
And warm at the heart, tho' her—manners are
*   rough:*
Like QUEEN BESS she disdains the resistance of
*   man,*
And knocks down a peer with the end of her fan;
Old Care knits his brows to coerce and impale her,
And eyes her with hatred but dares not assail her.
For social contumely cares not a fig,
For if none call her GREAT, all the world swears
*   she's big.*
She's a beef-lin'd adherent to thundering Rage,
And a prop of vast import to Wit and the stage;
But Bards have too potently season'd her song,
Which like garlic in soup makes the pottage too
*   strong;*
She's a stage-struck Silena, who raves and who
*   bellows,*
Like WESTON or WINDSOR when bilk'd by
*   their fellows;*
No precept—no labor can polish or tame her,
Not CHESTERFIELD'S page or the chissel of
*   DAMER!*
For by playing old furies so apt and so often,
No human device can the habitude soften;
Thus an erotic sapling we frequently see,
When engrafted by Art, become part of the tree.—
So poignant a mind in a vulgariz'd shell,

Resembles a bucket of gold in a well;
'Tis like Ceylon's best spice in a rude-fashion'd
*   jar,*
Or Comedy coop'd in a Dutch man of war.

Certainly when she essayed characters requiring subtler shadings she was not so effective. The most celebrated illustration of that
fact was her attempt at Falstaff in *1 Henry IV*
for her benefit on 21 July 1786. The *General
Advertiser* of the following morning disap-
proved: "Old Jack, instead of appearing with
all that easy, flowing, negligent facetiousness
which the poet has so inimitably pourtrayed,
assumed the part of moral solemnity, and
every joke was delivered with a sort of senten-
tious dignity that destroyed its natural impression."

Mrs Webb repeated many of her Edinburgh
roles in London, but some of them already belonged to jealous possessors. She continued to
be employed mainly in Glumdalca in *Tom
Thumb,* Mrs Grubb in *Cross Purposes,* Mrs Far-
dingale in *The Funeral,* Lady Rachel Mildew
in *The School for Wives,* and other eccentrics.
She was used constantly to help bolster with
her coarse fun some tottering trifle, but she
was also the original presenter of roles in several enduring comedy pieces.

Following, by season, are the characters
Mrs Webb "originated," as she alternated her
service from Covent Garden in the winter seasons to the Haymarket in the summers, from
the summer of 1778 through the fall of 1793:
Mrs Grogram in the elder George Colman's
comedy *The Suicide* at the Haymarket in 1778;
Lady Juniper in M. P. Andrews and W. A.
Miles's comic opera *Summer Amusements* and
Lady Oldcastle in Colman's comedy *The Separate Maintenance* at the Haymarket in 1779;
Dame Hearty in R. J. Goodenough's pastoral
afterpiece *William and Nanny* at Covent Garden in 1779–80; the Lady in the Balcony in
Colman's prelude *The Manager in Distress* and
Commode in Andrews's comedy *Fire and
Water!* at the Haymarket in 1780; Mrs High-
flight in Frederick Pilon's farce *The Humours of
an Election,* Mrs Tantrum in Henry Knapp's
farce *The Excise Man* (here even Mrs Webb's
efforts were insufficient, the *London Chronicle*
reporting that it "was not suffered to proceed
to its conclusion; and the actors were driven
from the stage"), and Elvira in Charles Dib-

Courtesy of the Garrick Club

MRS R[ICHARD?] WEBB, as Lady Dove
by De Wilde

din's comic opera *The Islanders* at Covent Gar-
den in 1780–81; Hebe Wintertop in John
O'Keeffe's comic opera *The Dead Alive* and
Mefrow VanBoterman in *The Baron Kinkver-
vankotsdorsprachengatchdern!* at the Haymarket
in 1781; Mrs Cheshire in O'Keeffe's musical
farce *The Agreeable Surprise* and Lady Dangle in
Richard Cumberland's comedy *The Walloons* at
Covent Garden in 1781–82; the Aunt in
Charles Dibin's farce *None Are So Blind as Those
Who Won't See* at the Haymarket in 1782; Mrs
Melpomene Sanguine in Leonard Macnally's *A
New Occasional Prelude* at Covent Garden in
1782–83; Mrs Henpeckt in John Dent's farce
The Receipts Tax at the Haymarket in 1783;
Winterbottom's Sister in Henry Knapp's mu-
sical farce *Hunt the Slipper* at the Haymarket in
1784; the Widow Grampus in Pilon's farce
Aerostation, Lady Bull in O'Keeffe's comic op-
era *Fontainebleau,* and Marcelina in Thomas
Holcroft's adaptation of *Le Mariage de Figaro*
called *The Follies of a Day,* Widow Winkle in

the anonymous farce *The Israelites,* and Honour in Leonard Macnally's *Fashionable Levities* at Covent Garden in 1784–85; the Landlady in the anonymous musical interlude *William and Susan* at the Haymarket in 1785; and Lady Mary Magpie in Elizabeth Inchbald's farce *Appearance Is against Them* at Covent Garden in 1785–86.

Still other parts introduced by Mrs Webb were Antonietta in O'Keeffe's comic opera *The Siege of Curzola* at the Haymarket in 1786; Mrs Poplin in James Cobb's farce *English Readings* at the Haymarket in 1787; Mrs Goodly in Mrs Inchbald's comedy *All on a Summer's Day* at Covent Garden in 1787–88; Amra in Richard Bentley's comic opera *The Prophet,* Katty Kavanaugh in O'Keeffe's comedy *The Toy,* the Taylor's Wife in O'Keeffe's farce *The Little Hunchback,* Mrs Syllabub in the anonymous entertainment *Saint George's Day,* and Lady Waitfor't in Frederick Reynolds's comedy *The Dramatist* at Covent Garden in 1788–89; the Baroness de Portsheim in the anonymous farce *The Swop,* Mrs Malmsey in the younger George Colman's farce *The Family Party,* and Lady Testy in Thomas Bellamy's comedy *The Comet* at the Haymarket in 1789; Catherine in *The Picture of Paris,* Di Clackit in Henry Bate's comic opera *The Woodman,* Lady Drowsy in E. J. Eyre's comedy *The Dreamer Awake,* and Mrs McNab in Wilson and Reeve's musical interlude *The Union* at Covent Garden in 1790–91; Lady Gander in Andrew Franklin's farce *The Mermaid,* Lady Acid in Reynolds's comedy *Notoriety,* Lady Oddly in Thomas Hurlstone's farce *Young Men, and Old Women,* and Diana Dupely in Mrs Inchbald's comedy *Cross Partners* at the Haymarket in 1792.

Mrs Webb's husband (called "Dicky" in John Barnard's *Retrospections*) had followed her to London from Edinburgh, and he acted at Covent Garden for three seasons. Larpent Manuscript 560 at the Huntington indicates that he lived at Blackheath in 1781. Mrs Webb was then in Bedford Street, so they may have been separated. The Argosy manuscript at Harvard asserts that he died in the King's Bench debtors' prison on 27 July 1784.

The Webbs were parents. The *Thespian Dictionary* (1805) tells an affecting story that "Mr. Webb, returning home late one night, found in the street a deserted female infant, and, calling a watchman to witness the poor babe's forlorn situation," he took her home, and the Webbs adopted her and raised her as their own. The story sounds suspiciously like many recounted in sentimental popular publications of the era. Yet, the writer continued, "Mrs. Webb introduced to the public, on her benefit at the Haymarket, 1788, her adopted daughter," as Leonora in *The Padlock,* and that fact is confirmed by the playbill of 30 July 1788. Perhaps the Webbs had a son as well. A Master Webb, of indeterminable age, appeared as a dancer in the chorus of *Blue Beard* at Covent Garden on 21 December 1791 and several nights afterward. He was several times in *The Enchanted Wood* at the Haymarket the following summer.

Mrs Webb lived with her family at No 15, Bedford Street, Covent Garden, from 1779 through 1782. She directed seekers of benefit tickets to her at No 22, "corner of Broad Court, Bow Street, Covent Garden," in 1787. She lived at No 19, Catherine Street, the Strand, in 1791.

A Folger Library manuscript dated 30 July 1793 reads, "Mrs. Webb has had the misfortune to be seized by a paralytic stroke." She died, aged 56, on 24 November 1793 and, according to the *Gentleman's Magazine* for December 1793, was buried at St Paul, Covent Garden. Her burial is not registered there, however, under Webb, Day, or Child.

A portrait by Samuel de Wilde of Mrs Webb as Lady Dove in *The Brothers* is in the Garrick Club (No 237). It was engraved by Audinet for *Bell's British Theatre,* 1792, and by J. Chapman (after H. Moses) as a plate to *British Drama,* printed by Cooke, 1808. James Gillray's caricature of her as Cowslip ("with a bowl of Cream") was published by Humphrey on 13 June 1797. A caricature by an unknown artist of Mrs Webb as Lucy and Mrs Edwards as Captain Macheath in *The Beggar's Opera* was published by Thomas Cornell, 1786, and is reproduced in this *Dictionary* 5:13. Another caricature by an unknown artist shows Mrs Webb in male attire, with her right hand inside her waistcoat and her left hand in her trousers pocket; it was published by A. Buengo in 1805 with the title "Ease and elegance."

Webb, Thomas *fl.* 1783–1814?,
boxkeeper, lobby keeper.

Thomas Webb is named as a boxkeeper and a lobby keeper at the King's Theatre in Lord Chamberlain's documents at the Public Record Office dated 1783, 1784, and 1785. He signed, with other servants belonging to that theatre, an affidavit addressed by Giovanni Gallini to Edward Jerningham in 1787. He may have been the Thomas Webb, "aged 47 years," buried at St Paul, Covent Garden, on 4 March 1807, or the Thomas Webb who was granted licenses by the Lord Chamberlain for plays and entertainments at the Haymarket for 20 January 1812 and for 14 February 1814.

Webb, William   *fl. 1787?–1794*, *violinist.*

A professional violinist named William Webb, of No 72, High Street, Marylebone, was cited in Doane's *Musical Directory* (1794) as a member of the New Musical Fund. There is a possibility that he was one of the several sons of the elder Samuel Webbe, composer of glees and bass singer. The surviving account of money paid to the band and singers employed for the 1787–88 concert season by the Academy of Ancient Music shows a "W. Webbe" receiving the sum of £6 6s. "for S. Webbe, Jr.," a "Tenor Voice."

Webbe, Mr   *fl. 1794*, *singer.*

The program of a concert offered for the benefit of the New Musical Fund by Signora Storace, Signor Rovedino, and others at the King's Theatre on 6 March 1794 included a "Song by Mr Webbe from Oxford."

Webbe, J.   *1787–1788 singer.*

A surviving account of money paid to musicians employed in the concerts sponsored by the Academy of Ancient Music during the 1787–88 season lists a J. Webbe, "Bass Voice," who was paid £12 12s. for his services. The notation is either a mistake for Samuel Webbe the elder or refers to one of his sons previously unrecorded. (The entry following that one in the list concerns £6 6s. paid "Per W. Webbe, for S. Webbe, Jr.," a "Tenor Voice.")

Webbe, Samuel   *1740–1816, composer, singer, organist, pianist.*

There are short notices for Samuel Webbe

the elder (often "Webb"), the remarkable composer of glees and church music, in *The Dictionary of National Biography* and the *New Grove Dictionary of Music and Musicians.* But both are silent about his career in performance.

The place of Webbe's birth is not known for certain. He is often said to have been born in Minorca, where his father died shortly after assuming a government post in 1740. But Samuel Webbe's obituary in the *Gentleman's Magazine* in 1816 seems to suggest that he had been born in London before his mother could join his father in Minorca.

Webbe's mother brought him up as a Roman Catholic and apprenticed him at age 11 to a cabinetmaker. He abandoned that trade when his articles expired and began copying music for Welcker in Soho. He studied music with Charles Barbandt, the organist at the chapel of the Bavarian ambassador. He found time also over the next few years to teach himself the rudiments of Latin, French, Italian, German, Greek, and Hebrew.

Webbe began composing vocal scores in 1763. In 1766 he won the first of his 26 medals from the Catch Club with his canon "O that I had wings." (Entries in *Grove's* fifth and earlier editions supply the titles of the other 25 pieces, the last of which was as late as 1794.)

We almost certainly encounter him in his capacity as bass singer at Marylebone Gardens in the summer of 1767. A surviving bill of 7 August lists a "Webb" with others singing catches and glees. That Webb sang music from Handel's *Solomon* for Thomas Lowe's benefit at the Gardens on 18 September following. "Webbe" was also one of 15 singers in the chorus of *Lycidas* when it was performed for the first time at Covent Garden Theatre on 4 November 1767. Webbe became a member of the Royal Society of Musicians on 5 April 1770.

We take Samuel also to have been the singer "Webb" who was mentioned in a letter William Bewley wrote from Houghton to Dr Charles Burney in 1771 saying that the Earl of Sandwich had arrived at the seat of the Walpoles accompanied by his mistress the amateur singer Martha Ray, "Mr Bates" (the organist and concert organizer Joah Bates, who was at that time Sandwich's secretary), and other

By permission of the Trustees of the British Museum

SAMUEL WEBBE

engraving by Skelton, after Behnes

singers. Among those others was a Mr Webb who, Bewley believed, Burney knew. The musicians had brought "with them ten or a dozen volumes of catches or canons & etc which they sing in such perfection that I believe they will put me out of love with instrumental music as long as I live."

In that same year, 1771, Samuel Webbe became a member of the Catch Club, no doubt as a result of his acquaintance with Sandwich, the Club's "soul," according to Charles Butler's *Reminiscences*. At the King's Theatre on 11 January 1774 a Webbe joined Fochetti, Schirolli, and other Italians performing some part unspecified in Casman's *La Contessina*, repeated once, on 15 January. Webbe may have sung in other operas that season; few casts are preserved.

In 1776, Samuel Webbe was organist of both the Portuguese and Sardinian Chapels. He also played on occasion at the Bavarian and Spanish Chapels. According to the manuscript Drury Lane account books in the Folger Library, when R. B. Sheridan produced his three-act version of Garrick's *Christmas Tale* on

18 October 1776, Webbe, bass, was one of the chorus, paid £1 5s. per week. The piece had an extended run. Webbe also assisted in the chorus accompanying *Macbeth at* Drury Lane, 25 November and following. Between 3 January 1778 and 14 November 1778 the account books show seven disbursements to him "for Chorus."

Samuel Webbe composed for and probably sang at Vauxhall Gardens. A surviving notice from that pleasure garden dated 10 May 1779 advertises the singing of new songs and glees and a "new catch called The Coachman set by Mr. Webb." The "Webb" who joined Reinhold, Vernon, Champness, R. Smith, Reynoldson, Simpson, Leoni, and "several other of the most eminent Performers" to sing "several of the most approved *Catches and Glees* (selected from the invaluable Collection of the Noblemen's and Gentlemen's Catch-Club)" at Covent Garden Theatre on 17 April 1779 was, then, Samuel Webbe.

Further, Samuel was the "Webb," bass, named by Burney as among the vocal performers at the Handel Memorial Concerts at Westminster Abbey and the Pantheon on 26, 27, and 29 May and 3 and 5 June 1784, for the entry for "Samuel Webb, Senr." in Doane's *Musical Directory* (1784) reads: "Composer, Organ, Prin[cipal] Bass, Royal Society of Musicians, Anacreontic Society, Abbey Westminster—grand performances . . ." Doane gives his address as "No 1, Great Sq, Gray's Inn," the address given also by Doane for "Webb, Jr . . . Tenor," the younger Samuel. The elder Webbe trained John Danby, Samuel Knyvett, and Vincent Novello and proposed Danby for the Royal Society in 1785. Samuel, senior, must also have been the Webb who sang for the benefit of one of the prominent oboists named Parke—either John or William his brother—at the Ancient Concert Rooms, Tottenham Street, on 8 April 1786. (William Parke would propose the younger Webbe for membership in the Royal Society of Musicians in 1790.)

Therefore, there is excellent reason to suppose that, when Anfossi brought out the pasticcio opera *Orfeo* at the King's Theatre on 12 May 1785, the "Director of and 1st Singer in the Chorus—Webb"—so advertised—was also Samuel Webbe the elder. He continued in those capacities for the rest of that season.

When the Glee Club was established in 1787 Samuel Webbe became its librarian and wrote for it the glee that was performed first at every meeting, his "Glorious Apollo."

Webb became secretary of the Catch Club in 1794 and held that office until 1814. He died at his chambers in Gray's Inn on 25 May 1816 and was buried in Old St Pancras churchyard. He was survived by several children, the eldest of whom, Samuel (1768–1843) was also a prominent London musician.

The *New Grove* contributes an extensive bibliography of his music published in London and a careful analysis of his importance as a composer.

A portrait of Samuel Webbe was engraved by W. Skelton, after W. Behnes, and published as a plate to the *European Magazine*, 1820.

Webbe, Samuel   *1768–1843, singer, instrumentalist, composer.*

The short account of the younger Samuel Webbe in the *New Grove* summarizes his career as organist and teacher and gives a good account of his composition but neglects his public performance.

He was the eldest son of the more important composer of glees and church music Samuel Webbe (1740–1816), under whom he studied organ and piano. He was born on 15 October 1768, according to an affidavit given to the Royal Society of Musicians by Father Ignatius John Wylde, "Apostolic Missionary and Chaplain in London to his most Excellent the Lord Legate to his Serene Highness, Duke of Bavaria." Webbe was baptized at the Bavarian Chapel on 2 November 1768, the "son of Samuel and Anne Webbe."

He was listed by Charles Burney—as "Webb (Jr)"—among that vast throng of singers in the Handel Memorial Concerts at Westminster Abbey and the Pantheon in May and June 1784. He was said to be a tenor. (His father was then listed as "Webb, bass.") A surviving list of payments to singers in the concerts sponsored by the Academy of Ancient music in 1787–88 shows him earning £6 6s. for that season.

The Minute Books of the Royal Society of Musicians record that "Samuel Webb, jr" was proposed for membership by the prominent oboist William Parke on 5 December 1790.

At that time he was unmarried and was organist at the Bavarian Chapel "at a salary of 24 guineas per ann." He was unanimously elected on 6 March 1791, signing the book of admission on 3 April following. "Sam Webb jr." was assigned by the Society to play trumpet at the annual benefit concerts for the clergy of St Paul's Cathedral on 10 and 12 May 1791. (He figures in the Minute Books again, in 1795 and 1796, as a violinist at St Paul's; in 1798 as a member of the Court of Assistants and as a violinist at St Paul's; in 1799 as an oboist but represented by a deputy at St Paul's; and in 1800 as a trumpeter at St Paul's.) Doane's *Musical Directory* of 1794 notes his membership in the Society and his participation both in the original and in more recent Handelian celebrations. It lists two of his areas of expertise—"Pia[no] Forte, Tenor"—and gives his address: "No 1, Great Square, Gray's Inn," which was also his father's place of residence.

In 1794 also, Webbe was awarded prizes from the Catch Club for a catch, "Ah, Friendship," and a canon, "Resonate Jovem," and in 1795 for a canon, "Come Follow Me." The *New Grove* attributes the music for the operatic farce *The Speechless Wife* (Covent Garden 22 May 1794) to the younger Samuel Webbe, but Hogan in *The London Stage 1660–1800* gives the work to the elder.

About 1798, according to the *New Grove*, Webbe settled in Liverpool as organist of the Unitarian Chapel, Paradise Street. The register of St John's, Liverpool, recorded his marriage on 7 October 1803 to Diana Smith, "a minor." He returned to London in 1817 to teach piano by the Logier system and to serve as organist at the Spanish Chapel. Some years afterward he returned to Liverpool as organist at St Nicholas Church. He was later organist of St Patrick's Chapel, Texteth Park, Liverpool.

Ten signatures of members of the Royal Society of Musicians attested on 3 July 1840 that Webbe, then 72, was in poor health, had suffered bankruptcy through "impropitious—tho' well advised—speculation," but had pursued his profession "steadily and industriously" for "upwards of 54 years." He was granted £5 5s. per week. He died in London on 25 November 1843.

Webber. *See also* WEBER.

Webber, Mr *fl. 1792–1818?*], *actor.*

When a mixed company of amateurs and country professionals gave a performance for the benefit of the Literary Fund at the Haymarket Theatre on 16 April 1792, a Mr Webber came on as Stanley in *Richard III*. It appears to have been his sole London performance. But it is possible that he was the Webber who was on a Manchester playbill of 24 March 1800 as Peter in *The Dramatist* and Idle in *The Son-in-Law*, and he may also have been the Webber who played Fag in *The Rivals* with the Richmond troupe at Harrogate on 1 August 1801 and Mancinus in *The Fall of Carthage* with the Richmond players at Whitby on 15 February 1802. He was also at York sometime in 1802. He was again at Whitby sometime in 1804. Perhaps he was the Webber who played at Harrogate in September 1818.

Webber, Antony *d. 1788, musician.*

Antony Webber became a member of the Royal Society of Musicians on 3 September 1762, and he was still a member in 1787, according to the Minute Books of the Society. He died before 3 August 1788.

Webber, John Francis *fl. 1739–1755*], *musician.*

John Francis Webber, of the parish of St James, Westminster, was an original subscriber to the Royal Society of Musicians of Great Britain. He was listed in the Declaration of Trust dated 28 August 1739. He was mentioned in the Society's records again in 1742, 1744, and 1755.

Webber, Peter *fl. 1739–1761*], *musician.*

Peter Webber was an original subscriber to the Royal Society of Musicians of Great Britain in 1739. He was still listed as a member in 1742 and 1744 and was on the Court of Assistants of the Society in 1761.

Weber. *See also* WYBER.

Weber, Francisco *fl. 1723–1728*], *lutanist.*

On 6 March 1723 Francisco "Weybough" played the lute at a concert at Hickford's Music Room. Lowell Lindgren has suggested to us that this musician was Francisco Weber (or Webber), who was given a benefit concert at the Haymarket Theatre on 22 April 1724 and another at Hickford's on 15 May 1728. At the latter he played the lute and a "Mandolino Concerto."

Webster, Mr *fl. 1728–1729*], *actor.*

An actor named Webster shared a benefit with the actors Sandham and Dove at the Haymarket Theatre on 11 February 1729. But he was first listed in a playbill on 25 February when he played both a Shepherd and a "Sylvan" in *The Humours of Harlequin*. On 29 March he played the Genius in *Hurlothrumbo*, repeated Shepherd and Sylvan on 26 May, and on 29 May was Cant in *The Beggar's Wedding*.

Webster, Mr *fl. 1780*], *actor, singer.*

The Webster who sang Sir William in *The Gentle Shepherd* at a specially licensed benefit for Walker and Stewart at the Haymarket Theatre on 23 September 1780 was not Anthony Webster, who had died in July. The members of the Haymarket group were probably Scots amateurs.

Webster, Mr *fl. 1793*], *equestrian.*

Mr Webster was one of a dozen equestrians named on the playbill for the performance of the spectacle called *The Disembarkation of the Night House* at Astley's Amphitheatre on 15 June 1793. But it had been performed from 20 to 27 May, when the bills did not name all the participants.

Webster, Anthony *d. 1780, actor, singer.*

Anthony Webster was the "son of Dr. Webster of St. Stephen's, Coleman Street," and "had just studied the Ecclesiastical Law, in order to be admitted a Doctor of Civil Law in Doctor's Commons," according to the recollection of the musician Richard John Samuel Stevens. But Webster then deserted law for the theatre.

We believe that his first attempt on the London stage was at the Haymarket Theatre on 15 October 1770, on the occasion of a special benefit for Thomas Weston, when a Mr Webster played Sir Richard Wealthy in *The Minor*. Certainly it was Anthony Webster who was introduced, as "A Young Gentleman," to the Covent Garden audience in the title role of *Douglas* on 15 January 1776. His name was revealed when he was given a benefit on 5 February. He drew a full review of his acting in the *Westminster Magazine* for January:

His person is rather elegant; his voice is full and harmonious, his pronunciation distinct and correct, and his delivery graceful and unembarassed. Those are his excellencies, and considering it was his first performance, he seems to possess them in a degree far superior to the various candidates for theatrical fame which the managers of both houses have brought forward for some years past. On the other hand he is aukward, and in some parts unanimated. His arms are too long, or he flung them about in a very disgusting manner. He seemed to express the sense of his author much better than his own feelings. His voice though full, wants variety and modulation; not but on some occasions he managed it with infinite grace and judgement. But if this want of variety of tones and extent of voice, which is so indispensibly necessary to constitute a first rate actor, be not the effect of Nature, the Public may behold with less anxiety their decayed veterans giving nightly proofs of their increasing infirmities, and quick approaching theatrical dissolution.

Evidently he improved rapidly enough to be awarded appearances during the rest of the spring of 1776 as Edgar in *King Lear,* Lothario in *The Fair Penitent,* and the title role in *Comus.* He was also in four repetitions of *Douglas.*

Stevens remembered that Webster had already begun living "in open adultery with" Elizabeth Battishill, the singer, wife of the musician Jonathan Battishill ("'If ever I meet that Rascal,' said poor Bat to some of his friends, 'I'll stick a knife in his heart.' Happily he never did. . . ."). In the spring of 1776 Webster and Mrs Battishill fled London for Ireland and acted first at Smock Alley Theatre and then at Crow Street, she appearing as "Mrs Webster." But, said the *Thespian Dictionary* (1805), Webster's vanity and his infidelities caused her to die "of a broken heart" at Cork in late October 1777.

John O'Keeffe in his *Recollections* says that Webster had been popular with Irish audiences. But in the fall of 1777 he was again in London, now at Drury Lane, where he was seen for the first time (in London, anyway) as Macheath in *The Beggar's Opera,* Lionel in *A*

ANTHONY WEBSTER, as Douglas
engraving by Thornthwaite, after Roberts

School for Fathers, Faulkland in *The Rivals,* and Young Meadows in *Love in a Village.* He was also the original Captain Melford in Thomas Holcroft's comic opera *The Crisis* and sang a "Principal Vocal Part" in *Acis and Galatea.* He returned to Drury Lane in 1778–79, where he added to his repertoire the original Young Boncour in Henry Fielding's newly discovered comedy *The Fathers* and repeated some of his former characters in comedy. In the oratorio season he had parts in *Judas Maccabaeus* and *Alexander's Feast.* Subscribers to his benefit on 6 April were sent for tickets to his lodgings at No 35, Upper Charlotte Street, Rathbone Place.

In Webster's last season of performance, 1779–80, he added Lord Aimworth in *The Maid of the Mill* and was the original William in R. B. Sheridan and the elder Thomas Linley's *The Camp.* In April 1779 was published *Nancy of the Dale. Sung by Mr. Webster in the*

ANTHONY WEBSTER, as Comus
engraving by Kingsbury, after Wheatley

Opera of The Camp. Webster seems not to have acted at Drury Lane after March and was probably ill. The *Morning Post* for 23 May 1780 reported that he had died at Brompton on 18 May but next day the newspaper retracted the statement. Joseph Reed's "Theatrical Obituary" manuscript in the Boston Public Library dates his death 12 July 1780, at Nine-Elms. The *Gentleman's Magazine* for July reported that he died that month.

Anthony Webster had at some point acquired a wife; whether or not she had to suffer his elopement with Mrs Battishill is not known. But the lines concerning the pair by Anthony Pasquin (John Williams) in *The Children of Thespis* (1786) are baffling, though plainly satirical:

> *When death seiz'd our Webster—his heav'n-born*
> *   wife,*
> *Sweet Grace, (whom he wedded and cherish'd*
> *   thro' life,*
> *Whose mild hallow'd influence led him along,*
> *Ennobl'd his action, and breath'd thro' his song:)*
> *Like a Persian bride, she survey'd his remains,*
> *As the pulses of horror beat high thro' her veins;*
> *And frowning on Fate, who had seiz'd all her*
> *   joys,*
> *With Misery laden, herself she destroys;*
> *Disdaining existence, his ashes she fir'd,*
> *Then mounted the pile, gave a sigh, and expir'd.*

A portrait by Francis Wheatley of Anthony Webster as Comus in *Comus* was engraved by H. Kingsbury and published by John Smith on 10 January 1781 with a dedication to the "Gentlemen of the Anacreontic Society." The original painting is untraced. An engraved portrait by Boyce of Webster as Comus was published as a plate to the *Ladies' Magazine.* An anonymous artist pictured him as Corporal William in *The Camp* in an engraving published by J. Bew, 1778. An engraving by T. Thornthwaite, after James Roberts, of Webster as Douglas in *Douglas* was published as a plate to *Bell's British Theatre,* 1778. A pencil drawing (profile left, head only), not in character, by James Roberts (acquired in a collection of drawings from Thomas Agnew, London, in 1976) is in the Harvard Theatre Collection.

Weedon, Mr *fl.* 1766₁, *actor.*
With Samuel Foote's troupe at the Haymarket Theatre Mr Weedon played a Spouter in *The Apprentice* on 26 June 1766 and an unspecified role in *Woman's a Riddle* on 31 July. With Barry's company at the King's Theatre Weedon acted Mezzano in *Venice Preserv'd* on 13 August.

Weedon, Cavendish *b. 1656, impresario, composer.*
Cavendish Weedon of the Inner Temple, a bachelor 30 years old, married Elizabeth Jackson of St Clement Danes, a spinster about 25, her parents deceased, on 11 December 1686. In 1702 Weedon turned impresario and presented a number of concerts of divine music at various places in London. On 6 January the concert was at Stationers' Hall, as were concerts on 31 January and 19 February. The *London Gazette* said of the February concert that it was a benefit for "decay'd Gentry, and the Maintenance of a School for Education of Children in Religion, Musick and Accompts." On 30 April 1702 the *Post Boy* noted that Weedon's concerts were to continue every Thursday until August at Stationers' Hall, but the other presentations of which we have a record were given elsewhere. At Somerset House Garden on 12 May music by Weedon and King was performed; Weedon's concert was at Chelsea College Hall on 21 May, and he held his concert of 2 July at York Buildings.

Weekley, Mrs *d. 1725, singer, actress.*
At Drury Lane Theatre on 29 January 1724 there was singing "In Italian by Mrs Weekly, who never sung in Publick before." She sang again on 1 February, and for her benefit on 10 April she acted Cherry in *The Stratagem.* She sang between the acts regularly during the 1724–25 season, usually in Italian, and the frequency of her appearances makes it clear that she was a very popular attraction. Mrs. Weekley had her benefit on 9 April 1725. The *Daily Post* reported that on 8 November 1725 "died in Child Bed Mrs. Weekly a famous singer in Drury Lane Playhouse."

Weeks, Mrs *fl. 1780₁, actress.*
Between 29 February and 19 April 1780 Mrs Weeks acted, at the Crown Inn, Islington, Lady Rusport in *The West Indian,* the Duchess of York in *Richard III,* the Nurse in *Romeo and Juliet,* Scentwell in *The Busy Body,*

Lucy in *The London Merchant,* Lady Sarah Swash in *The Camp,* Lady Bountiful in *The Beaux' Stratagem,* and Mrs Strickland in *The Suspicious Husband.*

Weeks, Master ₍*fl.* 1732–1740₎, *dancer.*

The "little Boy, who never appeared on the Stage before" who danced *The Pastorella* with Miss Rogers at Lincoln's Inn Fields Theatre on 28 February 1732 was Master Weeks. They were described as students of Sallé, and when they performed the dance again on 12 April, young Weeks was cited in the bill by name. The lad danced at Lincoln's Inn Fields and Covent Garden in 1732–33. When he appeared at the Goodman's Fields Theatre on 14 May 1733 he was identified as then a student of Dupré. At Covent Garden on 30 June Weeks offered a *Scottish Dance.* When Dupré shared a benefit at the same house on 8 May 1734 young Weeks assisted, dancing a turn called *Shepherd,* and on 20 May 1736 he performed at Miss Cole's shared benefit in a minuet and a rigadoon with her. Weeks was at Drury Lane in the fall of 1740, dancing in *Robin Goodfellow* as a Peasant and filling similar chorus parts in *Harlequin Shipwrecked, The Rural Sports,* and *The Fortune Tellers.* His last appearance seems to have been on 26 December 1740 in *Robin Goodfellow.*

Weeks, James ₍*fl.* 1729₎, *singer.*

James Weeks was a member of the "Lilliputian" troupe of young players who performed *The Beggar's Opera* at Lincoln's Inn Fields on 1 January 1729. Young Weeks was Crookfingered Jack and Wat Dreary, though the text must have been altered, for those two characters in the original are onstage together.

Weele, John ₍*fl.* 1800₎, *carpenter.*

At the trial of James Hadfield, who had attempted to assassinate George III at Drury Lane Theatre in 15 May 1800, John Weele appeared as a witness and identified himself as a carpenter at the theatre.

Weeley, Samuel *d. 1743, singer.*

The Mr Wheley who, according to the manuscript notes of Emmett L. Avery, sang at a concert at Epsom on 26 July 1708 was probably Samuel Weeley the court singer. In 1709

he spent 125 days attending the Queen at Windsor, and warrants in the Lord Chamberlain's accounts over the years through 1725 show that Weeley enjoyed many such assignments. He was active as a singing teacher as well, and concert bills from time to time cited him as being the master of some young singers; for instance, on 13 March 1712 at Stationers' Hall a benefit concert was held for an unnamed gentlewoman who had studied under Weeley.

On 29 October 1714 Weeley was sworn a Gentleman of the Chapel Royal, replacing Richard Elford; Weeley was described as a bass from St Paul's. He sang in March 1717 at two concerts at Stationers' Hall, on 11 January 1723 at Buckingham House, and on 2 February 1726 at the Inner Temple. On 28 August 1739 Weeley became one of the original subscribers to the Royal Society of Musicians. Samuel Weeley died on 2 November 1743; his post in the Chapel Royal was given to Thomas Vandernan. Administration of Weeley's estate was granted on 1 December to his nephew Samuel Weeley, his deceased brother's son. At his death our subject was living at Weeley Hall, Weeley, Essex. He died a bachelor.

Weichsel, Carl Friedrich *d. 1811?, oboist, clarinetist.*

Carl Friedrich Weichsel, a native of Freiberg in Saxony, was a professional musician working in London by 5 November 1752, the date he was admitted to the Royal Society of Musicians (but he was expelled for nonpayment in 1755). He was an oboist at the King's Theatre in London by 1757. On 17 April 1758 he received 8*s.* for playing in a performance of the *Messiah* at the Chapel of the Foundling Hospital. He also played in the Foundling Hospital performances in 1759, 1760, 1763, and 1769.

Sometime after 16 May 1764 and before 9 October 1765 Weichsel married the singer Fredericka Weirman. She had made her debut at Covent Garden Theatre on 18 October 1764 under her maiden name, and on 9 October 1765 she was advertised as Mrs Weichsel. For some 22 seasons Mrs Weichsel was a favorite singer at Vauxhall Garden; she died in 1786. Their daughter, Elizabeth Weichsel, born about 1765, married her voice teacher James Billington in 1783 and as Mrs Billing-

ton became one of the most celebrated sopranos in the history of the English theatre. A
son, Charles (Carl) Weichsel, born about
1768, became a leading violinist and for many
years accompanied his sister in her concerts.
Both of the elder Weichsel's children are noticed separately, as is his wife.

Carl Friedrich Weichsel was a principal
oboist at the King's Theatre and at Vauxhall
Gardens, according to his daughter's memoirs, but few records survive to document specifics. When the clarinet was introduced for
the first time in the Three Choirs Festival at
Worcester in 1763, Weichsel was one of the
players on that instrument. It is not known
how long his career lasted, but his daughter
stated that he and her brother accompanied
her and her new husband to Dublin in November 1783. (Mrs Billington's letters to her
mother in 1784 make no mention of her father, but by then Mrs Weichsel was reputedly
living with another man.) *The Royal Society of
Musicians of Great Britain List of Members
1738–1984* (1985) conjectures that the
younger Charles Weichsel died on 26 March
1811, but that conjecture is manifestly
wrong. The elder Weichsel, our subject, may
have died on that date.

FREDERICKA WEICHSEL
artist unknown

Weichsel, Mrs Carl Friedrich, Freder-
icka, née Weirman   *d. 1786, singer, ac-
tress.*

The soprano Fredericka Weirman, a pupil
of J. C. Bach, announced as making her first
appearance on the stage, played Andromeda
in the pantomime *Perseus and Andromeda* at
Covent Garden Theatre on 18 October 1764.
She appeared as one of the Witches and a
Shepherdess in *Harlequin Sorcerer* on 5 November. Though replaced in those latter roles on
15 January 1765, she returned to them on 15
February. On 16 May 1765 she was added as
one of the singers of the "Solemn Hymn" in
The Royal Convert.

Sometime after 16 May 1764 and before 9
October 1765 she married Carl Friedrich
Weichsel, a musician from Saxony who had
settled in London by 1752 and was a principal
oboist at the King's Theatre and Vauxhall
Gardens. (Reed's "Notitia Dramatica" in the
British Library identifies Weichsel's wife as
the former Miss Weirman.) Advertised as Mrs
Weichsel, she returned the next season to

Covent Garden, on 9 October 1765, as Andromeda. She helped swell the choruses of
Macbeth on 14 October and *Comus* on 22 October and sang a song in act III of *The Conscious
Lovers* on 13 November. She also sang during
that season in the "Solemn Dirge" in *Romeo
and Juliet.* She made her first appearance in a
featured speaking-singing role on 22 April
1766 when she played Sally in *Thomas and
Sally* for her own benefit. Two nights later she
appeared as Diana in *The Royal Chace.*

In the summer of 1766 Mrs Weichsel began
her association with Vauxhall Gardens, where
over the years she proved to be a very popular
vocalist. J. C. Bach wrote a set of songs for
her to sing there in 1766, as did Thomas
Pinto in later years. Numerous songs by other
composers are listed in the *Catalogue of Printed
Music in the British Museum* as sung by her at
Vauxhall.

She made other concert appearances but
sang in the London theatres infrequently. On
5 April 1769 she was a vocalist in the oratorio
Ruth at the King's Theatre, where she re-

turned on 24 March 1775 to sing a *duetto* with Signora Corri. At the Haymarket Theatre she sang in *Judas Maccabaeus* on 18 April 1769 and 12 April 1771 (on the latter date she also introduced a new song set by Hook) and in a concert of sacred music on 19 April 1733. She sang in the oratorios at Drury Lane in April 1771, March 1772, February 1773, and March 1775, and in those at Covent Garden in February 1776 and March 1778. At the latter house on 16 November 1775 she appeared as Mandane in *Artaxerxes.*

Other performances included singing in the *Messiah* at the Foundling Hospital in 1769 (for which she was paid £5 5s.), in the Handel oratorios at the Gloucester Three Choirs Festival of 1769, in *Ruth* at the Chapel of the Lock Hospital on 27 April 1771, as principal vocalist at the opening of the new building for the Incorporated Society of Artists on 11 May 1772, in concert recitals of the Reverend George Marriott's poem *The Jesuit* at the Crown and Anchor Tavern three nights in April 1773 and at Hickford's Room in Brewer Street on 18 May, and in *The Resurrection* at the Society of Artists Exhibition Room in the Strand on 23 January 1776.

In the Harvard Theatre Collection is a signed receipt from her to Jonathan Tyers, the Vauxhall proprietor, for payment to her of £52 10s. on account for her performances that season. About that time she lived at No 15, "Germin" Street. In 1784, when she received a series of letters from her daughter, she resided at No 42, St Martin's Lane, Charing Cross, and then at Mrs Haydon's, Vauxhall, Lambeth.

Mrs Weichsel died in London in January 1786—on the fifth, according to the *Town and Country Magazine,* or the sixth, according to the *Gentleman's Magazine,* which reported that she had performed at Vauxhall Gardens for 22 seasons.

She was the mother of the celebrated English soprano Elizabeth Billington (c. 1765–1818) and the violinist and conductor Charles Weichsel (b. c. 1768). Her husband Carl Friedrich Weichsel may have died as late as 1811. According to James Ridgway, author of the murky *Memoirs of Mrs Billington* published in 1792, by that time Mrs Weichsel lived with a "Mr R———l," who was "a common soldier, and made his mistress live, or rather *starve,* upon red herrings, till at last it was too well known, she died of want, and in the utmost penury."

A portrait of Fredericka Weichsel by an unknown engraver was published by J. Bew as a plate to the *Vocal Magazine* in 1778. Mrs Weichsel is shown singing to the Vauxhall audience from the front balcony of the Pavilion in a drawing by Thomas Rowlandson that is in the Yale Center for British Art. A large and "more highly finished" version, exhibited at the Royal Academy in 1784, is in the Victoria and Albert Museum. The latter version by Rowlandson was engraved by Robert Pollard (and acquatinted by F. Jukes) and published in 1785; it is reproduced in this *Dictionary* 3: 516.

Weichsel, Charles   *b. c. 1768, violinist, flutist, composer, conductor.*

Charles (Carl) Weichsel was born about 1768, the son of Carl Friedrich Weichsel, a native of Saxony who was working as a musician in London by 1752, and his wife Fredericka (née Weirman), a well-known singer at Vauxhall Gardens. Young Charles was a pupil of Wilhelm Cramer and no doubt was also instructed by his father. For his mother's benefit at the Haymarket Theatre on 10 May 1774 (not recorded in *The London Stage*) Master Weichsel and his elder sister Elizabeth played violin sonatas, and on 20 May 1777 the pair played at Hickford's Rooms with Samuel Wesley. On 6 March 1778 his sister played pianoforte and Charles rendered a violin concerto in a performance of sacred music at Covent Garden Theatre. Following the oratorio at Covent Garden on 18 March 1778 they joined the fine musicians Florio and Stamitz in a *quartetto,* and on 25 March young Charles and Stamitz played a *duetto* for violin and tenor.

The *Public Advertiser* of 13 March 1778 reported that Master Weichsel was ten years old. If that report is correct then he had been only about six when he made his debut in 1774. But it should be noted that *The Royal Society of Musicians of Great Britain List of Members 1738–1984* (1985) states that he entered that organization on 5 April 1761, a date that is manifestly incorrect unless there was another Charles Weichsel (and one who was not our subject's father). That source also provides the conjectural date of 26 March 1811 for his

By gracious permission of Her Majesty Queen Elizabeth II

A group of musicians: identified as WILLIAM SHIELD, PETER SALOMON, GEORGE FREDERICK PINTO, CHARLES WEICHSEL the younger, THOMAS LINLEY, WILLIAM THOMAS PARKE, and ANDREW ASHE

by Lane

death, which cannot be correct, for we still notice him in 1824.

Charles was still advertised as Master Weichsel when he played at the Smock Alley Theatre in Dublin in 1785–86. At Dublin he performed in concerts and accompanied his sister, by then the celebrated Mrs Billington, between 1785 and 1788. He visited Cork in 1786. On 7 April 1787 Charles made his first payment of 30*s.* and 3*d.* for a three-month subscription to the Irish Musical Fund, but he withdrew his name in 1788.

By the spring of 1790 Weichsel returned to London. Some of his music was played at Covent Garden on 8 March 1790 when Mrs Bil-

lington had a benefit and sang, and, no doubt, Weichsel accompanied her. Indeed, two nights later, on 10 March, Weichsel played a violin concerto in the oratorio at Drury Lane. It was reported that Weichsel, who had been heard before only at the Pantheon, had played a wonderful concerto, "with such rapidity of execution as to leave a doubt remaining whether it is possible for human excellence to go beyond it." He again played in the Drury Lane oratorios on 12 and 17 March. On 2 June 1790, back at Covent Garden, he accompanied Mrs Billington when she sang *Sweet Bird* (from Handel's *L'allegro ed il Penseroso*) for her benefit.

In 1790–91 Weichsel returned to Dublin as leader of the orchestra at the Crow Street Theatre, a position he held through 1792–93. After his benefit there on 21 January 1791 it was proclaimed, "His selection of Irish airs, solos, etc, was infinitely great, at once displaying a superior taste and finished excellence that evince for Mr Weichsell to be at least equal if not superior to any other performer in Europe."

During his tenure at Crow Street, he made several excursions back to London, to play in the oratorios on 30 March 1791 and for his sister's benefit on 28 February 1792 at Covent Garden. For the latter he composed a difficult aria, "When robbed of her mate, the poor bird," for Mrs Billington and played the violin obbligatos. He also performed for her second benefit at Covent Garden that season, on 22 May 1792. During that period he also played at the Orchard Street Theatre in Bath.

In 1794 Weichsel traveled with the Billingtons on their continental tour, playing solos and accompanying his sister's concerts for several years. He toured Italy with her, perhaps until 1799 when she married her second husband, a Mr Félissent, at Milan. We lose track of Weichsel for several years, though when Mrs Billington made her triumphant return to London in 1801–2 her terms with Covent Garden included the provision that he should lead the band on the nights she performed and that he should be paid £500 for the season.

Weichsel also became one of the leaders at the King's Theatre that season of 1801–2. His salary there in 1808 was £315. On 11 December 1814 he petitioned the Lord Chamberlain, complaining that at the beginning of the 1813–14 season he had been discharged as leader of the band because from time to time he gave leave to members of the orchestra to play elsewhere. He won his suit, for his name appeared as leader in the account books of the King's Theatre for another five seasons, through 1818. He also played flute many times at the Oxford Music Room early in the nineteenth century.

Weichsel was still alive in 1824 when the *Dictionary of Musicians* called him "an excellent violinist." Van der Straeten in his *History of the Violin* suggests that he did not die until after 1830.

Weichsel seems to have married twice. The *Oracle* on 15 April 1796 announced that Weichsel had married "lately" a Signora Vigano: "Mrs Billington is engaged for the Theatres of Verona and Bologna. Young Weichsel, her brother [who was with her in Italy] has entered into the holy state of matrimony with Signora VIGANO, a figurante. A correspondent says it may be termed *matrimony,* but it is not a matter—o'—money." Signora Vigano may well have been related to the Viganò family of dancers, several members of which performed in London in the 1790s, or to a Vigano who was a music copyist at Drury Lane in 1796. Weichsel's second wife was Stefania Rovedino, a singer, who had first appeared at the King's Theatre on 9 April 1799. She was the daughter of the singer Carlo Rovedino, and her mother probably was the singer Rosa Tinte, who was said to have married Rovedino after 1780. Both parents performed in London during the late eighteenth century. Weichsel's marriage to Stefania occurred sometime between 31 July 1804, when she appeared advertised as Rovedino, and 4 December following, when she was called "Weichsell." She performed as Mrs Weichsel at the King's Theatre until 1805–6.

Charles Weichsel's published music includes a set of variations for violin and pianoforte or violoncello and duets for violins. *A Favorite Solo for the Violin and Bass* was published about 1795. His contributions to *Orpheus and Eurydice,* a *pasticcio* performed at Covent Garden on 28 February 1792, were published that year. Van der Straeten cites two trios for two violins and bass that survive in manuscript.

Weichsel appears in a chalk drawing by William Lane, with a group of musical performers that includes Shield, Salomon, Pinto, Linley, Parke, and Ashe around a bust of Apollo on a pedestal. The drawing is in the Royal Library, Windsor Castle, and is a study for a picture of this scene that Lane exhibited at the Royal Acedemy in 1810 (No 544); that painting is untraced.

Weichsel, Mrs Charles, Stefania. *See* ROVEDINO, STEFANIA.

Weichsel, Elizabeth. *See* BILLINGTON, MRS JAMES.

Weideman, Charles Frederick   *d. 1782, flutist, oboist, composer.*

Charles Frederick Weideman (or Carl, Karl, Friedrich, Weidemann, Weidmann, Wiedeman) was born in Germany sometime in the early eighteenth century. The flutist, oboist, and composer was probably in England by 1724; Deutsch in his *Handel* suggests that Weideman may have been playing at the King's Theatre as early as October 1724. Weideman made a note in his oboe part of Handel's *Trio Sonatas* (now in the British Library): "Tamerlan 1725 which was the first Opera I play'd in &cc. C. W." *Tamerlano* had opened on 17 October 1724.

On 14 March 1729 at Stationers' Hall a benefit concert was held for Weideman; he played at Drury Lane on 26 March 1729; on 30 April 1729 he performed at Lincoln's Inn Fields Theatre; and at Stationers' Hall in March 1733 and March 1734 Weideman played the German flute, as he did again a year later. Similarly, on 16 March 1737 he performed at the Devil's Tavern. On 28 August 1739 he became one of the original subscribers to the Royal Society of Musicians. Weideman then lived in the parish of St George, Hanover Square. He participated in concerts at Hickford's Music Room on 16 January 1741, at the Haymarket Theatre on 3 February, and at Hickford's again on 27 February and 6 and 13 March. On 30 March 1743 he joined in the benefit for indigent musicians at the King's Theatre, as he did again on 28 March 1744. The 1745 benefit was at Covent Garden Theatre on 10 April; the 1746 concert was at the King's on 25 March. Perhaps he was the "Weidmar" who played in Norwich in 1750.

The frequency of Weideman's public appearances then diminished, but he was a productive composer in the period from 1746 to 1773. Soon after the accession of George III in 1760 Weideman was appointed Assistant Master of the King's Musick under William Boyce. He later became Composer of Minuets at the Court of St James and a member of the band of musicians at an annual salary of £100. As of 1763, when *Mortimer's London Directory* was published, Weideman was living in Angel Court, Windmill Street, near the Haymarket. Mortimer listed him as a teacher of the German flute (George III was one of his students).

Charles Weideman died in London on 24 May 1782. His will was made on 24 January 1781. He described himself as of the parish of St James, Westminster. Weideman had suffered an illness and had been cared for by his landlord Mr Billing and Billing's wife, to each of whom he made bequests. He left the bulk of his estate to Philip Peter Eiffert (the musician) of King Street, Soho. The will was proved on 5 June 1782.

Weideman is pictured playing the flute, at right, in plate 4 of Hogarth's *Marriage à la Mode* series ("The Countess's Morning Levée"). The original painting is in the National Gallery, London, and is reproduced in this *Dictionary* with the notice of Senesino. Hogarth also drew Weideman in "The Modern Orpheus," showing the flutist enrapturing an audience in the street; food, coins, and other objects fly through the air toward him.

Weidman or Weidmar. *See* WEIDEMAN.

Weippert, George   *fl. 1737–1738[1], musician?*

The manuscript Minute Book of the Royal Society of Musicians, under the date of 4 February 1738, cites a letter of thanks from George Weippert, presumably a musician, for a donation to his welfare granted at the Christmas meeting of the Society in December 1737. His relationship, if any, to the family of musical Weipperts later prominent in London is not known.

Weippert, John Erhardt   *1766–1823, instrumentalist, composer.*

John Erhardt Weippert (Weipart, Whippart) came of a German musical family and was father, grandfather, and uncle to numerous English musicians of the name. According to information in a legally attested deposition given by "Mr. John Lawrence Schmidt. First Minister of the principal Church at St. Johns," Weippert, "legitimate son of Mr. Bartholomew Weippert, citizen and musician . . . and his wife Ann Barbara née Rummert, was born on 15th June 1766 between 8 and 9 o'clock in the morning, in the Imperial Free City of Schweinfurt, in Franconia. Mr. John Erhardt Rummert, Citizen and Furrier of the same place was Godfather." The Reverend Georg

Drawn from life by R. Newton.

The Celebrated M.ʳ Weippert in the Ballad of Oscar & Malvina

Harvard Theatre Collection

JOHN EHRHARDT WEIPPERT
by Newton

Christopher Metz, Deacon of St John's, performed the baptism at the Weippert home.

Weippert had "Practised Music for his Livelihood upwards of Ten Years in England" when on 7 May 1797 the violinist John Mountain proposed him for membership in the Royal Society of Musicians. Weippert was said to be proficient "on the Violin, Tenor [viola], Violoncello, Clarinett, Horn, and Peddal Harp. Has great many Schollars on the Harp and engaged Temporary [i.e., from time to time for years] for that Instrument in Both the Covent Garden and Drury Lane Theatres."

The London Stage 1660–1800 mistakenly gives John Erhardt's nearly 50 performances on the pedal harp at London's patent theatres from 1791 through 1800 to John Michael Weippert (1775–1831), John Erhardt's younger brother, who does not seem to have performed in public in England until well after the turn of the century, if ever. When John Erhardt proposed John Michael to the Royal Society of Musicians in February 1802, he deposed that "His engagements being all private, such as Teaching etc., cannot well be inserted." (John Michael was rejected and not permitted to join the Society until July 1806.)

John Erhardt Weippert often teamed with the popular piper Denis Courtney until Courtney's death in 1794. One of their early (1792) collaborations was their accompaniment of Incledon and Mrs Mountain in a *Scotch Duetto*. But on an occasion (31 June 1792) when Courtney absented himself, "Weippert, with his harp, undertook the whole piece himself, with wonderful execution and taste."

Almost all of Weippert's patent-house appearances up until 1800 were at Covent Garden, only a few being at the Haymarket and, so far as the bills show, only one at Drury Lane—9 May 1799, a benefit for Miss Leak. (Weippert was often called upon to enliven benefits.) He continued irregularly at Covent Garden, playing several times a season until at least 1809–10 and probably later, at what appears to have been his standard fee of £1 11s. 6d. (British Library Add.MS. 29710). He accompanied the monologuist Collins's *Evening Brush* at the Lyceum on 27 March 1792 and was at the Lyceum again on a more regular basis in 1811–12. In 1801, 1803, and 1804 he appeared occasionally at the Royal Circus. Mee, in *The Oldest Music Room in Europe,* found performances by Weippert at Oxford early in the nineteenth century. Weippert's son wrote Sainsbury that his father had managed and performed at the Assembly Rooms at Margate for thirty years.

Weippert's principal—and almost exclusive theatrical—instrument was the pedal harp. But on at least a few occasions, such as his accompaniment of Mrs Billington's singing at Drury Lane in the season of 1801–2, he played the violin. And in several years he was on the list for the May charity concert of the Royal Society of Musicians at St Paul's playing either "tenor" (viola) or violin.

Weippert adapted "Cambro-British" folk songs to accompany Byrne's ballet *The Welsh Dairy; or Suitors in Abergavenny* according to the *Monthly Mirror* of May 1802. The *Catalogue of Printed Music in the British Museum* assigns to him the following compositions: *Absence. A Favorite Song for the Pedal Harp or Piano Forte* (words by T. A. Beckles) (1797?); *Ar Hyd y Nos, A Favorite Welsh Air, with New Variations . . . as . . . Perform'd on the Pedal Harp at . . . Drury Lane, in Harlequin Amulet* (1800); *God Save the King, with Variations for the Pedal Harp* (1800?); and *Four Sonatas for the Pedal-Harp, Harpsichord, or Piano-Forte; with an Accompaniment for the German Flute or Violin & Violoncello* (1796).

Various notations in the Minute Books of the Royal Society of Musicians, of which he was a Governor in 1818, show him to have been a charge on the Society from about 1820. He died, according to his son, on 1 April 1823, "Aged 56," and was buried "at St. Peter's in the Isle of Thanet."

John Erhardt Weippert married Mary Spence at St George, Hanover Square, on 28 December 1791. Their daughter Julia, born in 1792, married the actor William Lovegrove. She died in 1812. The Lovegroves had two children; one, a daughter, died a few months after her mother. The second child of John Erhardt and Mary Weippert, John Thomas Lewis Weippert, was born in 1798 and married Isabella Stevenson in 1821. Their children were John Charles (1822–1867), Sybil ("Sybell") Julia (b. 1824), Alfred Spring (b. 1825)—all recorded in the records of the Royal Society of Music—and Jessie and Rosine Elizabeth Baldwin Weippert, named in J. T. L. Weippert's will.

John Michael Weippert, with whom J. E. has been confused, was a younger brother, born 7 January 1775 in Schweinfurt. He had three children by his wife Lydia: George, born 1803; Nelson, born 1805; and Erhard (*sic*), born 1815. John Michael died in April 1831.

A portrait of Weippert playing on the harp, titled "The Celebrated Mr. Weippert in the Ballad of Oscar and Malvina," was engraved by R. Newton and published by him in 1797.

Weir, Thomas   *d. 1725?, trumpeter.*

The Lord Chamberlain's accounts show that on 20 (?) October 1725 the trumpeter

Thomas Weir was replaced in the King's Musick by William Harris. That probably meant that Weir had recently died. His annual salary had been £40.

Weirman, Fredericka. *See* WEICHSEL, MRS CARL FRIEDRICH.

Weiss, Carl   *fl. 1768?–1790?, flutist, composer.*

A musician named Weiss appeared in concert at the Assembly Room, Princess Street, Bristol, on 5 November 1768, along with (William?) Herschel, (John Abraham?) Fisher, and one of the Broderips. Weiss, who on that occasion shared the benefit with Fisher, was probably the flutist and composer Carl Weiss. According to the testimony of his son the composer Charles N. Weiss in a letter to the biographer Sainsbury in 1823, Carl Weiss had been "1st flute of the private concerts of their late Majesties King George the 3rd and the queen" and had made a "fortune" in England before returning to Mulhausen, in "German Switzerland," where the younger Weiss was born.

How Weiss obtained the "fortune" is not known. He played in a trio at the Concert Rooms, Hanover Square, on some date in 1790, but he is not known to have performed again in public in London.

The *Catalogue of Printed Music in the British Museum* lists several works by Carl Weiss, all with conjectural dating: *Trios for a German Flute, a Violin & Violoncello, etc.* (1775?); *Six Trios for a German Flute, Violin and a Bass . . . Opera II* (1780?); *Six Solos for the German Flute and Bass . . . Opera III* (1780?); and *Six Quartettos for a Flute, Violin or Two Flutes, Tenor and Bass . . . Op. IV* (1782?). Carl Weiss's relationship, if any, to the G. Weiss who is listed in the *Catalogue* as publishing music for the flute in London around 1790 is not known. It is possible that they were the same person.

Weitzenmiller. *See* MILLER JOHN WEITZEN.

Welch. *See also* WELSH.

Welch, Mr   *fl. 1794, organist, singer.*

Doane's *Musical Directory* of 1794 lists Mr Welch, of Newberry, as an organist and tenor (singer, presumably) who performed in the Handelian concerts at Westminster Abbey.

Welch, Mrs *fl. 1760–1762₁, dancer.*
References in the Covent Garden playbills and accounts in 1760, 1761, and 1762 to Miss Welsch, Miss Welch, and Mrs Welch all appear to concern one woman. We cannot be certain we have named her correctly above.

On a paylist dated 22 September 1760 she was listed as a dancer at £35 annually or 3s. 8d. daily, and in 1761 the accounts cited her as receiving £1 10s. per week. She danced in *Comus* on 11 December 1760 and again in September and December 1761. She was a Pandou in the comic ballet *The Hungarian Gambols* on 9 March and 21 September 1761. She shared with many others in a benefit on 25 May 1761, but there was a deficit, and she lost £3 14s. 3d. On 28 January 1762 she was a Follower of Daphne in *Apollo and Daphne*.

Welch, Miss *fl. 1792₁, performer?*
Covent Garden Theatre paid Miss Welch £10 10s. on account on 21 April 1792.

"Welch Will" *fl. 1699₁, wrestler.*
On 1 April 1699 at the new Red Theatre in Winchester Street, Southwark, was presented, along with music and dancing, "a Wrestling Match, between the famous Welch Will, of Kidwelly (who had the Honour last Year to divert the Elector of Bavaria) and Hugh Lammerton, Tinman, near Lestiethill, for Twenty Pounds." The full bill for this entertainment can be found in the entry of "Dapper Daniel" in this *Dictionary.*

"Welchman, The Little." *See* HOPKINS HOPKINS.

Weldon, John *1676–1736, organist, composer.*
John Weldon was born in Chichester on 19 January 1676 and was educated at Eton, where he studied music under the organist John Walter. Weldon later studied under Henry Purcell, and in 1694 he was appointed organist of New College, Oxford, succeeding Richard Goodson. Four years later Weldon contributed to Francis Smith's *Musica Oxoniensis,* and in 1700 he won first prize (£100) in a

competition for music to Congreve's *The Judgement of Paris,* defeating John Eccles, Daniel Purcell, and Godfrey Finger.

Weldon became a Gentleman of the Chapel Royal on 6 June 1701 (*The Dictionary of National Biography* mistakenly dates the appointment 6 January). He was given an unsalaried position at first, which may explain why he kept his New College post until 1702. In June 1702 he resigned his Oxford post and became organist at St Bride, Fleet Street. At the death of John Blow in 1708 Weldon was made organist of the Chapel Royal, and on 8 August 1715 he was appointed to the newly created position of second composer to the Chapel Royal. He was hired as organist of St Martin-in-the-Fields (a post that he shared with Maurice Greene from 1727).

Though Dr Burney found him a mediocre composer, Weldon was popular in his day for both sacred and secular music. His music was frequently heard at concerts, such as the ones at Hampstead on 27 June 1702, York Buildings on 17 December 1702, Drury Lane Theatre on 22 June 1703, and Richmond Wells on 12 August 1703. On the last occasion he and Elford performed several new songs composed by Weldon. Many of his pieces were published in musical periodicals such as *Monthly Masks* or in such collections as *Wit and Mirth* and *A Collection of the Choicest Songs & Dialogues.* Many songs composed by Weldon for the theatre were separately printed, as the *Catalogue of Printed Music in the British Museum* shows.

Plays for which Weldon wrote songs included *The Tempest, She Wou'd and She Wou'd Not, The Agreeable Disappointment,* and *The Fair Unfortunate,* and his music was still being used in such works as *Love in a Village* in the 1790s. Weldon published three books of songs in the first decade of the eighteenth century, and the title page of one that appeared about 1707 stated that the works were "Perform'd at his Consort in York Buildings." Six of his church anthems appeared in *Divine Harmony* about 1730, and other sacred pieces were included in various collections of church music.

Warrants among the Lord Chamberlain's papers show that Weldon spent some of his time attending the court at Windsor or Hampton Court from 1710 onward, often for two to three months at a time, usually during

Faculty of Music, Oxford

JOHN WELDON
artist unknown

the summers. His last discovered royal service in the Lord Chamberlain's accounts was at Windsor in the summer of 1725. John Weldon died on 7 May 1736 in London after a long indisposition. He was buried at St Paul, Covent Garden. William Boyce and Jonathan Martin succeeded to Weldon's posts as composer and organist to the Chapel Royal. The will of a John "Welldon" of St John the Evangelist, Westminster, was made on 27 November 1735 and proved on 10 May 1736; Weldon identified himself as a "Gentleman" and left his estate (unspecified) to his wife Susanna.

A portrait (canvas, $12\frac{1}{2}'' \times 9''$) of John Weldon by an unknown artist is in the Oxford University Music School.

Well, Mr   *fl. 1791₁,   dancer.*

Mr Well danced at the Haymarket Theatre on 24 October 1791.

Welldon, Mr   *fl. 1780₁,   actor.*

At the Haymarket Theatre on 13 November 1780 Mr Welldon played Landlord Blacklegs and Carmine in *The Detection* and James in *The City Association.*

Weller, Mr   *fl. 1703–1718₁,   actor.*

A Mr Weller acted at various London theatres between 1703 and 1718, making his first recorded appearance as Gaylove in *Different Widows* at Lincoln's Inn Fields Theatre about November 1703. At that theatre he acted a Lawyer in *Love at First Sight* on 25 March 1704, Pirotto in *Zelmayne* on 13 November 1704, the First Gentleman in *The Gamester* on 22 February 1705, and Corillo in *Cares of Love* on 1 August 1705. At the Queen's Theatre he played Agenor in *Ulysses* on 23 November 1705. At Drury Lane Theatre he acted in *Venice Preserv'd* on 22 April 1707 in a benefit he shared with Williams, Aegeon in *Oedipus* on 14 January 1710, a benefit in an unspecified role in *The Fair Quaker* on 25 March 1710, the Corporal in *The What D'Ye Call It* on 23 February 1715, and a member of the Mob in *The Contrivances* on 9 August 1715.

A memorandum (MS now in the Historical Society of Pennsylvania) in Barton Booth's hand, dated 20 October 1715, directs the treasurer of Drury Lane Theatre to discharge Weller and several other players on the "22 Instant." Weller, however, must have been reinstated soon, for his name is found in the Drury Lane bills on 6 December 1715 as Tyrrell in *Richard III*. He shared benefits in unspecified roles in *The Tempest* on 8 June 1716 and *Don John* on 31 May 1717 and 28 May 1718.

Weller, Mr   *fl. 1758–1768₁,   actor, dancer.*

The Mr Weller who acted at Norwich in 1758 was probably the person of that name who was paid £2 2s. on 29 December 1759 by Covent Garden Theatre for extra attendance "in getting the Fair ready." The pantomime *The Fair* had been revived there on the previous 10 December, but Weller's name did not appear in the bills. When it was played on 28 January 1760, however, Weller performed Pantaloon in place of Bencraft, and he continued in that role throughout the remainder of the season. He acted Bernardo in *Hamlet* on 18 March 1760. His other roles in 1759–60 were the Priest in *Love Makes a Man* on 12 May and Harlequin in *The Siege of Quebec* on 14 May.

In 1760–61 Weller returned to Covent

Garden at a salary of 3s. 4d. per day for playing primarily in pantomimes. He performed
numerous times that season as the Yeoman in
The Rape of Proserpine. On 25 March 1761 he
acted the Maid in a performance of *Rule a Wife
and Have a Wife* in which Shuter and Holtom
also played female roles. Other parts that season included Jack Ratling in *The English Tars
in America*, the Attorney in *Love à-la-Mode*,
Shorthose in *Wit without Money*, Scrip in *Phebe*,
and Oxford in *Richard III*.

Weller's association with Covent Garden
Theatre lasted for nine seasons, through
1767–68. In his final season his salary was 6s.
8d. per day, or £2 per week. His status and
line are shown in a selection of the roles he
performed: Clown in *Harlequin Statue* and a
Peasant in *The Pilgrim* in 1762–63; the
Watchman in *The Upholsterer*, Roger in *The
Squire of Alsatia*, Pedro in *The Wonder*, and Peter in *Romeo and Juliet* in 1763–64; Hussar in
Perseus and Andromeda and a Soldier in *The
Spanish Lady* in 1764–65; the Doctor in *The
Royal Chace* and Volumnius in *Julius Caesar* in
1765–66; the English Herald in *Henry V* in
1766–67; and Falconbridge in *King John* and
several roles in *A Peep behind the Curtain* in
1767–68. Over those seasons he also appeared
frequently in *Harlequin Dr Faustus* and as Pantaloon in *Harlequin Sorcerer*.

In the summer of 1762 Weller acted at Birmingham and he danced Harlequin in pantomimes at Bristol in the summer of 1767.

In *The Rational Rosciad* (1767) Weller was
not complimented:

> With a mean person and a feeble voice,
> Mistaken Weller made the stage his choice;
> In him sometimes the managers show wit
> And make him just the thing for which he's fit;
> A drowsy watchman, to excite a laugh,
> Sinking beneath his lanthorn and his staff,
> But still another watchman they must keep,
> Lest on the stage this watchman fall asleep.

Probably Weller was the husband of the
Mrs Ann Weller who was in the Covent Garden company in 1768–69 and perhaps earlier.
Her name appeared in no bills that season, so
she must have served in a supernumerary capacity. She signed her name with other Covent
Garden performers to an open letter to Colman that was published in the *Theatrical Monitor* on 5 November 1768. In a document in
the British Library (T. C. 38) specifying the
value of the women's wardrobe at Covent Garden Theatre in July 1769, Mrs Weller's is
listed at £5. A Mrs Weller sang in the opera
at Crow Street, Dublin, in 1776. Elizabeth
and Mary Weller, who performed in London
in the 1770s, were probably their children.

Weller, Ann ₍1768–1776₎ *actress, singer.*
See WELLER, MR *1758–1768*

Weller, Elizabeth   *1751–1770, actress,
singer.*
Announced as a pupil of Dr Arne and a
young gentlewoman making her first appearance on any stage, Elizabeth Weller played
Polly in *The Beggar's Opera* at Drury Lane Theatre on 8 January 1770. She was no doubt the
Miss Weller who had sung in the oratorio *Judith* at the Stratford Jubilee staged by Arne
and Garrick in September 1769. The *London
Evening Post* of 11 January 1770 was enthusias-
tic about her debut as Polly:

> A Pupil of Dr Arne and scarcely 19 years of age;
> her figure is that of the tallest of the middle size,
> well proportioned and at present possesses a dig-
> nity and grace which when habit brings her perfec-
> tion cannot fail of being universally admired. Her
> face is oval with an aquiline nose and though from
> the timidity of a first appearance the rest of her
> features lost that necessary animation, yet there
> were periods when she could dispossess herself of
> her confusion, that prognosticated great expression
> of countenance. Her voice was clear, commanding,
> and melodious, and her ear and manner both ex-
> cellent. She is that kind of singer that one can be
> pleased from looking at as well as from hearing—
> an excellence few vocal performers possess. Her
> acting abstracted from her voice would have done
> credit to a first appearance, as it was very pleasing
> and properly accompanied.

Miss Weller was no doubt the daughter of
the Mr and Mrs Weller who were performers
at Covent Garden Theatre in the 1760s. Her
sister Mary made her debut at Drury Lane on
22 September 1772, also as Polly.

Elizabeth Weller's promising career was
tragically cut short. On 12 March 1770 she
sang in a concert conducted by her master Dr
Arne at the Haymarket Theatre, and on 18
April 1770, in place of Mrs Baddeley, she performed Clarissa in *The School for Fathers* at
Drury Lane. On 7 May 1770 the *Public Adver-*

tiser reported that Miss Elizabeth Weller of Drury Lane Theatre had died on 5 May, at age 19, and Reed's "Notitia Dramatica" concurs. Other sources, among them a Winston manuscript in the Burney papers at the British Library, state that she died on 4 May. The St Paul, Covent Garden, registers record the burial of Elizabeth Weller, spinster, on 9 May 1770. Thirty-two lines of verse "On the Death of Miss Weller, a celebrated young Actress," by "W. E. W." appeared in the press, lamenting:

O Cruel death to dart thy fatal sting,
And chill the blossom in its early spring;
To crop at once Eliza's tender bloom,
Whose youth might promise length of years to come!

In his draft will made in 1770 after Elizabeth's death, Thomas A. Arne wrote that Elizabeth Weller "liv'd upwards of two years with me as an articled Apprentice and behav'd in so virtuous, true and affectionate a manner to me and mine, as to gain the love and esteem of everyone who had the happiness to know her. . . ." Consequently, Arne took Elizabeth's sister Mary as his apprentice.

Weller, Mary *fl. 1770–1779₁,* singer, actress.

In a draft will made by Dr Thomas A. Arne in the latter half of 1770 (and reported by Julian Harbage in *Musical Times,* February 1971) the composer praised his recently deceased apprentice Elizabeth Weller, whom he had introduced to Drury Lane audiences in January 1770 as Polly in *The Beggar's Opera.* Arne stated that in consequence of Elizabeth's premature death that year, he had taken under his protection her younger sister Mary Weller, who was bound his apprentice. In the will Arne expressed a desire that when he died Mary would not be "wrong'd of any part of the wearing apparel of what kind soever, or Trinkets or ornaments whatsoever, which were left to her by her said Sister, or since given by me." He hoped that Mary Weller would "not be wrong'd of her support and maintenance due for the remainder of her apprenticeship, with proper and sufficient Apparel." Mary and Elizabeth's parents were probably the Mr and Mrs Weller who performed at Covent Garden Theatre during the 1760s.

Mary Weller, advertised as making her first

By permission of the Trustees of the British Museum

MARY WELLER, as Polly

artist unknown

appearance on any stage, played Polly in *The Beggar's Opera* at Drury Lane on 22 September 1772. On the night of Miss Weller's debut the prompter Hopkins wrote in his diary that "Miss Wellers figure is very well for Polly but she wants Spirit & is apt to sing out of tune." Garrick did not use her again, and she seems to have been away from the London stage until 1775, when Foote engaged her for the summer at the Haymarket Theatre. She appeared there on 1 May 1775 as Pert in *The Sot,* under Arne's direction, and then was seen in an unspecified role in *The Devil upon Two Sticks* on 15 May and in subsequent performances of that piece. Her other roles at the Haymarket that season were an unspecified part in *The Waterman,* Sally in *Thomas and Sally,* Miss Sophie in *The Dutchman* on 21 August 1775, (when she was billed as "Mrs" Weller) Polly in *The Beggar's Opera,* and Jenny in *The Commissary.* When she played Polly again on 21 September she was again advertised as Mrs Weller.

That summer Arne tried to persuade Garrick to reengage her at Drury Lane for the fall, but the manager would have none of her, writing to Arne on 24 August 1775: "I try'd Mrs Bradford, Miss Weller . . . they did no credit to you or myself by appearing in a Piece which you obstinately insisted upon bringing out, though you knew it would be the means of making a coolness between us."

Miss Weller appeared infrequently over the next few years. At the Haymarket on 22 February 1776 she sang in *Phoebe at Court*, a new operetta produced by Arne. At Covent Garden on 16 March 1776 she performed a Pastoral Nymph and Sabrina in *Comus*. At the Haymarket on 18 September 1776 she played Mariana in *The Miser* and Nysa in *Midas*.

In 1778–79 Mary Weller returned to a winter theatre, this time to Covent Garden. On 18 September she appeared as Miss Dimity in the premiere of Dibdin's *The Wives Revenged*, a piece that was played a total of 13 times that season. On 17 October 1778 she appeared as Lucy in *The Beggar's Opera*. After that season she was not again seen on the London stage. Arne had died that year, on 5 March 1778. In his final will, drawn on 6 December 1777, he did not mention Mary Weller.

A portrait by an unknown engraver, of Mary Weller as Polly in *The Beggar's Opera*, was published as a plate to the *Vocal Magazine* by J. Bew, 1778.

Wellman, Mr   *fl.* 1726–1727₁, dancer.

At the Haymarket Theatre on 27 April 1726 Mr Wellman (or Welman) danced in a *Gardiner's Dance*, *Furies*, and *La Triomphante*. He had been in unnamed dances since the fourteenth. On 9 May he was seen in a new *Chacoon of All Characters*. The foreign troupe he was in had opened their engagement at the Haymarket on 24 March, and Wellman had probably danced then. The following fall, on 28 September, the same or another troupe began performing at the King's Theatre. Wellman danced on 17 December and probably earlier. He and Mrs Anderson offered a *Peasant Dance* on 16 March 1727, and he may have appeared regularly with the company through the end of their engagement on 10 May.

Wellman, Mr   *fl.* 1785–1799?₁,   actor, singer, manager?

Between 17 June and 27 July 1785 Mr Wellman performed the following roles at Hammersmith, sometimes essaying three characters per performance: Dick in *The Lying Valet*, Don Lopez in *The Wonder*, Lubin in *The Quaker*, Glenalvon in *Douglas*, Hodge in *Love in a Village*, Wingate in *The Apprentice*, a Witch in *The Death and Revival of Harlequin*, Shore in *Jane Shore*, Bundle in *The Waterman*, Sir John Trotley in *Bon Ton*, Farmer Giles in *The Maid of the Mill*, Sterling in *The Clandestine Marriage*, Dominick in *The Spanish Fryar*, the title role in *Midas*, Sir Jeffery Constant in *The Ghost*, Pantaloon in *Harlequin Skeleton*, Don Guzman in *The Follies of a Day*, Father Luke in *The Poor Soldier*, Tony Lumpkin in *She Stoops to Conquer*, Gaylove in *The Honest Yorkshireman*, a Fryar, an English Officer, and Pantaloon in *Robinson Crusoe*, and Horatio in *The Fair Penitent*. His wife also displayed a variety of roles. They shared a benefit on 15 July, when, in addition to playing Father Dominick and Midas, Wellman acted Mother Shipton and sang "Four and Twenty Fiddlers All in a Row." Tickets were available at No 20, Dorville's Row.

He was probably the Wellman who had a company that performed at Mr Thomas's theatre in Albrighton on 22 July 1799.

Wellman, Mrs   *fl.* 1785–1799₁,   actress.

With her husband, Mrs Wellman acted at Hammersmith from 17 June through 27 July 1785. Her roles were Kitty Pry in *The Lying Valet*, Isabella in *The Wonder*, Anna in *Douglas*, Alicia in *Jane Shore*, Miss Titup in *Bon Ton*, Miss Sterling in *The Clandestine Marriage*, Elvira in *The Spanish Fryar*, Colombine in *Mother Shipton*, Dorothy in *The Ghost*, Theodosia in *The Maid of the Mill*, Susan in *The Follies of a Day*, Arabella in *The Honest Yorkshireman*, Miss Hardcastle in *She Stoops to Conquer*, Colombine in *Robinson Crusoe*, Lavinia in *The Fair Penitent*, Charlotte in *The Apprentice*, Colombine in *Harlequin Skeleton*, and Colombine in *The Death and Revival of Harlequin*. She shared a benefit with Mr Wellman on 15 July. She was probably the Mrs Wellman who performed in Albrighton in July 1799.

Wellman, Mr _fl._ 1794–1795₁, dresser.

Mr Wellman was a dresser at Covent Garden Theatre in 1794–95 at a salary of 9s. 6d. weekly.

Wellman, Mlle _fl._ 1726₁, dancer.

In _Foreign Theatrical Companies_, Sybil Rosenfeld lists Mlle Wellman as a dancer in the foreign troupe that played at the Haymarket Theatre from 24 March to 11 May 1726. _The London Stage_ does not list any bills in which the young lady's name appeared, though the dancer Wellman (her father?) was cited several times.

Wellman, Mrs _fl._ 1717₁, performer?

Mrs Wellman, who may have been a performer, shared a benefit with three others at Lincoln's Inn Fields Theatre on 28 May 1717.

Wells, Mr _fl._ 1723?–1730₁, actor.

The Wells who played the Duke in _Venice Preserv'd_ in a special benefit performance for James, Eyre, and Mrs Ratcliff at the Haymarket Theatre on 13 February 1723 may have been the Wells who performed there in the winter season of 1729–30. That season, a Wells was the original Brush in the anonymous "Dramatick Opera" _Love and Revenge; or, The Vintner Outwitted_, Cant in _The Beggar's Wedding_, Dologodelmo and Soaretherial in _Hurlothrumbo_, the original Don Manuel in O. S. Wandesford's tragedy _Fatal Love; or, The Degenerate Brother_, Gibbet in _The Stratagem_, Molly in _The Metamorphosis of The Beggar's Opera_, Culverin in _The Half-Pay Officers_, the original Nobody in Henry Fielding's _The Author's Farce_, Quill in _Rape upon Rape_, and Dr Churchyard in _Tom Thumb_. He also played some unspecified part in the opening performances of _The Cheshire Comicks; or, The Amours of Lord Flame_ by Samuel Johnson of Cheshire, and he sang some role in _The Village Opera_. In playbills in which his son (or younger brother?) figured, our subject was called "Wells, Sr."

In the summer of 1730 the elder Wells engaged at the fairs, playing Churchyard again at Reynolds's booth on 4 September at Bartholomew Fair and once again, during Southwark Fair, at the Great Theatrical Booth in Bird-Cage Alley.

Wells, Mr _fl._ 1729–1730₁, actor.

A young actor named Wells, doubtless related to the older actor Wells in the same company, acted at the Haymarket Theatre at least five times in the winter of 1729–30. On 18 December he played Darno in _Hurlothrumbo_, the first time his name was seen in the playbills. Thereafter that season he was noticed as the original Pizarro in _Fatal Love_, a tragedy by Osborne Sidney Wandesford, Jasper in _The Half-Pay Officers_, and the original Blotpage in Henry Fielding's _The Author's Farce_. He does not seem to have returned to the London boards after that season.

Wells, Mr _fl._ 1774–1805₁, house servant.

A Mr Wells shared benefit tickets with a long list of other Covent Garden servants at the end of each season from 1774–75 through 1781–82. He (or another) Wells was being paid 12s. per week at Covent Garden in 1793–94, according to the Folger Library account books of the theatre (MS W. b. 436). A British Library pay sheet (Add MS 29949) identifies Wells as a doorkeeper earning a salary of 12s. per week in 1794–95, an amount that remained steady through 1801–2 but which dropped to 10s. in 1802–3. A document tipped into a copy of Kirkman's _Memoirs of the Life of Charles Macklin_ in the Harvard Theatre Collection specifies Wells as a boxkeeper as of 17 June 1805.

Wells, Mr _fl._ 1792₁, puppeteer.

A puppet show was conducted by a Mr Wells at Bartholomew Fair in 1792.

Wells, Master _fl._ 1796–1798₁, actor.

Master Wells first came to notice as Young Marcius in _Coriolanus_ at Drury Lane Theatre on 1 October 1796. Presumably he was the Master Wells who played the Count's Son in the premiere of Benjamin Thompson's drama _The Stranger_ at Drury Lane on 24 March 1798 and who had some part in John O'Keeffe's new interlude _The Eleventh Sylvester Daggerwood_ on 5 June 1798. He was probably the son of J.

Wells, who was a dancer and actor at Drury Lane during the period.

Wells, Mrs Ezra, Mary Stephens, née Davies, later Mrs Joseph Sumbel
1762–1829, actress, singer.

Most of what is known of the early years of Mary Stephens Wells (who was characterized by one of her contemporaries as "a noted and infamous woman") derives from her three-volume autobiography, *Memoirs of the life of Mrs. Sumbel, late Wells* . . . (1811). Even "The Manager's Note-Book," a source itself known to be cavalier about facts and imaginative with anecdotes, cautions that Mrs Sumbel's narrative contains a good deal of romance and was written by a person whose mind was not "always perfectly, collected."

Mary Davies was born on 16 December 1762, one of the daughters of Thomas Davies, a woodcarver and gilder in Birmingham who was employed by Garrick to dig up the root of the celebrated mulberry tree at Stratford-upon-Avon and fashion a box from it. It seems that Davies's partner, a Mr Griffith, having designs on Mrs Davies, manipulated Davies into prison and eventually into a madhouse where he died. At that time Mary Davies was about six. Her mother was soon driven out by Griffith and became a keeper of a tavern frequented by actors. Yates, the Birmingham manager, gave the mother a benefit in which she attempted Indiana in *The Conscious Lovers* but suffered extreme stage fright. Mrs Davies had a modest provincial career, playing at Bath, York, and Gloucester in the 1770s.

It was at Birmingham that Mary Davies made her stage debut, as the Duke of York in *Richard III,* and played Prince Arthur in *King John,* Cupid in *A Trip to Scotland,* and similar juvenile roles. In 1776, at the age of 14, Mary Davies acted at York in Wilkinson's company. At Gloucester she performed Juliet to the Romeo of an actor named Ezra Wells, whom she married on 22 November 1778 at St Chad's, Shrewsbury. The register recorded her full name as Mary Stephens Davies. Shortly afterwards Wells deserted her, leaving her with her mother at Cheltenham. (He acted in Dublin between 1783 and 1787, and according to the *Thespian Dictionary* he "gave his heart and name to another, who also became an actress" and was engaged with him in Dublin. So far

as we can determine, Ezra Wells never appeared on the London stage.)

Mary played singing leads in 1778 and 1779 at Bristol and in the summer of 1780 at Plymouth (where on 19 July she appeared as Donna Louisa in *The Duenna* and Nancy in *Three Weeks after Marriage*). Announced as from the Theatre Royal, Exeter, and making her debut on the London stage, Mrs Wells played Margery in *Love in a Village* and Mrs Cadwallader in *The Author* at the Haymarket Theatre on 1 June 1781. The next day the *Morning Chronicle* wrote of "a beautiful young Actress of the name of Wells, who has for some time been the Thalia of the West . . . her vocal powers are her slightest recommendation; and in her person and her acting consist her chief excellence." That month's *Westminster Magazine* believed that "when her *manières* have acquired a little more urbanity, she will be a very good performer." That summer she repeated both parts several times and on 26 June 1781 she acted Jenny in *Lionel and Clarissa.* On 28 August the bills offered additional entertainments: "Speaking, Singing, Sneezing, Yawning, Acting and Pantomime, particularly The Military Exercise by Mrs Wells." On 4 September 1781 she was the original Cowslip in O'Keeffe and Arnold's *The Agreeable Surprise,* in which her acting, according to Genest, could not be exceeded. The nickname "Cowslip" stuck with her for many years, and sometimes she was called "Becky" Wells. At short notice she replaced Mrs Cargill as Macheath on 14 September 1781 in a production of *The Beggar's Opera* in which men and women exchanged roles.

At the conclusion of the Haymarket season she was engaged at Drury Lane Theatre, where she made her first appearance on 25 September 1781 as Nancy in *The Camp.* That season at Drury Lane she also appeared numerous times as Jenny in Tickell's adaptation of Ramsay's *The Gentle Shepherd,* and she was seen as Flora in *She Wou'd and She Wou'd Not,* Inis in *The Wonder,* Widow Brady in *The Irish Widow,* Kitty Pry in *The Lying Valet,* and Jacintha in *The Suspicious Husband.* She went over to Covent Garden Theatre on the evening of 4 May 1782 to act Filch in *The Beggar's Opera* for Mrs Catley's benefit. At her own benefit at Drury Lane on 30 April she played Mrs Oakly in *The Jealous Wife* and Widow Brady;

MARY WELLS, as Mrs Page
by Hamilton

tickets could be had of her at No 417, the Strand, and the net receipts after house charges amounted to about £164.

In the summer of 1782 Mrs Wells returned to the Haymarket Theatre, adding to her summer repertoire Molly in *The English Merchant*, Bridget in *The Chapter of Accidents*, Slipshod in *The Female Dramatist*, Comfit in *The Dead Alive* (for her benefit on 23 August), and Nell in *The Devil to Pay*. She returned in the autumn to Drury Lane, where she remained for three more seasons. For her benefit on 30 April 1783 she made her initial essay in tragedy playing the title role in *Jane Shore*. Her second tragic role was Isabella in *Isabella*, again for her benefit on 30 April 1784 when tickets could be had from her at No 5, York Street, Covent Garden. Among her new roles in 1783–84 were Fainlove in *The Tender Husband*, Audrey in *As You Like It*, and Anna in the premiere of M. P. Andrews's Comedy *Reparation* on 14 February 1784.

In 1784–85 she added Imogen in *Cymbeline*, and for her benefit on 15 April 1785, when tickets were available from her again at No 417, the Strand, she presented herself as Captain Macheath and was the original Laura in *The Fool*, a farce by Edward Topham, who became her avowed admirer. Though the latter piece was silly, her acting was commendable. In that line, according to "The Manager's Notebook," she had no superior: ". . . her voice, action, and manners beautifully combined to give a true picture of simplicity." When she acted Isabella on 30 October 1784 the *Public Advertiser* compared her favorably with Mrs Siddons: "Both these actresses possess a quality which no other actresses have on the English stage—they are *always*, whether speaking or not speaking, in their part."

While engaged during winters at Drury Lane she continued to appear at the Haymarket in summers, playing the original Mrs Ragan in O'Bryen's *A Friend in Need, Is a Friend Indeed!* on 5 July 1783. There in 1784 she also created Fanny in Mrs Inchbald's *A Mogul Tale* on 6 July and Maud in O'Keeffe's *Peeping Tom* on 6 September. In the latter summer she made her first appearance as Lady Randolph in *Douglas* on 13 August 1784. On 16 June 1785 she was the original Nancy Buttercup in O'Keeffe's *A Beggar on Horseback*.

In 1785–86 Mrs Wells went over to Covent Garden Theatre where she was engaged at £7 per week. Her appearance there was delayed several months until 14 December 1785, when she acted Jane Shore with Alexander Pope as Shore and Holman as Hastings; she also acted Laura in *The Fool*. A repetition of her performance as Jane Shore on 20 December was prevented by her illness, and Mrs Kennedy was obliged to fill the role. Mrs Wells was sufficiently recovered by 29 December to act Lady Randolph. After appearances as Isabella, Imogen, and Andromache in *The Distrest Mother* in January, she made her first appearance as Rosalind (with the "Cuckoo Song") in *As You Like It* on 7 February 1786 and Portia in *The Merchant of Venice* on 18 February. She was Mrs Conquest in *The Lady's Last Stake* on 4 March, Fidelia in *The Plain Dealer* on 18 April, and the original Eugenia in *The Bird in a Cage* on 24 April, when she spoke an epilogue provided by Edward Topham. On 11 May 1786 she appeared for her benefit in Topham's farce *Small Talk; or, The Westminster Boy*. Because, as the *Town and Country Magazine* reported that month, "An old and established rule among the youth of Westminster will not permit any exhibition on the stage reflecting on their body," a large group of Westminster boys, assuming that Topham intended to ridicule them, mustered and dispersed throughout the boxes. When in the second act Mrs Wells appeared in the dress of a Westminster scholar, they made such an uproar that the rest of the piece "was prevented from being heard." Despite the rioting Mrs Wells cleared about £177 from tickets that had been available from her at No 188, Oxford Street. In the last weeks of the season she also acted Statira in *Alexander the Great*, Mrs Euston in *I'll Tell You What*, and Jenny in *The Deserter*.

After another summer at the Haymarket in 1786, she returned to Covent Garden, still at £7 per week, to appear in 1786–87 as Charlotte in *The Gamester*, Belinda in *The Provok'd Wife*, Harriet in *He Wou'd be a Soldier*, Lady Percy in *1 Henry IV*, the Lady in *Comus*, Lady Easy in *The Careless Husband*, Violetta in *The Brothers*, Sophia in *Bonds without Judgement* (another farce by Topham), Ann Lovely in *A Bold Stroke for a Wife*, Julia in *The Midnight House*, and Fatima in *Cymon*.

Mrs Wells was one of the numerous players

Courtesy of the Garrick Club

Mary Wells, as Anne Lovely
by De Wilde

engaged by John Palmer for his new Royalty Theatre in Wellclose Square. She was scheduled to appear as Rosalind in *As You Like It* on that theatre's opening night on 20 June 1787, but the Covent Garden manager Harris prevented her and others of his employees from performing at the East End theatre, and Rosalind was taken over by Mrs Bellfille. The authorities closed Palmer down for most of the summer. In September Mrs Wells did manage to appear at the Royalty Theatre, performing on the third and two nights thereafter in a scene called *Ourselves; or, The Realities of the Stage,* in which she gave "Extracts from some of the principal Female Performers."

At Covent Garden in 1787–88, now earning £8 per week, she appeared for the first time on 17 September 1787 as Mrs Page in

The Merry Wives of Windsor. Other new roles that season included Angelina in *Love Makes a Man,* Rose in *The Recruiting Officer,* Hermione in *The Winter's Tale,* and on 8 April 1788 Clara in the premiere of Lady Wallace's comedy *The Ton; or, Follies of Fashion.* At her benefit on 25 April (when tickets were available at No 15, Beaufort Buildings, where she now lived with Topham), she acted Widow Brady in *The Irish Widow* and offered those *Dramatic Imitations* in which she mimicked Mrs Siddons, Mrs Wrighten, Sga Sestini, Mrs Abington, Mrs Martyr, and Mrs Crawford, among others. Total receipts were £337 17s. 6d., and the usual house charge of £105 seems not to have been levied.

She remained engaged at Covent Garden for the next four seasons, with her salary in 1788–89 raised to £9 per week and to £10 the following season. A Covent Garden pay sheet for 1791–92 (now in the Harvard Theatre Collection) indicates she received £181 13s. 4d. for that season. She was the original Marianne in Reynolds's *The Dramatist,* which she brought on for her benefit on 15 May 1789, when tickets again could be had at Beaufort Buildings. For her benefit the following season on 29 April 1790 the anonymous comedy *The Female Adventurer* was introduced, but she apologized for not appearing in it because of "the Fatigue of going through various and numerous Imitations." Her address had changed to No 12, Weymouth Street, Portland Place, where she was the following year also. She acted Betty in *The Clandestine Marriage* on 27 November 1789 and Macheath to Mr Johnstone's Lucy and Mr Bannister's Polly on 13 April 1790.

Returning to the Haymarket for the first time in four years she played Mrs Cadwallader in *The Author* on 15 June 1790. That summer she also appeared there as Maud in *Peeping Tom,* Molly in *The English Merchant,* Fanny in *A Mogul Tale,* and Cowslip in *The Agreeable Surprise.*

Back at Covent Garden she was the original Lucy in Holcroft's *The School for Arrogance* on 4 February 1791, when the critic in the *Gazetteer* of 9 February hoped that "Mrs Wells could be prevailed upon to *speak out,* so that the audience might hear her." Other original roles were Jane in O'Keeffe's *Wild Oats* on 16 April 1791 and Clerimont in Simon's *National Prej-*

udice for her benefit on 10 May 1791. Her performance in the latter was marred by imperfect lines, and her imitations, though some were "tolerably true," were becoming outrageous caricatures. "She is now deficient in *tone* and *emphasis*," reported the *Oracle* on 11 May; "all is *shiver* and *sob*." She acted Lady Anne in *Richard III* on 15 October 1792.

For several summers Mrs Wells played in the provinces, performing in Cheltenham and Weymouth in 1788 and 1789 to large audiences. She acted at Richmond, Surrey, in August 1790 and in July 1792 and at Birmingham, "for that night only," on 28 July 1791.

By the late 1780s Mrs Wells had developed a reputation for unconventional and sometimes eccentric behavior, some of it brought on by incipient insanity and some of it by drink. In 1789 at Weymouth she caused a sensation and some embarrassment when she failed in her attempts to attract the attention of their Majesties on the esplanade, and, according to James Winston's *Theatric Tourist*, she paid ten guineas a week for the hire of a yacht "to follow them to Plymouth, a gun mounted on the deck, on which she sat astride, singing 'God save the King.'" In the summer of 1790 at the Haymarket, according to the same informant, she announced for her benefit a one-act piece called *Mrs Nonsuch's Nonsense*, "which she had written for the purpose of introducing Miss Edwin on the stage." But she was obliged to explain in a statement to the papers that Stephen Kemble had withdrawn from a leading role only two days before the scheduled opening and had written her a letter that began "Madam,—I think nothing can exceed your impertinence in offering me any part in your absurd piece. . . ." Either Kemble's timing and the manner of his resignation were unconscionable, or Mrs Wells was fabricating a story to cover up the hopelessness of her play. (The unfortunate Miss Edwin did not make it to the London stage that season. She perhaps was Elizabeth Edwin [fl. 1784–1797], the sister of the elder John Edwin, but that actress had appeared at the Haymarket on 10 February 1785; or she could have been the daughter of the John Edwin who died in 1793.)

At about that time Mrs Wells's relationship with Captain Edward Topham (1751–1820) was fast winding down. A successful officer who became known as "the tip-top adjutant" (he is noticed in *The Dictionary of National Biography*), Topham by the 1780s was a conspicuous figure in fashionable London. He was a close friend of Frederick Reynolds and was often seen in the company of Horne Tooke, the elder Colman, and Sheridan. His farce *The Fools,* in which Mrs Wells had appeared in April 1785, was published the following year with a dedication to her. His *Small Talk* was written to promote her benefit on 11 May 1786, and she also appeared in his *Bonds without Judgement,* which she introduced for her benefit on 1 May 1787.

Mrs Wells lived with Topham in his house at No 15, Beaufort Buildings, producing four children by him. On 1 January 1787 Topham set up *The World,* a daily paper the principal purpose of which was to puff Mrs Wells, whom he never did marry. Topham's colleagues in the venture were Miles Peter Andrews, the Reverend Charles Este, and the publisher John Bell. In that paper the Della Cruscans, headed by the poetaster Robert Merry, presented their fantastic works. Topham contributed some articles under the title of "The Schools," and Este was the editor until 1790. According to Winston "the conduct of the paper was principally left to Mrs Wells," who, it is said, regularly attended the Hastings trials and sent reports to *The World*.

After five years Topham sold his paper, left Mrs Wells for another woman, and took his three surviving daughters off to Wold Cottage, his place about two miles from Thwing in the East Riding of Yorkshire. Mrs Wells quickly fell upon hard times. The author of *A Pin Basket to the Children of Thespis* in 1796 protested that "The ingratitude of Mr. Topham to poor Wells, must receive the marked detestation of every honest man. After living upon her salary, and exhausting her finances, even to the last farthing, he deserted her to want and misery. . . ." But much of Mary Wells's distress had been caused by her indiscretion in backing the considerable debts of Emanuel Samuel, husband of her sister Anna Davies, who made her debut at the Haymarket Theatre on 28 July 1786 and acted for several seasons at Drury Lane. Mrs Wells had bailed Samuel out of Fleet Prison by paying his debts of £60 in 1789 and then arranged an appointment for him in the West Indies and

JOHN EDWIN as Lingo and MARY WELLS as Cowslip
by Downman

provided him with money for the journey. The indignities she was compelled to suffer on Samuel's account are related in her memoirs.

Apparently she was obliged to evade her creditors in the summer of 1792 by fleeing to Calais for several months. She returned when Topham took care of some debts, and she began the 1792–93 season at Covent Garden on 28 September 1792 playing Jacintha in *The Suspicious Husband,* followed by such roles as Lady Anne in *Richard III,* Lady Touchwood in *The Belle's Stratagem,* Marianne in *The Dramatist,* and Angelina in *Love Makes a Man.* Her performance of 28 December 1792 as Jane in *Wild Oats* turned out to be her last of that season and her final appearance as a regular member of a London company.

The following several years of her life seem to have been passed either in prison or in avoiding prison. In August 1792 at Brighton she first announced her intention to publish by subscription "Mrs. Wells' Life, written by Herself, in Four Pocket Volumes, price One Guinea," but the project was delayed almost 20 years. Soon afterward she was imprisoned for a while, liberated about March 1793, and driven to France by her creditors but driven back to England by the Reign of Terror. After only a few weeks, spent in Chelsea, she was carried to the King's Bench.

She managed, however, to get herself to Dublin in 1794–95 (she had acted at Cork the previous summer). According to her memoirs, at Dunglaire, where she lodged in the spring of 1795, she was arrested for one of Samuel's old debts but managed a compromise and left Ireland for London, where, she wrote, she arrived in April. But she was already in London that March, for the bills at the Haymarket Theatre on 20 March announced that she would be making her last appearance on the stage in *The Thespian Panorama,* a variety show composed of "Matter, Musical, Rhetorical, and Imitative." The *Morning Herald* the next day reported that "the chief novelty was the Imitations of Mrs Wells, which were given in a very admirable stile." The press announced on 7 April 1795 (clipping in the Folger Shakespeare Library) that she was going to perform in Edinburgh and thereafter in Glasgow. But she was back in London by 6 May once more to present her imitations, this time

at Covent Garden, in what was billed as "positively" her last appearance in public.

Soon after, the press reported that during her retirement from the stage Mrs Wells had taken up residence at Kenyon Lodge in St Giles in the Fields: "This salubrious Retreat is rendered the more pleasing by the kind & flattering Attentions of a *Hibernian Captain.*" He was the Captain Blackwood who had befriended her when both were lodging in the King's Bench, according to the colorful narration in the *Memoirs,* and having purchased her the liberty of the Rules, invited her to walk out with him. They lived together for a while (in Merton according to Winston's version), but when he was ordered to join his regiment in the West Indies she remained in England, not wishing to part from her children. Topham, however, had removed them to Yorkshire. The author of *A Pinbasket to the Children of Thespis* in 1796 was distressed that

the town is deprived of the excellent powers of Mrs Wells on the stage, than whom a more engaging actress never graced its boards; and she, whose generous hand, when competent, was to the indigent world, in its bounty, as universal as the sun, who never rose but to pity and relieve, is now so much reduced as to need others charity and commiseration.

By April 1796 Mrs Wells was back in the King's Bench and was in August removed to the Fleet. While at the Fleet she met Joseph Haim Sumbel, a Moorish Jew and former secretary to the ambassador from Morocco. The Sumbel family had had a checkered history. The father, Samuel "Sumbal," was many years a Minister of Affairs to the Sultan of Morocco and had served as his ambassador to Denmark in 1751. After 30 years of service the elder Sumbal was imprisoned for embezzlement. Though he managed to escape to Gibraltar, he died in the autumn of 1782, apparently a victim of poisoning.

Winston characterized Joseph Haim Sumbel as "rich, young, and handsome; but haughty, irascible, and jealous, to the greatest degree." He had been educated in France, traveled to Holland, and in 1794 was appointed Moorish Envoy to the Court of St James, a position often held by Moroccan Jews. When Mary Wells met him, Sumbel

MARY WELLS as Betty Blackberry and JOHN EDWIN as Jemmy Lumps
engraving after O'Keefe

was being confined in the Fleet for contempt of court, having refused to answer interrogatories concerning a large quantity of diamonds in his possession.

On October 1797 in the Fleet Mrs Wells married Sumbel in a wedding of "Eastern grandeur," solemnized, as Winston put it, with all the *"Jewish magnificence."* They made their way from the Fleet within a few weeks and first took a house in Orchard Street, Portman Square, and then one at No 79, Pall Mall, next door to the Duke of Gloucester. The new Mrs Sumbel, now converted to Judaism and having taken the name of Leah, lived "in splendid misery." Sumbel proved to be a man of vicious and irrational tempera-

ment who often locked her up without food and apparently kept a harem. After his plot to have her carried away on a ship failed, he threatened her with a pistol one night, firing at her and missing. In December 1798 she left his house and lodged a complaint against him, signing her name as Leah Sumbel. On the fourteenth of that month Sumbel advertised that Mary Wells had no right to use his name and that he would not pay any debts contracted by her. A silly exchange of charges followed concerning whether or not Mary was really a Jewess. According to certain stories in the press the marriage had not been a legal Jewish ceremony and she had broken the "Sabbath and the Holy Feast" by running away from Mr Sumbel in a post chaise and eating *"forbidden fruit*—namely, *pork griskin and rabbits."*

Sumbel sought an annulment, which was denied. In the hearing at the King's Bench his counsel Thomas Erskine argued that Sumbel was not a Jew but a Moslem and that accordingly the marriage in the Fleet was invalid. After a series of legal events, Sumbel suffered a penalty of £25, but he refused to pay, and, having procured a passport from his friend the Duke of Portland, he left England to take up residence in Altona, near Hamburg. He died at Altona in November 1804 and was buried in the local Jewish-Portuguese cemetery. In the middle of the nineteenth century, a talmudic school was founded at Altona by a "Sumbal," probably the product of one of Joseph Sumbel's liaisons after his relationship with Mary Wells.

Though Mary continued to call herself Mrs Sumbel (and published her memoirs in 1811 under that name), she renounced Judaism, writing: "I am now once more received into the bosom of Christianity as a repentant sinner, fully confident, as such, that the Almighty will pardon my transgressions."

On 25 February 1779 Mary returned to the Haymarket Theatre to act Bridget in *The Chapter of Accidents* for the benefit of the younger John Palmer. That night she also offered imitations of Mrs Siddons, Mrs Jordan, Mrs Crawford, and Mrs Martyr in various characters. Winston in "The Manager's Notebook" claimed that at the Haymarket the next month she also acted Jane Shore and other roles, "and the whole of her exertions were crowned with universal and deserved applause," but those performances are not to be found in *The London Stage.* That spring she advertised that she would give "Sublime Readings" four nights in Passion Week at Villeneuve's Rooms in Newman Street at 12s. for the series, but these and other readings in April were prevented by the Lord Chamberlain after the intervention of the Bishop of London. On 17 April 1799 she acted Portia in *The Merchant of Venice* at the Haymarket for the benefit of "an Infant Orphan family." The bills listed her as Mrs Sumbel, late Mrs Wells, and stated that she had "generously volunteered her services for that Evening." At Covent Garden on 12 June 1799 she presented her

Imitations in a performance by singers and actors for the benefit of the General Lying-In Hospital in Bayswater.

She offered her *Imitations* for Palmer's benefit at the Haymarket, a performance that was postponed until 8 November 1799 because she could not obtain her release from the Fleet, and then it was altogether canceled. She was for a while in and out of prison and for a time kept a shop at No 55, in the Old Bailey, where she gave some performances of her *Imitations.*

About 1799 or 1800 her sister and brother-in-law returned to England from the West Indies to take up residence in Hammersmith, where Mrs Sumbel lived with them for about a year and a half. Joseph Sumbel agreed to settle a guinea a week upon her to alleviate her distressed situation, but after several years of "irregular payments" he withdrew the allowance in 1805. On 29 August 1807, for Liston's benefit at the Haymarket, she returned to the stage to give her "celebrated Imitations" and in the following month repeated her program at a small theatre in Catherine Street, the Strand.

In 1809 she claimed on the Covent Garden Theatrical Fund, and in 1811 published her *Memoirs of the Life of Mrs. Sumbel, late Wells, of the Theatre Royal Drury Lane, Covent Garden, and Haymarket, written by herself* in three volumes. A document in the Public Record Office records the granting of a license to Mrs L. W. Sumbel for a play and entertainment at the Haymarket in 1812, with the specific period unstated. Thereafter the details of her life are few. Winston called her "unquestionably insane," and in her *Memoirs* she spun some extraordinary adventures related mainly to travels in search of her children.

On 4 December 1815 at the Haymarket a benefit was played for an old lady of 84, who, it was revealed, was the mother of Mary Sumbel. Mary had promoted the event and delivered her *Imitations.* She was at that time 53. That year, according to a letter in the Smith collection in the Garrick Club, her address was No 16, Buckingham Street, the Adelphi, in the Strand.

Receiving an annuity of £55, she passed her last years in the lodging house of a Mrs Bellini in Cavendish Street, Portland Chapel. Mrs Wells's generosity seems to have continued to

Private collection, London

MARY WELLS (when Mrs Topham) and her three children

by Russell

the last, when she raised money on her annuity to aid her landlady, to whom she had become very much attached. She also supported her mother. To her she gave up her bed and was her constant companion, sleeping in an armchair by her side, during a terminal illness of 17 weeks. Such sacrifices brought on an eye complaint and a disorder in her legs from which Mrs Wells never fully recovered. Her mother died in January 1827 at age 95. Mrs Wells and Mrs Bellini were now "even poorer than the poor," but their distresses were alleviated by an inheritance from Mrs Bellini's sister-in-law. Thereafter they lived comfortably and happily, according to Winston's account—"in perfect harmony, jointly partaking of the sunshine which came so opportunely."

Mrs Wells died on 23 January 1829 at age 67 and was buried in her mother's grave in the old churchyard of St Pancras.

Mary Wells had three daughters by Edward Topham (who died at Doncaster on 26 April 1820). According to F. Ross, *Celebrities of the Yorkshire Wolds* (1878), they were reckoned "the best horsewomen in Yorkshire." They were Juliet, who on 4 May 1803 married the Reverend Timothy Fish Foord, who proceeded M.A. at Trinity College, Cambridge, in 1802, and later adopted the surname Bowes; Harriet, who married John Arthur Warsop of Brandesburton, near Beverley, Yorkshire, and died at the age of 23 at Doncaster in 1810; and Maria Cowslip, who in January 1805 married Peter Acklom of Beverley (he died in April 1827 at the age of 45).

On 30 July 1834 Maria Arthur Warsop, daughter of J. A. and Harriet Warsop, married Capt W. H. Trollope at Landford, Wiltshire; their son, born in 1837, became Rear Adm Anthony Trollope, who was for some time owner of a picture by J. Russell of Mrs Wells and her three daughters (see iconography, No 8).

Mrs Wells was a very good actress in comedy and respectable in tragedy. She was often praised in the press and enjoyed considerable popularity during her years on the stage. She no doubt would have enjoyed a greater career had she not suffered a mental condition that caused great aberrations in her behavior. Frederick Reynolds described her as the most beautiful woman on the stage, though not the best. John Williams (as Anthony Pasquin) in *The Children of Thespis* (1792) wrote of her:

> For 'tis WELLS, the resistless, who burst on the
>   sight,
> To wed instant Rapture, and strengthen De-
>   light.—
> When she smiles, Youth and Valour their trophies
>   resign:
> When she laughs she enslaves, for that laugh is
>   devine.

Her best role was Cowslip in *The Agreeable Surprise*. She was highly regarded as well for her portrayal of such rustics as Maud in *Peeping Tom*, in which character she was described by one poetaster in the *Morning Chronicle:*

> If rustic beauty, in one mortal dwells,
> Fame's trump must sound it in the name of Wells.

Portraits of Mary Wells include:

1. By William Beechey. Full-length, standing in landscape. Long dress, long veil from head down over right shoulder; right hand up to head. Last known with Knoedler & Co, formerly with A. Tooth, and previously with Mrs Nathaniel Witt. Photograph in Witt Library.

2. By John Downman. Drawing 8½" × 6½", signed and dated 1791. Sold at Sotheby's on 14 November 1945, buyer unknown.

3. By John Downman. Drawing 8½" × 6½", signed and dated 1795. In white dress with pink sash and large black hat trimmed with pink ribbons. Sold at Christie's on 16 June 1938, bought by Hogan for £29 8s.

4. By John Downman. Undated miniature, sold at Sotheby's on 17 November 1954.

5. By George Engleheart. Miniature called Mrs Topham, 1795. Owned by Mrs W. M. Philips when it was exhibited at the Victoria and Albert Museum in May and June 1929.

6. By Joshua Reynolds. She sat for Reynolds in 1787 but the portrait has not been traced.

7. By George Romney. Canvas 50" × 40". Seated under a tree, nearly full face; cream-colored dress with pink stripes, her hands in a gray-black muff. In the possession of the Right Honorable E. P. Bouverie in 1875; purchased by H. G. Marquand and sold in his sale at the American Art Association in New York on 23 January 1903 (lot 34). Present location unknown.

8. By John Russell. Mrs Topham and her three children. Pastel 39" × 49½". When exhibited at the Royal Academy in 1791 (lot 90) it was called "Portrait of a Lady and Three Children," but Mrs Wells's identity was revealed in the *Morning Chronicle* of 2 May 1791. The picture was "Done for Mr. Ford Bowes to order." It was in the collection of Rear Adm Trollope, London, in 1891 and owned by J. Pierpont Morgan in 1907. On 22 April 1948 it was in the Slater sale at Parke-Bernet, New York. It (or another version, signed and dated 1791) appeared at Christie's on 7 July 1967 and was bought by Parks for 180 guineas; it was again at Christie's on 16 December 1969, when it was bought by Coulter for 130 guineas. (The latter catalogue reported "Another version of the pastel is in the Pierpont Morgan Library," but that library claims not to have it.) The picture was with Spink & Son in June 1977, when it was advertised in *Burlington Magazine*. It was again at Christie's on 24 November 1978 (lot 66), when it was bought for £1700 by a private collector in London.

9. By unknown artist. Oil on canvas 30" × 25". Half-length, facing right, low-

cut dress, and strand of pearls or beads around neck. Unsigned and undated, this portrait has been attributed erroneously to Francis Cotes, according to Edward Johnson's book on that artist (1975). In the Lady Lever Collection, Port Sunlight.

10. Engraved portrait by W. Ridley, after Naish. Published as a plate to Parsons's *Minor Theatre,* 1794.

11. As Anne Lovely in *A Bold Stroke for a Wife.* Painting by S. De Wilde. In the Garrick Club (No 265). Engraving by Leney as a plate to *Bell's British Theatre,* 1791. A copy of the engraving was published as a plate to *British Drama,* 1817.

12. As Belinda, with Patty Ann Bates as Lady Brute and Thomas Ryder as Sir John Brute, in *The Provok'd Wife.* Drawing by T. Stothard in the British Museum. Engraving after Stothard published as a plate to *Lady's Magazine,* 1783.

13. As Betty Blackberry, with John Edwin as Jemmy Jumps, in *The Farmer.* Engraving after O'Keefe. Published by Laurie & Whittle, 1794.

14. As Charlotte, with Alexander Pope as Beverley, Elizabeth Pope as Mrs Beverley, and Thomas Hull as Jarvis, in *The Gamester.* Painting by M. Brown. In the Garrick Club (No 446). Reproduced in this *Dictionary* with the notice of Alexander Pope.

15. As Cowslip in *The Agreeable Surprise.* Sketch by S. De Wilde. In the Yale Center for British Art.

16. As Cowslip, with John Edwin as Lingo. Drawing by John Downman, 1787, exhibited at the Royal Academy, 1788. Sold from Lady Currie's collection at Christie's on 30 June 1906 for 820 guineas; sold from the E. M. Hodgkins collection at Christie's on 29 June 1917; eventually passed through Agnew, Knoedler, Mrs P. Daingerfield, and Mortimer Brandt (New York, 1966). Now in the Yale Center for British Art. Engraving (in reverse) by Hugh Downman (n.d.).

17. As Cowslip, with John Edwin as Lingo. Engraving by E. Scott, after H. Singleton. Published by I. Birchall, 1788.

18. As Cowslip. Engraving by J. R. Smith. Published by the artist, 1802.

19. As Hebe. By James Northcote, signed and dated 1805. Exhibited at the Royal Acad-

emy, 1806. In the Art Gallery of Ontario, Toronto, the bequest of J. J. Vaughan, 1965. Reproduced in *Burlington Magazine,* December 1936, when it was the property of Messrs Leger & Sons, London.

20. As Imogen in *Cymbeline.* India ink drawing by J. H. Ramberg. In the British Museum. Engraving by C. Sherwin, printed for J. Bell, 1786. Ramberg's drawing was in the sale of the Bell collection of original drawings ("which have distinguished Bell's various editions") at Christie's on 27 March 1793 (lot 94).

21. As Jane Shore. Engraving by J. G. Wooding, on the same plate with a portrait of Mrs Inchbald. Published as a plate to the *New Lady's Magazine,* 1786.

22. As Juliet, with William Diamond as Romeo. Engraving by F. Bartolozzi, after C. Sherriff, 1796.

23. As Laura in *The Fool.* Pencil and watercolor study by John Downman, 1784. Fulllength, standing outdoors, with hat perched on head. Sold at Christie's on 16 July 1974; bought by Walker for 350 guineas (illustrated in the catalogue); again at Christie's on 8 June 1976, and sold for 300 guineas to an unknown buyer.

24. As Lavinia in *Titus Andronicus.* India ink drawing by J. H. Ramberg. In the British Museum. Two drawings by Ramberg of Mrs Wells as Lavinia were in the sale of the Bell collection of original drawings at Christie's on 27 March 1793 (lot 85).

25. As Lavinia. Engraving by Thornthwaite, after Hamilton. Published as a plate to *Bell's Shakespeare,* 1785.

26. As Mrs Page in *The Merry Wives of Windsor.* Chalk and watercolor drawing by John Downman. In the British Museum. Probably this is the picture noted in one of Downman's sketchbooks (4th series, vol XI) at Butleigh Court: "23. Mrs Wells, the Actress, 1787, as one of the Merry Wives of Windsor." Engraving by Walker & Cockerell.

27. As Mrs Page. Painting by William Hamilton. In the Picture Gallery of the Royal Shakespeare Theatre, Stratford-upon-Avon. Probably the picture sold by the artist at Phillips's, London, on 20 May 1802.

28. Drawings on a whole sheet (9″ × 12¾″) in pen and ink and colored

chalks by S. De Wilde depict various head studies of actors and actresses, including Mary Wells. At Sotheby's on 20 April 1972 (lot 1). Now in the Yale Center for British Art.

Wells, Henry ₁fl. 1735₁, trumpeter.

Henry Wells was a trumpeter in the King's Musick in 1735, according to the Lord Chamberlain's accounts.

Wells, J. ₁fl. 1794–1816₁, dancer, actor.

A Mr Wells began to dance occasionally at Drury Lane for 3s. 4d. per day toward the beginning of the 1794–95 season, according to acccounts in the Folger Library (Mss W. b. 297–309). Those accounts and others in the British Library (Add Ms 29710) show Wells as a regular member of the theatre's dance corps from 1797 through the season of 1815–16.

Though his presence in the theatre was constant during those years, Wells apparently was assigned no featured roles. He was always one among many: in the tribe of Indians in *The Cherokee*, in the throng of Furies in *Harlequin Captive*, or one of numerous Villagers in *The Scotch Ghost* or Peasants in *Richard Coeur de Lion*.

By 1802–3 Wells was drawing a salary of £1 per week. By 1805–6 his pay had risen to £1 5s. In a September 1804 entry in the Drury Lane accounts, he was called J. Wells. In 1808–9 "Mr Wells and Wife" danced for £2 5s. per week. By 1811–12 Mrs Wells had departed from the roster, and Wells was earning £1 5s. alone, as he did until his disappearance from the accounts in 1816. Mr and Mrs J. Wells may have been the parents of the juvenile actor Master Wells (fl. 1796–1798).

Wells, John Wilmot d. 1810, actor, singer, manager.

John Wilmot Wells and his first wife were familiar to provincial theatregoers from Margate to Dublin and Brighton to Edinburgh, but so far as we know only the husband acted in London or environs, and he only a few times. He may have been the Wells who played at Richmond, Surrey, in the summers of 1776 and 1777, and he was probably the Wells whom Henry C. Porter records in *The History of the Theatres of Brighton* (1886) as per-

forming under Buckle's management at Brighton in 1783.

Each year, 1784 through 1787, John Wilmot Wells played at the Theatre Royal, Shakespeare Square, Edinburgh, from late January to early summer. There he unfolded a repertoire of some 70 important secondary and tertiary characters in comedies, tragedies, melodramas, and ballad operas, including Hardcastle in *She Stoops to Conquer*, Peachum in *The Beggar's Opera*, Justice Guttle in *The Lying Valet*, Claudius in *Hamlet*, Priuli and Renault in *Venice Preserv'd*, Major Sturgeon in *The Mayor of Garratt*, Strickland in *The Suspicious Husband*, Sir Anthony Absolute in *The Rivals*, Sir Oliver Surface in *The School for Scandal*, and Sir Tunbelly Clumsy in *A Trip to Scarborough*. Mrs Wells did not begin to act in Edinburgh until 1785, but she was to remain there longer than her husband.

The couple acted also at Norwich early in 1784, and the *Hibernian Journal* of 27 December 1784 said that they were "from Norwich" when on that date they made their debut at the Fishamble Street Theatre in Dublin.

Nothing is known of the activities of Wells and his wife for several years after 1787, except that Mrs Wells had continued to perform at Edinburgh, where she was popular in leading roles in both comedy and tragedy through the spring of 1791. On 18 June 1791 the *Newcastle Courant* reported that she had died in Edinburgh on 8 June.

Also in 1791, Wells was appointed manager of the Margate Theatre by its proprietor, Grubb, according to James Winston in *The Theatric Tourist* (1805). Evidently Wells retained some connection with the Edinburgh Theatre as well, for the "Recorder's Book" of the Calton Burying Ground in Edinburgh bears the notation under the date of 15 March 1792: "Daughter of William Welcot [sic] Wells Comedian from Canal Street Died of the Smallpox Buried 3 p 2 feet SE from the SE C[orner] of Ann Gells Stone aged 4 years."

A poetic "Address" written by "Mr Meyel of Bath" (doubtless William Meyler) was spoken by Wells on the "opening of the New Theatre, at Stockbridge, May 1, 1793." He played some roles at the theatre in Richmond, Surrey, in the summer season of 1796, and the *Monthly Mirror* for August commended his "good figure" and "very respectable" action.

Wells's only known appearance in a major London theatre was on 17 December 1798 when a special benefit was held at the Haymarket for the senior Willoughby Lacy. On that occasion Wells played Major Oakly in *The Jealous Wife*.

About 1797 Wells had been married to one Sarah Pass, according to a supplement to the *Gentleman's Magazine* in 1807, but the marriage was for some reason considered irregular. The couple remarried at St John's, Margate, on 8 October 1807. The *Gentleman's Magazine* for July 1810 reported the death of John Wilmot Wells in London "lately."

Wells, Robert *fl.* 1785?–1794₁, singer, engraver.

Robert Wells, of No 10, Greenhill Rents, West Smithfield, a member of the New Musical Fund, a music engraver, and a tenor singer, had sung in at least one of the later Handelian celebrations at Westminster Abbey (1785, 1786, 1787, or 1791), according to his entry in Doane's *Musical Directory* of 1794.

Wells, William *d.* 1721?, performer, proprietor?

On 8 September 1702 the *Post Man* carried a notice that William Wells and other strolling performers were required to pay town constables 2s. daily. The strollers had presumably been performing in the London area. Wells was possibly the proprietor of the bear garden at Hockley in the Hole and then the bear garden at Marylebone. That Wells died in 1721, and Dan Singleton wrote an epitaph quoted by Malcolm in his *Anecdotes*:

> Shed, O ye combatants, a flood of tears;
> Howl, all ye dogs; roar, all ye bulls and bears!
> Ye butchers, weep! for ye no doubt are grievers,
> And sound his loss with marrow-bones and cleavers.
> Wells is no more! Yet death has been so kind
> That he hath left the bulls and bears behind.

Malcolm also quoted a newspaper notice:

> By the decease of Mr. Wells, the original Beargarden in Hockley in the Hole is now likely to be thronged, especially since all the old gamesters are resolved to bait every Monday and Thursday; and the gladiators have promised frequently to try their skill there; the brutes to box; the furmity and hasty-pudding eaters, to cobble down their hot guttage at Madam Preston's, and at no other place.

Wells, William *d.* 1725?, violinist.

William Wells was sworn a musician in ordinary in the royal musical establishment on 17 January 1709. On 23 February 1713 he shared a benefit concert at Stationers' Hall with Kenny, as he did again on 22 February 1714 and 2 May 1715. His basic income of £40 annually, however, came from his service at court. He earned £30 as a violinist in the Academy of Music opera orchestra in 1720, according to the Portland papers at Nottingham. On 29 December 1725 James Nichols replaced Wells at court; that may have meant that Wells had died recently, though there is no certain evidence of that.

Welman. *See* WELLMAN.

Welsch, Miss. *See* WELCH, MRS.

Welsh. *See also* WELCH.

Welsh, James *fl.* 1792–1806₁, singer, actor, pianist.

Mr Welsh, whose first name is given as James by *The London Stage*, first appeared with the Drury Lane Company playing at the King's Theatre on 21 November 1792 in the chorus of *The Pirates*. Also in the company that season was Master Thomas Welsh, and the theatre's account books for 26 April 1793 identified them as brothers. James Welsh was old enough to receive adult billing. That season he was heard in numerous performances of *The Pirates*, and on 16 January 1793 he acted a Gentleman to Petruchio in *The Chances*. At the Haymarket Theatre on 15 March 1793 he sang in the *Messiah*.

He began his second season as a Soldier in *Royal Clemency* at the Haymarket on 10 October 1793. He moved with the company to the new Drury Lane Theatre in the spring, where he sang in *The Pirates* again and played Ralph in *Catherine and Petruchio*. In 1794 Doane's *Musical Dictionary* listed him as a player on the pianoforte and a bass singer who was employed at Drury Lane and had sung in the Oxford Meeting in 1793. His address was given as No 2, Parliament Square, Westminster, the same as his brother's.

James Welsh's engagement with Drury Lane paralleled his younger brother's through 1796–97, but James was not so prominent a member of the company. While his salary in 1793–94 was £4 per week, Thomas's was £9, and the latter also enjoyed a benefit. James's modest assignments in 1794–95 included singing in the choruses of *Lodoiska*, *The Mountaineers*, and *The Cherokee*. On 6 February 1795 he played Nimming Ned in *The Beggar's Opera*. He appeared as a Footman in *The Wheel of Fortune*, a Knight in *King Lear*, James Guerney in *King John*, and a Bailiff in *The Plain Dealer* in 1795–96; and in the choruses of *The Prisoner*, *Robinson Crusoe*, and *A Friend in Need* in 1796–97. In the latter season he also acted Camarzin in *Lodoiska* a number of times and played Dorcas in *Linco's Travels* on 24 May 1797.

Though his name did not appear in the bills after 1797, James Welsh continued at Drury Lane as a chorus singer until at least 1806. On 21 January 1800 he and his brother were paid a total of £4 16s. 8d. for five days' salary. In 1801–2 James was paid £4 9s. 8d. per week, and his name was on company lists (without salary specified) through 1805–6.

Welsh, Thomas   *c. 1780–1848, singer, actor, pianist, composer.*

Thomas Welsh was born about 1780 at Wells, the son of John Welsh. There is no evidence for the assertion in *The Dictionary of National Biography* and the *New Grove* that his mother was a daughter of the elder Thomas Linley. Of the Linley daughters who survived to some degree of maturity, only Charlotte could be eligible as Thomas Welsh's mother, but little is known of her except that she was born about 1768, died about 1788, and would have been barely 12 at the time of Thomas Welsh's birth. Welsh's early career, however, was connected with Linley and R. B. Sheridan, Linley's son-in-law.

At the age of six, Welsh became a chorister at Wells Cathedral. Master Welsh's lovely voice as a choirboy soloist drew Sunday crowds to Wells from Bath, Bristol, and Bridgewater. Sheridan heard him sing at Wells and recommended him to Linley. On 24 February 1792, Master Welsh sang in the oratorio *Redemption* at the King's Theatre, where the Drury Lane company was residing that year. His selections included Handel's "Angels ever bright and fair" from *Theodora* and "Where is this stupendous stranger?" from

Alcina. He sang in the oratorios at the King's again on 29 February and several times in March of that season. On 23 May 1792 he appeared as Ascanius in the masque *Neptune's Prophecy*, his first stage role. By the end of the season the masque was performed five times at the conclusion of Hoare's dramatic opera *Dido Queen of Carthage*, and Welsh seems to have been paid 10s. for each performance. He also sang in the first performance of Giardini's *Ruth* on 22 May 1792 at Ranelagh Gardens, along with Mrs Crouch, Miss Poole, Mrs Bland, James Bartleman, and Michael Kelly, in the presence of Haydn, at which time Welsh was reported to be about 12 years old.

The *Wolverhampton Chronicle* of 18 April 1792 had announced that "Mr Linley has engaged young Welsh for five years certain at a salary of £600. He is to be thirty weeks in London, the remainder of the year . . . at Wells, under the care of Perkins." As a member of the Drury Lane company in 1792–93 Welsh appeared at the King's Theatre as Narcisso in the premiere of Rose and Attwood's *The Prisoner* on 18 October 1792 (a piece evidently written to exhibit the boy's talents), as Carlos in *The Regent* on 7 January 1793, and as Cupid in *Cymon* on 23 January. During the last half of the season the company played at both the King's and the Haymarket; Welsh performed in the oratorios and as the Boy in the premiere of Hoare's *The Prize* on 11 March and a Sea Boy in the premiere of Birch's *The Mariners* on 10 May, and he occasionally sang specialty numbers. For his benefit on 27 May 1793, Welsh offered a new song by Percy; tickets were available from him at No 2, Parliament Street, Palace Yard, and receipts were £263 11s., less £167 3s. house charges. Also joining the Drury Lane company in 1792–93 was James Welsh, who sang in the various choruses. The Drury Lane account books at the Folger Library record the payment on 26 April 1793: "Welsh 7/10/0 & Brother 3/6/8/." James, then, was presumably the elder and of sufficient age to be billed as Mr Welsh. The younger Thomas, however, made the higher salary, receiving £9 per week to James's £4.

In 1793–94, when his salary was £9 per week (a substantial sum considering that Moody's and Mrs Bland's salaries were £8), Master Welsh sang Handelian selections in the oratorios that inaugurated the new Drury

Lane Theatre on 12 March 1794 and several performances thereafter in March and April. On 21 April 1794, he was in the chorus of Witches and Spirits in *Macbeth*, Kemble's production, the first dramatic event at the new theatre. On 30 May 1794 he played Ralph in *Catherine and Petruchio*, and on 9 June 1794 he was a Page in the premiere of Kemble's *Lodoiska*. Doane's *Musical Dictionary* in 1794 listed Master Thomas Welsh of No 2, Parliament Street, Westminster, as a soprano who performed in the Concert of Ancient Music and at Drury Lane; Doane also reported that Welsh sang at the Oxford Meeting in 1793 and in the Handelian concerts at Westminster Abbey.

Master Welsh first sang at Vauxhall Gardens on 3 June 1795 and appeared there over the next several years. Numbers of songs were printed during that period as sung by him at Vauxhall. Also published were songs composed by him, including *This is the House that Jack. Composed by Master Welsh* (1796), *Fair Mary, a Favorite Song, composed & sung by Master Welsh at Vauxhall Gardens* (1796), and *The Gentle Shepherdess, written by Mr Cunningham, composed & sung, by Master Welsh, at the Academy of Ancient Music* (1796).

He continued to appear as Master Welsh at Drury Lane through 1796–97, playing Henry in Cobb's *The Cherokee* on 20 September 1794, the Boy in Brick's *The Adopted Child* on 1 May 1795 (when his address was No 9, Margaret Street, Westminster, and his benefit receipts were £226 10s. free of charges), a Page in *Jack of Newbury* on 6 May 1795, Arthur in *King John* (a role taught him by Kemble who thought he had potential as an actor) on 18 December 1795, Edward in *The Smugglers* on 13 April 1796, Narcisso in *The Prisoner* on 29 September 1796, and a Child in Hoare's *A Friend in Need, is a Friend Indeed!* on 9 February 1797. For his benefit on 18 May 1797, when he still lived at No 9, Margaret Street, Welsh played Narcisso and sang several specialty numbers. Benefit tickets totaled £219 11s. free of house charges.

Thomas Welsh's last juvenile appearance seems to have been as Juba in *The Prize* on 13 June 1797. When young William Heather made his stage debut at Drury Lane on 15 October 1798 as Edward in *The Smugglers*, he was described by the *Monthly Mirror* as "an admi-

THOMAS WELSH

engraving by Holl, after Wivell

rable substitute for Welsh, who has not only outgrown those characters, but whose voice, on account of the approach of manhood, is at present defective." The same journal reported in June 1798: "A short time ago, in the Court of King's Bench, the father of Welsh the singer recovered 900l. 2s. 4d. from Mr. Westley, one of the proprietors of Drury Lane theatre, under an agreement signed by Mr. Sheridan."

Welsh then began to study with Johann Cramer, C. F. Horn, and Baumgarten. He was paid £50 by Drury Lane in May and June 1799 for writing a medley of songs. On 28 September 1799 he received 10s. 6d. for coaching the Drury Lane chorus one day. For a similar service he was paid £3 3s. on 19 November 1801.

On 13 May 1801 Jane Porter went to a rehearsal at the Haymarket for Dr Busby's concert and stood on the stage while "young Welsh practiced one song." As she wrote in her diary, she "was not pleased with his voice, as it is now." J. P. Kemble recorded in his memorandum book that "Mr. T. Welsh engaged for three years at ten Pounds a week" at Drury Lane. When he sang in the comic opera

Algonah on 4 May 1802 the bills advertised the event as "Being His Second Appearance these Five Years." In that year, by which time his high coloratura had deepened into a powerful bass, he was admitted to the Chapel Royal. Though he had been one of the outstanding boy sopranos of his time, he enjoyed little professional success as an adult singer. Probably he was the Welsh whose name appeared in the Drury Lane paylist through 1808–9 at £4 per week from September 1806.

Later he wrote music for *Twenty Years Ago* at the Lyceum on 21 July 1810, *The Green-eyed Monster; or, How to Get Your Money* at the Lyceum on 14 October 1811, *Up to Town* (with Reeve and others) at Covent Garden on 6 November 1811, *Kamtchatka* at Covent Garden on 16 October 1811, *For England Ho!* at Covent Garden on 15 December 1813, and *Is He Jealous?* at the Lyceum on 2 July 1816. In 1825 at London he published the *Vocal Instructor, or The Art of Singing Exemplified in 15 Lessons Leading to 40 Progressive Exercises*. Welsh also wrote some sonatas for piano (1819) and some songs, glees, and duets.

Most of his later professional life was occupied by successful teaching and publishing. Among his pupils were C. E. Horn, John Sinclair, Catherine Stevens, and Mary Ann Wilson. (Miss Wilson made her debut at Drury Lane on 18 January 1821 and soon gained a great deal of money but lost her voice from overwork.) Welsh took Horn and Miss Wilson to Dublin and Cork for a series of concerts in 1822. Welsh remained in Dublin for six months as pianist in the orchestra of the Hawkins Street Theatre and performed at numerous concerts, including one in St Patrick's Cathedral for the benefit of "the poor peasantry."

About 1825 Welsh and William Hawes took over a music publishing business from the Royal Harmonic Institution, in the Argyll Rooms, No 246, Regent Street. On 14 April 1827 Welsh and Horn narrowly escaped death when a gas explosion occurred at the Argyll Rooms, knocking Welsh senseless for two days. After the partnership was dissolved in 1828, Welsh continued the music selling business at that address until the Argyll Rooms were destroyed by fire in February 1830. He then removed to No 234, Regent Street, for a while until the premises at the Harmonic Institution were rebuilt.

On 9 June 1827 Welsh had married Mary Ann Wilson, and their only child became the wife of the cellist Alfredo Pratti.

Thomas Welsh died at Brighton on 24 January 1848. An engraved portrait of Welsh by B. Holl, after A. Wivell, was published in 1831. C. Phillips's engraved portrait, after T. Wageman, was published as a plate to volume 8 of *The Apollo*.

"Welsh Ambassador, The." *See* HOWELL, JAMES.

"Welsh Will." *See* "WELCH WILL."

Wendling, Johann Baptist *c. 1720–1797, flutist, composer.*
Johann Baptist Wendling was born in Rappoltsweiler in Alsace about 1720, served as a flutist in the court chapel at Zweibrücken and then, beginning in 1754, at the Mannheim court chapel. The *New Grove* notes that Wendling visited London in 1771, but references to him in advertisements all stem from the spring of 1772. At a concert at the Haymarket Theatre on 30 March he played a solo on the German flute, and for his benefit on 6 April he accompanied some singers in a performance of *Endimione*. He performed again at the Haymarket on 27 April. Wendling was described in bills as a musician to the Elector Palatine.

Wendling returned to Mannheim, where he met Mozart in 1777. He went with Mozart to Paris in 1778, appearing at the Concert Spirituel, as he had done in 1751–52 and as he did again in 1780. Wendling composed a number of sonatas and duets for flute. His wife, Dorothea, born Spourni (1737–1811), was a singer and teacher. The Wendlings had a daughter, Auguste, who became one of the Elector's mistresses and died of consumption. Johann Baptist Wendling died in Munich on 27 November 1797.

Wenpicollo, Mr *(fl. 1728), actor.*
A man with the unlikely name of Wenpicollo played Pantaloon in *The Rivals* with Mme Violante's troupe at the Haymarket Theatre on 21 February 1728. He shared a benefit with two others on 3 April.

Wentworth, Mr   ₍fl. 1791–1802₎,   actor, singer.

A Mr Wentworth and his wife were itinerant actors by 1791, when on 31 January their names appeared on a bill at Prescot as Antonio and Miranda in *The Tempest* and the Constable and Kitty in *The Village Lawyer*. That year they also acted on Tate Wilkinson's York circuit. In October 1793 and June and December 1794 Wentworth was a member of the company at Manchester.

On 23 November 1795 Wentworth appeared at Drury Lane Theatre in the chorus of *Alexander the Great*. Also in the chorus accompanying Alexander's triumphal entry into Babylon, was Miss S. Wentworth, his daughter. He sang in *Harlequin Captive* on 18 January 1796, acted Sir Anias Paulet in *Mary Queen of Scots* on 15 February, sang in the chorus of *The Iron Chest* on 12 March, was an Attendant in Ireland's Shakespearean forgery *Vortigern* on 2 April 1796, played an Officer in *Coriolanus* on 18 April, acted a character in *Almeyda, Queen of Granada* on 20 April, took a role in *Mahoud* on 30 April, and appeared as Ferguson in *Julia* on 2 May. On 11 May 1796 he shared benefit tickets with seven other minor personnel.

In the summer of 1796 the Wentworths went strolling once more. At Worthing on 29 September 1796, the occasion of Mrs Wentworth's benefit, he acted the Master of the Madhouse in *The Noble Pilgrim* and Apollo in *Midas*; in the latter piece Mrs Wentworth played Mysis and their daughter Nysa.

All three were members of the Drury Lane company in 1796–97 when Wentworth earned £1 10*s*. per week. He did not reappear until 26 October 1796, when he played the Second Gentleman in *Isabella*, and then he was seen or heard as the Taylor in *The Trip to Scarborough*, Sir James Blount in *Richard III*, an unspecified character in *The Conspiracy*, the Watchman in *The Apprentice*, a Sailor in *Robinson Crusoe*, a Singer in the chorus of *The Honey Moon*, an Officer in *The Wheel of Fortune*, a vocal part in *Theodosius*, Mirvan in *Tamerlane*, a Chairman in *The Suspicious Husband*, a voice in the chorus of *A Friend in Need*, a Captive in *The Children in the Wood*, a Chairman in *The Heiress*, and an Arcadian in *Linco's Travels*.

After a summer at Richmond, Surrey, where his wife and daughter also acted, Went-worth returned to Drury Lane to fill a similar line of tertiary and chorus roles at least through 1801–2 at a constant £1 10*s*. per week. In 1800 he also was at the Theatre Royal, Manchester; on 24 March he acted John in *The Son-in-Law* and the Prompter in *Sylvester Daggerwood*.

Wentworth died by 1806, the year in which the *Authentic Memoirs of the Green Room* reported that Miss Wentworth now supported her mother. His wife and daughter are noticed separately.

Wentworth, Mrs   ₍fl. 1791–1806₎,   actress, singer.

Mrs Wentworth, wife of the Drury Lane player and mother of the singer Miss S. Wentworth, was acting at Prescot by 1791. On 31 January of that year she appeared there as Miranda in *The Tempest* and Kitty in *The Village Lawyer*, pieces in which her husband acted Antonio and the Constable, respectively. The same year they also performed on the York circuit. At Worthing on 29 September 1796 she had a benefit and acted Mysis in *Midas*; her husband played Apollo and her daughter Nysa. About six weeks later, on 9 November 1796, she sang in the chorus of Knights and Ladies in *Harlequin Captive* at Drury Lane Theatre, a pantomime that was performed only four times that season. Her husband and daughter, also members of the company, were busier. Mrs Wentworth appeared at Covent Garden Theatre on 21 June 1797 in the title role of *The Duenna*, with Braham as Carlos and Sga Storace as Clara, for the benefit of the General Lying-In-Hospital.

In the summer of 1797 the three Wentworths were with Haymes's company at Richmond, Surrey. The name "Mme" Wentworth appeared on Drury Lane bills over the next several years, but maybe her daughter, Miss S. Wentworth, who was a regular chorus singer at that theatre, was intended. Those appearances, in any event, included singing in the choruses of *The Tempest* on 9 December 1797, *Aurelio and Miranda* on 29 December 1798, *Pizarro* on 24 May 1799, and *De Montfort* on 29 April 1800.

Mrs Wentworth was with her husband at Manchester in 1800; she played Letty in *The Dramatist* on 24 March. She was still alive in 1806, being supported by her daughter.

Wentworth, Miss *fl. 1772₁*, *actress, singer.*

As a member of Foote's summer company at the Haymarket Theatre in 1772, a Miss Wentworth acted Lucy in *The Virgin Unmask'd* on 18 May. Since she was announced as making her first appearance on that stage, presumably she had had some previous experience. She acted Miss Biddy in *Miss in Her Teens* on 27 May and performed Charlotte in *The Apprentice* on 3 July, Dorcas in *The Mock Doctor* on 6 July, Arethusa in *The Contrivances* on 10 July, Frichetta in the premiere of Gentleman's *Cupid's Revenge* on 27 July, Wheedle in *The Miser* on 4 August, a role in *The Rehearsal* on 10 August, Silvia in *The Old Bachelor* on 8 September, and an unspecified role (with songs in character) in *Madrigal and Truletta* on 17 September.

Wentworth, Miss S. *fl. 1795–1806₁*, *singer, actress.*

On 23 November 1795, Miss S. Wentworth made her debut at Drury Lane Theatre singing in the chorus of *Alexander the Great*. Also in the chorus that night was her father, who worked at that theatre until at least 1802. Miss Wentworth was employed there, mainly as a chorus singer, through at least 1804–5 at a salary of £1 10s. in the last year and £1 5s. prior to 1802–3. She signed as S. Wentworth on an 1804 pay ledger (now in the Folger Shakespeare Library).

Her contributions were usually to choruses in *The Mountaineers, Harlequin Captive, The Iron Chest,* and *Mahoud* in 1795–96; *The Honey Moon, A Friend in Need,* and *Linco's Travels* in 1796–97; *Richard Coeur de Lion, The Tempest,* and *Blue-Beard* in 1797–98; *The Captive of Spilburg, The Surrender of Calais, Aurelio and Miranda, Feudal Times, The Secret, Macbeth,* and *Pizarro* in 1798–99; and *Lodoiska, The Egyptian Festival,* and *De Montfort* in 1799 and 1800.

According to the *Authentic Memoirs of the Green Room* (1806), upon her initial engagement at Drury Lane Miss Wentworth had been promised opportunities for advancement, but she remained little known, being principally employed as a chorus singer. She advanced on occasion to better roles. Her Drury Lane credits included Louisa in *No Song No Supper* on 2 December 1796, 23 February 1797, and several times thereafter, including once at Covent Garden on 14 June 1797; Agnes in the *Follies of the Day* on 8 February 1797, 23 December 1797, and 11 January 1800; Titania in *The Fairy Festival* on 13 May 1797; Charlotte in *My Grandmother* on 18 September 1798; Viletta in *Don Juan* on 13 June 1798; the Prince of Wales in *Richard III* on 25 September 1798 and 7 October 1799; Ursula in *Much Ado about Nothing* on 4 July 1799 and 12 October 1799; Mrs Godfrey in *The Liar* on 5 July 1799; Josephine in *The Children in the Wood* on 26 September 1799; and Clara in *Rule a Wife and Have a Wife* on 13 November 1799. On 9 June 1800 she acted Laura in the second performance of Prince Hoare's *Indiscretion*, replacing Miss Heard, who had played it at the premiere the previous 10 May.

On 11 June 1800, at very short notice, Miss Wentworth replaced the indisposed Mrs Bland in the featured role of Agnes in *The Mountaineers*. The *Dramatic Censor* reported that she acquitted herself "to general satisfaction," though she was not competent in the songs. According to the *Authentic Memoirs of the Green Room*, she studied the character "scene by scene, as she proceeded," and went through "with astonishing success." In 1804–5 she rescued a performance of *Love in a Village* by stepping in as Rosetta for the ill Miss Stephens and succeeded once more, to the chagrin of several other actresses who attended in hopes of seeing her fail. The audience was "unbounded" in its applause.

In September 1796 she had acted at Worthing with her parents and was with them again in 1797 in the company at Richmond, Surrey.

In 1804–5 she was still singing in the Drury Lane chorus. Though she did little, claimed the *Authentic Memoirs*, she had the "credit of doing little well." She was described as "neat, genteel and pleasing" and still "very young" in 1806. As small as her salary was (£1 10s. per week), she supported her mother "in a style of comfort and respectability," a remark suggesting that by that year her father was dead.

Werner, Anthony *fl. 1739–1755₁*, *musician.*

On 28 August 1739 Anthony Werner became one of the original subscribers to the

Royal Society of Musicians. He was still active in 1755.

Werner, ₁Francis?₁ ₁*fl. 1768–1785?*₁, *harpist.*

In *The Pleasure Gardens of London* Wroth reports that a Mr Werner, harpist, performed in 1768 at Marylebone Gardens for two guineas weekly. Perhaps he was Francis Werner, who is represented in the *Catalogue of Printed Music in the British Museum* by a number of collections of dances published from about 1775 to 1785. Almost all the dances call for a harp.

Werrit. *See* WHERRIT.

Wescomb, Mr ₁*fl. 1733–1735*₁,   *actor.*
When Mr Wescomb made his first appearance at Drury Lane Theatre he was hailed as from Edinburgh, though we know none of his Edinburgh roles before his London debut. On 1 October 1733 he played the title role in *The Mock Doctor*, and he repeated it on 5 October. By 5 November he was back in Edinburgh, playing Bajazet in *Tamerlane*. His other Edinburgh parts through 19 November 1735 were Gibby in *The Wonder*, Hob in *Flora*, Jobson in *The Devil to Pay*, Lovegold in *The Miser*, Pero in *The Perplex'd Polander*, and Sir Wilful Witwoud in *The Way of the World*.

Wesley, Charles   *1757–1834, organist, composer.*
Charles Wesley was born at Bristol on 11 December 1757, the eldest son of the Reverend Charles Wesley (1707–1788), the divine and hymn writer, and his wife Sarah (1726–1822), third daughter of Marmaduke Gwynne of Garth, Beconshire. The younger Charles was one of the three of his parents' children (with Samuel and Sarah) to survive infancy. He was the nephew of John Wesley (1703–1791), the evangelist leader of Methodism. Both of Charles's parents were fond of music. His father's hymns are rich in melody, and, as *The Dictionary of National Biography* describes them, "in the best of them there is a lyrical swing and an undertone of mystical fervour." His mother had considerable vocal talent and played the harpischord in a pleasing manner.

In his *Journal* (edited by Thomas Jackson, 1849), the elder Charles Wesley gave an account of his two musical sons, Charles and Samuel, in which he describes Charles as an extraordinary musical prodigy by the age of four. John Stanley, the blind composer and well-known London organist, "expressed his pleasure and surprise at hearing him, and declared he had never met one of his age with so great a propensity to music." The Vauxhall organist John Worgan thought that Charles would become "an eminent master, if he was not taken off by other studies." An offer by the talented theatre vocalist John Beard to have Charles admitted as one of the boys of the Chapel Royal was declined by his father who "then had no thoughts of bringing him up a musician." That was an unfortunate decision, for Charles then was obliged to receive his early tuition in Bristol instead of London where he might have proved the distinguished musician that his talent promised.

At the age of six Charles was given for instruction to a Bristol organist named Rooke, who failed to impose any discipline and let Charles "run on *ad libitum*." His father wrote, "I saw no likelihood of my ever being able to procure him the first masters, or of purchasing the most excellent music, and other necessary means of acquiring so costly an art." Charles continued on his own, "with the assistance of nature," to study his favorite composers, Handel and Corelli.

About 1771 the elder Wesley moved his family to London, where they occupied a house at No 1, Chesterfield Street, Marylebone, which was allowed him, with furnishings, for over 20 years by his benefactress Mrs Gumley. Though urged by some to send Charles abroad for his further education, upon the advice of William Bromfield, the first surgeon at the Lock Hospital, the elder Wesley placed him with Joseph Kelway, organist of St Martin-in-the-Fields. Under Kelway he learned the lessons of Handel, Geminiani, and Scarlatti, and in the performance of Scarlatti's sonatas he became distinguished. It was becoming clear, wrote his father, that Charles's particular bent was to church music, and "his chief delight was in the oratorios," all of which he heard for three seasons, especially concentrating on those by Handel. These he learned to play by heart. Advertisements in the Bristol newspapers record one of his performances: on 31 March 1774 Master Charles

Royal College of Music

CHARLES WESLEY

artist unknown

Wesley played a concerto on the organ between the parts of the *Messiah* at Bristol Cathedral. He was tutored in composition by William Boyce, and in 1776 he dedicated a set of six string quartets to Dr Boyce. Upon his master's death, young Wesley wrote an elegy, words to which were provided by the elder Wesley. Beginning in 1779 and lasting through 1785, Charles and his brother Samuel gave concerts in their music room in the house in Marylebone that were subscribed to by many of the nobility.

Wesley became a sound and practical musician who had failed to fulfill the promise of his youth. Perhaps, as has been suggested, his personality prevented him from obtaining the more important positions. He was somewhat withdrawn and unsociable, and he was not resourceful. One commentator, perhaps exaggerating, doubted "whether through the entire course of his life he was able to dress himself without assistance; if left to himself he was apt to appear with his wig on one side, his waistcoat buttoned awry or the knot of his cravat opposite one of his shoulders." As noted by Erik Routley in *The Musical Wesleys* (1968), the Wesley name was also an impediment to his career and worked against his applications for appointments as organist at St Paul's, Westminster Abbey, the Charterhouse, and Gresham College. He was told by the Chapter at St Paul's, "We want no Wesleys here."

In 1794 Doane's *Musical Directory* listed him as a composer and organist of the South Street Chapel and living at No 1, Chesterfield Street, the family home. By then he had also served as organist of the Surrey Chapel.

On 19 March 1794, announced as making his first appearance in public, Wesley played a concerto on the organ at the end of the second part of the oratorio at Covent Garden Theatre. That seems to have been his only appearance in a London theatre; there is no indication that he ever played in any of the concert rooms.

After 1794 he served as organist at various places, including Welbeck Chapel, Chelsea Hospital, St George, Hanover Square, and, finally, Marylebone Parish Church.

Wesley never married, and he lived in the family home with his parents until their deaths and then with his sister Sarah. A woman of culture and a member of the literary society of her day, Sarah Wesley died at Bristol, unmarried, on 19 September 1828 at age 68. Charles's younger brother Samuel, also a musician, is noticed separately. Five other siblings died in infancy.

Charles Wesley died at London on 23 May 1834. In his will, signed on 18 May 1831, he gave his address as No 20, Edgeware Road. His bequests included £300 to his brother Samuel Wesley, £10 to Samuel's son Charles, and £50 each to Samuel's other son and his daughter Emma, £200 to his cousin Francis Baldwyn of Edgeware Road, and £20 to Miss Jane Jeffrys of Manchester Street, Marylebone. To Francis Baldwyn he also gave 20 volumes of travel books and one of the two silver cups that had been presented to him by the Royal Starmount Institution of Bath. The other cup and all his other books went to his cousin Elizabeth (last name illegible) of Edgeware Road, who also received £200. The will was proved at London on 21 July 1834.

Wesley's published music included *Six Concertos for the Organ or Harpischord* (1780?); *God save the King, with New Variations for the Organ or Harpischord* (1798?); *Six Hymns . . . Composed by Charles Wesley, with a Hymn by the last Dr. Boyce* (1795?); *Six Quartettos for two Violins, a Tenor, and Violoncello* (1779); and several collections of songs, duets, glees, hymns, and anthems. Evidence of the precocity of Charles Wesley and his brother Samuel is given in Daines Barrington's *Miscellanies* (1781).

A portrait of Charles Wesley by an unknown artist is at the Royal College of Music; it was never engraved.

Wesley, Samuel   *1766–1837, organist, violinist, composer.*

Samuel Wesley was born at Bristol on 24 February 1766, the son of the Reverend Charles Wesley (1707–1788), the divine and hymn writer, and his wife Sarah (1726–1822), third daughter of Marmaduke Gwynne of Garth, Beconshire. The evangelist John Wesley (1703–1799) was his uncle. Samuel was one of eight children, five of whom died in infancy. His elder brother Charles is noticed separately on these pages. His sister Sarah, born in 1760, moved in literary society and died unmarried on 19 September 1828 at age 68.

Samuel exhibited extraordinary musical

gifts at an early age, though not then so re-markable as those of his brother, whom he eventually outshone in musicianship. Accord-ing to his father's *Journal* (edited by Thomas Jackson, 1849), at between four and five years of age Samuel taught himself to read music by studying the oratorio *Samson*, and soon after-ward he taught himself to write music. Before he was six he had composed in his mind his oratorio *Ruth* and at eight wrote it down, causing Dr Boyce to exclaim to the father, "Sir, I hear you have got an English Mozart in your house." The manuscript of the *Ruth* ora-torio, finished on 26 October 1774, is in the British Library (Add MS 34997). Daines Bar-rington's *Miscellanies* (1781) contains accounts of the precocious activities of the brothers Wesley.

Wesley began to study the harpsichord at the age of seven with David Williams, organ-ist at the Bristol Church of St James, Barton. Violin he learned from Bean, Kingsbury, and W. Cramer, but it appears that he was mostly self-taught and received little or no instruc-tion in the theory of music. At the insistence of his father he received a fine classical educa-tion and had knowledge of several modern languages.

About 1771 (and probably not as late as 1778, the date given by the *New Grove*), the elder Charles Wesley took his family to Lon-don, to live in a leasehold house at No 1, Chesterfield Street, Marylebone, which his patron Mrs Gumley had provided, furnished, for the remainder of the lease—over 20 years. In the music room there, which contained two organs, Samuel and his brother gave concerts, beginning in 1779 and lasting through 1785, which were subscribed to by many of the no-bility. In the British Library is a transcript list (Add MS 35017) of the subscribers' names, concert programs, refreshment expenses, and payments to performers. In 1777 Samuel's *Eight Lessons for the Harpsichord* was published.

About 1783 Samuel made a clandestine conversion to Roman Catholicism, the news of which, kept for some time from his father, se-verely distressed the evangelist when he heard of it. Samuel seems to have been drawn to his conversion not so much by religious convic-tion as by his attraction to the music at the Portuguese Chapel in South Street (now South Audley Street). Apparently Samuel had been

setting Roman texts to music as early as 1780, and he celebrated his conversion by compos-ing a *Missa de Spiritu Sancto*, which he dedi-cated and sent to Pope Pius VI and for which he received thanks. About that time he also composed his motet *In Exitu Israel*. His devo-tion was not permanent. He became a Free-mason on 17 December 1788, and in 1793 he married in the Church of England. He wrote later, "If Roman doctrines were like the Ro-man *music* we should have heaven on earth" and was reported to have said, "For excom-munication I care not three straws."

Wesley suffered a serious accident in 1787 at the age of 21, when, passing along Snow Hill one night, he fell into a deep building excavation. Insensible, he was not discovered until midnight. A doctor suggested trepan-ning to relieve pressure on his brain, but Wes-ley refused and the wound eventually healed. It is sometimes assumed that this accident was the cause of the irritable and manic-depressive behavior he exhibited for the rest of his life, and that his consequently eccentric habits be-came a severe liability to his creative talents. Erik Routley in *The Musical Wesleys* (1968) points out, however, that Wesley survived for 50 years after that injury, and in his autobio-graphical manuscript (British Library, Add MS 27593) he never mentioned the accident. Percy Scholes writes that the accident incapac-itated Samuel for seven years, a statement re-jected by Routley, who argues that he was "anything but inactive during the years 1787–94" and that there was no discernible diminution in the quality of his music after the incident. Samuel had an unstable temper-ament from the first. He once wrote, "I hate public life: I always did." Though he loved music, he considered the profession of music to be a "trivial and degrading business," which he regretted having been pushed into by his father.

Indeed, Wesley's professional activities and appointments were not extensive though he was an extremely prolific composer. Doane listed him in his *Musical Directory* (1794), de-scribing him as an organist and composer liv-ing at No 1, Chesterfield Street, the family home; however, no professional appointments were noted. Wesley made one appearance of record at Covent Garden Theatre, on 22 Feb-ruary 1799, when at the end of the first part

Royal College of Music

SAMUEL WESLEY, at age 11

by Russell

of the oratorio *Acis and Galatea* an *Ode on St Cecilia's Day* was performed with music by him set to a text by the Reverend Samuel Wesley (1622–1735), his grandfather. As an introduction to the ode Wesley played Handel's "third organ concerto."

After he failed in his application for the position of organist at the Foundling Hospital in 1798, he seems, as the *New Grove* informs us, "to have made little attempt to gain a perma-

nent salaried position." Christian Latrobe wrote on 7 February 1799 to Dr Burney, "It is a shame to the nation, that such a man, & his brother Charles, pass unheeded when a Dibdin rides triumphant upon his Asses Ears of the town." In November of that year Wesley's address was at the 5th Milestone, Highgate.

Perhaps Wesley's greatest interest was "the vigorous propaganda" for the works of Johann Sebastian Bach, and the *New Grove* credits him as having been "the central figure in the early revival of Bach's music in England." His enthusiasm for Bach developed about 1800, and soon he enlisted C. F. Horn, Vincent Novello, and Benjamin Jacob in the cause. During 1808 and 1809 he wrote a number of letters to Jacob, the organist of the Surrey Chapel, which were edited by his daughter Eliza Wesley. (The originals, bound together with programs of organ concerts at the Surrey Chapel, are in the library of the Royal College of Music.) At some of Jacob's concerts Wesley played Bach's violin sonatas. He also corresponded with Dr Burney about his Bach project. (A series of letters to Burney are in the Osborn Collection at Yale, with copies at McGill University.) Writing from No 27, Arlington Street, Camden Town, on 12 April 1808, Wesley asked Burney's opinion of his plan to bring out a new edition of Bach's preludes and fugues, which had become, according to Wesley, exceedingly scarce in England and almost unobtainable.

Several months later, on 23 June, he wrote: "Now what I request of you is to give me an Order how to proceed:—Shall I immediately issue Proposals about *Lecturing*, or about *publishing* Sebastian with annotations & an Explication?—Or is it too late to make any Noise about it till next Season?" From a letter written on 1 July 1808 we learn that at the recent Cambridge commencement Wesley had conducted the choruses in a selection from Haydn's *Creation* on the occasion of Carnaby's taking his doctor's degree. At the end of the year, on 20 December, he expressed his concern to Burney over his forthcoming lectures and asked to rehearse his first lecture before him; Burney replied that he was confident that Wesley had language, eloquence, and science in his fingers: "you will yourself to be not only a great Musician but a Scholar & a man of letters, & we have not the least doubt that you will be called for at the royal Institution" (letter in the Berg Collection, New York Public Library). At his "Morning Musical Party" on 3 June 1809, Wesley introduced to an English audience Bach's cantata "Jesu, priceless treasure."

In conjunction with Horn, he published Bach's six organ trios in 1809 and the first English edition of *Das vohltemperierte Clavier* in installments that appeared between 1810 and

1813. Beginning in 1811, as Burney had predicted, Wesley began to lecture on music at the Royal Institution, and elsewhere. He also gave frequent concerts; in one at the Hanover Square Rooms on 19 May 1810, he performed his motet *In Exitu Israel* for the first time, and the rest of the program consisted mainly of Bach's music. In addition to teaching music, he conducted and played solo organ at the Birmingham Festival in 1811. He was in demand to play recitals in many parts of the country. In September 1813 he became an associate of the Philharmonic Society and was a member from 1815 to 1817. He was honorary Grand Organist to the Ancient Lodge of Freemasons from 1813 to 1818.

In 1816 Wesley suffered an acute depression that incapacitated him professionally until 1823. In 1824 John Sainsbury was embarrassed by the report in his *Dictionary of Musicians* that "S. Wesley died about the year 1815," prompting a humorous denial by Wesley in *The Times* of 12 October 1824 that concluded, "My *living* residence is now at No 16, Euston-street, Euston-square, New-rood, St. Pancras." The mistake provided an opportunity for several exchanges of letters between Wesley and Sainsbury in the press and for commentaries in the monthly journals. (Details of the letters and a discussion of biographies of musicians of that period are given by Lawrence I. Ritchey, "The Untimely Death of Samuel Wesley; or, the Perils of Plagiarism," *Music & Letters*, vol 60 [1979].) He was appointed organist of Camden Chapel (now St Stephen's Parish Church) in 1824, but in that year was unsuccessful in his application at St George's, Hanover Square.

At the Fitzwilliam Museum in Cambridge in 1826 Wesley found three of Handel's settings for his father's hymns, which he published. In the next several years Wesley composed a large number of hymns. In 1830 he suffered a return of his depression and thereafter seldom played in public. The small annuity he shared with his brother from the Wesleyan Conference for the copyright of their father's hymns was not sufficient maintenance. He was reduced to copying music for a living at times and was so destitute that he was once sent to debtor's prison. He received some relief in 1830, when Vincent Novello organized a subscription for his benefit.

At a concert of the Sacred Harmonic Society, Exeter Hall, on 7 August 1834 he made one of his last public appearances when he accompanied the anthem "All go unto one place," which he had composed upon his brother Charles's death. On 1 January 1837 the Governors of the Royal Society of Musicians approved a donation to him of £3. He last ventured from his house on 12 September 1837, to hear Mendelssohn play the organ in Christ Church, Newgate Street; and Wesley was also prevailed upon to play.

Samuel Wesley died a month later, on 11 October 1837, at Islington, and was buried in the churchyard of the old St Marylebone Church in the grave with his parents and near other relatives. There is a memorial window for him in Bristol Cathedral.

At Ridge, a small village in the south of Hertfordshire, Wesley had married (according to the Church of England rites) on 5 April 1793 Charlotte Louisa Martin, daughter of Captain Martin of Kensington. She was an assistant teacher in a private school in Marylebone. They lived for a brief time in Ridge but then moved to Camden Town. The marriage lasted only two years, and in 1795 Samuel wrote to his sister of their separation. Their marriage produced a son, Charles (1793?-1859), who attended St Paul's School, entered the Church, was appointed in 1833 chaplain to the King's household at St James's Palace, and later became sub-dean of the Chapel Royal. According to J. T. Lightwood, *Samuel Wesley; Musician* (1937), Samuel and his wife also had two other children, John William and Emma Francis, though nothing is known of them.

Before his marriage, Wesley had come under the influence of Martin Madan, who had been dismissed from his ministry at the Lock Hospital because of his sexual eccentricities, and his publication of a tract entitled *Thelyphthora*, in which he argued for bigamy. While still living with his wife, Wesley began an affair with his housekeeper Sarah Suter. It is not clear when Mrs Wesley moved from the house.

The liaison with Sarah Suter, whom he did not marry, produced four children, the eldest of whom was Samuel Sebastian Wesley (1810–1876), born on 14 August 1810, who became "the greatest composer in the English

Cathedral tradition between Purcell and Stanford," according to the *New Grove*, where he receives an extensive notice. Their daughter Eliza Wesley was born in 1819, served as organist of St Margaret Pattens, and died, unmarried, in 1895. She published her father's *Letters referring to the Works of J. S. Bach* in 1875. Another son, Robert Glen Wesley, was for some years organist at Wesley's Chapel, City Road, London. Matthias Erasmus Wesley, another son, followed business but remained a lover of music; for several years he was treasurer of the College of Organists, retiring from that office in 1894. Wesley's wife Charlotte, whom he never divorced and who survived him, died on 5 February 1845 at 84 and was buried in Highgate Cemetery. The cemetery register records her as the "relict of Samuel Wesley, the celebrated composer."

In his fine article on the Wesleys in the *New Grove*, Nicolas Temperley calls Samuel Wesley "incomparably the finest English organist of his day" and provides a discussion of his music which concludes that Wesley's "importance and individuality as a composer is only beginning to be fully recognized." A very extensive list of his compositions is given by Temperley.

Wesley was also an accomplished violinist when young. In a letter to Dr Burney on 4 September 1809 he stated that he had played the violin very well some 30 years ago, but when he lost a favorite violin in a hackney coach and then could not find another that suited his hand and fancy, he "turned sulky at the whole *Genus*, which you will say is acting very like an Ideot." His work on Bach, however, regenerated his liking for the instrument and he told Burney that he had taken up "my wooden Box once more" and that he felt confident enough to be the accompanist at a forthcoming concert at Chelsea College in the event Salomon could not be engaged.

Despite the apprehensions expressed to Dr Burney, Wesley also proved a polished lecturer and writer. Some original manuscripts of his lectures on music delivered between 1811 and 1830 are in the British Library (Add MSS 35014–15). In addition to the publications mentioned above, he published a translation of Rinck's *Practical School for the Organ* (edited by John Bishop, London, n.d.) and a number of review and critical articles in various journals, including an "Impartial and Critical Re-

National Portrait Gallery, London

SAMUEL WESLEY
by Jackson

view of Musical Publications" that appeared in the *European Magazine* from July 1813 to December 1816.

Wesley has been the subject of many articles, dissertations on his music, and several books, including W. Winters, *An Account of the Remarkable Musical Talents of Several Members of the Wesley Family* (1874); J. T. Lightwood, *Samuel Wesley, Musician* (1937); and Erik Routley, *The Musical Wesleys* (1968, reprinted 1976).

Wesley was a man of keen and unconventional wit, with a warm heart and an acute mind that often betrayed him into psychotic lapses. His unbalanced personality was described by Mrs Vincent Novello, wife of his close friend:

I knew him unfortunately too well. Pious catholic, raving atheist; mad, reasonable; drunk and sober. The dread of all wives and regular families. A warm friend, a bitter foe; a satirical talker; a

flatterer at times of those he cynically traduced at others; a blasphemer at times, a purling methodist at others.

A full-length portrait in oil of Samuel Wesley at age 11 was exhibited by John Russell at the Royal Academcy in 1777. In 1894 the painting was in the possession of M. E. Wesley of Holland Park, London. It is now in the Royal Academy of Music. Russell's portrait was engraved by W. Dickinson and published by J. Walker on 26 January 1778. Wesley's portrait by John Jackson was in the artist's family for many years; it was owned in 1826 by the artist's nephew, the Reverend John Jackson of Higher Broughton, and was sold in 1924 by Sydney P. Jackson to the National Portrait Gallery (No 2040). The picture is unfinished and has not been engraved. A three-quarter-length oil of Wesley by J. J. Masquerier was painted for Sir Charles Forbes; its location is unknown. Masquerier's small pencil drawing showing Wesley in profile as an old man with curly white hair inscribed "sketched at Brighton by J. M." was at Christie's on 9 April 1974. A pencil drawing of Wesley by an unknown artist is in the British Library (Add MS 31764.f.3) and was reproduced in the *Listener* of 3 March 1937.

West, Mr [fl. 1724–1727], *house servant?*

The Lincoln's Inn Fields accounts show that a West, probably a house servant, was at that theatre as early as 21 December 1724; on that date he was paid £1 1s. for his "attendance this season." On 2 January 1725 he was on the paylist for 10s., and on 26 May 1726 a Mr West shared a benefit with three others. On 16 September 1726 he received 5s., and on 7 June 1727 he was paid 5s. for three days and on 14 June 1727 3s. 4d. for two days.

West, Mr [fl. 1734], *actor, singer.*

A Mr West acted Clodio in *Love Makes a Man* at Goodman's Fields Theatre on 19 January 1734. On 31 January he sang a vocal part in *Macbeth*. On 11 February he played a Royal Attendent in the premiere of *Britannia; or, The Royal Lovers*, an entertainment that was popular that season and the next. In the autumn of 1734 West was again listed in *Britannia*, as a Grenadier. He was replaced, however, by Rosco on 11 December 1734.

West, Mr ₁*fl. 1742*₁,   *boxkeeper?*

Tickets for Signor Fausan's benefit at Drury Lane Theatre on 1 February 1742 could be had from Mr West at the Green Door in Duke's Street, Lincoln's Inn Fields, or from Mr Bradshaw at the King's Arms in Russell Street near the theatre. For Signora Fausan's benefit on 24 February tickets and places for the boxes were "to be had only of Mr. West, at the Green Door in Duke Street. . . ." The regular boxkeeper that season was Bradshaw. West was either a temporary boxkeeper or was performing a service for the Fausans.

West, Mr ₁*fl. 1795*₁,   *equestrian.*

In April and May of 1795 a Mr West performed in equestrian exercises at the Royal Circus, London.

(It is possible that this person was James West, who by 1802 began to appear at Astley's Amphitheatre and became a leading rider and manager in the first quarter of the nineteenth century. James West went to America in 1816–17, leading a troupe to New York, Philadelphia, Boston, and elsewhere. Returning to England he became Andrew Ducrow's co-manager at Astley's in 1825 and retired in 1832. His wife also was a circus performer. His son William West [1812–1890] managed at Astley's after his father and was also a leading performer. For information on the nineteenth-century Wests see Arthur Saxon, *The Life and Art of Andrew Ducrow* [1978] and Stuart Thayer, *Annals of the American Circus* [1976].)

West, Charles. *See* DIGGES, WEST DUDLEY.

West, D. ₁*fl. 1758–1781*₁,   *actor, dancer, singer.*

Mr D. West was a minor performer at Drury Lane Theater by 1758–59. On 28 May 1759 he shared benefit tickets with other journeymen personnel and also played Filch in *The Beggar's Opera*. He remained at Drury Lane at least through 1766–67, sharing benefit tickets annually, playing modest roles, and mostly dancing, it seems, in the chorus. His salary in 1764–65 was 2*s.* per day, or 12*s.* per week, among the very lowest in the company. It was still at that level in 1766–67. His

name was in the bills for dancing in *The Magician of the Mountain* on 3 January 1763 and several other times that season. He danced in *The Hermit; or, Harlequin at Rhodes*, a pantomime that premiered on 6 January 1766, and he also performed in a new farce called *The Hobby Horse* on 16 April 1766.

Our subject was probably the West who with Mrs West was in Roger Kemble's company at Worcester in 1771 and 1772. From about November 1773 to February 1774, West and a son and daughter performed at Richmond, Surrey. He was at Brighton between 1774 and 1776 and at Bath in 1775–76. Between 13 October and 20 December 1776 West earned £1 10*s.* per week at Liverpool.

His surname and first initial are found with those of members of his family in the records of the York company from 1775 to 1781. Dorothy Eshleman, editor of *The Committee Books of the Theatre Royal, Norwich 1768–1825*, identified the Mr West who earned one guinea per week there in 1783 as D. West, but we believe that person more likely was James West, the actor who later went to America and played at Charleston, South Carolina, in 1794. It is probable that James West was one of D. West's sons.

West's wife acted with him at Worcester in 1771 and 1772 and at York in 1776, when her name was recorded as Mrs D. West. Perhaps she was the Mrs West who performed at Kilkenny in February 1773. We also believe that she was the Mrs West who with Miss West and Master Williamson danced in *The Shoemaker* at the Haymarket Theatre on 17 May 1771.

The Wests had at least three children, and possibly four, who became performers. Their son William West began to appear in London as Master West by 1768 and had a career as a dancer and deviser of pantomimes that extended for over 55 years throughout the three kingdoms. A daughter, Louisa Margaretta, danced on the London stage as Miss West from 1768 to 1779; in 1781 she married the actor Richard Suett and retired. Another daughter, recorded as Miss D. West, performed at York and Edinburgh in 1779 and at York in 1780; she was at the Royalty Theatre, London, in July 1787. It is also possible, as mentioned above, that the provincial performer James

West was a son. A James West witnessed the marriage of Louisa West to Richard Suett on 8 September 1781 at St Michael le Belfrey, York. James West went to America in 1794; he married the widow of the Charleston manager John Bignall in June 1795, and he died at Charleston on 8 July 1805 at the age of 42. His wife had died at Richmond, Virginia, on 20 January of the same year.

West, Mrs D. *fl. 1768–1776₁*, actress. See WEST, D

West, Miss D.? *fl. 1779–1787₁*, dancer.
A Miss West danced a Country Girl in the pantomime *Hobson's Choice* at the Royalty Theatre, London, on 3 July 1787. Perhaps she was the Miss D. West who danced with her parents, Mr and Mrs D. West, at York in 1779 and 1780. On a trip from Edinburgh to London, Miss D. West and her sister Miss Louisa West (later Mrs Richard Suett) performed at York on 2 April 1779, for that night only. In 1780 at York Miss D. West had a benefit on 15 March 1780.

West, J. *fl. 1795?–1827?₁*, dresser.
On 19 December 1795 a Mr West was put on the Drury Lane Theatre paylist as a dresser at a salary of £1 6s. per week. Our subject was perhaps one of the two persons named West who were dressers at that theatre in the nineteenth century. A J. West, dresser, was paid 9s. per week from 1815–16 through 1819–20, and a Mr W. West, also a dresser, received a similar sum for approximately the same period. A Mr West was dresser at the Liverpool Theatre Royal in 1818–19 and 1819–20 at 9s. per week.

Indeed, at Drury Lane in the early years of the nineteenth century there was a numerous family of Wests, who occupied positions as dressers, messengers, chorus singers, and sweepers. A Mr West was a messenger from 1800–1801 at least through 1812–13 at a salary varying from £1 4s. to £1 16s. per week. A Mr West was a sweeper from 1812–13 through 1816–17 at 12s. per week.

In his *Remarkable Persons*, Caulfield described a West, formerly a footman to the actor Robert Baddeley, and an "Applebee" who "are the present [presumably nineteenth cen-

tury] persons who conduct the calls of Drury-Lane theatre, and pick up many stray shillings and half-crowns from the performers on several occasional services they render them." Probably he was the West noted by James Winston in his diaries as a servant at Drury Lane from 1823 to 1827.

West, Joseph *fl. 1794₁*, singer.
Joseph West was listed in Doane's *Musical Directory* in 1794 as a bass singer and a member of the Choral Fund and the Handelian Society, living at No 1, Cumberland Street, Middlesex Hospital.

West, Louisa Margaretta, later Mrs Richard Suett *1754–1832, dancer.*
Louisa Margaretta West, who in 1768–69, at the age of 14, began dancing at Drury Lane Theatre, was the daughter of D. West (fl. 1758–1781), a minor performer at Drury Lane, and his wife, Mrs D. West (fl. 1768–1776), also a sometime London performer. She was the sister of William West (b. c. 1757), a dancer who had a career of over 55 years on the London stage and throughout the three kingdoms. James West (d. 1805), a provincial player who went to perform in America in 1794, was probably her brother also; he married the widow of the manager John Bignall in June 1795 at Charleston, South Carolina. Louisa's sister, called Miss D. West (fl. 1779–1787), was also a dancer; she performed at least once in London, at the Royalty Theatre on 3 July 1787, and was seen at York in 1779 and 1780.

On 27 September 1768 Louisa West's name appeared in the Drury Lane bills for dancing with Giorgi, Miss Rogers, and Miss Collett. Leading the dancers was Giuseppe Grimaldi, teacher of Louisa and her brother William. At Drury Lane the following season, on 4 October 1769, she again danced with Grimaldi and others. On 2 May 1770 she and Master West (her brother William), announced as pupils of Grimaldi, danced an allemande. On the sixteenth of that month she made her debut at the Haymarket Theatre, dancing *The Pedlar* with Master West. On 21 May they performed *The Cowkeeper*, on 11 June *The Nosegay*, and on 4 July a double hornpipe, and then were seen in similar dances throughout the summer until 15 September 1770. She and her brother returned to dance at the Haymarket regularly in the summer of 1771.

With her brother and her father, Miss West was a member of the company performing at Richmond, Surrey, from about October 1773 to February 1774. She also danced with her brother at York in 1772 and 1773, Bath in 1773–74, and Birmingham in the summer of 1774, by which time her brother was being called Mr West.

On 19 September 1774 she and her brother returned to London to appear for the first time at Covent Garden Theatre, in *The Italian Gardeners*. Then for several years Miss West seems to have been on tour with the family. She was at York the entire season of 1775. At the Birmingham Theatre Royal between 12 October and 20 December 1776 she earned £1 10*s*. per week. She also performed again at York in 1776. It was at York that Mrs Sumbel, as she related in her *Memoirs*, first learned dancing from Miss West, "who kindly taught me gratuitously: she was then the principal dancer in the theatre, and taught in the city."

On 27 May 1777 Miss West was back in London dancing at Sadler's Wells. She played Colombine in *Harlequin Doctor Faustus* at Edinburgh in December 1777. In April 1779 she stopped to perform at York on the way from Edinburgh to London. She was also a member of the York company in March 1780, when she had a benefit on the fifteenth, and again in 1781. With her brother she appeared at Derby between 20 December 1780 and 14 January 1781 in *The Iroquois*, a dance that the advertisements proclaimed the pair had performed before their Majesties at Kew Palace.

On 8 September 1781 Louisa West married the actor Richard Suett at St Michael le Belfrey in York. She then, according to Tate Wilkinson in his *Wandering Patentee*, retired, never again to appear on the stage. Writing in 1795, Wilkinson described her as a homebody, who "combs the lap-dog, scolds the servant—(not her husband)—and it is her own fault in every respect she is not a contented woman." In terms which suggest that Wilkinson *had* heard something, he concluded, "I never heard to the contrary—so I hope they will live long and happy together."

But they did not. Suett died in a small public house in Denzell Street, Clare Market, in July 1805 and was buried on the north side of St Paul's churchyard. In his will made on 16 June 1805, a few weeks before his death, he left one shilling to "Louisa Suet my Wife who at this time is separated from me and who I verily believe at this time and for a long time lives in a state of adultery with Mr Grindal a distiller in St Giles's."

Mrs Suett died on 13 May 1832 and was buried in the Doncaster Parish Church. Her full name and dates are recorded in Charles W. Hatfield's *Historical Notices of Doncaster*. By Richard Suett she had two sons: John Suett, born in 1785, died on 11 October 1848 and was also buried at Doncaster; the other son, Theophilus, who died on naval service in the Mediterranean on 28 April 1817. Theophilus Suett was the "Young Gentleman" who made his debut at Covent Garden Theatre as Wilford in *The Iron Chest* on 23 April 1799, the night his father made his only appearance at that theatre, as Samson in the same piece. Richard Suett mentioned neither son in his will, but left his estate and property to Lucy Wood, of Clare Market, spinster, who proved the will on 8 July 1805. No doubt she had been living with him.

West, Thomas Wade *1745–1799, actor, manager.*

Thomas Wade West, born in 1745, was described by Edward Cape Everard in his *Memoirs* as "a natural son of Lord Somebody's." In her dissertation on the Charleston Theatre, Julia Curtis suggests that he was the West who was performing with Roger Kemble's company at Worcester in August 1771. But that West already had a teenage son and daughter who were on the provincial stage in the 1770s, and we believe the Worcester player to have been Mr D. West (fl. 1758–1781), who is noticed on these pages. So far as we can determine, Thomas Wade West was not connected to that family.

Most likely, however, Thomas Wade West had provincial experience before, at about the age of 30, he acted Bassanio in *The Merchant of Venice* at the Haymarket Theatre on 23 March 1775. That night he also spoke the prologue and acted an unspecified role in *The Snuffbox; or, A Trip to Bath*. Probably he was the West who performed Sir Hearty in *The Jealous Wife* at the same theatre on 2 May 1776.

Thomas Wade West was a member of a company that performed 12 nights at China Hall, Rotherhithe, from May until October 1776 under the management of William Bailey. West delivered the address on opening night, 25 May 1776. On 7 August, Mrs West, the sister of the dancer and actor Matthew Sully, acted Honoria in *Love Makes a Man*. Throughout the season husband and wife appeared in leading roles. On 23 August West played Edward in *Edward and Elivera*, and the *Morning Post* on 26 August printed a letter form someone who had seen the performance: ". . . I was much surprised at Mr West's coming forward and apologizing for the badness of his dress, at the same time acquainting the audience that the manager would allow no better: I was happy to find the audience protected West and censur'd the manager for his scandalous behaviour. . . ." That correspondent reported that West spoke the part of Edward well, "but for a disagreeable whine, which with a little care he might soon get rid of." West acted the Earl of Richmond in *Richard III* on 4 October 1776, and on 7 October he played the title role in *Alexander the Great* and Sir Charles Racket in *Marriage à la Mode*. That night was for the benefit of Mrs West, who acted Lady Racket, and tickets could be had of West at the Ship, near the Seven Houses, Rotherhithe.

When China Hall was closed by the authorities soon after, the Wests probably went into the country. They reappeared in London on 11 February 1777 when West shared a benefit at the Haymarket Theatre and acted Hotspur in *1 Henry IV*. Tickets could be had from him at the Black Lion, Russell Street. His wife, announced as making her first appearance "in Town," played Lady Percy. At the Haymarket on 1 May 1777 West acted Petruchio in *Catherine and Petruchio* and Captain Dormer in *A Word to the Wise*. They returned to China Hall in June, but the season was aborted on 23 July by armed authorities. In that year and the next West made other occasional appearances at the Haymarket, playing Sir William in *The Gentle Shepherd* on 13 October 1777, Lorenzo in *The Spanish Fryar* on 26 January 1778, Lord Hastings in *Jane Shore* on 9 February, Petruchio again and Oakly in *The Jealous Wife* on 23 March, an occasional prologue to *Richard III* and Colonel Tamper (with prologue) in *The*

Deuce Is in Him on 24 March, and Sir John Melvil (with prologue) in *The Clandestine Marriage* and Captain Cape in the *The Old Maid* on 30 April. For his benefit on 24 March 1778 tickets were available from him at No 4, Stanhope Street, Clare Market.

In the summer of 1778 West returned to China Hall with a company of actors that included Everard and the young George Frederick Cooke to play 14 nights beginning on 25 May when West acted Colonel Briton in *The Wonder* and spoke the prologue to *The Lying Valet*. The season was marred by a fire, the work of an arsonist, that destroyed China Hall on 26 June, and the company struggled on in a makeshift tent before the authorities shut them down six weeks later. West's roles that summer also included Lord Randolph in *Douglas*, Bruin in *The Mayor of Garratt*, Hastings in *She Stoops to Conquer*, Petruchio, Sir George Airy in *The Busy Body*, Sir John Melvil in *The Clandestine Marriage*, Squire Robert in *The Mock Doctor*, Captain Cape in *The Old Maid*, Uncle in *The London Merchant*, Romeo in *Romeo and Juliet*, Jaffeir in *Venice Preserv'd*, Essex in *The Earl of Essex*, Thomas Bevil in *Cross Purposes*, Aubrey in *The Fashionable Lover*, Sparkle in *The Miser*, Thomas in *The Irish Widow*, the Earl of Richmond in *Richard III*, and the Bastard in *King Lear*. The *Morning Chronicle* on 19 June reported that his portrayal of Jaffeir on 15 June was "far from despicable, though we cannot rank him among the Barry's and Smith's of the stage."

For over a decade West then worked in the provinces, evidently in East Anglia for several seasons and at Birmingham in the summer of 1779. He also was with Whitley's company touring from 1780 to 1782 in Gloucester, Worcester, Shrewsbury, and Stamford. According to James Winston and the *Thespian Dictionary*, West also became the circuit manager for theatres at Gainsborough, Louth, Rotherham, and Mansfield.

Early in 1790, at the age of 45, West, with his wife Margaretta, sailed for the United States. They were accompanied by their children and John Bignall, their son-in-law, who was married to their daughter Ann. The Bignalls had acted in the English provinces, but evidently never performed in London. West and Bignall were to become important pioneers in the development of theatre in the American South.

By September 1790 the Wests and Bignalls were in Philadelphia, hoping for engagements with Hallam and Hodgkinson's Old American Company at the Southwark Theatre. Finding opportunities there slight, West declined an offer of two guineas a week, and the Wests and Bignalls set off for Richmond, where they formed the Virginia Company. In August 1790 they were offering the entertainment *The Evening Brush* at Quesnay's Academy, renamed the New Theatre, on Shockoe Hill. Few bills survive to record the company's activities in 1790–91. Surviving advertisements reveal performances of *Know Your Own Mind* and *The Farmer* on 18 October 1790. In the former, West acted Dashwood, his wife Lady Bell, Bignall Millamour, and Mrs Bignall Miss Neville. In the latter, West played Captain Valentine, and the Bignalls acted Jimmy Jump and Betty Blackberry; Mrs West was not listed. On 24 November the local *Independent Chronicle* lavishly praised the talents of the Bignalls and Wests, writing of the latter:

The theatre demands our praise supreme;
Ah! may my song be equal to my theme.
And hark! a second Siddons charms each heart,
Nature in her is closely link'd with art—
The name of West should every tongue employ,
She comes to give us pain which leads to joy.
Nor less his merit claims the muse's art,
Whose talents are imprinted on each heart.
The husband's vocal power attention gain,
Soft as the accent of Thalia's strain.

Advertisements for actors placed by the new Virginia managers in the London press brought ridicule in the *Morning Chronicle* of 23 June 1791: "Among the eccentricities in the advertising line, is that of a Company of Players wanted in Virginia!—A vessel now lies at Liverpool ready to transport your Hamlets, Richards, Alexanders, and other Princes and Potentates—passage free." Two days later that paper jibed that any recruits might have to accept tobacco as salaries.

The company, however, expanded and prospered. Soon it was joined by Mrs West's brother, Matthew Sully, and his large family. West and Bignall built a theatre in Norfolk in early 1792. By May 1792 they announced

their plans to build a new theatre in Charleston, South Carolina. They then went to Philadelphia to play a brief engagement with Hallam and Hodgkinson at the Southwark Theatre. After spending seasons again at Richmond and Norfolk, they opened their new Charleston Theatre—which the press claimed could not be "surpassed in neatness and elegance"—on 11 February 1793 with Mrs Inchbald's *The Adventures of a Shawl*, in which the Wests did not appear, and O'Keeffe's comic opera *The Highland Reel*, in which West acted Sergeant Jack. Mrs West's performance of Lady Randolph in *Douglas* on 15 February evoked effusive verses in the *City Gazette*, and on 25 February she acted Charlotte in the first Charleston production of Tyler's *The Contrast*. She acted Queen Elizabeth in *Richard III* on 11 March, when the London actor A. A. Chambers (who several months later married Miss Charlotte Sully) appeared in the title role. In that first successful season, when they called themselves the South Carolina Company, West was seen as Crabtree in *The School for Scandal*, Polonius in *Hamlet*, and Stephano in *The Tempest*, among other roles. On 13 May 1793 his daughter Harriet West made her debut as Polly Fairlop in *The Woodman*. The season closed on 31 May with a production of *Romeo and Juliet*, in which Mrs West acted Juliet for her benefit. On 3 June 1793, after about 100 performances at Charleston with few repetitions, the Wests and Bignalls sailed in the packet *Swift* for Norfolk.

In his next season at Charleston in 1794 (during which he lived at No 78, Tradd Street) West managed to weather the keen competition from John Joseph Legar Sollée and Alexandre Placide at the rival City Theatre in Church Street, but he lost his partner and son-in-law John Bignall, who died 11 August 1794. In May 1795 Mrs Bignall married James West, a singer-actor who had joined the company in 1794 but was not a blood relation. To further complicate the West family genealogy, another of Thomas Wade West's daughters, Harriet West, who made her Charleston debut in 1793, later married Isaac Bignall, who joined the company from England in 1794. He was, according to Julia Curtis's study of the Charleston Theatre, the stepson of Mrs Bignall, and thus the son of

John Bignall by an earlier marriage presumably. Moreover, the name of Mr T. West began to appear in the Charleston bills in October 1794, along with those of T. W. West and James West. T. West was perhaps Thomas Wade West's son. He acted, maybe for the first time, Jeremy in *She Stoops to Conquer* on 8 October 1794, when West played Diggory and James West Hastings.

At the end of the 1796 season in Charleston, which had been plagued by disastrous fires in the city and a yellow fever epidemic, West gave up his theatre there to concentrate on his ventures in Virginia. In 1797 he had theatres under construction in Fredericksburg and Alexandria and was managing theatres in Norfolk, Richmond, and Petersburg. While the company was playing at the Richmond Theatre, it was ravaged by fire in the middle of the night of 23 January 1798. The loss of scenery, costumes, and properties, perhaps because of arsonists, amounted to an estimated $15,000. West, undaunted, continued to operate the remaining theatres.

In the summer of 1799 West moved his family into the still-unfinished theater in Alexandria. Something apparently disturbed his sleep in the early hours of 28 July and he began to search the stage area and suffered a fatal accident. The *South Carolina State Gazette* of 10 August 1799 reported:

Alexandria, July 29. Yesterday morning departed from this transitory world, in the 54th year of his age, THOMAS WADE WEST, Esq. . . . Having lately sustained material injury from the destructive ravages of fire, he had risen from his bed under the apprehension of again experiencing a disaster of a similar nature, and, while with anxious solicitude he was examining the theatre, unfortunately fell from the painting gallery (of the same height as the front gallery of the house) to the stage. He survived but a few moments.

West was buried with Masonic honors the next day in the cemetery of Christ Church in Alexandria, where his gravestone still stands.

Details of West's substantial contributions to the early American theatre are in Suzanne K. Sherman's "Thomas Wade West, Theatrical Impresario, 1790–1799," *William and Mary Quarterly* (January 1952), where we find:

The assumption that Thomas Wade West was in possession of much more money than was usual for provincial theatre managers is based upon: the Deeds of Norfolk, Richmond, Petersburg, Fredericksburg, and Alexandria, which show that he bought land in each of these cities and put up at least part of the money for the theatres in each; . . . tax returns from Norfolk, Richmond, Petersburg, Fredericksburg, and Alexandria; inventory of his personal property at his death which included among other items: a mahogany sideboard, dining table and eight chairs, 2 sofas, an easy chair, card table, a pier of glasses, 185 oz. of silver, 4 decanters, a desk, bookcase, horse, harness, and chair; deed in Fredericksburg in 1818, which shows that his descendants were still inheriting property which he had left; Mutual Assurance Company records in which the two houses he owned in Norfolk were described; an advertisement in the Fredericksburg *Virginia Herald* (August 21, 1798) in which he offered five pounds reward for the return of a silver tankard "weighing nearly forty ounces;" and upon the size and calibre of the acting company he maintained, the long advertisements he ran in the newspapers, and the elaborate productions he offered his audiences.

West's wife died at Norfolk on 6 June 1810. His daughter Ann, who was married to John Bignall and then to James West, died at Richmond on 20 January 1805, when the *Richmond Inquirer* of 22 January described her as "the most distinguished ornament of the Virginia stage." Her husband James West died at Charleston on 9 July 1805 at the age of 42. Thomas Wade West's other daughter, who married Isaac Bignall, and his son T. West probably continued as actors on the southern circuit of the United States.

West, Mrs Thomas Wade, Margaretta, née Sully *d. 1810, actress.*

Margaretta Sully, whose real family name was O'Sullivan, was probably born in the village of Long Crendon, where the family had roots for generations. Her uncle, John O'Sullivan, served as aide-de-camp to Prince Charles in Scotland in 1746. Her brother, Matthew Sully, turned actor against their father's wishes, and after a career in the minor theatres of London took his wife Sarah (née Chester) and a large family to Charleston, South Carolina, in 1792. Margaretta, it seems, actually took to the stage before her brother.

No doubt Margaretta acted in the provinces

before she came to London in 1776 with her husband, the actor Thomas Wade West, who at that time was 31 years old. They were engaged with William Bailey's company at China Hall, Rotherhithe, from May until October of that year. She was first noticed in the surviving advertisements as acting Honoria in *Love Makes a Man* on 7 August 1776. Throughout the season she and her husband appeared in leading roles. She acted Anne Bullen in *Henry VIII* on 25 September, the Masked Lady in *A Bold Stroke for a Wife* on 30 September, the Landlady in *A Trip to Scotland* on 2 October, Arabella in *The Honest Yorkshireman* on 4 October, Lady Racket in *Marriage à la Mode* for her benefit on 7 October, Cleora in *The Life and Death of Tom Thumb the Great* on 9 October, and Melinda in *The Recruiting Officer* on 18 October 1776.

The Wests were back in London on 11 February 1777 when, announced as making her first appearance "in Town," she acted Lady Percy and he played Hotspur in *1 Henry IV* at the Haymarket. At that theater on 1 May 1777 they appeared in the title roles in *Catherine and Petruchio*. After an aborted summer season at China Hall they made occasional appearances at the Haymarket, where she acted Elvira in *The Spanish Fryar* on 24 January 1778, Harriet in *The Jealous Wife* and Catherine again on 23 March, Florival in *The Deuce Is in Him* on 24 March, and Betty in *The Clandestine Marriage* on 30 May 1778. They were again at China Hall in the summer of 1778 in a season marred by a fire that destroyed the theatre on 26 June, after which the company played in a makeshift tent before the authorities shut them down six weeks later. Her roles included Iris in *The Wonder*, Melissa in *The Lying Valet*, Lady Anne in *Douglas*, Mrs Bruin in *The Mayor of Garratt*, the Maid in *She Stoops to Conquer*, Lady Loverule in *The Devil to Pay*, Betty in *The Clandestine Marriage*, Florival in *The Old Maid*, a character in *Comical Courtship*, the Maid in *The Fashionable Lovers*, Emily in *Cross Purposes*, and Wheedle in *The Miser*. On 17 September 1778 Mrs West acted Regan in *King Lear*, in which her husband played Edmund.

For the next 12 years she acted in the provinces with her husband, who became manager of the circuit that included Gainsborough, Louth, Rotherham, and Mansfield.

Early in 1790 the Wests and their children left for America, accompanied by John Bignall, a provincial actor who was married to their daughter Ann. After arriving at Philadelphia in September 1790, the group set off for the South and established the Virginia Company at Richmond, where Mrs West is known to have acted Lady Bell in *Know Your Own Mind* on 18 October 1790. The local press dubbed her "a second Siddons." The company expanded, having recruited the Sullys, and West and Bignall built a theatre at Norfolk early in 1792, and then on 11 February 1793 opened a new theatre in Charleston, South Carolina. Effusive verses in the *City Gazette* paid tribute to Mrs West's Lady Randolph in *Douglas* on 15 February, and on 25 February she played Charlotte in the first Charleston production of Tyler's *The Contrast*. On 11 March 1793 she appeared as Queen Elizabeth in *Richard III*.

Thereafter Mrs West's career was closely allied to her husband's, as he continued to manage at Charleston through 1796 and to build theatres in the Virginia cities of Fredericksburg, Petersburg, and Alexandria. Her other known roles at the Charleston Theatre in 1794 included the Countess of Rutland in *The Earl of Essex*, Milwood in *George Barnwell*, Cleopatra in *All for Love*, Rosetta in *The Foundling*, Mrs Hardcastle in *She Stoops to Conquer*, and Mrs Slammekin in *The Beggar's Opera*.

In 1795–96 at Charleston her roles were Cordelia in *King Lear*, Belvidera in *Venice Preserv'd*, Julia in *The Rivals*, and Amelia in *The Robbers*, among others. At the end of that season the Wests gave up their Charleston establishment to concentrate on their Virginia theatres. She was living with her husband in Alexandria in 1799 when on 28 July he fell to his death from a carpenter's gallery in the unfinished theatre. What little is known of Mrs West's family is related in her husband's notice. Presumably Mrs West continued to act until her death at Norfolk on 6 June 1810. In her obituary in the *Charleston Times* on 14 June 1810 she was described as "Margaret West, Proprietor of the Norfolk Theatre . . . a Member of the Charleston Theatre about 14 years ago."

Previously Published